American Writers
Before 1800

AMERICAN WRITERS BEFORE 1800

A Biographical
and Critical Dictionary

G–P

EDITED BY James A. Levernier AND Douglas R. Wilmes

GREENWOOD PRESS
WESTPORT, CONNECTICUT
LONDON, ENGLAND

Library of Congress Cataloging in Publication Data
Main entry under title:

American writers before 1800.

  Bibliography: p.
  Includes index.
  1. American literature—Colonial period, ca. 1600-
1775—History and criticism. 2. American literature—
Revolutionary period, 1775-1783—History and criticism.
3. American literature—1783-1850—History and criticism.
4. American literature—Colonial period, ca. 1600-1775—
Bio-bibliography. 5. Authors, American—18th century—
Biography. 6. Authors, American—To 1700—Biography.
I. Levernier, James A. II. Wilmes, Douglas R.
PS185.A4   810'.9'001   82-933
ISBN 0-313-23477-9 (lib. bdg. : v. 2)   AACR2

Library of Congress Catalog Card Number: 82-933
ISBN 0-313-22229-0 (set)
        0-313-23476-0 (vol. 1)
        0-313-23477-9 (vol. 2)
        0-313-24096-5 (vol. 3)

First published in 1983

Greenwood Press
A division of Congressional Information Service, Inc.
88 Post Road West
Westport, Connecticut 06881

Printed in the United States of America

10 9 8 7 6 5 4 3 2 1

In Memory of
Theodore Hornberger

Contents

Preface

This book is designed to provide a convenient source of information about the lives and works of a large number (786) of early American writers. Each writer is discussed in an individual entry that includes primary and secondary bibliographical references, a brief biography, and a critical appraisal of the writer's works and significance. The entries are arranged alphabetically and are followed by appendixes (classifying the writers by date of birth, place of birth, and principal place of residence and presenting a chronology of important events from 1492 to 1800) and by a general index.

A noteworthy feature of this reference tool is its wide scope and broad principles of inclusion, enabling us to include entries on a variety of minor writers. Although we have also provided entries on the major writers of the period, which should prove useful and informative in their own right, we have recognized that treatments of authors such as William Bradford, Benjamin Franklin, Cotton Mather, and Edward Taylor are available in a variety of readily accessible reference formats. However, convenient accessibility of information does not prevail when one turns to the study of the many early American writers who are not well-known or highly valued in strictly literary terms but who are nevertheless worthy of our attention. As microform reproductions of practically all texts published in colonial and early national America are now available, the need for widely inclusive reference tools is all the more apparent. In an effort to meet this need, we have included entries on a large number of lesser-known writers, many of whom are discussed and evaluated here in some detail for the first time.

Students of early American culture will be aware of the vitality and scope of current scholarly interest in early American writing. It would be impossible to summarize briefly and fairly the development of this body of scholarship; a thorough survey would note the many biographies and works of criticism focusing on major writers, but it would also note the appearance of a number of anthologies and histories or interpretations founded in wide-ranging appreciations of the pluralism and multiplicity of early American writing. Works such as

The New England Mind by Perry Miller, the anthology of Puritan writing edited by Miller and Thomas H. Johnson, the anthologies of early American poetry edited by Harrison T. Meserole and Kenneth Silverman, the writings of Sacvan Bercovitch and Richard Beale Davis, and many other distinguished contributions have immeasurably broadened and deepened our knowledge of the substance and import of the lesser-known voices of early American culture.

In fact, our early literature has always—by its nature—demanded of its students an acquaintance with minor voices. In 1878, when Moses Coit Tyler wrote the preface to his pioneering literary history of the colonial period, he was careful to define his subject broadly, as inclusive of those "early authors whose writings, whether many or few, have any appreciable merit, or throw any helpful light upon the evolution of thought and of style in America, during those flourishing and indispensable days." The history of twentieth-century scholarship in early American studies has validated Tyler's approach, and this reference work is based upon a similar reluctance to define narrowly the matter of early American literature.

A reference tool's success is measured by its practical, utilitarian ability to perform the task for which it is designed. We have kept this principle firmly in mind when preparing these volumes, and it has informed two areas of our responsibility that merit particular explanation. These areas are the method by which we selected writers for inclusion and the format of the entries.

SELECTION OF ENTRIES

The writers included in *American Writers Before 1800* are not necessarily the 786 "best" writers of the period. We have not, in other words, selected writers by applying any original definition of literary quality. Such a methodology would have presupposed an ability to form a widely useful and acceptable objective definition of literary quality, which has important subjective components. Moreover, to apply such a definition to a project of this size would require encyclopedic knowledge, and the book would become in part an argument for the validity of the definition and for the accuracy of its application.

Therefore, the selection of writers for this volume was not based upon our individual and personal judgments of their merit. Rather, we have worked inductively from the evidence of a selection of anthologies, literary and cultural histories, and bibliographies of the period. In the first instance, writers have been included in these volumes by virtue of their appearance in secondary works likely to be read or used by scholars and students of early American literature. This array of writers—which we believe includes most writers of works with clearly significant literary merit—forms the backbone of the book. It has been expanded upon in two additional ways. First, in some areas we included some very minor figures in order to provide a representative coverage of certain subgenres, such as the Puritan elegy or early nature reportage. Second, we have sought the advice of experts in certain specialized fields, such as Quaker writing, German pietism, and black literature, to ascertain whether we had included significant and representative writers from those fields.

In examining the results of this process of selection, other scholars will undoubtedly discover sins of omission and commission. As a matter of individual judgment, one might wish for an entry on one writer at the expense of another. Stepping beyond the limits of this equation, we would regard the sin of omission as the more serious and the more to be regretted but also as an inevitable result of limitations of space and human fallibility. There are certainly many more early writers who deserve at least the kind of preliminary and limited discussion and evaluation that our format allows. On the other hand, we are not persuaded that we have included writers who are not worth even the brief discussion they have received in these volumes.

In every regard, our selection is founded upon a considered estimation of the practical uses to which this reference book may be put. We hope, for example, to have met the needs of readers of anthologies, histories, or critical analyses of early American literature who discover passing references to minor writers and want to obtain a sense of who those writers were and what they wrote. Our method of selection should ensure that these volumes will meet such needs in many cases. Furthermore, although the book has a literary bias, its scope is broad enough to accommodate the needs of many constituencies within the field of early American studies. Finally, practical considerations have led us to avoid any prescriptive limitation that might make the book less useful. We have not, for example, interpreted the meaning of "American writers" narrowly. The world of early America obviously had important transatlantic dimensions, and we have therefore included entries on a number of temporary residents or visitors to America who could not themselves be considered "American." In a few instances, we have included entries on writers who themselves never visited America but whose writings concern America and influenced, in some significant way, the development of an American literary heritage and cultural self-identity. In every case, we have asked whether or not the entry would benefit the student of early American culture; we have allowed no consideration to outweigh this central concern.

ENTRY FORMAT

In keeping with our intention to provide information on a variety of lesser-known writers, we have not scaled the length of the entries in proportion to the importance of the writer being discussed in a given entry. Although in some cases minor writers have received a relatively shorter treatment and major writers a relatively longer treatment, in general we have tried to maintain a fairly constant length. Thus a minor writer will often receive more attention than that writer might otherwise have gained, and a major writer less attention, on the principle that the reader may easily obtain further information and critical analyses of the major figures in early American literature. First references within each entry to other writers included in the book are indicated by cross-references (q.v.).

Each entry has been divided into four sections, which organize the content in a predictable and convenient manner:

Works: Each writer's major publications are listed in chronological order. Works are listed by short title, and each title is followed by the date of publication. Significant delays between composition and publication have been indicated when possible. Unpublished material is included where appropriate. In general, we have excluded writers whose work exists only in manuscript, but we have made a few exceptions to this rule where future publication of such material is expected. Although the focus of this book is not primarily bibliographical, we have attempted to ensure that these primary bibliographies are as complete and accurate as possible. In a very few instances, a complete listing of the writer's major publications has not been practicable; in these instances, the reader is directed to appropriate bibliographies or sources. Both American and European imprints are listed; in most cases, the titles will have been published in America, and texts may be obtained by using Charles Evans's *American Bibliography* or the *National Index of American Imprints Through 1800: The Short-Title Evans* (1969), by Clifford K. Shipton and James E. Mooney. Texts listed in these bibliographies may be read in microprint in the Early American Imprints Series. Further references to modern printings or reprintings are included in the "Works" or "Suggested Readings" sections of the entry as appropriate.

Biography: A brief summary of the salient features of the writer's life is included in the second section. In some instances, very little is known about the writer's biography, but in every instance, the entry provides an overview of the writer's life and social context within the limitations of present knowledge.

Critical Appraisal: The third section of the entry is devoted to a summary of the writer's work and a critical estimation of its value. Depending on the nature of the writing, the appraisal may place the writer's work into the context of intellectual, religious, social, or political history. This section of the entry is judgmental and offers opinions; however, an attempt has been made to present each writer in a positive light, without being misleadingly uncritical. Since a vast variety of writing is discussed in these volumes, the kinds of analyses made in the critical appraisals will necessarily vary. But in each case, the appraisal supplies a critical introduction to the writer and serves as a guide to further readings in the original texts.

Suggested Readings: The final section of each entry is devoted to a secondary bibliography. References to standard sources (such as the *Dictionary of American Biography* [DAB] and the *Dictionary of National Biography* [DNB]) are listed first in abbreviated form, followed by fuller references to other sources.

These suggested readings do not in any way pretend to be inclusive or exhaustive, and in the cases of major writers, they are highly selective. Their purpose is solely to direct the reader to sources that the authors of entries in these volumes found particularly useful or informative when they wrote their essays.

The entries in this book have been contributed by some 250 scholars of early American culture and literature. These volumes are thus a collective effort and do contain many voices and many points of view. The format has been designed to maintain a productive tension between the consistency of form required in a reference tool and the variety of content implicit in the individuality of the writers selected for inclusion and of the scholars who have interpreted and judged them.

James A. Levernier
Douglas R. Wilmes

Acknowledgments

In organizing and undertaking this project, we have incurred professional debts far too numerous to list in these acknowledgments. For their invaluable assistance in helping us review the entries to be included in these volumes and/or seek appropriate contributors, we are especially indebted to Ronald Bosco of the State University of New York at Albany; Hennig Cohen of the University of Pennsylvania; Michael Lofaro of the University of Tennessee; Pattie Cowell of Colorado State University; David S. Wilson of the University of California at Davis; Sacvan Bercovitch of Columbia University; Richard Beale Davis, late of the University of Tennessee; and Philip Barbour, late of the Early American Institute in Williamsburg, Virginia.

In addition, we wish to acknowledge a special debt of gratitude to the following individuals for their willingness to assume responsibilities well above and beyond the call of duty for entries that we requested them to research and write: Douglas M. Arnold of Yale University; Dorothy and Edmund Berkeley of Charlottesville, Virginia; Steven Kagle of Illinois State University; Daniel F. Littlefield, Jr., of Little Rock, Arkansas; Julian Mason of the University of North Carolina at Charlotte; David Minter of Emory University; Irving N. Rothman of the University of Houston; John Shields of Illinois State University; Frank Shuffelton of the University of Rochester; James Stephens of Marquette University; and Marion Barber Stowell of Milledgeville, Georgia.

We wish also to thank the editorial staff at Greenwood Press, particularly Cynthia Harris, Anne Kugielsky, Maureen Melino, Mildred Vasan, and James T. Sabin, for their strong commitment to this project, from its inception through to its publication, and for their patient and always helpful advice, commentary, and attention. In this capacity, we likewise wish to thank Mary DeVries for the painstaking attention she gave to copy-editing the completed manuscript. Our thanks also go to the many friends and colleagues, especially David Jauss, Mary De Jong, Frank Parks, Julian Wasserman, and Bruce Weigl, who gave us their tireless encouragement and support. To these individuals we owe an immeasurable debt; without their assistance and confidence we could not have completed this project.

In addition, we wish to thank the following institutions and their staffs for allowing us access to their resource materials and holdings: The Boston Public Library, The Newberry Library, and the libraries at Alliance College, Harvard University, Northwestern University, the Pennsylvania State University, Rice University, the University of Arkansas at Fayetteville, the University of Arkansas at Little Rock, the University of Connecticut, the University of Pennsylvania, Wesleyan University, Westminster College (New Wilmington, Pennsylvania), Yale University, and Youngstown State University. In this capacity, we wish to express particular gratitude to Shirley A. Snyder, librarian, and Eric R. Birdsall, associate director for academic affairs, both of the Pennsylvania State University, the Shenango Valley Campus.

Finally, we wish to thank the Donaghey Foundation and the faculty research committee at the University of Arkansas at Little Rock for a grant that helped defray expenses related to this project, and we wish to thank all of our contributors for their patience, cooperation, and support.

J.A.L. and D.R.W.

Abbreviations

STANDARD REFERENCE SOURCES

BDAS	Clark A. Elliott, *Biographical Dictionary of American Science: The Seventeenth Through the Nineteenth Centuries* (Westport, Conn., 1979).
CCMC	Frederick Lewis Weis, *The Colonial Churches and the Colonial Clergy of the Middle and Southern Colonies, 1607-1776* (Lancaster, Mass., 1938).
CCMDG	Frederick Lewis Weis, *The Colonial Clergy of Maryland, Delaware and Georgia* (Lancaster, Mass., 1950).
CCNE	Frederick Lewis Weis, *The Colonial Clergy and the Colonial Churches of New England* (Lancaster, Mass., 1936).
CCV	Frederick Lewis Weis, *The Colonial Clergy of Virginia, North Carolina and South Carolina* (Boston, Mass., 1955).
DAB	*Dictionary of American Biography*, ed. Allen Johnson and Dumas Malone, 20 vols. (New York, 1928-37; Seven Supplements, 1944-1965).
DARB	Henry Warner Bowden, *Dictionary of American Religious Biography* (Westport, Conn., 1977).
Dexter	Franklin Bowditch Dexter, *Biographical Sketches of the Graduates of Yale College*, 6 vols. (New York, 1885-1912).
DNB	*The Dictionary of National Biography*, ed. Leslie Stephen and Sidney Lee, 21 vols. and 1 supplement (London, 1882-1900; Six Supplements, 1901-1950).
FCNEV	Harold S. Jantz, *The First Century of New England Verse* (Worcester, Mass., 1944; 1962; 1974).

LHUS	*Literary History of the United States*, ed. Robert E. Spiller et al., 2 vols. (New York, 1948; 4th ed., 1974).
NAW	*Notable American Women, 1607-1950: A Biographical Dictionary*, ed. Edward T. James et al., 3 vols. (1971-1980).
P	*Princetonians: A Biographical Dictionary* (Vol. 1: *1748-1768*, ed. James McLachlan; Vol. 2: *1769-1775* and Vol. 3: 1776-1783, ed. Richard A. Harrison, Princeton, N.J.).
Sibley-Shipton	John L. Sibley and Clifford K. Shipton, *Biographical Sketches of Those Who Attended Harvard College* (Vols. 1-3: 1642-1689, Boston, Mass., 1873; Vols. 4-17: 1690-1771, Boston, Mass., 1933-1975).
Sprague	*Annals of the American Pulpit*, ed. William B. Sprague, 9 vols. (New York, 1857-1869; 1969).
T_1	Moses Coit Tyler, *A History of American Literature During the Colonial Period, 1607-1765*, 2 vols. (New York, 1878; 1897; 1898).
T_2	Moses Coit Tyler, *The Literary History of the American Revolution, 1763-1783*, 2 vols. (New York, 1897).

JOURNALS AND PERIODICALS

AC	*American Collector*
AEST	*American Ethnological Society Transactions*
AGR	*American German Review*
AH	*American Heritage*
AHAAR	*American Historical Association Annual Report*
AHR	*American Historical Review*
AJHQ	*American Jewish Historical Quarterly*
AJP	*American Journal of Physics*
AL	*American Literature*
AM	*Atlantic Monthly*
AMH	*Annals of Medical History*
AmR	*American Review*
APSR	*American Political Science Review*
AQ	*American Quarterly*
AS	*American Speech*
ASJ	*Alchemical Society Journal*
BB	*Bulletin of Bibliography*
BC	*Baptist Courier*
BEM	*Blackwood's Edinburgh Magazine*
BFHA	*Bulletin of the Friends' Historical Association*
BHM	*Bulletin of the History of Medicine*
BHSP	*Bulletin of the Historical Society of Pennsylvania*

Biblioteca	*Biblioteca Sacra*
BJHH	*Bulletin of the Johns Hopkins Hospital*
BNYPL	*Bulletin of the New York Public Library*
Bookman	*The Bookman*
BPLQ	*Boston Public Library Quarterly*
BQ	*Baptist Quarterly*
BrHP	*Branch Historical Papers*
BRPR	*Biblical Repertory and Princeton Review*
BSMHC	*Bulletin of the Society of Medical History of Chicago*
BSP	*Bostonian Society Publications*
BSPNEA	*Bulletin of the Society for the Preservation of New England Antiquities*
CanHR	*Canadian Historical Review*
CanL	*Canadian Literature*
CGHS	*Collections of the Georgia Historical Society*
CH	*Church History*
CHer	*Choir Herald*
CHR	*Catholic Historical Review*
CHSB	*Connecticut Historical Society Bulletin*
CHSC	*Connecticut Historical Society Collections*
CJ	*Classical Journal*
CLAJ	*College Language Association Journal*
CM	*The Connecticut Magazine*
CMaineHS	*Collections of the Maine Historical Society*
CMHS	*Collections of the Massachusetts Historical Society*
CNHamHS	*Collections of the New Hampshire Historical Society*
CNYHS	*Collections of the New York Historical Society*
CR	*Church Review*
CRevAS	*Canadian Review of American Studies*
CS	*Christian Spectator*
CUQ	*Columbia University Quarterly*
DAI	*Dissertation Abstracts International*
DalR	*Dalhousie Review*
DBR	*De Bow's Review*
DedHR	*Dedham Historical Review*
DiaN	*Dialect Notes*
DN	*Delaware Notes*
EAL	*Early American Literature*
ECS	*Eighteenth-Century Studies*
EIHC	*Essex Institute Historical Collections*
EN	*Essex Naturalist*
ES	*Economic Studies*
ESQ	*Emerson Society Quarterly*
ESRS	*Emporia State Research Studies*

EUQ	*Emory University Quarterly*
GHQ	*Georgia Historical Quarterly*
GHR	*Georgia Historical Review*
HER	*Harvard Educational Review*
HGM	*Harvard Graduates' Magazine*
Historian	*The Historian*
HL	*Historica Linguistica*
HLB	*Harvard Library Bulletin*
HLQ	*Huntington Library Quarterly*
HM	*The Historical Magazine*
HMagPEC	*Historical Magazine of the Protestant Episcopal Church*
HTR	*Harvard Theological Review*
HTS	*Harvard Theological Studies*
HudR	*Hudson Review*
HumLov	*Humanistica Lovaniensia: Journal of Neo-Latin Studies* (Louvain, Belgium)
IHSP	*Ipswich Historical Society Publications*
IUS	*Indiana University Studies*
JA	*Jahrbuch für Amerikastudien*
JAH	*Journal of American History*
JAmS	*Journal of American Studies*
JD	*Journal of Documentation*
JHI	*Journal of the History of Ideas*
JHS	*Johns Hopkins University Studies in History and Political Science*
JLH	*Journal of Library History*
JNH	*Journal of Negro History*
JPH	*Journal of Presbyterian History*
JPHS	*Journal of the Presbyterian Historical Society*
JQ	*Journalism Quarterly*
JR	*Journal of Religion*
JRUL	*Journal of the Rutgers University Library*
JSAH	*Journal of the Society of Architectural Historians*
JSBNH	*Journal of the Society for the Bibliography of Natural History*
JSCBHS	*Journal of the South Carolina Baptist Historical Society*
JSH	*Journal of Southern History*
JSR	*Jackson State Review* (Mississippi)
Judaism	*Judaism: A Quarterly Journal of Jewish Life and Thought*
LCR	*Lutheran Church Review*
MagA	*The Magazine of Art*
MagH	*Magazine of History*
MdHM	*Maryland Historical Magazine*
MH	*Methodist History*
MHSP	*Memoirs of the Historical Society of Pennsylvania*

MichH	*Michigan History*
MiH	*Minnesota History*
MLN	*Modern Language Notes*
MQ	*Mississippi Quarterly*
MR	*Massachusetts Review*
MusQ	*Musical Quarterly*
MVHR	*Mississippi Valley Historical Review*
Nation	*The Nation*
NCarF	*North Carolina Folklore*
NCF	*Nineteenth-Century Fiction*
NCHR	*North Carolina Historical Review*
NEG	*New England Galaxy*
NEHGR	*New England Historical and Genealogical Review*
NEM	*New England Magazine*
NEQ	*New England Quarterly*
NHB	*Negro History Bulletin*
NHR	*Narragansett Historical Review*
NJHSC	*New Jersey Historical Society Collections*
NJHSP	*New Jersey Historical Society Proceedings*
N&Q	*Notes and Queries*
NYGBR	*New York Genealogical and Biographical Review*
NYH	*New York History*
NYHSQ	*New York Historical Society Quarterly*
NYTBR	*New York Times Book Review*
OC	*Open Court*
OCHSC	*Old Colony Historical Society Collections*
OHSQ	*Oregon Historical Society Quarterly*
OntHSPR	*Ontario Historical Society Papers and Records*
PAAS	*Proceedings of the American Antiquarian Society*
PAH	*Perspectives in American History*
PAHS	*Papers of the Albemarle Historical Society*
PAJHS	*Publications of the American Jewish Historical Society*
PAPS	*Proceedings of the American Philosophical Society*
PBosS	*Proceedings of the Bostonian Society*
PBSA	*Papers of the Bibliographical Society of America*
PCSM	*Publications of the Colonial Society of Massachusetts*
PennH	*Pennsylvania History*
Phaedrus	*Phaedrus: An International Journal of Children's Literature Research*
Phylon	*Phylon: The Atlanta University Review of Race and Culture*
PIHS	*Publications of the Ipswich Historical Society*
PM	*Presbyterian Magazine*
PMHB	*Pennsylvania Magazine of History and Biography*
PMHS	*Proceedings of the Massachusetts Historical Society*

PMichA	*Papers of the Michigan Academy of Sciences, Arts, and Letters*
PMLA	*PMLA: Publications of the Modern Language Association of America*
PMPJ	*Philadelphia Medical and Physical Journal*
PNHCHS	*Papers of the New Haven Colony Historical Society*
PNYHS	*Proceedings of the New York Historical Society*
PQ	*Philological Quarterly*
PRev	*Princeton Review*
PSR	*Political Science Review*
PULC	*Princeton University Library Chronicle*
PWASA	*Proceedings of the Wisconsin Academy of Sciences and Arts*
PWHS	*Proceedings of the Wesley Historical Society*
QH	*Quaker History*
QMIMS	*Quarterly Magazine of the International Musical Society*
QQ	*Queen's Quarterly*
RACHSP	*Records of the American Catholic Historical Society of Philadelphia*
RALS	*Resources for American Literary Study*
RIH	*Rhode Island History*
RIHSC	*Rhode Island Historical Society Collections*
RP	*Register of Pennsylvania*
RS	*Research Studies* (Pullman, Washington)
RSCHS	*Records of the Scottish Church History Society*
SAQ	*South Atlantic Quarterly*
SatR	*Saturday Review*
SB	*Studies in Bibliography: Papers of the Bibliographical Society of the University of Virginia*
SCBHSP	*South Central Baptist Historical Society Proceedings*
SCHM	*South Carolina Historical Magazine*
SChR	*Scottish Church Review*
SCLR	*South Carolina Law Review*
SCM	*South Carolina Magazine*
SCN	*Seventeenth-Century Notes*
SEJ	*Southern Economic Journal*
Serif	*The Serif* (Kent, Ohio)
SF	*Social Forces*
Signs	*Signs: Journal of Women in Culture and Society*
SLitI	*Studies in the Literary Imagination*
SLJ	*Southern Literary Journal*
SLL	*Studies in Language and Literature*
SoPR	*Southern Presbyterian Review*
SP	*Studies in Philology*
SRC	*Studies in Religion and Culture*
SS	*Scandinavian Studies*

SSS	*Studies in the Social Sciences*
TA	*Theatre Annual*
TAAS	*Transactions of the American Antiquarian Society*
TAPS	*Transactions of the American Philosophical Society*
TCSM	*Transactions of the Colonial Society of Massachusetts*
TennSL	*Tennessee Studies in Literature*
ThS	*Theatre Survey*
TMHS	*Transactions of the Moravian Historical Society*
TQHGM	*Tyler's Quarterly Historical and Genealogical Magazine*
TR	*Texas Review*
TRSC	*Transactions of the Royal Society of Canada*
UCC	*University of California Chronicles*
UMS	*University of Missouri Studies*
USCHM	*United States Catholic Historical Magazine*
VC	*Virginia Cavalcade*
VELM	*Virginia Evangelical and Literary Magazine*
VMHB	*Virginia Magazine of History and Biography*
VMM	*Virginia Medical Monthly*
WHQ	*Western Historical Quarterly*
WL	*Woodstock Letters*
WMH	*Wisconsin Magazine of History*
WMQ	*William and Mary Quarterly*
WPHM	*Western Pennsylvania Historical Magazine*
YR	*Yale Review*
YULG	*Yale University Library Gazette*

Biographical and Critical Dictionary

G

CHRISTOPHER GADSDEN (1724-1805)

Works: *Observations on Two Campaigns Against the Cherokees* (1762); *Second Letter* (1762); essays number 5, 15, 17, *The Letters of Freeman, Etc.* (1771); *Few Observations* (1797); Richard Walsh, ed., *The Writings of Christopher Gadsden* (1966).

Biography: Christopher Gadsden was born in Charleston, S.C., on Feb. 16, 1724. After receiving his education in Eng., Gadsden clerked for a Philadelphia merchant and served in the royal navy. In the late 1740s, he returned to Charleston, where he established himself as a successful merchant and planter. In 1757 he was first elected to the Commons House of Assembly and within a few years became one of that body's most active and outspoken members. Although a member of Charleston's elite, Gadsden allied himself with the city's artisans and mechanics, who formed the core of the Revolutionary Sons of Liberty. Gadsden represented S.C. in the Stamp Act Congress and the First Continental Congress, and in 1780 he remained in Charleston when the government fled. As vice-president of the state, he was captured and later exiled and imprisoned in St. Augustine. Exchanged, he returned home but declined election as governor. Becoming less radical, he favored moderation and compassion in dealing with former Loyalists. This stance, coupled with his outspoken criticism of the Charleston mob, alienated his former supporters. Gadsden married three times: Jane Godfrey, Mary Hasell, and Ann Wragg. Following a fall near his home in Charleston, Christopher Gadsden died on Aug. 28, 1805.

Critical Appraisal: The published writings of Christopher Gadsden consist of three pamphlets and a number of newspaper essays. Most of his writings are political and resulted from controversies in which he was intimately involved. In 1756, for example, Gadsden became captain of a militia unit that eventually participated in the Cherokee campaigns of 1760 and 1761. Considerable ill will existed between the colonial troops commanded by Thomas Middleton and the British regulars commanded by James Grant. Upon the return of the expedition to Charleston, Grant made derogatory comments about the bravery and competence of the militia, and Gadsden responded with a spirited defense of the colonials in an essay signed "Philopatrios," which appeared first in the Dec. 18, 1761, issue of the *South-Carolina Gazette* and was later printed as a pamphlet titled *Observations on the Two Campaigns Against the Cherokee Indians*. About this time, Henry Laurens, a Charleston merchant, circulated a manuscript signed "Philolethes" that took strong exception to Gadsden's essay, and Gadsden responded with a second pamphlet, *Some Observations on the Two Campaigns . . . in a Second Letter*. As was his nature both in person and in prose, Gadsden not only defended the militia and Middleton but also made snide references about Laurens.

During 1762 Gadsden became embroiled in another controversy that once again resulted in his taking his view to press. When Governor Thomas Boone refused to administer the necessary oaths of office to Gadsden as a member of the Commons House of Assembly, the House protested the governor's violation of their rights and privileges and refused to attend to the business of the colony. As a result, government ground to a halt. Not all Carolinians, however, agreed with the actions of the Commons House. In an essay titled "To the Gentlemen Electors of The Parish of St. Paul, Stono," published in the Feb. 5, 1763, issue of the *South-Carolina Gazette*, Gadsden defended the actions of the Commons House and discussed the history of the elections laws in S.C., English precedents, and, significantly, the rights and liberties of English subjects.

In 1765, at Gadsden's urging, the Commons House sent three delegates, Gadsden among them, to the Stamp Act Congress. This experience had a strong impact on the future of Gadsden's thinking and writing, for after the 1765 meeting, he made frequent references not only to the rights of the colonists but also to the idea of "America": "There ought to be no New England man, no New Yorker, *etc*. . . but all of us Americans." In the decade between the Stamp Act Congress and the Revolution, he developed this attitude to the point where he viewed virtually every action of the British government with a "jaundiced eye," and he ably expressed his ideas in what are now regarded as his finest essays, those he composed during the Non-Importation Controversy of 1769.

In Jul. 1769 a Charleston committee agreed to establish a Non-Importation Association to protest the passage of the Townshend duties. William Henry Drayton (q.v.) and William Wragg, members of two of the colony's most prominent families, opposed the association as a violation of individual rights. The planter, John Mackenzie, and Gadsden defended the association, and the resulting debate in the *South-Carolina Gazette* was the liveliest since the controversies surrounding George Whitefield (q.v.) and the Great Awakening some thirty years earlier. In his three essays about the controversy, Gadsden proved a shrewd propagandist, one who could address himself to small farmers as well as planters and to merchants as well as mechanics. Throughout, he appealed to his fellow Carolinians for unity in the face of British tyranny: "And the present ministry have at last. . . brought us to such a pass, that, for the recovery of our most essential rights, we have nothing, absolutely nothing, left to depend upon, but our own union, prudence, and virtue."

The style and structure of these essays were more sophisticated and consequently more effective than those in his previous essays. Although Gadsden resorted to *ad hominem* attacks on Drayton and Wragg, his attacks were far more deft than those on Grant and Laurens and his education and careful reading habits more evident. Among the many writers and works that Gadsden used to advantage in these essays are Juvenal, Horace, and Cicero; Addison, Pope, and Swift; Richardson and Sterne; English law and precedent; and Scriptures. There was no question about who won the debate, for Drayton was so undone that he retired briefly to London, where he had the entire series of essays printed as *The Letters of Freeman, Etc.*

During the next twenty years, Gadsden published occasional essays in the Charleston papers. These essays indicated a growing conservatism and—as with all his writings—concerned actions in which he was a participant. Of particular note is a series of three essays that appeared in 1784 and were signed "A Steady and Open Republican." In these essays, Gadsden defended the state government against charges leveled by Alexander Gillon, who had succeeded Gadsden as the darling of the Charleston mob. By this time, Gadsden maintained that the threat to American liberties came not from tyrannical government but from the lawlessness that wracked Charleston and much of the state and that this lawlessness severely endangered republican institutions established during the Revolution.

Following the presidential election of 1796, Gadsden published yet another pamphlet, *A Few Observations on Some Late Public Transactions*, that in characteristic fashion he signed "A Steady Federalist." Although it supported the presidency of John Adams (q.v.), this pamphlet was written after the election and therefore was not campaign literature. After dismissing Thomas Paine (q.v.), whose *Common Sense* he had published in Charleston in 1776 in support of independence, as a man whose forte was "*pulling down*," Gadsden launched into an impassioned defense of the Constitution, which included warnings against the intrigues of foreigners (notably the French) who might want to interfere in the country's internal affairs and which concluded with a paragraph about his own role in the cause for independence. Although he openly supported candidates of the Federalist party (and was himself an elector for Adams in the 1800 election), Gadsden still considered himself a "true republican," one who supported the actions of the government "once constitutionally carried, whether by a single, or a number of votes." By the end of his career, S.C.'s hotspur of the Revolution had become a firm supporter of the establishment.

A Few Observations was followed three years later by three essays in support of the reelection of John Adams. In these and in *A Few Observations* Gadsden's style and method of making his point are similar to those in the *Freeman* essays. Like the latter, these are adroitly written and studded with references to Juvenal, Pope, and others. Following the election of 1800, Gadsden retired from public life, and his literary career came to a halt.

Christopher Gadsden wrote as he acted in politics. As one biographer explained, he was "a violent enthusiast in the cause," one of the "most determined leaders and tribunes of the people," and a "plain, blunt, hot and incorrect, though very sensible" debater.

Suggested Readings: DAB. *See also* Walter B. Edgar and N. Louise Bailey, *The Biographical Directory of the South Carolina House of Representatives* (1977), II, 259-263; Jack P. Greene, "The Gadsden Election Controversy and the Revolutionary Movement in South Carolina," MVHR, 46 (1959), 469-492; F. A. Porcher, *A Memoir of General Christopher Gadsden* (1878); Richard Walsh, *Charleston's Sons of Liberty* (1959), passim; Robert M. Weir, ed., *The Letters of Freeman, Etc.* (1977).

Walter B. Edgar
University of South Carolina

HUGH GAINE (1726-1807)

Works: *The New-York Mercury* (Aug. 3 or 8, 1752-Nov. 10, 1783); *The New-York Pocket Almanack* (by Theophilus Grew, 1755; by Poor Tom, 1756-1757; by Grew, 1758-1759); *The New-York Royal Sheet Almanack* (1759-1767); *Gaine's New Memorandum Book; or, The Merchant's and Tradesman's Daily Pocket Journal* (1774); *Gaine's Universal Register* (1775-1782, 1787, 1793); *Gaine's Universal Sheet Almanack* (1775, 1776, 1778, 1780, 1788-1790); *Gaine's Universal Register, or American and British Kalendar* (1777, 1780, 1781); *Gaine's Universal Register; or, Columbian Kalendar* (1786, 1791); *Journals* (edited and published posthumously in 1902).

Biography: Printer and almanac maker, Hugh Gaine was born in 1726 in Portglenone in the Parish of Ahoghill, Ire. At age 14, he was apprenticed for six years to Samuel Wilson and James Magee in Belfast at the Sign of the Crown and Bible. In 1744 he sailed for America and in 1745 became a journeyman for James Parker (q.v.) in New York City, where he worked until 1752. From 1753 until 1800, Gaine had his own printing company, the "Bible & Crown." When the British evacuated N.Y. in 1783, Gaine, who could switch his political allegiance at will, removed the crown and left only "the Bible." In 1759 he married Sarah Robbins, by whom he had two daughters and one son: Elizabeth (1761), John R. (1762), and Anne (1765). A second marriage, in 1769, to Mrs. Cornelia Wallace also produced two daughters, Cornelia A. and Sarah.

In 1768 Gaine became public printer for the province of N.Y. and printer to the city of New York. During the Revolution, Gaine was both Tory and Whig. Although self-interest clearly motivated his change in politics, his journal entries suggest that his later loyalty to the British was sincere. His newspaper, however, survived, no matter which side was in power. In 1773 Gaine became part owner in a paper mill. Although he gave up printing in 1800, he continued to operate his bookstore. A wealthy man when he died on Apr. 25, 1807, Hugh Gaine was buried at Trinity Church, where he had been a vestryman. He was also a Mason and a member of the St. Patrick Society (then Protestant).

Critical Appraisal: Hugh Gaine's most important publications were his almanacs and *The New-York Gazette; and the Weekly Mercury* (until 1768 called *The New-York Mercury*), published from 1752 to 1783. He printed every style of almanac: the broadside or sheet, the register, and the pocket almanac, in addition to a regular type of farmer's almanac by John Nathan Hutchins, Yale University professor, from 1755 to 1800, as well as a Low Dutch-language almanac in 1755 and 1775. The pocket almanacs were small reference works of, in one case, 84 pages (1775). His register for the same year had 168 pages and was chiefly a compendium of lists and tables.

An almanac printer was generally responsible for much of the miscellaneous content as well as the format. Gaine usually kept his varying political views out of his almanacs, but in the 1778 *Universal Register* he expressed surprise that any "thinking Mind" could consider that a "Parent State" that had "lavished...so much Expence upon its Provinces...should be desirous of their Destruction" and cited specific expense amounts as "An unequivocal Testimony of her Affection and Regard, and a full Refutation of the slandering Falsehoods of a licentious Congress!"

Gaine vacillated between Tory and Whig, though he printed nothing against the American cause in the beginning of the Revolution. His attempts to be impartial incurred the anger of the Whigs, but he was still in fairly good standing in 1775. In 1776, when finally forced to take a stand, he chose America. Before the British moved into N.Y., he moved part of his press to Newark, N.J., but returned after one and a half months when the American cause seemed doomed. He then printed pro-British material during the occupation. While in Newark, Gaine printed seven issues as a Whig; yet his regular newspaper in N.Y. (managed by Ambrose Serle) continued to appear as a Royalist organ under Sir William Howe's supervision.

Gaine's popular newspaper was printed for about thirty years. Because he was Anglican (rather than Presbyterian), Gaine was involved in religious as well as political conflicts, especially regarding the proposed King's College (later Columbia Univ.). He ably defended himself for publishing both sides of the controversy in the midfifties. Later, however, his bias surfaced as he printed only the Episcopalian side in another conflict between the two factions.

Daily during the Revolutionary years, Gaine made diary entries. These journals, published posthumously, show that he dealt mostly with trivia. The importance of the diaries is that they reveal much more information than was given to the public. For example, Gaine mentioned Burgoyne's surrender in his diary a month before he mentioned it in his newspaper, at which time he simply printed the articles of surrender without comment. He also noted other significant events regarding Gens. Burgoyne, Benedict Arnold (q.v.), and Cornwallis, while keeping his readers ignorant. In fact, his private comments sometimes contradicted the accounts he published in his newspapers. His journals, as records of war activities from Jan. 1757 through Dec. 1798, are extremely valuable. They include, among other information, comments on two years of the French and Indian War, five years of the Revolution, and two years of John Adams's (q.v.) presidency.

An amusing, rollicking, and ironical rhyme by Philip Freneau (q.v.) (first printed in 1783) has ensured Hugh Gaine's fame. Called "Hugh Gaine's Petition to the New York Assembly" (and also "Hugh Gaine's Life"), the rhyme satirizes Gaine's duplicity with an offer to turn against the British and return to the fold: "And I always adhere to the sword that is longest, / And stick to the party that's like to be strongest."

Suggested Readings: DAB; T₂. *See also* Clarence S. Brigham, "Bibliography of American Newspapers 1690-1820," PAAS, 27 (1917), 423, 456; Paul L. Ford, ed., *The Journals of Hugh Gaine*, 2 vols. in 1, biography and journals (c. 1902, 1970); A. L. Lorenz, *Hugh Gaine: A Colonial Printer-Editor's Odyssey to Loyalism* (1972), pp. xi, 5, 7, 24, 53-55, 127-130, 143-144; F. L. Patee, ed., *The Poems of Philip Freneau* (1902), II, 208.

Marion Barber Stowell
Milledgeville, Georgia

ALBERT GALLATIN (1761-1849)

Works: Reports, speeches, and so on in the Pa. House of Representatives, *Pennsylvania House Journal* (1790-1795); *Speech on the Validity of the Western Elections* (1795); speeches in U.S. House of Representatives, *Annals of Congress* (w. 1795-1801; pub. 1834); *A Sketch of the Finances of the United States* (1796); *Speech upon the Constitutional Powers of the House with Respect to Treaties* (1796); *An Examination of the Conduct of the Executive* (1797); "Autobiography, 1798," *Maine Historical Society Collections*, VI; *Speech upon the Foreign Intercourse Bill, 1st March, 1798* (1798); *The Speech of Albert Gallatin on the Alien and Sedition Laws* (1799); *Substance of Two Speeches on the Bill for Augmenting the Navy Establishment* (1799); *Views of the Public Debt* (1800); *Annual Reports of the Commissioners of the Sinking Fund* (1801-1813); *Annual Reports of the Secretary of the Treasury on the State of the Finances* (1801-1813); *Special Reports* and *Communications* of the secretary of the Treasury to Congress (1801-1813); "Letter to the *National Intelligencer*, dated 21st April, 1810," *National Intelligencer* (Jul. 18, 1810); "Speech at the Reception of La Fayette at Uniontown, Pa., 26th May 1825," *National Intelligencer* (Jun. 11, 1825); "Letter to S. D. Ingham, Secretary of the Treasury, on the Relative Value of Gold and Silver. 31st Dec. 1829," *Senate Documents, XXIst Congress, 1st Session*, II, no. 135 (1830); *Considerations on the Currency and Banking System of the United States* (1831). *American State Papers*, published by Gales and Seaton under authority of Congress, contain the following: "Campbell's Report, 22d Nov., 1808"; "Letter to D. M. Erskine, 13 Aug., 1809"; correspondence as commissioner for negotiating a treaty of peace with G.B., 1814; correspondence as commissioner for negotiating a treaty of commerce with G.B., 1815; correspondence while minister to Fr., 1816-1823; correspondence as joint commissioner with Mr. Rush to negotiate the treaties of 1818 with G.B.; correspondence while minister to Eng., 1826-1827 (all pub. 1832); *Memorial of the Committee Appointed by the "Free Trade Convention" Held in Philadelphia in September and October, 1831* (1832); *Report of the "Union Committee"* (with others; 1834); *Synopsis of the Indian Tribes within the United States East of the Rocky Mountains, and in the British and Russian Possessions in North America* (1836); "Letter to Leonard Maison on Restrictions upon Currency and Banking, 20th Dec., 1836," *New York Evening Post* (Jan. 13, 1837); *The Right of the United States of America to the North-Eastern Boundary Claimed by Them* (1840); *Suggestions on the Banks and Currency of the Several United States* (1841); "Inaugural Address Delivered Before the New York Historical Society, 7th Feb., 1843," PNYHS, (1843); "Memoir on the North-Eastern Boundary in Connection with Jay's Map," PNYHS (1843); "Letters to D. D. Field on the Treaty-making Power and the Admission of Texas. Dec. 17, 1844, and Feb. 10, 1845," *Niles's Register* (Dec. 28, 1844, and Mar. 15, 1845); "Letter to Commodore Stewart in Regard to His Comments on J. R. Ingersoll's *History of the War of 1812*, Oct. 16, 1845," *Niles's Register* (Dec. 20, 1845); "Letter to Edward Coles on Commodore Stewart's Publication and on the Naval Policy of President Madison and His Cabinet in 1812. 24th Nov., 1845," *Niles's Register* (Dec. 20, 1845); *Notes on the Semi-Civilized Nations of Mexico, Yucatan, and Central America* (1845); *The Oregon Question, with an Appendix on War Expenses* (1846); *Peace with Mexico* (1847); "Introduction to 'Hale's Indians of North-West America,' " AEST (1848); *War Expenses* (1848).

Biography: Abraham Alfonse Albert Gallatin was born in Geneva, Switz., on Jan. 29, 1761. His family, which had been among that city's ruling elite for more than two centuries, expected young Albert to conform, but he refused to perpetuate aristocratic tradition. Before graduation from the Geneva Academy in 1779, he had been attracted by Rousseau's arguments for freeing oneself from civilized conventions through a return to nature, which he attempted by journeying to America.

In Oct. 1781, after a year at Machias on the Maine frontier, Gallatin moved to Boston, where he began speculating in western lands and soon acquired title to 60,000 acres on the upper Ohio River. In 1784 he established his home, Friendship Hill, in western Pa.'s Fayette County. From there he launched his public career in Sept. 1788, serving as a delegate to the Harrisburg Convention and calling for drastic revision of the centralizing features of the new U.S. Constitution. The following year, he attended the convention to revise the Pa. constitution, and from 1790 to 1795, he was a representative to the state legislature.

With his election to the U.S. House of Representatives in 1794, Gallatin began a thirty-two-year national service career. In 1797 he became House minority leader. Specializing in national monetary and fiscal policy, he permanently revived the Ways and Means Committee to ensure that the secretary of the Treasury would remain strictly accountable to Congress. In 1801 President Thomas Jefferson (q.v.) appointed Gallatin secretary of the Treasury, and Gallatin served continuously in this position until 1813, when he traveled to St. Petersburg, where unsuccessful efforts were under way to secure Russian mediation in the War of 1812. In 1814 he became one of five U.S. commissioners at the Anglo-American peace negotiations in Ghent. The following year, he went to London to assist John Quincy Adams and Henry Clay in obtaining favorable commercial agreements with G.B. From 1816 to 1823, he was ambassador to Fr. In 1826 he returned to Eng. to negotiate continuing problems in Anglo-American trade, as well as U.S.-Can. boundary disputes.

Following his retirement from public service in 1827, Gallatin lived in New York City. In 1831 he began an eight-year term as president of the National Bank in N.Y. During the same year, he became a founder and the first president of the council of the University of the City of New York. In 1842 he founded and became first president of the American Ethnological Society, and the following year he was chosen president of the New York Historical Society. After a rather lengthy illness and the death of Hannah, his wife of fifty-five years, Gallatin passed away on Aug. 12, 1849, at his daughter Frances's Long Island country home.

Critical Appraisal: Albert Gallatin's early writings established his commitment to Jeffersonian Republicanism and demonstrated his marked analytical abilities. Both were evidenced in his *Speech on the Validity of the Western Elections* (1795) and *Speech upon the Foreign Intercourse Bill, 1st March, 1798*, in which he advocated the principle of strict construction with respect to the Pa. and U.S. Constitutions. In the earlier speech, he opposed a Pa. House resolution to void the 1794 election results in the state's western counties, site of the Whiskey Rebellion. Since the people had "not deemed it expedient to entrust either house with the power of judging" elections but had instead specified trial by a special committee, he reasoned that any attempt to employ the "theoretical doctrine of inherent power" to justify illegal legislative actions would agitate an undesirable and destructive "party spirit." In the Mar. 1798 speech, he favored reducing the size of the U.S. diplomatic corps through adjustments in congressional appropriations. Relying upon the concepts of separation and balance of powers, he emphasized the strict delineation and equal distribution between presidential power to appoint ambassadors and congressional power to appropriate funds for their salaries. Consequently, he labeled as novel and absurd the Adams administration's argument that any diplomatic appointment automatically required funding. He said that this argument, which rested upon executive usurpation of legislative power, would enhance presidential patronage powers at the expense of the public treasury, increase the risk of entangling foreign alliances, and certainly encourage a raging party spirit detrimental to the Union's stability.

Gallatin relied upon the long-recognized appeal of Whiggish conspiracy theories to discourage Americans' passive acceptance of growing executive power. In the 2nd edition of the *Speech upon the Foreign Intercourse Bill*, he denied being the "high priest of the constitution, assuming the keys of political salvation," but he reminded readers of Hampden's, Sydney's, and other early radical English Whigs' clarion calls for popular vigilance to preserve liberty. Earlier, in a sixteen-letter series titled *An Examination of the Conduct of the Executive* (1797), he had exhorted citizens to "have the torch of investigation ever in a blaze," lest foreign commitments in violation of existing treaty agreements lead to foreign war and loss of American liberty. Especially concerned about Francophobic sentiments, he chastised "Pacificus," Secretary of the Treasury Alexander Hamilton (q.v.), for displaying base "talents at riddle and perversion" and condemned other members of the Adams administration as an "insidious and ambitious group of pro-British stockjobbers, stockholders, bank directors and brokers." This particular "antidote" to the "circulating poison" of the Anglophiles belied the author's professed "dispassionate and unprejudiced" temper.

Gallatin's most important work before 1800 was *A Sketch of the Finances of the United States* (1796). In Mar. 1796, when concern over the national debt escalated, Jefferson had expressed the hope to James Madison (q.v.) that Gallatin might render the accounts of the U.S. "as simple as those of a common farmer, and capable of being understood by common farmers." By Nov. 1796 Gallatin had produced a very thorough, highly analytical critique of Federalist financial practices. Relying heavily upon the definitional and conceptual work in Adam Smith's *Wealth of Nations* but applying them carefully to America's unique circumstances, the emergent wizard of Jeffersonian finance castigated the Federalists for overspending on frontier defense, naval armaments, and suppression of the Whiskey Rebellion. That, as well as wholesale adoption of Hamilton's debt assumption and funding programs, had caused the government to incur expenses at a much faster rate than it accumulated revenues; the obvious result was a rapidly increasing national debt. He convincingly demonstrated that foreign loans, secured at exorbitant and uncertain interest rates, compounded the nation's financial malaise when used for extravagant consumption rather than capital improvements. The author saw the solution in frugality coupled with a new, direct tax on land to increase federal revenues. Read in its entirety, the *Sketch of the Finances of the United States* affords an excellent example of the statistical mode of expression that became increasingly popular in discussions and assessments of national vitality after the American Revolution.

Gallatin's briefer pamphlet, *Views of the Public Debt* (1800), offered fewer statistics than the *Sketch of the Finances* but was technically superb propaganda. Appearing in Jul. 1800, for the purpose of influencing the upcoming national elections, *Views of the Public Debt* charged the Federalists with covering up their mismanagement of public finances through fallacious methods. Although its author termed the pamphlet "a hasty production...imperfect in its general arrangement," the Jeffersonian press delighted in its timeliness.

Throughout his career, Gallatin championed the notion of a carefully regulated national banking system. In *A Sketch of the Finances*, he labeled the bank a useful and necessary institution for moderately increasing the rate of monetary circulation and simultaneously reducing the national debt. But he also believed that the Federalists had turned the bank into a "political engine" from which the government borrowed too freely and for which private citizens paid dearly. By 1830 his experiences while ambassador to Fr. had convinced him that bimetallism (free circulation of gold and silver) furnished the key to American as well as French monetary stability and that a national banking system provided the best means for accomplishing free circulation. He presented this viewpoint on "Banks and Currency" in the Dec. 1830 *American Quarterly Review*, which was reprinted with additions as *Considerations on the Currency and Banking System of the United States* in Feb., 1831. His subsequent *Suggestions on the Banks and Currency of the Several United States* (1841) presented a detailed description of the banking crises of the late 1830s and a lucid explanation of causes, effects, and cures. Through scrupulous application of Adam Smith's "sound principles," the ideas of Jean Baptiste Say, and careful observations on America's unique circumstances, Gallatin established his place among the founders of American economic thought.

Gallatin advocated laissez faire commercial principles in his *Memorial of the Committee Appointed by the "Free Trade Convention" Held in Philadelphia in September and October, 1831* (1832). His opposition therein to the high protective tariff of 1828 marked the first consequential challenge to Henry Clay's American system and prompted Clay to condemn Gallatin for being an alien at heart. Of course he was not, and, as secretary of the Treasury, he had created the base for another pillar of Clay's American system with the noteworthy *Special Report on Internal Improvements (Roads and Canals)* in 1808. That work determined the parameters of the debate on national transportation policy well into the 1830s.

By the 1840s his extensive diplomatic experience entitled Gallatin to a role as political oracle on foreign policy problems. As such, he consistently opposed "calamitous and expensive" military solutions to border disputes, because they drained the public treasury without generating commensurate rewards and threatened the purity of America's world mission. That position underlay *The Right of the United States of America to the North-Eastern Boundary Claimed by Them* (1840). It was reiterated in his four essays during 1846 on *The Oregon Question*, in which he accused President Polk of courting war with G. B. by abrogating treaty provisions in a fit of passionate impatience. In the 1847 essay on *Peace with Mexico*, he condemned the U.S. for waging an unjust, aggressive, and "lamentable war," which ignored our providential role as a model Republic with unsurpassed intellectual and moral energies. These works amply demonstrated his superb ability to weave cold statistics and a heated sense of justice into convincing expositions.

Gallatin believed he lacked talent to achieve a lasting place in American letters and science. In 1842 he informed a correspondent, "All my writings... adhere to my political career and have only a local and transitory importance." One recent biographer assessed his writing style as "informed, lucid, never felicitous." Despite his handicap on the latter score, his study of American Indians led to publication of several widely acclaimed surveys. When the first of these, *A Synopsis of the Indian Tribes Within the United States East of the Rocky Mountains*, appeared in Nov. 1836, historian George Bancroft told the author, "You are our guide and teacher." The massive 422-page tome contained ethnological data on eighty-one tribes with technical analysis, including detailed grammatical tables, of their languages. In 1849 Edward Everett Hale praised it as "the most valuable treatise which has been attempted on the Indian language of the continent." The sequel, *Notes on the Semi-Civilized Nations of Mexico, Yucatan, and Central America* (1845), prompted European scholars to remark that Gallatin had "added something to the literary reputation" of the U.S. In each of his scientific studies, he relied heavily on a clearly conceived comparative methodology, which set a valuable precedent for future ethnologists. Long after his death, he continued to draw praise for his anthropological contributions, as evidenced by John Wesley Powell's statement in 1886: "As Linnaeus is to be regarded as the founder of biologic classification, so Gallatin may be considered the founder of systematic philology relating to the North American Indians." Nearly a century after Gallatin's passing, anthropologist Clark Wissler mused, "All subsequent papers have done no more than elaborate his statements, usually without recognizing his claim to priority for the first comprehensive statement." Most assuredly, Gallatin had a far more significant and enduring impact upon American scholarship than he imagined.

Suggested Readings: DAB; LHUS. *See also* Henry Adams, ed., *The Writings of Albert Gallatin*, 3 vols. (1879); idem, *The Life of Albert Gallatin* (1879); Alexander Balinky, *Albert Gallatin: Fiscal Theories and Policies* (1958); E. James Ferguson, ed., *Selected Writings of Albert Gallatin* (1967); James Gallatin, *The Diary of James Gallatin, Secretary to Albert Gallatin, a Great Peace Maker, 1813-1827* (1916); Frederick Merk, *Albert Gallatin and the Oregon Problem* (1950); John Austin Stevens, *Albert Gallatin* (1884); Gayle Thornbrough, ed., *The Correspondence of John Badollet and Albert Gallatin, 1804-1836* (1963); Raymond Walters, Jr., *Albert Gallatin: Jeffersonian Financier and Diplomat* (1957, 1969); George Washington Ward, *The Early Development of the Chesapeake and Ohio Canal Project* (1899), pp. 19-30, contains a discussion of Gallatin's ideas on internal improvements of roads and canals.

Rick W. Sturdevant
University of California, Santa Barbara

JOSEPH GALLOWAY (c. 1731-1803)

Works: *To the Public* (1764); *Die Rede* (1764); *The Speech of...* (1764); *Advertisement* (1765); *A Receipt to Make a Speech* (1766); *A Candid Examina-*

tion of the Mutual Claims of Great Britain and the Colonies (1775); *A Reply to an Address* (1775); *The Examination of Joseph Galloway, Esq.* (1779); *A Letter to the Rt. Honourable Viscount H—e* (1779); Letters to a Nobleman on the Conduct of the War in the Middle Colonies (1779); *Cool Thoughts on the Consequences to Great Britain of American Independence* (1780); *Historical and Political Reflections on the Rise and Progress of the American Rebellion* (1780); *Observations on the Fifth Article of the Treaty with America* (1783); *The Claim of the American Loyalists Reviewed and Maintained* (1788); *A Short History of the War in America* (1788); *Brief Commentaries upon...Revelation and other Prophecies* (1802); *The Prophetic...History of the Church of Rome* (1803).

Biography: Joseph Galloway—lawyer, colonial statesman, and British Loyalist—was born sometime around 1731 near West River, Anne Arundel County, in Md., into a family of well-known merchants who also owned large estates in Pa. Shortly after his father's death during the mid-1730s, Galloway moved to Philadelphia, Pa., where he eventually became a lawyer, rising to eminence while still relatively young. In Oct. 1753 Galloway married the daughter of Lawrence Growden, one of the richest and most influential men in the province, but despite the wealth his marriage brought him, he sought political office for the additional power and influence it would provide. In 1756 Galloway was elected to the Pa. Assembly, where, with the exception of the 1764 session, he held office until 1776, when he fell from favor at the outbreak of the Revolutionary War. As a member of the Assembly, Galloway participated in prosecuting the war against Fr. In May 1764 both he and Benjamin Franklin (q.v.) petitioned the crown to substitute royal control for proprietary government in Pa. The petition failed, contributing significantly to the defeat of both men in the 1764 Assembly elections.

From 1766 to 1775, however, Galloway was annually elected to the speakership, and in his additional role as chairman of the Assembly's committee to correspond with the agents of the colony in London, he helped restore harmony, for a time, between Britain and the colonies. Although he understood the Crown's need to derive revenues from the colonies, Galloway disapproved of parliamentary taxation and of burdensome restrictions on American commerce. In 1774 Galloway was selected a delegate from Pa. to the First Continental Congress, where his major contribution was a plan for an imperial legislature designed to provide the British Empire with a written constitution. Although the Congress voted six states to five to postpone consideration of Galloway's Plan of Union, the narrow margin was misleading, for the proposal was too impractical ever to adopt. Subsequent to this reversal, Galloway's political base rapidly eroded: the Pa. legislators removed Galloway from the speakership, and the congressional delegates expunged his Plan of Union from the *Congressional Journal*.

In defense of himself and his plan, Galloway published *A Candid Examination of the Mutual Claims of Great Britain and the Colonies* (1775), which severely arraigned the First Congress and further eroded Galloway's popularity. Finally, when Galloway refused to recognize the Second Congress, he was forced to flee

Philadelphia for the safety of his country estate. In 1776 Galloway accepted a proclamation of indemnity from Gen. William Howe, and he joined Howe's army. Following upon the capture of Philadelphia by British forces in Sept. of 1777, he was appointed magistrate of police and superintendent of the Port. Upon recapture of the city by Continental troops in 1778, he fled with his daughter to Eng., where he quickly became a principal spokesman for the American Loyalists and their interests. In 1779 Galloway testified before Parliament on the conduct of the war, and he arraigned the Howes, both in this forum and in print, for their general incompetence. As a result, Galloway's estates in America were confiscated, and he became dependent upon a pension from the British government. In 1793 he petitioned the Pa. authorities for permission to return to the colony but was refused. After twenty-five years of exile, Galloway died in Eng. at Watford, Hertfordshire, on Aug. 29, 1803.

    Critical Appraisal: Joseph Galloway's published works reflect his professional concerns. Until 1766 Galloway's public career was that of lawyer and politician, but following the reorganization of G.B.'s colonial system, Galloway assumed the role of an imperial spokesman. In this capacity, he guarded colonial rights of self-government, while simultaneously sympathizing with significant strands of British imperial thought. Although he disapproved of parliamentary taxation, for example, he never questioned the right of Parliament to govern the colonies, steadfastly believing that the conflict between the two powers was essentially constitutional and strongly advocating a written empirewide constitution as a solution.

    At the time of the First Continental Congress of 1774, Galloway still favored direct American representation in the British Parliament, but he realized that such a plan was generally impractical. The central part of Galloway's Plan of Union provided for a subsidiary American legislature with concurrent powers with Parliament over American affairs. Viewed in the abstract, Galloway's plan for reconciliation and union between G.B. and the colonies is not unimpressive in the reasoned argument it makes. Nevertheless, a fundamental flaw resides in Galloway's purely constitutional definition of the conflict between Britain and the colonies, for he apparently conceived of the Continental Congress as fundamentally a constitutional convention. In fact, however, it was an assembly of desperate urgency, which had been assembled to deal with what most delegates considered foreign invasion—the presence of British troops in Boston. Galloway's seeming blindness to the felt urgency of the situation was a radical weakness of his presentation, and when the Congress voted to expunge all reference to Galloway's plan from its minutes, the best chance for a negotiated settlement of the conflict was eliminated.

    In his *Candid Examination of the Mutual Claims of Great Britain and the Colonies*, published in 1775 after Galloway refused to participate in the Second Congress, Galloway distinguished between justifiable and unjustifiable resistance to G.B. As his argument develops, the presentation also becomes an *apologia* for Galloway's own activities. He argued, for example, that although the convening of a congress was justified, the actual assembly had failed in its legitimate purpose: the drafting of an equitable constitutional settlement. As a consequence of this failure, the individual colonies must, according to Galloway, renounce the Congress and its promulgations to negotiate with G.B. for settlement of their differences. He concluded this work by advocating that the individual colonies dissolve the Revolutionary committees and dismantle the government framework erected by the First Congress.

Galloway's subsequent tenure as civil administrator in Philadelphia under the protection of Gen. Howe's occupying army proved short-lived. Upon his flight to Eng., he was called to testify before Parliament on the ill-fated British conduct of the war (*The Examination of Joseph Galloway Before the House of Commons*, 1779), and he published pamphlets representative of American Loyalist sentiment against the Howes and what the Loyalists viewed as grossly incompetent prosecution of the war. Even in exile, Galloway persisted in his attempt to achieve reconciliation of the conflict on the basis of a written constitution between the two warring parties, setting forth his views in two works published in 1780: *Historical and Political Reflections on the Rise and Progress of the American Rebellion* and *Cool Thoughts on the Consequences to Great Britain of American Independence*.

In the last decade of his life, Galloway became increasingly interested in religion, most especially in the biblical prophecies, and he published two elaborate volumes that put forth his views of two matters he had come to seek as interlinked: The Book of Revelation and that work's prophetic foretelling of the rise of Roman Catholicism.

Suggested Readings: DAB; DNB; LHUS; T$_2$. *See also* Julian P. Boyd, *Anglo-American Union: Joseph Galloway's Plans to Preserve the British Empire* (1941); Robert M. Calhoon, *The Loyalists in Revolutionary America: 1760-1781* (1973), pp. 85-89, 391-396, 481-482; Oliver C. Kuntzleman, *Joseph Galloway, Loyalist* (1941); William H. Nelson, *The American Tory* (1961), pp. 8-10, 46-48, 50-69, 135-139, 177-179.

Robert Colbert
Louisiana State University in Shreveport

ALEXANDER GARDEN (c. 1685-1756)

Works: *Regeneration* (1740); *Six Letters to the Rev. George Whitefield* (1740); *Take Heed How Ye Hear* (1741); *The Doctrine of Justification* (1742); *A Brief Account of the Deluded Dutartres* (1762).

Biography: Alexander Garden was born in Scot. sometime around 1685. After attending Aberdeen University, he served as curate of the Barking Church in Eng. In 1720 Garden appeared in Charleston, S.C., where he began work at St. Philip's Church. However, owing to the anticlericalism associated with the 1719 overthrow of proprietary government, Garden was not elected rector of St.

Philip's until 1725. In 1729 Garden was appointed the bishop of London's commissary for the Anglican Church in S.C., an office he held until 1748. As commissary, Garden played an important role in strengthening the Church of England in S.C. He convened an ecclesiastical court that suspended one clergyman guilty of drunkenness, and in less formal ways, he exercised a salutary discipline. Although earlier commissaries had fought against the power of the Anglican laity and the privileges of the dissenters, Garden accepted the particular nature of the established church in S.C. and helped it become an indigenous institution. Garden's greatest challenge, however, came during the Great Awakening, when George Whitefield (q.v.) won the support of both dissenters and Anglicans in S.C. During the ensuing controversy, Garden successfully attempted to discipline Whitefield through an ecclesiastical court, and he attacked Whitefield in both the *South Carolina Gazette* and published sermons. When he retired in 1753, Garden was thoroughly respected and loved. He died in Charleston on Sept. 27, 1756, at age 71.

Critical Appraisal: The literary reputation of Alexander Garden rests on materials he published during the Great Awakening to weaken the appeal of George Whitefield's contention that the Church of England preached salvation through good works rather than through faith. In *Six Letters* Garden responded that although the cause of salvation was faith, faith had to be "true and lively," for only a "true and lively" faith could produce "good Fruits or Works," which were the "necessary *Condition*" of justification. In addition, Whitefield challenged the authority of southern Anglicans by claiming that a spiritual deadness permeated the South and was evident in the harsh treatment of slaves, their refusal to convert to Christianity, recent epidemics, and a slave rebellion. To counter Whitefield, Garden noted that although no workable method of instruction had yet been found, the Church of England advocated the education and baptism of slaves. Garden also defended the planters: "The Generality of Owners use their Slaves with all due Humanity, whether in respect of *Work*, of *Food*, or *Raiment*."

In the prolonged debate over predestination, original sin, and the nature of salvation sparked by Whitefield's Calvinism, Garden played a leading role. Probably "Arminius," the author of a series of articles in the *South Carolina Gazette* on the Anglican view of the debate, Garden also published several sermons under the collective title of *Regeneration*, in which he used the Bible, Anglican doctrine, and common sense to justify the Arminian position of good works. When Garden's works were reprinted in Boston and Andrew Croswell of Conn. published an attack on his views, Garden responded with *The Doctrine of Justification*, in which he took up Croswell's strictures one by one and thereby carried the debate with Whitefield beyond the South to New Eng.

Even more important than Garden's theology was his attack on the emotion of the Great Awakening. In the preface to *Regeneration*, Garden asserted that the excitement of the revivals stemmed less from divine grace than from Whitefield's voice, "that enchanting Sound, the natural and a lone Cause" of "all the

Passion and Prejudice, that prevailed 'mong some (the *weaker* some indeed)."
Garden's sermon, *Take Heed How Ye Hear*, explicitly attacked excessive emotion or enthusiasm. Enthusiasm, according to Garden, was evidenced by "itching
of ears," which led people to new preachers, hoping to "hear Things that will
rouse their Passions, as Children do Stories of Ghosts and goblins." After he
mentioned historical instances of enthusiasm, Garden illustrated the dangers of
emotional excess with an account of the Dutartre family of S.C., an incident that
had created a sensation in 1724. Stimulated by the doctrines of an itinerant
preacher from Europe, this improvident French family of eight children and
several in-laws believed itself chosen by God as Noah had been. One of them
claimed to be a prophet and convinced the family he was divinely ordered to
leave his wife and cohabit with her younger, virginal sister. Refusing to recognize civil authority, the Dutartres eventually clashed with the law, killed a peace
official, and were jailed. Three of them went to the gallows, predicting until the
last their resurrection in three days.

Although his published writings are polemical, occasionally bitter, but always
clearly written and logically argued, Garden was one of the more effective
opponents of the Great Awakening, and although he broke no new theological
ground, he defended Anglican doctrines ably, particularly when he drew on his
own experience, as in the case of the Dutartres materials.

Suggested Readings: CCV; LHUS; Sprague (II, 39-43); T₁. *See also* Sidney
Charles Bolton, "The Anglican Church of Colonial South Carolina: A Study in Americani-
zation" (Ph.D. diss., Univ. of Wis., 1973), chs. vi-vii; Richard Beale Davis, *Intellectual
Life in the Colonial South, 1585-1763* (1978), II, 710-711, 755-756; Alan E. Heimert,
Religion and the American Mind (1966) pp. 20, 35-37, 92, 167, 393; Quentin Begley
Keen, "The Problems of a Commissary: The Reverend Alexander Garden of South
Carolina," HMag., PEC, 20 (1951), 136-155.

S. Charles Bolton
University of Arkansas at Little Rock

DR. ALEXANDER GARDEN (1730-1791)

Works: "An Account of the Gymnotus Electricus," *Transactions of the Royal
Society of London* (1775), LXV, 102-110; "An Account of the Indian Pink,"
Essays and Observations, Physical and Literary (1771), III, 145-153; William
Darlington, ed., *Memorials of John Bartram and Humphry Marshall* [Garden's
letters to and from John Bartram] (1849), pp. 390-400; "The Description of a
New Plant," *Essays and Observations, Physical and Literary* (1756), II, 1-7;
James Edward Smith, ed., *A Selection of the Correspondence of Linnaeus* [Gar-
den's letters to Linnaeus and John Ellis] (1821), I, 282-605.

Biography: Dr. Alexander Garden was the son of the Church of Scotland
minister of the parish of Birse near Aberdeen. He served a medical apprentice-

ship while attending Marischal College and spent two years as a surgeon's mate in the royal navy. After a year at the University of Edinburgh, he immigrated to S.C. in 1752, practicing first outside Charleston and later becoming one of that city's most popular doctors.

He was not content with confining his interests to medicine, but examined his new environment methodically, sending his observations to two of his Edinburgh professors. Having received no encouragement from them and finding little local interest in such matters, he wrote to Dr. John Huxham, the Reverend Stephen Hales, and William Shipley in Eng. In 1754 Garden spent several weeks in the north for his health. There he met others interested in natural history: Cadwallader Colden (q.v.) and his daughter Jane, in N.Y., and John Bartram (q.v.) and Benjamin Franklin (q.v.) in Philadelphia. Returning home, he found letters from John Ellis and Henry Baker in Eng., soliciting his correspondence. He wrote to them as well as to his new northern friends and John Clayton (q.v.) in Va. While in the north, he had read letters to his friends from J. F. Gronovius in Holland and Carolus Linnaeus in Swed., and he wrote to the two Europeans as well. His studies were not confined to botany but included zoology, climatology, and mineralogy. He supplied Linnaeus with eighty-seven fish specimens, forty of which were mentioned by the latter as either types or cotypes. He sent several amphibians, sixteen snakes, and a number of insects, all of which were included in various editions of the *Systema Naturae*. A grateful Linnaeus named the *Gardenia* in the doctor's honor and saw to his election to the Royal Society of Arts and Sciences at Upsala. Garden was the first corresponding member of London's Royal Society of Arts and subsequently was elected to the American Philosophical Society, the Royal Society of London, and the Royal Society of Edinburgh. He returned to Eng. after the Revolution when all Loyalist sympathizers were forced to leave Charleston. Little is known of the remaining years of his life other than his appearances before the Loyalists' Commission in an attempt to receive compensation for his lost property in S.C. and his attendance at many meetings of the Royal Society.

Critical Appraisal: Garden's publications were few, the major portion being his letters appearing in the *Correspondence of Linnaeus*. His facility in writing and excellent education exhibited in them suggest how unfortunate it was that he did not write more for publication. This is particularly well demonstrated in his lengthy description of S.C. windstorms included in the *Supplement* to Thomas Pennant's *Arctic Zoology* (1784, II, 41-44). In this work, Garden's meticulous choice of words and detailed attention to minor incidents engender in the reader a breathless feeling of suspense and horror.

The majority of Garden's letters to Linnaeus were in Latin and consequently formal and dependent upon the translator for style. Typical of the times, they are replete with Classical allusions and excessive courtesy. In spite of this, Garden did not refrain from argument on scientific points as he addressed "the favoured priest of Nature," and his later letters are full of discussion and description of the specimens that he was sending.

His letters to Ellis are more relaxed and entertaining and even sometimes a bit presumptuous as when Garden went so far as to inquire what specifications the Royal Society required for new members. His criticism of others could be caustic, as it was of Mark Catesby (q.v.) and Sir Hans Sloane, for example. Garden was a perfectionist and very intolerant of what he considered careless work. He did not hesitate to test his theories of natural phenomena on Ellis as he felt isolated from the intellectual world and dependent upon books and correspondents as stimuli to his spirit of inquiry. His attitude toward many Carolinians, his frustration at the confines of his life, and his sense of humor are all apparent in a note to Bartram, who was then exploring Florida: "Think that I am here, confined to the sandy streets of Charleston, where the ox, where the ass, and where men as stupid as either, fill up the vacant space, while you range the green fields of Florida." Garden's letters make absorbing reading as they range from science in general to shrewd analyses of Indian character and behavior, discussion of French strategy, promotion of a friend's poetry, and a detailed account of John Bartram's visit. Altogether, they give an excellent picture of the scientific community in G.B.'s colonies as well as the relationship between them and European scientists.

Suggested Readings: BDAS; DAB; T₁. *See also* Edmund Berkeley and Dorothy Smith Berkeley, *Dr. Alexander Garden of Charles Town* (1969); Richard Beale Davis, *Intellectual Life in the Colonial South, 1585-1763* (1978), II, 861-864; Raymond Phineas Stearns, *Science in the British Colonies* (1970), pp. 599-619; Dr. Joseph Ioor Waring, *A History of Medicine in South Carolina, 1670-1825* (1964), pp. 221-235.

Dorothy Smith Berkeley
Edmund Berkeley
Charlottesville, Virginia

LION GARDINER (1599-1663)

Works: "Leift Lion Gardener His Relation of the Pequot Warres" (w. 1660; pub. in CMHS, 3rd ser., 3 [1833], 131-160).

Biography: Lion Gardiner (also spelled *Gardener* and *Gardner*) was born in Eng. in 1599. Like many enterprizing young men of his day, he sought his fortune in the Neth., where he served in the military under Sir Thomas Fairfax. According to his own account, Gardiner was working in "the Low Countries" as "Engineer and Master of works of Fortification" when in 1635 he was persuaded by John Davenport (q.v.) and Hugh Peters (q.v.), who were acting in the interests of the Conn. patentees, to come to New Eng. and assist "in the drawing, ordering and making of a city, towns or forts of defence." To aid him in this task, Gardiner was to receive the help of "300 able men" and to be paid 100 pounds a year.

Having accepted this offer, Gardiner and his wife, Mary (Wilemson) Gardiner, set sail from Holland to Eng., and then from Eng. to Boston, where they arrived in Nov. of 1635. Under the supervision of John Winthrop, Jr. (q.v.), Gardiner took his wife to the mouth of the Connecticut River, where he later directed the building of the fort at Saybrook. Gardiner soon discovered, however, that life in New Eng. was not what it had been presented to be. Help from Boston was not forthcoming, and he was left to defend Saybrook from hostile natives with only a few men and scant provisions. To make matters worse, the government of the Bay Colony sent John Endecott on an unsuccessful mission to destroy the Pequot Indians. Instead of subduing the Indians, Endecott only antagonized them. Enraged at all Englishmen, the Pequots began indiscriminate warfare on the English settlers of the region, and during one of their raids, Gardiner himself was severely wounded.

The entire conflict came to a bloody climax in May of 1637, when John Mason (q.v.), after joining forces at Saybrook with John Underhill (q.v.), attacked and then butchered the Indian inhabitants of a Pequot fortification at Mystic. Although he counselled against war with the Pequots, Gardiner is said to have helped plan Mason's victory, and when Mason returned in triumph to Saybrook, Gardiner welcomed him "with many great Guns" and "many Courtesies." After the War, Gardiner purchased the Isle of Wight (known as Gardiner's Island), where he lived with his family until 1753, when he removed to Long Island. A trusted friend of the "great Sachem" Wyandanch, Gardiner was influential in maintaining peaceful relations between the Indians and whites of the area, and had his Indian policies been followed by the authorities of New Eng., King Philip's War might very well have been averted.

Lion Gardiner died in Long Island in the latter part of 1663. In addition to his exploits as an Indian fighter and negotiator, he is credited with having founded the first permanent British settlement in the state of N.Y. His son David (born at Saybrook in 1636) was probably the first British child born in Conn., and his daughter Elizabeth (born on Gardiner's Island in 1641) was probably the first British child born in New York.

Critical Appraisal: Lion Gardiner's "Relation of the Pequot Warres" has the distinction of being one of only four contemporary accounts of the first major conflict between the Indians and the British in New Eng. The other three extant narratives of the war are John Underhill's *Newes from America*, Philip Vincent's (q.v.) *A True Relation of the Late Battell Fought in New-England*, and John Mason's *Brief History of the Pequot War*. Unlike these other narratives, which saw publication during the seventeenth century, Gardiner's "Relation" remained in manuscript until the nineteenth century when it was published by the Massachusetts Historical Society. The exact reasons why the "Relation" was never published along with the other accounts remain uncertain, but they may very well center around the fact that Gardiner was quite forthright in blaming the causes of the Pequot conflict as much on the deliberate provocations of the British as on the hostility of the Pequots. In a prefatory letter published along with the "Relation," Gardiner describes his narrative as "a piece of timber scored and forehewed" but in need of "somebody to chip it and smooth it lest the splinters should prick some men's fingers." He also comments that although to the best of his knowledge he has "written nothing but the truth," the truth "must not be spoken at all times," and he counsels that before his manuscript becomes public it should perhaps be shown to John Winthrop, Jr., and to Major Mason for their approval and corrections. On the basis of evidence such as this, it has been suggested that Gardiner's version of the war may have been deliberately suppressed, perhaps even by Winthrop or Mason, both of whom had profited politically from the uprising.

Although he states that he wrote his "Relation" to illustrate "the passages of God's Providence at Seabrooke in and about the time of the Pequit War" and to leave posterity with his version of what actually happened during the war, Gardiner's narrative is above all the memoirs of an old soldier reminiscing with bluntness, candor, nostalgia, humor, and not a little regret on the historical events that he witnessed and helped to shape. Moving easily from the practical to the philosophical to the spiritual, Gardiner emerges as an individual who gained wisdom from life and who wished to give that wisdom to others. Unlike Mason, Gardiner takes little delight in the glories of war. He believed that the war was fought for "the glory of God, and honour of our nation," but he remained horrified at its waste and destructiveness: "I think the soil hath almost infected me...I hope I shall not live so long..., for I am old and out of date."

Instead of seeking out conflict, Gardiner avoided it whenever possible. He was, for instance, extremely irritated at John Endecott's bold and heartless Indian policies: "You come hither to raise these wasps about my ears, and then you will take wing and flee away." His main goal was to die peacefully and with dignity:

> And now I am old, I would fain die a natural death, or like a soldier in the field, with honor, and not to have a sharp stake set in the ground, and thrust into my fundament, and to have my skin slayed off by piece-meal, and cut in pieces and bits, and my flesh roasted and thrust down my throat.

And he was by no means incapable of noting the various ironies which sometimes determine history. He records, for example, that unlike the English, the Indians did not make it a practice "to kill women and children," and about the causes of the Pequot war in general he points out that it was the act of a single Indian in the company of an Englishman that ultimately triggered the fighting: "Thus far I had written in a book, that all men and posterity might know how and why so many honest men had their blood shed, yea, and some slayed alive, others cut in pieces, and some roasted alive, only because Kichamokin [Cutshamequin], a Bay Indian, killed one Pequit." As for himself, Gardiner far preferred to fight "Capt. Hunger" than any human antagonist.

Although it ultimately lacks the spiritual intensity and literary finesse of the other accounts of the Pequot war, Gardiner's "Relation" is nonetheless well worth reading. Based on the premise that life is both a "tragical story" and yet a "comedy," Gardiner's narrative is, in the end, perhaps the most human of the

Pequot war stories. In addition to providing insights into the war not available in the other accounts, Gardiner's "Relation" reveals the personality of an individual who was in many ways quite remarkable for his times, and as such his narrative is a refreshing contrast to the more stridently pietistical interpretations of the war we would otherwise have received.

Suggested Readings: DAB; T₁. *See also* Alexander Gardiner, "Lion Gardiner," CMHS, 3rd Ser., 10 (1849), 173-185; C. C. Gardiner, *Lion Gardiner and His Descendants* (1890); idem, *The Papers and Biography of Lion Gardiner* (1883); Francis Jennings, *The Invasion of America: Indians, Colonialism, and the Cant of Conquest* (1975), pp. 186-227; Richard Slotkin, *Regeneration Through Violence: The Mythology of the American Frontier, 1600-1860* (1973), pp. 69-70; Alden T. Vaughan, "From White Man to Redskin: Changing American Perceptions of the American Indian," AHR, 87 (1982) 917-953; idem, *The New England Frontier: Puritans and Indians, 1620-1675* (1965), pp. 138-154; idem, "Pequots and Puritans: The Causes of the War of 1637," WMQ, 3rd Ser., 21 (1964), 256-269; idem, "A Test of Puritan Justice," NEQ, 38 (1965), 331-339; Wilcomb E. Washburn, "The Moral and Legal Justification for Dispossessing the Indians," *Seventeenth-Century America: Essays in Colonial History* (1959), ed. by James Morton Smith, pp. 15-32.

James A. Levernier
University of Arkansas at Little Rock

EBENEZER GAY (1696-1787)

Works: *Ministers Are Men* (1725); *Discourse* (1728); *Duty of People* (1730); *Well-Accomplished Soldiers* (1738); *Ministers Insufficiency* (1742); *Untimely Death* (1744); *Character and Work* (1745); *The True Spirit* (1746); *Alienation of Affections* (1747); *The Mystery* (1752); *Jesus Christ the Wise Master-Builder* (1753); *The Work of a Gospel Minister* (1755); *The Levite* (1756); *Natural Religion* (1759); *Evangelical Preacher* (1763); *Beloved Disciple* (1766); *St. John's Vision* (1766); *Soveraignity of God* (1767); *Call from Macedonia* (1769); *The Devotions* (1771).

Biography: Called the "father of American Unitarianism," Ebenezer Gay was born in Dedham, Mass., on Aug. 15, 1696, the son of Nathaniel and Lydia (Lusher) Gay. He studied at Harvard, where he received a B.A. in 1714 and later M.A. and doctor of divinity degrees. After teaching in grammar schools in Hadley and Ipswich, Gay made a concentrated effort to master the Scriptures. He was, consequently, invited to preach at First Parish in Hingham, Mass., where he was ordained in 1718. In 1728 Gay delivered the Artillery Election Sermon, and in 1745 he preached the General Election Sermon, indications that he was well respected by the ministers and leaders of his day. He also delivered the distinguished Dudleian Lecture at Harvard for 1759 and was a popular preacher at New Eng. ordination ceremonies.

A friend of most of the leading religious figures of his time, including Nathaniel Appleton (q.v.), Charles Chauncy (q.v.), Jonathan Mayhew (q.v.), and Cotton Mather (q.v.), Gay was noted for his ability to solve disputes without compromising his own integrity on the subjects under debate. During the Great Awakening, he sided against the New Light teachings of George Whitefield (q.v.) and his followers, yet he was respected for the moderation and tact with which he expressed his views. Despite his Tory leanings, Gay managed to maintain the respect of the patriots, including John Adams (q.v.), during the American Revolution when other ministers such as Mather Byles (q.v.) were reviled for their British sympathies.

Gay's liberal theological views have led some commentators to see in his career the beginnings of American Unitarianism. While it is true that Gay avoided excessive emphasis on the doctrine of predestination, he never fully espoused the more liberal views of Jonathan Mayhew, with whom he is frequently associated because of his defense of Mayhew after the latter's death. According to Clifford K. Shipton, Gay was "nearer to that gentle Calvinist, Benjamin Colman" (q.v.), than he was to Mayhew, and "one must make reservations to the statement that Gay was the founder of Unitarianism in America."

Gay died in Hingham on Aug. 19, 1787, after a ministry of some seventy years. According to Shipton, "the dry, good humored wit which marked his private conversation" has made Gay "one of the traditions of Hingham," where he was long remembered by his parishioners with "affection and reverence."

Critical Appraisal: During the years of the Great Awakening and afterwards until the Revolution, American clergymen such as Ebenezer Gay, Jonathan Mayhew, and Charles Chauncy struggled to subdue what they considered to be the overly enthusiastic and unlearned preachings of the evangelists. Far from united in their efforts to quell the fervor of the Great Awakening, however, these men were divided between the two major strains of the Rationalist movement current in G.B. On one side, the monarchistic philosophy of Thomas Hobbes, held by Chauncy, opposed the other, more democratic view of John Locke, for whom Mayhew was a spokesman. Ebenezer Gay, in an interesting exercise in moderation, wrote with a clarity of style and force of metaphor to combine the two ideologies into a single theology that greatly influenced the course of religious thought during his day.

In his sermons, Gay emphasized the need for complete obedience to God and to the sovereign (whom Gay believed to be a ruler by divine right) as well as the necessity of exercising reason as a means for determining the limits of personal duty. Gay's philosophy is perhaps best articulated in his *Natural Religion*, a lecture he presented for the Dudleian Lecture at Harvard on May 9, 1759. In this lecture, Gay sought to synthesize the theories of Hobbes and Locke. For Hobbes, man in his natural state is not only incapable of governing himself, he is unable to make moral decisions unaided by a governing ruler. Locke believed, as did Hobbes, that the natural state of man is social, and that man should be governed by an elected few. Man has the right, Locke believed, is even required, to watch that elected authority and to change the government if that authority is not performing its job properly. What Gay did, and why it is so remarkable an achievement, was take the two philosophies and accept the principles of both while convincing us that they not only can exist together but that they do exist dependent on each other.

Gay began his lecture by distinguishing between "revealed" and "natural" religions. *Revealed religion*, Gay explained, is God's word, God's message as told by the prophet. The ultimate explanation of life, Gay insisted, is Christian Revelation as written in the Bible. Gay claimed that revealed religion first demands faith in the truth of the Bible as the word of God. This belief is not a matter of reason but of faith, and it is very much a by-product of Hobbes's view that members of a society must delegate their rights to a sovereign; if they do not, Hobbes said, man will be left to his natural state, which is a state of war. *Natural religion* is "that which bare Reason discourses and dictates." Thus just as Locke emphasized that man's natural state is freedom and equality, Gay said that if one uses reason, one's moral obligation is clear. This type of thinking is reminiscent of John Tillotson's sermon *The Usefulness of Consideration*. Tillotson argued that man is given reason so that man may "consider" his life and avoid damnation. Gay expanded Tillotson's notion of "consideration" into Gay's concept of "Natural Conscience." The "Natural Conscience" is, simply, God's voice telling man his duty. Man is not "so much lumpish Matter, or a *mechanical* Engine, that moves only by the Direction of an impelling Force; he hath a Principal of Action within himself, and is an Agent in the strict and . . . proper sense of the Word."

The "strict and proper sense" of "Agent" is the key to understanding how Gay synthesized his natural and revealed religions into a coherent whole. First, reason is put into action by the religion that is already within man. This religion becomes part of man's conscience only when revealed to him by an external force such as the Bible or directly from God. In this initial stage, reason is relatively useless and not nearly so effective as Revelation. Gay told us that "had Man with all his natural Endowments in their perfect Order and Strength been placed in this World, and no Notice given him of it's [sic] Maker, might he not have stood wondering some Time . . . before he would have thence, by Deductions and reason, argued an invisible Being, of Eternal Power?" Gay explained that Revelation is necessary because the Fall weakened man's otherwise "perfect" faculties. Man's need for Revelation, therefore, becomes an intrinsic part of man's nature. Thus it is within man's "common Nature" to have a compulsion to worship.

After Revelation, man is potentially an agent of God's word. Although man has potential, he must depend solely upon himself to become an agent. Natural religion, or reason, becomes the second phase of man's development. Gay's ontology does not see natural religion as secondary, but rather as a second stage. Without the use of his ability to reason, Gay said, man would not know what was expected of him, and "Absurdities and Contradictions . . . are not to be obtruded on our faith." Gay answered the evangelists who held that religion was purely a question of belief: "to run down natural Religion as mere *Paganism*, derogates from the Credit of revealed, subverts our Faith in it, dissolves our Obligation to practice it." Without reason, man would not be a proper vessel for God's love, because man would be no better than a beast and would have no desire, or means, to worship a god. Finally, Gay concluded that one must not have too strong a zeal for either natural or revealed religion. Here, again, Gay spoke to the evangelists, as he did in his sermon *Evangelical Preacher*, warning them not to use "airy speculation" when teaching God's word, lest the minister lose the attention and loyalty of his congregation.

Gay provided his age with the theological compromises it needed to face the theological complexities of the times. He was a man with enough vision to see that moderation is the lasting approach in dealing with volatile issues, and without being either too dogmatic or too pedantic, he managed to synthesize two antithetical polemics. As a result, he made a significant contribution to colonial thinking, theology, and writing.

Suggested Readings: CCNE; Sibley-Shipton (VI, 59-66); T$_2$. *See also* Alan Heimert, *Religion and the American Mind* (1966).

Jeanne Merle
University of Houston

JOSHUA GEE (1698-1748)

Works: *Israel's Mourning for Aaron's Death* (1728); *The Strait Gate and the Narrow Way* (1729); *A Letter to the Rev. Mr. Nathaniel Eells* (1743).

Biography: Joshua Gee was born in Boston, Mass., on Jun. 29, 1698, to Joshua Gee, a shipbuilder, and his wife, Elizabeth (Thatcher) Gee. Fulfilling the expectations of his father (who, incidentally, had once been enslaved in Algiers), Gee was educated at Harvard College, where he graduated in 1717. After receiving overtures from several nearby churches, Gee accepted a call from his family congregation, and on Dec. 18, 1723, he was ordained as colleague minister for the Old North, or Second, Church, then under the direction of Cotton Mather (q.v.), a friend of Gee's father. Gee married three times: Sarah Rogers (1732), Anna Gerrish Appleton (1734), and Sarah Gardiner (1740).

A man of paradoxical talents, Gee was a dull preacher with no passion for writing, but he excelled at witty and poetical conversation. The major controversy of Gee's tenure at the Old North Church concerned the Great Awakening. Gee brought in George Whitefield (q.v.) to preach, and in the backlash that enabled the Old Lights to censure the revival movement, he actively supported the New Light cause in *A Letter to...Nathaniel Eells*. Although the general discord in New Eng. during the 1740s was reflected in the conflicts within Gee's Second Church, he maintained his position as minister even though that meant a break with the Mather dynasty. At his death on May 22, 1748, Gee left behind a sympathetic congregation, a household of stepchildren and children, and ample worldly goods, the fruits of the family estate he had inherited and maintained.

Critical Appraisal: Joshua Gee reputedly disliked polishing his sermons for publication and consequently published little of his work. However, the few pieces by Gee that were printed illustrate the main concerns of New Eng. ministers during the middle years of the eighteenth century: the revival within the church manifested in the "Great Awakening," the concern for the upright lives and saved souls of their congregations and the passing of the second generation of Puritan saints in the death of Cotton Mather. In *A Letter to the Rev. Mr. Nathaniel Eells* (q.v.), Gee supported the evangelical movement headed by Whitefield; in manner, the letter is urgent but not quarrelsome, clear in its defense of the revivalists, but not condemnatory of those who feel otherwise. In *The Strait Gate and Narrow Way*, a pair of doctrinal sermons, Gee took the familiar images of the broad and narrow ways and elucidated in total orthodoxy the options man has in this world and the necessary reward of each choice. In *Israel's Mourning*, he offered a eulogy to Cotton Mather, whom Gee saw as illustrative of all that is valuable in the New Eng. ministerial spirit. Gee's writings reveal none of the wit for which his conversation was renowned; rather, his prose mirrors the conventional sentiments and old-fashioned doctrines that mark the sermons and writings of those New Eng. ministers who stand in the shadow of the great theologians and rhetoricians of their day.

Suggested Readings: CCNE; Sibley-Shipton (VI, 175-183); Sprague (I, 312-314). *See also Appleton's Cyclopaedia of American Biography* (1892), II, 622.

Roslyn L. Knutson
University of Arkansas at Little Rock

ELBRIDGE GERRY (1744-1814)

Works: Russell W. Knight, ed., *Elbridge Gerry's Letterbook: Paris, 1797-1798* (1966); C. Harvey Gardiner, ed., *A Study in Dissent: The Warren-Gerry Correspondence, 1776-1792* (1968).

Biography: Elbridge Gerry was born in Marblehead, Mass., on Jul. 17, 1744. After graduating from Harvard College in 1762, Gerry entered his father's shipping business, where he worked until 1772, at which time he was elected to the Mass. General Court and first came under the influence of Samuel Adams (q.v.). In Aug. 1774 Gerry was elected to the Essex County Convention and later that year to the Provincial Congress, where he was appointed to the Committee of Public Safety. While serving on the committee, Gerry worked closely with John Hancock and John Adams (q.v.), and he began to develop his patriotic sentiments.

In Jan. 1776 Gerry was elected to the Continental Congress, where he served through 1780, returning in 1783, but leaving again in 1785 to take a seat in the Mass. House of Representatives. As a member of the Continental Congress, Gerry signed both the Declaration of Independence and the Articles of Confederation. In 1787 Gerry was elected a delegate to the Constitutional Convention; from 1789 to 1793, he served as a member of the House of Representatives during the first Congress.

In 1797, after supporting John Adams for the presidency, Gerry was appointed, along with John Marshall and Charles Pinckney (q.v.), to the XYZ Mission to Fr. When the American delegation refused to pay an exorbitant bribe to Talleyrand for the privilege of a meeting with the French Directory, Talleyrand proposed negotiations with Gerry alone. Outraged, Marshall and Pinckney left Paris, but Gerry remained in the hope that his presence would prevent a war between the two countries. Eventually recalled by Adams, Gerry was sharply criticized by the Federalists for his conduct in Fr. As a result, Gerry ran four unsuccessful campaigns for the governorship of Mass. before he was finally elected to that office in 1810. As governor, Gerry became famous for a bill he signed on Feb. 11, 1812, that redistricted the state to give the Republicans a disproportionately large number of representatives. Afterwards, similar practices were termed *gerrymanders*, in reference to Gerry and the salamander shape of the newly redrawn map of Essex County.

Although he lost a bid for reelection in 1812, Gerry was nominated to run for the vice-presidency with James Madison (q.v.). The Madison-Gerry ticket was elected, and from Mar. 4, 1813, until his death, en route to the Senate Chamber, on Nov. 23, 1814, Gerry served as vice-president. He was survived by his wife, Ann Thompson, whom he had wed in 1786, and by three sons and four daughters.

Critical Appraisal: Although Elbridge Gerry is remembered today as a secondary figure of the American Revolution, his extant published correspondence sheds considerable light on the early years of the Republic. Although a number of historical journals have published certain of Gerry's letters and speeches, the two collections of letters from 1776 to 1792 and 1797 to 1798, edited by C. Harvey Gardiner and Russell W. Knight, respectively, are the most accessible and, textually, the most reliable.

The Gardiner edition contains the correspondence between Gerry and two of his fellow Mass. Revolutionaries, James Warren and his wife, Mercy Otis Warren (q.v.), and consists of sixty letters by James Warren, eight by Mercy Otis Warren, and twenty-four by Gerry. Together, these letters reveal the political evolution and gradual disenchantment of three prominent and like-minded individuals with the direction the new Republic was taking. Unlike Gerry, who was a national figure, James Warren served as speaker of the Mass. House in 1775, was a member of the Navy Board in 1777, and worked for American freedom on a state level. Mercy Otis Warren, sister of James Otis (q.v.), was a playwright who promoted the Revolution through her writings, particularly through her massive three-volume *History of the Rise Progress and Termination of the American Revolution* (1805). Read together, the early letters of these individuals indicate a mutual depth of commitment to separation from Eng., a country whose government and people James Warren described in one letter as "corrupt and totally destitute of Virtue." Perhaps the most valuable of these letters, however, are those written after the Revolution in which Gerry explained the doubts that led him to refuse to sign the Constitution on Sept. 17, 1787. Throughout the convention, Gerry was quite active and so outspoken in his distrust of the Federalists that he addressed the delegates 119 times. A letter dated Mar. 22, 1789, in which Gerry discussed his growing feeling of anti-Federalism with James Warren, is particularly revealing:

> A federalist I always was, but not in their Sense of the word, for I abhor now as much as ever the corrupt parts of the constitution, but I am bound on honor to Support a government ratified by the majority untill it can be amended, for to oppose it would be to sow the seeds of a civil War and to lay the foundation of a military tyranny.

During this same period, Mercy Otis Warren anonymously wrote *Observations on the New Constitution and on the Federal and State Conventions*, a nineteen-page pamphlet she published in 1788 as "A Columbian Patriot." Although authorship of this pamphlet has been traditionally attributed to Gerry (see DAB and LHUS), historians such as Gardiner and George Billias now concur that the literary style of *Observations*, as well as the specific points of contention in the pamphlet, points to Mercy Warren, and not Elbridge Gerry, as the author, and a careful reading of their letters further indicates this point.

The second published collection of Gerry's letters (those written from 1797 to 1798), comprises Gerry's version of his role in the XYZ Affair. This edition presents thirty-three letters Gerry wrote from Paris and five miscellaneous letters dating from July 1799 to Jan. 1801. Not as useful to an understanding of Gerry's negotiations with Talleyrand as might be hoped, many of the items in this collection are letters written to family members about personal matters. When these letters do deal with Gerry's mission to Paris, their content is essentially itineraries and administrative details. In sum, this edition, which is not without its errors in the editorial annotations, tells us more of Gerry the man than Gerry the statesman and thus has a more limited historical value than Knight's introduction would lead one to believe. Other of Gerry's letters have been published in his son-in-law's biography, *Life of Elbridge Gerry* (1827-1828), but their text is unreliable.

Elbridge Gerry's contribution to the development of this nation resides primarily in his successful work in promoting the Revolution and his unsuccessful work in developing a constitution he could accept; many of the convictions he held during this period, which reflected the intellectual tenor of a significant portion of the American population, are evidenced in his published letters. Thus, as Gardiner pointed out, "Close study of such successful-unsuccessful revolutionaries can validate the necessity, the indispensibility of dissent in the early political as well as military moments of our nation."

Suggested Readings: DAB; LHUS; Sibley-Shipton (XV, 239-259); T$_2$. *See also* James T. Austin, *Life of Elbridge Gerry* (1827-1828); George Athan Billias, *Elbridge Gerry: Founding Father and Republican Statesman* (1976).

Francis J. Bosha
Marquette University

HENRY GIBBS (1668-1723)

Works: *The Right Method of Safety* (1704); *Bethany; Or, The House of Mourning* (1714); *The Certain Blessedness* (1721); *Godly Children Their Parents Joy* (1727).

Biography: Henry Gibbs was born on Oct. 8, 1668, in Boston, Mass. The son of Robert and Elizabeth (Sheate) Gibbs, he was educated at Harvard College, where he received an A.B. degree in 1685. Gibbs began his ministerial career as assistant to the Rev. John Bailey, the minister of Watertown, Mass. When Bailey retired in 1692, a long-standing controversy erupted between the western and eastern parts of the town concerning the location of the town's meetinghouse. In 1697, after a new meetinghouse had been built near the center of the town, the western faction chose Samuel Angier (1645-1719) as minister, but the eastern faction chose Gibbs, who remained in the old meetinghouse and retained the church records. On Oct. 6, 1697, the day for Gibbs's ordination, the western party barred Gibbs from entering the new church, and the ordination ceremony was held outside. Not until 1720, with the death of Angier, did the controversy finally close.

Remarkably, however, Gibbs managed to retain the respect of all sides during this prolonged turmoil. Described as a man of "real kindness of feeling and simple rectitude of conduct," Gibbs did not judge others harshly. In fact, he was one of the few New Eng. ministers who expressed serious doubts about the 1692 witchcraft proceedings at Salem. In 1704 Gibbs was invited to deliver the Artillery Election Sermon, and he was proposed by Samuel Sewall (q.v.) as a compromise candidate for the General Election Sermon of 1720. In addition, Gibbs was active in the affairs of Harvard College, was appointed an officer of the corporation in 1700, and according to the diaries of Samuel Sewall and Joseph Baxter was present at Arrowsic Island in the Kennebec River, Me., when Governor Shute forced the treaty upon the Indians that ultimately led to the general uprising of 1721. Gibbs died on Oct. 21, 1723, and was buried in Watertown. His son-in-law Nathaniel Appleton (q.v.) composed his epitaph.

Critical Appraisal: The events of Henry Gibbs's life are more striking than his writings. Only four of his sermons were published and are noteworthy for their plain style and lack of rhetorical ornamentation. In the preface to Gibbs's last published sermon, *Godly Children*, Benjamin Colman (q.v.) praised "Such a plain, Scriptural, serious, methodical and applicatory way of Preaching" as "infinitely preferable to that of a general and short *Harangue*."

The Certain Blessedness is a fine example of Puritan dialectical logic. The topic of the sermon is forgiveness of sin, defined by Gibbs as "the Removal of Guilt from a Sinner, by an act of free Grace thro Christ Jesus." Although guilt is "a necessary consequent of Sin," only those can be forgiven, stated Gibbs, who are "truly Blessed," that is, elected by God for "free Grace." This doctrine could have become paradoxical if Gibbs had developed the idea of providence as a temporal process: "blessedness," the state of those forgiven, would have to precede in time the guilt that is a consequent of sin. One would be both sinning and blessed at the same time. Gibbs deftly avoided the fallacy of temporal priority. According to Gibbs, forgiveness changes neither the nature of the sin nor the nature of the sinner; rather, forgiveness changes the relationship between the sin and the sinner. The nature of this relationship, not the temporal history of the sinner, is the plan of God's providence. By such logical definitions and distinctions, the sermon develops into a discussion of the covenant, mediatorial nature of Christ, and doctrine of election. A careful and sensitive application of these doctrinal matters and logical methods to practical advice on the spirit of forgiveness concludes the sermon.

In the Artillery Election Sermon, *The Right Method of Safety*, Gibbs condemned most wars as unlawful: "The Wars of Sovereign Princes, and of free States, what are they for the most part better than a more plausible and powerful sort of Piracie?" Yet war in itself is not unlawful. Against "Enthusiasts" and "Rational Religionists," Gibbs defended the idea of the Christian soldier as the preserver of order and justice. *Bethany*, a funeral sermon for the wife of a friend, also balanced human uses and God's glory by integrating feelings of loss with the doctrine of providence. "Christianity does not teach us a Stoical Apathy, or wholly stifle our affections, but approves mourning agreeable to the Dictates of righted Reason: Else we could neither be benefitted by them, nor Glorify God with them." His last sermon, *Godly Children*, identified practical uses with God's glory: "True Wisdom is true Piety or Godliness. . . . True Piety engages to the pursuit of the best and highest end." This sermon provides an excellent summary of Gibbs's fundamental attitude: "Without knowledge the heart can't be good or wise."

Suggested Readings: CCNE; Sibley-Shipton (III, 327-334). *See also* Henry Bond, *Genealogies of the Families. . .of Watertown*, vol. II (1885); Convers Francis, *An Historical Sketch of Watertown* (1830), pp. 58-77; Josiah W. Gibbs, *Memoir of the Gibbs Family* (1879), pp. 13, 21, 39; "Indian Treaties," CMaineHS (1853), III, 361-375; "Journal of the Rev. Joseph Baxter," NEHGR, 21 (1867), 45-59; Charles E. Nash, *The Indians of Kennebec* (1892), pp. 45-47; Josiah Quincy, *The History of Harvard College*, vol. I (1860), passim.

William J. Irvin
New York, New York

CHRISTOPHER GIST (1705-1759)

Works: *First Journal* (1750-1751); *Second Journal* (1751-1752); *Third Journal* (1753-1754).

Biography: Christopher Gist (his grandfather had changed the family name from *Guest*) was born in Baltimore, Md., in 1705. He was a merchant there until the early 1740s and then briefly an Indian trader in the Yadkin River country of

N.C. In 1750 Gist was hired by Va.'s newly formed Ohio Company to explore the Ohio Valley and to select a site for the company's settlement, and for almost five years, he was the dominant figure on the Ohio Valley frontier, where he is remembered as the area's first permanent settler.

Gist made three important journeys—two for the Ohio Company and one with young Col. George Washington (q.v.), in the process producing his three noted journals and describing and surveying much of what is now western Pa. and W.Va., as well as portions of Ky. and Ohio. When his settlement was wiped out by the French during the opening days of the French and Indian War in 1754, Gist moved to Winchester and served until 1759 as Indian agent for the southern colonies. He died on Jul. 25, 1759, of smallpox, on the road home from Williamsburg.

A great-grandson, B. Gratz Brown, was governor of Mo. and Greeley's vice-presidential running mate in 1872. A granddaughter, Violet, was the wife of the noted journalist-politician Francis P. Blair, owner of Washington's famed Blair House. Their son Montgomery was attorney for the plaintiff in the *Dred Scott* case and later Lincoln's postmaster general. Another son, Francis P., Jr., was Seymour's running mate in 1868.

Critical Appraisal: Evaluation of Christopher Gist's journals is to be found not so much in formal literary criticism as in a universal appreciation of his work by contemporaries and by historians who continue to cite his precision and accuracy. The journals are the most reliable picture we have of the area between the Alleghenies and the Ohio during the 1750s. Bailey described Gist as unusually well educated for his time, accomplished as a surveyor and mathematician; but it is as a writer that his real value is best realized. At a time when most frontier chronicles and adventure sagas were semiliterate at best, Gist's journals are in consistently spelled and grammatically correct simple prose. The same is true of the extensive correspondence by Gist found in the papers and orderly books of contemporaries such as Jeffrey Amherst, Henry Bouquet, Edward Braddock, George Washington and Robert Dinwiddie and in the journals of Va.'s Council and Burgesses.

Finally, Gist's maps and journals were major components of Thomas Jefferson's (q.v.) *Notes on the State of Virginia*, and his descriptions of Indian villages and of the virgin forest were comparable to those of far better-known colonial personages. He ranks high among those who by 1763 had moved the political emphasis from the coast to the Ohio, and he contributed as much to the British domination of North America as did any other individual, Washington included. In fact, Gist's *Third Journal*, recording their trip to Fort LeBoeuf in the grip of winter, parallels the diary of Washington and is the better of the two by virtually any standard. It was Washington's record of this 1753 adventure that preserved our clearest picture of Gist, referring to his "rare fortitude and modesty" and describing Gist's frozen fingers and general physical distress when he saved the young colonel from death in the icy waters of the Allegheny, an event barely mentioned in Gist's account.

Suggested Readings: DAB. *See also* Kenneth Bailey, *Christopher Gist, Colonial Frontiersman, Explorer, and Indian Agent* (1976); William M. Darlington, ed., *Christopher Gist's Journals* (1893); Jean Muir Dorsey and Jay Maxwell Dorsey, *Christopher Gist of Maryland and Some of His Descendants, 1679-1957* (1969); Don Marshall Larrabee, *The Journals of George Washington and His Guide, Christopher Gist, on Their Historic Mission to the French Forts in 1753* (1950); Lois Mulkearn, ed., *George Mercer Papers Relating to the Ohio Company of Virginia* (1954); Isaac Rupp, *Early History of Western Pennsylvania* (1846); Sylvester R. Stevens and Donald H. Kent, *Papers of Col. Henry Bouquet,* Part I (1941); David B. Trimble, "Christopher Gist and the Indian Service in Virginia, 1757-1759," VMHB, 64 (1956), 143-165; idem, "Christopher Gist and Settlement on the Monongahela, 1752-1754," VMHB, 63 (1955), 143-165; James Veech, *Monongahela of Old* (1858-1892).

Donovan H. Bond
West Virginia University

MARY KATHARINE GODDARD (1738-1816)

Works: *The Maryland Journal and Baltimore Advertiser* (editor, publisher-printer; May 17, 1775-Jan. 2, 1784); *Mary K. Goddard's Pennsylvania, Delaware, Maryland, and Virginia Almanack* for 1779 (1778) and 1785 (1784); *The Maryland, Virginia and Pennsylvania Almanack* for 1779 (1778) and 1780 (1779); *The Maryland, Delaware, Pennsylvania, Virginia, and North-Carolina Almanack* for 1781 (1780); *The Maryland and Virginia Almanack* for 1782 (1781); *The Pennsylvania, Delaware, Maryland, and Virginia Almanack* for 1782 (1781 and 1782), 1783-1786 (1782-1785).

Biography: Mary Katharine (or Katherine) Goddard, America's first postmistress and editor for almost ten years of Baltimore's first weekly newspaper, was born in New London or Groton, Conn., on Jun. 16, 1738, the elder child of Dr. Giles Goddard and Sarah Updike Goddard. Mrs. Goddard, one of the best educated women of her time, probably taught her daughter at home. In 1762 Mary Katharine, with her mother, moved to Providence, R.I., to help her younger brother William in his print shop. In 1765 he left for Philadelphia to publish *The Pennsylvania Chronicle,* leaving *The Providence Gazette* in the hands of his mother and sister. Mary Katharine, already a competent and reliable printer, worked for "Sarah Goddard and Company."

In 1768 William again sent for the two ladies. When Mrs. Goddard died in 1770, Mary Katharine was in complete charge of the *Chronicle* in Philadelphia while her brother attended to business elsewhere. In 1773 he began *The Maryland Journal* in Baltimore. In 1774, when William was appointed to organize the Constitutional Post Office, Mary Katharine went to Baltimore to operate his printing business and, in 1775, began to use her own name in the colophon. Goddard ran a bookstore and a bookbinding business, and she may have had part interest in a paper mill. From Aug. 1775 until Nov. 1789, Goddard was postmistress of Baltimore. Dismissed because she was a woman and (allegedly) unsuited for some traveling that the job required, she fought in vain to be reinstated.

Mary Katharine and William were never friendly after 1784, issuing rival almanacs for 1785 and exchanging harsh words. She never married and gradually withdrew from public life to manage her bookstore. Although William Goddard was still alive when Mary Katharine died on Aug. 12, 1816, she willed her property to her female Negro slave, whom she also freed.

Critical Appraisal: Printer, newspaper publisher, and almanac compiler, Mary Katharine Goddard—unlike other women printers before 1800—worked because she chose to, not because she needed financial support for herself and a family. An active printer in Providence, Philadelphia, and Baltimore, Mary K. or M. K. Goddard (as her colophons read) is best known for her work in Baltimore. Many newspapers that she actually edited and published were printed under her brother's name. For example, she published *The Pennsylvania Chronicle* for nearly four years and edited as many issues as her brother William did. Although she did not replace her brother officially as editor until May 17, 1775, her responsibility for *The Maryland Journal* actually began in Feb. 1774, and she was probably responsible for writing the last page (condensed and softened) of William Goddard's "The Prowess of the Whig Club" (1777).

M. K. Goddard's *Maryland Journal* claims two major distinctions. It was the first American newspaper to publish the official copy (authorized for publication by the new government) of the Declaration of Independence, including the names of the signers. The *Journal* was also the only newspaper printed in Baltimore from Jul. 5, 1779, through May 16, 1783, and one of the few in the country that, despite paper shortages and other vicissitudes, continued publication regularly during the Revolution. This newspaper equaled all of its rivals in editorial excellence and was as extensively read as any others in the colonies. M. K. Goddard not only wrote, edited, and supervised; she also performed the manual labor required to operate a successful printshop.

Goddard, like other printers, found the publication of almanacs lucrative. Her series ran from 1779 to 1786 (1778-1785). The first two were calculated by David Rittenhouse, America's foremost astronomer and member of the Royal Society. Andrew Ellicott, prominent astronomer and surveyor, calculated the others. As printer and publisher, Goddard was responsible for much of the almanac content. The calculators usually did only the calculations—a notable exception, of course, being Benjamin Franklin (q.v.) and his *Poor Richard*.

Goddard's almanacs were of relatively high literary quality. For example, her 1782 edition contained a serious and formal preface; eclipses; "Explanation of the Type of the Transit of Mercury," accompanied by an illustration; an advertisement that offered (from the printer) cash and merchandise in exchange for rags and "empty vials"; an "Account of the Allegany Philosopher"; fables, anecdotes, maxims; "Some remarkable Observations and Reflections on that Remarkable Bird the STORK"; "A Concise Character of the Indians from Capt. Carver's Travels"; "An Account of the River Mississippi"; and verse.

A graceful style saved Goddard's almanac prefaces from the prevailing pomposity of many of her contemporaries. For example, in 1783, she wrote:

One year passeth away and another cometh—so likewise 'tis with Almanacks—they are annual productions.... In performances then of so transient a nature, it is no wonder, when they become Old Almanacks, that we frequently see them made use of by the pastry-cook, or flying in the tail of the school-boy's kite.—The works of greater authors meet with the same fate... many a system of metaphysics may be seen in the bottom of old trunks.

A fair test of Mary Katharine's printing skill is a comparison of the Ellicott almanacs, also printed by William Goddard. Mary K. Goddard's calendar pages, a real test of the printer's craft, were neater and clearer than her brother's. Spelling and capitalization were generally consistent, an unusual accomplishment for any printer of that period. Furthermore, unlike her brother, she never quarreled with the eminent astronomer Andrew Ellicott. Her almanacs also had more literary merit than her brother's. In addition to the usual almanac fare, she included travel accounts, verse (English originals and translations from the French), and one of the few attempts in early American literature to create a literary character—her "Allegany Philosopher," a regular feature. She was the only colonial woman printer to use her name as part of her almanac title, an uncommon practice even among male printers.

Having administrative and technical skill as well as initiative M. K. Goddard was admirably prepared to assume her brother's duties as he relinquished them for one reason or another. Ambitious and intellectual, she excelled in every business she undertook. She refused to take sides in local political arguments and adamantly believed in freedom of the press. She was greatly respected (as attested by the 230 Baltimore citizens who signed her petition for reinstatement as postmistress), and she served her community remarkably well during the Revolution.

Suggested Readings: NAW. *See also* Leona M. Hudak, *Early American Women Printers and Publishers, 1639-1820* (1978), pp. 318-396 (including list of imprints); Ward L. Miner, *William Goddard, Newspaperman* (1962), pp. 91-94, 139-194, 321; Ellen Oldham, "Early Women Printers of America," BPLQ, 3 (1958), 150-153; Marion Barber Stowell, *Early American Almanacs* (1977), pp. 125-132, 155-156; Joseph Wheeler, *The Maryland Press, 1777-1790* (1938), pp. 10-18; Lawrence C. Wroth, *History of Printing in Colonial Maryland, 1686-1776* (1922), pp. 144-145.

Marion Barber Stowell
Milledgeville, Georgia

THOMAS GODFREY (1736-1763)

Works: *The Court of Fancy* (1762); *Juvenile Poems on Various Subjects* (1765).

Biography: Thomas Godfrey was born in Philadelphia, Pa., on Dec. 4, 1736. His father, also Thomas, was an original member of Benjamin Franklin's (q.v.) Junto and a widely respected although formally untrained mathematician; he is credited with inventing the *quadrant*, a navigational device, that was finally named for Hadley. Although his formal relationship to the Academy and College of Philadelphia is unclear, young Godfrey became a protégé of Provost William Smith (q.v.) of that school. Smith encouraged Godfrey in the arts and literature and introduced him to the painter Benjamin West as well as to Nathaniel Evans (q.v.) and Francis Hopkinson (q.v.). Through Smith's aid, Godfrey received a commission in the Pa. militia and fought briefly in the French and Indian War. In 1759 he took a job as a factor in Wilmington, N.C., where he spent most of the rest of his life. He died of a fever there in 1763, leaving his play *The Prince of Parthia* unpublished and unperformed. The play was added to some of his verse, both published and unpublished, to form *Juvenile Poems on Various Subjects*, posthumously collected by his friend Evans in 1765.

Critical Appraisal: Thomas Godfrey's principal literary achievement is his play *The Prince of Parthia*, which is rightly credited with being both the first tragedy written and published by a native-born American and the first American-written play performed on the professional stage. Godfrey was familiar with the stage through the English company led by David Douglass that played in Philadelphia; indeed, he prepared *The Prince of Parthia* for that group's 1759 season. Unfortunately, the play was not ready in time and was not performed until after Godfrey's death, when it was staged by the Douglass company at the New Theatre, Southwark, Philadelphia, in 1767.

The play is a five-act, blank-verse tragedy loosely based on events of Parthian history as recounted by historians such as Tacitus. It relies heavily on Renaissance dramatic conventions and themes, especially revenge. The forty scenes of the piece make it bumpy in plot and character development, but the speeches are of occasionally powerful force and give the whole a moderate level of actability.

Recent scholarship has documented in detail the widely held assumption that Godfrey both knew and appreciated Shakespearian drama. Close parallels in language and characterization to *Othello, Lear, Macbeth*, and especially *Hamlet* illustrate Godfrey's debt to Shakespeare. For all its roughness and borrowings, *The Prince of Parthia* manages to achieve a certain strength and appeal probably best ascribed to Godfrey's natural but unpolished literary talents.

The twenty-two poems included with the tragedy in *Juvenile Poems on Various Subjects* exhibit something of the same roughness but, with rare exceptions, little of the dramatic power of the play. The elegies, pastorals, and songs that make up most of Godfrey's poetry are undistinguished. They address conventional themes in conventional forms. The longest and most interesting is *The Court of Fancy* (first published in 1762). Like the play, the poem borrows heavily—this time from Chaucer and Pope—for theme and plot. Godfrey's success in *The Prince of Parthia* and, to a lesser degree, in *The Court of Fancy* suggests that his strength lay in dramatic and narrative, not lyric, composition.

Suggested Readings: DAB; DNB; LHUS; T_1; T_2. *See also* William E. Carron, *A Bicentennial Edition of Thomas Godfrey's The Prince of Parthia, with a Critical Introduction* (1976); Albert Frank Gegenheimer, *Thomas Godfrey: Protégé of William Smith* (1943); A. H. Quinn, *History of the American Drama from the Beginning to the Civil War* (1923); Henry B. Woolf, "Thomas Godfrey: Eighteenth-Century Chaucerian," AL, 12 (1941), 486-490.

William D. Andrews
Philadelphia College of Textiles and Science

SARAH GOODHUE (1641-1681)

Works: *The Copy of a Valedictory* (1681).

Biography: Sarah Whipple Goodhue, the youngest daughter of John and Susannah Whipple, was born in Ipswich, Mass., in 1641. Having settled in the community by 1638, her father became an eminent citizen and merchant, who served at various times as both deacon and ruling elder. On Jul. 13, 1661, Sarah married Joseph Goodhue (1639-1697), oldest son of William and Margery (Watson) Goodhue. Sarah's father-in-law had come to Ipswich in 1635 and had become the settlement's first deacon and one of its leading merchants. Joseph Goodhue was also active in local affairs: he served as moderator, selectman, assessor, deputy to the General Court, and deacon. According to the title page of her work, Sarah Goodhue died on Jul. 23, 1681, "three Days after she had been delivered of two hopeful Children, leaving ten in all surviving."

Critical Appraisal: Anticipating that she might die in childbirth or shortly afterwards, Sarah Goodhue addressed a "valedictory and monitory writing" to her relatives and friends. She had not shared her premonition of death even with her husband, for she wanted to spare him "needless trouble." Through her "valedictory," she bid farewell to her family and friends, told them that she accepted death as providential, and encouraged them with thoughts of God's grace.

She asked her husband to give three of their children to relatives whom she specified, lest the widower be overwhelmed by the responsibilities of their "great family." Then she took up religious and moral concerns, urging her readers to trust God—and to prepare themselves for eternity. After exhorting her brothers, sisters, and friends to make sure they had no cause to fear death, she called upon her children, remarking that a parent's "dying words" sometimes leave "a living impression." As they are "by nature, miserable sinners, utterly lost and undone," she said, "the best counsel that a poor dying mother can give [them] is, to get a part and portion in the Lord Jesus Christ." They must avail themselves of the means of grace—especially sermons, which have meant a great deal to her. They must believe that God will keep his covenant and be merciful if they "seek his face in truth." Goodhue also admonished them to love and obey their father and to be pious and modest, avoiding "the pride of life, that now too much abounds."

Goodhue closed with a tribute to her "tender hearted, affectionate, and intire loving husband," who for twenty years had cheerfully helped and sympathized with his "weakly natured" wife. She had often been unable to attend meetings, but Joseph, her spiritual mentor, had read Scripture to her, copied and repeated sermons for her, and prayed with her. She encouraged him to keep his faith and his "affectionate heart" alive and not, in his sorrow, to be deflected from "the right way."

Born and married into prosperous families, Goodhue doubtless had more opportunities for learning than most women. A grammar school for boys had been set up in Ipswich by 1636. It failed, but another opened in 1642; John Whipple was named to the school board in 1652. Whipple's will, made in 1669, lists books as part of his estate. As a girl, Sarah Whipple may have had the benefit of highly literate company: Thomas F. Waters has suggested that her father was visited by some of the colony's leading citizens—Ezekiel Cheever (q.v.), John Winthrop, Jr. (q.v.), Thomas Dudley (q.v.), Simon Bradstreet, and Anne Bradstreet (q.v.). Whatever her educational opportunities may have been, her occasional use of balance and antithesis indicates an awareness of rhetoric. She warned her children and friends to use their time wisely, "for you know not how soon your health may be turned into sickness; your strength into weakness; and your lives into death." Her husband was assured that, through Christ, "thy loss" would be "my gain" and reminded that the realization of God's will had constantly been "my desire and thy prayer." She addressed a few rough lines of verse to Joseph and four of their children. Although she did not cite Scripture, the piece is imbued with her knowledge of the Bible. She alluded to Christ's parable of the wedding feast to make her point that believers must be ready to die.

Reprinted twice in the eighteenth century and two more times in the nineteenth, Goodhue's work is valuable for the light it sheds on roles and relationships within the Puritan family. Her first child was born in 1662, the year of the Half-Way Covenant; Goodhue's writing expressed concern that her offspring "own and renew [their] covenant" and so become "fit" for redemption. Although she apparently expected to share in Christ's kingdom, Goodhue portrayed herself as "weak" and "unworthy." It was her husband—a paragon, by her testimony— who, by his experience of grace, had led her and would guide their children "in God's ways." Goodhue gently reproved some of the children for not appreciating patriarchal wisdom. She asked the older ones to observe "how careful [their] father is when he cometh home from his work, to take the young ones up into his wearied arms"; in this demonstration of affection, they should "behold as in a glass" his concern for each of them.

The "saints" of seventeenth-century New Eng. believed that body and soul were beset by dangers. During the Goodhues' own childhood, Ipswich was troubled by wolves; its citizens were often called upon to defend neighboring communities against Indian attacks. In 1652 Ipswich built a jail and disciplined a man for consorting with the devil. Like many devout Puritans, the Goodhues took seriously their responsibility to prepare their children for grace.

Suggested Readings: Pattie Cowell, *Women Poets in Pre-Revolutionary America, 1650-1775: An Anthology* (1981), pp. 195-196; William R. Cutter, *Genealogical and Personal Memoirs Relating to the Families of Boston and Eastern Massachusetts*, 4 vols. (1908), III, 1669; Edmund S. Morgan, *The Puritan Family: Essays on Religion and Domestic Relations in Seventeenth-Century New England*, 2nd ed. (1956), pp. 45-61, 78-83; Elias Nason, "Ipswich" in *Standard History of Essex County, Massachusetts* (1878), pp. 203-204; Thomas F. Waters, *The John Whipple House in Ipswich, Mass. and the People Who Have Owned and Lived in It*, PIHS, 20 (reprints Goodhue's work; 1915), 12-17; idem, *Ipswich in the Massachusetts Bay Colony: A History of the Town from 1700 to 1917* ([reprints Goodhue, I, 519-524;] 1905, 1917), I, 57, 80, 149-150, 325, 471, 491, 494.

Mary De Jong
The Pennsylvania State University

DANIEL GOOKIN (c. 1612-1687)

Works: *To All Persons Whom It May Concern* (1656); *Historical Collections of the Indians in New England* (w. 1674; pub. 1792); *An Historical Account of the Doings and Sufferings of the Christian Indians in New England in the Years 1675, 1676, 1677* (w. 1677; pub. 1836). *Historical Collections* was published separately in 1792 as well as in CMHS, 1st ser., I (1792), 141-226. *An Historical Account* was first published in TAAS, II (1836), 423-534.

Biography: Daniel Gookin was born in either Kent, Eng., or County Cork, Ire., and was raised in the latter place. In 1630 he arrived in Va. to manage his father's plantation. Although a burgess, militia captain, and judge for Upper Norfolk County, Gookin moved to Mass. when Va. banned religious nonconformity in 1643. A zealous Puritan, he was chosen to important offices, including deputy to the General Court; assistant to the Court, and major-general. In 1655 Oliver Cromwell appointed Gookin to seek New Englanders to settle in Jam. A frequent dealer in land, Gookin helped found Worcester, Mass. In 1656 and from 1661 until his death in 1687, Gookin served as superintendent of those Indians who had submitted to the Bay colony. In this capacity, he cooperated closely with John Eliot (q.v.), New Eng.'s renowned missionary to the Indians. During King Philip's War, Gookin's defense of Christian Indians angered many colonists, and he lost his position as assistant to the General Court, but during the 1680s, he regained public favor by refusing to compromise with the king's commissioners on the matter of charter rights and by opposing submission to Parliament's trade regulations. Gookin died in Cambridge, Mass., on Mar. 19, 1687. His eldest son, Daniel Gookin, Jr. (q.v.), was the Congregational minister at Sherborn and preached to the Indians at Natick.

Critical Appraisal: Daniel Gookin wrote his two major works—the first at the height of success of the missions, the second immediately after their near total destruction—to promote religious conversion of the Indians of whom he had charge. In these works, Gookin expressed the view that, if converted, Indians could and should be assimilated into English civilization. Although Gookin sent both works to London to the Society for the Propagation of the Gospel in New England, which had supported John Eliot's endeavors, neither treatise saw print in Gookin's time.

Originally intended as the second chapter of a history of New Eng., Gookin's *Historical Collections of the Indians in New England* was sent to London as a separate work along with a prospectus for the broader study, the manuscript for which was supposedly destroyed by fire in 1742. When the manuscript for *Historical Collections* was finally published in 1792, its title was modified from the more appropriate "Indians Converted, or Historical Collections," the title Gookin intended, to its present form. Indeed, the work is primarily about the Praying Indians and prospects for further expanding the mission enterprise among the Indians of New Eng. Catering to the scientific interests of his potential audience in Restoration Eng., Gookin used his extensive knowledge of New Eng.'s Indians to provide the most complete and accurate description of their ethnography then available. From careful personal observation, he described the religious, political, and social institutions of New Eng.'s natives; their methods of warfare; their tools, food, clothing, and art; and their borrowings from English material culture. In addition, he provided a detailed account of the history and current state of missions in New Eng., including an explanation of his role as superintendent of the project. Arguing throughout that Praying Indians who were settled in towns and leading an ordered way of life under organized political authority should be recognized as a civilized society, Gookin ended his tract with suggestions for improving the missions: a nationwide collection, to be authorized by the king; integrated education of red and white children; and apprenticeship of Indian children in white families.

In *An Historical Account of the Doings and Sufferings of the Christian Indians*, Gookin revealed the injustice, imprisonment, exile to islands in Massachusetts Bay, and premeditated murder of Praying Indians by whites during King Philip's War, when white settlers throughout New Eng. turned their vengeance on all Indians, hostile or otherwise. In addition, he underscored the unreasonableness of the popular frenzy by recounting the contributions of the Praying Indians to the English war effort, first in warning of Philip's plans, then in spying and scouting, and finally in fighting for and defending their white brethren. As such, Gookin's *Historical Account* is a major source for the history of King Philip's War and stands in marked contrast to other accounts of the war like those by William Hubbard (q.v.) and Increase Mather (q.v.), which largely ignored the plight of New Eng.'s friendly Indians. An able defense of the Praying Indians as constant to the English and true to Christianity, Gookin's work provides an apologia for them as a civilized people. The works of Daniel Gookin, then, are worth reading as historical sources, literature, and sincere attempts to address the problems of Indian assimilation into the white society of New Eng. during the latter part of the seventeenth century.

Suggested Readings: DAB; DNB; T₁. *See also* Frederick William Gookin, *Daniel Gookin, 1612-1687* (1912); Guy Loran Lewis, "Daniel Gookin, Superintendent and Historian of the New England Indians: An Historiographical Study" (Ph.D. diss., Univ. of Ill. at Urbana-Champaign, 1973).

Michael J. Crawford
Naval Historical Center, Research Branch

DANIEL GOOKIN, Jr. (1650-1718)

Works: *Upon the Death of the Reverend, Pious, Incomparably Learned, and Faithful Servant of Christ, in the Works of the Ministry Mr. Urian Oakes* (1681); *A Few Shadie Meditations Occasioned by the Death of the Deservedly Honoured John Hull, Esq.* (1683).

Biography: Born on Jul. 12, 1650, in Cambridge, Mass., Daniel Gookin, Jr., was the eldest son of Molly (Dolling) and Daniel Gookin (q.v.), John Eliot's (q.v.) associate among the Praying Indians. After graduating from Harvard in 1669, Daniel Gookin, Jr., served as an instructor on the faculty from 1673 to 1681. In 1682 Gookin married Elizabeth Quincy, and about the same time, he began preaching to the Christian Indians at Natick, a decision of "great consolation" to his father. Three years later, Gookin, whom John Eliot described as "a pious and learned young man," received a call to be pastor of the church at Sherborn, Mass., where he ministered—as well as assisting the Indian minister at Natick—until his death on Jan. 8, 1718.

Critical Appraisal: Both of Daniel Gookin's published works are poems delivered as funeral elegies and printed as broadsides. A parishioner in Urian Oakes's (q.v.) congregation at Cambridge, Gookin was probably chosen to deliver the elegy for Oakes because they had worked together on the Harvard faculty. Gookin's relationship to John Hull (q.v.) is clearer: an inscription on the manuscript identifies Hull as Gookin's uncle. Since both poems were written when Gookin was in his early 30s at a time when he had no position or influence, Gookin probably wrote and published these elegies (his only ones to be published) as much for advancing his reputation and career as for remembering the deceased.

As funeral elegies, Gookin's verse reflects the Calvinist theology of late seventeenth-century Puritan Mass., particularly the themes of predestination, the service of the sainthood to God, and the omnipresence of death. As poetry, however, neither work parallels the accomplishment of Oakes's own elegy to Thomas Shepard (q.v.), a work generally considered among the best American poems from the period. Although Gookin's elegies suffer from overtly artificial theological imagery, poor rhyming, and unusual metrical variations, they are, nevertheless, in the words of one commentator, "a good example of the theological poetry of the period."

Suggested Readings: CCNE; FCNEV; Sibley-Shipton (II, 277-283). *See also* Clarence Brigham, "Elegy on Urian Oakes, 1681, by Daniel Gookin, Jr.," PCSM, 20 (1918), 247-252; Frederick William Gookin, *Daniel Gookin, 1612-1687, Assistant and Major General of the Massachusetts Bay Colony, His Life and Letters and Some Account of His Ancestry* (1912); J. Wingate Thornton, "The Gookin Family," NEHGR, 2 (1948), 167-174.

Richard L. Haan
Hartwick College

WILLIAM GORDON (1728-1807)

Works: *A Discourse Preached Dec. 15th, 1774* (1775); *A Discourse Preached in the Morning of Dec. 15th, 1774* (1775); *A Sermon Preached Before the Honourable House of Representatives* (1775); *The Separation of the Jewish Tribes* (1777); *The Doctrine of Final Universal Salvation* (1783); *The History of the Rise of the United States*, 3 vols. (1789); *The Plan for a Society* (1792).

Biography: Born in Hitchin, Hertfordshire, Eng., sometime in 1728, William Gordon was educated at a Dissenter academy conducted by the Rev. Zephaniah Marryat at Plasterer's Hall in London. From 1752 until 1770, Gordon held successive pastorates in the Tackett Street Meeting House in Ipswich and the Gravel Lane Meeting House in Southwark. Due to personal and political differences resulting from his support for the American cause, Gordon eventually left the Southwark congregation and moved to Roxbury, Mass., where he arrived in 1770 and immediately accepted the pastorate of the local Congregational Church. Preceded by his pro-American reputation, Gordon was cultivated by the political elite of nearby Boston, who quickly rewarded his political activities on behalf of the colonies with appointments to the Harvard Board of Overseers and the chaplaincy of the Mass. General Court and with a series of honorary degrees: A.M. (Harvard, 1772; Yale, 1773) and doctor of divinity (Princeton, 1777).

Sometime during the course of the Revolutionary War, Gordon determined to write a general history of the event based upon a careful examination of documents and interviews. Dissatisfied with the leadership in America after the war, Gordon returned in 1786 to Eng., where he spent the next several years writing and publishing his multi-volume *History* and where he died on Oct. 19, 1807, at age 80. At the time of his death, Gordon was living in Ipswich, where he was impoverished and generally ignored.

Critical Appraisal: Although he published several sermons, including the General Election Sermon for 1775, William Gordon's literary reputation rests almost entirely upon his massive *History...of the United States*. Published in London in 1788 and in N.Y. the following year, this work is written in the form of an epistolary exchange, beginning in Dec. 1771 and continuing through Jun. 1783, between an anonymous American and his anonymous English friends. Despite the fact that its value and accuracy were determined by patriots like Ebenezer Hazard (q.v.) and David Ramsay (q.v.), contemporary eighteenth-century readers were by and large distressed by the pro-British sentiments they found in the *History*, and many readers dismissed it as nothing more than a scurrilous attack on the Revolution, which they attributed to Gordon's gradual disillusionment with the course of American leadership after the war.

In fact, Gordon's *History* does indeed possess a somewhat pro-British tone, but this tone stems more from Gordon's difficulty in finding a British publisher for his work than it does from any personal antipathy he might have harbored toward America. In addition, Gordon's reputation as a historian and writer has suffered unduly from unfair comparisons between his work and more recent histories of the Revolution, which make Gordon seem insufficiently analytical and overly reliant on contemporary sources. It should be remembered, however, that at the time when Gordon was writing, the historian had yet to discover the footnote and similar appurtenances of "scientific" history and was generally permitted considerable leeway in the use of sources. As a result, Gordon, like his contemporaries, freely borrowed from the works of others, and that Gordon did so makes his work neither inaccurate nor imperceptive. Generally accurate in his description of the events leading to the outbreak of the Revolution in Mass., Gordon was actually modern in his discussion of popular forces behind the war, particularly the ambivalent role played by the New Eng. merchants, and some of his accounts (e.g., the Boston Massacre and subsequent trial) have been superseded only by the publication of the *Adams Family Papers* some two centuries later. Above all, the *History* combines and effectively transmits the passions and immediacy of Revolutionary America while striking a surprisingly modern and sophisticated tone.

Suggested Readings: CCNE; DAB; T$_2$. *See also* L. H. Gipson, *The British Empire Before the American Revolution* (1967), XIII, 321-326; Zoly Zoltán Haraszti, "More Books from the Adams Library," BPLQ, 3 (1951), 119-122; Orin G. Libby, "Critical Examination of Gordon's History," AHAAR (1800), I, 367-388; "Some Pseudo Historians of the American Revolution," PWASA, 13 (1900), 419-425; George William Pilcher, "William Gordon and the History of the American Revolution," *Historian*, 34 (1972), 447-464.

George W. Pilcher
Ball State University

SIR FERDINANDO GORGES (c. 1566-1647)

Works: *A Briefe Relation of the Discovery and Plantation of New England* (1622); *A Briefe Narration of the Original Undertakings of the Advancement of Plantations into the Parts of America* (pub. in Ferdinando Gorges, *America Painted to Life*; 1659).

Biography: Although he never set foot in North America, Sir Ferdinando Gorges is often called "the father of American colonization" because of his indefatigable efforts between 1607 and 1647 to establish settlements in New Eng. The Gorges family name was derived from a lower Normandy hamlet near Carenton, and Ferdinando Gorges was the nineteenth in descent from Ranolph de Gorges, a Norman in the train of William the Conqueror in 1066. Although the Gorges family lands in Wraxall date from the time of Edward II, it is supposed that Ferdinando Gorges was born in 1566 at Clerkenwell, Middlesex County, Eng., the second son of Edmund and Cicely Gorges. While a youth, Gorges probably studied both military science and navigation at Oxford, and he may have put his knowledge to use in service against the Great Armada and the Spanish forces in Portugal in 1589. During these years of political and religious wars, Gorges distinguished himself on the field at Rouen in 1591, where he was knighted by the earl of Essex (Robert Devereux). By 1596 Essex's influence and Henry of Navarre's advice to the queen resulted in Gorges's appointment as commander of the strategic coastal port of Plymouth in Devonshire. Gorges was to continue in this capacity for the major part of his life, although for one year (1601), he was jailed at Gatehouse for suspected complicity in the ill-fated Essex rebellion against Queen Elizabeth.

Restored to his command at Plymouth upon the accession of James I to the throne, Gorges was present in Plymouth when Capt. George Weymouth landed there is 1605 on his return trip from North America. Of the five native Americans brought to Eng. by Weymouth, Gorges took charge of three, and his subsequent discussions with the natives, one of whom was perhaps Squanto, fired his imagination with the prospects of colonizing North America. In 1606 he and other Plymouth-area merchants and noblemen formed the Plymouth Company, which was granted a charter to colonize the area of "Northern Virginia," a domain ranging from what is now Philadelphia to Nova Scotia. From 1606 to 1620, the Plymouth Company sponsored trading, fishing, and colonizing expeditions, but little success resulted from their efforts because of inclement weather, insufficient finances, and often insubordinate sea captains.

In 1620 Gorges and a few of his partners reorganized the Plymouth Company into the Council for New England and petitioned the Privy Council for an exclusive charter. After a lengthy debate over the question of fishing privileges, the Council granted the charter to the Council for New England in 1621. Becoming with this action the sole owners of North American lands between forty and forty-eight degrees North latitude, the Council thus controlled the organization, government, and apportionment of the territory. Gorges's personal dream was to establish a manorial system in North America modeled after the feudal English model, and throughout the 1630s, his alternative vision of the New World's future worried the Massachusetts Bay Colony leaders, who learned in 1623 that Gorges's son Robert held the patent for Mass. Since the Massachusetts Bay colonists had bypassed the Council for New England and had their petition approved by the king, Gorges attempted to annul the Puritans' charter by enlisting the help of, among others, Thomas Morton (q.v.) and Archbishop Laud. By 1639, after engineering a series of political moves that resulted in the recall of the Puritan charter, Gorges was appointed governor-general of New Eng. However, before the 73-year-old man could capitalize on his victory, his partner John Mason died, his finances gave out, John Winthrop (q.v.) refused to return the charter, and the English Civil War began. During the last years of his long and active life, Gorges supported the king during the Civil War. When he died in 1647, his eldest son was bequeathed the patent to the province of Maine; when John Gorges died in 1656 his will gave the patent to Gorges's grandson Ferdinando, who in 1677 sold the title to Massachusetts Bay and relinquished his family's claims to the New World.

Critical Appraisal: Sir Ferdinando Gorges's two major literary efforts narrate the history of the author's attempts to organize numerous expeditions to colonize the New World. Each work briefly comments on the failure of the Plymouth Colony's ventures to establish a lasting settlement, discusses the opposition the company's ventures received in London, outlines Gorges's proposed plan of government in the province he controlled, and presents the potential benefits to be gained from colonization. Viewed in this light, *A Briefe Narration*, published after Gorges's death, would seem merely an expanded version of the earlier *A Briefe Relation* (1622) discussion of events such as Captain John Smith's (q.v.) 1614-1615 expeditions to North America.

Although nominally concerned with similar subjects, *A Briefe Relation* was written, unlike the later work, to raise money for future colonization and to argue for the author's right to a charter virtually giving him and his group a monopoly over the disposition of the New Eng. territory. Written and published during the years when rival claimants and the London Company were contesting Gorges's group's claims, Gorges's narrative opens with objections to those suspecting him of forming a monopoly and to those desiring to profit from New World trading and fishing without having faced the initial hardships of the Plymouth Company. Given the company's financial losses between 1606 and 1620 and the lawless and corrupt activities of English traders then in New Eng., Gorges argued that his group deserved the new charter, because they alone should reap the benefits of their previous efforts and because they alone had an organized system for colonizing the area so as to gain the friendship of the natives and to prevent the Dutch and French from taking over New Eng. In part II of *A Briefe Relation*, Gorges discussed how temperate air, fertile soil, rich fisheries, and tractable natives made New England "the most commodious country for the benefit of our Nation, that ever hath beene found."

On the eve of realizing some profits, finally, from his continued support of colonization, Gorges persuasively made his case by appealing both to practical and spiritual benefits to be had in the New World and to audience sympathy at the series of reverses his company experienced. Given the hardships he encountered, it is surprising that Gorges's firm prose did not dwell longer on fiascos such as John Smith's service to his company; however, Gorges's stoic tone reveals a man confident that any "business [that] was in itself just and righteous" would triumph in the end. Gorges's *A Briefe Narration*, on the other hand, written in the knight's later years, more often discloses the realizations of a man who became resigned to the succession of failures that greeted all of his attempts to colonize New Eng. Divided into two books, *A Briefe Narration* is less a polemic than a serene justification of Gorges's attempts "to make perfect the thorough discovery of the Countrey" so others would benefit. More willing here to relate when the deaths of friends and the failure of his colonists made him "resolve never to intermeddle in any of those courses" again, Gorges's later work is at times a poignant effort by the author to discover the workings of providence within a fabric of disappointment and renewed hope in the future of a land he never visited except in the imagination.

Suggested Readings: DNB. *See also* James P. Baxter, *Sir Ferdinando Gorges and His Province of Maine* (1890); Henry S. Burrage, *Gorges and the Grant of the Province of Maine, 1622* (1923); Raymond Gorges, *The Story of a Family* (1944); John E. Pomfret, *Founding of the American Colonies, 1583-1660* (1970), pp. 168-171, passim; Richard A. Preston, *Gorges of Plymouth Fort* (1953); *Publications of the Gorges Society*; Alfred L. Rowse, *The Elizabethans in America* (1959), pp. 104-122, passim; John Seelye, *Prophetic Waters* (1977), pp. 162-168, passim; Lyon G. Tyler, *England in America, 1580-1642* (1969), pp. 204-209, passim; Alden T. Vaughan, *New England Frontier: Puritans and Indians, 1620-1675* (1965), pp. 9-10, passim; Louis B. Wright, *The Atlantic Frontier* (1959), pp. 104-105, passim.

Stephen Tatum
University of Utah

SAMUEL GORTON (c. 1592-1677)

Works: *Simplicities Defence Against Seven-Headed Policy* (1646); *An Incorruptible Key* (1647); *Saltmarsh Returned from the Dead* (1655); *An Antidote Against the Common Plague of the World* (1656).

Biography: Born about 1592 in Gorton, Eng., Samuel Gorton later established himself in London as a clothier. In 1636/7 he arrived in Boston, Mass., but soon removed to Plymouth and then to R.I., where he and his followers established their own settlement at Shawomet (later called Warwick). Because of his radical theological and political views, Gorton frequently ran afoul of the various colonial governments under whose jurisdiction he found himself, even arousing the ire of the usually tolerant Roger Williams (q.v.). These difficulties grew more severe in 1643, when Gorton was summoned to Boston to answer the complaint of two Indian sachems who charged that he had seized their lands illegally. Gorton refused to answer the charges, and after he had sent the Bay magistrates several immoderate letters (included in his *Simplicities Defence*), he was arrested by an expeditionary force led by Edward Johnson (q.v.), who later recorded the event in his *Wonder-Working Providence* (1654). Brought to Boston for trial as heretics and enemies to civil order, Gorton and a number of his followers were forced to explain their theological views in writing and then were sentenced to chains and hard labor in the towns surrounding Boston. Within a few months, however, the General Court overturned its sentences and freed the Gortonists, at which time Gorton himself sailed for Eng. to bring a formal complaint against Mass. for detaining him and his followers. Between 1644 and 1648, Gorton joined in the activities of Eng.'s radical underground by publishing several books that display an ideology similar to that of groups such as the Ranters and Levellers and by preaching in and around London to large audiences who found his theology compelling. In 1648 Gorton returned to Warwick, where he spent the remainder of his life. Until his death in 1677, he continued his support for radical causes by encouraging groups such as the Quakers to settle in the area, and as one report has it, he even met with the renowned Quaker leader George Fox when he traveled to that colony in the early 1670s.

Critical Appraisal: Samuel Gorton's primary importance in American history is as a representative of the complex Antinomian culture that emerged in Eng. in the 1620s and 1630s and continued to leaven radical politics during the English Civil Wars. The central doctrine of Gorton's theology—apparent in all of his writings, but particularly evident in *Simplicities Defence*—was a belief in the indwelling of the Holy Spirit in all men and a willingness to follow its dictates over the demands of any human ordinances. From this belief sprang Gorton's resistance to the various New Eng. governments under whose jurisdiction he lived, as well as his open contempt for the civil and ecclesiastical power of the Puritan clergy. Moreover, his belief in the animating presence of the Holy Spirit in all men fostered an antiauthoritarianism that linked him to the Levellers in Eng. and that made the Mass. authorities fear the potentially anarchic effects of his social philosophy.

Although Gorton never openly declared himself a Ranter, Leveller, or Quaker, his published works suggest that in his own idiosyncratic theology, he borrowed elements from each group. What now is apparent, however, is that he was not explicitly a "Familist," as he so often was labeled by his New Eng. enemies. He denounced critics who leveled such charges at him, and as the title of one of his works suggests, he preferred to be identified with the teachings of men like John Saltmarsh and William Dell, whose conceptions of Free Grace were similar to his and who were instrumental in developing some of the views later expressed by the Quakers. Gorton's brief return to Eng. at the height of the Civil War and the favorable reception afforded his writings and preaching seal the testament to his radical affinities.

In addition to presenting a historical narrative of Gorton's difficulties with the New Eng. Puritans, *Simplicities Defence* contains much theological and political discourse that enables historians to locate his ideological connections to the English Puritan underground. The New Eng. Puritans were sufficiently troubled by this book to have it answered by their agent in London, Edward Winslow (q.v.), in *Hypocrisie Unmasked* (1647). *An Incorruptible Key* further defines

Gorton's radical beliefs; in this work, he ostensibly answered John Cotton's (q.v.) exposition of the same psalm, but he also clarified his belief—akin to Roger Williams's—that civil magistrates have no right to meddle in affairs of conscience. In his two later works, sent to London from Warwick, Gorton explicitly invoked the spirit of John Saltmarsh and demonstrated that, even after the failure of the radical reordering of English society, Gorton himself still believed in the importance of the English radicals' political goals.

The New Eng. Puritans' deep resentment of Gorton stemmed from more than the ideological implications of his mysticism, for his presence in New Eng. threatened to broadcast to the Protestant world that the pure Congregational polity they had established in the New World offered a spawning ground for aberrant doctrines such as his. Gorton's writings—published at a time when the American Puritans were particularly sensitive to criticism in Eng.—lent support to the English and Scotch Presbyterians' charge that English Puritans had to institute a more structured ecclesiastical polity than the one established by the Cambridge Platform in New Eng. Like Anne Hutchinson, John Wheelwright (q.v.), and others, Gorton played a significant role in altering the New Eng. Puritans' conception of their mission in Protestant history.

Suggested Readings: DAB; DNB; T₁. *See also* Charles Deane, "Notice of Samuel Gorton," NEHGR, 4 (1850), 201-220; Philip F. Gura, "The Radical Ideology of Samuel Gorton: New Light on the Relation of English to American Puritanism," WMQ, 3rd ser., 36 (1979), 78-100; Lewis Janes, *Samuel Gorton: A Forgotten Founder of Our Liberties* (1896); John M. Mackie, "Life of Samuel Gorton, One of the First Settlers of Warwick, in Rhode Island," in *Library of American Biography*, ed. Jared Sparks, 2nd ser., 5 (1864), 317-411; Kenneth W. Porter, "Samuel Gorton: New England Firebrand," NEQ, 7 (1934), 405-444; William R. Staples, Introduction, *Simplicities Defence*, by Samuel Gorton, RIHSC, 2 (1835).

Philip F. Gura
University of Colorado, Boulder

JOHN GRAHAM (1694-1774)

Works: *The Oligations* (1725); *A Ballad Against the Church of England* (1732); *The Christian's Duty* (1733); *Some Remarks upon a Late Pamphlet* (1733); *The Duty of Renewing* (1734); *Some Remarks upon a Second Letter* (1736); *Such as Have Grace* (1746); *The Sufficiency of a Worm* (1746); *The Spiritual Watchman* (1750); *An Answer to Mr. Gale's Pamphlet* (1759); *A Letter to a Member of the House of Representatives of...Connecticut* (1759); *A Few Remarks on the Remarker* (1760).

Biography: John Graham was born in Edinburgh, Scot., in 1694. He studied medicine at Glasgow University, taking a degree in 1714. In 1717 he immigrated to America, landing in N.H., then moving on to Conn. Later he studied theology, and in 1723 he was ordained as the first minister of Stafford, Conn. In 1731 Graham obtained his dismissal on grounds of insufficient support, and two years later he settled in Southbury, Conn., where he was again ordained as the town's first minister. Graham was an ardent New Light and an enthusiastic exponent of experimental religion, and in defense of his principles, he engaged in a series of polemical disputes with Old Lights, Quakers, and Anglicans. In 1737 Graham received an honorary M.A. from Yale College. He died in Southbury in 1774.

Critical Appraisal: John Graham's zealous devotion to the doctrines of revivalist religion is evident in all of his writings. Thus in his ordination sermons of the 1740s (*Such as Have Grace, The Sufficiency of a Worm, The Spiritual Watchman*), he seized the opportunity to reassert the necessity that ministers themselves experience the motions of saving grace. More commonly, Graham's commitment to his cause expressed itself in aggressive polemical exchanges with opponents.

In 1733 Graham composed his *Ballad Against the Church of England in Connecticut*. Samuel Johnson (q.v.), the most prominent Anglican in the colony, chose to respond in print to what he termed a "scurrilous Paper of Verses." Graham happily replied to the response, and the controversy persisted through 1736 with Johnson's persistence gaining him the last word (Graham's further contributions being *Some Remarks upon a Late Pamphlet* and *Some Remarks upon a Second Letter*). Graham's essential object was to prove "the Presbyterian Government truly apostolic," but he was aware that this discussion of ecclesiastical polity might serve as an Anglican diversion from the more important differences in doctrine. The level of the debate was not always elevated: Johnson disparaged Graham as a "sour-tempered Gentleman" and an "unaccountable Man," and Graham at one point curiously undertook to demonstrate that during the English Civil War, the Presbyterians had been guilty neither of intolerance nor regicide.

Graham's argument with the Quakers (*The Christian's Duty*) proved little more than his unwavering commitment to his own creed, but his involvement in the controversy concerning Thomas Stephen Clap (q.v.), the New Light president of Yale, led him to make certain radical propositions in the field of politics—arguing essentially that voters should select representatives whose principles accorded with their own, rather than merely approve the most eminent men in the community.

Graham's style is often as enthusiastic as his principles. He sometimes writes with a vigor that might have made Swift grin. His sermon, *Such as Have Grace*, begins with a challenge to linguistic as well as theological decorum:

> However the atheistical Scoffers of a degenerate Age may ridicule experimental Religion, as *Enthusiasm*, and resolve all the Experience of the Godly into no better Original than an over-heated Brain, disorder'd Imagination, and Confusion in mere animal Nature, improved by a Spirit of fanatick Delusion, on purpose to lead men into the Fogs and Quag-mires of Error; yet the most thinking, sober and judicious Sort of Men, to wit, real Christians, find that Reality and Sweetness in it, which is to their Souls more precious than Ten Thousand Such Worlds as This.

Suggested Readings: CCNE; Sprague (I, 314-316). *See also* Richard L. Bushman, *From Puritan to Yankee* (1967); Joseph J. Ellis, *The New England Mind in Transition* (1973).

J. Kenneth Van Dover
Lincoln University

ELLIS GRAY (1715-1753)

Works: *The Design* (1741); *The Fidelity of Ministers* (1742).

Biography: Ellis Gray was born in Boston, Mass., on Sept. 7, 1715, the son of Hannah (Ellis) and Edward Gray, a wealthy rope manufacturer. Educated at Harvard College (B.A., 1734; M.A., 1737), Gray was ordained the third minister of the New Brick Congregational Church (also called the North Brick or Seventh Church), in Boston on Sept. 27, 1738. Gray was the third minister in the history of the New Brick Church, not the second one, as Clifford K. Shipton erroneously states (the first minister was William Waldron, who died in 1727). On Sept. 20, of the following year, Gray married Sarah Tyler of Boston, who became known for her efficiency and frugality in the management of their household; they had five children, one of whom (their first-born, a son) died in infancy. In Jun. 1742, when James Davenport, one of the most erratic of the Great Awakening revivalists, accused a Congregational minister at Charlestown of being unconverted, Gray was among sixteen ministers who signed a statement rebuking him for his impulsive excesses and closing their churches to him. Although Gray had initially favored George Whitefield (q.v.) and the Great Awakening, he became increasingly disturbed by the excesses of the revivalists, and when Whitefield visited Boston in 1745, Gray refused to invite him to preach at his church. In 1749 Gray preached the Artillery Election Sermon. He died in Boston on Jan. 7, 1753, the same year as his copastor at the New Brick Church, William Welsteed. According to Samuel Mather (q.v.), who preached the funeral sermon, Gray was remembered as a man of "gracious calm, a Divine Composure, [and] an Heavenly satisfaction in his own Mind."

Critical Appraisal: When the third anniversary of Ellis Gray's ordination fell on a Lord's Day, Sept. 27, 1741, he took as his topic for his morning sermon that day his views concerning the ministry. With Paul's defense before King Agrippa (Acts 26) as his point of departure, Gray in *The Design* interpreted Christ's commission to Paul as "the Design of the Institution of the Gospel-Ministry," given not just to Paul but also to ministers of the Gospel in all ages. Gray pointed to Paul as an example of fidelity to the commission of Christ and also as an example of gratitude to "the Power and Grace of GOD in him and with him, especially in preserving him."

In the controversies about the Great Awakening, some revivalists accused their critics of being unconverted, in the sense of lacking deep, personal experience of spiritual regeneration. This sort of argument "poisoned the wells": if the critics were unconverted, then anyone—even a minister—who spoke out against the excesses of the revivalists risked being written off as unconverted and unregenerate. Gilbert Tennent (q.v.) precipitated the Presbyterian schism of 1741 with his abusive sermon *The Danger of an Unconverted Ministry* (1740), which Gray may have read in its Boston reprint (1742); and Gray certainly remembered Davenport's accusation against the minister at Charlestown. Near the beginning of *Fidelity*, Gray affirmed his belief in the importance and the expediency of a converted ministry, but he also sought to allay the fears of those who, influenced by various revivalists, wonder whether some ministers are indeed unconverted and unregenerate. Gray argued that the view that only a converted person can be instrumental in begetting souls to God and carrying on the work of grace derogates from God's honor and ascribes

> too much of the Glory of converting Grace to a poor weak Instrument . . . the entire Glory of it is to be ascribed to the Grace and Sovereignty of God. . . . Now when a Person regularly introduc'd into the Ministry, clearly explains, and urges, and enforces the great Doctrines and Duties of the Gospel, though perhaps all the while he may be destitute of an experimental Knowledge of, and Acquaintance with these Things, to say that God will never own the Ministry of such an one, is . . . altogether without any Warrant from the Word of God.

The Fidelity of Ministers is an ordination sermon, preached on Nov. 3, 1742. From Paul's solemn charge to the elders at Ephesus (Acts 20:28), Gray unfolded the character of a faithful minister of the Gospel, and he discussed the motives and arguments with which Paul's charge to the Ephesian elders—and to all succeeding generations of ministers—is enforced. In contrast to the complete absence of such references in *Design*, preached thirteen months earlier, there are occasional passing references to the Great Awakening in *Fidelity*. Perhaps some of the events of the intervening year, such as Davenport's conduct at Charlestown, convinced Gray that it was time to speak out, or perhaps he felt more free to criticize the Great Awakening while preaching an ordination sermon elsewhere (at Kingston, Mass.) than he did in his own church, which remained neutral about the Awakening. Near the end of *Fidelity*, Gray acknowledged that God's grace has been at work in the land, truly converting many persons.

> But Oh at the same Time the busy Adversary has been very active in sowing his Tares the Seeds of Discord and Division in our Churches . . . the Characters of some of our most aged, faithful and experienc'd Guides . . . have been injuriously struck at. And Oh the lamentable Divisions that seem to be prevailing in many Churches of the Land!

Gray called on his fellow Christians neither to overlook the substantial and valuable things that have taken place nor to "put the divine Stamp upon those Things which will give the Scoffer Occasion to speak reproachfully of our most holy Religion, & which cannot without the greatest Dishonour be attributed to the Holy Spirit."

Regrettably, the topics of Gray's two published sermons did not provide him with much scope for originality: in his day, it was commonplace for anyone preaching about the ministry to stick close to what Paul had declared about it. Nonetheless, Gray's preaching skills and personal piety were probably great sources of satisfaction to his congregation. He could occasionally get worked up enough about some controversial issue to take a·stand on it, and in his brief critical comments on the Great Awakening, he contributed to New Eng. literature on that movement.

Suggested Readings: CCNE: Sibley-Shipton (IX, 400-404). *See also* Emerson Davis, *Biographical Sketches of the Congregational Pastors of New England*, typescript, from a nineteenth-century ms., deposited in the Congregational Library, Boston, I, 163-164; Edwin S. Gaustad, "Society and the Great Awakening in New England," WMQ, 3rd ser., 11 (1954), 576; Harold Field Worthley, *An Inventory of the Records of the Particular (Congregational) Churches of Massachusetts Gathered, 1620-1805*, HTS, 25 (1970), 77. For the text of the Boston/Charlestown ministers' statement about Davenport (1742), see *Christian History*, II (1745), pp. 406-407. Tennent's sermon, *The Danger of an Unconverted Ministry*, is reprinted in *The Great Awakening*, ed. Alan Heimert and Perry Miller (1967), pp. 71-99. Samuel Mather, *The Walk of the Upright* (1753), is a funeral discourse on the deaths of Gray and his co-pastor, William Welsteed.

Richard Frothingham
University of Arkansas at Little Rock

ROBERT GRAY (fl. 1609)

Works: *A Good Speed to Virginia* (w. 1609; rep., 1864, 1937).

Biography: Virtually nothing is known of the author of *A Good Speed to Virginia*, although he was probably the Robert Gray who served as rector of St. Bennet's Sherehog, London, 1606-1612, and who published a sermon, "An Alarum to England," in 1609. *A Good Speed* was the third major work published on Va., after Capt. John Smith's (q.v.) *True Relation* (1608) and Robert Johnson's (q.v.) *Nova Britannia* (1609), on which Gray's argument relies heavily. *A Good Speed* has little of substance to add to the great debate on British imperialism, but its emphasis on colonizing as a patriotic duty and a guarantee of immortality surely affected popular response to the project.

Critical Appraisal: In comparison with most other works in its mode, *A Good Speed* is well-written and cogently argued. It is so polished a piece of promotion, in fact, that one reader, J. Payne Collier, has argued seriously that the mysterious "Robert Gray" was no less a person than Sir Walter Raleigh (*Illustrations of Early English Popular Literature* [1864], pp. 1 ff.). Constructed as a sermon, the work states its thesis plainly: "it is everie man's dutie to travell both by sea and land, and to venture, either with his person or with his purse, to bring the barbarous and savage people to a civil and Christian kinde of government." To defend this unoriginal, but still much argued, notion, Gray first made a logical point and then followed quickly in each case with citations from the Bible designed to prove beyond doubt that God agrees: Eng., for example, is a prosperous but overcrowded Christian nation. Something must be done to relieve the pressures for preferment and opportunity. Yet we cannot employ the powers of civil law to reduce the population, nor is it either Christian or wise to make war on sparsely populated nations in order to create new openings for the young. Still, as the children of Israel said to Joshua, "we are a great people, and the lande is too narrow for us." It is apparent, therefore, that we must be "both prudent and politicke," avoiding "impudent" rejection of "profitable and gainful expectation." In fact, it is our duty to act as Christian militants, gathering "the pleasures and riches of the earth," so that they are never again usurped by beasts and wild men. Rich nations are taught their special obligations by the events of the Old Testament: they must regard it as holy to "reclaim an idolator" and seize the world from "odious" tribes of savages. We will, in short, make advancement for ourselves possible by teaching barbarians how to save their own souls. As for Va.: its Indians are known to be particularly bestial but also "desirous to embrace a better condition"; no true Englishman will ignore the opportunities Va. presents.

After such hyperbolical, if not unpersuasive, sermonizing, Gray attempted to meet head-on some of the stronger objections to expansion. His characteristic mixture of shallow biblical exegesis and shrewd good sense never failed him: "It is true, for example, that we seek to deprive of their inheritance men who have provoked us in no way. Yet what men they are!" Residing as the wild beasts reside, they surely have "no particular proprietie." They "range and wander up and downe the Countrey, without any law or government," save that of "their owne lusts and sensualitie." The Bible has taught Christians to be politicians, to make war on barbarians. To a further objection against expansion—that it is not profitable—Gray took another tack by quoting Proverbs on the theme of building for posterity. For those concerned chiefly for their own profit, he provided a reminder from Job 18: "They that do not provide for eternitie, can have no assured hope of eternitie, and they which onely are for themselves, shall die in themselves."

Finally, Gray compiled a list of rules for future colonists. Attempting to imitate Joshua's exhortation to his people, he urged that debate and delay be replaced by a combination of art and industry. If Englishmen use both muscle and wit to "cast out those Idolatrous Cananites" in Va., they may also prevent popery from spreading to America. Eng. will prove to all of the world not only that it is blessed, but that it knows how to fend for itself in a world of heathens.

A Good Speed to Virginia, although apparently not sponsored by the Virginia Company, is typical of the promotional literature then being written on the colony's behalf. Its ethics, if dubious, are at least candidly expressed and practical, and both its style and argument make it more readable than the usual defense of colonizing.

Suggested Readings: Howard Mumford Jones, *O Strange New World: American Culture: The Formative Years* (1964), pp. 179-185; *The Oxford Companion to American Literature* (1941), p. 288; Louis B. Wright, "A Western Canaan Reserved for England," *Religion and Empire: The Alliance Between Piety and Commerce in English Expansion: 1558-1625* (1943), pp. 84-113.

James Stephens
Marquette University

ALEXANDER GRAYDON (1752-1816)

Works: *Memoirs of a Life, Chiefly Passed in Pennsylvania, within the Last Sixty Years* (w. 1811; first pub. 1822; repub. as *The Life of an Officer*, 1828; and as *Memoirs of His Own Time*, ed. by John Stockton Littell, 1846 [this edition was republished in 1969 by *The New York Times*]).

Biography: Revolutionary War Veteran and author, Alexander Graydon was born in Bristol, Pa., on Apr. 10, 1752, to Alexander and Rachel (Marks) Graydon. The elder Graydon—a merchant, lawyer, and colonel in Pa.'s provincial army—had emigrated from Ire. to Philadelphia in 1730 and is described further as a recognized leader of that city's social and business worlds as well as a well-known habitué of its coffeehouses. Mrs. Graydon was of German and Scottish ancestry.

Alexander Graydon attended David James Dove's school and at the age of 8 was sent to the College and Academy of Philadelphia. Although forced by his father to study law at age 16, Graydon was more interested in poetry, metaphysics, wine, and women and soon gained a reputation as a skillful fencer and enthusiastic taverngoer.

When the Revolution began, Graydon volunteered for service in Philadelphia but was soon disillusioned by the Patriots' treatment of two Loyalists, Dr. Kearsley and Isaac Hunt (q.v.). He later wrote of a sense of truth and justice instilled in him at an early age that "prevented his becoming a patriot, in the modern acceptation of the word." Commissioned by Congress as a captain on Jan. 6, 1776, he recruited and drilled a battalion before being sent on an expedition to join Gen. Philip Schuyler at Lake George in May. He then rejoined the Continental troops in N.Y., covering George Washington's (q.v.) retreat from Long Island to New York City during the Battle of Long Island. During the Battle of Harlem Heights, the British captured him at Fort Washington and he was taken to N.Y. Transferred to Flatbush on Long Island in Jan. 1777, he was paroled eight months later. He returned to Philadelphia, after stopping at American camps in Morristown and Reading, and although officially exchanged in the spring of 1778, he did not return to the army. He did, however, get married that year to a Miss Wood of Berks County, who died six years later.

Although not an active politician, Graydon was elected prothonotary of Dauphin County in 1785 and moved to Harrisburg. A firm advocate of the federal Constitution, he was elected as a member of the state convention to ratify it. His term of service as prothonotary ended in 1799 with Thomas McKean's election as governor, Graydon's federalism being in direct opposition to the republicanism espoused by McKean.

Graydon retired to a small farm near Harrisburg with his second wife, Theodosia Pettit, and spent most of his time in writing. He contributed articles to literary and political journals, including "Notes of a Desultory Reader" in the Philadelphia *Port-Folio* and contributions to John Fenno's (q.v.) *Gazette*. In 1811 he composed his autobiography in Harrisburg. Titled *Memoirs of a Life, Chiefly Passed in Pennsylvania within the Last Sixty Years; with Occasional Remarks upon the General Occurrences, Character, and Spirit of the Eventful Period*, it has been described as one of the most valuable (and undervalued) historical sources of the period. In 1822 Graydon's *Memoirs* was edited by John Galt for publication under a different title by Blackwood's in Edinburgh. Galt called it "perhaps, the best personal narrative that has yet appeared relative to the history of that great conflict which terminated in establishing the independence of the United States." Despite the opinion of the *Quarterly Review* (vol. 26, p. 364), which ventured "to pronounce [it] to be in matter almost worthless, and in manner wholly contemptible," Blackwood's republished it in 1828 under a modified title. Although Graydon had suffered from political realities, his book remains relatively free from political bias but is rich in humor, opinion, anecdotes, shrewd character observation, and considerable literary charm. Graydon spent the last two years of his life in Philadelphia to be closer to the literary and publishing world and died there on May 2, 1816..

Critical Appraisal: In nearly 400 pages, Alexander Graydon, in his *Memoirs*, gives the reader more than just "occasional remarks" concerning the "occurrences, character, and spirit" of his time. His intent, he stated in the introduction, was to "relate incidents within the scope of ordinary life" and his excuse was that he "lived and was an author." He provided the reader with a personal glimpse of society, individuals, and events of the Revolutionary and early national period that is both vivid and entertaining.

Graydon began his account with a background of his family's history and his early days at David James Dove's unorthodox school and John Beveridge's (q.v.) Latin school. These early chapters of schoolboy days are followed by a description of figures in Philadelphia society in the pre-Revolutionary era. His account of his legal education and all of the things that distracted him from it, from women to the novels of Richardson, offer amusing insight into colonial life.

Before the Revolution, Graydon finally became a lawyer, but he soon turned the attention of the narrative to the political events brewing at the time and began his tale of military life and the Revolution. He quickly dispelled the notion that 1776 saw a groundswell of patriotism and described the "cradle of liberty" as a faction-ridden place indeed. He characterized the soldiers from New Eng. with whom he came in contact as corrupt nepotists and detailed his part in the battles in N.Y., his capture by the British, and his just treatment in their hands. Along the way, he provided character sketches of people he met such as Philip Schuyler, Thomas Mifflin, Robert Howe, Israel Putnam, Nathanael Greene, Ethan Allen (q.v.), George Washington, Alexander Hamilton (q.v.), Anthony Wayne, and Benjamin Franklin (q.v.). The post-Revolutionary period is concerned with his views of the problems of the new government under Washington, John Adams (q.v.), and Thomas Jefferson (q.v.) including the Whiskey Rebellion and the intrigues of Br. and Fr.

The memoirs are narrated in a lively style and with a contagious enthusiasm. For someone who led what he described as an "ordinary life," Graydon detailed a wealth of extraordinary experiences and was in the right place at the right time often enough to write first-hand impressions of many historical figures. His opinions on the politics of the time are forthright but never doctrinaire. Moreover, his work is an excellent study in the manners of social life of his time, especially those of pre-Revolutionary Philadelphia. One might certainly agree with John Stockton Littell that the book is too neglected. It offers a fine contrast to the memoirs and autobiographies of the more famous, who have a greater stake in self-aggrandizement. Graydon's tale is more often history than outright autobiography and is all the more invaluable as a study of his period.

Suggested Readings: DAB. *See also* Robert Reed Sanderlin, "Alexander Graydon: The Life and Literary Career of an American Patriot" (Ph.D. diss., Univ. of N.C., (1968).

Randal A. Owen
St. Mary's Dominican College

JACOB GREEN (1722-1790)

Works: *Christian Baptism* (1766); *Spiritual Inability* (1767); *A Vision of Hell...by Theodorus Van Shermain* (1767); *An Inquiry into the Constitution and Discipline of the Jewish Church* (1768); *A Reply to the Rev. Mr. George Beckwith's Answer* (1769); *A Small Help Offered to Heads of Families* (1771); *Observations on the Reconciliation of Great-Britain and the Colonies* (1776); *A Sermon Delivered at Hanover* (1779); *A Sermon on Persons Possessing the Iniquities of Their Youth in After Life* (1780); *A View of the Christian Church* (1781). Green also wrote several newspaper essays, including a series of noteworthy contributions to the *New Jersey Journal*: "Letters on Our Paper Currency" (Nov.-Dec. 1779); "On Liberty" (May 3 and May 10, 1780); and "Negro Slavery" (Jan. 31, 1781). Jacob Green's autobiography, titled "Sketch of the Life of Rev. Jacob Green, A.M.," was published serially by his son, Ashbel Green, in the *Christian Advocate* (Aug. 1831-May 1832).

Biography: Clergyman, politician, and reformer—Jacob Green was born in Malden, Mass., on Jan. 22, 1722. His father, also named Jacob, died shortly after Green's birth. Until age 14, Green lived with his mother and her second husband, John Barret, in Killingly, Conn., spending the remaining time before he entered college with various relatives. In 1740 Green began studying at Harvard, where he was graduated with the class of 1744. During his stay at Harvard, Green was influenced by the preaching of Gilbert Tennent (q.v.), the famous evangelist, and he showed an inclination to enter the ministry.

After teaching school for a short period of time in Sutton, Mass., Green was asked by George Whitefield (q.v.) to head his proposed orphanage in Ga. That plan did not work out, but Green received a license to preach, and in 1746 was ordained pastor of the Presbyterian church in Hanover, Morris County, N.J. He remained there until his death on May 24, 1790, serving his congregation as both minister and physician. Appointed a trustee of the College of N.J. (now Princeton University), Green held that position, along with his other duties, from 1748 until 1764. After the death of Jonathan Edwards (q.v.) on March 22, 1758, Green, then acting as vice-president of the college, assumed the responsibilities of administering the institution until the new president, Samuel Davies (q.v.), arrived in July of the following year.

At the time of the American Revolution, Green was an outspoken advocate of American independence, and in May of 1776, he was one of five, from a group of twenty-nine candidates, elected to serve on the newly formed Provincial Congress of New Jersey. As a member of the Congress, Green chaired the committee which drafted the state's constitution, for which he has been suggested as a primary author. Throughout his career Green championed the rights of black slaves. Arguing publicly for the abolition of slavery in N.J. and the colonies, he was for a time extremely unpopular with the many slaveholders in his community. In 1780 Green and several other ministers left the Presbyterian Church and founded the Associated Presbytery of Morris County. Green's main problem with the Presbyterians involved the centralized authority which synods maintained over individual congregations.

Green was twice married: to Anna Strong in 1747 and, after her death in 1756, to Elizabeth Pierson, the granddaughter of Abraham Pierson (q.v.), the first president of Yale College. Among Green's ten children was Ashbel Green, a future president of the College of N.J. According to the inscription on his tombstone, Green "was a man of temper, even, firm and resolute; of affections, temperate, steady and benevolent; of genius, solid, inquisitive and penetrating; of industry, active and unwearied; of learning, various and accurate; of manners, simple and reserved; [and] of piety, humble, enlightened, fervent and eminent."

Critical Appraisal: A reformer by both inclination and decision, Jacob Green made numerous contributions to the theological, political, and social debates of his day. In his religious concerns, Green stood somewhere between the Presbyterians and the older forms of Congregationalism. He believed, for example, in Presbyterian ordination, but he preferred the independent church structure of the Congregationalists. Like Jonathan Edwards, by whom he was influenced, Green adopted a Calvinistic view of God as an absolute sovereign, and on the issue of predestination he wrote that "God has a Right to take some into Favour, redeem and save them, and to leave others to perish in their sins." Concerning church participation, Green argued that only the saved should be admitted to communion, a view which he defended in a pamphlet debate with George Beckwith (q.v.), who advocated a less stringent admission policy. Many of Green's theological opinions were popularized in his most famous work, *Visions of Hell*. Artfully told through the persona of a "Theodorus Van Shermain" and frequently reprinted, *Visions of Hell* consists of a conversation, theoretically overheard by the writer, between Satan and various other devils about their current problems in catching souls. Chief among Satan's favorites in this world were the Rogerenes, the Conn. followers of the heretic John Rogers (q.v.), who had argued in favor of personal inspiration and against ministerial salaries.

In the area of politics, Green was one of the most successful and influential of the patriot preachers of the Revolution. His outspoken advocacy of the inevitability and justice of American independence, as expressed in his *Observations on the Reconciliation of Great-Britain and the Colonies*, did much to further the cause of the Patriots at a time when reconciliation still seemed a desirable possibility, even to someone like John Dickinson (q.v.). Green's vision of an independent America as a "land of liberty" and "an asylum for all noble spirits and sons of liberty from all parts of the world" shares much in common with the patriotic writings of men such as Thomas Paine (q.v.) and J. Hector St. John de Crèvecoeur (q.v.), with whom he has sometimes been compared. Throughout the war, Green remained faithful to his country's cause, even when the British invaded N.J. and his opinions brought him into personal danger. His widely circulated newspaper essays "On Liberty," for example, helped to bolster the morale of the American populace in the face of British victories, and his "Letters on Our Paper Currency," also published in a newspaper, pointed out the deleterious effects on the American cause of an inflated monetary system overly dependent on the fiscally irresponsible production of unsound paper money.

Ultimately, however, Green's most important writings may very well have been those arguing for an end to the institution of slavery both in N.J. and the other colonies. Like his Quaker contemporary and fellow New Jerseyite, John Woolman (q.v.), Green believed that "slavery [was] one of the great and crying evils" of his day, and he sincerely hoped that in time "the guilt of slavery would be banished from us." According to Green, who wrote and preached tirelessly on the subject, "the slavery of human creatures who are naturally free" was "an unnatural evil and one of the greatest injuries that can be done to human nature." Believing that slavery was incompatible with true Christianity, he made it a point of policy not to "admit into our Church any that hold persons in slavery as slaves during life, unless in some particular cases,...[as] when aged slaves ought to be taken care of and supported during life." Green was also among the first to note the "dreadful absurdity" in the "shocking consideration that people who are so strenuously contending for liberty should at the same time encourage and promote slavery!" Green even went so far as to see the war and the victories of the

British during the war as a punishment from God on the colonies for refusing to abolish slavery. In his *Sermon Delivered at Hanover* on a "day of public fasting and prayer throughout the United States of America," for example, Green stated, "I cannot but think our practising Negro Slavery is the most crying sin in our Land, and that on this account more than any other, God maintains a controversy with us." A major voice in his country's struggle for human liberty, Green deserves more attention than he has received.

Suggested Readings: CCMC; DAB; Sibley-Shipton (XI, 405-416); Sprague (III, 135-139); T₂. *See also* Robert M. Benton, "The Preachers" (pp. 87-104), and Elaine K. Ginsberg, "The Patriot Pamphleteers" (pp. 19-38), in Everett Emerson, ed., *American Literature, 1764-1789: The Revolutionary Years* (1977); Joseph F. Tuttle, "Rev. Jacob Green, of Hanover, N.J., as an Author, Statesman and Patriot," NJHSP, 2d ser. 12 (1893), 189-241.

James A. Levernier
University of Arkansas at Little Rock

JONAS GREEN (1712-1767)

Works: *Maryland Gazette* (editor; 1745-1767); "Lugubrus Cantus," *Maryland Gazette* (with others; 1751); "Properties of a Gardiner," *Maryland Gazette* (1758)."Anniversary Ode, 1754" (1975).

Biography: The descendant of two generations of New Eng. printers, Jonas Green was baptized in Cotton Mather's (q.v.) church in Boston, Mass., on Dec. 28, 1712, and grew up in New London, Conn., serving an apprenticeship under his father, "Deacon" Timothy Green. At age 23, Green joined his oldest brother's firm, Kneeland and Green, in Boston, but by 1736 he was in Philadelphia working for either Benjamin Franklin (q.v.) or Andrew Bradford (q.v.). In Apr. 1738, Green married Anne Catherine Hoof at Philadelphia and the following month was invited to become the public printer in Md. Green moved to Annapolis in 1738 and began operating his press the following year. In 1745 Green established the second *Maryland Gazette*, a weekly that, except for an interruption during the Revolution, was continued by members of his family until 1839. From 1758 until 1766, Green's partner in the printing business was William Rind. Thomas Sparrow, the first Md. engraver, made engravings for the press. At various times, Green held the positions of alderman and postmaster of Annapolis, vestryman and registrar of St. Anne's Parish in that city, auctioneer of the Anne Arundel County venues, clerk of entries for the Annapolis races, and secretary of the local lodge of Masons. Of the fourteen children born to him and his wife between 1738 and 1760, eight died in childhood. Fondly remembered as a witty, whimsical, and good-natured friend, Green died in Annapolis on Apr. 11, 1767.

Critical Appraisal: As yet unpublished, most of Jonas Green's works were prepared between 1748 and 1756 for the Tuesday Club of Annapolis

(1745-1756), a sophisticated coterie of wits who imitated the Scottish comico-literary societies. In the club, Green was known as "Jonathan Grog." His puns, conundrums, odes, club songs, and jokes are scattered through the club papers kept by Dr. Alexander Hamilton (q.v.). This substantial humorous output, with its emphasis on the ribald and the burlesque, its pastoral-maritime-gastronomic metaphors, and clever imitation of the British satirists, offers some of the most enjoyable samples of early American comic literature.

In all, Green wrote six anniversary odes, three mock epics, and a variety of other pieces of varying lengths—eulogies, odes for different occasions, a poetic entry for the minutes of the club, an acrostic in verse, and two "Poetical Speeches." Several of the odes, cleverly modeled on similar verse by the English dramatist-laureate Colley Cibber, were set to music by the club and performed in concert, but none was published in his time; the Ode for 1754, however, appeared in the *Maryland Historical Magazine* (Summer 1975), 70:147-148. His last long poem, titled "A Tragical and Heroic Episode on the Club Tobacco Box," was presented to the Tuesday Club on Sept. 2, 1754. Written with others and published in 1751, "Lugubrus Cantus" is a parody of Spencer that laments the illness and absence of the club president Charles Cole. A mock epic in three cantos, "A Heroic Poem," delivered to the club in Oct. 1752, jokingly recounts the history of the group through the somewhat inconsequential adventures of the president. The incongruity of lazy Charles Cole in the role of the heroic Odysseus or Vergil's Aeneas pokes fun at the absurdities of provincial American social-cultural life. It followed another long poem of Aug. 1751, by the same title, an even more pointed travesty on the pretensions of British society that facetiously re-counts a robbery at the president's house.

Green's self-mockery and his technique of burlesquing a grand theme for a trifling occurrence were typical forms of humor of the Tuesday Club. In recogni-tion of the publisher's wit and in imitation of Alexander Pope's 1742 ridicule of Colley Cibber ("The king had his poet and also his fool"), Green was chosen poet laureate of Annapolis Wits in 1748 and granted the added titles of purveyor, punster, punchmaker general, printer, and poet. Green's earliest critic, Dr. Ham-ilton, noted that he served the club with "acute wit and lively imagination," excelling "in that sort of poetry which is called Doggerell."

According to one source, Green's verses, especially the parodies that lampoon both the form and ideals of English society, may have been refused publication by English magazines because of its very sophistication. His unique contribution to the forms of American literature is the satiric elegy, which, according to another source, "is so entirely different... from New England graveyard verse that it marks a separate genre in America... secular..., pastoral in form and imagery... with mocking or ironic overtones."

It was through the *Maryland Gazette*, however, that Green most affected the development of colonial American literature. As editor of the *Gazette*, Green encouraged local essayists and versifiers to submit pieces to the newspaper and provided a forum for political and social polemics. The literary output of the first three years was alone large enough to merit a critical commentary by his friend, Dr. Hamilton. Green himself contributed a few of the paper's humorous punning pieces. His "Properties of a Gardiner" essay appeared in 1758; the burlesque verse "Lugubrus Cantus" was published in 1751; and he was responsible for the satirical comments printed in the *Gazette* on the Stamp Act of 1765. In addition, Green is probably the author of "Memorandum for a Sein-Hauling, on the Severn River," a poem in the manner of Matthew Prior, and probably contributed to the literary war in verse that took place in the *Gazette* in 1745 between the Annapolis Wits and the Baltimore Bards.

As a printer, Green's fame rests on what has been described as the "typographical monument" of early America—*The Laws of Maryland*, compiled by Thomas Bacon (q.v.) and completed in 1766. He also printed sermons, broadsides, political tracts, almanacs, and the official happenings in the provincial legislature, using his limited equipment "with a serious and thoughtful craftsmanship." From 1758 to 1766 William Rind was his partner in the printing business. Thomas Sparrow, the first Md. engraver, although not of special renown, was also associated with Green and made the engravings for the press. After Green's death in 1767, his press continued in existence until 1845, under the control successively, and sometimes in combination with, his wife, three sons, and a grandson.

Suggested Readings: DAB. *See also* Richard Beale Davis, *Intellectual Life in the Colonial South* (1978), III, 1383-1386, 1466-1469; William C. Kiessel, "The Green Family," NEHGR, 104 (1950), 81-83 (corrects Isaiah Thomas's account of the family [*History of Printing*]; J. A. Leo Lemay, "Hamilton's Literary History of the *Maryland Gazette*," WMQ, 3rd ser., 23 (1966), 273-285; idem, *Men of Letters in Colonial Maryland* (1972), pp. 193-212; Douglas C. McMurtrie, *History of Printing in the United States* (1936), II, 114-117, 423-426; *National Cyclopedia of American Biography*; David C. Skaggs, "Editorial Policies of the *Maryland Gazette*," MdHM, 59 (1964), 341-349; Lawrence C. Wroth, *A History of Printing in Colonial Maryland* (1922), pp. 75-94.

Elaine G. Breslaw
Morgan State University

JOSEPH GREEN (c. 1705-1780)

Works: *Parody of a Psalm by Byles* (1733); *The Poet's Lamentation for the Loss of His Cat* (1733); *The Disappointed Cooper* (w. 1743; pub. 1974); *Entertainment for a Winter's Evening* (1750); *A Mournful Lamentation for the Sad and Deplorable Death of Mr. Old Tenor* (1750); *The Grand Arcanum Detected* (1755); *An Eclogue Sacred to the Memory of. . .Jonathan Mayhew* (1766); *Epitaph on John Cole* (1789); *Fragments* (1829).

Biography: The poet and wit Joseph Green, sometimes known as "Josey" Green or "Stiller Josey," was born in Boston, Mass., sometime around 1705.

Although his record was marred by more than usual departures from the college rules, Green received an M.A. from Harvard in 1729. After graduation, rather than pursuing a career in the ministry, Green became a merchant, beginning as distiller (hence "Stiller Josey") and eventually acquiring considerable land and other business interests. Even though Green's reputation rests mainly on his verse satires, he also wrote several prose satires about then Governor Jonathan Belcher that appeared in Boston newspapers.

Complementing Green's lighter side was his appreciation for culture and learning. A fine Classical scholar, he was known for his comprehensive knowledge. It is said that, before his departure from America in the winter of 1774-1775, he had accumulated one of Boston's largest personal libraries. Despite the fact that much of his verse is bawdy (called "filthy" by one of his critics), Green was a man of strong religious commitment; he was also a charter member of the Society for Propagating Christian Knowledge among the Indians of North America.

In 1761 Green married Elizabeth (Cross) Austin, a widow. The couple had no children, but from the date of his marriage, Green's business activities increased markedly. In 1774, when Green's Loyalist sympathies forced him to leave Mass. for Eng. he took with him some 25,000 pounds in cash and stocks. After several years of retirement, Green died in London on Dec. 11, 1780.

Critical Appraisal: The majority of Joseph Green's surviving works are verse satires on a variety of subjects. In his *Entertainment for a Winter's Evening* and its less popular sequel *The Grand Arcanum Detected*, Green satirized the Boston Brotherhood of Masons, whose parading about in full regalia provided the occasion for a bawdy burlesque replete with irreverent humor and good-natured fun. In *The Poet's Lamentation for the Loss of His Cat*, Green satirized Mather Byles (q.v.), who was known for his attachment to a cat named Muse. Speaking as Byles himself, Green asserted that Byles depended on the cat as the source of inspiration for his poetry; but sometimes, "when my dulness has too stubborn prov'd" and when not even his feline's musical purring could give sustenance, "Oft to the well-known volumes have I gone, / And stole a line from Pope or Addison."

In what may be called a low burlesque allegory upon the name of Cooper, Green is at his bawdy best. The Rev. William Cooper (q.v.), a prominent New Light leader of the Great Awakening, came under Green's satirical scrutiny, because Green's religious sympathies lay with the Old Lights and because Cooper had published a virulent attack upon another minister who had censured the revivalist movement. At the time, Cooper had recently married a red-haired maid half his age. Throughout the poem, Green poked fun at the revivalist movement by applying ingenious analogies of the cooper's trade (barrel making) to the New Lights. Recalling the young Mrs. William Cooper, the refrain reads, "But his credit will lost—lost how? do ye ask? / Why he put an old bung in a new red-oak cask." As such, Green became, as has been pointed out, "the first of a long line of American writers to satirize revivalistic ministers by identifying their emotionalism with sexuality."

Green was, however, not always bawdy and satirical. At times he wrote poetry imbued with deep, religious feeling. *An Eclogue Sacred to the Memory of the Rev. Doctor Jonathan Mayhew* is both a devotional poem and one of the earliest pastoral elegies written in America. The subject of the poem is, of course, Jonathan Mayhew (q.v.), the radical Old Light forerunner of Unitarianism and a close friend of Green. In this poem, Green demonstrated a mastery of the form and conventions of the pastoral elegy, including an invocation to the muse, an expression of grief at the loss of a friend, a procession of mourners (Mayhew's "flock"), a consolation in which the speaker (or speakers) submits to the inevitable and confirms a strengthened belief in immortality, a digression that makes the elegy conform to the structure of the Puritan elegy, and a host of other minor conventions.

Closing the *Eclogue* is a twelve-stanza "Ode" that expresses "a Submission to the Will of Heaven" and effectively syncretizes Classical paganism with Christianity. A writer capable of producing both whimsical satires and serious literary productions that bespeak a wide breadth of reading and no little creativity, Green was an accomplished poet whose works deserve more attention than they have received.

Suggested Readings: DAB; LHUS; Sibley-Shipton (VIII, 42-53); T_1. *See also* Thomas V. Duggan, "Joseph Green—the Boston Butler" (M.A. thesis, Columbia Univ., 1971); George Duyckinck and Evert Duyckinck, *Cyclopaedia of American Literature* (1855), I, 130-133; Samuel Kettell, *Specimens of American Poetry* (1829), I, 139 (for texts of "Fragments" and of "Mr. Old Tenor"); J. A. Leo Lemay, "Joseph Green's Satirical Poem on the Great Awakening," RALS, 4 (1974), 173-183 (for text of "The Disappointed Cooper" with notes and discussion). For titles of Green's alleged prose pieces, see J. A. Leo Lemay's *A Calendar of American Poetry* (1972).

John C. Shields
Illinois State University

ISAAC GREENWOOD (1702-1745)

Works: *A Friendly Debate* (1722); *An Experimental Course of Mechanical Philosophy* (1726); *Arithmetick Vulgar and Decimal* (1729); "A New Method for Composing a Natural History of Meteors," *Philosophical Transactions of the Royal Society of London* (1729), 390-402; "A Brief Account of Some of the Effects and Properties of Damps," *Philosophical Transactions of the Royal Society of London* (1729), 184-191; "An Account of an Aurora Borealis Seen in New-England on the 22nd of October, 1730," *Philosophical Transactions of the Royal Society of London* (1731), 55-69; *A Philosophical Discourse Concerning the Mutability and Changes of the Material World* (1731); *Apparatus Mathematicus* (1731); *Explanatory Lectures on the Orrery* (1734); *A Course of Mathematical Lectures and Experiments* (1738); *A Course of Philosophical Lectures* (1739).

Biography: Isaac Greenwood was born in Boston, Mass., on May 11, 1702. A 1721 graduate of Harvard College, Greenwood possessed a strong interest in poetry, mathematics, and science. His principal tutor and adviser at Harvard was Thomas Robie, the compiler of annual almanacs. After graduating from college, Greenwood became a principal participant in the smallpox inoculation controversy of 1721 and at age 19 published his first literary work, a tract titled *A Friendly Debate* which defended Zabdiel Boylston (q.v.) and Cotton Mather (q.v.) and satirized William Douglass (q.v.) and John Williams (q.v.). From this tract, Greenwood gained the friendship of Cotton Mather, under whom he studied divinity in the fall of 1722.

In Jun. 1723 Greenwood voyaged to Eng., where he was introduced to several members of the Royal Society of London, including William Derham, William Whiston, Francis Hauksbee, and Isaac Newton. While in London, Greenwood continued his research into inoculation and was befriended by the renowned scientist John Desaguliers, who became his adviser and tutor in mathematics and natural philosophy. Desaguliers was the Royal Society's curator of scientific instruments and was a prominent lecturer on popular science. Greenwood attended Desaguliers's lectures, assisted him, and even substituted when his tutor was ill. During this time, Greenwood also met Thomas Hollis, the Harvard benefactor who became interested in endowing a mathematics chair for Greenwood at Harvard.

Prodded by the prospect of being a Harvard professor, Greenwood left London for Boston on Oct. 20, 1726, and to ingratiate himself with the Harvard Corporation, he gave the first lecture course on science in New Eng. In May 1727, after the course ended, Greenwood was elected Hollis professor of mathematics and natural philosophy. In this capacity, Greenwood was the first native-born American to teach differential calculus at the college level.

After several years of teaching, Greenwood left Harvard and in 1738 set up a School of Mathematical and Experimental Philosophy, modeled after Desaguliers's schools in Eng. In the spring of 1739, Greenwood offered another school, and in 1740 he went to Philadelphia, where he met Benjamin Franklin (q.v.), who subsequently arranged for him to give a course of scientific lectures at a room next to the Library Company. On Nov. 10, 1742, Greenwood enlisted in the British navy as a chaplain on board the frigate H.M.S. *Rose* under Capt. Thomas Frankland. Two years later, Frankland returned to Eng., and Greenwood shipped on board H.M.S. *Alborough*, finished a tour of duty with her, and was discharged from the service on May 22, 1744, in Charleston, S.C., where he died on Oct. 12, 1745.

Critical Appraisal: Isaac Greenwood's importance to the American intellectual historian can be seen in his involvement in the inoculation controversy and his subsequent close friendship with Cotton Mather; his mentorship under John Desaguliers and the English Newtonians of London; his *Experimental Course of Mechanical Philosophy*, the first course of its kind in the colonies; his other public lectures on Newtonian science; his teaching of the Newtonian calculus; his

Arithmetick, the first written in English by a native American; his papers to the Royal Society on weather charting, mine damps, Aurora Borealis, and Dighton Rock; and his friendship with and influence on Benjamin Franklin.

During the first few years of his professorship, Greenwood published several articles in the *Philosophical Transactions of the Royal Society of London*. His first paper, "A New Method for Composing a Natural History of Meteors" (1729), proposed that the Royal Society of London and the French Academy of Sciences collect wind and weather reports from merchantmen at sea to create a network of world weather observations. His second paper, "A Brief Account of Some of the Effects and Properties of Damps," was printed in the Dec. 1729 issue of the *Philosophical Transactions*. Two days after its occurrence, Greenwood sent a third paper to the Royal Society of "An Account of an Aurora Borealis Seen in New England on the 22nd of October, 1730." Greenwood's last communication to the Royal Society was an account of an Indian inscription on Dighton Rock in the Taunton River sent to John Eames, an English archaeologist, on Dec. 8, 1730. In addition, Greenwood published his *Arithmetick Vulgar and Decimal* in May 1729. The first mathematics text written in English by an American, it was used extensively for a number of years at Harvard and Yale.

Greenwood's most important literary work, *A Philosophical Discourse Concerning the Mutability and Changes of the Material World* was occasioned by the death on Jan. 20, 1731, of Thomas Hollis, the English merchant and Harvard benefactor who endowed the chairs of divinity and mathematics at the college. It was delivered on Wednesday, Apr. 7, at the Harvard College Hall a day after Edward Wigglesworth (q.v.) delivered his funeral sermon, *The Blessedness of the Dead*, on behalf of the deceased Hollis. Greenwood's *Discourse* describes the unity existing between God and man, man and nature, and man and his immortal soul, all subject to and governed by mechanical laws of perpetual variation and motion. Using ideas from contemporary astronomy, meteorology, geology, and biology, Greenwood discussed the mutability of the sun, planes and stars; the atmosphere, surface, and internal regions of the earth; and animated nature, including man. To support his Deistic view of nature, Greenwood transformed the physicotheological notions of the English Newtonians into a completely materialistic paradigm in which mechanical law rather than Divine Providence governs the cosmos. Thus despite the mutability of the natural objects in the material world, Greenwood found consolation for death in a belief in the transformation and regeneration of matter according to the laws of Newtonian science.

Suggested Readings: BDAS; DAB; Sibley-Shipton (VI, 471-482). *See also* David C. Leonard, "Harvard's First Science Professor: A Sketch of Isaac Greenwood's Life and Work," HLB, 29 (1981), 135-168; Raymond Phineus Stearns, *Science in the British Colonies of America* (1970), pp. 446-455.

David C. Leonard
Georgia Institute of Technology

HANNAH GRIFFITTS (1727-1817)

Works: Manuscript poems, letters, and essays in the Historical Society of Pennsylvania. Pattie Cowell's *Women Poets in Pre-Revolutionary America* (1981) contains selections from Griffitts's verse, pp. 55-70.

Biography: Little can be learned of Hannah Griffitts from sources other than her own voluminous collection of manuscript poems, letters, and essays. She was born in 1727 to Thomas Griffitts, an important public official in Philadelphia, and Mary Norris, member of a prominent Pa. Quaker family. The extent of Griffitts's formal education is unknown, but her manuscripts suggest that some care was taken to provide basic skills. She apparently began writing poetry as a child, dedicating her work to religious purposes even at the age of 10: "the Muse long banished and disused / I now will consecrate to thee."

Griffitts remained single all of her life, a factor that may be at least partially responsible for the financial difficulty she experienced in later years. In fact, poverty may very well have forced her to stay in Philadelphia during the British occupation of 1777-1778. Despite her Quaker pacifism, Griffitts seems to have taken sides in the Revolutionary War: in a letter to Gen. Anthony Wayne dated Jul. 13, 1777, she declared herself "so good a whig that of Consequence [she] must be a little of a politician." She confided to Wayne that in such troubled times "every Woman is desirous of being acquainted with what interests her Country." Outliving the fervor of Revolutionary times by nearly forty years, Griffitts died in Philadelphia on Aug. 24, 1817. Remaining mentally alert throughout her 90 years, she wrote poetry even when her eyesight began to fail.

Critical Appraisal: The correspondence of Hannah Griffitts portrays a retiring person, firm in her opinions but reluctant to share them with others. Some of her letters, particularly those to Susanna Wright, Elizabeth Graeme Fergusson (q.v.), and Deborah Logan, reveal an informal network of Pa. women poets with whom Griffitts exchanged verses. The anonymity of much of Griffitts's work was protected by her pseudonym "Fidelia." Although she was willing to circulate her manuscripts among friends, Griffitts resisted publication. Her wish has been observed: even to this day only a small handful of her more than 200 manuscript poems are in print.

As one might expect of so prolific a writer, Griffitts's poetry is diverse in subject and form. Her initial commitment to religious poetry led her to explore themes of salvation, sin, and divine omnipotence. But Griffitts developed secular themes as well. Political events, social occasions, tributes to friends, satiric attacks on prominent patriots—all fell within the range of her pen. Thomas Paine (q.v.), for example, seemed to elicit nothing but scorn: "Paine—tho / thy tongue may now run glibber, / Warm'd with thy independent glow, / Thou art indeed the coldest fibber, / I ever knew, or wish to know." John Roberts and Abraham Carlisle (Quaker martyrs to American nationalism) aroused a different response: "And you, the guiltless victims of the day / (Who to a timid city's late reproach /

And blush of its inhabitants) have fallen, / A prey to laws, disgraceful to the man /
...Long shall your names survive the brutal deed, / And fair, transmitted down
to better times / Stand the reproach of ours." These few examples can hardly
suggest the breadth of Griffitts's poetic interests or the extent of her skill.
Evidence of continued revision in her manuscripts testifies to her concern for the
right word or the most effective rhythm.

But even as she worked and reworked, Griffitts acknowledged to herself that
poetry should never become too important in a woman's life: letters to friend and
poet Susanna Wright make it clear that poetry for Griffitts was "design'd but as
amusement to [her] own melancholy hours." Emphasizing that although her
poems "sometimes divert a dull hour," she hoped she had never "visited the
muses when the stockin' ball was so much more necessary." Deliberately subordinated to more traditional concerns, Griffitts's verse remains apprentice work,
but its variety and wit offer a look at colonial Philadelphia that may make us
wonder why it has been so little read.

Suggested Readings: Carl Bridenbaugh and Jessica Bridenbaugh, *Rebels and
Gentlemen* (1962), p. 125; Pattie Cowell, *Women Poets in Pre-Revolutionary America*
(1981), pp. 55-70; Linda DePauw and Conover Hunt, *Remember the Ladies: Women in
America, 1750-1815* (1976), p. 86; Samuel Hazard, RP, 8 (Sept. 17, 1831), 178; M.
Katherine Jackson, *Outlines of the Literary History of Colonial Pennsylvania* (1906), pp.
153-154; F. W. Leach, "Genealogies of Old Philadelphia Families," typescript, Historical
Society of Pennsylvania, p. 25; PMHB, 17 (1893), 28; 27 (1903), 109-111; 39 (1915),
286-287; 75 (1951), 199; John F. Watson, *Annals of Philadelphia in the Olden Times*
(1845), I, 559; Anne Wharton, *Through Colonial Doorways* (1893), pp. 54-55.

Pattie Cowell
Colorado State University

STANLEY GRISWOLD (1763-1815)

Works: *A Statement of the Singular Manner* (1798); *A Funeral Eulogium
Pronounced at New Milford* (1800); *Truth Its Own Test* (1800); *The Good Man's
Prospects in the Hour of Death* (1801); *Overcoming Evil with Good* (1801); *The
Good Land We Live In* (1802); *Infidelity Not the Only Enemy of Christianity*
(1803); *The Exploits of Our Fathers* (1813).

Biography: Stanley Griswold was born in Torrington, Conn., on Nov. 14,
1763. After graduating from Yale College in 1786, he continued his theological
studies with David McClure of East Windsor, Conn., and was ordained and
installed as pastor in New Milford, Conn., on Jan. 20, 1790.

For the next twelve years, Griswold served in New Milford, but under increasing pressure to resign. Ostensibly, the opposition to his ministry that he received
from groups such as the Litchfield South Association of Ministers stemmed from
his Latitudinarian tendencies, but his theology could not be easily divorced from

his distaste for the Federalists and his unpopular support for Thomas Jefferson (q.v.). With the support of his congregation, however, Griswold continued in his office until 1802, when he finally resigned. His political sympathies were clearly elaborated in a series of sermons he published after 1800, and apparently he saw that such views made his position untenable.

As a result, at the age of 39, Griswold began a new career. In Nov. 1803 he became the first editor of *The Political Observatory* in Walpole, Mass., a Jeffersonian newspaper designed to counter the popular *Farmer's Weekly Museum* in that same town. The newspaper first appeared on Nov. 19, 1803, and ran until Mar. 20, 1809. But Griswold's life was not yet settled and indeed never would be. On Mar. 1, 1805, Jefferson appointed him secretary to the Michigan Territory, a position he held until 1808. During Governor William Hull's absence in 1805-1806, Griswold also served as acting governor. In 1809, after the resignation of Edward Tiffin as U.S. senator of Ohio, Griswold was appointed to fill out his term, and in 1810 he was appointed by President James Madison (q.v.) to serve as a federal judge in the Illinois Territory, a position of great responsibility in the territory as it made the transition to statehood.

On Aug. 21, 1815, Stanley Griswold died of a fever at Shawneetown (Ill.) and despite his many important positions and his involvement in a number of important controversies during the Jeffersonian era, he has been virtually forgotten.

Critical Appraisal: When Stanley Griswold preached the funeral sermon for Nathanael Taylor, his long-time colleague at New Milford, he praised him for his piety, which was "neither stiff nor ostentatious," as "a friend to justice, order and peace," and above all as an enemy to bigotry whose "sentiments were of a liberal cast" and who was often heard to say that even "some of the *Heathens* might be saved." For Stanley Griswold, these points were the essential Christic values of charity, mercy, and humility, and they were the qualities of character he personally valued.

Such views may seem innocent enough—even the Latitudinarian belief that some nonbelievers will be saved. Had they been privately held, Griswold would never have been pressed to defend them. Even when expressed in a published funeral sermon, they might have been condoned by his stricter Congregational colleagues. But when in the late 1790s and early 1800s he insisted more and more forcefully and publicly that his professional critics (and Federalists in general) lacked precisely these gentle Christic qualities, they thought he had gone too far. Expelled from the Litchfield South Association of Ministers, Griswold was forced to resign from his pastorate.

Griswold was a rarity among the New Eng. Congregational clergy of his time—a Jeffersonian who preached a "mild" Christianity. Like Ezra Stiles (q.v.) a generation earlier, he believed that diverse opinions and "free toleration" promised religious *and* secular improvement. "The time is not far off in my view," he explained in *The Good Land We Live In*, "when the HONEST of all sects will unite in fellowship and brotherly communion, tho' they may still retain that variety of worship which we may suppose is not unpleasing to the Father of the universe." The danger to such happiness, as he went on to explain, rested in excessive concern with *"institutions and old institutions and traditions"* at the expense of "practical religion, judgment, mercy, charity and all the peaceful graces which form and adorn the Christian."

For Griswold, these excessive concerns with form at the expense of substance— and the resulting evil of bigotry—characterized both the Congregationalists of his time and the Federalists: both had been infected by "party spirit." What is more, the two had become even more dangerously intertwined as Congregationalism began to identify itself with Federalist politics (and *vice versa*). "The question with many," he wrote in *Infidelity Not the Only Enemy*, "seems to be, not so much what GOD a man serves, as what *party*—not so much what SAVIOUR he believes in, as what *President!*" Griswold feared that the church in America was recapitulating the history of Christianity in the third century: sacrificing its primitive spiritual responsibilities for secular sophistications and political power.

Griswold's argument in these sermons is brilliant and effective. Himself a victim of "bigots," he turned to them in charity, warning them of the dangers they faced and offering to forgive them. Of course, each such offer was more infuriating than the last, prompting additional persecution. The passive aggression of Griswold's rhetoric did not seem to be calculated, nor was his offer to heal the wounds insincere. Nevertheless, he himself came to exemplify in his career the fate of his friend Nathanael Taylor's gentle Christianity in a society torn by faction. In the end, Griswold publicly embraced Jeffersonian politics as the surest way to support toleration and social justice and still maintain the separation of church and state.

After Griswold left the pulpit and became active in politics, his writing virtually ceased. As an editor, he provided an effective but relatively restrained platform for the Democrats, and in his many later public roles, he apparently worked hard but without recognition. Two of the rare views of his later life are instructive. He appeared briefly as "a decided friend" to the Bible Society missionaries who visited him in 1814, distributing their Bibles for them and generally demonstrating that Christian values had spread even to the territories. Griswold also appeared in Governor John Reynolds's *Pioneer History of Illinois* (1852), where his career in the Northwestern Territories is again very briefly acknowledged. Although Reynolds gave him scant praise, Griswold might well have accepted his words as a fittingly modest epitaph after his controversial and far-flung career: "Stanley Griswold was a correct, honest man; a good lawyer; paid his debts and sung David's psalms."

Suggested Readings: DAB; Dexter (IV, 476-481). *See also* Samuel J. Mills and Daniel Smith, *Report of a Missionary Tour* (1815), pp. 11, 13; Samuel Orcutt, *History of the Towns of New Milford and Bridgewater* (1882), pp. 256-273; John Reynolds, *The Pioneer History of Illinois* (1852), p. 337.

Barry R. Bell
Washington State University

MOLLY GUTRIDGE (fl. 1778)

Works: *A New Touch on the Times* (c. 1778).

Biography: Author of a single eighty-four-line verse broadside, Molly Gutridge left no other materials from which to reconstruct her life. Accounts of birth and family are unavailable, but we know from *A New Touch on the Times* that she lived in Marblehead, Mass., during the turmoil of the American Revolution. As Gutridge's verse makes clear, the Revolutionary years were particularly difficult for residents of seaport communities: "The world is now turn'd up-side down." Like most of the Marblehead women described in the broadside, Gutridge was probably married to a seaman, perhaps to one of the many Marblehead men serving in the marine division of the Continental Army. Left behind in Marblehead, Gutridge and her neighbors were virtually impoverished, perhaps because the value of the Continental notes in which the army was paid had depreciated enormously: "For money is not worth a pin....Takes 20 weight of sugar for two foot of wood....Nothing now-a-days to be got, / To put in kettle or in pot."

Despite the critical shortages of food and fuel that furnish the occasion for *A New Touch on the Times*, Gutridge's byline—"By a Daughter of Liberty"—implies her support for the Revolutionary cause. Her patriotic sympathies seem qualified, however, by her conventional religious interpretation of their plight: "For sin is all the cause of this, / We must not take it then amiss, / Wan't it for our polluted tongues / This cruel war would ne'er begun." These meagre details of Gutridge's situation—her poverty, politics, and faith—are all that remain for her biography. The date and place of Gutridge's death are unknown.

Critical Appraisal: The hardships described in Molly Gutridge's *A New Touch on the Times* were so common in Marblehead from 1776 to 1780, that the work is difficult to date. Worthington Chauncey Ford's checklist of Mass. broadsides places it in 1778 (although Ford's "List of Illustrations" for the checklist contains a 1779 attribution). The problem of dating is further complicated because only one extant copy of the broadside is known, in the collection of the New York Historical Society. Given the perishable nature of most broadside publication, that circumstance yields little occasion for surprise, nor does the broadside itself. In fact, Gutridge's piece is typical of much contemporary broadside verse, both in its close attention to local issues and in the roughness of its technique.

In *A New Touch on the Times*, Gutridge explored three closely related topics. The opening lines note the absence of most of Marblehead's male population during the Revolution and record the feelings of helplessness and loneliness experienced by the women left behind: "Our best beloved they are gone, / We cannot tell they'll e'er return." The second topic area, comprising nearly half the poem, is a detailed description of the economic hardships facing Marblehead's remaining residents: "It's hard and cruel times to live, / Takes thirty dollars to buy a sieve." The concluding lines attribute these hardships to the will of "a

gracious God," who is repaying humankind for its sins but who will one day
"cause to cease, / This bloody war and give us peace!" As the excerpts quoted
above indicate, Gutridge's tetrameter couplets are rough, straining for rhyme and
rhythm often to the detriment of sense, but despite her inexperienced handling of
poetic form, the detail of Gutridge's descriptions and the directness of her expression provide much of value to historians and readers of American poetry.

Suggested Readings: Elizabeth Cometti, "Women in the American Revolution,"
NEQ, 20 (1947), 335; Worthington Chauncey Ford, *Broadsides, Ballads &c. Printed in
Massachusetts, 1639-1800* (1922), pp. 299, 300; Ola Elizabeth Winslow, *American Broad-
side Verse* (reprints the broadside in facsimile; 1930), pp. 190-191.

Pattie Cowell
Colorado State University

JOHN GYLES (c. 1678-1755)

Works: *Memoirs of Odd Adventures, Strange Deliverances, Etc., in the
Captivity of John Gyles, Esq.* (1736).

Biography: John Gyles was born in Pemaquid, Maine, probably in 1678,
shortly after the conclusion of King Philip's War, in which the Indians of New
Eng. had waged fierce warfare against the English settlements as far south as
Conn. and as far north as Maine. With the beginning of King William's War in
1689, the French in Can. began a systematic program of Indian raids along the
New Eng. frontier. Because of its location on the Atlantic coast and its close
proximity to the Canadian border, Maine was particularly vulnerable to French
and Indian attacks. During an invasion of Pemaquid, Gyles and his brothers and
sisters were taken captive by an Indian war party. For nearly six years, until his
ransom in 1695 by a Frenchman, Gyles remained a captive among the Indians,
sharing their life-style and observing their customs firsthand. In 1698, when
King William's War drew to a close, Gyles was allowed to return to New Eng.,
where he lived out the remainder of his life. He died in 1755, at the age of 77.

Critical Appraisal: One of the most popular works in the colonial genre
known collectively as the Indian captivity narrative, the *Memoirs of Odd Adventures, Strange Deliverances, Etc., in the Captivity of John Gyles* is a good
example of why early American audiences, restricted for their entertainment to
historical narratives of war and adventure, made captivity narratives an important
part of their reading. A lively narrative in the tradition of Mary Rowlandson's
(q.v.) *The Soveraignty and Goodness of God* and John Williams's (q.v.) *Redeemed Captive*, Gyles's *Memoirs* both titillates and horrifies the sensibilities of
his audience. Ostensibly written to excite "in our offspring a due sense of their
dependence on the Sovereign of the universe," the *Memoirs* is less a religious
tract than an attempt to fashion an engaging and entertaining narrative from the
factual occurrences in an unusual autobiographical experience, by its very nature

designed to arrest the imaginations of eighteenth-century American readers, who took great interest in the tales told by Indian captives.

A precursor of the frontier romances of James Fenimore Cooper, William Gilmore Simms, and Robert Montgomery Bird, Gyles's *Memoirs* contains all of the makings of good fiction, including dialog, plot, characterization, and suspense. Beginning with Gyles's capture during the Indian attack on his family's home, the narrative proceeds through a series of adventures, enlivened by frequent digressions about battles and tortures and culminating in Gyles's ransom by the French and his return to civilization. Within the context of these events, the Indians become villains, and Gyles becomes a hero whose ingenuity and courage triumph over adversity and evil. As such, the narrative forms a ritual pattern of capture and escape, a pattern of initiation and experience that appears with great frequency in later American literature.

Finally, Gyles's *Memoirs* is valuable for the perspective it gives us on British colonial attitudes toward the French during King William's War and for information it provides about Indian culture and the interior of the North American continent before it was settled by the English. Like many of his contemporaries, Gyles viewed the Indians as the instruments of Satan, an attitude he also projected onto the French, whose Roman Catholic affiliations he blamed for the ongoing perpetration of Indian atrocities during the French and Indian conflicts.

Suggested Readings: Phillips D. Carleton, "The Indian Captivity," AL, 15 (1943), 169-180; Emma Lewis Coleman, *New England Captives Carried to Canada* (1925), I, 168-172; Roy Harvey Pearce, "The Significances of the Captivity Narrative," AL, 19 (1947), 1-20; Richard VanDerBeets, ed., *Held Captive by Indians* (for the text of Gyles's *Memoirs* accompanied by both scholarly and critical commentary; 1973); idem, " 'A Thirst for Empire': The Indian Captivity Narrative as Propaganda," RS, 40 (1972), 207-215.

James A. Levernier
University of Arkansas at Little Rock

H

JOHN HALE (1636-1700)

Works: *A Modest Enquiry into the Nature of Witchcraft* (1697).

Biography: John Hale was born on Jun. 5, 1636, at Charlestown, Mass. His father, Robert Hale, was a blacksmith by occupation who probably arrived in New Eng. with John Winthrop (q.v.) and who was a founder and deacon of the church at Charlestown. Graduated from Harvard College with an A.M. in 1657, Hale began his career as a preacher sometime around 1664. In the same year, he married Rebecca Byley; the couple eventually had two children: Rebecca (1666) and Robert (1668). After his first wife died in 1683, Hale married Sarah Noyes, with whom he fathered four more children: James (1685), Samuel (1687), Joanna (1689), and John (1692). When his second wife died in 1695, Hale married Elizabeth Clark.

In 1664, when the first Congregational Parish of Beverly was established, Hale was elected its first pastor, in which capacity he served until his death on May 5, 1700. In 1690 Hale was invited to be one of the chaplains in Sir William Phip's expedition against Can., and although his parishioners did not approve, he accepted the charge. Apparently, however, Hale remained on good terms with the members of the congregation, for when his wife, Sarah, was later accused of witchcraft, they rallied to his support, and their efforts, together with his and his wife's good reputation, prevented a successful prosecution of the charges.

Earlier, Hale had himself participated in the prosecution of several people suspected of witchcraft, including several members of his own congregation, but when the tide of accusations turned toward his wife, he reversed his previous position on the nature of evidence needed to convict someone of practicing witchcraft, and he lamented "the errors and mistakes" he had "unwittingly" encouraged through his participation in the events of 1692.

Critical Appraisal: The single work upon which the literary reputation and life of John Hale rests is *A Modest Enquiry into the Nature of Witchcraft*, published in 1697. Another work, the General Election Sermon for 1684, was authorized for publication by the General Court but was probably never printed. No copy of it has been found. Ironically, Hale's book on witchcraft apologizes for the endorsement he gave the witchcraft trials before his wife was accused of sorcery. Assuming some responsibility for the "errors and mistakes" of 1692, Hale gave as reasons for his reversal a desire "to clear the names of innocent sufferers" and to reveal the "unsafe principles" under which the prosecutions were carried out.

However he felt about the "unsafe principles" upon which those suspected of witchcraft were prosecuted, Hale had difficulty defining what he meant by *unsafe*. Ultimately, he simply transferred the causes of witchcraft from man to Satan. In his discourse, Hale listed several signs by which witchcraft was mistakenly identified. Some supposed evidence proceeded from natural causes and some by abnormal deformities or infirmities. Of most interest in the work, however, is the logic used to refute Hale's earlier convictions of the reality of witchcraft. In general, he assumed two possible answers to the suspicion of, or the delusion involved in, witchcraft. Either he blamed the actions directly on Satan, or he found causes that have a natural origin in physical deformity or an explicable origin. According to Hale, Satan has no "tenderness of conscience" to restrain him in affecting mankind's destruction; he is driven by malice to oppose both man and God.

Whatever aspects of witchcraft Hale analyzed, he found natural explanations for behavior that in 1692 would have been accepted by the court as positive evidence of possession. He left open the possibility that man's sinful nature might permit possession by Satan, but he also stated that man's sinful nature might make him wicked but not necessarily a witch. If A *Modest Enquiry* may be defined as a kind of confession, the statement of a man who regrets his errors and mistakes, then it has an ethical value. As a treatise exploring a state of mind and the condition of the age, it has historical value. As a clear, intellectual statement of a principle and fact, it has perhaps less value, but it nonetheless remains important for the light it sheds on the New Eng. witchcraft hysteria of the 1690s, and it was used by Cotton Mather (q.v.) as a source for his writings on the subject.

Suggested Readings: CCNE; Sibley-Shipton (I, 509-520); T$_1$. *See also* Chadwick Hansen, *Witchcraft at Salem* (1969), passim.

George Craig
Edinboro State College

CLEMENT HALL (c. 1699-1759)

Works: *A Collection of Many Christian Experiences, Sentences, and Several Places of Scripture Improved* (1753).

Biography: Born sometime around 1699 in Eng. (probably in Coventry), Clement Hall was living in N.C. in 1731, at which time he purchased 104 acres for himself, his brother, and their mother, who had apparently immigrated with him to the colony. In 1739 Hall became a justice of the Perquimans County Court. In addition, he acted, in the absence of a regular Anglican clergyman, as a lay reader. With a certificate of recommendation from several prominent N.C. dignitaries, Hall returned in 1743 to Eng., where he was ordained the following year. With financial support from church authorities in Eng., Hall returned to N.C. and began a period of effective service to the northern counties of the colony. Making his home near Edenton, Hall not only held services at St. Paul's Church but also made regular visits elsewhere, traveling more than 2,000 miles annually. Sometimes his congregation numbered more than 600, and during the thirteen years of his ministry, he baptized more than 10,000 people. Hall's extensive travels, however, took their toll, and he died in Jan. 1759, survived by his wife, five daughters, and a son.

Critical Appraisal: While riding horseback around the colony, Clement Hall wrote a fifty-one-page book titled *A Collection of Many Christian Experiences, Sentences, and Several Places of Scripture Improved*, which he referred to as "a Pocket-Companion . . . to keep my Thoughts employed on good Subjects; which I believe most People find are naturally apt to be vain and wandring when we are alone, notwithstanding our greatest Care." About this work, he also wrote, "considering that it might also be of some Use to others, who have a Desire to improve their Time upon the like Occasions, or when on a Winter's Night or a rainy Day they have Leisure to peruse it, instead of Drinking, Gaming, or telling of an idle or slandrous Tale; I have ventured to put this my small Mite into the Treasury."

The first twenty-one pages of Hall's work contain "A Miscellaneous Collection of many Christian Experiences, &c." consisting largely of quotations or paraphrases from Ecclesiastes, Proverbs, Job, and Psalms and from the New Testament books of Matthew, Luke, John, Corinthians, and Timothy. Most of the entries in the book consist, however, of proverbs, many of which, according to the title page, were "Collected and Composed . . . by C.H." himself. Others of the pithy sayings were probably derived from Benjamin Franklin (q.v.); one is from Tertullianus and another from Thomas Fuller. With a separate title page, Hall reproduced the eleven-page text of *Serious Advice to Persons Who Have Been Sick*, published anonymously by Hall but actually written by the Rt. Rev. Edmund Gibson, bishop of London, who had ordained Hall in London. Hall's concluding contributions to the book include several prayers, various forms of a grace to be said both before and after meals, and some prayers for children. Although several of these items are clearly derived from the *Book of Common Prayer*, some may well have been original compositions by Hall. Hall's book was the first written and published in N.C., for although James Davis had established a printing press in New Bern in 1749, not until the appearance of Hall's book had anything but official material been printed.

Suggested Readings: CCV. *See also* Edgar L. Pennington, *The Church of England and the Reverend Clement Hall in Colonial North Carolina* (1937); William S. Powell, ed., *Clement Hall, A Collection of Many Christian Experiences, Sentences, and*

Several Places of Scripture Improved, A Facsimile of A North Carolina Literary Landmark (1961).

William S. Powell
University of North Carolina at Chapel Hill

ELIHU HALL (1714-1784)

Works: *The Present Way of the Country in Maintaining the Gospel Ministry by a Publick Rate or Tax Is Lawful, Equitable, and Agreeable to the Gospel* (1749).

Biography: Elihu Hall was born in Wallingford, Conn., on Feb. 17, 1714. His father, the Hon. John Hall, was a governor's assistant from 1722 until 1730, and his brother Samuel was the first pastor of the Congregational Church in Wallingford. Graduated from Yale College in 1731, Hall was licensed to practice law by the New Haven County Court in the same year. As early as 1743, Hall represented Wallingford in the General Assembly, and by 1744 he was king's attorney for the county. In addition, he was a colonel in the colonial militia, and he served as one of four special commissioners of the General Assembly whose job it was to meet with the other colonies in 1757 to plan an expedition to invade Can. During the Revolutionary War, Hall fought with the British and eventually was forced to seek refuge in Eng., where he died in the early part of 1784 at the age of 70.

Critical Appraisal: Elihu Hall's only published work, *The Present Way*, is an essay-dialog written in the tradition of Plato and Bunyan. At the time when Hall published *The Present Way*, Congregationalism was the official religion of Conn. As a result of the Great Awakening, however, other sects began to seek official acceptance, and as these groups withdrew from the Congregational Church, resentment arose over the practice of using taxes to support a church other than one's own. In *The Present Way*, two fictional characters—Thomas Casuisticus and John Queristicus—argue the validity of taxing the public as a means of supporting the clergy. When Casuisticus learns that his friend Queristicus has been speaking publicly against this tax and has been attending "enthusiastic lay teaching" at a Separate Church, he tries to persuade Queristicus to return to the established church. In their conversation, Casuisticus explains that supporting the clergy by means of a public tax is both lawful and scripturally valid. Queristicus, however, argues otherwise, but in the end Casuisticus convinces Queristicus that it is "Christ's will that ministers shall not work" and that a public tax is the proper "covenant" between a minister and the people he serves.

Although Hall signed his work "E.H.M.A." and his authorship of it was in doubt until the end of the nineteenth century, *The Present Way* did not go unanswered. In 1750 Ebenezer Frothingham (q.v.) published *The Articles of Faith and Practice with the Covenant*, a strong argument in defense of the belief that the clergy should be supported by contribution rather than taxation, and in 1763 Joseph Bolles addressed Hall's work directly with *An Answer to a Book Entitled: The Present Way*, in which he refuted Hall's scriptural argument verse by verse. Bolles, however, made no mention of the church-state issue. Instead, he distinguished between the "travelling" minister who must be supported, and the "settled" minister who is capable of supporting himself. His reasoning is that the "settled" minister need not be excused from labor on the assumption he needs time to study, because ministers preach by revelation from God.

A significant historical work of America's pre-Revolutionary period, *The Present Way* and the controversy that surrounded it reflect the transformation of America's political thought regarding the relationship between religion and society that ultimately resulted in Article VI and the First Amendment to the Constitution.

Suggested Readings: Dexter (I, 154-155; 427). *See also* Joseph Bolles, *An Answer to a Book Entitled: The Present Way* (1763); Jerald C. Brauer, ed., *Religion and the American Revolution* (1976); Goldwin French, "Religion and Society in America's Revolutionary Era: Some Preliminary Reflections" in *The Varied Pattern: Studies in the 18th Century* (1971), pp. 321-331; Ebenezer Frothingham, *The Articles of Faith and Practice with the Covenant, That Is Confessed by the Separate Churches of Christ in General in This Land* (1750); Edwin S. Gaustad, *The Great Awakening in New England* (1957); James H. Trumbull, *List of Books Printed in Connecticut, 1709-1800* (1904), p. 90.

Mary Hall Patton
University of Houston

PRINCE HALL (c. 1735 [or 1748] - 1807)

Works: *A Charge Delivered to the Brethren of the African Lodge on the 25th of June, 1792 . . . in Charlestown* (1792); *A Charge, Delivered to the African Lodge, June 24, 1797, at Menotomy* (1797).

Biography: Until recently, it was accepted that Prince Hall was born in 1748 at Bridge Town, Barbados, British W.I., son of an Englishman and a free black of French descent, and that he came to this country in 1765. More recent evidence suggests an earlier birth, place unknown, and that he was a slave in Boston in the late 1740s, joined the Congregational Church in 1762, and was given his freedom in 1770. All agree that he became a leather worker, was reasonably well educated, owned property, and was a Methodist minister. There also is agreement that he was the most prominent black leader in Boston during the period of the Revolution and the early Republic, organizing blacks to petition for military service in the Revolution, safety, rights, freedom, and education. Hall is also recognized as the founder and leader of the first Masonic Lodge for blacks, African Lodge No. 1, established in Boston on Jul. 3, 1776.

He later helped establish lodges elsewhere in Mass. and in Philadelphia and Providence.

Critical Appraisal: Although a number of petitions and letters survive of which Prince Hall was at least partial, if not full, author, apparently only two items by him were published, both of them Masonic addresses. Unlike many of his fellow ministers, Hall did not have his sermons published. However, the two Masonic addresses partake heavily of homiletics in form, tone, method, message, and evidence—which is not surprising given both his background and also the nature of Masonic belief with its biblical supports. The 1792 address (of thirteen pages) is taken up primarily with his "endeavour to shew the duty of a Mason" through admonition, instruction, and historical and biblical examples. Along the way, he noted the inadequate education available for blacks in the Boston area, compared to Philadelphia, and he advocated perseverance. He gave a brief history of the beginnings of Masonry, and ended by advocating upright living according to "the square of justice, [and] the level of truth and sincerity." Each of his addresses closes with a quotation from a poem.

The 1797 charge (of eighteen pages) is much more sermonic. It begins by alluding to the 1792 one and quickly moves on to take up its primary theme, "that it is our duty to sympathise with our fellow men under their troubles," no matter of what color, party, or place they may be. He painted the grievous troubles of slavery and of being vilely discriminated against even as free blacks. He also pointed to signs of change, including reference to recent events in Haiti. However, Hall's method is never inflammatory, instead reflecting patience coupled with insistent perseverance under the faith and optimism that God's will must be done. On the other hand, in his writings and in his other activities, Hall did not ignore wrongs or fail to advocate their correction, often pointing to the interdependence of all men. "Worship God," he said, "but worship [and fear] no man." The blacks of Boston were fortunate to have such an articulate and successful leader, whose writing, although not exceptional, was evenhanded and at least equal in quality to most of that of the day. Undoubtedly, it gained for their causes respectful consideration that they might not so easily have had otherwise.

Suggested Readings: *Afro-American Encyclopedia* (1974), IV, 1114-1115; Harry E. Davis, "Documents Relating to Negro Masonry in America," JNH, 21 (1936), 411-432; Philip S. Foner, *History of Black Americans from Africa to the . . . Cotton Kingdom* (1975), pp. 559-561, 577-578; Thomas R. Frazier, ed., *Afro-American History: Primary Sources* (1970), pp. 46-52; Lorenzo J. Greene, *The Negro in Colonial New England* (1968), p. 315; Sidney Kaplan, *The Black Presence in the Era of the American Revolution, 1770-1800* (1973), pp. 181-192; Dorothy Porter, ed., *Early Negro Writing, 1760-1837* (1971), pp. 63-78; Benjamin Quarles, *The Negro in the American Revolution* (1961); William H. Upton, *Negro Masonry* (1902); Harold van Voorhis, *Negro Masonry in the United States* (1940); Carter G. Woodson and Charles H. Wesley, *The Negro in Our History*, 12th ed. (1972), pp. 143-144.

Julian Mason
University of North Carolina at Charlotte

ALEXANDER HAMILTON (1757-1804)

Works: *The Federalist* (1788); Harold C. Syrett, ed., *The Papers of Alexander Hamilton* (1961-   ).

Biography: Alexander Hamilton was born in the W. Ind. on the island of Nevis in 1757. His family was marked by financial misfortune, and the death of his mother in 1768 left him virtually an orphan, since his father was unable to provide for his support. His mother's family lived on St. Croix, where Alexander received his early education and learned to speak French fluently. The generosity of his aunts made it possible for him to attend Frances Barber's Grammar School at Elizabethtown, N.J., after which he entered Kings College (now Columbia Univ.) in the fall of 1773.

The coming of the Revolution, however, interrupted Hamilton's college education, and he turned his writing skills to defending the cause of the Patriots in anonymous pamphlets. During the Revolutionary War, Hamilton commanded an artillery company authorized by the provincial convention from which he had received his commission, and attracted the attention of George Washington (q.v.), who made him first a secretary and later aide-de-camp with the rank of lieutenant colonel.

In 1780 Hamilton married Elizabeth, the second daughter of Gen. Philip Schuyler. At the end of the Revolutionary War, Hamilton returned to Albany and after less than five months' study was admitted to the bar. After serving a term in the Continental Congress beginning in 1782, Hamilton retired to devote himself to the practice of law, opening an office in N.Y. on Wall Street. Hamilton later served in the commercial convention at Annapolis in 1786, and he was responsible for the proposal to meet in Philadelphia at what was to become the federal Constitutional Convention. Although Hamilton was kept from active participation in the convention by his legal practice as he alternated between N.Y. and Philadelphia, he alone signed the new document for the state of N.Y., and he quickly entered into a spirited defense of the document and planned the Federalist series that argued the case for the new Constitution in the N.Y. press.

Hamilton is perhaps most justly remembered for his able fight in N.Y. for the adoption of the Constitution. Hamilton sat again in the Continental Congress in 1788, and following Washington's inauguration, he became head of the Treasury Department. He gave the country a bank, a mint, and a policy to protect infant industries. Although Hamilton left the government in 1795, he continued to advise Washington and assisted him in the preparation of his Farewell Address. Perceiving himself snubbed by President John Adams (q.v.), Hamilton authored a belligerent letter that was widely circulated and, after a copy was obtained by Aaron Burr, repeatedly printed. As a result of Hamilton's continued opposition, Burr sought revenge and, seizing upon a slur by Hamilton, challenged him to a duel. Mortally wounded during the duel, Hamilton died in 1804.

Critical Appraisal: Of the eighty-five *Federalist Papers* published in 1788, seventy-seven originally appeared in three N.Y. newspapers between Oct. 27, 1787, and Apr. 4, 1788. The essays appeared under the collective pseudonym "Publius" that served Alexander Hamilton, John Jay (q.v.), and James Madison (q.v.). The name for the collection, Hamilton's best-known and most significant literary project, was appropriated by proponents of the Constitution, distinguishing them from those who adhered to the Articles of Confederation. John Jay authored only five of the essays, and his contact with the Constitution was the least of the three, since he had not been a delegate to the Convention. Madison, who played a prominent role in the Convention, combined an intimate and exacting knowledge of the Convention and Constitution supported by his unofficial notes on the Convention, which were of great assistance to the project, since Hamilton had been away from the Convention frequently to tend to his law practice. Hamilton's legacy in the *Federalist* is a lucid exposition of constitutional republican government. In taste and convictions, Hamilton was a high Tory. His disdain for social concerns and the people whom he called the "great beast" was frequently evident in his exposition of constitutional centralization.

Suggested Readings: DAB; LHUS; T₂. *See also* Douglas Adair, "The Authorship of the Disputed Federalist Papers," WMQ, 3rd ser., 1 (1944), 97-122, 235-264; Bower Aly, *The Rhetoric of Alexander Hamilton* (1941); Broadus Mitchell, *Alexander Hamilton*, 2 vols. (1947, 1962). The two best editions of *The Federalist* are edited by Benjamin F. Wright (1961), and Jacob E. Cooke (1961).

L. Lynn Hogue
Georgia State University at Atlanta

DR. ALEXANDER HAMILTON (1712-1756)

Works: *Itinerarium* (w. 1744; pub. 1907, 1948); "A Discourse Delivered from the Chair in the Lodge-Room at Annapolis" (pub. in the Rev. John Gordon, *Brotherly Love Explained and Enforc'd*; 1750); *A Defence of Doctor Thomson's Discourse on the Preparation of the Body for the Small-Pox* (1751); J. A. Leo Lemay, ed., "Hamilton's Literary History of the *Maryland Gazette*," WMQ, 3rd ser., 23 (1966), 273-285 (this is Hamilton's essay of Jan. 29, 1748).

Biography: Alexander Hamilton was born in Edinburgh, Scot., on Sept. 26, 1712, the sixth son of the Rev. William H. Hamilton, professor of divinity and principal of the University of Edinburgh. Given the best education available in the early eighteenth century, Hamilton studied pharmacy in the shop of the surgeon David Knox and then followed his older brother John into the medical school at the University of Edinburgh. Having received his medical degree in 1737, Alexander Hamilton immigrated to Md. in early 1739, where his brother had been residing since 1721. In Md. Hamilton very quickly became one of the colony's most distinguished physicians and a popular member of aristocratic society. His marriage in 1747 to Margaret Dulany, daughter of Daniel Dulany the Elder (q.v.), allied Hamilton with one of the richest and most powerful Md. families. A Scots Presbyterian who converted to Anglicanism, Hamilton served from 1749 to 1752 as a vestryman of St. Ann's Church in Annapolis. He held the elected position of common councilman of Annapolis from 1743 until his death, and he served one term (1753-1754) in the Lower House of the Assembly. In 1749 Hamilton organized and subsequently served as grand master of a Freemason's society. Throughout his residence in Md., Hamilton was plagued with poor health, probably tuberculosis, which claimed his life prematurely on May 11, 1756, at the age of 44.

Critical Appraisal: One of the ablest belletristic writers in the colonial South, Alexander Hamilton dominated the literature of mideighteenth-century Md. but has not been adequately represented in American literary history because most of his writing is either in manuscript or in the extant copies of the *Maryland Gazette* and other colonial newspapers. A widely read, cultivated, urbane, witty writer, Hamilton was a skilled satirist, particularly in his depiction of social and intellectual life in the Chesapeake colonies, which reveals the reactions of this aristocratic, highly educated Scotch-American gentleman to his American acculturation.

The only major work of Hamilton's to be published since the eighteenth century is his *Itinerarium*, a travel diary of a trip from Annapolis, Md., to York, Maine, and back during four months in 1744. J. A. Leo Lemay has said that the *Itinerarium* is "the best single portrait of men and manners, of rural and urban life, of the wide range of society and scenery in colonial America." Hamilton's special skill in characterization and caricature and his ability to view colonial life with cool detachment make the book especially valuable as a chronicle of mideighteenth-century American society. Although *Itinerarium* is basically a straightforward travel narrative, Hamilton's penchant for satire permeates the material in the form of irony and wit, burlesque exaggeration, and incorporated tall tale, especially with regard to the many individuals he encountered on the road and in taverns and whom he took great delight in caricaturing: the would-be gentleman, tavern keeper, bully, quack, and exasperating inquisitive rustic.

In addition to an eye for character, Hamilton also possessed an eye and an ear for natural scenery, dialect, and folklore. In fact, Hamilton is perhaps the earliest American so thoroughly to appreciate American scenery in prose. His fascination with the picturesqueness of scenery and his interest in romantic, melancholic scenery are anticipatory of early nineteenth-century Romanticism, and his unique ability to capture in prose the intricacies of dialect (Negro, Scottish, or Dutch), colloquial idioms, and rustic dialog, makes his rendition of these elements a vital part of the *Itinerarium*. The book also includes folklore in the form of proverbs, folk sayings, anecdotes, and American versions of archetypal tales, such as those about quacks and a colonial version of the snipe hunt.

Widely read and thoroughly competent as a literary critic, Hamilton wrote highly allusive prose that indicates an extensive knowledge of Classical, Renaissance, and contemporary authors. While on his journey to and from Maine, Hamilton read Henry Fielding's *Joseph Andrews*—published only two years earlier—and wrote a perceptive critical evaluation of the novel. Hamilton published perhaps the colony's ablest belletristic essay in the *Maryland Gazette* of Jan. 29, 1748. A critical survey of the Md. writers and writing that had appeared in that periodical since its founding in 1745, Hamilton's essay is a compilation of several literary genres skillfully fused together: dream vision, Lucianic satire, a Dantesque tour through hell, and the dialog genre of question and answer. Hamilton's criticism of Md. authors is perceptive and fair and is carried out with good-natured humor.

Throughout the *Itinerarium* and other writings, Hamilton demonstrates an extensive knowledge of medical and scientific books and theories. In Nov. 1750 his friend and colleague Adam Thomson delivered a lecture in Philadelphia, "A Discourse on the Preparation of the Body for the Small-Pox," that generated a flood of attacks by Philadelphia physicians. Thomson attacked the empirical school, proposed the "American method" of inoculation, and suggested that legislatures appoint examining bodies to prevent unqualified physicians from practicing. Alexander Hamilton answered Thomson's critics with *A Defence*, an able assemblage of the facts and arguments for Thomson's proposal and a devastating attack on unqualified doctors.

On May 14, 1745, Hamilton organized the Tuesday Club of Annapolis in the tradition of the eighteenth-century British coffeehouse club. One of the most brilliant clubs in an age of clubs, the Tuesday Club had as its members the bright, influential leaders of Md., who acted out a mock-heroic commentary on government, history, society, and manners through an elaborate structure of mock officials and ceremonies. Hamilton was the leading spirit of the club. As its secretary, he produced three manuscripts: the minutes of the meetings, the "Record of the Tuesday Club," and the "History of the Tuesday Club"—works that provide a fascinating glimpse into eighteenth-century American club life.

From his thorough minutes, Hamilton prepared the "Record," a work that exhibits its author's self-conscious literary craftsmanship. He revised and expanded the minutes, added poems that were declaimed at the club, and produced a number of pencil and ink portrait drawings of individual members and of group meetings. The "Record" is an elaborate, unified production, with references to past and future meetings that indicate that it was deliberately organized. An appendix contains the club music composed by the Rev. Thomas Bacon (q.v.) and the favorite songs used by the club.

It is the "History of the Tuesday Club," however, that is Hamilton's major belletristic work and the one—when it is published—that will make him a major American author of neo-Classical prose. This elaborate, highly allusive mock-heroic work is one of the finest humorous works in colonial America. Filled with complex, highly sophisticated burlesques of serious genres, burlesques worthy of comparison to models in British literature such as Alexander Pope's *Dunciad* and Fielding's *Tom Jones*, the "History" is extant in two versions, the second of which is much more elaborate than the first, revealing a skilled artist at work. Perhaps even more revealing of Hamilton's craftsmanship as an artist, however, are the differences between the "History" and the "Record." Whereas the "Record" is a straightforward reporting of the club's activities, the "History" has all of the machinery of elaborate literary satire that constitutes art. Hamilton also invented facetious names for the members ("Loquacious Scribble, M.D." for himself), included new poems probably by himself, wrote criticism of Md. literature, and developed complete characterizations for the members of the club. One of Hamilton's "asides" is a satiric mock play containing local allusions.

Hamilton's contemporary manuscripts on the Tuesday Club are in the Library of Congress ("Record of the Tuesday Club," vol. II); the Maryland Historical Society ("Record of the Tuesday Club," vol. I, and two fragments of manuscript volumes in the Dulany Papers from the "Record" and the "History"); and Johns Hopkins University ("Annapolis Md. Tuesday Club Record Book," being the minutes taken in and shortly after the meetings of the club and the three volumes of "The History of the Ancient and Honourable Tuesday Club," which contains in vol. III a portion of the earlier draft of the "History").

Suggested Readings: DAB. *See also* Anonymous, "The Tuesday Club of Annapolis," MdHM, 1 (1906), 59-65 (this is the third chapter of the tenth book of the "History of the Tuesday Club"); Carl Bridenbaugh, *Gentleman's Progress: The Itinerarium of Dr. Alexander Hamilton, 1744* (1948); Richard Beale Davis, *Intellectual Life in the Colonial South, 1585-1763,* 3 vols. (1978), passim; Sarah Elizabeth Freeman, "The Tuesday Club Medal," *The Numismatist,* 57 (1945), 1313-1322; Albert Bushnell Hart, ed., *Hamilton's Itinerarium* (1907); J. A. Leo Lemay, *Men of Letters in Colonial Maryland* (1972), pp. 213-256; Albert Matthews, "Rattlesnake Colonel," NEQ, 10 (1937), 341-345 (for a discussion of one of Hamilton's colloquialisms); Anna Wells Rutledge, "A Humorous Artist in Colonial Maryland," AC, 16 (1947), 8-9, 14-15.

Homer D. Kemp
Tennessee Technological University

BRITON HAMMON (fl. 1747-1760)

Works: *A Narrative of the Uncommon Sufferings and Surprising Deliverance of Briton Hammon* (1760).

Biography: Nothing is known about Briton Hammon outside what his *Narrative* reveals. According to his only known work, Hammon served as a slave in the household of Gen. John Winslow (1703-1774), an officer in the colonial army who once led a company in the West India expedition. Since Hammon observed that he had visited Jamaica before the beginning of his autobiography (1747), one can assume that he had either accompanied Winslow on his expedition or that Winslow had seized him there.

Although it is not explicitly stated, Winslow apparently hired out Hammon on Christmas day of 1747 to sail on a voyage back to Jamaica. Hammon encountered little difficulty on the voyage until his ship, out from Jamaica fifteen days, "cast away on Cape Florida." Two days later, still moored in the sand, the captain and his crew were captured by Indians, and all save Hammon were slaughtered. After remaining with the Indians for about five weeks, Hammon escaped when, by "the Providence of God," a Spanish captain whom Hammon had earlier met in Jamaica happened upon the Indians and rescued him. For about a year afterward, Hammon served in the "castle" of the governor of Cuba in Havana, but when the authorities in Havana tried to press him into service on board one of the Spanish king's ships, Hammon refused to serve and was subsequently "confin'd almost five years in a close dungeon." Eventually discovered and released into the governor's custody, he finally escaped from Cuba on an English man-o'-war. After having sailed for London, Hammon shipped on several different English war vessels. By sheer chance, he eventually encountered Gen. Winslow while the general was in London on business. It was after their return to Boston, thirteen years after his departure, that Hammon set down these extraordinary events. The details of Hammon's death are unknown.

Critical Appraisal: Briton Hammon's *Narrative* is an important document in the history of early American black letters. Not only is his *Narrative* the earliest publication in America by a black author, it is also the earliest prose work written by a black American and is definitely the oldest black American autobiography to have survived. In addition, it is one of the few Indian captivity narratives written by a black, and it is one of the first and most significant of the American slave narratives.

Like the authors of the early Indian captivities, Hammon stressed his extreme sufferings and his eventual reward "thro' the Divine Goodness," but unlike most of the Indian captives, he was a black man who called himself a slave and who drew attention to his condition on the title page, where he publicly identified himself as "A Negro Man,—Servant to General Winslow." Moreover, Hammon underscored his servitude in a brief note, "To the Reader," where he remarked that since his "capacities and condition in life are very low," he would refrain from expressing opinions and "only relate matters of fact." This refusal to reflect on his sufferings is in stark contrast to later slave narratives, many of which are little more than propaganda tracts attempting to speed abolition. One may only guess that Hammon's motive derives from the deference he asserted in the piece toward "my good master," Gen. Winslow, and to the fact that Hammon's *Narrative* was one of the earliest in the genre.

Nonetheless, despite Hammon's preferred obeisance to an apparently benevolent master, he gave several clues of his displeasure with other, less understanding masters and, by implication, the institution of slavery in general. One of the verbs Hammon most used in his short piece is *confin'd*, always attendant on a description of enslavement or imprisonment. In the conclusion, he remarked, "I have been most grievously afflicted." Concerning his capture by the Indians, he hinted that they did not kill him because he was the only black man among the captives. (A crewman whom Hammon previously identified as a "Mulatto" was probably grouped by the Indians with the white men or taken for a Spaniard). But Hammon's high visibility may well have piqued the Indians' curiosity, for when he was later enslaved by the Spanish, they treated him miserably and he escaped three times before succeeding. Thus Hammon's *Narrative*, with or without its author's expressed opinion, may be read as an aggressive protest against inhuman and unjust treatment of a human being, who had received such treatment because of his color and low condition in life.

Suggested Readings: Frances S. Foster, "Briton Hammon's *Narrative*: Some Insights into Beginnings," CLAJ, 21 (1977), 179-186; Vernon Loggins, *The Negro Author: His Development in America* (1931), pp. 30-31, 95, 271, 373, 411; Dorothy Porter, *Early Negro Writing: 1760-1837* (1971), pp. 515-516, 522-528 (for a modern reprint of "Narrative"); Theressa G. Rush, Carol F. Myers, and Esther S. Arata, *Black American Writers, Past and Present* (1975), I, 352; Roger Whitlow, *Black American Literature: A Critical History* (1973), p. 24.

John C. Shields
Illinois State University

JUPITER HAMMON (1711-c. 1800)

Works: *An Evening Thought. Salvation by Christ, with Penetential Cries: Composed by Jupiter Hammon, a Negro Belonging to Mr. Lloyd, of Queen's-Village on Long Island* (1760); *An Address to Miss Phillis Wheatly, Ethiopian Poetess, in Boston, Who Came from Africa at Eight Years of Age, and Soon Became Acquainted with the Gospel of Jesus Christ* (1778); *A Winter Piece: Being a Serious Exhortation, with a Call to the Unconverted* (1782); *An Evening's Improvement. Shewing, the Necessity of Beholding the Lamb of God* (c. 1785); *An Address to the Negroes in the State of New-York* (1787).

Biography: Jupiter Hammon lived his entire life as a slave in N.Y. and Conn. He is remembered today as the first black to publish a poem in America. His *An Evening Thought*, published in broadside format in 1760, appeared a year before Phillis Wheatley (q.v.) was brought to Boston from Africa.

In comparison with the more famous black poetess, little is known of Hammon's life. His birth date, Oct. 17, 1711, has only recently been established, and his date of death remains unknown. Most of what we do know about Hammon's life is derived from his own writings and from the records of the Lloyd family, Hammon's owners. The Lloyds were a prominent Long Island family who had acquired considerable wealth as landlords and merchants. When Hammon's first master, Henry Lloyd, died in 1763, Hammon was bequeathed to Joseph, one of Henry's four sons. Joseph Lloyd, an ardent Patriot, left Long Island for Hartford, Conn., when the British invaded N.Y. following the outbreak of the Revolutionary War. Joseph committed suicide in 1780, having received a false report of a British victory at Charlestown. Hammon then became the property of John

Lloyd, grandson of his original owner, and returned to Long Island, where he probably lived the rest of his life.

Hammon's duties as a slave are unknown, but he stated in his old age that he was still "able to do almost any kind of business." His writings suggest that the Lloyds were relatively kind masters, that they allowed him a rudimentary education and access to books, and that they encouraged and helped to arrange publication of his poetry and prose. Hammon was powerfully affected by the evangelical revivals of the eighteenth century, and he probably served as a slave exhorter or minister. Religion was the dominant force in his life and motivated all his writing.

Critical Appraisal: Jupiter Hammon's extant writings include four poems, two sermons, and the *Address to the Negroes in the State of New-York. An Essay on the Ten Virgins* was advertised in the *Connecticut Courant* in 1779, but no copy has been discovered. Hammon is also said to have written a poem celebrating the 1782 visit of Prince William Henry, later King William IV, to the Lloyd estate. Like the *Essay on the Ten Virgins*, no copy of this poem has survived.

Of the published poetry, *An Evening Thought* and *An Address to Miss Phillis Wheatly* appeared in broadside, and "A Poem for Children with Thoughts on Death" and "A Dialogue Entitled the Kind Master and the Dutiful Servant" were printed with Hammon's sermons. Hammon's poems employ the ballad stanza, reflecting the influence of Methodist hymns; another possible influence is Michael Wigglesworth's (q.v.) *The Day of Doom*. All of the poems have religious themes and imagery, and two are glossed with biblical references. Because of the poems' powerful rhythmic effects and their frequent use of repetition to emphasize key words, they are best appreciated if read out loud.

Hammon's two sermons, both published in Hartford, show a familiarity with traditional sermon structure, in which the text and the doctrine derived from it are followed by illustrations and applications of the doctrine. Hammon's theological arguments are somewhat lacking in coherence, although they establish his themes with sufficient clarity. His religious beliefs are absolute, and they dominate all secular considerations: "If we be slaves it is by the permission of God, if we are free it must be by the power of the most high God."

Hammon's final work, *An Address to the Negroes*, is more rigorously structured than the sermons. The promise of eternal salvation is paramount in Hammon's consolatory argument, but he does comment on the worldly aspirations of his listeners: "That liberty is a great thing we may know from our own feelings, and we may likewise judge so from the conduct of the white people in this war. . . . I must say that I have hoped that God would open their eyes, when they were so much engaged for liberty, to think of the state of the poor blacks, and to pity us." The *Address* was reprinted in 1787, at the request of the Pennsylvania Society for Promoting the Abolition of Slavery, and again in 1806, after Hammon's death.

Hammon's religious impulse and his position as a slave enforced a secular neutrality: "I have never said, nor done anything, neither directly nor indirectly, to promote or to prevent freedom." In his later years, he stated that he was personally willing to remain a slave. It is perhaps for this reason that he was all but forgotten until rediscovered by Oscar Wegelin in the early twentieth century. Yet Hammon could express his beliefs powerfully in a variety of literary forms. His achievement as a writer is significant and of more than historical interest.

Suggested Readings: Bernard W. Bell, "African-American Writers" in *American Literature, 1764-1789*, ed. Everett Emerson (1977), pp. 176-180; Sidney Kaplan, *The Black Presence in the Era of the American Revolution, 1770-1800* (1973), pp. 171-178; Roderick R. Palmer, "Jupiter Hammon's Poetic Exhortations," CLAJ, 18 (1974), 22-28; Stanley A. Ransom, Jr., *America's First Negro Poet: The Complete Works of Jupiter Hammon of Long Island* (1970); William H. Robinson, *Black New England Letters* (1977), pp. 117-120; Oscar Wegelin, *Jupiter Hammon, American Poet: Selections from His Writings and a Bibliography* (1915; rep., 1969).

Douglas R. Wilmes
The Pennsylvania State University

JOHN HAMMOND (fl. 1634-1663)

Works: *Hammond vs. Heamans* (1655); *Leah and Rachel: Or, The Two Fruitfull Sisters Virginia and Mary-Land* (1656).

Biography: Little is known of John Hammond's life, and nothing is known of the period before his immigration to Va. In *Leah and Rachel* (1656), which was written after his return to Eng., he reported that he had lived in the colonies twenty-one years. It seems likely, therefore, that he immigrated to Va. from Eng. sometime about 1634, at what age we do not know, although he was at the time unmarried. Having settled in Va., he married a woman named Ann, with whom he had one daughter, also named Ann, and three sons, Mordecai, Bernard, and Daniel. In addition, he became involved in public affairs and acquired both substantial property and an unsavory reputation. In 1652, when he was elected to the House of Burgesses, Hammond was promptly expelled on grounds that his "scandalous" reputation made him unfit to serve.

Embarrassed by his expulsion, Hammond sold his property and moved his family to Md., where he bought a small plantation in St. Mary's County near Newton. In addition to running his plantation, Hammond again gravitated toward public affairs—first as a lawyer practicing before the Provincial Court of Md. and then as an ally of Lord Baltimore in the Md. wars. After the Puritan victory at the Battle of Severn (Mar. 25, 1655), Hammond fled to Eng. There, looking back on the battles he had fought and the land he had come to love, he became a writer, first of a political pamphlet, *Hammond vs. Heamans*, and then of a celebration of the New World called *Leah and Rachel*. By 1661 Hammond was back in Md., where he died in the late winter or early spring of 1663.

Critical Appraisal: *Hammond vs. Heamans* is a sharp, sometimes witty polemic in which Hammond responded to accusations made by Capt. Roger Heamans, who had fought on the Puritan side in the Battle of Severn. A pamphlet rather than a book and a work of very limited interest, *Hammond vs. Heamans* serves primarily as a reminder that colonists poured considerable interest into both local controversies and political tracts.

Leah and Rachel is a far more important work, in part because it engages larger issues and in part because it is better written. Having returned to the land of his birth, Hammond apparently found himself homesick for his adoptive land: "it is that country in which I desire to spend the remnant of my days, in which I covet to make my grave." But as *Leah and Rachel* clearly shows, it was not only the thought of his adoptive home but also two features of Eng., and especially London, that inspired Hammond to write. On one hand, he saw crowds of people who lived poorer lives than those of "the meanest servant in Virginia." On the other, he heard pernicious reports of the New World as an unhealthy land inhabited by rogues. Convinced that the false reports were designed to discourage the people who most needed to emigrate, Hammond took it upon himself to set things straight. *Leah and Rachel* constitutes, then, a direct appeal to Eng.'s dispossessed. It not only urges them to see their hapless, hopeless existences for what they are; it also urges them to undertake the difficult journey to the New World—"a place of pleasure and plenty" where "all things necessary for Humane subsistence" are found in abundance.

Suggested Readings: LHUS; T₁. *See also* Freda A. Stohner, "John Hammond" in *Southern Writers: A Biographical Dictionary*, ed. Robert Bain et al. (1979), pp. 198-199.

David Minter
Emory University

LAWRENCE HAMMOND (c. 1640-1699)

Works: *Diary of Lawrence Hammond* (w. 1677-1694; pub. 1892); *To the King's Most Excellent Majesty, the Humble Address of Divers Subjects, Inhabiting in Boston, Charlestown and Places Adjacent, Within Your Majesties Territory and Dominion of New-England, in America* (1691).

Biography: Although his name appears regularly in *The Genealogical Register of the First Settlers of New England*, little is recorded about Lawrence Hammond before Sept. 1662, when he married the first of his four wives, Audria Eaton, who had come to Charlestown, Mass., from London the year before. Hammond became a freeman on May 23, 1666. His personal life was marked by illness and death: with his first three wives, who died of childbirth or "feaver," he had four daughters and one son; with his fourth wife, two sons. By 1689 all three sons were dead; of the daughters, only two survived.

Hammond became a lieutenant in the local artillery company, rising to the rank of captain of militia by 1672. From that year until 1678, he was representative of Charlestown to the General Court of Mass. in Cambridge. In 1686 he became clerk of the peace, of General Quarter-Sessions, and of the Court of Inferior Common-Pleas, as well as recorder of Middlesex County, Mass., a position that required him to keep records of deeds, probations, and various other civic events, including weddings, births, and deaths. Hammond died on Jul. 29, 1699, in Boston.

Critical Appraisal: During his lifetime, Lawrence Hammond's only publication was an address to William and Mary requesting arms and ammunition. Published in 1691 in *Black-Fryars* along with several letters from Hammond concerning the lack of royal response, this address is signed by others in Charlestown, including the more well-known John Hammond, who was no relation to Lawrence.

Lawrence Hammond is remembered for his personal diary, a hand-written journal of forty-three pages covering the years 1677 to 1694, that was given to the Massachusetts Historical Society in 1858 by a descendant of the early historian of N.H., Jeremy Belknap (q.v.). Although the complete diary was published in the society's *Proceedings* in 1892, by that time several leaves, covering a period of thirteen years, were missing from the original manuscript. The diary is in only rough chronological order, sometimes covering a dozen days in a row, sometimes skipping from month to month. The individual entries form the following categories: everyday happenings (diseases, weather, family records); herbal recipes for sickness; political pre-Revolutionary events (uprising of people in Boston led by Nathan Wade against Governor Edmund Andros on Apr. 18, 1689); lists of constables and selectmen from Charlestown; folk stories; and remarkable scientific anecdotes ("An Eminent Deliverance of Mr. Jn° Hale Minister of Beverly from Lightning," or "A Remarkable Experiment Tryed upon a Deaf & Dumb Man").

Portions of the diary are written in cipher, an increasingly necessary precaution as the diary grows more politically oriented each year and includes an account of a seizure of letters being delivered by Col. Potter to the governor of Va., after which "Som have been called to acco^t for w^t they writ, & other expect ye like." The coded entries, which were translated for the Historical Society using Thomas Skelton's alphabet, seem so bereft of political content as to suggest they were written in both cipher and code.

Many of the entries in Hammond's diary are unintentionally humorous because of juxtaposition of subject matter, writing style, and naiveté. The experiment with the deaf man, for instance, begins with this description: "Wee pricked a knife's point...into ye belly of a Harpsicot, causing him to hold ye haft in his Teeth, then two of us severally played in his sight, ye one Harmonically som Tunes, ye other afterward struck a Confused Discord, clashing many of ye keyes at once." The point of this experiment, according to Hammond, was to prove "a probability y^t ye mouth is not devoid of a power of perceiving sound; & y^t by ye tender nerves of ye teeth."

According to William Matthews, Lawrence Hammond's diary is of "some linguistic interest" because of its "amusing antiquarian material." Because of its erratic nature, frequent misspellings, and missing pages, the diary is not a reliable document. But it is useful for what it is: the random record of the dailiness of an ordinary American in late seventeenth-century New Eng.

Suggested Readings: "Diary of Lawrence Hammond," PMHS, 2nd ser., 7 (1892), 144-161; Richard Dorson, ed., *America Begins: Early American Writing* (prints folkloric anecdote from diary; 1950); John Farmer, ed., *Genealogical Register of First Settlers of New England* (brief account of Hammond's life; 1964); Elizabeth Deering Hanscom, ed., *The Heart of the Puritan: Selections from Letters and Journals* (prints selected herbal recipes from the diary; 1917); Frank R. Holmes, ed., *Directory of the Ancestral Heads of New England Families* (1923); William Matthews, comp., *American Diaries: An Annotated Bibliography of American Diaries Written Prior to the Year 1861* (1945).

Timothy Dow Adams
McMurry College

JOHN HANCOCK (1702-1744)

Works: *The Instability of Humane Greatness* (1738); *A Memorial of God's Goodness* (1739); *The Danger of an Unqualified Ministry* (1743); *A Discourse upon the Good Work* (1743); *The Examiner, or Gilbert Against Tennent* (1743); *An Expostulatory and Pacifick Letter* (1743).

Biography: John Hancock was born on Jun. 1, 1702, at Lexington, Mass., where his father John (1671-1752) was pastor. Like his father, Hancock was educated at Harvard College, receiving an A.B. in 1719 and serving as the college's librarian between 1723 and 1726. Following employment as a teacher at the Lexington and Woburn schools and unsuccessful candidacies for pulpits at Westborough and at Portsmouth, N.H., Hancock was called to the First Church of Braintree (later Quincy), Mass. There he was ordained on Nov. 2, 1726, and there he would serve until his early death on May 7, 1744.

When Hancock's father stood before the Braintree congregation to deliver his son's ordination sermon, he emphasized the themes of ministerial authority and power that had distinguished his own career: ministers "must have power to *rule*, as well as power to *preach*." Hancock followed the example and exhortations of his father. Like the elder Hancock, he would in time be castigated as a "bishop" by those who defined the minister's role in less authoritarian terms. Thus Hancock's opposition to the Great Awakening was as predictable as it was vehement. By attacking the spiritual sincerity and authority of the established ministry, the itinerant revivalists challenged the tenets of pastoral responsibility and leadership that Hancock had inherited from his father and exemplified in his own ministry. Hancock's response to this challenge in his sermons and tracts of 1743 established his reputation as one of the most resolute opponents of intemperate Awakeners such as James Davenport, Gilbert Tennent (q.v.), and George Whitefield (q.v.).

Having married Mary Hawke Thaxter in 1733, Hancock left a young family of a daughter and two sons when he died at the age of 41. His eldest son John, later governor of Mass. and a signer of the Declaration of Independence, was raised by Hancock's brother Thomas, a Boston merchant.

Critical Appraisal: Most of John Hancock's writings were implicitly or explicitly polemical. Against the forces of enthusiastic revivalism, he advanced arguments that were often passionate but always balanced by his confidence in his own pastoral responsibility, which depended on a sober, orderly vision of the legacy of the traditional New Eng. way. Thus in light of Hancock's attacks on the Great Awakening in 1743, his early sermons of 1738 and 1739 may be seen as illustrating the values he believed the Awakening threatened. In *The Instability of Humane Greatness*, a funeral sermon commemorating the death in London of Edmund Quincy, Hancock portrayed Quincy's distinguished public career as typifying the qualities of the good ruler, who would exercise his power with *"Wisdom* and *Prudence."* As a soldier, judge, councilor, and colonial agent, Quincy had lived a life of service and piety that confirmed the traditional social values of responsibility and order. Similar concerns appear in *A Memorial of God's Goodness*, two sermons preached to mark the hundredth anniversary of the Braintree church. Hancock insisted on the stability of a historical imperative, reminding his congregation of "strong Obligations to answer the pious Design of your Transplantation into the *Wilderness."* That Braintree in 1739 was no wilderness highlighted Hancock's rhetorical intention. In words solemnized by the congregation's renewal of the church's original covenant, he drew an unbroken connection through history to the eight founding members of the actual wilderness congregation at Braintree. From a perilous beginning, the church had prospered for a century. History had validated the enduring truth of the "Design," and its filiopietistic lessons remained relevant: "Now it should be our great Care to *stand fast in the Liberty* of our Fathers, and remember their great Errand into this Wilderness." Such lessons were all the more important because of "the Decay of vital Piety" in New Eng. and the emergence of "fierce Contentions" in its churches, which Hancock ascribed to "the depreciating Nature of the Bills of Credit" that exposed ministers to financial hardships and conflicts with their congregations.

But the itinerant preachers of the Great Awakening soon opened far more serious fractures in the foundations of the established ministry. Of these itinerants, Gilbert Tennent particularly incensed Hancock. Tennent's Nottingham sermon of 1740, which accused his fellow ministers of spiritual hypocrisy, his notably successful tour of New Eng. in the winter of 1740-1741, and his copious publications during this period drove Hancock to reply in words scarcely less restrained than those of the fiery Tennent. In *A Discourse upon the Good Work*, a Tuesday lecture sermon preached in the fall of 1742, Hancock attacked both the instruments and the agents of the revival. Emphasizing the "growing progressive

Nature" of grace, Hancock summarized the conversion process in terms that implicitly contrasted to the dramatic excesses of the revivalists' harvests of conversions. Turning upon the harvesters, Hancock accused them of vanity in presuming to judge the spiritual states of others while themselves pretending to "extraordinary Sanctity." "It is well," he noted, "if the present unbounded License in preaching, doth not end in Libertinism."

There is little doubt that Hancock had Tennent in mind as he made these charges, for in 1743 he repeatedly criticized the Awakening in general and Tennent in particular, identifying Tennent as "the grand Instrument of promoting those animal Convulsions" that the Awakening had encouraged in its more enthusiastic converts. In Jul. Hancock delivered his judgment on the general efficacy of the Awakening in *An Expostulatory and Pacifick Letter*. In Sept. he launched a frontal attack on his archenemy, preaching *The Danger of an Unqualified Ministry* at Ashford, Conn. Finally, writing as "Philalethes," he published *The Examiner, or Gilbert Against Tennent*, to which Tennent replied with *The Examiner, Examined, or Gilbert Tennent, Harmonious*.

Hancock's *Letter* emerged from the controversy surrounding the May 1743 annual meeting of the Mass. ministers at Boston, which had led to a public split within the ministry over the Awakening. Referring to "Antinomian and Familistical Errors, gross Delusions, and scandalous Disorders of various Kinds," Hancock left little doubt that he stood solidly with those who opposed the Awakening, however much he might decry "the Prevalency of a Party-Spirit" in the ministry. In *The Danger of an Unqualified Ministry*, an ordination sermon echoing the similar title of Tennent's Nottingham sermon (*The Danger of an Unconverted Ministry*), Hancock used the requirements of the occasion—which normally mandated a discussion of the prerequisites for membership in the ministry—to attack his opponent's "outrageous Sermon." Influenced by Tennent, the established ministry was failing to adequately control entrance into their ranks, thus "prostituting the holy Ministry to every bold Intruder." Fearing an unconverted ministry, Tennent had seemed to ignore the dangers of an unqualified ministry. To Hancock, the errors and disorders attendant on the latter far outweighed the unknowable possibility of the former. The argument was finally epistemological: might one's own call to the ministry be a chimera born of "Pride and Self-Conceit"? Might one's condemnations of others have equally disreputable origins? Hancock claimed that there was no way to answer such questions with confidence; it was "Presumption" to aspire to the certain knowledge that seemed to animate the strident claims of Tennent and his followers. Hancock's criticisms of Tennent in *The Danger* were sustained and occasionally intemperate, but his fiercest attacks were reserved for *The Examiner*. In this tract, Hancock compared Tennent's statements in the Nottingham sermon with seeming contradictions in his later writings. By placing such contradictory statements in parallel columns, Hancock managed to land some telling blows, as Tennent seems to have recognized. His reply to Hancock's 32-page pamphlet ran to 146 pages. But to the modern reader, the bitterness of Hancock's prose may be the best measure of the passions aroused by the Great Awakening: "[Tennent's] Progress thro' this Province favour'd more of worldly Pomp and Grandeur, than the Humility of the meek and lowly *Jesus*: He came eating and drinking, galloping over the Country with his *Congregatio de propagandâ*, &c...with a Troop of 20 or 30 Horse, entring into *other Men's Labours*, and *devouring their Livings, having all Things in common.*"

The horror of chaos, of disruptions that threatened an orderly, stable world governed by a long established "pious Design," was the key to Hancock's passionate rejection of the Great Awakening. His own father had participated in his ordination; the continuity of the past had been visible in his own entrance into the ministry. Like many other ministers, Hancock believed that the Great Awakening and its self-appointed apostles threatened both the institutions of the ministry and the very identities of its members.

Suggested Readings: CCNE; Sibley-Shipton (VI, 316-319); Sprague (I, 240-241). *See also* Edwin Scott Gaustad, *The Great Awakening in New England* (1968), pp. 36, 63-66, 71, 91; Ebenezer Gay, *The Untimely Death of a Man of God Lamented* (1744); John Hancock, *A Sermon Preached at the Ordination of Mr. John Hancock* (1726).

Douglas R. Wilmes
The Pennsylvania State University

CHARLES HANSFORD (c. 1685-1761)

Works: "On the Conquest of Cape Breton" (1745); "Of Body and of Soul"; "Some Reflections on My Past Life and the Numberless Mercies Receiv'd from My Maker"; "Barzillai"; "My Country's Worth" (all w. 1749-1752; pub. 1961).

Biography: Little is known of Charles Hansford's life except the few autobiographical details to be gleaned from his poems (especially "Some Reflections..." and "Barzillai") and a very brief memoir of him by his friend and fellow poet Benjamin Waller (q.v.), a prominent Williamsburg attorney. From these documents, it appears that Hansford was largely self-educated and worked variously as a blacksmith, schoolteacher, tavern keeper, yeoman farmer, and, quite probably, seaman. But, according to Waller, smithing was his primary trade, at which he worked "as long as his strength would permit." A licensed lay reader in the established (Anglican) church, Hansford was deeply religious, a characteristic evident in his poems. Hansford is also one of the very earliest native-born southern colonials whose verses are extant, his grandfather having come to Jamestown in the early days of settlement. His writings are likewise unique in that, although almost all that survives from the colonial South is from a planter's or a preacher's pen, Hansford was a distinctly middle-class artisan. His poems were evidently the products of old age, written to while away the hours when deafness had robbed him of the pleasures of conversation. If, as has been convincingly claimed, the poem "On the Conquest of Cape Breton, by An

Honest Tar," published in the *Virginia Gazette* of Aug. 29, 1745, and reprinted a few weeks later in the *Boston Post Boy*, is Hansford's work, it appears to be the only poem he published in his lifetime. The remaining four poems (nearly 1,900 lines for which the editors supplied all but one of the titles) were discovered in 1960 at Tower Hill (near Waverley, Va.), the plantation home of Hansford's descendants, in a manuscript copy made by the poet's son in 1765 and containing, as well as Waller's memoir and occasional emendations, three appreciative verses by Richard Hewitt, John Dixon, and Waller himself. Hansford died in Va. in 1761.

   Critical Appraisal: Hansford's verses are rough-hewn heroic couplets and triplets that have both historical and literary significance. Although his poems contain numerous forced rhymes, many lines that do not quite scan, and frequent passages that are simply rhymed prose, the sentiments expressed in all of his poems are genuine and deeply felt. The patriotic praise heaped upon Sir Peter Warren for his capture of Fort Louisbourg in "On the Conquest of Cape Breton" is no less sincere for its being delivered in conventional tropes with a *laus Deo* conclusion. The poet's spirited defense of the orthodox Christian doctrine of a literal resurrection of the body, in "Of Body and of Soul," is interesting as an indicator of how deeply into colonial Virginian life Deistic heterodoxies had already penetrated. Hansford's most felicitous lines are to be found in "Barzillai," a heavily autobiographical meditation on a minor Old Testament patriarch (in II Samuel 19:31-39) whose condition the poet sees as paralleling his own. His least accomplished, although most personal and pious, poem is the one he titled "Some Reflections on My Past Life..." The final poem in the Tower Hill manuscript, "My Country's Worth," is a lengthy survey of the plantation oligarchy of Va. and some of their vices—gambling chief among them—as well as their penchant for relying on chattel slavery, which Hansford regarded as a dangerous, if not an immoral, institution. The chance survival of even one manuscript copy of the several that apparently circulated among the poet's friends suggests a tantalizing possibility that Hansford may have written other poems that are not now extant and, yet more, that there were others like him in the southern colonies of whose versifying we may never have an inkling.

   Suggested Readings: Robert Bain, Joseph M. Flora, and Louis D. Rubin, Jr., eds., *Southern Writers: A Biographical Dictionary* (1979), pp. 199-200; J. A. Leo Lemay, "A Poem Probably by Charles Hansford," VMHB, 74 (1966), 445-447; J. A. Servies and C. Dolmetsch, eds., *The Poems of Charles Hansford* (1961).

Carl Dolmetsch
The College of William & Mary

ELIZABETH HANSON (1684-1737)

   Works: *God's Mercy Surmounting Man's Cruelty* (1728).
   Biography: Most of what is known of Elizabeth Hanson is recorded in the narrative of her captivity among the Indians. Born in 1684, she was 40 at the

time of her capture. Because she was married to John Hanson, a Quaker who adhered to his sect's pacifism, their farm, located at Cocheco in Dover Township, N.H., was undefended when attacked by the French and their Indian allies on Aug. 27, 1724. After five months with the Indians and one with the French, she was returned to her husband along with three of their children and a maid at Port Royal in 1725. Her eldest daughter, however, remained in captivity, later marrying a Frenchman. Elizabeth Hanson died in 1737.

Critical Appraisal: Elizabeth Hanson's narrative occupies an important transitional position in the history of the Indian captivity narrative. Its publication brings to an end a period dominated by New Eng. narratives such as those of Mary Rowlandson (q.v.) and John Williams (q.v.) and heralds a concern for "literary refinement." It relies on the traditional elements of its New Eng. counterparts—scorn mixed with surprised admiration for Indian ways, children killed before their parents' eyes, biblical quotations cited to illuminate and justify great physical hardship. Because she was a Quaker, Hanson's narrative focuses on the personal aspect of her experience rather than the communal emphasis common to other examples of New Eng. captivity narratives that precede hers. She delivered no jeremiad to warn backsliders, as did John Williams in *The Redeemed Captive* (1707), but merely stated that she hoped to "have given a short but true account of some of the remarkable trials and wonderful deliverances...that I hope thereby the merciful kindness and goodness of God may be magnified, and the reader hereof provoked with more care and fear to serve Him in righteousness and humility."

Hanson's narrative has a complex publication history. Published in 1728 in the Quaker city of Philadelphia rather than in Boston, the first American edition contains a three-paragraph introduction by an unknown person who interviewed Hanson, suggesting the possibility that someone else wrote or at least helped compose the narrative, despite the occurrence of the initials E. H. on the final page. Another American edition followed in 1754. The noted English Quaker preacher Samuel Bownas visited Hanson during his trip to America in 1727 but never claimed to have had a hand in the various American editions. English editions of the Hanson narrative were published in 1760, 1787, and 1791; the editors of these three versions did not alter its content but certainly treated the material to coincide with the prevailing taste for sentimentality common to the second half of the eighteenth century.

The fact that she was harshly treated and had given birth to a child (common among female captives) only two weeks before her capture proved too enticing for Hanson's English editors to ignore. The first American edition, for example, tells of her distress in a factual, straightforward manner, "By this time, what with fatigue of spirits, hard labor, mean diet, and want of natural rest, I was brought so low that my milk was dried up, my babe very poor and weak, just skin and bone." In contrast, the English edition of 1760 substitutes the word *reduced* for *brought*; thus through this type of subtle stylistic change, the rhetorical emphasis shifts, inviting the reader to identify more intensely with Hanson's suffering.

God's Mercy Surmounting Man's Cruelty marks an important turning point in the development of the captivity narrative as a literary genre, moving away from factual detail and communal concern toward literary effect and an emphasis on the individual. It points the way for sentimentalized accounts such as the fictional *History of Maria Kittle* (1797) by Anne Eliza Bleecker (q.v.) and eventually to the dime novels of the nineteenth century.

Suggested Readings: R.W.G. Vail, *Voice of the Old Frontier* (1949), 216-218, 248, 272, 274, 309, 313, 336, 362-363; Alden T. Vaughan and Edward W. Clark, eds., *Puritans among the Indians* (1981), 23-24, 229-224, rep. of 1728 American edition; Richard VanDerBeets, ed., *Held Captive by Indians* (1973), 130-150, rep. of 1760 English edition.

Edward W. Clark
Winthrop College

THOMAS HARIOT (1560-1621)

Works: *A Briefe and True Report of the New Found Land of Virginia* (1588); *Artis Analyticae Praxis* (1631).

Biography: Born in Oxford, Eng., probably in Nov. 1560, Thomas Hariot (also spelled *Harriot*) attended the university there, receiving a B.A. in 1580. Soon thereafter he was in the service of Sir Walter Raleigh, to whom he taught navigation and cosmography and helped prepare for the first Roanoke expedition. Hariot was among the 108 men who sailed in 1585 to "Virginia" (Roanoke Island, N.C.) under the command of Sir Richard Grenville. During the eleven months he sojourned in the New World, Hariot collected specimens and took copious notes, most of which were cast overboard by Sir Francis Drake's sailors during a storm on the return voyage. After 1593 Hariot was a pensioner of Henry Percy, ninth earl of Northumberland. At the time of the Gunpowder plots, Hariot was briefly imprisoned but was later freed when he pleaded that he never meddled "in matters of state" and was "contented with a private life for the love of learning." After Northumberland's arrest, Hariot often visited him in the Tower of London, where Raleigh was also incarcerated. At the Tower, Hariot was one of only three persons given free access to Raleigh, whom Hariot aided in the writing of his *History of the World*. A skeptic who had consorted with Christopher Marlowe, Hariot was on good terms with Ben Jonson, John Donne, and George Chapman, who in the preface to his translation of Homer acknowledged the assistance of Hariot, "whose judgment and learning in all kinds, I know to be incomparable, and bottomless." In the field of optics, Hariot corresponded with Johannes Kepler on refraction and on the causes of the rainbow. He also studied the chemistry of metals and dabbled in physics and philosophy, and his interest in astronomy led to the construction of a telescope by means of which he first detected sunspots and was able to draw the earliest map of the moon showing "seas" and craters. Some of the mathematical symbols he devised are still in use.

For relaxation, Hariot played word games and deciphered codes, and he continued his scientific experiment until his death on Jul. 2, 1621, at Isleworth, Northumberland's estate near London.

Critical Appraisal: The first English book about America by one who had lived there, Thomas Hariot's *A Briefe and True Report* has been described as "the most delectable of Americana" and as "a classic of scientific and anthropological observation by the most original and wide-ranging of Elizabethan scientific intellects." Hariot was Raleigh's official naturalist, cartographer, and historian on Roanoke Island. His directive was to study the aborigines and to make a survey of economic resources for use by future settlers. Quickly recognizing that a colony, to survive, must be populated by artisans and farmers—not "gentlemen" and wealth seekers—Hariot wrote his *Report* for two reasons: to deny the "slaunderous and shamefull" rumors that the colony had not been a success and to attract "planters" and investors for subsequent expeditions. As a promotional tract, Hariot's *Report* became a model for similar books to follow. The first section dealt with those "Merchantable commodities" that, transported into Eng., would "enrich your selues and prouiders": grass silk, flax and hemp, tar and turpentine, wine, furs, skins, pearls, dyes, and others. In the second part was information about foods and other commodities to sustain the settlers: maize, beans and peas, melons and gourds, potatoes, nuts and berries; deer and bears; rabbits and squirrels; turkeys and geese; crabs, oysters, and fish. The third part described the amicable and impressionable natives: their clothes, weapons, houses, towns, wars, and religion. No colony, wrote Hariot, could fail in a region where planting and harvesting were so easily managed and where the air was "so temperate and holsome, the soyle so fertile, and yeelding such commodities as I haue before mentioned." In addition, Hariot wrote of an herb the natives called *vppówoc* (tobacco), the leaves of which

> being dried and brought into pouder, they use to take the fume or smoke thereof by sucking it through pipes made of claie, into their stomacke and heade; from whence it purgeth superfluous fleame & other grosse humors, openeth all the pores & passages of the body...wherby their bodies are notably preserued in health & know not many greeuous diseases wherewithall wee in England are oftentimes afflicted.

Included in Richard Hakluyt's *Principall Navigations* (1589), Hariot's book was later published in Frankfort by Theodor de Bry in a multilingual edition (Latin, German, French, and English) as *Americae Descriptio* (1590) with handsome engravings of the John White drawings. In some form, Hariot's account appeared in about two dozen editions over the next several decades and was more widely read on the Continent than any other book by an Englishman.

Artis Analyticae Praxis (1631), a seminal work, influenced Descartes and is, according to a historian of mathematics, "less rhetorical and more symbolic than perhaps any other algebra that has ever been written." Thousands of Hariot's unpublished papers, including metaphysical verse and a number of poems about algebra and navigation, are in the British Museum and other depositories.

Suggested Readings: DNB; LHUS. *See also* John Aubrey, *Brief Lives, 1669-1696* (1898); David Beers Quinn, ed., *The Roanoke Voyages, 1584-1590*, vol. 1 (1955); A. L. Rouse, "Elizabethan Heterodox," NYTBR (Apr. 18, 1971); Muriel Rukeyser, *The Traces of Thomas Hariot* (1971); John W. Shirley, ed., *Thomas Hariot: Renaissance Scientist* (1974); Henry Stevens, *Thomas Hariot* (1900).

Richard Walser
North Carolina State University, Raleigh

BENJAMIN HARRIS (fl. 1673-1711)

Works: *An Appeal from the Country to the City, for the Preservation of His Majesty's Person and the Protestant Religion* (1679); *The Protestant Tutor* (1685); *The New England Primer* (1687-1690); *Public Occurrences* (1690); *The London Post* (1702-1705); *The Protestant Post-Boy* (1711).

Biography: Although neither his birth date nor place is known, Benjamin Harris was a well-known figure in the printing and publishing worlds of New Eng. and London throughout the late seventeenth and early eighteenth centuries. His political and religious principles were never in doubt; he was a stout-hearted Protestant, a firm supporter of the Hanoverian succession, and a champion of the freedom of the press. For his principles, he on more than one occasion found himself seized by the government; although never detained for long periods, Harris nevertheless suffered considerable economic and professional losses.

Little is known of his early life, but by 1673 Harris already was established as a small bookseller in Bell Alley in Coleman Street, London. Throughout the 1670s, he printed and sold tracts as well as news sheets defending the Protestant religion, but it was not until 1679 that the government acted against him for printing and distributing *An Appeal from the Country to the City*. Over the next three years, Harris was brought to trial and was forced to find security for his good behavior. Never one to lose an opportunity, Harris printed an account of his own trial, which did little to endear him to the authorities, who were even more angered in 1681 by the appearance of a *Protestant Petition*. Harris again was arrested, tried, fined 500 pounds, and put in the pillory. With the political and religious climate so hostile to his own interests and inclinations, he wisely left London for New Eng. between 1684 and 1686.

In Boston, Harris once again turned to his trade as a bookseller, but here he again was unable to remain at peace with the authorities. His *Public Occurrences*—the first newspaper printed in America—was issued without official approval and was immediately suppressed. His *The New England Primer* appeared sometime between 1687 and 1690, but it was not until after the Glorious Revolution of 1688 that he was in harmony with constituted authority. In 1691, in partnership with John Allen (q.v.), he became printer to the governor and Council, but by 1695 he had resolved to return to London, where the publishing trade was booming and where he also would be at the center of political and religious activity.

From 1696 Harris enjoyed all of the advantages not only of a less censored press but also of a highly charged, partisan atmosphere that encouraged and used his abilities as a printer and publisher. In the reign of Queen Anne, he emerged as printer of *The London Post* from 1702 through 1705 and of *The Protestant Post-Boy* in 1711 with Sarah Popping. Indeed, Harris's last great public appearance was in keeping with his history, for in early Dec. 1711, he was taken into custody by the Tory government for printing *The Protestant Post-Boy*. With this final challenge to authority, Harris disappeared from public view.

Critical Appraisal: Although neither a great nor a renowned figure in the literary and printing history of his age, Benjamin Harris played a minor role in the advancement of the press in New Eng. and in London. His move to Boston brought to Mass. the latest printing and publishing ideas and techniques, and it is fitting that the first newspaper in the colonies should be his contribution to America. In Eng. Harris resolutely defended the causes of Protestantism and limited monarchy, but he was neither a strong writer nor a reckless printer. In trouble with the authorities both before 1688 and during the Tory government of 1710-1714, he most often was willing to abide by the reasonable rules of responsible government. It was only the determined attacks of government that brought him to trial. Overall, he was a constant and interesting man open to new ideas and well equipped to hold his own in the fascinating new world of printing and publishing that followed the lapsing of the censorship laws in the reign of William III.

Suggested Readings: DAB. *See also* J. A. Downie, *Robert Harley and the Press* (1979); W. R. McLeod, and V. B. McLeod, *A Graphical Directory of English Newspapers and Periodicals, 1702-1714* (1981); R. S. Mortimer, "Biographical Notices of Printers and Publishers of Friends' Books up to 1750: A Supplement to Plomer's *Dictionary*," JD, 3 (1947-1948), 107-125; Henry R. Plomer, *A Dictionary of the Printers and Booksellers Who Were at Work in England, Scotland and Ireland from 1668 to 1725* (1922, 1968).

W. R. McLeod
West Virginia University

LEVI HART (1738-1808)

Works: *The Christian Minister* (1771); *The Duty and Importance of Preaching* (1772); *The Excellence of Scripture* (1775); *Liberty Described* (1775); *The Description of a Good Character* (1786); *The Earnest Desire* (1786); *The Perfection of Saints* (1786); *The Resurrection of Jesus Christ* (1786); *A Christian Minister Described* (1787); *The Important Objects* (1788); *A Sermon on the*

Sacred Obligations (1789); *The Evangelical Ministry and Pastoral Office* (1790); *The War Between Michael and the Dragon* (1790); *God the Unfailing Source* (1792); *The Importance of Parental Fidelity* (1792); *The Religious Improvement* (1798); *Religious Improvement* (1800); *A Discourse at the Funeral of the Rev. Samuel Hopkins* (1805).

Biography: Levi Hart, eighth and youngest son of Deacon Thomas Hart, was born in Southington, Conn., on March 30, 1738. Immediately following graduation from Yale College in 1760, Hart began studying theology under Dr. Joseph Bellamy (q.v.) of Bethlehem, Conn., and Jonathan Edwards (q.v.). On June 2, 1761, the Hartford North Association of Ministers licensed Hart to preach, and in August of 1763 he accepted the call of the Second, or North, parish in Preston, Conn., in the present township of Griswold, where his ministry continued until his death on Oct. 27, 1808. During his residency and study in the Bellamy household, Hart married his instructor's second daughter, and the couple had four children. After the death of his first wife in 1788, Hart married the widow of Nathaniel Backus of Norwich.

In addition to his ministerial duties in Preston, Hart was deeply committed to the Revolutionary struggle and actively sympathized with the cause of liberty. As early as 1744, he delivered a sermon entitled "On Liberty," which dealt with his nation's subjugation to Eng. In Aug. of 1775, Hart visited the rebel camp at Roxbury, Mass., where he preached to Col. Pearson's regiment, and in 1783 he delivered a sermon at Fort Griswold, in Groton, Conn., commemorating the slain revolutionaries of the battle of 1781. One of Hart's finest sermons—delivered Dec. 29, 1799—is a eulogy to George Washington (q.v.), that "great and good man." Hart pursued his missionary work with no less zeal than his patriotic duties. As early as 1769, he spent six weeks in the Maine woods preaching to the settlers and Indians, and he was a founder and director of the Missionary Society of Connecticut. In 1800, Princeton College recognized his evangelical efforts by conferring upon him an honorary Doctor of Divinity.

In 1847, the Rev. Samuel Nott recollected that "few ministers in New England...had so much to do as [Hart] in training men for the ministry." Hart's interest in education led to his election to the Corporation of Dartmouth College from 1784 to 1788 and to that of Yale College from 1791 to 1807, the year before he died. Hart lent his prestige to healing the estrangement between the General Association of Connecticut and the General Assembly of the Presbyterian Church, and in 1801 he served as a delegate to the General Assembly from the General Association. Furthermore, from its commencement in 1808, Hart edited *The Connecticut Evangelical Magazine*. His diary, unpublished and housed at the Congregational Library in Boston, spans almost fifty years and records his piety and devotion.

Critical Appraisal: The seventeen published sermons of Levi Hart, never collected, indicate his indebtedness to the New Light of the Great Awakening. While neither his style nor erudition is exceptional, they both corroborate the influence upon Hart of Jonathan Edwards and his associates, Joseph Bellamy and

Samuel Hopkins (q.v.). Like Edwards, Hart disdained man's rational faculties. In *The Duties and Importance of Preaching* he points out the "exceeding stupidity and madness of man; his total alienation from God, and utter aversion to his return." If rationality cannot be trusted, Hart believed that affections could, and he sought to rouse the emotions of his audience and kindle a sense of fear. He pictures, for example, the "vile and odorous condition of man," "the emptiness of the world," and "the vanity of earthly prospects." And in a direct allusion to Edwards's famous Enfield sermon of 1741, Hart's *A Sermon on the Sacred Obligations* reminds Christians that they "are sinners in the hand of an angry God, that because [they] love darkness rather than light [their] condemnation must be exceedingly dreadful."

If the Great Awakening swelled the number of the faithful in America, it also diluted traditional Calvinist dogma, especially regarding predestination and the role of grace. Like Edwards, Bellamy, and Hopkins, Levi Hart condemned free will and the heresy of Arminianism that such a reliance encouraged. According to Hart, man is powerless before God, and only by God's grace may his preordained salvation occur. Consequently, a 1775 sermon warns that "the true penitent looks for pardon and salvation alone by free grace in the Mediator," and a 1786 message reminds Hart's audience of "the sovereign freedom of divine grace in the salvation of sinners." And one of Hart's final published sermons, *Religious Improvement*, signals his continued adherence to the conservative doctrines he learned as a young man from Dr. Bellamy.

Paradoxically, while Hart's theology spurned reason, his prose style (like that of Jonathan Edwards) was a product of the age of reason. Simple, lucid, precise, and correct, it shuns any superfluity of figures, extravagance of conceit, or artificiality of balance. His reasoning is likewise forceful and close, vigorous and intelligent, but not clothed in rhetorical splendor. According to Hart, a good preacher "made use of no deceitful glosses, double meanings, or designing ambiguities of expression" but relied upon "a plain and intelligible manner." Hart followed his own advice. His sermons are modest, unadorned, cogent, logical in argument and rational in form. In short, what Hart's theology denies, his style implies: man is a reasonable being.

Suggested Readings: CCNE; Dexter (II, 656-661); Sprague (I, 590-595).

John R. Schell
University of Arkansas at Little Rock

OLIVER HART (1723-1795)

Works: *The Character of a Truly Great Man* (1777); *Dancing Exploded* (1778); *An Humble Attempt to Repair the Christian Temple* (1785); *America's Remembrancer* (1791); *A Gospel Church Portrayed* (1791); *Extracts of the Diary of the Rev. Oliver Hart* (1896); *A Copy of the Original Diary of Rev. Oliver Hart*

(1949); *Oliver Hart's Diary to the Backcountry* (w. 1775; pub. in JSCBHS; 1975).

Biography: By far the most influential Baptist minister of Revolutionary South Carolina, Oliver Hart was born in Pa. on Jul. 5, 1723. Strongly influenced in his youth by the revivalism of George Whitefield (q.v.), Gilbert Tennent (q.v.), and William Tennent II (q.v.), Hart was "called" to preach in 1746. In 1748 he married Sarah Brees and after ordination a year later moved to Charleston, S.C., where he became pastor of the Charleston Baptist Church in 1750. In Charleston for thirty years, Hart ushered in a time of stability and growth in the aftermath of the doctrinal controversies of the 1730s and 1740s. With industry and strong organizational skills, he founded in 1751 the first Baptist Association in the South. Largely self-taught, he stressed the value of an educated clergy, establishing a fund and a school for ministers. In 1769 Hart received an M.A. from Rhode Island College (now Brown Univ.).

Throughout his career, Hart labored for interdenominational cooperation and for a unified system of church discipline, but his influence greatly expanded in the 1770s. Widowed for two years, he married the former Mrs. Charles Grimball in 1774. With the imminence of war, Hart's reputation as a patriot led to his commission by the Charleston Council of Safety to accompany William Henry Drayton (q.v.) and the Rev. William Tennent III (q.v.) as an emissary to the backcountry. His three-month mission was to gain support for the patriotic cause among the suspicious and often hostile dissenters of the back settlements. This decade also saw the publication of Hart's best-known sermons: the funeral oration for William Tennent III and the attack on dancing. In 1778 and 1779, Hart also firmly supported the disestablishment cause. With the British conquest of Charleston in 1780, Hart was forced to flee north, where in 1780 he became pastor of Hopewell Baptist Church in N.J. Refusing two requests to return to Charleston, Hart remained at Hopewell, publishing sermons in Philadelphia and Trenton, until his death in Hopewell, N.J., on Dec. 31, 1795. He was buried at Southampton, where he was honored for his contributions to the Baptist church and to the American Revolution.

Critical Appraisal: The work of Oliver Hart represents an important aspect of colonial American culture, the union of evangelical religion and Revolutionary politics. Although only five of Hart's sermons were published, they reveal an unadorned, logically developed style, a recurrent emphasis on personal piety, and a well-rounded, if modest, learning, and they indicate the existence of a strong southern Puritanism in the waning years of the Great Awakening and the persistence of that tradition even in the tidewater region. Hart's central position in this movement resulted from his organizational achievements, his eminent reputation among evangelicals, and his vigorous support of the Revolution.

Reflecting a respectable knowledge of Classical authors, of theology, and of science, Hart's work refutes the frequent criticism that colonial Baptists were illiterate and ignorant. Theologically, Hart remained a consistent Calvinist, emphasizing the doctrines of Free Grace, original sin, and rebirth, and his exhortations to repentance and piety recall the sermons of Jonathan Edwards (q.v.). In fact, Hart's domination of the Charleston Baptists, in the pulpit and within the organization, has earned him the title of "Bishop of the Baptists." Combining his religious influence with his patriotism, Hart supported both church and state with a militancy characteristic of the leaders of the Great Awakening.

Illustrative of this militancy is the best-known sermon of Hart's Charleston period, his 1778 *Dancing Exploded*, reprinted in 1860. Written in a time of Revolution, this sermon openly attacks the social amusements of Charleston society. Using the current war as evidence of life's seriousness, Hart argued that the times required piety, sobriety, and militant devotion to the causes of liberty and religion. Thus, in a city famous for its balls and assemblies, Hart declared a "vigorous war" on the "sinful diversions of the age." Drawing upon Classical and biblical sources, he condemned dancing as a vice of frivolity and dissipation and as inappropriate to a life of seriousness. His extensive argument detailed thirteen reasons for this censure, chief among them the premises that dancing is secular, wasteful of time and money, and conducive to more harmful vices. He ridiculed the claims of "society" and urged a rejection of the "vanities of life." His language is direct and dramatic, and the sermon is overall a valuable example of controlled evangelicalism, a call for piety and spiritual militancy.

From Hart's later period is his *America's Remembrancer*, a sermon delivered in 1789 and published in Philadelphia in 1791. Given on an occasion of public thanksgiving, Hart's work commemorates the American Revolution from an evangelical perspective. In plain, animated language, Hart essentially reiterated and updated the Puritan vision of the New World as fulfilling a messianic destiny. The successful Revolution is but the most recent evidence of the providential order of American history. From the discovery, settlement, and political development of the country, Americans have enjoyed special favor as the chosen people of God. American progress is thus a religious process, the inevitable triumph of God's will over the sins of man. The new country is blessed with "liberty of conscience" and with a pure, or evangelical, gospel ministry. It is also a natural paradise, a garden of health and fertility. Hart's Christian version of the Revolution provides a striking contrast to the more rational, secular attitudes of the American Enlightenment. As such, with all of its emphasis upon piety and providence, Hart's sermon admirably represents a significant colonial attitude toward the emerging nation.

Although unpublished for over a century, the diaries of Oliver Hart warrant attention for their historical and biographical importance. The diaries exist in two forms—actual daily entries and lengthier entries, apparently recorded from memory at a later date. An example of the former is Hart's diary of the backcountry Commission of 1775. Written partly in a protective code, this work was published in 1975 and is a valuable record of important political events. The other type of journal, written in 1780 and published in slightly different versions in 1896 and 1949, records Hart's concerns with family, work, and the Revolution. Other diaries, still in manuscript, record several trips to the North and to the frontier settlements. As a whole, these works provide a useful insight into the life and attitudes of one of the South's most influential evangelical clergymen.

Suggested Readings: CCMC; CCV; Sprague (XI, 47-50); T_2. *See also* Richard B. Davis, *Intellectual Life in the Colonial South* (1978), II, 760; Richard Furman, *Rewards of Grace* (1796); Joe King, *A History of South Carolina Baptists* (1964), pp. 17-20; Loulie Latimer Owens, *Oliver Hart* (1966); William Rogers, *A Sermon Occasioned by the Death of the Rev. Oliver Hart* (1796); Leah Townsend, *South Carolina Baptists* (1935), pp. 14-25, 282; David Wallace, *A Short History of South Carolina* (1951), pp. 212-213, 279; B. W. Whilden, "Rev. Oliver Hart," BC, 9 (1893), 1-7.

Tony J. Owens
Greenville, South Carolina

JASON HAVEN (1733-1803)

Works: *The Duty of Thanksgiving* (1759); *A Sermon Delivered at a Private Meeting in Framingham* (1761); *A Sermon Preached to the...Artillery Company* (1761); *A Sermon Preached...at the Ordination of the Rev. Mr. Edward Brooks* (1764); *A Sermon Preached Before His Excellency, Sir Francis Bernard* (1769); *A Discourse Occasioned by the Death of Mrs. Hannah Richards* (1770); *A Sermon Preached...at the Ordination of the Rev. Mr. Ephraim Ward* (1771); *A Sermon Preached...at the Ordination of the Rev. Mr. Joseph Avery* (1775); *A Sermon Preached...at the Ordination of the Rev. Mr. Moses Everett* (1775); *A Sermon Preached...at the Funeral of the Rev. Mr. Samuel Dunbar* (1783); *A Sermon Preached...When the Rev. Stephen Palmer Was Ordained* (1793); *A Sermon Preached in the First Society in Dedham* (1796).

Biography: Born on Mar. 2, 1733, to Deacon Moses and Hannah (Walker) Haven of Framingham, Mass., Jason Haven attended Harvard College (class of 1754) and was ordained on Feb. 5, 1756, at the First Church in Dedham. In Oct. of the same year, he married Catherine Dexter, the oldest of his predecessor's daughters, and she bore him five children. The two youngest children, Samuel and Catherine, outlived their parents, the latter marrying Stephen Palmer, whom Haven ordained to the church at Needham in 1792. Throughout much of his ministry, Haven's health was poor. He suffered severe headaches, but this infirmity did not appreciably diminish his value to or devotion from the Dedham congregation. Despite his health, Haven fulfilled numerous demands for occasional sermons, especially ordinations, five of which (including his son-in-law's) were published. In his house a number of young ministers were trained in their life's calling. Often a guest in the surrounding parishes, Haven hosted numerous visitors in return, as the diary he kept from 1769 to 1796 documents; for many years, he corresponded with the Rev. Dr. John Joachim Zubly (q.v.) in Savannah, Ga., and the Rev. Dr. Knox of St. Croix in the W. Ind. During the War of Independence, Haven adjusted his political allegiances from Loyalist to patriot but was never particularly outspoken or activist. In theological matters, however, Haven remained thoroughly orthodox and conservative. Long after many of his colleagues had adopted milder positions, Haven continued to preach the Calvinist doctrine of man's depravity and the inefficacy of merit to account for man's life on the Day of Judgment. After 1798 Haven's health declined rapidly, and he died on May 17, 1803.

Critical Appraisal: The style of preaching and the theological concerns of Jason Haven are ably conveyed in the variety of his published sermons. His political speeches—an artillery sermon (1761) and an election sermon (1769)—show an interest in the human dimension of war and government. Granting the obligations of the soldiers to defend their land, Haven looked forward to a time of peace when the members of the Artillery Company could return to their proper work of agriculture; speaking to the leaders of the community, he urged that they become a political priesthood, encouraging religion through the troubled years ahead. In his five ordination sermons, Haven followed the conventional format: the characteristics of an ideal gospel minister, the direct address to the new pastor, the charge to the congregation, and the closing remarks to the audience in general. These sermons, close variants of one another, contain practical advice to the new minister: he should consider the variety of ages, intellects, education, and receptivity in his audience and should avoid a monotonous and overly pompous delivery. Indicative of his rather conservative reliance on the doctrines of faith and repentance, Haven ended by reminding his listeners that at the day of judgment they would be accountable for the quality of their lives. In the sermons to his own congregation, Haven preached on more conventional issues: doctrine, funerals, and the progress of the congregational unit. Uniformly conservative in his religious views, Haven occasionally revealed specific, homey details; for example, in the funeral sermon for Hannah Richards, he quoted some of the deceased's writings and commented sympathetically on her patience while enduring a lingering death, even though she had readied herself—and wished for—a speedy end. Furthermore, in a kind of "state of the congregation" message at Dedham (1796), which incidentally mentioned that the size of his congregation was 142 members, Haven examined his own ministry. Enumerating the responsibilities he had borne and expressing his regret that illnesses had too frequently kept him from the pulpit, Haven decided that, compared to the hardships St. Paul faced, the American pastor had a relatively easy ministry.

Haven's writing style is direct and incisive. In the ordination sermons, he described the appropriate manner of sermons, and his own are illustrative examples: "a plain easy and familiar style; free from vain flourishes of words, on the one hand; and a slovenly incorrectness on the other." The minister's discourses, he said, should not be "crowded with a great variety of sentiments."

The number and variety of Haven's sermons show him to have been a revered member of the religious community. An old-fashioned reliance on the central doctrines of faith and regeneration, and a rejection of the doctrine of merit did not make Haven such an archaism that his presence and wisdom were not sought outside of Dedham for ordinations and political sermons, including the Dudleian Lecture in 1789. In the zeal of his beliefs and the solid craftsmanship of his prose, he joins the ranks of those well-educated, dedicated, selfless gospel ministers of eighteenth-century New Eng. who were honorable shepherds within and beyond their communities.

Suggested Readings: CCNE; Sibley-Shipton (XIII, 447-455); Sprague (I, 557-559).

Roslyn L. Knutson
University of Arkansas at Little Rock

SAMUEL HAVEN (1727-1806)

Works: *Preaching Christ* (1760); *The Supreme Influence* (1761); *Joy and Salvation* (1763); *A Guard Against Extremes* (1767); *A Sermon Preached...at the Ordination of the Rev. Mr. Jeremy Belknap* (1767); *A Sermon on the Knowledge of Christ* (1768); *Slothful Servants* (1771); *An Election Sermon* (1786); *A Funeral Discourse* (1791); *The Reasonableness and Importance of Practical Religion* (1794); *An Ode Occasioned by the Repairing of the South Church* (1798); *Poetic Miscellany* (1798); *The Validity of Presbyterian Ordination* (1798); *An Oration, Spoken at Dedham,* (1799); *The Disinterested Benevolence of Gospel Ministers* (1800); *A Statement of the First Church and Parish in Dedham* (1819).

Biography: The great-grandson of Richard Haven (who settled in Lynn, Mass., in 1636), Samuel Haven was born on Aug. 4, 1727, to Joseph and Mehetabel (Haven) Haven, a family of substantial means. From 1745 to 1749, Haven attended Harvard College, where in his first year, he was fined for obtaining and drinking "prohibited liquors." By the time he graduated, Haven had yet to decide his life's calling. After two years of teaching, he eventually settled on the ministry and began studying under the Rev. Ebenezer Parkman of Westborough. By 1752 Haven had accepted a unanimous call from the South Church in Portsmouth, N.H., where he was ordained that same year. On Jan. 11, 1753, Haven married Mehitable Appleton; the couple had eleven children, of whom seven survived. After his wife's death in 1777, Haven married Margaret Marshall, a widow with two children, who bore him an additional six children.

A dedicated pastor, Haven learned medicine so that he could minister to those in need. He joined the war movement both by marching to the defense of his town and by supporting the distressed and widowed. An ardent supporter of George Washington (q.v.), he welcomed the general for the town in 1789. Involved in the growth of Dartmouth College, Haven was the recipient of a doctor of divinity degree from that institution in 1773; he had been similarly honored by the University of Edinburgh in 1770. In addition, he was often in demand for ordinations and other such occasions. Theologically, Haven became increasingly more lenient in his views of election, not being able to reconcile

God's paradoxical condemnation of and love for man. In his preaching style, he showed the influence of George Whitefield (q.v.), and in his penchant for the rhetorical and sentimental, he was thought archaic by those who favored a less impassioned and more modern speaking manner.

Before his death on Mar. 3, 1806, Haven had endured almost ten years of very poor health. His wife, Margaret, apparently in good health as she attended Haven's final illness, died within thirty-six hours and was buried with her husband. An old-fashioned man in his emotional style and frugality, Haven distinguished his ministry not only by the competence of his religious activities and the partisanship of his civic works but by the charity that led him to share all that he had, including his inheritance, with the poor and desolate of Portsmouth.

Critical Appraisal: In *Poetic Miscellany* (1798), a volume of twenty-two occasional poems and lyrics, Samuel Haven demonstrated a special competence with hymnic verse and epigrams. The volume also includes a variety of literary forms (ode, epigram, complaint, meditation, epistolary lyric) and metrical patterns (folk meter, elegiac quatrains, heroic couplets), as well as several nonce forms. In the latter category is Ode V, "On Thanksgiving Morning," which has two introductory stanzas followed by eight verses that vary from four to twelve lines and address blessings such as "Life," "Table," "Peace," and "Prayer." Although many of the poems express conventional sentiments, several show genuine strength of talent and perception. Of them, "The Aged Doubting Christian's Complaint and Prayer" movingly conveys the religious struggles of the persona: " 'Lord, I believe, oh! help my unbelief.' "

The fascination with literary rhetoric and figurative devices is also a mark of Haven's sermon style. Several of the works are typological; *Preaching Christ* (1760) and *Joy and Salvation by Christ* (1763), the latter opening with the repeated phrase, "all praise to him." In the published ordination sermons (for Jeremy Belknap [q.v.] and Timothy Alden, the latter intended to be Haven's successor), Haven followed the conventional form of such pieces, stressing the mutual obligations of the gospel minister and his congregation. *Preaching Christ*, occasioned by the Annual Convention of Congregational Ministers, is a variant of the ordination form, wherein Haven enumerated for his audience the business of the ministry, ending with an exhortation that their work be extended to the "aboriginal tribes of this land." In the funeral orations (for Henry Sherburne and Benjamin Stevens), he likewise followed typical form, but his own moving style intensifies a subject inherently freighted with emotion. In one passage, for example, Haven illustrated the linguistic richness of his prose: "The world, indeed, is a great theatre of human nature, which first displays upon the stage the follies and afflictions of a frail life, and then the scene is closed with the sorrowful tragedy of death." Several of Haven's sermons, occasioned by political circumstances, illustrate a benevolent theocracy: God's hand in the survival of Protestants, the accrued benefits of successful wars, and the contract between governments and the governed are fully illustrated in *Joy and Salvation by Christ, The Supreme Influence*, and the 1768 election sermon.

As the variety and number of the published sermons indicate, Haven was a preacher of considerable popularity. Each of the sermons is carefully adapted to the audience and to the accepted form of such addresses; yet each is marked by Haven's very personal, rhetorical style. For example, in *Slothful Servants*, Haven, although not speaking to his home congregation, established a confidential rapport with the audience by addressing them directly as "dear immortal souls." After asking them to consider several points about the status of their faith, he turned to the excuses sinners use to remain unregenerate. In a fine passage that shatters the excuse that "God will save me out of his uncovenanted grace—even though I am a sinner," Haven rang all of the appropriate changes, ably demonstrating why he was such a revered and effective watchman over the souls of his congregation.

Suggested Readings: CCNE; Sibley-Shipton (XII, 382-392); Sprague (I, 495-497); T₁. *See also Appleton's Cyclopaedia of National Biography* (1892), III, 118.

Roslyn L. Knutson
University of Arkansas at Little Rock

ANNA TOMPSON HAYDEN (1648-1720)

Works: "Upon the Death of the Desireable Young Virgin Elizabeth Tompson" and "Verses on Benjamin Tompson" (written in the ms. journal of Joseph Tompson, Billerica, Mass. and published in Kenneth Murdock, ed., *Handkerchiefs from Paul* [1927]).

Biography: Anna Tompson Hayden was born in Braintree (now Quincy), Mass., in June of 1648. She was the one child of the Rev. William Tompson by his second wife, Anna Crosby, and was the half-sister of Benjamin Tompson (q.v.) and Joseph Tompson, in whose journal Hayden's poems appear. As with so many other colonial women, biographical information about Anna Tompson Hayden is sparse. By 1678 she had married Ebenezer Hayden of Boston and Braintree, by whom she had a child in 1679. Although she wrote only two poems, her mention of the pleasant conversations she and her brother frequently enjoyed proves that Hayden must have been an intelligent and educated woman, for Benjamin Tompson was one of the most talented and educated poets, physicians, and educators of his day.

Critical Appraisal: Anna Tompson Hayden's elegiac poems reveal how a cultured Puritan woman perceived and handled grief. Compared to the comforts and safety of Eng., most Puritan settlers found seventeenth-century Mass. a hostile environment, where death was a frequent, harsh reality; as a result, they confronted and accepted death in terms of theological doctrines that ordered human existence according to the strict Calvinistic beliefs of the times. Therefore, because death was part of God's universal plan for man, grief was handled piously, and even didactically, by the living as a way to comprehend God's greater purpose in the event itself.

In "Upon the Death of the Desireable Young Virgin Elizabeth Tompson," Hayden explored the lesson in piety that the untimely death of her niece, a particularly young girl, provides. Thus, while commemorating the goodness and purity of the deceased, Hayden framed Elizabeth's exemplary virtue as a model others could wisely follow in preparing for their demise. Hayden retained the same basic concept in the elegy she composed for her brother, with the exception that the tone of the poem is slightly more personal, probably owing to the more intimate relationship she had with the deceased. Particularly noteworthy is her comment that "Many a time we walk't together / & with discorce haue pleasd each other," for it reveals that despite the limitations placed on the role of women in Puritan New Eng., Hayden and her brother enjoyed a mutually complementary intellectual relationship that extended over a long period.

Along with other elegies commemorating various family members, Hayden's elegies were transcribed into the manuscript journal of Joseph Tompson. Accompanying the verse is a critical commentary, apparently written by Joseph Tompson, that praises the poems for their "Christian Spirit." For the modern reader, Hayden's poems are particularly valuable as some of the earliest verse written in America by a woman writer.

Suggested Readings: Kenneth B. Murdock, *Handkerchiefs from Paul* (1927), pp. xv-xxi, xxx, xxxvi-xxxviii, 6, 20; Emily Stipes Watt, *The Poetry of American Women from 1632 to 1945* (1977), pp. 21, 23-25.

Mindy Janak
Maurice Duke
Virginia Commonwealth University

ESTHER HAYDEN (c. 1713-1758)

Works: "Composed About Six Weeks Before Her Death, When Under Distressing Circumstances" (pub. in *A Short Account of the Life, Death and Character of Esther Hayden*; 1759). This volume was omitted from Charles Evans's *American Bibliography* and the Shipton-Mooney *National Index of American Imprints through 1800*. It can be found in the Harris Collection at Brown Univ.

Biography: Born about 1713, Esther Hayden was the daughter of Samuel Allen. She married Samuel Hayden of Braintree, Mass., and bore nine children, eight of whom survived her. An account of her life by "a near Relative" describes her as a devout woman who "strove for Grace and Holiness, / That *Christ* might be her Part," a woman who in the process of caring for others "Appear'd a precious Saint." Hayden's "Relative" suggests that her saintliness extended to temporal affairs as well: she had been "a true faithful Wife:—/ So saving, diligent

and neat, / She well adorn'd her Place." Her death on Feb. 14, 1758, at age 45
was preceded by more than a year of serious illness. These sketchy details are all
that remain of her life.

Critical Appraisal: Esther Hayden's only extant verse is printed in *A
Short Account of the Life, Death and Character of Esther Hayden*, published in
1759 apparently as a memorial. This slim volume contains a brief prose testimonial by an anonymous author, a longer verse tribute "by a near Relative," and a
167-line deathbed message in verse that Hayden had composed for her family
and friends. Like most contemporary deathbed statements, Hayden's verse treats
her concern for her family's religious condition. But she is even more concerned
with her own. However convinced her "near Relative" may have been of the
godliness behind her "meek and quiet Sp'rit," Hayden seemed unsure. Her verse
continually returns to her fear of death and her struggle to believe in her salvation: *"O that JEHOVAH would appear, / And satisfy me with / His Loving-
kindness! so that I / Mayn't fear the Pow'r of Death:—/ And oh! that I Assurance
had / Of any Grace in me!"* Hayden's poem is not the work of an experienced
poet; it may be the only piece she composed. But the fear and uncertainty it
reveals make it a more poignant memorial than her family seemed to recognize.

Suggested Readings: Pattie Cowell, *Women Poets in Pre-Revolutionary America*
(prints excerpts from the verse; 1981), pp. 237-239; Emily Stipes Watts, *The Poetry of
American Women from 1632 to 1945* (1977), pp. 21, 25.

Pattie Cowell
Colorado State University

LEMUEL HAYNES (1753-1833)

Works: *The Character and Work of a Spiritual Watchman Described* (1792);
The Important Concerns of Ministers (1798); *The Influence of Civil Government
on Religion* (1798); *The Nature and Importance of True Republicanism* (1801);
Universal Salvation: A Very Ancient Doctrine (1807); *Mystery Developed* (1820);
The Sufferings, Support, and Reward of Faithful Ministers, Illustrated (1820).

Biography: Lemuel Haynes was born at West Hartford, Conn., Jul. 18,
1753. Son of a white mother and black father, he was abandoned as an infant and
was bound out at the age of five months to David Rose of Granville, Mass., in
whose household he was treated almost as a member of this family from whom
he gained an early affinity for and insights into Christianity. Haynes assisted
Rose in carving a farm from the forest and tilling it. He also gained all of the
formal education his situation could provide and supplemented that at night. The
eager young Haynes was encouraged to pursue his fascination with theology, and
he began providing sermons while still a youth. In 1774 he enlisted as a minute-
man and later was involved at the siege of Boston and in the battle of Ticonderoga.
In 1779 he was invited to live in Canaan, Conn., for the purpose of furthering his

education toward the ministry. He served as a teacher at Wintonburg and learned Latin and Greek. In 1780 he became the minister of a white congregation in Middle Granville. Three years later, he married Elizabeth Babbitt, a white schoolteacher, and they eventually had ten children. In 1785 Haynes became the first officially ordained black Congregational minister. He continued in this work for the rest of his life, the first black to serve white congregations on a regular basis, holding pastorates at all-white churches at Torrington, Conn. (1786-1787), at Rutland, Vt. (1788-1818), at Manchester, Vt. (1818-1822), and at Granville, N.Y. (1822), until his death there on Sept. 28, 1833. He also was called on for backwoods, evangelistic missionary work. During his long ministry, he became well known and highly respected among New Eng. leaders in education and religion, and in 1804 the trustees of Middlebury College conferred on him an honorary M.A., the first bestowed on a black in America.

Critical Appraisal: The writing of Lemuel Haynes is characterized by clarity, reason, keen intelligence, and wit. Most of his publications are sermons, sometimes making good use of irony (even satire), and always reflecting his thorough knowledge of the Bible and current theology as well as his directly challenging homiletical style. Like the approaches of Jonathan Edwards (q.v.) and George Whitefield (q.v.), his approach to religion tends more toward philosophical abstraction than toward specific problems of this world; and unlike the writings of most of his black contemporaries who were published, his writings seldom even reflect the phenomena of slavery and racial discrimination. However, he was not hesitant to enter either religious or political controversy. Indeed, his persistent open advocacy of Federalist positions finally ended his long pastorate at Rutland. Haynes was a man who read widely, and an unusually good memory led to use in his sermons and oratory of much that he had read. Timothy Cooley reported that "At the age of fifty he could repeat nearly the whole of [Edward] Young's *Night Thoughts*, [John] Milton's *Paradise Lost*, [Isaac] Watts's *Psalms and Hymns*, and large unbroken passages from different authors, and more of the scriptures than any man I knew." He also was much influenced by the works of Jonathan Edwards; Royall Tyler (q.v.) was a personal friend.

The pronouncements of Haynes were influential and much in demand, both "in the flesh" and in print; and those that were published usually went through various reprintings. His 1805 sermon skillfully refuting the doctrine of universal salvation brought him his widest fame, both here and abroad. It was published the next year in a volume containing other material about the dispute; and as a separate item, it was in a 6th edition in 1807, a 9th in 1814, and a 10th in 1821, being reprinted widely and as late as 1860. Perhaps increasing the demand for it was its dependence on subtle humor woven throughout what otherwise is a strong and reasoned espousal of Puritan theology. The 1820 *Mystery Developed*, relating and expounding upon events surrounding a sensational trial and convictions for a murder that (it turned out) never took place, contains a separate narrative, sermon, and report and was a best-seller for a decade (the sermon having been reprinted as late as 1848). In this three-part work, one finds both vivid detail and imaginative response, with the reader held more by suspense than by moral. Finally, Haynes's Federalist Fourth of July sermon on true Republicanism in 1801 not only praises the Revolution and the rights of men but also provides one of the few instances where Haynes castigated slavery and its effects.

Suggested Readings: Sprague (II, 176-187). *See also* Richard Bardolph, *The Negro Vanguard* (1959), pp. 40-41; Richard Barksdale and Kenneth Kinnamon, eds., *Black Writers of America* (1972), pp. 226-229; Timothy M. Cooley, *Sketches of the Life and Character of the Rev. Lemuel Haynes, A.M.* (with writings by Haynes not published elsewhere; 1839); Philip S. Foner, *History of Black Americans from Africa to the... Cotton Kingdom* (1975), pp. 541-542; Sidney Kaplan, *The Black Presence in the Era of the American Revolution, 1770-1800* (1973), pp. 102-108; Vernon Loggins, *The Negro Author* (1931), pp. 117-126, 419-420; *The National Cyclopaedia of American Biography* (1904), XII, 256-257; Dorothy Porter, ed., *Early Negro Writing, 1760-1837* (1971), pp. 448-454; Job Swift, *Discourses on Religious Subjects* (1805), pp. 23-32; Carter G. Woodson and Charles H. Wesley, *The Negro in Our History*, 12th ed. (1972), pp. 157-158.

Julian Mason
University of North Carolina at Charlotte

EBENEZER HAZARD (1745-1817)

Works: *Proposals for Printing by Subscription, A Collection of State Papers Intended as Material for an History of the United States of America* (1791); *Historical Collections*, 2 vols. (1792, 1794); "Remarks on Mr. Schermerhorns Report Concerning the Western Indians," CMHS, 2nd ser., 3 (1815), 65-69; miscellaneous travel diaries from 1777 to 1778 (edited by Fred Shelley and pub. in MdHM, 46 (1951), 44-54; VMHB, 62 (1954), 400-423; GHQ, 41 (1957), 316-319; PMHB, 81 (1957), pp. 83-86).

Biography: Ebenezer Hazard was born in Philadelphia, Pa., on Jan. 15, 1745, the first child of Samuel Hazard, a prominent businessman and publisher, and his wife, Catherine. Educated at the New Light academy conducted by his uncle, the Rev. Samuel Finley (q.v.), in West Nottingham, Md., and later at the College of New Jersey (now Princeton Univ.; A.B., 1762; A.M., 1765), Hazard became a bookseller in Philadelphia and in 1762 commenced his collection of historical documents and publications. These *Historical Collections* were a chronological arrangement of documents concerned with the discovery and settlement of the American colonies (Vol. I) and the United Colonies of New Eng. (Vol. II). Between 1775 and 1785, Hazard held a series of government posts culminating in the position of postmaster general for the Confederation government, which he held from 1782 until 1789. In 1789 political disagreements surrounding the ratification of the Constitution forced Hazard from the government, and he became an investor and broker. Best known for his participation in the organization of the Insurance Company of North America, Hazard eventually curtailed his business activities and generally devoted much of the seventeen years before his death promoting and encouraging historical writing. He died at his home on Arch Street in Philadelphia on July 13, 1817, after a trip to the Alabama Territory.

Critical Appraisal: Ebenezer Hazard's literary importance is less as an author than as a collector and publisher of historical documents and a promoter of the works of others. Intended as the first of many volumes of basic source material for future histories of American culture, Hazard's *Historical Collections* extends only to 1664, for even though he had the public support of many Revolutionary personages and governmental leaders, uncertain finances prevented Hazard from continuing the series.

Like many American thinkers of the post-Revolutionary period, Hazard was particularly concerned with the establishment of an American nationality and identity. The preface to the *Historical Collections* succinctly stated his desire for a history of the American nation transcending the parochial histories of individual colonies or states. He frankly hoped "to induce others to prosecute a Work which he conceives is not devoid of either Utility or Entertainment." In this respect, Hazard was successful. The two volumes of his *Historical Collections* that were published in 1792 and 1794 much influenced Jeremy Belknap (q.v.), who found them useful when he compiled his own history of the United States.

Suggested Readings: DAB; P. *See also* Ralph Blodgett, "Ebenezer Hazard" (Ph.D. diss., Univ. of Colo., 1971); Marquis James, *Biography of a Business, 1792-1942, Insurance Company of North America* (1942); L. S. Mayo, "Jeremy Belknap and Ebenezer Hazard, 1782-84," NEQ, 2 (1929), 183-198; Fred Shelley, "Ebenezer Hazard: America's First Historical Editor," WMQ, 3rd ser., 12 (1955), 44-73.

George W. Pilcher
Ball State University

MOSES HEMMENWAY (1735-1811)

Works: *Seven Sermons* (1767); *A Vindication* (1772); *Remarks on the Rev. Mr. Hopkins's Answer* (1774); *A Discourse on the Nature . . . of . . . Baptism* (1781); *A Sermon Preached Before His Excellency John Hancock* (1784); *A Discourse to Children* (1792); *A Discourse Concerning the Church* (1792); *A Sermon Delivered at Somersworth* (1792); *A Sermon Delivered December 5, 1792* (1793); *Remarks on the Rev. Mr. Emmons' Dissertation* (1794); *A Sermon Preached at the Ordination of Mr. Jonathan Calef* (1795); *A Discourse Delivered at Wells* (1800); *A Sermon Preached at York* (1810).

Biography: Moses Hemmenway was neither a charismatic preacher nor a profoundly original theologian; yet in his time he was well loved as a minister and highly regarded as a thinker. Born in Framingham, Mass., in 1735, Hemmenway attended Harvard College (A.B., 1755; doctor of divinity, 1785), where he earned the lifelong respect and friendship of his classmate John Adams (q.v.).

After teaching school for three years, Hemmenway accepted a call to the Congregational Church in Wells, Me., where he served as minister from 1759 to 1811. At intervals, he published his contributions to current religious discussions, generally adopting a moderate line and attempting to liberalize the implications of Edwardsian doctrine without himself falling into the heresies of Arianism or Socinianism.

During the Revolutionary period, Hemmenway was politically active, adhering to the Whig view. In 1788 he was sent to the federal Constitutional Convention, and he worked for ratification. Hemmenway continued to preach until 1810, the year before his death from cancer. He was survived by his wife and ten children.

Critical Appraisal: Moses Hemmenway's most important works appeared in two series; both elicited responses from articulate opponents; and in both instances, Hemmenway chose to yield the advantage of last word. *Seven Sermons*, Hemmenway's first publication, was a substantial treatise that proposed to modify the rigor of Jonathan Edwards's (q.v.) Calvinist views on free will and predestination. This document led to an exchange with the New Light, Samuel Hopkins (q.v.). Hemmenway waited until 1774 to publish his *Remarks on the Rev. Mr. Hopkins's Answer*, and he made no rely to Hopkins's further response. The second controversy into which Hemmenway was reluctantly drawn began with the publication of *A Discourse Concerning the Church*, in which he took a liberal stand on the requirements of church membership. On this occasion, he was now attacked by the strict Calvinist, Nathaniel Emmons (q.v.). Hemmenway replied directly with *Remarks on the Rev. Mr. Emmons' Dissertation*, but again he chose not to consider his opponent's further attacks.

A Discourse has been called "one of the most amusingly dialectical discussions of New England religious literature," but the prose of none of these works bears much impress of Hemmenway's unpretentious personality, which was known by his contemporaries for its eccentric disregard for proprieties. Even the occasion of the death of Gen. George Washington (q.v.) in 1800 provoked from Hemmenway nothing more than a routinely pious sermon (*A Discourse Delivered at Wells*).

A Discourse to Children is perhaps Hemmenway's most attractive work, because the nature of his audience demanded some modulation of his normally pedestrian tone. Even here he resorted to a conventional format. Following the biblical epigraph, he began: "Will you attend now to a few observations on the text you have heard read?" He then proceeded to elaborate in sequence four propositions. Still, this address to children concerning Jesus's love for them makes a pleasant composition (the work is further embellished with two engravings and a somewhat touching parable of the conversion and death of a poor man). The work went through six printings before Hemmenway's death.

Hemmenway's other popular publication was *A Discourse on the Nature . . . of. . .Baptism*. In this work, the object was once again a defense of liberal principles. Hemmenway allowed the validity of adult baptism, but he asserted the equal legitimacy of infant baptism. *A Discourse* was printed separately in four editions. In an abridged form, it was adopted as a doctrine by the Methodist Episcopal Church in America and was consequently reprinted in the various editions of the church's *Form of Discipline* between 1790 and 1797.

Suggested Readings: CCNE; Sibley-Shipton (XIII; 609-618); Sprague (I, 541-547). *See also* Frank Hugh Foster, *A Genetic History of the New England Theology* (1907; rep., 1963); Joseph Haroutunian, *Piety Versus Moralism* (1932).

J. Kenneth Van Dover
Lincoln University

DANIEL HENCHMAN (1677-1708)

Works: *Lamentations upon the Death of Sir William Phips, Knight Governour. Who Expired in London February 18, 1694,5* (1695). No copy of the broadside is known to exist, but Samuel Sewall's contemporaneous copy is printed in Harold Jantz, "The First Century of New England Verse," PAAS, New Series, 53 (1943), 387-390.

Biography: Daniel Henchman, son of a schoolmaster and famed Indian fighter in King Philip's War, was born in Boston, Mass., on Jun. 16, 1677. He was admitted to Harvard College as a member of the class of 1696, but inattention to his studies and continued disorderly conduct led to his expulsion without a degree at the end of his senior year. His family then sent him to join a colony of New Englanders recently established in S.C. Their leader, Joseph Lord, a minister and ardent naturalist, was perhaps responsible for Henchman's interest in the fauna and flora of his new home. He appears to have written on the subject and to have corresponded and exchanged specimens with James Petiver, fellow of the Royal Society. His scientific writings, however, have not come to light. After Henchman's death, Lord received permission from his wife to copy them for Petiver, but this apparently was never done. The only other notice of Henchman occurs in 1705, when, acting as agent for Governor Nathaniel Johnson, he attested the treaty of alliance between S.C. and the Creek Indians. He died of a stroke in 1708.

Critical Appraisal: Daniel Henchman's only extant work is the elegy on Sir William Phips, written at the age of 17, at a time when his other activities somewhat contradict such a performance. There is at least the possibility that the true author was Daniel's older half-brother Richard Henchman (q.v.). Samuel Sewall (q.v.) knew various members of the Henchman family; he exchanged verses with Richard on several occasions, among them verses by Richard that are akin in style and spirit to the "Lamentations." Sewall, often a careless copier, may have written "D. Hincsman" instead of "R." when he transcribed the elegy in his commonplace book.

Whoever the author, the "Lamentations" is one of a handful of Puritan funeral elegies to show neo-Classical influence before the turn of the century. This influence appears not only in the relatively smooth versification, with a tendency toward closed couplets, and in the generalizing vocabulary, but even more noticeably in the worldly spirit of the lines. Entirely without the details of personal piety that characterize elegies in the "plain" Puritan tradition, the poem is more in the vein of formal public compliment, closer to ode than elegy, and its praise is primarily for secular achievement.

All facets of Phips's career are celebrated: his early success in recovering 300,000 pounds worth of sunken Spanish silver; his exploits at Port Royal and Quebec in the French and Indian Wars; his knighthood and appointment as first governor under the new charter; even his projected new expedition to recover Spanish treasure—"Safe since He's laid under the Earth asleep, / Who learn't where thou dost under water keep." Adventurousness and military skill, although certainly appreciated in Puritan society, were seldom "remembered" in elegies as resoundingly as in Henchman's for Phips: "Thunder his Musick; Sweeter than the Spheres / Chim'd Roaring Cannons in his Martial Ears. / Frigats of Armed men could not withstand / 'Twas tryed, the force of his one Swordless Hand." These details, furthermore, do not give rise to exhortation of survivors to profit from Phips's example but, uncharacteristically, to an attack on "Dead, Pale Envy": "On him vain Mob, thy Mischeiefs cease to throw; / Bad but in this alone, the times were so." In these lines and in the sixteen or so like them, there is a touch of satirical dryness and general social criticism that is unlike the prophetic denunciations and the laments for New Eng.'s religious decline that are typical of the "plain" Puritan elegy. Phips's faithfulness as a husband and his childlessness are mentioned, and there are warnings to New Eng. to see a portent of disaster in his death; but the elegy is weakest in just those places where it wavers and falls back on homely detail and conventional admonition. Its strength is in its tribute to Phips as a secular "Publick Spirit,...To England often blown, and by his Prince / Often sent laden with Preferments thence."

Suggested Readings: FCNEV; Sibley-Shipton (IV, 297-298). *See also* Robert Henson, "Form and Content of the Puritan Funeral Elegy," AL, 32 (1960-1961), 11-27.

Robert Henson
Upsala College

RICHARD HENCHMAN (c. 1655-1725)

Works: "In Consort to Wednesday, Jan. 1st. 1701 Before Break of Day" (w.c. 1701); "Vox Oppressi" (n.d.); "Sewall Our Israel's Judge and Singer Sweet" (w.c. 1712).

Biography: Born in Boston, Mass., sometime around 1655, Richard Henchman was the son of Capt. Daniel Henchman, a schoolmaster and a hero of the bloody King Philip's War. Nothing is known of Henchman's early life or educational background. Although his brother Daniel Henchman (q.v.) was admitted to Harvard as a member of the class of 1696 and was later dismissed for "continued disorderly conduct," there is no record that Richard Henchman ever attended college. In 1686 Henchman became a schoolmaster in Yarmouth. He returned to Boston, however, in 1697, and on Nov. 1, 1700, he became master of the North Writing School, a position he held until his retirement in 1719.

Henchman seems to have spent his later years writing poetry, reading extensively, and corresponding. Mentioned frequently in Samuel Sewall's (q.v.) diary, Henchman appears to have been closely associated with the judge, often exchanging poetry with him, and dedicating at least two poems to Sewall. Upon Henchman's death on Feb. 15, 1725, Sewall made the following entry in his diary: "Mr. Richard Henchman died about 3 p.m. I sent him 20s by his cousin our Deacon...dies of the palsey which invaded his well side." In "cold, dry weather" on Feb. 18, 1725, Richard Henchman was buried in Boston "at the North."

Critical Appraisal: Perhaps Henchman's most carefully written work, "In Consort to Wednesday, Jan. 1st, 1701 Before Break of Day" was dedicated to Sewall and was obviously inspired by Sewall's own "Wednesday, Jan. 1st, 1701." Predominantly iambic, with several metrical variations, the poem is 100 lines long and includes several biblical and mythological allusions. Continually alternating between images of darkness and light (he contrasted, for example, the Indians' existence outside of God's will in the "Darker woods" to the "fair morning" of the "prophesies," and "Darkness and death's shadow" that surrounds our mortal lives to the overwhelming power of the "prayer of truth and light" that is the promised salvation), the poem's primary message is every man's potential for salvation and a place in the afterlife. Although the poem may seem heavy-handed and unnecessarily allusive, Henchman's language is surprisingly rich and musical at times. That Henchman considered this poem a work of art as opposed to simply an opportunity to moralize is clear from the revised, finished condition of the poem.

Dedicated to Mary (Spencer) Hull Phips, wife of Sir William Phips, the first royal governor of Mass., "Vox Oppressi" was written in response to a gift of silver from Mrs. Phips. Like his other work and like the majority of early New Eng. poetry, this poem is for the most part iambic. Apparently Henchman was moved by Mrs. Phips's gift; he compared the silver to "Jacob's staff," a staff carried by pilgrims to the tomb of the Apostle James the elder, and to "Gunter's Scale," a measuring device invented by the English mathematician Edmund Gunter (1581-1626) and used to solve problems in navigation. Notable throughout the poem is Henchman's paradoxical use of the word *oppressed*. In the first few lines, the poet posited the notion that it is possible to be oppressed simultaneously by joy and sorrow, joy because he had received a gift and sorrow because he felt inept (comparing himself to Palinurus, the mythic helmsman of Aeneas who fell asleep at the wheel, fell overboard, and was drowned), unworthy of the gift, and unable to return the gesture except in the form of the poem, which ends in a blessing: "May Those Fresh Roses, ever in their Bloom, / Unto her latest Breath, retain their June; / And typify, when Death hath clos'd her Eyes, / What she shall, at the Resurrection, rise." Unusual for a Puritan sensibility, Henchman's notion of the simultaneity of good and evil and his attempt in the poem to embrace both poles of human experience in order to better understand himself and his place in the world are remarkably modern.

Further evidence of his close friendship with Samuel Sewall ("Sewall Our Israel's Judge and Singer Sweet") is simply a translation of Nehemiah Hobart's (q.v.) fifty-five-line Latin poem written in praise of Sewall.

Suggested Readings: FCNEV. *See also* Harrison T. Meserole, ed. *Seventeenth-Century American Poetry* (1968), pp. 467-475; Kenneth Silverman, ed., *Colonial American Poetry* (1968), pp. 160-163.

Bruce Weigl
Old Dominion University

SAMUEL HENLEY (1744-1815)

Works: *A Sermon Preached at Williamsburg* (1771); *The Distinct Claims of Government and Religion* (1772); *A Candid Refutation* (1774); *A Discourse Delivered in the Chapel of William and Mary College* (1776); *A Dissertation upon the Controverted Passages in St. Peter and St. Jude* (1778); *Observations on the Subject of the Fourth Ecologue* (1788).

Biography: Samuel Henley was born on Nov. 23, 1744, in Devonshire, Eng. He attended Caleb Ashworth's Dissenting Academy at Daventry for four years, after which Ashworth certified that Henley's studies and behavior befitted a candidate for the ministry. In 1768 eight dissenting ministers testified to his character, abilities, and education and received him into the ministry. Shortly thereafter Henley chose to conform to the Thirty-Nine Articles of the Church of England. Upon appointment to a professorship in moral philosophy at the College of William and Mary, Henley signed his bond with Richard Terrick, bishop of London, and arrived in Williamsburg, Va., in Apr. 1770. Henley's five years in Williamsburg were filled with acrimonious public debate, much of which resulted from his unsuccessful bid for the rectorship of Bruton Parish in Williamsburg. Soon after his return to Eng. in 1775, Henley became assistant master at Harrow School and, a few years later, rector of Rendlesham in Suffolk. In 1805 he became principal of the East India College in Hertfordshire, a post he held until shortly before his death on Dec. 29, 1815.

Critical Appraisal: A man of wide-ranging intellectual and literary interests, Samuel Henley was a poet, commentator, translator, and, according to one critic, "learned Orientalist." His published American writings, however, were primarily polemical, dealing with church polity, religious establishment, theological controversy, and educational reforms. Although his published American works included several sermons and a pamphlet, Henley aired his controversial views most frequently in the *Virginia Gazette*.

In Jun. 1771 Samuel Henley joined with Thomas Gwatkin, a fellow clergyman and professor at William and Mary, in a formal protest against the proposed American episcopate. For months after this joint protest appeared in the *Virginia Gazette*, Henley and various critics filled the pages of the newspaper with theological disputation and personal invective. Neither clergy nor laymen in Va. gave broad support to the American episcopate. What distinguished Henley from most of Va.'s Anglican opponents to the naming of an American bishop was his implicit questioning of the institution of episcopacy and his explicit condemnation of the accepted theory underlying the church-state alliance.

These views led Henley into open conflict with Robert Carter Nicholas (q.v.), treasurer of Va. and staunch lay supporter of Va.'s religious establishment. Because Nicholas, an important vestryman of Bruton Parish in Williamsburg, had kept Henley from a permanent appointment as rector of the parish, Henley challenged Nicholas in May 1773 to bring his charges into the open. Once again the *Virginia Gazette* became the principal vehicle for impassioned theological disputation with Samuel Henley as a key participant.

At the heart of the Nicholas-Henley debate were the ideas contained in a sermon that Henley had preached to the House of Burgesses in Mar. 1772. This sermon, *The Distinct Claims of Government and Religion*, was the finest of Henley's American writings, carefully reasoned and free of the contumely that characterized his *Gazette* publications. At the time of the delivery of the sermon, the burgesses were giving serious consideration to a bill that provided for a limited religious toleration. Henley's sermon was a philosophical treatise on the origin and interrelationships of society, the state, and religion. While the House of Burgesses was considering a minor modification of the existing religious establishment, Samuel Henley questioned in toto the concept of a church-state alliance.

Nicholas's objections to Henley included not only the latter's views on episcopacy and religious establishment but also his doctrinal latitudinarianism. Nicholas quoted witnesses who accused Henley of denying the divinity of Christ and the existence of hell and the devil. Henley defended himself and made counterattacks in the newspaper and in a pamphlet, *A Candid Refutation of the Heresy Imputed by Ro. C. Nicholas, Esquire to the Reverend S. Henley*, and he prolonged the controversy until his departure for Eng. in May 1775.

After his return to Eng., Henley's wide interest in books, inscriptions, and languages led to his election as a fellow of the Society of Antiquaries. He corresponded with various scholars on literary and antiquarian subjects, wrote essays, and edited and translated literary works. No longer the gadfly of his youthful Williamsburg days, Henley was involved in only one controversy of note after his return to Eng. In 1786 he published his translation of William Beckford's romance, *Vathek*, without authorization and without acknowledging Beckford's authorship.

Although he spent but a few years in America, Samuel Henley is deserving of recognition as a minor American writer because of his participation in the important pre-Revolutionary debates on the American episcopate and on the role of religion and religious establishment in society.

Suggested Readings: CCV; DNB. *See also* Mellen Chamberlain, "Rev. Samuel Henley, D.D.," PMHS, 15 (1878), 230-241; Ray Hiner, Jr., "Samuel Henley and Thomas Gwatkin; Partners in Protest," HMagPEC, 37 (1968), 39-50; E. Alfred Jones, "Two Professors of William and Mary College," WMQ, 1st ser., 36 (1918), 221-231; Fraser Neiman, *The Henley-Horrocks Inventory* (1968); idem, "The Letters of William Gilpin to Samuel Henley," HLQ, 35 (1972), 159-169; George W. Pilcher, "Virginia Newspapers and the Dispute Over the Proposed Colonial Episcopate, 1771-1772," *Historian*, 23 (1960-1961), 98-113; Mary E. Quinlivan, "From Pragmatic Accommodation to Principled Action: The Revolution and Religious Establishment in Virginia," SSS, 15 (1976), 55-64; Robert P. Thomson, "The Reform of the College of William and Mary, 1763-1780," PAPS, 115 (1971), 187-213.

Mary E. Quinlivan
University of Texas of the Permian Basin

JOHN HEPBURN (fl. 1715-c. 1745)

Works: *The American Defence of the Christian Golden Rule* (1715).

Biography: Information about John Hepburn's life is fragmentary. The dates of his birth and death are unknown. Those facts that do exist have been pieced together from public records by the American Antiquarian Society. Hepburn, who also spelled his name *Haburne* and *Hebron* on various documents, came to America from Scot. as an indentured servant. He arrived in N.J. on Dec. 5, 1684, to serve "Robert Barclay of Urie, governor of the province." N.J. allotted thirty acres of land to each indentured servant upon his arrival; Hepburn deeded the land to his master and thus apparently freed himself.

Described as a tailor in subsequent deeds and documents, Hepburn proceeded to acquire property around the Raritan River in Middlesex County and also in Monmouth County. Sometime before 1695, he married Ann or Anna Laurie (*Lowry, Lawry*), daughter of Thomas Laurie, also a tailor. The date of the marriage is unknown but must have been before 1695, the year Anna Laurie signed her name Anna Hebron when witnessing a Quaker marriage in Shrewsbury, N.J. The couple had four children: James, John, Jr., Naomi, and Elizabeth. John, Jr., died in Jan. 1744/45, leaving provision in his will for the care of his father and surviving brother and sisters. From this information, it is probably safe to assume that Anna was dead and that John Hepburn lived well into old age.

Although there is no record of his membership in any of the N. J. Friends meetings of his day, strong evidence exists that John Hepburn was a Quaker. Both he and his wife are on record as having witnessed Quaker weddings at Shrewsbury in Sept. 1695 and in 1706/7. On May 31, 1709, Hepburn witnessed a will at Perth Amboy, "attesting and affirming according to Act of Parliament," rather than taking an oath. On Apr. 1, 1721, he again witnessed a will by affirmation. Here the executor of the will specifically stated, "John Hepburn, being as he says of the people called Quakers" affirmed, rather than swore, when giving his deposition. His son John married one Sarah Laing in Mar. or Apr. 1734, "after the manner of Friends." In addition, Hepburn's antislavery treatise, his use of "first month" and "fifth month" as dates on letters, and his salutation to a "Water-baptist" as "Friend Silby" all indicate close affiliations with the Society of Friends.

Critical Appraisal: Only two copies of *The American Defence of the Christian Golden Rule* are extant, a complete copy of ninety-four pages at the British Museum and a fragmentary one of the first forty pages at the Boston Public Library. The complete copy consists of Hepburn's antislavery treatise of forty-four pages; his father-in-law's treatises against election, outward baptism, and infant damnation; and Hepburn's letter to Silby, supporting Lawry (*Lowry, Laury*) in his refutation of water baptism.

Subtitling his work "An Essay to Prove the Unlawfulness of Making Slaves of Men," Hepburn declared that he "loves the Freedom of the Souls and Bodies of all men." He apologized for his thirty-year silence on the subject, explaining that ever since his arrival in America, he had hoped his betters would undertake the work. Since they had not, he would then speak out. He hoped his work would reach Br. and that the British would "admonish their American Brethern for this affront to the Blessed Messiah and his glorious Gospel." This foreign admonition was needed because slavery is an "enriching sin" and would not be easily abandoned by the "negro-masters" who had profited from their evildoing. To deprive the slaves of dignity as well as freedom, the negro masters gave their human property the same names they gave to dogs and horses. The animals, however, were treated well, but the slaves were starved, beaten, and hung by their thumbs if they displeased their masters.

The negro masters' earthly blessings were gained through the slaves' spiritual damnation; slavery forced the slave to break all ten of the commandments. Hunger forced the slave to steal; separation from his wife forced him to commit adultery; separation from his parents forced him to lose respect for his mother and father; misery forced him to suicide, which is a form of murder; poverty forced him to envy and covet what little his neighbor owned; assent to his own wretched condition forced him to bear false witness against himself each time he said, "Yes, master." But the slave was not responsible for his own sins. The negro master, true author of all of this evil, would surely be the one to answer for it before God.

Having thus depicted the slaves' wretched condition, Hepburn set up a dialog between a negro master and a "True Christian": The negro master argues that slavery has brought Christianity to heathens. But they are not freed once this blessing has been conferred upon them, answers the True Christian. The negro master declares that slavery is sanctioned by the Old Testament. So are concubinage and polygamy, the True Christian responds. The negro master offers many such spurious explanations for slavery; the True Christian refutes them all.

The negro master saves his heaviest argument for last. Even Quakers, the best and holiest people among us, keep slaves. True Christian laments this sad fact. Quakers became corrupted in 1711, when they participated in an anti-French military foray into Can. They have thus lost their claim to holiness, all except the Germantown, Pa., Quakers, who have remained free of all militaristic or slave-owning taint. If we are to model ourselves after Quakers, they are the ones to emulate. The negro master cannot exculpate himself by citing the sins of others. His only hope for salvation lies in freeing his slaves and sharing all of his temporal property *and* his "portion in Glory" with those whom he has robbed and driven to sin.

Twenty syllogistic arguments against slavery followed. According to Hepburn, it is unlawful to use labor without pay; slavery is the use of labor without pay; therefore, slavery is unlawful. To imprison those who break no law is wrong; slavery imprisons those who have broken no laws; therefore, slavery is wrong, and so on. There are also nine objections and answers and twenty motives for keeping slavery and suggestions for dealing with these motives, all in dialog form. Again, the negro masters' arguments are shown to be meretricious and self-serving.

The question-and-answer form of Hepburn's treatise may lack elegance and cohesiveness, but it strikes the reader's soul more forcibly than would a smoother, more literary style. Lacking formal doctrine and set dogma, independent Quaker meetings compose their own informal catechisms. These *Guides to Faith and Practice* describe the concerns of a particular meeting by employing a series of "queries." They are not rules but questions that each Friend must answer in his own heart and to the satisfaction of his own conscience. This popular Quaker form seems to have been Hepburn's model for *The American Defence of the Christian Golden Rule*.

Suggested Readings: PAAS, 59 (1949), 90-112.

Zohara Boyd
Appalachian State University

ALEXANDER HEWAT (c. 1740-1824)

Works: *An Historical Account of the Rise and Progress of the Colonies of South Carolina and Georgia* (1779); *The Firm Patriot* (1795); *Religion Essential to the Being and Happiness of Society* (1796); *Sermons on Various Subjects* (1803-1805).

Biography: Alexander Hewat was born in Scot. sometime around 1740. After attending the University of Edinburgh, Hewat was called by the Scots (First Presbyterian) Church in Charleston, S.C., and was in the colony by Nov.

1763. As the minister of one of the leading dissenting congregations in S.C., Hewat met and associated with the colony's elite, including William Bull II, lieutenant governor of S.C.; John Stuart, superintendent of Indian affairs; and Robert Wells, editor of the *South-Carolina and American General Gazette*. These men and others like them had either witnessed or participated in many of the events that had helped shape S.C.'s history. In 1777 Hewat refused to take an oath of allegiance to the state government and fled to Eng. for his safety. In 1780 the University of Edinburgh awarded him an honorary doctor of divinity degree. His claims for property lost in the Revolution were eventually denied and he lived on a small government pension until his death on Mar. 3, 1824.

Critical Appraisal: Alexander Hewat's reputation rests primarily on *An Historical Account of the Rise and Progress of the Colonies of South Carolina and Georgia*. Despite its title, this work is concerned essentially with S.C., for the material on Ga. is incidental and comprises only a very small portion of the book. Hewat's sermons, "chiefly on duties rather than doctrines," were published in London.

An Account showed the influence of the eighteenth-century Scottish school of historical writing in which history was supposed to provide moral instruction, not simply chronicle events. In following the example of William Robertson and others, Hewat strove for accuracy. As a result, he included lengthy verbatim transcriptions of various documents. A contemporary critic in *The Monthly Review* of London dismissed the book as "extremely deficient in the graces of historical composition" but did allow that because of its detail, it would "probably be preserved as a valuable collection of materials."

It is precisely this attention to detail that makes Hewat's history so important. Although late eighteenth- and nineteenth-century American historians tended to denigrate Hewat because of his loyalty to the crown, they used him time and again in their own histories. David Ramsay (q.v.), William Gilmore Simms, James Rivers, and Edward McCrady all turned to Hewat for historical information about S.C. Ramsay's *History of South Carolina* contained page after page of material lifted directly from Hewat. Rivers was not as blatant, but he, too, liberally mined Hewat for his *History*. Even the staunchly Whiggish Simms resorted to *An Account* as a source. McCrady, the best nineteenth-century historian of the state, was more critical and careful in his use of Hewat as a source. McCrady found errors in Hewat (which earlier authors had repeated), but he commented that when "Dr. Hewat speaks from tradition he does so from the very best source of information." In the twentieth century, David Duncan Wallace, a neo-Whig, dismissed Hewat as "that interesting but often inaccurate writer." Wallace's assessment was not only biased, it was unjust.

Hewat began writing in the 1770s in the midst of the unsettled years before the Revolution and completed his work in exile in London. Given those circumstances, he produced not only an interesting account of S.C., but also a dispassionate one, and those biases that emerge in the work are more a product of the times than a willful distortion of fact. He extolled the economic benefits that

742   HICKS, ELIAS

S.C. derived from the imperial system—benefits, incidentally, that recent historians have confirmed. His comments on the lords proprietors and the Church of England were generally critical, and those on the dissenters and their activities were always favorable.

Political and religious events aside, the descriptive passages on life in the colony (notably Chapter XI) make his history worthwhile. Hewat traveled widely in S.C. and Ga. Whether in the country or at home in Charleston, he was a keen observer of his surroundings. In addition, Hewat's acquaintance with S.C. leaders gave him access to documents and records otherwise unavailable. With such positive attributes, it was little wonder that *An Historical Account of the Rise and Progress of the Colonies of South Carolina and Georgia* long served as the major source for colonial S.C. history.

Suggested Readings: CCV; DAB; Sprague (III, 251-253). *See also* George Howe, *History of the Presbyterian Church in South Carolina*, 2 vols. (1870-1883), passim; Elmer D. Johnson, "Alexander Hewat: South Carolina's First Historian," JSH, 20 (1954), 50-62; Geraldine Meroney, "Alexander Hewat's *Historical Account*" in *The Colonial Legacy*, vol. I: *Loyalist Historians*, ed. Lawrence H. Leder (1971), pp. 135-63.

Walter B. Edgar
University of South Carolina

ELIAS HICKS (1748-1830)

Works: *Observations on the Slavery of the Africans and Their Descendants* (1811; rev. 1814, 1823); *A Series of Extemporaneous Discourses* (1825); *The Substance of Two Discourses, Delivered in New York, 17 Dec. 1824* (1825); *The Quaker, A Series of Sermons*, 4 vols. (1827-1828); *The Answers, by Elias Hicks, to the Six Questions* (1831); *Journal of the Life and Religious Labours of Elias Hicks* (1832); *Letters of Elias Hicks* (1861).

Biography: Born in Hempstead Township, Long Island, N.Y., on Mar. 19, 1748, Elias Hicks was the son of John and Martha (Smith) Hicks, who shortly before Elias's birth had become members of the Society of Friends. Although he acquired little formal education, he possessed a fine mind and became at an early age an avid reader. In 1771 he married Jemima Seaman, daughter of Jonathan Seaman of Jericho, Long Island, whose farm he managed for the rest of his life. At 26, Hicks became much concerned about religious matters and in 1778 was recorded as a Quaker minister. During the next fifty years, he traveled some 40,000 miles, attending religious meetings from Me. to Va. and as far west as Ind.

Hicks was sensitive to all forms of suffering, both human and animal, and was outspoken on what he considered the vices of his day: intemperance, horse racing, war, and, most of all, slavery. Theologically, he had an inclination toward Quietism. He distrusted theological dogma and the authority of the elders

The   one-third   of of the society, believing that one should rely on the Inner Light of God within the soul. In the 1820s, when he was already an old man, these beliefs often brought him into conflict with the minority of elders who ruled the society. By 1827, when the great separation occurred in the Society of Friends, Hicks had become identified as the leader of the liberal cause, and the terms *Hicksite* and *Orthodox* were widely used to differentiate between the two branches of the society. Throughout these acrimonious disputes, Hicks maintained an inviolable self-assurance and continued to travel and expound his religious views until just a few weeks before his death on Feb. 27, 1830.

Critical Appraisal: Between managing his farm at Jericho and traveling thousands of miles to preach at Quaker meetings, Elias Hicks must have had little time to devote to serious writing. Many of his sermons appeared in print from 1825 on, but most of them were taken from shorthand transcriptions at the time of their delivery and published without Hicks's consent. They are, by and large, lucid accounts of Hicks's Inner Light theology, written in a plain style and heavily dependent on biblical quotations to support doctrinal points. His letters reveal a man of deep feelings who could convey his ideas with conviction.

One work that Hicks did see through the presses himself and in which he took a firm and uncompromising stance was his *Observations on the Slavery of the Africans*. After a brief introduction, Hicks in a series of nineteen "Queries and Answers" condemned both slavery and those who purchased products manufactured by slaves. He concluded his essay with a sketch in which he vividly laid before his readers what the appalling consequences would be if the slave traders were forced to obtain their slaves on the banks of the Delaware and the Hudson. *Observations* was undoubtedly as vigorous and impassioned a statement against slavery as had ever come from a Quaker pen.

But Elias Hicks's literary reputation must rest mainly on his *Journal*, which he finished a few months before his death and which was published posthumously, after substantial editorial tampering, in 1832. Hicks was a reluctant author, believing that too much historical material already existed and that the insights of one generation were likely "to cloy and shut up the avenue of better instruction" to a succeeding one. However, the Quaker separation of 1827-1828 in which he figured so prominently might have prompted him to record the consistency of his views over his long ministry as well as the support he had from other Friends.

Apparently Hicks's *Journal* was composed from some thirty or more travel journals that he kept on his journeys and from a home journal that covers the years 1813 to 1819. In the travel journals, Hicks recorded the miles he traveled, his expenses, where he lodged, the meetings he attended, and some situations he encountered. The home journal is much more comprehensive. In it he included, in addition to the many meetings, matters such as funerals and weddings attended, problems with managing his farm, disputes among neighbors he attempted to settle, and advice he gave to those enmeshed in sin. As a consequence of relying on these two different sources, almost two-thirds of a journal supposedly covering his entire life is devoted to the years 1813-1819. The one-third of the *Journal* covered by the travel journals contains very few of the illuminating anecdotes and anguished soul searching that have become hallmarks of the better Quaker journals. There are, though, some exceptions. His account of how he gradually became aware of the viciousness of killing for sport may be favorably compared to similar accounts by John Woolman (q.v.) and Henry David Thoreau. His observations on Quakers who were offered money for billeting English troops and the dangers encountered when attempting to cross the lines between opposing camps provide insight into the moral dilemmas and physical dangers the pacifistic Quakers faced during the Revolutionary War.

The portion covering the years 1813-1819 contains some of the same cataloging of meetings attended, miles traveled, and people visited as the other one-third of the *Journal*, but Hicks in this part commented much more often on his theological beliefs and the details of his daily life. One of the more interesting aspects of this section of the *Journal* is the recurring conflict between the spiritual and the secular worlds. Hicks's main concern was the state of his and other people's souls, but time and again the management of his farm and other business matters intruded upon his spiritual interests, creating a tension within this man of God that engages the reader's sympathy.

However, the *Journal* provides little insight into the social concerns of Hicks's time. So steadfastly are his eyes fixed on his religious duties that we see little of the broader social context within which he moved. Even the dramatic and bitter separation of 1827-1828, in which he played so important a part and which should have been fresh in his memory, fails to come alive in his pages. Hicks seldom provided vivid descriptions or dramatic anecdotes as did, for instance, John Woolman in his journal. Nor did Hicks project the sincerity, tolerance, and humility of Woolman. At times he even seemed a bit self-righteous and vain, expressing indignation with those ministers whose doctrinal positions differed from his and continually emphasizing the size of the crowds who came to hear him preach.

Still, Hicks's *Journal* is valuable for what it tells us about the life of a Quaker minister of the late eighteenth and early nineteenth centuries and the religious doctrines that he and many other Quakers held. His style is, like that of most Quakers, basically plain, embellished only by biblical figures and allusions; yet he employed a variety of sentence rhythms well modulated to convey his passion, or lack of it, toward the subject at hand.

Suggested Readings: DAB; DARB; LHUS. *See also* Robert W. Doherty, *The Hicksite Separation* (1967); Thomas E. Drake, *Quakers and Slavery in America* (1950), pp. 114-118; Bliss Forbush, "Elias Hicks—Prophet of an Era," BFHA, 38 (1949), 11-19; idem, *Elias Hicks: Quaker Liberal* (1956); idem, "The Newly Discovered Manuscript Journal of Elias Hicks," BFHA, 39 (1950), 16-26; Rufus M. Jones, *The Later Periods of Quakerism* (1921), I, 435-487; Walt Whitman, *Complete Poetry and Prose* (1948), II, 469-487; Henry W. Wilbur, *The Life and Labors of Elias Hicks* (1910).

Don Mortland
Eastern Kentucky University

FRANCIS HIGGINSON (1587-1630)

Works: *A True Relacion* (1629); *New Englands Plantation* (1630).

Biography: Born on Aug. 6, 1587, into a clerical family, in Claybrooke, Leicestershire, Eng., Francis Higginson was educated at Cambridge (A.B., 1610; A.M., 1613) and was ordained at York in Dec. 1614. After 1615, having accepted a living at Claybrooke, Higginson fell under the influence of the famous nonconformist recruiter, Arthur Hildersam, and by the 1620s he was a leader among the Leicester Puritans and in frequent difficulty with the establishment. In 1627 Archbishop William Laud suspended Higginson for his Puritan beliefs, and he was deprived of the pulpit at St. Nicholas, Leicester.

In 1629 the Massachusetts Bay Company hired Higginson as its minister and appointed him to its governing council. In the spring of that year, he sailed to New Eng. with his family, arriving in Salem that Jun. At Salem he and his colleague Samuel Skelton formed a controversial covenanted Congregational Church that served as a model for future Mass. ecclesial polity. After only a year in the colony, Higginson contracted a fever and died on Aug. 6, 1630, leaving a widow and eight children, the eldest of whom, John Higginson (q.v.), became pastor of his father's church in 1660.

Critical Appraisal: Francis Higginson wrote his two major works, *A True Relacion of the Last Voyage to New England* (1629) and *New Englands Plantation* (1630) to encourage Puritan migration to Massachusetts Bay. He set out in a lively and convincing style to counter the growing suspicion in Eng. that New World colonies, beset by disease, Indians, and Spaniards, were doomed to failure. By all accounts, his efforts were a popular success; his *New Englands Plantation* went through three editions the year it was published in London.

Higginson's works, however, should not be dismissed as mere promotional literature. According to Moses Coit Tyler, "there was no braver or more exquisite spirit" than Higginson among the first settlers, and, consequently, his prose still has an appealing immediacy and power born of Puritan conviction and unfeigned delight in a new, unspoiled landscape. More significantly, Higginson, being one of the first and most popular of the American Puritan writers, developed themes that became characteristic of colonial culture generally.

The *True Relacion* is essentially a journal of a harrowing ocean voyage that culminated in a joyous summer landfall. For the author, the episode is a metaphoric recapitulation of the passage of the Hebrews through the Wilderness to Canaan. Higginson, thus, was among the first to envision Mass. as a New Israel. Presaged by masses of flowers floating in a calm sea, the landfall sought was "our new paradise of New England," a phrase redolent of regenerative meaning to persons weary of political and religious travail in Eng.

New Englands Plantation is a description of the "Commodities and Discommodities of that Country" carefully organized in true Renaissance fashion around the four Classical elements of earth, water, air, and fire. The advantages include fertility of land and sea, abundant fire wood, cleared land, and a generally wholesome climate. The disadvantages mentioned are mosquitoes, relative severity of winter, snakes, and the sparseness of English settlement. Obviously the "Commodities" outweigh the "Discommodities." There follows a brief section on the Indians, designed to allay English fears and conscience qualms, and a concluding discourse on the "present condition of the Plantation." This pamphlet, then, is a more specific elaboration on the Promised Land theme in the *True Relacion* and the central message of both is encapsulated in the last sentence of *New Englands Plantation*: "And thus wee doubt not but God will be with us, and if God be with us, who can be against us?"

Finally, Higginson's metaphor of a Chosen People in a New Israel would grow into the great agrarian myth of America. Significant elements of that myth are already present in Higginson's observation that: "great pitty it is to see so much good ground for Corne & for Grasse as any is under the Heavens, to ly altogether unoccupied, when so many honest Men and their Families in old England through the populousnesse thereof, do make very hard shift to live one by the other."

Francis Higginson's promotional pieces were intentionally ephemeral, but by coming so early in American experience and by being so widely read by emigrating Puritans, they proved seminal. No student of early American culture should ignore them.

Suggested Readings: CCNE; DAB; DARB; DNB; Sprague (I, 6-10); T_1. *See also* Cotton Mather, *Magnalia Christi Americana* (1702), III, sec. 2, ch. 1; Richard P. Gildrie, "Francis Higginson's New World Vision," EIHC, 106 (1970), 182-189; *New Englands Plantation* (1630; rep. in Edmund S. Morgan, ed., *The Founding of Massachusetts: Historians and the Sources* [1964], pp. 138-149, which also contains a letter of advice to immigrants from Higginson, pp. 154-157); *A True Relacion* (1629; also pub. in PMHS, 62 [1930], 281-299).

Richard P. Gildrie
Austin Peay State University

JOHN HIGGINSON (1616-1708)

Works: *The Cause of God* (1663); *A Direction for a Publick Profession* (1665); *Our Dying Saviours Legacy* (1686); *A Testimony to the Order of the Gospel* (with William Hubbard; 1701).

Biography: Born on Aug. 6, 1616, at Claybrooke, Leicestershire, Eng., John Higginson was the eldest son of Francis Higginson (q.v.), the celebrated Puritan clergyman who settled at Salem, Mass., in 1629. The elder Higginson died the following year, leaving a widow with eight children. Educated for the ministry under the supervision of John Winthrop (q.v.), John Cotton (q.v.), and other prominent figures in early Mass., Higginson served as chaplain at Saybrook

Fort from 1636 to 1640. In 1641 he was "sometime a school-master" at Hartford, Conn., and in 1643 he became assistant pastor of the church at Guilford and married the pastor's daughter. In 1659 Higginson and his family sailed for Eng., but contrary winds drove their ship to Salem, where he was "by a strong hand of Providence brought and settled in the ministry" in the town of his boyhood, and where he died on Dec. 9, 1708, much revered as one of New Eng.'s oldest ministers and strongest defenders of old-line Puritan orthodoxy.

Critical Appraisal: John Higginson, educated in a wilderness and denied the polish of formal university training, made diligent use of what talents he had. Besides publishing his own sermons and tracts, he transcribed and edited for publication more than 200 sermons of Thomas Hooker (q.v.) and Samuel Stone (q.v.). He wrote introductions to more than half a dozen other works, among them the "Attestation" to Cotton Mather's (q.v.) monumental history of New Eng., *Magnalia Christi Americana* (1702). Praised in the nineteenth century as "incomparably the best writer, native or foreign, who lived in America during the first hundred years," Higginson wrote good—but certainly not extraordinary—prose, and his simple, direct style, unadorned by metaphors and imagery, is plainer than most examples of the Puritan "plain style."

Higginson's 1663 election sermon, *The Cause of God*, was the first election sermon printed in New Eng. and is the best example of his writing. Written in the accepted Puritan form, with "doctrines," "reasons," and "applications" methodically set forth, the sermon pleads for a return to the purity of early New Eng. religion and reminds a worldly generation that the "cause of God" is not "the getting of this World's good." Cotton Mather quoted this work in Higginson's funeral sermon, and it was excerpted in *Elijah's Mantle* (1722), a pamphlet on the purity of the early New Eng. churches.

Although Higginson supported the Half-Way Covenant in the 1660s, he was a staunch conservative when it came to the autonomy of the Puritan churches as set forth in the Cambridge Platform of 1648. His concern for preserving religious orthodoxy can be seen in *Our Dying Saviours Legacy* (1686), a volume consisting of two long sermons on Puritan devotions and spiritual exercises, and in *A Testimony to the Order of the Gospel*. This work, written "by the two most Aged Ministers of the Gospel yet Surviving in the Country," was an endorsement of Increase Mather's (q.v.) book, *The Order of the Gospel* (1700), a defense of New Eng. Congregationalism. Higginson's touch can be seen in the homely but powerful imagery of *A Testimony*: "We have taught our Children in the *Catechism*, called *Milk for Babes.*...And it cannot but be grievous unto us, as well as unto all serious Christians, for any *Children* of *New-England*, Scornfully to vomit up their *Milk*." John Wise (q.v.) reprinted this work in 1717 as an addition to his treatise *A Vindication of the Government of New-England Churches*. This model of conservative Puritan ideology apparently found an appreciative audience, and it appeared in a 2nd edition as late as 1772.

Suggested Readings: CCNE; DNB; Sprague (I, 91-93); T₁. *See also* S. Austin Allibone, *A Critical Dictionary of English Literature and British and American Authors*

(1900), I, 843; S. E. Baldwin, "Rev. John Higginson, of Salem," PMHS, 36 (1902), 478-521; Thomas Wentworth Higginson, *Descendants of the Reverend Francis Higginson* (1910); "Higginson Letters," CMHS, 27 (1838), 196-222; "Letters, &c., of John Higginson," CMHS, 38 (1868), 269-287; Cotton Mather, *Nunc Dimittis Briefly Descanted* (1709); "Part of Mr. John Higginson's Letter, of Guilford, dated 25 of the 8th Month, 1654, to his Brother the Rev'd Thomas Thacher of Weymouth," CHSC, 3 (1895), 318-320; "Rev. John Higginson's Advice to his Children, called His Dying Testimony," EIHC, 2 (1860), 97-99; "Testimony and Counsel of the Rev. John Higginson, of Guilford" in *Papers Relating to the Controversy in the Church in Hartford, 1656-59*, CHSC, 2 (1870), 93-100.

Virginia Bernhard
University of St. Thomas

THOMAS HINCKLEY (1618-1706)

Works: *Mr. Thomas Walley, The Reverend Pastor of the Church of Christ at Barnstable* (1678; no copy of this broadside has come to light, but a contemporaneous copy in Samuel Sewall's [q.v.] commonplace book is pub. in Harold Jantz, "First Century of New England Verse," PAAS, New Series, 53 [1943], 361); "Upon the Death of the Honourable and Highly Esteemed Josiah Winslow" (1680), Ms.a., Boston Public Library, pub. in CMHS, 4th ser., 5 (1861), 53-55; "Verses on the Death of His Second Consort, Mary Smith Hinckley, 1703," Ms.a., pub. in NEHGR, 1 (1847), 92-95.

Biography: Thomas Hinckley, sixth and last governor of Plymouth colony, was born in Eng. in 1618. He was with the family when his father, Samuel, was made pastor at Scituate in 1635. In 1639 the family moved to Barnstable, a town later rent by schism and dissension, to which Thomas Walley (q.v.) came as peacemaker. There Hinckley was admitted a freeman in 1645. In the following year, he held his first public office as deputy to the General Court. He served frequently in that capacity until 1658, when he was elected an assistant. In 1681 he was chosen to succeed Josiah Winslow as governor and was reelected annually, except during the Andros regime, until Plymouth was joined to Mass. by the charter of 1692. He had already served as a commissioner of the United Colonies; after the union he acted as councillor to the province of Mass. Twice married and the father of seventeen children, he died in Barnstable on Apr. 25, 1706.

Critical Appraisal: Thomas Hinckley's three long funeral elegies belong squarely in the tradition of the "plain" Puritan elegy. In this tradition—well established by 1677, the date of Hinckley's earliest elegy—sincerity of utterance had been elevated to a principle and was allowed to compensate fully for any deficiency in art. In Urian Oakes's (q.v.) popular elegy on Thomas Shepard (q.v.), which Hinckley quoted in "Thomas Walley," no less than fifteen stanzas are devoted to establishing the claims of spontaneity and plainness over "Poetick Raptures." Clearly, Hinckley was of this persuasion. Despite often-awkward handling of versification, reliance on well-worn figures of speech—all scriptural in origin, and pious digressions that pull the elegies out of shape, Hinckley fearlessly circulated his efforts among family and friends and in one case had a broadside printed for more general consumption. The thought behind the gesture was sure to forestall any criticism or ridicule.

In form, Hinckley followed a pattern that had long since been adapted by Puritan elegists from funeral sermons, religious biographies, and prose eulogies. The life of a "saint," whether housewife or governor, was seen as exemplifying the pattern set forth by St. Paul in *Romans* 8:29-30. Some or all of the steps from vocation to salvation formed the heart of the portraiture in the elegy, but especially details illustrating the combination of zeal and loving kindness that proved sanctification and argued election. To portraiture was added exhortation, by means of which survivors were urged to grasp the meaning of death (most often a warning to New Eng. to mend its ways) and to remember and emulate a well-spent life.

Hinckley uses the portrait-exhortation pattern consistently and in one case— the elegy on his second wife—exhaustively, carrying her from early calling as a Christian through daily acts of sanctification to undoubted salvation with "that blest company / Who thro' their faith and patience now possess / The full completion of the Promises." Along the way, one learns that Mary Hinckley was an only child, that the marriage had lasted forty-three years despite early opposition by her relatives, that she conducted household worship when her husband was away, that she suffered sharp pain "allmost constantly for six weeks before she died," and that her last words were: "Come dear Lord Jesus, Come / And take me quickly to thy Bosom home." Such details give the elegy on Mary Hinckley a certain expressiveness that only "plainness" can give. Hinckley's elegies on his minister at Barnstable and on his predecessor as governor of Plymouth, although weighting different parts of the portrait-exhortation pattern, also contain passages that individualize both the elegist and the elegized and go far to compensate for lack of technical skill.

Suggested Readings: FCNEV. *See also* Robert Henson, "Form and Content of the Puritan Funeral Elegy," AL, 32 (1960-1961), 11-27; Hinckley Papers, CMHS, 4th ser., 5 (1861), 1-308.

Robert Henson
Upsala College

ENOS HITCHCOCK (1744-1803)

Works: *A Discourse on Education* (1785); *A Discourse on the Causes of National Prosperity* (1786); *An Oration Delivered July 4, 1788* (1788); *The*

Parent's Assistant (1788); *Memoirs of the Bloomsgrove Family* (1790); *A Discourse Delivered at the Ordination of. . .Abel Flint* (1791); *A Discourse Delivered at the Ordination of. . .Jonathan Gould* (1793); *The Farmer's Friend* (1793); *An Oration, in Commemoration of. . .Independence* (1793); *An Answer to the Question* (1795); *A Discourse Delivered at the Dedication of the New Congregational Meetinghouse* (1795); *A New-Year's Sermon* (1797); *A Sermon Delivered at Wrentham* (1799); *A Discourse, on the Dignity. . .of. . .Washington* (1800); *A Funeral Sermon, Occasioned by the Death of Mrs. Sarah Bowen* (1800).

Biography: Clergyman and patriot, Enos Hitchcock was born in Brookfield, Mass., on May 7, 1744, the son of Pelatiah and Sarah (Parsons) Hitchcock. After graduating from Harvard in 1767, Hitchcock undertook theological studies that culminated in 1771 with his ordination as a Congregationalist minister. Hitchcock's first clerical assignment was at the Second Congregational Church in Beverly, Mass., where he was assistant to an aging pastor. During the Revolutionary War, Hitchcock served as a chaplain in the Continental Army at Valley Forge. After the war, he became pastor of the Benevolent Congregational Church in Providence, R.I., a position he held until shortly before his death.

As a clergyman and a citizen, Hitchcock was noted for his interest in the community. For Hitchcock, religion was an instrument of social welfare. Less doctrinal than those of his contemporaries, his sermons stress "the virtues of the Christian" and the peace that these virtues afford society. An ardent supporter of the federal government, Hitchcock was particularly effusive in his praise of George Washington (q.v.). In addition, he cultivated a lifelong interest in public education, writing warmly in its defense. In fact, all of his books examine the requirements of an American education. Hitchcock's concern for community gained the respect of his contemporaries. He was awarded an M.A. from Yale College in 1781 and an honorary doctor of divinity degree from Brown in 1788. Shortly before his death in Providence on Feb. 26, 1803, Enos Hitchcock bequeathed 2,500 dollars for the support of the ministry.

Critical Appraisal: The title page of the *Memoirs of the Bloomsgrove Family* describes the central purpose of Enos Hitchcock's major writings: to develop "a mode of domestic education suited to the present state of society, government and manners in the United States." In keeping with this purpose, Hitchcock's two fictional narratives, *The Bloomsgrove Family* and *The Farmer's Friend*, take the form of extended educational treatises. Such fictional devices as happily-ever-after endings and imaginary characters were clearly secondary to his didactic purposes, and even though he claimed to be writing fiction, Hitchcock distrusted his own vehicle. He repeatedly criticized most fiction, usually because it excites the passions, and gave even Richardson's *Pamela* only cautious acceptance.

Hitchcock's first extended narrative, *The Bloomsgrove Family*, is epistolary in structure, with all letters written by the same writer. The narrative has two thrusts: to describe the three stages of a child's education as exemplified in the Bloomsgrove children, Ossander and Rozella, and to argue for a change in the character of female education. The three stages of Hitchcock's education—"the period of impressions," the burgeoning of reason, and the cultivation of understanding—take the child from cradle to marriage, at which point he is presumably safe from the snares of the world. The goal of this education is to teach *"how to think,"* not *"what to think."* For this reason, Hitchcock rejects many of the features of a traditional education, especially Latin. Hitchcock's central metaphor, the garden, defines the character of education and indicates the role of the parent. The parent-gardener cultivates "the little plant of reason," his child, to enhance natural virtues and to guard against any passions that might pervert the fruits of reason. For Hitchcock, traditional female education was unnatural, because it placed too much emphasis on artificial concerns such as fashion, manners, and the "female arts." Since he conceived the marital relationship as a balance of power, he believed that women should receive an education that would enable them to maintain that balance. Such an education is of necessity practical, training the woman in the "economy and domestic employments" necessary to be an American wife.

The Farmer's Friend is an eighteenth-century self-help book that directs the reader to see "the progressive steps whereby others have arisen from obscure poverty, and disastrous conditions, to easy circumstances." For Hitchcock, the action of his tale is subordinate to the lessons that can be drawn from that action. For example, lest the reader miss the implications of an episode that details the domestic economies of the protagonist's wife, the narrator moralizes: "This saving the effects of industry from devouring jaws of carelessness and squandering, does not imply the least degree of parsimony or stinginess; but the most prudent use and application of what we have acquired." In *The Farmer's Friend*, the narrator guides the reader, never allowing for the possibility of misinterpretation. To reinforce his didactic purpose, Hitchcock arranged his characters allegorically, the characters' names—Charles Worthy, Mr. Slack, and Mr. Gruff—calling attention to the didactic schema.

When Hitchcock said a minister should "offer his hearers useful sentiments, and practical truths" rather than "amuse them with paradoxes and systems of contrivance," he described the purpose of his own sermons, orations, and pamphlets. His writer's stance is always commonsensical and practical. For example, in his pamphlet on the Lord's Supper, "An Answer to the Question," Hitchcock avoided the controversy in the Congregational Church over the nature of the rite in order to emphasize that communion is commemorative of Christ's death, to describe the practical results of its reception, and to allay fears about the attitude necessary for participation. Similarly, in a sermon dedicating a new Congregational meetinghouse, Hitchcock stressed the respectability that accompanies the building of a church and that leads to the town's "happiness and prosperity." For Hitchcock, the writer—whether preacher or novelist—should help the individuals in an audience to live happier, more useful lives.

Although Hitchcock's goal of adapting education to the demands of a new nation is laudable, it limited his achievement as a writer. Because he never came to trust his own fictional vehicle and because his ideas of education now seem anachronistic, his writings are dated. Nonetheless, they deserve attention as representatives of early American fiction and as documents in the life of federalist America.

Suggested Readings: CCNE; Sibley-Shipton (XVI, 475-484). *See also* Herbert Ross Brown, *The Sentimental Novel in America: 1789-1860* (1940), passim; Tremaine McDowell, "Sensibility in the Eighteenth-Century Novel," SP, 24 (1927), 383-402; Henri Petter, *The Early American Novel* (1971), pp. 67-68, 77-79; Arthur Hobson Quinn, *American Fiction: An Historical and Critical Survey* (1936).

David M. Craig
Clarkson College

GAD HITCHCOCK (1719-1803)

Works: *A Sermon Preached in the 2d Precinct in Pembroke* (1757); *A Sermon Preached at the Ordination of...Enos Hitchcock* (1771); *A Sermon Preached Before His Excellency Thomas Gage* (1774); *A Sermon Preached at Plymouth* (1774); *Natural Religion* (1779).

Biography: The first son of Capt. Ebenezer and Mary Hitchcock, Gad Hitchcock was born in Springfield, Mass., on Feb. 12, 1719. After graduation from Harvard in 1742, he remained in residence there for two years, "riding out to preach when opportunity offered." Although some financial issues nearly prevented his appointment, Hitchcock became the first minister of the First Congregational Church of Hanson, newly formed in the district of Tunk in Pembroke, Mass. He remained in this position for the rest of his life. A popular preacher frequently called upon to participate in ordination ceremonies, Hitchcock was awarded a doctor of divinity degree from Harvard in 1787. Hitchcock preached the Artillery Election Sermon for 1765 and the General Election Sermon for 1774. In addition, he delivered the Dudleian Lecture at Harvard in 1779. During the Revolutionary War, Hitchcock served as a chaplain in the armed forces and was a representative to the Mass. Constitutional Convention of 1779. In that same year, he was struck by paralysis while delivering a sermon, and he never preached again. He died in Hanson on Aug. 8, 1803, at the age of 83.

Critical Appraisal: As a champion of personal liberty, Gad Hitchcock wrote and preached sermons addressed to both civil and religious topics. As early as 1757, in *A Sermon Preached in the 2d Precinct*, Hitchcock likened the role of the soldier in earthly armies to that of the soldier for Christianity. He skillfully asserted that the principle of self-preservation is God's law as well as nature's, giving man the responsibility of protecting his country against "unreasonable and unpeaceable men." Hitchcock endeavored to prove with the story of David and Saul that God commands man to take up arms as a religious responsibility to protect personal liberty.

Before Hitchcock was to deliver the election speech for 1774, *A Sermon Preached Before His Excellency*, he was encouraged by excited Whigs to change his comments in light of the governor's presence in the audience. Their pleading was in vain. Hitchcock delivered his sermon without changes, illustrating his belief that civil leaders need religious guidance to perform at their best and to keep their subjects content. Present-day government must correct its course, he cautioned, for "religion is one quality wanted in a ruler." Probably Hitchcock's most memorable sermon, this work provoked some of his parishioners into accusing him of playing politics—a charge he denied. With customary wit, Hitchcock was said to have judged it a moving sermon because of the number of people who got up and walked out. The sermon is typical of Hitchcock's style and concerns; he did not threaten hell and brimstone, only exhorted Christians to their finest behavior, as examples to all. This behavior includes the right to change leaders, since the people, stated Hitchcock, "are the only source of civil authority on earth."

Although Hitchcock's style of writing is plain, it is frequently embellished, according to the traditions of the time, with scriptural metaphor: "The brave soldier is as bold as a lion." He often compared the colonial Americans to the oppressed Jews. His rhetorical style has considerable grace and force as it develops an argument point by point, adding examples for clarity. His style is most ringing when addressing issues of freedom and liberty during the years approaching the American Revolution. Later his style took on the more philosophical and sedate tones of maturer, more introspective thought.

Hitchcock's concern with civil matters deemphasizes the religious viewpoint of his works but shows him to be a spokesman of his time, addressing issues of political concern to the people. His final sermon, given as the Dudleian Lecture for 1779, concerns itself with "the mental furniture" of the first man, and human progress toward reason. In this same sermon, Hitchcock denied the concept of innate ideas and espoused the Lockean focus on the acquisition of knowledge as the basis of all understanding.

Beloved by the people of his church, Hitchcock was remembered by them after his death by a pair of "handsome gravestones" voted by the parish to be purchased for him and his wife, who had died in 1792. One of his contemporaries, William Bentley, wrote of Hitchcock in his diary: "He may be ranked among the most useful men of his times."

Suggested Readings: CCNE; Sibley-Shipton (XI, 231-236); Sprague (VIII, 30-31).

Patricia F. Clark
University of Houston

LEONARD HOAR (c. 1630-1675)

Works: *Index Biblicus* (1668; rev. 1672); *Catalogus* (1674); *The Sting of Death* (1680).

Biography: Leonard Hoar was born in Gloucestershire, Eng., sometime around 1630, the son of Charles and Johanna (Hinksman) Hoar. After the death of Charles Hoar in 1638, Leonard's mother decided to relocate her family to Braintree, Mass., probably as a consequence of Archbishop William Laud's persecution of the Rev. John Workman, of whom the Hoar family had been devoted followers. After graduation from Harvard College (A.B., 1650; A.M., 1653), Hoar left Mass. for Eng., where he received an incorporated A.M. from the Univ. of Cambridge in 1654. Pursuing an interest in science, Hoar cultivated an acquaintance with some of the leading scientific figures of the day, and at their urging the Univ. of Cambridge awarded him an M.D. in 1671.

Unable to preach in Eng. because of his refusal to conform, Hoar left Eng. in 1672 for Mass., where he had been asked to share the pulpit of the Old South Church with Thomas Thacher (q.v.). Having heard that Harvard might soon be in need of a new president, Hoar brought with him a letter from thirteen prominent nonconformist British ministers suggesting that he would make a suitable candidate for the position, and in 1672 Hoar was selected to succeed Charles Chauncy (q.v.) as Harvard's new president, the first Harvard graduate to ascend to that office.

Although Hoar brought plans to Cambridge, Mass., intended to make Harvard an international seat of learning, his term of office was plagued with difficulties, and in 1675 he was forced to resign. Not even Hoar's closest friends could understand the exact cause of his unpopularity among the students and faculty at Harvard. Cotton Mather (q.v.), who was a student at Harvard during Hoar's tenure there, wrote that a conspiracy existed between "*some* that made a Figure in the Neighbourhood" and "the *Young Men* in the Colledge...to ruine his Reputation, as far as they were able." Although some historians have suspected that Urian Oakes (q.v.), one of Hoar's rivals for the Harvard presidency, may have been the driving force behind Hoar's ouster, it is more generally concluded that Hoar's strict disciplinary policies and drive for academic excellence may very well have led students and faculty to work toward his resignation.

Broken in spirit, Hoar retired to Boston, where he died on Nov. 28, 1675, at age 45. Hoar's wife, Bridget (Lisle) Hoar, the daughter of the regicide John Lisle, lived until May 25, 1723. The couple had three children. One of Hoar's kinsmen, John Hull (q.v.), perhaps best summarized Hoar's unfortunate career. According to Hull, "Would those that accused him had but countenanced and encouraged him in his work, he would have proved the best president that ever yet the college had."

Critical Appraisal: Leonard Hoar is the author of only three published works: an abridged version of "The Historical Books of the Holy Scripture" which he published in 1668 and revised for a subsequent edition in 1672; a funeral sermon "Preached on the occasion of the Death of the truely noble and virtuous The Lady Mildmay" and titled *The Sting of Death*; and a catalog of the graduates of Harvard College which he drew up and published in 1674, while he was still president of that institution. Although Hoar would undoubtedly have considered his *Index Biblicus* to be his most important contribution to posterity, it is ironically through his *Catalogus* that he has entered the records of colonial literary history.

Printed as a small broadside with a Latin verse inscription at the end, President Hoar's *Catalogus* for 1674 listed the names of all Harvard graduates according to year of graduation and academic ranking. Subsequent degrees from other institutions were likewise listed after the name of each graduate. Although the *Catalogus* was probably compiled in an effort to strengthen student morale at Harvard during the difficult time of Hoar's presidency by reminding the students of the illustrious company they kept, it established several important academic traditions which have become a permanent part of university and college life across the country. According to Samuel Eliot Morison, "President Hoar's little broadsheet of 1674 set a fashion that American universities have, in the main, followed to this day." By listing graduates according to the year when they received their A.B. degrees, Hoar stressed the overall importance of that degree over other degrees. In addition, by listing students together according to class, he helped to instill in Harvard students the importance of class unity. Finally, Hoar provided a relatively accurate record of the graduates of Harvard. Without this record, much of the information contained might not have survived. As Morison explains, "A century ago, the Harvard or the Yale Triennial Catalogues, or both, were on the desk of every gentleman and scholar in New England."

Ending in the Latin lines, *"Macti estote pii juvenes; atque edite fructus / Condignos vestro semine, Rege, Deo., [Advance then, pious youth! And put forth fruits worthy your ancestry, your King, your God.],"* Hoar's twenty-two-line poem titled *"En Regis Magni Diploma Insigne Jacobi!"* ["Behold the Charter of the Great King James"] was probably printed, states Morison, to attract an audience from overseas. A tribute to the founding of New Eng. and of Harvard College in particular, this poem illustrates that like his successors at Harvard, Urian Oakes and John Rogers (q.v.), Hoar was no stranger to the pleasures of poetry.

Suggested Readings: CCNE; DAB; DNB; FCNEV; Sibley-Shipton (I, 228-252). *See also* Cotton Mather, *Magnalia Christi Americana* (1702), IV, 129; Perry Miller, *The New England Mind: The Seventeenth Century* (1939; rep. 1954), pp. 103, 119-120; Samuel Eliot Morison, *The History of Harvard University* (1935), II, 390-414; Josiah Quincy, *The History of Harvard University* (1840), I, 31-38.

James A. Levernier
University of Arkansas at Little Rock

NEHEMIAH HOBART (1648-1712)

Works: *An Almanack. . .for. . .1673* (1673); *Martij 27. 1712* (1712); *The Absence of the Comforter Described* (1717).

Biography: Nehemiah Hobart was born at Hingham, Mass., on Nov. 21, 1648, the son of the Rev. Peter Hobart, the first Congregational minister of

Hingham, and Rebecca (Ibrook) Hobart. Educated at Harvard College (B.A., M.A., 1667), Hobart began preaching in 1672 at the First Congregational Church of Cambridge Village (now Newton), Mass., where he was ordained on Dec. 23, 1674. After the death of Hobart's predecessor in 1668, the church where Hobart preached had become badly divided, but Hobart was so successful at restoring harmony that he became known as "the Repairer of Breaches." In all, Hobart's ministry at Newton lasted forty years, counting the two years when he preached there before his ordination.

On Mar. 21, 1678, Hobart married Sarah Jackson of Cambridge Village; six daughters were born to the couple. Hobart was a fellow of Harvard College from 1681 to 1692 and again from 1697 to 1712. In 1707 he was nominated to serve as Harvard's vice-president, and in 1686 he preached the Artillery Election Sermon. Hobart died at Newton on Aug. 25, 1712. Both before and after his death, Hobart was held in high esteem by his contemporaries. In his *Diary* for May 25, 1700, Cotton Mather (q.v.) called Hobart "holy and humble." After Hobart's death, Samuel Sewall (q.v.) referred to him as "A very worthy Minister...a very good old Friend," and Eliphalet Adams (q.v.) wrote not only of Hobart's "Excessive modesty" but also of his "Exemplary Conversation & Exact Walking with God."

Critical Appraisal: Although other authors of the annual Cambridge Press almanacs for New Eng. often included specimens of poetry, chiefly their own, Hobart did not, and his *Almanack...for...1673* thus sheds no additional light on his development as a poet or his attitudes toward the art of poetry itself.

Regrettably, no copy of a poem known to have been written by Hobart about the Great Fire of 1711 ("Lines...on the Dreadful Fire at Boston") is known to exist, and his only surviving poem is *Martij 27. 1712* (Mar. 27, 1712), a tribute in Latin to the virtues and achievements of Samuel Sewall, who in 1712 was in his twentieth year of unbroken service as a justice of the Superior Court of Mass. The poem's title suggests New Year's season reflections (New Year's Day was Mar. 25 on the Julian calendar). Significantly, Mar. 27, 1712, was exactly one month after the funeral of Hobart's wife, who died on Feb. 26, 1712, and was buried the next day. Duties at court kept Sewall from attending Mrs. Hobart's burial, but Hobart dined with him on Mar. 6 and undoubtedly heard words of comfort from Sewall on that occasion. Near the beginning of the poem, Hobart referred to his friend's absence from Boston: Sewall was away from the city from Mar. 22 to Mar. 29, at which time he was conducting court business in Plymouth. Sewall arranged for *Martij 27. 1712* to be published as a broadside, adding at the end a pious distich of his own (initialed "S.S."), which he had composed independently and entered, with minor variations in punctuation and capitalization, in his *Diary* for May 16, 1711.

Although generally undistinguished, Hobart's poem is nonetheless written in fair to good Latin, closer in style to Medieval than to Classical Latin: "O, tibi quae, faciam! compresbyterique / Partibus addicti, faciant [Kata prosklisin ouden]. / Felices! si sint cum judice presbyter instar / Numinis Aeterni, quem munera nulla movebunt." Richard Henchman's (q.v.) translation, which has been called "excellent," enlarges on Hobart's Latin, is somewhat more eloquent, and has thus enhanced Hobart's reputation as an early eighteenth-century versifier: "O, that myself and fellow-Presbyters / Might do what You to do This Poem stirrs: / That wee from th' Byas of all *Faction* clear / Might by th' impartial Rules of Justice steer. / How happy would our Bench and Pulpit be, / If like to Heaven from Bribes and Parties free."

Hobart's only other published work, *The Absence of the Comforter Described*, was probably adapted from a series of sermons on Lamentations 1:16. In this text, the biblical writer alludes to the desolation of Jerusalem, deserted by God because of her sins. In the tradition of the New Eng. jeremiad, Hobart began his discourse along similar lines, lamenting the sins that have caused God to withdraw his spirit from the inhabitants of New Eng. and giving a systematic account of God's withdrawal from sinners, after which he sought to reconcile this situation with the doctrine of God's presence everywhere in his creation. Commenting on I Corinthians 1:12, Hobart declared: "Joy arising primarily from our doings, is not the Joy of the Holy Ghost. Our depending on Justification hereupon, is so far a Sign of his Withdrawing from us." Hobart objected to the "very rash and false Assertion, that men must be brought to that pass as to be Willing to be Damned, before they can be true Believers and Receive true Comfort." Although Hobart acknowledged that we are condemned by God's law, he held that "this is quite another thing from being willing to undergo Damnation, which includes in it a full & perfect Enmity against God and Christ, which no man should be willing to."

The Absence of the Comforter also reveals the talent for selecting effective imagery and phrasing that no doubt contributed to Hobart's popularity as a preacher. He described, for example, "the Means of Grace...as the Chariot, by which the Holy Spirit Rides Triumphantly into the Soul." Commenting on Isaiah 3:9, he reflected: "Men dig deep to hide their Counsels, their Works are in the dark, and they say who seeth them? And indeed as to man it may be answered, None seeth them; yet they are all in the light of God's countenance, It were Atheism to imagine otherwise." On persons who are merely reformed in character rather than truly converted, he warned: "They are but on the outside of the Ark: unless they get within it, the Waves will Dash them off, and they Perish Miserably." On the brevity of vain and mad mirth, he commented, "They make a great Blaze to little purpose... the Blaze of it instead of warming doth but scorch & singe...it is quickly over & gone; not like a fire of Coals or sollid Wood which is more serviceable & durable."

The Absence was published posthumously. More than likely its editor, Eliphalet Adams, was mistaken in his assertion that Hobart modestly wrote this long discourse "for Private Use, without any thought or Design of Communicating it to the Publick." Had such been the case, Hobart could just as easily have left these materials in the form of the separate sermons from which they were gathered. Rather, his copious use of exhortation suggests that he hoped that there would eventually be readers for this discourse.

Suggested Readings: CCNE; FCNEV; Sibley-Shipton (II, 235-238). *See also* Francis Jackson, *A History...of Newton* (1854), pp. 122, 308-309; Samuel Eliot Morison, *Harvard College in the Seventeenth Century* (1936), I, 132-138, 216-219; Henry K. Rowe, *Tercentenary History of Newton* (1930), pp. 20, 44-46; George Parker Winship, *The Cambridge Press: 1638-1692* (1945), pp. 76-81; Harold Field Worthley, *An Inventory of the Records of the Particular (Congregational) Churches of Massachusetts Gathered, 1620-1805*, HTS, 25 (1970), 426-427. Hobart's poem is reprinted, with Henchman's translation, in Samuel Sewall, *Letter-Book*, CMHS, 6th ser., 1 (1886), 315-317.

Richard Frothingham
University of Arkansas at Little Rock

NOAH HOBART (1706-1773)

Works: *Ministers of the Gospel* (1747); *A Serious Address* (1748); *Civil Government* (1751); *A Second Address* (1751); *A Congratulatory Letter* (1755); *The Principles of Congregational Churches* (1759); *A Vindication of the Piece* (1761); *An Attempt to Illustrate* (1765); *Excessive Wickedness* (1768).

Biography: Remembered as "the great protagonist of eighteenth-century Connecticut Congregationalism," Noah Hobart was born at Hingham, Mass., on Jan. 12, 1706. His father was David Hobart, and his grandfather was Peter Hobart, the first pastor at Hingham. The nephew of Nehemiah Hobart (q.v.), Noah Hobart attended Harvard (A.B., 1724; A.M., 1729), and after graduation he taught school for a time in either Duxbury or Marshfield. For a short period of time he assisted Jedidiah Andrews at the First Presbyterian Church of Philadelphia.

In 1733 Hobart succeeded Joseph Webb (q.v.) as pastor of the First Congregational Church in Fairfield, Conn., where he remained for the rest of his life. In 1750 Hobart preached the Connecticut Election Sermon, and in 1752 he became a fellow at Yale. Throughout Hobart's ministry, he engaged in a series of printed debates of an ecclesiastical nature. Hobart married twice: to Ellen Sloss in 1735 and to Priscilla Lothrop (a widow) in 1753. His son by his second wife graduated from Yale and became a U.S. senator. Hobart died peacefully on Dec. 6, 1773. An inscription on his tombstone states that "He served God and his generation with Fidelity, and Usefulness." Noah Welles (q.v.), whose ordination sermon Hobart had preached, delivered Hobart's funeral sermon. About Hobart, Welles commented that "The mild Affability of his Temper, and the friendly Benevolence of his Heart, made him easy Access to all who sought his Conversation and Company, from which few ever parted without sensible Pleasure and Improvement."

Critical Appraisal: During the Great Awakening, Noah Hobart distinguished himself, through two series of pamphlet debates, as one of the leading Old Light spokesmen against the New Light itinerant preachers and the clerics of the Church of England in the American colonies. The first of these debates began in 1746 when Hobart preached *Ministers of the Gospel* at the ordination of Noah

Welles. In this sermon, Hobart incidentally attacked the "Arrogance" of itinerant preachers and Church of England ministers who challenged the validity of Congregational and Presbyterian churches to decide ecclesiastical matters on a local rather than centralized basis. In response to these charges, James Wetmore (q.v.) published *A Vindication* of the Episcopal position, to which Hobart further replied with his *Serious Address*, a document which denied the authority of British law over matters of church polity in New Eng. and drew attention to the meddling of S.P.G. missionaries in areas of New Eng. where Hobart felt they had no valid reason for preaching.

Angered by Hobart's *Serious Address*, John Beach (q.v.) escalated the controversy by publishing his *Calm and Dispassionate Vindication*, in which he not only lambasted the very basis of Congregational principles but openly attacked Hobart's character as well. To add authority to his argument, Beach appended to his pamphlet a preface by Samuel Johnson (q.v.) which also contained *ad hominem* attacks on Hobart's integrity. In consequence of Beach's pamphlet, Hobart in turn published *A Second Address to the Members of the Episcopal Separation in New-England*, in which he drew further aspersions on the work of the S.P.G. missionaries, and in response to Hobart's pamphlet, Beach published a *Continuation* of his earlier pamphlet, in which he continued to argue the authority of the Church of England over the Congregational churches of New Eng. As a result of these controversies, Hobart became something of a local celebrity, having made it appear that Eng. was over-zealous in maintaining control over all aspects of colonial life, political as well as theological. According to a contemporary, Hobart became "so popular that all his Books are taken up" and immediately sold.

Known as the "Wallingford Controversy," the second of Hobart's pamphlet debates began when Joseph Noyes, pastor at Yale where Hobart had recently become a fellow, was accused of Arminianism, and Hobart, Solomon Williams (q.v.), and President Thomas Clap (q.v.) of Yale attempted to have him removed from a position of influence over the students. Opposed to this action, the congregation at neighboring Wallingford selected the liberal cleric James Dana (q.v.) as its minister, an action intended as a direct insult to Clap and Hobart, who preferred a more conservative choice. In so doing, the Wallingford congregation brought to public attention one of the fundamental weaknesses in the Congregational system. By virtue of its governing authority, an individual congregation could, if it so chose, subvert the conservative nature of the system and select someone whom the other churches in the area might dislike, provided that it could locate three ministers who would agree to serve at the ordination. In an attempt to explain and restore the integrity of the original system, Hobart wrote a series of pamphlets: *The Principles of Congregational Churches, A Vindication of the Piece Entitled "The Principles of Congregational Churches,"* and *An Attempt to Illustrate and Confirm the Ecclesiastical Constitution of the Consociated Churches in the Colony of Connecticut*. Before the debate subsided, it attracted the attention of church leaders throughout New Eng., including Joseph

Bellamy (q.v.), Robert Sandeman (q.v.), Jonathan Todd (q.v.), and Roger Wolcott (q.v.).

As one of the leading theological spokesmen of his day, Hobart did much to defend New Eng. Congregationalism against the various tides of change and reform which threatened to overwhelm it. Although even his admirers acknowledged that Hobart was "a poor Speaker" who "made a very indifferent Figure in the Pulpit," he nonetheless possessed a lively and well-educated intellect which he used to advantage in his writings. Throughout the 1740s and 1750s, pamphlets such as those written by Hobart helped to refine and sharpen the rhetoric and form which would later culminate in the spirited pamphlets written by American patriots at the time of the Revolutionary War. In fact, it has been suggested that in drawing public attention to Church of England efforts to regulate the ecclesiastical affairs of New Eng. Hobart himself "did more to alienate Connecticut from England than did the Stamp Act."

Suggested Readings: CCNE; Sibley-Shipton (VII, 359-368); Sprague (I, 375-376). *See also* Alan Heimert, *Religion and the American Mind* (1966), pp. 119, 171, 367, 375; Ezra Stiles, *The Literary Diary of Ezra Stiles*, ed. Franklin B. Dexter (1901), I, 425; Noah Welles, *Discourse Delivered at Fairfield* (1774).

James A. Levernier
University of Arkansas at Little Rock

JOHN HODGKINSON (c. 1766-1805)

Works: *A Narrative of His Connection with the Old American Company, from 5 September, 1792 - 31 March, 1797* (1797); *The Man of Fortitude; Or, The Knight's Adventure* (1807).

Biography: John Hodgkinson was born near Manchester, Eng., as John Meadowcroft (also spelled *Meadowcraft*) sometime around 1766 or 1767. He adopted his mother's maiden name of Hodgkinson, he began playing in provincial circuits, and he then took leading roles in theatres in Bath and Bristol. He wrote to Lewis Hallam and John Henry, managers of the American Company in N.Y., requesting a position. He married Miss Britt and with her, her mother, and her sister, he journeyed to America. His first performances were in Philadelphia, where he appeared in 1792; he quickly became the leading actor of the Old American Company, centered primarily in N.Y. He was joint manager of the company with Hallam for the 1794-1795 season. In the 1795-1796 season, William Dunlap (q.v.) joined the partnership, and Hallam had dropped out by 1798. A short while later, Hodgkinson left the N.Y. company to form his own in Boston. He returned to N.Y. as an actor, then moved on to Charleston, where he was both actor and manager. He applied to lease the Park Theatre in N.Y. but died Sept. 12, 1805, before he could take over.

He was the finest actor America had yet seen. He had amazing versatility and a huge range of parts. His fine singing voice made him much sought after in concerts of the time.

Critical Appraisal: John Hodgkinson was the author of several trifles for the theatre, including a prologue to Mrs. Hatton's *Tammany*; a one-act pasticcio, *The Launch* (with music assembled by Pelissier); an adaptation of an English comic opera; and a play, *The Man of Fortitude; Or, The Knight's Adventure* (first performed Jun. 7, 1797, and first published in 1807), a drama he expanded into a full-length work after reading William Dunlap's one-act version.

The Man of Fortitude is a weak play but a good example of the sort of drama that actors used as novelties to gain an audience for a benefit. It is in three acts. It begins on a gloomy heath where Sir Bertrand is traveling with his servant Carlos on a political mission. He has been fighting for three years in an attempt to forget that on his wedding night, Hortensia, his bride, was stolen from him. Eventually, he and Carlos find shelter in a castle that seems haunted by fiends. The fiends turn out to be kind-hearted bandits whose leader is in love with a female captive. It is discovered that the captive is Hortensia and that the bandits have killed her abductors. The piece ends happily with Sir Bertrand and Hortensia reunited and Sir Bertrand promising to try to achieve pardons for all. The high-flown passages are all in stodgy blank verse, and the comic passages (primarily involving Carlos) are in prose. Hodgkinson acted Sir Bertrand, and Mrs. Johnson performed Hortensia in the first performance, thereby assuring some sort of audience for the popular Mrs. Johnson's benefit. The piece was only rarely performed thereafter.

The most important work left to us by Hodgkinson was not a play at all, but his *A Narrative of His Connection with the Old American Company, from 5 September, 1792-31 March, 1797* (1797). While much of the text deals with his difficulties with Mrs. Hallam, leading to his temporary resignation from the Old American Company, most of this booklet deals with the management of a theatre in eighteenth-century America—the musicians, rehearsals, stage management, benefits, and decisions about repertory and casting. Hodgkinson's *Narrative* is an invaluable primary source for those attempting to understand the early theatre in America.

Suggested Readings: DAB. *See also* William Dunlap, *Diary*, (1930) I, 1786, 1788, 1797-1798; idem, *A History of The American Theatre* (1832), pp. 181-191; Billy J. Harbin, 1-43; "Hodgkinson's Last Years: At The Charleston Theatre, 1803-05," ThS, 13 (Nov. 1972), 20; idem, "Hodgkinson and His Rivals at the Park: The Business of Early Romantic Theatre in America," ESQ, 20 (1974), 148-169; Julian Mates, *The American Musical Stage Before 1800* (1962), pp. 108-110; G.C.D. Odell, *Annals of the New York Stage* (1927), I, 315ff; II, passim; William C. Young, *Famous Actors and Actresses of the American Stage: Documents of American Theatre History* (1975), I, 525-530.

Julian Mates
Long Island University

JOHN HOLME (fl. 1685-1701)

Works: *A True Relation of the Flourishing State of Pennsylvania* (w. 1696; pub. 1848).

Biography: Virtually nothing is known about John Holme before his arrival in America in 1685 except that he was born in Eng. According to his own testimony in *A True Relation*, Holme lived in the Barbados before setting foot on the Continent. Soon after his arrival in America, he settled in Philadelphia, where he purchased the first house built on the Schuylkill. In his poem, Holme unabashedly stated he was not a Friend: "I am not Quaker, nor can I / With their mistakes at all comply." Even so, he praised the Quakers and their thriving enterprise in the New World.

Holme fared well politically in William Penn's (q.v.) experiment in toleration, serving from 1687 until 1690 as one of Philadelphia's magistrates. Early in 1690, he, along with four other prominent Philadelphians, petitioned the Provincial Council to prepare a suitable defense of the city against the French, who were then at war with the English and who had stationed hostile troops within striking distance of Philadelphia. In the conclusion of his poem, written six years later, Holme summarily condemned the destructiveness of war and urged those who would escape its ravages to come to Pa. With the French threat apparently thwarted, the poet affirmed that the colony's residents could "bide and safely hide / Whilst Europe broils in war." Perhaps, nonetheless, the intermittent build-up of French forces on the frontier moved Holme to leave his beloved Philadelphia and relocate in Salem, N.J., where he died in 1701.

Critical Appraisal: Written in 1696, Holme's *A True Relation of the Flourishing State of Pennsylvania* did not appear in print until 1848. Moses Coit Tyler, implying that the poem probably should never have been published, assessed the piece as scarcely rising to the puerile; indeed, he remarked, it "approach[es] the idiotic." Tyler's judgment, however, appears to have been made from a hasty reading, for the poem is a pleasant and energetic celebration of the many fine qualities of Pa. that recommend it to prospective émigrés. Holme's penchant for cataloging practically everything the colony offered from good soil and fruits to shipbuilders and block makers prefigures the poetry of Walt Whitman. *A True Relation* is hardly great poetry, but neither is it "idiotic."

The weakest point of *A True Relation* lies in its design. Holme delayed statement of his objective in writing the piece until the section preceding his conclusion. In these penultimate verses, he declared "My business. . . is to. . .disprove / Those lying tongues. . .Brought ill report on this good land." The poet arranged his confutation of "Those lying tongues" into an "Introduction" followed by forty-five separately named sections varying from four to seventy-one lines and concluding with an eight-stanza hymn. The basis for the order appears to be completely desultory, one section titled "The Praise of Quakers," for example, immediately followed by "Of Precious Stones." The arrangement of the named sections resembles what one may guess mirrors the order of composition, an activity perhaps stretching over many days and weeks. Although Holme tried his hand at three variations of verse—tetrameter couplets, pentameter couplets, and the already identified hymn or common stanza—he definitely preferred the faster paced, simpler tetrameter couplets, which compose well over half the piece. One triplet, a variation commonly used during the time, strikingly echoes today's idiom; describing the kind of strong drink available in the colony, the poet counseled, "Some men have made a little wine, / Whose good endeavors may in time / Make many tuns right superfine."

The two themes that recur with some consistency and that link an otherwise unruly arrangement identify the colony as a land of plenty and opportunity, particularly for the poor, but only if they are willing to work. The poet especially emphasized the production of surplus grains; here Holme suggested inchoate agricultural capitalism. Some sections are worthy of note because of what they suggest about American social history. "Barbados," which names the island country Holme visited before he came to America, tells of the severe oppression of the lower class of whites by an indifferent aristocracy. This section also reveals, early on in the history of slavery, that the upper class's black slaves "their masters fain would kill, / And all the white people's blood spill." Here may be traced the beginnings of white fear of blacks that resulted in the close legal control of slaves (e.g., denial of an education) before the Civil War and gave way to the Jim Crow laws afterwards. Holme promised the poor whites equal treatment under the law in Pa. but offered nothing of improvement for blacks. In another section, "The Laws," the poet averred that, in the colony, "Each man here freely serves his God / Free from the persecutor's rod." In "Of Schools," Holme related that free schools are maintained by the generous for the poor; doubtless he has here described one of the first American experiments in public education.

Although Holme's rhymes are not always perfect, *A True Relation* is more noteworthy than many American poems of the time. His observations on early Pa. urban society have something to tell historians, and his attitude of celebration regarding the colonial experiment and his energetic, capacious cataloging of many aspects of colonial life bespeak qualities that are distinctly American.

Suggested Readings: T₁; T₂. *See also Appleton's Cyclopaedia of American Biography* (1887), III, 239; *Colonial Records of Pennsylvania* (1852), I, 334; J. Thomas Scharf and Thompson Westcott, *History of Philadelphia: 1609-1884* (1884), I, 124, 143; John F. Watson, *Annals of Philadelphia and Pennsylvania* (1870), I, 52. The complete text of *A True Relation* can now be found only in BHSP, (1848), 161-180; other selections appear in *Colonial American Poetry*, ed. Kenneth Silverman (1968), pp. 19-27.

John C. Shields
Illinois State University

ABIEL HOLMES (1763-1837)

Works: *Sermon on Freedom and Happiness of America* (1795); *Sermon for National Thanksgiving* (1795); *A Family Tablet* (1796); *Life of Ezra Stiles* (1798); *Sermon . . . After Interment of Increase Sumner* (1799); *Sermon . . . at Ordina-*

tion of Jonathan Whittaker (1799); *Sermon Preached at Brattle-Street Church* (1799); *The Counsel of Washington* (1800); *Sermon Preached at Cambridge* (1800); *American Annals* (1805, 1829, 1837); *Discourse Before Society for Propagating the Gospel Among Indians* (1808); *Discourse on Validity of Presbyterian Ordination* (1810); *Address Before Washington Benevolent Society* (1813); *Address Before American Antiquarian Society* (1814); *Discourse at Opening New Almshouse* (1818); *Two Sermons on Thirty-Seventh Anniversary of Abiel Holmes' Installation* (1829).

Biography: John Holmes, owner of a saw and fulling mill and possibly a surveyor, moved the Holmes clan from Milton, Mass., to Woodstock, Conn., in 1686, where his grandson David, a pious man nicknamed "Deacon," grew up and later served as captain in the French and Indian War (1758) and then as regimental surgeon for four years in the Revolutionary War. David Holmes married Temperance Bishop from Norwich, Conn., and they had two daughters and eight sons; one son became a general, one a doctor, and their second child, Abiel, born on Dec. 24, 1763, became a minister, historian, and father of Oliver Wendell Holmes. As did his son after him, Abiel Holmes credited his maternal side, the Bishops and Hewets, with his intellectual stimulation. When Abiel was 15, his father moved the family from Woodstock to Yale (New Haven) probably so that his sons could better afford college.

John Holmes died in 1779, the same year Abiel enrolled at Yale, where he was a conscientious student of conservative theology, and graduated in Sept. 1783 "with honour and a respectable part at commencement." On Sept. 15, 1785, he was ordained with the keynote sermon delivered by Levi Hart (q.v.). For seven years, Abiel served as evangelical minister in Ga., returning to New Eng. in 1792 for installation as pastor of the First Church (Congregational) of Cambridge, home of the former Provincial Congresses and the Committee of Safety. In 1790 he had wed Mary Stiles, daughter of Ezra Stiles (q.v.), president of Yale; together and with her sisters, they produced a collection of poems called *A Family Tablet*, written in the mock-epic style of the Connecticut Wits, with Holmes adopting the nom de plume MYRON. A portrait of Abiel by Edward Savage for 1795 depicts him as a handsome, youthful-looking man.

Abiel's serious writing career began with Mary's death in 1795, when he published two sermons and began the *Life of Stiles*, emphasizing his father-in-law's intellectual leadership and conservative open-mindedness. On Mar. 26, 1801, Holmes married Sarah Wendell, daughter of a rich and powerful family that counted the Quincys, Cabots, and Bradstreets among their ancestors, and they had five children. Abiel continued to publish, and his magnum opus was *American Annals; Or, A Chronological Survey of America, from Its Discovery in 1492* for which Thomas Jefferson (q.v.) had loaned his *Mémoires de L'Amerique*; this history was praised by the London *Quarterly Review*, and its author was awarded an honorary degree by Edinburgh University.

An otherwise peaceful life was disrupted by the schism of 1827-1829 when Holmes's flock complained of his outdated orthodoxy and criticized his oratorical style for being "as placid as the preacher looked." Holmes quarreled with his wife over a woman he had excommunicated for "contumacious behavior," and, in 1829, when all but sixty members of his congregation left in protest, he lost his church. Holmes was a man who had outlived his era, and it is no surprise that he saw himself as the antiquated oddity portrayed in his son's poem "The Last Leaf"; he would have recognized the brand of theology parodied in his son's "The Deacon's Masterpiece, or The One-Hoss Shay." In "The Vanity of Life," one of his last essays before his death on Jun. 4, 1837, Holmes commented on this phenomenon not so much apologizing for his outdatedness as warning America in its Jacksonian Age that the country "was growing too fast for its heart." Oliver Wendell Holmes refused to permit his father's biography to be written because he felt a fair, impartial one was impossible in the shadow of the recent church schism, a suspicion that subsequent biographies appear to confirm. Abiel's wife survived him until Aug. 19, 1862.

Critical Appraisal: Abiel Holmes was primarily a minister in the Puritan tradition that reached out for authority in politics, education, and daily life as well as in religion. For example, the two main points of one sermon are political: that Union is essential and that America should avoid "those overgrown military establishments which are particularly hostile to republican liberty." Before 1800 Holmes called for a national religion, saying one should dare to be "a Christian in an unbelieving age and before a scoffing world" and cited three contemporary heresies—that the Supreme Being is no other than nature uncreated and uncreatable, that man when free wants no other divinity than himself, that reason dethrones both the kings of earth and the kings of heaven. After 1800 he emphasized scholarship and thus, although an anomaly in liberal Cambridge, could be made overseer and teacher of ecclesiastical history at Harvard as well as trustee of Andover Seminary. His most significant work, *American Annals*, is of great merit especially in its thorough scholarship, but it runs two risks. Its historicism borders on *antiquarianism*, an amassing of facts not united by an impelling idea, and its tendency to conservative bias is demonstrated by its failure in later editions to mention events such as Henry Ware's appointment at Harvard as the first nonorthodox professor of divinity. Although called "liberal for a Connecticut man," Holmes was a staunch public defender of a theological and political tradition that was, as his son later argued, collapsing; yet his private views may have been less chauvinistic, since what he accented in his *Life* is Ezra Stiles's skepticism, Arminianism, Deism, and racial tolerance.

His poetry—sentimental, secular, decorous, witty—is not original, but in his discourses, which he distinguished from essays for having greater "unity of design," he attempted to abjure the abstract, abstruse, and metaphysical in favor of more concreteness and simplicity of style, because he blamed the current disinterest in sermons on the Puritans' obsession with convoluted methodology— "the ramified heads, the negative and positive propositions, the exegetical and elenchtical divisions, the doctrines, inferences, uses, and applications, which encumber and disfigure the sermons of our forefathers." Yet his style remained old-fashioned, full of quotations from poets, the Classics, and the Bible, while he himself remained a lucid, orderly, and well-researched man of letters, a New Eng. patriot, and a Federalist who believed strongly in reason, saying of the Salem witch trials that they represented an outbreak of passion that "sound philosophy and useful knowledge" could repress. His life's model was Ezra Stiles who, Holmes believed, proved that ultimately "the union of piety with learning forms the sublimest human character."

Suggested Readings: DAB; Dexter (IV, 277-285); Sprague (II, 240-246); T$_2$. *See also* C. D. Bowen, *Yankee from Olympus* (1944); E. P. Hoyt, *The Improper Bostonian* (1979); E.M. Tilton, *Amiable Autocrat* (1947).

Henry Golemba
Wayne State University

WILLIAM HOOKE (1601-1678)

Works: *New-Englands Teares* (1641); *New-Englands Sence* (1645); Preface, *The Saints*, by John Davenport (with Joseph Carlyl[e]; 1661); *The Privilege of the Saints* (1673); *A Discourse Concerning the Witnesses* (1681).

Biography: William Hooke was born in 1601 to wealthy parents in Southampton, Eng. He entered Trinity College, Oxford, in 1616 and received a B.A. in 1620, and an M.A. in 1623. He then took orders in the Church of England and served as vicar at Axmouth in Devonshire before being forced to flee for his nonconformity. Hooke probably arrived in New Eng. in 1636; in 1637 he was appointed minister of the newly settled town of Taunton, Conn. In 1644 Hooke left Taunton for New Haven, where he spent the next twelve years as a teacher under John Davenport (q.v.).

In 1656 Hooke sailed back to Eng., where he obtained the mastership at Savoy hospital, Westminster; and, partly through the influence of his wife of forty-five years, Jane Whalley Hooke, who had returned to Eng. in 1654, he was appointed Oliver Cromwell's domestic chaplain. Whalley was Cromwell's cousin, sister of Cromwell's Gen. Edward Whalley, and a noted benefactress to the Regicides. During the rest of Cromwell's reign, Hooke was a powerful influence in Eng., but after the Restoration, he was ejected from Savoy and lived the rest of his life as a silenced minister in obscurity. He died in or near London on Mar. 21, 1678, at age 77 and was buried in the London cemetery Bunhill Fields. A table in Centre Church, New Haven, commemorates his life and services.

Critical Appraisal: The works that appeared near William Hooke's death are as conventional as their titles, and the preface he wrote with Joseph Carlyle is equally unremarkable. His reputation as one of the most polished and ornamental writers in New Eng. rests on his two early occasional sermons, *New-Englands Teares* and *New-Englands Sence*. Their stylistic peculiarity immediately stands out, for Hooke made good on the promise of the preface to *New-Englands Teares* that the reader should "expect not eare-pleasing, but heart-affecting phrases in it." The author's goal is not to "inform the judgement" but to "worke upon the affections" by rendering the saints' spiritual war against the reprobate in a series of vividly realized battle scenes replete with cannons that belch fire and smoke, terror and death; men struck dead in the twinkling of an eye; and a parade of dismembered soldiers horrifying the widows and children who look on. Hooke returns to his battle images in the even more sensationalistic *New-Englands Sence*, which begins with a tirade against those "monsters among men that the Prelates are, trained up by Tygers, whom no incestuous offspring of Lot can parallel by a thousand degrees!" Hooke's wrath grows even more violent as the sermon proceeds, and the concluding section on the Catholic persecutions in Ire. ascends to a rhetorical climax that rivals even most exaggerated evangelical hysteria of the 1700s: "Oh those incarnate *Irish* Devils! let them be often in our sight. Their blasphemies, their burnings, their robberies, their rapes, their rostings, their strippings, rippings, hangings, drownings, dis-memberings, butcheries."

In addition to their military metaphors and hyperbolic collections of outrages, Hooke's sermons offer a more subtle insight into the complicated emotional dilemma of men caught between their traditions as English churchmen and their fate as New Eng. Puritans. The address to the reader in *New-Englands Teares* is a proclamation of the colonists' love "to a Countrey left," and it raises the difficult questions of the New Englanders' responsibility to the mother country they have fled. The author of the preface dismissed these questions, but they persist in a series of letters that Hooke wrote from Eng. to leading Puritan divines in Plymouth and Boston after the Restoration. Writing under the pseudonym "D.G." and addressing the letters in an elaborate code, Hooke described the virulent attacks on Puritanism in the period and praised the "crosse Capers" with which the exiled dissenters continued to harass the new monarch. But joined with his admiration for the New Englanders is a bitter, self-recriminating admission of his own silence in the immediate presence of the abuses he described that offers us an intimate record of the geographical and political complexities of a Puritan conscience in the latter part of the seventeenth century.

Suggested Readings: CCNE; Sprague (I, 104-106); T₁. *See also* Leonard Bacon, *Thirteen Historical Discourses* (1839); William Bradford, *History of Plymouth Plantation* (1856; rep., 1912), II, 261-262; Samuel Hopkins Emery, *The Ministry of Taunton* (1853); CMHS, 4th ser., 8 (1868), 260-268, 298; Cotton Mather, *Magnalia Christi Americana* (1702; rep., 1855), III, pt. iv, ch. 1, pp. 586-587; Charles M. Segal and David C. Stineback, *Puritans, Indians, and Manifest Destiny* (1977), p. 112; Benjamin Trumbull, *History of Connecticut* (1797).

Michael P. Clark
University of Michigan

SAMUEL HOOKER (1635-1697)

Works: *Righteousness Rained from Heaven* (1677).
Biography: Samuel Hooker was a son of the Rev. Thomas Hooker (q.v.), one of the leading ministers of early New Eng. and a founder of Hartford, Conn.

Born in Cambridge, Mass., in 1635, Hooker grew up in Conn. A member of the class of 1653 at Harvard College, he became a fellow of the college the following year. As early as 1657, he began to preach but for four years was without a settled pastorate, having declined in 1659 an offer from the Springfield church. In 1661 Hooker became the minister at Farmington, Conn., where he remained until his death on Nov. 6, 1697. Hooker was a vocal opponent of the Half-Way Covenant, which allowed baptized members of congregations who had not had conversion experiences to have their own children baptized, and he was a member of the Conn. commission sent to New Haven in 1662 to negotiate the union of the two colonies. Hooker delivered the election sermon in Conn. in 1677 and 1693, but only the former was printed, and it represents his sole published work.

Critical Appraisal: When Hooker addressed the Conn. voters in 1677, many New Eng. ministers believed that the Puritan colonies faced a number of problems. These clergymen believed that the settlers of the second generation were not as religious as the first generation had been. The "declension" from the founders' piety was evident, it was thought, in the people's pursuit of wealth and the lack of respect accorded ministers and religious rituals. After 1660 the clergy often pointed out these alleged failures to the settlers and called for reformation; such sermons have come to be called *jeremiads*.

Righteousness Rained from Heaven is not the best of the jeremiads, but it includes in clear prose the central message of that type of sermon and a number of the usual themes. The preacher ascribed the sufferings of the settlers to God's wrath directed against them for their sins, finding evidence of God's displeasure in the recently concluded King Philip's War with the Indians and the effects of sickness on the colonists and drought, caterpillars, and mildew on the crops. Hooker emphasized that these afflictions were not reasons for despair. "You are chastened but not destroyed," he told his listeners; "you have a breathing time yet left." He assured the people that God still cared for them; however, he insisted that they must turn to God. Just as the dry fields needed rain, the parched souls of the settlers needed a shower of grace from heaven. Although the people could not earn that grace by their own actions, unless they sought to abide by God's laws, the Lord would surely punish them further. In Hooker's words, the only hope for New Englanders was for them to become "a God-omnifying, Christ-admiring, Sin-hating, Self-denying, World-despising people."

The distinctive feature of Hooker's sermon is his frequent and skillful use of the images of rain and crops. According to the Farmington pastor, the first-generation Puritans planted the wilderness with vines and choice wheat, which represented the second generation. Just as crops cannot grow without rain, young New Englanders cannot mature in faith without the Holy Spirit poured on them from above. Just as farmers cannot produce rain by their own efforts, the colonists cannot earn grace. Like farmers, the settlers needed to be aware of their great limitations and their dependence on God for what they required. If the colonists sought after God's grace, they would be successful, because the Lord still considered them his people.

Suggested Readings: CCNE; Sibley-Shipton (I, 348-352). *See also* Emory El-liott, *Power and the Pulpit in Puritan New England* (1975), pp. 109-110; Paul R. Lucas, *Valley of Discord* (1976), pp. 127-129; Perry Miller, "Declension in a Bible Common-wealth" in *Nature's Nation* (1967), pp. 14-49; Robert Pope, *The Half-Way Covenant* (1969), pp. 123-124.

Timothy J. Sehr
Indiana University Archives

THOMAS HOOKER (1586-1647)

Works: *The Poore Doubting Christian* (1629); *The Soules Preparation* (1632); *The Soules Humiliation* (1637); *The Soules Implantation* (1637); *Foure Learned and Godly Treatises* (1638); *The Properties of an Honest Heart* (1638); *The Sinners Salvation* (1638); *The Soules Exaltation* (1638); *The Soules Ingrafting* (1638); *The Soules Possession* (1638); *The Soules Vocation* (1638); *Spiritual Thirst* (1638); *Spirituall Munition* (1638); *The Stay of the Faithfull* (1638); *Three Godly Sermons* (1638); *The Unbeleevers Preparing* (1638); *The Christians Two Chiefe Lessons* (1640); *The Paterne of Perfection* (1640); *The Soules Implanta-tion into the Naturall Olive* (1640); *The Danger of Desertion* (1641); *The Faithfull Covenanter* (1644); *A Briefe Exposition of the Lords Prayer* (1645); *An Exposi-tion of the Principles of Religion* (1645); *Heavens Treasury Opened* (1645); *The Saints Guide* (1645); *A Survey of the Summe of Church Discipline* (1648); *The Covenant of Grace Opened* (1649); *The Saints Dignitie and Dutie* (1651); *The Application of Redemption...the First Eight Books* (1656); *A Comment upon Christs Last Prayer* (1656); *The Application of Redemption...the Ninth and Tenth Books* (1659).

Biography: Thomas Hooker was born in Jul. 1586, at Marfield, Leicestershire, Eng. He went to the Market Bosworth grammar school and from 1604 until 1618 was at Queens and Emmanuel Colleges, Cambridge, where he took a B.A. in 1608 and an M.A. in 1611. At Emmanuel, where he was variously a Dixie fellow, lecturer, and catechist, Hooker underwent a religious conversion and dedicated himself to the ministry. After leaving the university, he was rector of St. George's in Esher, Surrey, then a lecturer at St. Mary's in Chelmsford, Essex, where he also maintained a school in the nearby village of Little Baddow. When William Laud, then bishop of London, began to restrict and remove nonconforming ministers in the late 1620s, Hooker fled to Holland, but not before consulting with the associates of the Massachusetts Bay Company. He was invited in 1631 by a faction of the English church in Amsterdam to assist in the ministry, but John Paget, the pastor, opposed his appointment and engaged him in controversy. He then went to Delft as an assistant to John Forbes but in 1633 left for New Eng., arriving on the same ship with John Cotton (q.v.) and Samuel Stone (q.v.).

In New Eng. Hooker and Stone organized a church at Newtown (now Cambridge), where a group of Essex supporters had previously settled, and where he became embroiled in disputes between Thomas Dudley (q.v.) and Governor John Winthrop (q.v.) and was also caught up in the controversies raised by Roger Williams (q.v.) and John Endicott. In 1636 Hooker and a large part of his congregation disposed of their Newtown holdings and immigrated to Hartford, Conn. When the General Court of Conn. first met in May 1638 to draw up its Fundamental Orders, Hooker delivered an important sermon outlining the relationship between the people and their magistrates. Although the notes of this sermon were formerly cited as evidence for his democratic attitudes, this view is no longer commonly accepted. He returned to Boston in Aug. 1637 to serve as one of the moderators of the Antinomian Synod, and he returned once again in 1645 to an assembly of ministers called to consider responses to the Presbyterian-oriented Westminster Assembly. The first of these meetings signaled the triumph of the preparationist theology of Hooker and his colleagues as a nearly official view of the process of salvation. At the later meeting, Hooker presented for inspection and comment a draft of his *Survey of the Summe of Church Discipline*, which became one of the definitive statements of the New Eng. way. The finished draft was lost at sea while en route to Eng., and he was apparently still polishing the rewritten manuscript at his death. Hooker died at Hartford on Jul. 7, 1647.

Critical Appraisal: Along with John Cotton and Thomas Shepard (q.v.), Thomas Hooker was one of the most influential ministers of the first generation in New Eng. and was probably the one with the greatest share of literary talent. His sermon collections examining the various stages that the soul passes through in the conversion process have been widely reprinted, and they are marked equally by his significant literary and rhetorical gifts and by his compassionate attention to the doubts and anxieties of souls caught up in the difficulties of spiritual rebirth. His *Survey of the Summe of Church Discipline* is also remembered for its masterly defense and explanation of the independent congregational church order of New Eng.

Hooker's most important writings on the psychology and theology of conversion include the series, all with similar titles, beginning with *The Soules Preparation* and concluding with *The Soules Possession*, the two volumes on *The Application of Redemption*, which go over the same material, and *The Poore Doubting Christian, The Unbeleevers Preparing*, and *The Christians Two Chiefe Lessons*. The earliest printed of these documents, *The Poore Doubting Christian Drawne unto Christ*, is the most popular of his works, going into at least twenty-three printings by 1975, and it also reveals most effectively his literary skills and his central concerns. This work is in fact the "use" section of a sermon later printed in full in *The Soules Vocation*, and set apart from the usual sermonic structure, it points up the strongly practical direction of Hooker's writing. It takes the form of a debate with a soul doubting his own conversion, a doubting soul, possibly modeled after Joanna Drake, the wife of Hooker's first patron;

with gently persuasive arguments, lively prose, and a rationally organized approach to Scripture and meditation, it leads the distressed soul over the hindrances it raises to its own salvation. The concern with meditation is a characteristic of Hooker, and he dealt with the subject more fully in *The Soules Preparation, The Christians Two Chiefe Lessons*, and *The Application of Redemption*, among others.

Hooker drew upon his academic training in rhetoric and faculty psychology as organizing forces in his sermons, moving upon the errant heart by first correcting the understanding and impressing the memory, but the style of the sermons was framed for a popular audience. Colloquial, dramatic, drawing from a wide range of everyday activities and situations for their illustrative tropes, the sermons on the stages of conversion were effective in calling out the sinner lurking "behinde the Pillor," awakening him "asleep in his Pue." Hooker's moral homilies such as *The Faithful Covenanter* and those contained in *The Saints Guide* and *The Saints Dignitie and Dutie* vigorously exhorted the reprobates to examine their ways and reminded the saints of their responsibilities to their faith.

The *Survey of the Summe of Church Discipline*, a scholarly treatise rather than a sermon, was, however, intended for a learned audience. The *Survey* is at once a theological justification of the form of church government developed in New Eng., a complete model of this government, and a closely reasoned, detailed refutation of Presbyterian critics like Samuel Rutherford. Hooker's concern for church order also appears in *The Covenant of Grace Opened*, a refutation of anabaptism. Other works of special significance include *The Danger of Desertion*, his sermon preached on leaving Eng. for the Netherlands; *The Paterne of Perfection*, a consideration of the nature of God's image in man; and *A Comment upon Christs Last Prayer*, on the union of the saints with God through Christ.

Suggested Readings: CCNE; DAB; DARB; DNB; Sprague (I, 30-37); T₁. *See also* Sargent Bush, Jr., *The Writings of Thomas Hooker* (1980); Cotton Mather, *Piscator Evangelicus* (1695); Perry Miller, "Thomas Hooker and the Democracy of Connecticut," NEQ, 4 (1931), 663-712; Norman Pettit, *The Heart Prepared* (1966); Frank Shuffleton, *Thomas Hooker, 1586-1747* (1977); George H. Williams et al., *Thomas Hooker: Writings in England and Holland, 1626-1633* (1975).

Frank Shuffleton
University of Rochester

WILLIAM HOOPER (1702-1767)

Works: *Christ the Life of the True Believers* (1741); *The Apostles* (1742); *Jesus Christ the Only Way to the Father* (1742); *On the Truth and Reasonableness of the Christian Religion* (1747); *A Sermon Preached at the Funeral of Thomas Greene, Esq.* (1763).

Biography: William Hooper was born near Kelso, Scot., in 1702 and was educated at Edinburgh Univ. He assumed the pastorate of West (Congregational)

Church of Boston in 1737 and remained there until 1746. In that year, disturbed by the liberalizing influences upon the Congregational Church of the Great Awakening, he embraced the Church of England. After going to Eng. for his ordination, he returned to Boston and became rector of Trinity Church, where he remained until his death in 1767.

Hooper married Mary Dennie, daughter of Boston merchant John Dennie. His will listed the names of five children, including William Hooper (1742-1790), a signer of the Declaration of Independence.

Critical Appraisal: Although William Hooper published few of his sermons, he was, according to Nathaniel Henchman, an intelligent and forceful preacher who stood "high in the Esteem of Gentlemen of Figure." Like most other Congregational ministers, he wrote in the plain style, and his earliest surviving sermon, *Christ the Life of the True Believers* (1741), is marked by a laboriously self-conscious structure, as he lays out the "heads" that he will treat and "proofs" them one by one. Despite this method, no doubt an influence of his schooling at the University of Edinburgh and his desire to demonstrate the rational nature of his argument, there is, however, a certain grace in his expression in this sermon, and his later sermons maintain the same plain, unaffected diction while displaying a suppleness of structure.

Christ the Life of the True Believers is particularly important to an understanding of Hooper, because it sets forth a conservative, even literal, interpretation of the New Testament, maintaining that at the "end of the world" Christ "will descend from Heaven in all his Glory sitting on a cloud. . ., with a vast and numberless Army of Angels." At that time, our bodies will be raised from the graves, he continued, "freed from all Seeds of Mortality and Corruption." Hooper's conservative bent can also be seen in *Jesus Christ the Only Way to the Father*, where he argued that Christ is the "only Creature capable of restoring man to his sanctity and delivering him to God." According to Hooper, philosophers, politicians, and lawgivers are incapable of leading man to God, and his congregation should "not with open eyes run into everlasting Destruction."

But Hooper was not one to call up strong emotions in his efforts to persuade his congregation to "conform" to Christ like "so many copies of this divine Original." Rather his method, stipulating the correctness of the Scriptures, was to insist upon the use of reason to prove the validity of the Christian faith. Consequently, as early as 1742, in his sermon *The Apostles neither Imposters nor Enthusiasts*, he enumerated the reasons that would convince any "serious and considerate" person of the truth of Christianity, including the "Sublimity of his Doctrines," "speedy Propagation of the Gospel," and "exact Accomplishment of the prophecies." This sermon was directed both at the enthusiasts of the Great Awakening who were undermining traditional religious values and the ideas of the Enlightenment, which by the 1740s had begun to influence the thought of ordinary Christians. He especially argued against the validity of faith based upon superficial enthusiasm and a faith embraced because one had been born into a churched family or because it was the custom of a time and place.

Eventually, Hooper left the Congregational Church because of his disgust with the enthusiasm that was, for him, tainting it, taking with him many of his former parishioners when he became the minister of Trinity Church. In addition, his move to the Church of England probably reflects his political sympathies. With the exception of his eldest son, William Hooper the signer, all members of his family were Loyalists and otherwise politically conservative. Even his son William was called the greatest Tory in the Continental Congress by Thomas Jefferson (q.v.), and after the Revolutionary War, the younger Hooper was an advocate of "gentle treatment" of Tories.

Suggested Readings: CCNE; DAB; Sprague (V, 122-126). *See also* Edwin A. Alderman, *Address on the Life of William Hooper, the Prophet of American Independence* (1894); *Appleton's Cyclopaedia of American Biography* (1887), III, 252; Alan Heimert, *Religion and the American Mind* (1966), p. 51; Nathaniel Henchman, *A Letter to the Reverend Mr. William Hobby* (1745).

Joseph H. Harkey
Virginia Wesleyan College

LEMUEL HOPKINS (1750-1801)

Works: *The Democratiad* (1795); *The Guillotina* (1796); *The Anarchiad* (contributor; 1786-1787, 1856); *The Political Green-House* (1799); *The Echo* (1807).

Biography: Three of the Connecticut Wits practiced medicine as well as poetry and one of them, Lemuel Hopkins, was, in both professions, preeminent. Hopkins came from a long line of Conn. farmers but turned to the study of medicine as a result of his susceptibility to tuberculosis, a disease whose treatment he came to specialize in. Hopkins served briefly as a volunteer in the Revolution, then established a reputation in Litchfield as an idiosyncratic but effective doctor. By 1784 he had transferred his practice to Hartford, where he was accepted into the circle of the Wits. Hopkins was known for his prodigious memory, his medical innovations, and his intolerance of quackery. He was awarded an honorary M.A. from Yale in 1784, and he was a founder of the Connecticut Medical Society. Although willing to provide ideas and lines to his friends and occasionally to finish a piece of poetry for anonymous publication, Hopkins never published anything in his own name. He became ill early in 1801 and died in Hartford at the age of 51.

Critical Appraisal: It has been usual to observe that Lemuel Hopkins hated sham and quackery as much in poetry and politics as in medicine. He is commonly called the most caustic of the Wits, and his several contributions to their collaborative publications are often identifiable on this basis.

Most of Hopkins's verse appeared in two of these joint efforts: *The Anarchiad*— with Joel Barlow (q.v.), David Humphreys (q.v.), and John Trumbull (q.v.)—

and *The Echo*—with Richard Alsop (q.v.), Mason Fitch Cogswell (q.v.), Theodore Dwight (q.v.), and Elihu Hubbard Smith (q.v.). *The Anarchiad* took form as a series of polemical newspaper verse (Oct. 1786-Sept. 1787), advocating a unified nation and an orderly fiscal policy and denouncing the forces of chaos as embodied in paper money, Shays' Rebellion, and the Democrats. The conception of the series—with its elaborate editorial apparatus and its "looking backwad" conceit—is variously attributed to Hopkins or to Humphreys, but it is generally agreed that Hopkins became chiefly responsible for its execution. Some of *The Anarchiad's* quarrels may now seem parochial, but it evidently did act to encourage the conveners of the Constitutional Convention. On the day before the convocation of the Convention, *Anarchiad* X (attributed to Hopkins by Parrington) ended with the "warning cry": "YE LIVE UNITED, OR DIVIDED DIE!"

The sharp sarcasms of *The Anarchiad* suited Hopkins's temperament. He brought a similar edge to the otherwise somewhat less militant satire of *The Echo*. Here certain of his contributions may be confidently identified. *Echo* XVIII first appeared in *The American Mercury*, Sept. 8, 1794. It was published separately as *The Democratiad* in 1795 before finally being included in the 1807 collected *Echo*. *The Guillotina* ("By the Author of the 'Democratiad' ") underwent similar transformations. In both works, Hopkins used a defense of John Jay's (q.v.) commercial treaty with G.B. as the occasion for slashing attacks on the principles and the persons of the Democrats. He made little use of the burlesque "Echo" device; instead, his contributions (including also "New-Year's Verses" [1795] and, with Alsop and Dwight, *The Political Green-House* [1799]) are characterized by a relish for direct, ad hominem assaults. Hopkins disdained the transparencies of initials and asterisks, and consequently, his verse at times achieves a concrete and focused indignation comparable to that of his English model Churchill.

Hopkins's uncompromising judgments and his forceful, unadorned style are clearly present in highly regarded short poems such as "On General Ethan Allen" and "Epitaph on a Patient Killed by a Cancer Quack." The former is a sharp rebuke to the Deist who "tell[s] the world the bible lies"; the latter is a pointed fable against trust in miracle cures to trivial ailments. Immune to the temptation of magniloquence, Hopkins produced a few strong satires on important political and social issues of his time.

Suggested Readings: DAB; LHUS. *See also* William K. Bottorff, ed., *The Anarchiad* (1967); Benjamin Franklin V, ed., *The Poetry of the Minor Connecticut Wits* (1970); idem, "The Published Commentary on the Minor Connecticut Wits," RALS, 8 (1978), 157-167; Leon Howard, *The Connecticut Wits* (1943); Vernon Louis Parrington, *The Connecticut Wits* (1926, 1969).

J. Kenneth Van Dover
Lincoln University

SAMUEL HOPKINS (1721-1803)

Works: *A Bold Push in a Letter to the Author of "Fair Play"* (1758); *Sin . . . an Advantage to the Universe* (1759); *An Enquiry Concerning the Prom-*

ises of the Gospel (1765); *The Life of the Late Rev. Jonathan Edwards* (1765); *The Importance and Necessity of Jesus Christ* (1768); *Two Discourses* (1768); *The True State and Character of the Unregenerate* (1769); *Animadversions on Mr. Hart's Late Dialogue* (1770); *Rare Observations* (1770); *An Inquiry into the Nature of True Holiness* (1773); *A Dialogue Concerning the Slavery of the Africans* (1776); *An Inquiry Concerning the Future State of Those Who Die in Their Sins* (1783); *A Dialogue Concerning the Slavery of the Africans* (1785); *A Discourse upon the Slave-Trade* (1793); *The System of Doctrines* (1793); *A Treatise on the Millennium* (1793); *The Life and Character of Miss Susanna Anthony* (1796); *Memoirs of the Life of Mrs. Sarah Osborne* (1799); *Twenty-one Sermons* (1803); *A Dialogue Between a Calvinist and a Semi-Calvinist* (1805); *Sketches of the Life of Samuel Hopkins, Written by Himself* (1805); *Timely Articles on Slavery* (1854).

Biography: Founder of the influential Hopkinsian school of theology, Samuel Hopkins was born in Waterbury, Conn., on Sept. 17, 1721. Hopkins graduated from Yale in 1741 and following in the footsteps of his well-known, Indian missionary uncle, Samuel Hopkins (1693-1755) of West Springfield, Mass., Hopkins decided to study for the Congregational ministry. Impressed with Jonathan Edwards's (q.v.) address at the Yale Commencement of 1741, Hopkins moved to Northampton, Mass., several months after graduation to pursue theological studies under the eminent Calvinist divine. Licensed to preach in 1742, Hopkins was ordained at the frontier town of Housatonic (now Great Barrington), in 1743. When Edwards settled in nearby Stockbridge in 1750, Hopkins renewed the close friendship and theological discipleship that had begun in Northampton a decade earlier. Hopkins remained in Great Barrington until 1769, when dwindling financial support and opposition to his Edwardsian theology and ecclesiastical policies led him to request a dismissal from his church. A year later, he was ordained over the First Congregational Church of Newport, R.I., where he preached until his death on Dec. 20, 1803, and where his theological concerns became increasingly focused on social reform—particularly the antislavery movement.

Critical Appraisal: The most distinguished student of Jonathan Edwards, the first biographer of the brilliant theologian, and the editor of his manuscripts, Samuel Hopkins was one of the major Calvinist intellectuals in late eighteenth-century New Eng. An original theologian, Hopkins upheld but also modified his teacher's thought, and he contributed three original doctrinal interpretations to the New Divinity, the school of theology that grew from the teachings of Edwards. In *Sin, Thro' Divine Interpretation, an Advantage to the Universe* (1759), Hopkins stressed divine sovereignty over creation, arguing that God does not merely permit sin in the world, He wills it into existence for good ends. Hopkins advanced another provocative theological interpretation in *An Inquiry into the Promises of the Gospel* (1765), where he depreciated the role of means (prayer, Bible reading, and church attendance) in regeneration and insisted that the more an outwardly moral but unconverted person used these means, the more such an individual appeared detestable in God's sight.

Hopkins's third and major theological contribution to the New Divinity derived from his efforts to reinterpret Jonathan Edwards's ethical theory. In *An Inquiry into the Nature of True Holiness* (1773), Hopkins formulated a highly original and influential doctrine of disinterested benevolence. He defined *true virtue* as disinterested love of "Being in general," that is, God and humankind. He stressed that true Christians should not be preoccupied with saving their own souls; they must lose themselves in a cause higher than their own salvation, namely, the temporal and eternal well-being of others. Hopkins's emphasis on the central place of selflessness in Christian social ethics led to the most famous tenet of his theological system: a Christian must be willing to be damned for the glory of God. "He therefore cannot know that he loves God and shall be saved," Hopkins argued in *A Dialogue Between a Calvinist and a Semi-Calvinist*, published posthumously in 1805, "until he knows he has that disposition which implies a willingness to be damned, if it be not most for the glory of God that he be saved." In other words, one could not avoid damnation except by being willing to be damned.

The selfless idealism of Hopkins's doctrine of disinterested benevolence influenced New Eng. religious reformers in the late eighteenth and early nineteenth centuries. It inspired Hopkins's own assault on slavery and the slave trade during the Revolutionary era. In the early 1770s, Hopkins preached to his congregation on the iniquity of the slave trade, and he published his first important antislavery tract, *A Dialogue Concerning the Slavery of the Africans*, in 1776. This work was dedicated to the Continental Congress, from which he sought reassurance that a 1774 resolution prohibiting the slave trade issued "not merely from political reasons; but from a conviction of the unrighteousness and cruelty of that trade and a regard to justice and benevolence." He urged the Congress not only to abolish slavery but also to launch a "thorough reformation" of all "public sins." Hopkins saw the evils of slavery and the slave trade in the context of a social order rooted in self-interest rather than true virtue. His *Dialogue* expressed the utopian hope that the Revolution and the antislavery movement would lead to broad social regeneration that would establish a truly Christian society held together by the cement of disinterested benevolence.

Hopkins persevered in the antislavery cause from the early 1770s until his death thirty years later. He also continued his theological efforts during these years of social activism. He spent a decade working on his magnum opus, *System of Doctrines* (1793), a comprehensive, 1,100-page explanation of the New Divinity. Hopkins synthesized Edwards's thought, his own "improvements" upon Edwards, and the work of other New Divinity ministers and created a complete doctrinal system of evangelical Calvinism. His *System of Doctrines* remains the fullest expression of the New Divinity, or what has often been referred to as "*the* New England school of theology*.*"

Hopkins is best understood as a transitional figure in this theological movement. Although he upheld aspects of Edwards's high Calvinism and formulated novel hyper-Calvinistic interpretations of his own, he also stressed social ethics and modified Edwards's thought in ways that foreshadowed the watered-down Calvinism of the nineteenth century. In another respect, Hopkins was a bridge between the eighteenth and nineteenth centuries. He became a hero to many antebellum New Eng. abolitionists, who recalled his early reform efforts and who read his idealistic pronouncements against slavery, and he was the hero of Harriet Beecher Stowe's novel, *The Minister's Wooing*. In 1854, long after the demise of the New Divinity, all of Hopkins's antislavery writings were reprinted under the title *Timely Articles on Slavery*.

Suggested Readings: CCNE; DAB; DARB; Dexter (II, 210-212); Sprague (I, 428-435). *See also* Joseph A. Conforti, "Samuel Hopkins and the New Divinity: Theology, Ethics, and Social Reform in Eighteenth-Century New England," WMQ, 34 (1977), 572-589; idem, "Samuel Hopkins and the Revolutionary Antislavery Movement," RIH, 38 (1979), 38-49; Oliver Wendell Elsbree, "Samuel Hopkins and His Doctrine of Disinterested Benevolence," NEQ, 7 (1935), 534-550; Joseph Haroutunian, *Piety versus Moralism: The Passing of the New England Theology* (1932); David S. Lovejoy, "Samuel Hopkins: Religion, Slavery and the Revolution," NEQ, 40 (1967), 227-243; Edwards A. Park, *Memoir of the Life and Character of Samuel Hopkins, D.D.* (1854).

Joseph Conforti
Rhode Island College

STEPHEN HOPKINS (1707-1785)

Works: *A True Representation of the Plan Formed at Albany* (1755); *Having Been Honored by My Countrymen* (1757); *Governor Hopkins's Vindication of His Conduct* (1762); *In Memory of Obadiah Brown* (1762); *To the Freemen of the Colony* (1763); *Essay on the Trade of the Northern Colonies* (1764); *To the Inhabitants of the Colony of Rhode Island* (1764); *The Rights of Colonies Examined* (1765); "A Vindication of a Late Pamphlet," *Providence Gazette* (Feb. 23, Mar. 2, Mar. 9, 1765).

Biography: Stephen Hopkins was born in Scituate, R.I., outside Providence, on Mar. 7, 1707, the son of William Hopkins, a farmer. In 1732 Hopkins became town clerk of Scituate and in 1735 president of the Town Council. He served in a number of other offices, including speaker of the General Assembly and chief justice of the Superior Court, before his election as governor of R.I. in 1755. In 1754 Hopkins, along with Martin Howard, Jr. (q.v.), represented his colony at the Albany Congress where he supported Benjamin Franklin's (q.v.) Plan of Union, support he dropped when it became apparent that the R.I. Assembly opposed any possible encroachment on their autonomy.

From the mid-1750s until the 1770s, Hopkins led a faction that engaged in a prolonged struggle against Samuel Ward of Newport and his supporters for control of R.I. This struggle was political, not ideological, and both factions were attacked by a Newport Tory "junto" of which Martin Howard, Jr., was a member, one of whose arguments was that the colony's charter, because it allowed such factionalism and petty politics, should be revoked.

Hopkins represented R.I. at both the First and Second Continental Congresses, and he signed the Declaration of Independence. In debates on the Articles of Confederation, he argued for equal votes for all states: "every Colony is a distinct person." John Adams (q.v.) remembered Hopkins's "wit, humor, anecdotes, science, and learning," and the Rev. Ezra Stiles (q.v.) described him as a man "of Penetration and Sagacity." In addition to being active politically, Hopkins was active in commercial ventures, helped establish a public subscription library, helped found the *Providence Gazette*, for which he wrote regularly, and was the first chancellor of Rhode Island College (now Brown Univ.). Hopkins married twice and had seven children. He died on Jul. 13, 1785.

Critical Appraisal: Stephen Hopkins's early writings included a report of the Albany conference at which he and Martin Howard, Jr., represented R.I. in discussions concerning a union of the colonies for mutual defense, cooperation, and regulation of the settlement of North America. Hopkins defended his role in presenting the plan to the R.I. Assembly, which evidently did not receive it warmly. Other published writings include several defenses of his actions in various public roles. In early 1764 his *Essay on the Trade of the Northern Colonies* was printed in two parts in the *Providence Gazette*, reprinted in several other colonial newspapers, and published as a pamphlet in London. It was a successful and comprehensive statement of the problems peculiar to those colonies and the harm that would be caused by the new parliamentary regulations. Hopkins may also have written a dream allegory satirizing the Stamp Act that was printed in the *Providence Gazette* on Nov. 10, 1764. This effective allegory equates with "branded asses" those who submit to the stamp tax.

Hopkins's pamphlet *The Rights of Colonies Examined*, published in Dec. 1764 (but dated 1765), provoked a pamphlet war involving Hopkins, Martin Howard, Jr., and James Otis (q.v.). In his pamphlet, Hopkins argued that colonies and citizens of colonies are entitled to all privileges and rights enjoyed by and in the mother state. Acknowledging that although the colonial legislatures are responsible for internal matters, there are some general matters, including the commerce of the entire empire, that must be regulated by Parliament, he maintained that Parliament could not tax the colonists, because such a tax would require them to relinquish property without the agreement of their own duly elected representatives. Hopkins failed, however, to resolve the ambiguities and contradictions in his argument, which hinted at a theory that G.B. is "an imperial state, which consists of many separate governments each of which hath peculiar privileges." He refused to face the question of whether the colonies should be represented in Parliament. What he did deal with forcefully and convincingly is the effect that the Stamp Act, the Sugar Act, and the new Vice-Admiralty Regulations would have on the trade of the colonies.

When Martin Howard, Jr., quickly attacked the weaknesses in Hopkins's arguments, Hopkins responded with a three-part series in the *Providence Gazette* titled "A Vindication of a Late Pamphlet" (Feb. 23, Mar. 2 and 9, 1765). In the series, Hopkins did not explain his former arguments but instead retreated slightly, protesting that although he believed that Parliament had no right to tax the colonies, if Parliament should proceed to tax them, it was their duty to obey cheerfully. Hopkins dismissed Howard's theories as "unmeaning jargon" and attacked Howard personally: the author of such trash must be a "madman (for he can be no better)...Drunk with rage at some disappointment, he has retired into the dark, and, grasping the dagger in his assassin hand, seems at a stand whether he shall plunge it into his country's bowels or into his own."

Called by some scholars one of the ablest propagandists of the American Revolution, Hopkins is most interesting for the way he conveyed vehemence of feeling and clarity of purpose despite his inconsistencies in political philosophy.

Suggested Readings: DAB; T₁; T₂. *See also* Bernard Bailyn, *Pamphlets of the American Revolution* (1965), I, 499-522; William E. Foster, *Stephen Hopkins, a Rhode Island Statesman* (1884); Merrill Jensen, *Tracts of the American Revolution, 1763-1776* (1967), pp. 4-18, 42-62; David S. Lovejoy, *Rhode Island Politics and the American Revolution, 1760-1776* (1958), passim.

Elaine K. Ginsberg
West Virginia University

FRANCIS HOPKINSON (1737-1791)

Works: *An Exercise* (1761); *A Collection of Psalm Tunes* (1762); *Science: A Poem* (1762); *Errata; Or, The Art of Printing Incorrectly* (1763); *A Psalm of Thanksgiving* (1766); *The Psalms of David* (1767); *A Pretty Story* (1774); *The Battle of the Kegs* (1779); *Account of the Grand Federal Procession* (1788); *An Ode* (1788); *A Set of Eight Songs* (1788); *Judgments in the Admiralty of Pennsylvania* (1789); *An Oration* (1789); *Ode from Ossian's Poems* (1794).

Biography: The eldest of eight children, Francis Hopkinson was born in Philadelphia, Pa., on Oct. 2, 1737. His father, Thomas Hopkinson, had come to Philadelphia from London in 1731 and was a member of the governor's Council. After he graduated from the College of Philadelphia in 1751, Hopkinson took up law and in 1761 was admitted to the Supreme Court of Pa. In 1766, at the advice of his family, Hopkinson left for Eng., where he hoped to gain employment, but after only a year abroad, he decided to return to America.

During the Revolutionary War, Hopkinson gained prominence as an elected official and as a man of letters. In 1776 he was elected to represent N.J. in the Continental Congress, and he voted for and signed the Declaration of Independence. He also served as chairman of the Continental Navy Board, treasurer of loans, and judge of Admiralty for Pa. In addition, Hopkinson is credited with having designed the American flag, as well as the seals for the American Philosophical Society, the state of N.J., and the University of Pennsylvania. His many inventions include a ship's log, a shaded candlestick, and a pick for the harpsi-chord. After a long and illustrious career, Hopkinson died suddenly on May 9, 1791, while he was resting at his home.

Critical Appraisal: Poet, politician, musician, judge, scientist, and artist—Francis Hopkinson excelled in so many activities that his contributions to Ameri-can culture defy easy classification. More than any other event, however, the Revolutionary War shaped Hopkinson's interests and career, and it is with the war, both as a diplomat and a man of letters, that he is associated today.

Not the least of Hopkinson's accomplishments were the many poems and essays he wrote in support of his country's decision to separate from G.B. His verses, most of which satirized the British and praised the Americans, were light, humorous, and deft. Although not the stuff of great poetry, they accomplished what they were intended to do. Easily set to music, they lifted the spirits of American soldiers who sang them at the front, and they helped to demoralize the British by good-naturedly ridiculing their cause. Hopkinson's most famous poem, *The Battle of the Kegs*, recounts in ballad form how the British, unfamiliar with explosives, battled relentlessly with a flotilla of mines that American patriots had ingeniously floated in kegs down the Delaware River toward their camp. Other famous poems written by Hopkinson during the Revolutionary War include "A Camp Ballad," "The Toast," and "Tory Medley." Together these poems made Hopkinson one of the most popular American poets of his day. So great was their fame that many of Hopkinson's poems, despite their anti-British sentiment, were read and praised even in Eng.

Equally popular were the prose essays and tracts that Hopkinson directed against the British. From Arbuthnot, Swift, and Addison, Hopkinson developed a fondness for satire, particularly when it was couched in the form of allegory or fabrication. Like his verse, Hopkinson's prose was extremely effective propa-ganda. Written in the form of a lighthearted allegory, *A Pretty Story* describes the events that led the colonies to declare their independence. In "A Prophecy," also an allegory, Hopkinson uses the persona of a biblical prophet to predict the establishment of a new and prosperous government in North America.

Although Hopkinson frequently contributed poems and essays to periodicals such as the *American Magazine*, *Columbian Magazine*, and *Pennsylvania Maga-zine*, his writing before and after the war lacked the vigor that the conflict with Eng. had inspired in him. With the possible exception of "My Days Have Been So Wondrous Free" (1759), a work that is thought to be the oldest American song known, his early and late poetry, for the most part dull and uninteresting, is rarely read today. His letters are more profitable because he corresponded with the most important statesmen of the day, including George Washington (q.v.), Benjamin Franklin (q.v.), and Thomas Jefferson (q.v.). *The Miscellaneous Es-says and Occasional Writings of Francis Hopkinson* (1792), collected by Hop-kinson himself, contains only a small portion of his total literary output. Many of his writings, particularly those written for periodicals, have yet to be collected.

Suggested Readings: DAB; LHUS; T$_2$. *See also* G. E. Hastings, "Francis Hopkinson and the Anti-Federalists," AL, 1 (1930), 405-418; idem, *The Life and Works of Francis Hopkinson* (1926); A. R. Marble, "Francis Hopkinson: Man of Affairs and Letters," NEM, 27 (1902), 289-302; Dixon Wecter, "Francis Hopkinson and Benjamin Franklin," AL, 12 (1940), 200-217.

James A. Levernier
University of Arkansas at Little Rock

MARTIN HOWARD, JR. (fl. 1730-1781)

Works: *A Defence of the Letter from a Gentleman at Halifax* (1765); *A Letter from a Gentleman at Halifax* (1765).

Biography: Most of the details of Martin Howard, Jr.'s birth and early life are unknown. His father was active in political life, serving as a member of the Newport, R.I., Town Council. Martin Howard, Jr., studied law with James Honyman, Jr., and by the 1740s was a prominent lawyer in Newport, representing shipowners and merchants. In 1754 he was chosen to represent R.I. at the Albany Congress. He made a brief appearance as a candidate for attorney general in 1761 but did not otherwise participate in public affairs until about 1763, when, as a member of a Tory "junto," he began openly defending Eng.'s new policies and attacking the factionalism and democratic tendencies of R.I.'s leadership.

In 1765 Howard published two urbane and witty tracts. The first answered Governor Stephen Hopkins's (q.v.) *The Rights of Colonies Examined*; both Hopkins and his friend James Otis (q.v.) answered Howard, who defended himself in a second "Letter," which was again answered by Hopkins and Otis. In Aug. 1765 Howard's effigy was dragged through the streets, hanged, and burned. After fleeing to Eng., he was rewarded for his loyalty with the chief justiceship of N.C., where he quickly became as unpopular as he had been in R.I. When independence was declared, Howard fled again to Eng., where he died in 1781.

Critical Appraisal: As a member of the Tory Newport Junto, Howard contributed regular articles in the *Newport Mercury* in 1764 and 1765. The group argued that the present R.I. charter gave too much power to the people and too little to the crown, creating parties and factions that in turn led to disorder. They argued the necessary submission of the colonies to Parliament, criticized the opposition to the Sugar Act, and urged the revoking of the colony's charter.

In early 1765, Howard published *A Letter from a Gentleman at Halifax to His Friend in Rhode-Island*, an attack on Stephen Hopkins's *The Rights of Colonies Examined*. Howard's *Halifax Letter* (Halifax, Nova Scotia, was the seat of the new Vice-Admiralty Court created by the Sugar Act) presented three basic arguments: first, that the rights of the colonists were the same as those of all Englishmen but that they were limited and defined by the charters that created the colonial governments; second, that Parliament's power "is attached to every English subject, wherever he be"; it is not divisible but "transcendent and entire"; and finally, on the subject of representation, that the colonists are represented as much, or as little, as the citizens of the Isle of Man, Guernsey, or Scot. Howard also included personal attacks on Hopkins, calling the latter's work "a labored, ostentatious piece" and its author "totally unacquainted with style or diction."

Howard's *Letter* provoked angry responses from both Hopkins and James Otis. Objectively, Howard seems to have gotten the better of the argument, for both Hopkins and Otis, despite their personal and vicious attacks on the author of the *Letter*, were forced to back off from their former illogical positions and insist that they were not questioning either the authority or the absolute sovereignty of Parliament.

Howard then followed with his *Defence of the Letter from a Gentleman at Halifax*. The *Defence* begins intelligently and rather temperately by reviewing some of the pamphlets and newspaper essays opposing the Stamp and Sugar Acts but accuses Hopkins's essay of being "ostentatious, in the manner and execution, and in the matter, disrespectful and unthankful to the mother country." Howard then attempted to prove the latter charges and, in addition, once again to demonstrate the illogicality and contradictory nature of Hopkins's positions on parliamentary power and authority. This section of the pamphlet is followed by a mocking response to James Otis's answer to the first *Halifax Letter*, pointing out Otis's changes of position and contradictions. Taken together, Howard's two pamphlets constitute the most important and articulate defenses of parliamentary authority written by an American before 1774.

Suggested Readings: T_2. *See also* Bernard Bailyn, *Pamphlets of the American Revolution* (1965), I, 524-544; Philip M. Davidson, *Propaganda and the American Revolution* (1941), pp. 261-271, 302; David S. Lovejoy, *Rhode Island Politics and the American Revolution* (1958).

Elaine K. Ginsberg
West Virginia University

SIMEON HOWARD (1733-1804)

Works: *A Sermon Preached to the Ancient and Honorable Artillery-Company* (1773); *A Discourse Occasioned by the Death of Mrs. Elizabeth Howard* (1777); *Christians No Cause to Be Ashamed* (1779); *Discourse at Boston* (1779); *A Sermon on Brotherly Love* (1779); *A Sermon Preached Before the Honorable Council* (1780); *A Sermon Preached at Boston* (1791).

Biography: Simeon Howard was born on Apr. 29, 1733, in West Bridgewater, Maine, the son of David and Bethiah (Leonard) Howard. After attending Harvard College (class of 1758), Howard held a teaching position in Boston until 1763. Following a brief move to Nova Scotia for his health, he returned to

Boston and accepted a call from the West Church, lately in mourning for Jonathan Mayhew (q.v.); Howard was ordained on May 11, 1767. In 1771 Howard successfully challenged a parishioner, Province Treasurer Harrison Gray, for the hand of Mayhew's widow, Elizabeth Clarke, whom he married on Dec. 3. She died six years later in childbirth with their third son, Jonathan Mayhew, who died in infancy. In 1790 Howard married Jerusha Gray, aged 55.

Howard's pastorate was marked by an estrangement from his fellow ministers, the disruptions of the Revolutionary War, and a bond of mutual regard with his congregation. In the early years of his ministry, Howard was shunned by his pastoral colleagues because of his Arian and Arminian beliefs. However, over the years, the local ministers became more moderate, and Howard demonstrated that he was no theological threat. In time Howard received the acceptance he had earlier been denied or had avoided; for example, he joined the Boston Association of Ministers and delivered the Dudleian lecture in 1787. Along with these troubles, Howard endured the pressures of a wartime pastorate. At the beginning of the hostilities, he was bullied by the regulars, who dismantled the steeple of West Church. He removed to Nova Scotia with his parishioners for fifteen months, returning in 1776. Even though the congregation was unable to pay him during the war, Howard served on, living off voluntary contributions, until the church was reestablished at the war's close. Throughout his ministry—despite the trouble with fellow ministers and the Revolution—Howard enjoyed the high regard of his congregation. He was not an abrasive, obstreperous man, and his participation in civic and charitable organizations endeared him to the community. He did not insist that his congregation adopt his own religious views, a stance that defused controversy and enabled his parishioners to become more liberal as the times allowed. At his death in Boston on Aug. 13, 1804, Howard was sincerely mourned.

Critical Appraisal: Of Simeon Howard's six published sermons, two are political. His artillery sermon argued for the necessity of civil defense, and it justified a war to protest the liberties of a people; his election sermon, discussing the relationship of government to the happiness of the governed, defended the popular selection of civil officials and described the qualifications of such rulers. Three of the sermons concerned the appropriate attitudes of Christians. The *Sermon on Brotherly Love*, preached before the Masons, spoke of the special obligations of the audience to be charitable toward the families of soldiers in the recent war. A favorite theme of Howard, evident both in *Christians No Cause to Be Ashamed* and the ordination sermon for the Rev. Thomas Adams, is the high esteem in which Christians should hold their religion. In the latter piece, Howard expressed his belief that the minister's supreme obligation is to preach the truth as he perceives it in the Scriptures, that text being his sole authority. The most emotional and moving of the sermons is the funeral elegy for his wife, Elizabeth Howard. After a prefatory inquiry into the scriptural meaning of death and the evidence for the doctrine of salvation, Howard substituted a personal essay on grief for the more traditional eulogy of the deceased. He confided to his congregation the depths of his bereavement but consoled them and himself with the assurance that God acts in wisdom and for the good of his worshippers.

Like the most able and competent of his colleagues, Howard had absolute control over his medium. In the ordination sermon for Thomas Adams, he described his sense of the ideal sermon style, which his own works admirably illustrate: "to speak of so noble and sublime a subject in language, and in a manner becoming its dignity and importance, that he [the minister] may produce in others the same esteem of it, which he feels in himself." For Howard, successful prose was simple and intelligible, and he relied so little on rhetorical flourishes, decorative devices, and allusion that a reference to Shakespeare's *The Tempest* in the conclusion to the election sermon of 1780 is all the more effective. In the years of Howard's pastorate, 1767 to 1804, the West Church enjoyed the services of an accomplished prose stylist; if this qualification does not distinguish Howard from the dozens of literary craftsmen who were his professional contemporaries, it is only for the reason that the level of excellence among the preachers in eighteenth-century America was high indeed.

Suggested Readings: CCNE; Sibley-Shipton (XIV, 279-289), *See also Appleton's Cyclopaedia of National Biography* (1892), III, 278; Everett Emerson, ed., *American Literature, 1764-1789: The Revolutionary Wars* (1977), p. 83; Alan Heimert, *Religion and the American Mind* (1966), pp. 290, 418-419.

Roslyn L. Knutson
University of Arkansas at Little Rock

JOHN HOWE (fl. 1753-1812)

Works: *The Journal Kept By John Howe While He Was Employed as a British Spy; Also, While He Was Engaged in the Smuggling Business* (w. 1775-1812; pub. 1827).

Biography: An Englishman born in 1753, John Howe was 22 years old when Gen. Thomas Gage, then military governor of Mass., asked him "to go as a spy to Worcester...and to see which was the best route...to take an army to destroy the military stores deposited there." Dressed as a civilian, he left Boston on the morning of Apr. 5, 1775, and successfully returned a week later. Early on the morning of Apr. 19, the same time Maj. Pitcairn left on his fateful march to Concord, Howe was again sent on a spy mission, this time to warn Loyalists that the conflict was starting and to warn Pitcairn what preparations were being made to stop his force. But Howe's sympathies were already shifting. By the time he returned, he "was determined to leave the British Army and join the Americans." Escaping Boston in disguise, he proceeded to Albany, where he enlisted in the Continental Army. After the war, he became a fur trader around the Great Lakes, successfully preaching and trading among the Indians. At the outbreak of hostilities in 1812, he again became a spy, but now for an American commander, Gen.

Hull. He was betrayed when Hull surrendered him and the rest of the American army to the British. Disgusted with both Americans and British, Howe returned to New Eng. and became a smuggler, bringing goods across the Canadian border. After several successful adventures, he left America for Mex. to search for his stepson and was never heard from again. His private journal was found and published in 1827.

Critical Appraisal: John Howe remains today as elusive a figure as he was while employed as a British spy during the American Revolution and later while self-employed as a smuggler during the War of 1812. Accustomed to disguises and elaborate lies, he moved about early America in a variety of roles: British spy, Continental soldier, wilderness settler, frontier trader, Indian preacher, American spy, and smuggler. Although brief and badly edited, Howe's *Journal* offers valuable insights into unusual areas of American history.

For a few dramatic days during the spring of 1775, John Howe played a central role in the American Revolution. Consequently, the first section of his *Journal* is of considerable historic interest, offering a unique and intimate perspective on the final days and hours before the first shots were fired. As Gen. Gage's most successful spy, Howe saw both the American and British preparations for the war and described the entire range of sympathies, from contemptuous British officers to rebellious farm boys.

Before taking action against the colonists, Gage sent a British officer and Howe out to examine the roads and towns around Boston, gather information concerning rebel forces and supplies, and contact Tories. In spite of his disguise, the officer was immediately recognized, and Howe, who in all probability was an infantryman sent along to accompany the officer, continued alone. After traveling throughout the countryside and visiting both Worcester and Concord, he returned with information that shaped Gage's final decision. When asked "how large an army will it take to go to Worcester, and destroy the stores there," Howe answered with great insight that if "they should march ten thousand regulars and a train of artillery to Worcester... that not one of them would get back alive." When Gage next asked about Concord, the young spy replied that "five hundred mounted men, might go... and return safe, but to go with one thousand foot, to destroy the stores, the country would be so alarmed that the greater part of them would get killed or taken." Unfortunately for Gage, he had no cavalry to send and a week later ordered Maj. Pitcairn and a force of 800 on foot to Concord.

Although lacking any discussion of the political issues, Howe's *Journal* also contains memorable descriptions of the people and places he encountered in and around Boston: a 77-year-old man cleaning his gun and preparing to hunt "a flock of red coats," the old man's wife sorting through drawers looking for his bullets, a black serving woman treating a British officer with contempt and scorn, a Tory living in constant fear of his neighbors, and Gen. Gage and his staff drinking shortly after breakfast. The people of the countryside are tense, anxious, and determined, an overwhelming majority of them angry and rebellious. The *Journal* describes how Gage was governor in name only and how the

Revolution began long before Pitcairn and his troops confronted the militia at Lexington.

Between Howe's years as a spy and his later years as a smuggler, there is an unfortunate break, leaving the *Journal* in two disjointed parts. The first printer, Luther Roby, claimed that the sections describing Howe's war experiences were "very much worn and out of order." Instead, Roby inserted a brief outline, stating that during the war "few men [have] done more in the American cause than Mr. Howe." Obviously more interested in the sensational and criminal areas of Howe's life, Roby included nothing of the frontier experience either, only mentioning that "he grew rich" in the fur trade and was "a great help in civilizing the Indians." In addition, Howe's adventures as an American spy in Can. are only briefly outlined, and the *Journal* resumes only after Howe had been betrayed by Gen. Hull, who surrendered Fort Detroit without firing a shot.

After his release, Howe was a bitter man, feeling no loyalty to any state or government. He returned to New Eng., where he became a smuggler, and the rest of the *Journal* is filled with his adventures attempting to deceive various customs inspectors. But Howe's rogue adventures are not without historical importance. The narration of his excursions offers a rare glimpse of the New Eng. smuggling network. After years of practice under British rule, many Boston merchants preferred smuggling to paying the new American duties. The smugglers that Howe met and conspired with are not depraved criminals but respectable merchants, tavern keepers, working men, and traveling families. Most people did not hesitate to help or offer advice. Howe carefully invested in his schemes. His clever disguises and devices required preparation and assistance: a fake coffin complete with a corpse, a hollow sleigh, and a borrowed family complete with a dog.

Finally, the *Journal* is not without literary merit. Originally intended as a record of his life for friends, it nonetheless is entertaining reading, and Roby's editing proves that its publication was intended less as a tribute to American history than to satisfy a certain craving among readers for sensation and adventure. Howe is an elusive, intelligent man, always self-reliant, always disdainful of authority. Although he did not try to defend his actions, it is hard to blame him for either his spying or smuggling. He is a kind of picaresque hero, relying on his cleverness to keep two steps ahead of the hangman's noose or a bucket of tar and a handful of feathers. Ultimately, Howe's *Journal* is frustrating, but frustrating because of its strengths and not its weaknesses. The value and quality of the existing sections make the loss of the middle parts much lamented.

Suggested Readings: Allen French, *General Gage's Informers* (1932); idem, *The Day of Concord and Lexington* (1925); Robert A. Gross, *The Minutemen and Their World* (1976), pp. 111-112.

Daniel E. Williams
Abteilung Für Amenkanistik
Universität Tübingen

REDNAP HOWELL (fl. 1750-1787)

Works: "When Fanning First to Orange Came" (w. c. 1765; pub. 1826); "Song" (w. 1768; pub. 1826); *A Fan for Fanning and a Touchstone to Tryon* (1771).

Biography: Rednap Howell's date of birth is not known. In fact, little is known of Howell's activities outside his involvement in the so-called N.C. Regulator movement, a pre-Revolutionary rebellion. *Appleton's Cyclopaedia*, however, claims that Rednap was the brother of Richard Howell, governor of N.J. (1794-1801), whose father was a N.J. farmer and who lived from 1753 until 1802. Even though later biographies of Richard do not include Rednap as a member of the family, Rednap probably was Richard's older brother because in his *A Fan for Fanning*, Rednap identified himself as "the eldest Son of a reputable Farmer" and because it is known that Rednap came from N.J. A final fact suggesting Rednap's kinship to Richard is worth mentioning. Richard's parents were originally Quakers (although they later became Anglicans); Herman Husband (q.v.), to whom the name of Rednap Howell is invariably justaposed in many surviving documents pertaining to the N.C. Regulators (these two are usually identified as the movement's ringleaders), is also known to have himself been a Quaker, perhaps suggesting the affinity of social views obviously shared by these two men.

Rednap came to N.C. as an itinerant schoolmaster. Apparently Howell's tenancy as schoolmaster was not typical, for it is said that he even taught his students to sing the forty or so protest lyrics he composed to incite resistance against royal injustices. The year before his *A Fan for Fanning* was published in Boston in 1771, Howell participated in an act of open insurrection against the royal court of Orange County in Hillsborough. He was one of 150 Regulators, along with Herman Husband, who broke into the court and dragged out allegedly offending Royalist officials and whipped them. In the following years, the inflammatory language and immediate style of *A Fan for Fanning* doubtlessly gained a sympathetic audience and probably contributed to the general arousal to unity among the colonies, which began to be noticeable in the early 1770s.

Howell's role in the Regulator movement came to a head at what must be called the "Battle" of Alamance Creek on May 16, 1771, when Governor Tryon launched an attack of 1,100 militia against a comparable number of the Regulators and won the battle. On Jun. 9, 1771, Governor Tryon issued a Proclamation in which he declared the leaders of the rebellion, naming Howell and Husband among others, were "Outlawed and liable to be shot by any Person whatsoever [so] that they may be punished for the Traiterous and Rebellious Crimes they have committed." Tryon offered a reward of 100 pounds and 1,000 acres of land to anyone who could bring him, dead or alive, just one of the named leaders. Howell prudently sought refuge in Md. but died in N.J. in 1787 after the Revolution, probably under the protection of his brother Richard. An assessment of Howell and his Regulators is given by William Fitch in *Some Neglected History of North Carolina*: "Of the forty-seven sections in the present Constitution of North Carolina...thirteen of them, or one-fourth, are the embodiment of reforms sought by the Regulators."

Critical Appraisal: Surprisingly, Rednap Howell is remembered primarily as the author of some forty songs and ballads of patriotic fervor directed at injustices imposed on him and his fellow colonists by royal officials, only two of which survive, rather than for his pamphlets on Fanning and Governor Tryon, eight of which are extant. It is said, however, that these songs were favorites among the colonists who passed them on to succeeding generations. But if they were as popular as commentators claim, why have only two survived? One source called Rednap "the bard of the Regulators." Another observed that Howell's popular poems "were indeed well calculated to stir the disaffected and warm them up to patriotic ardor." The two known songs (which may be found in the *Raleigh Register* for Jun. 2, 1826) are ballads, one ridiculing Fanning (of the pamphlets) and the other celebrating a minor victory of the Regulators. Howell recorded of Fanning that he was penniless when first he came to Orange County, "But by his civil robberies, / He 'as lac'd his coat with gold." The other ballad tells of Hamilton's forcing Fanning (the victim once again of Howell's acrimonious pen) to wade across the Eno River to negotiate with a band of men who threatened Hillsborough with violence: "At length their headmen they sent out / To save their town from fire; / To see Ned Fanning wade Eno, / Brave boys you's all admire."

Although his ballads show a flare for telling a story in immediate, simple, and satirical words arranged into rhythmical lines, Howell's pamphlets should also interest literary students of today. Collected in the book *A Fan for Fanning and a Touchstone to Tryon*, these pamphlets were written not merely as tools of protest, but also as a means of defense for Howell's actions, as well as for those of others involved in the Regulator movement. At the beginning of the collection, Howell boasted that a professor of the University of Glasgow had pronounced his character to be "a remarkable and almost singular instance of disinterestedness." In the first pamphlet, Howell particularly objected to what he believed to have been Fanning's collusion with Governor Tryon (the pun on the governor's name in Howell's title for the book is surely obvious by now) in the collection of excessive taxes that both the author, who called himself, appropriately, Regulus, and other Regulators believed were paying for the building of Tryon's "palace" at New Bern.

The second pamphlet is more specific, less satirical, and certainly more inflammatory. In it Howell identified one of the major abuses against the colonists as the overcharging of legal fees by Royalist lawyers and courts. At one strategic point, Howell uttered this threatening outburst: "If these things [the overcharging] were absolutely according to Law, they are enough to make us throw off all submission to such tyrannical Laws; for were such things tollerated, it would rob us of the means of living; and it were better *to die* in defence of our Privileges than to perish for want of the means of subsistance." Howell's disposition to rebellion predicted Patrick Henry's fiery speech of Mar. 23, 1775, before the Va. House. Continuing in the same vein, Howell declared, "But as these practices are contrary to Law, it is our duty to put a stop to them before they quite ruin our Country; and before we become Slaves to these lawless Wretches, and hug our Chains of Bondage." Significantly, Howell carefully avoided using the words *rebellion* or *revolution* to describe his recommendations. Rather, he was careful, at a time when he was curiously not careful of much else, to employ the term *reformation* as his prescription for change.

In "No. V," Howell listed the "New Set of Articles by the Regulators," which is actually a document setting down specific grievances lodged against the unjust government; this listing in writing of specific grievances prefigures the Declaration of Independence. "No. VII" presents a defense of the Regulators as agents of law and order trying to prevent acts of violence: "the wise men among the Regulators [not the least of which was Howell], had all their influence exercised in moderating the People, and keeping them from violent out-breakings." Since Howell and other Regulators did eventually participate in violent actions (the fracas at the court in Hillsborough and in the "Battle" of Alamance Creek, which some have called the first battle of the Revolution), the reader is invited to examine the relevant documents and make up his own mind about Howell's "moderating" influence. But there can be little doubt that Howell's songs and pamphlets speak the minds of many early Americans who were becoming increasingly dissatisfied with British domination in colonial affairs. If Howell did not directly influence future pamphleteers, his writing provides an accurate mirror of the times.

Suggested Readings: T₂. *See also Appleton's Cyclopaedia of American Biography* (1894), III, 285; John S. Bassett, "The Regulators of North Carolina (1765-1771)," AHAAR (1895), pp. 157, 198-199; R.D.W. Connor, *History of North Carolina* (1919), I, 304-305; William Edwards Fitch, *Some Neglected History of North Carolina* (1905), pp. 124-125, 167-171, 180-181, 227-228, 295-297; Hugh T. Lefler and William S. Powell, *Colonial North Carolina: A History* (1973), pp. 222-223; William S. Powell et al., compilers and eds., *The Regulators in North Carolina: A Documentary History, 1759-1776* (1971), pp. xvi, xxi, 97, 113-121, 124-125, 127, 155, 199, 356, 373-374, 398, 473, 489, 536-537, 563-564; Blackwell P. Robinson, ed., *The North Carolina Guide* (1955), p. 69.

John C. Shields
Illinois State University

WILLIAM HUBBARD (1621-1704)

Works: *The Happiness of a People in the Wisdome of Their Rulers* (1676); *A Narrative of the Troubles with the Indians* (1677); *A General History of New*

England (w. 1682; pub. 1815, 1848); *The Benefit of a Well-Ordered Conversation* (1684); *Quaestiones Discutiendae* (1688); *Testimony to the Order of the Gospel* (with John Higginson; 1701).

Biography: William Hubbard, Puritan minister and historian, in many ways formed a bridge between the first- and second-generation Puritans. Although he was born in Eng. in 1621 and came to New Eng. with his father and his family in 1635, Hubbard was shaped primarily by his New Eng. experience. A member of the first graduating class (1642) of Harvard College, Hubbard married Margaret Rogers in 1646 and became a freeman in 1653. It is not clear whether Hubbard came to the ministry reluctantly or whether he simply had the same difficulties in finding a suitable post as did many of the second generation, but he did not accept a call to join Thomas Cobbet (q.v.) at the Ipswich church until 1656, and he was not ordained to the ministry until 1658.

By the 1670s, perhaps Hubbard's most influential decade, he was becoming known as a champion of moderation and order, a political realist who could be counted on by the civil authorities, especially the magistrates. In 1671 he joined in protesting the General Court's censure on the ministers for innovation and apostasy in connection with the founding of the Third Church in Boston. By the mid-1670s, Hubbard had become the major challenger to Increase Mather's (q.v.) bid for spiritual leadership in the Bay Colony, and together they conducted their contest for power through election sermons and histories of King Philip's War. Although Mather eventually triumphed, Hubbard remained an important figure throughout the 1680s, writing his *General History*, providing pragmatic political theory in his published sermons, and leading the Ipswich opponents of taxation by the Andros government in 1687. He served as temporary president of Harvard in 1684 and was rector there in 1688 while Mather was in Eng. trying to save the charter.

During the 1690s, Hubbard continued to pursue his principles of moderation and toleration. He apparently opposed the witchcraft trials, aided a potential victim, and in 1703 joined with several other Essex ministers in petitioning the General Court on behalf of several individuals still under legal disabilities because of the trials. In the 1690s, Hubbard also astonished his parishioners by marrying his housekeeper, his wife, Margaret, having died some years earlier. In 1701 he published a brief tract with John Higginson (q.v.) in support of Increase Mather's and Cotton Mather's (q.v.) position against the emerging faction that rejected elements of New Eng. Congregationalism such as congregational ordination and the doctrine of the gathered membership. Hubbard left his pastorate in 1702, and he died on Sept. 14, 1704.

Critical Appraisal: Along with Nathaniel Morton (q.v.) and Increase Mather, William Hubbard is best remembered as a major second-generation New Eng. historian. In fact, because of his interest in the underlying natural causes of events and his departures from the more traditional "providential" interpretations of history, Hubbard is often considered the most "modern" of the Puritan historians and is thought to have been more rational in his approach to issues such as the role of the civil government in a religious commonwealth, the necessity of finding a balance between excessive tolerance and intolerance, and the need to adapt the ideals of the first generation to meet the challenges facing the second generation. Always concerned about the possible loss of the charter, for example, Hubbard preferred to compromise rather than risk losing the charter completely.

The two major pieces on which Hubbard's reputation rests are his election sermon of 1676, *The Happiness of a People*, and his *Narrative*, published in 1677. *The Happiness of a People*, labeled by Perry Miller as the "finest prose of the decade," contains, among other things, a celebration of peace and order, a plea for at least limited religious tolerance, a call for restraint from oppression (Hubbard is thought to have had the Anglican merchants in mind), and veiled criticism of the handling of King Philip's War, which at the time was not going well for the colonists. In searching for the causes of God's displeasure in bringing such a visitation upon New Eng., Hubbard dismissed the more superficial sins, such as excessive drinking or the wearing of periwigs, that were often cited by more fanatical reformers and stressed the failure of the colony to deal with the growing problems of land greed and an obsession with the letter of the law. A year later, Hubbard published his *Narrative*. Although there were inaccuracies in Hubbard's account, as even his contemporaries noted, it was then considered the best of the war narratives and is still highly valued by historians as a source of information on events and on the view of the war favored by Bay Colony officials. It is a fast-paced story of the exploits and sufferings of Puritans and the treacheries of the Indians, for Hubbard shared the general Puritan conception of the Indians as children of the Devil. Even so, it is possible to find praise for an Indian sympathetic to the colonists' cause or condemnation of the poor judgment of a militia leader. Again, in rejecting declension as a possible cause of the war, Hubbard made his account particularly welcome to a government trying to save its charter. Throughout, natural causes as well as providences play an important role in Hubbard's interpretation of events.

Hubbard's final major work, his *General History of New England*, is more controversial as well as more uneven in quality. It is richest in detail and style in the years from the first planting to the 1640s, primarily because Hubbard had the manuscripts of John Winthrop (q.v.) and William Bradford (q.v.) at his disposal. Even for this period, however, Hubbard recorded events with a remarkable sense of detachment. The later years (parts of the narrative extend to 1682) are lacking in both detail and insight. Although the General Court voted the sum of fifty pounds to Hubbard for the work in 1682, it is not clear whether Hubbard received any of that sum. The manuscript remained unpublished until 1815, when a 1st, incomplete edition was issued by the Massachusetts Historical Society. A 2nd, more complete edition followed in 1848.

Hubbard has been criticized by some historians for his heavy borrowing from other writers, but he has also been defended or even applauded for his use and thus preservation of those accounts. Writing with remarkable objectivity of the whole Puritan attempt to found a religious commonwealth and making the first attempt at a comprehensive history of the New Eng. colonies, Hubbard seems secure in his reputation as the foremost second-generation historian of New Eng.

Suggested Readings: CCNE; DAB; LHUS; Sibley-Shipton (I, 54-62); Sprague (I, 148-150); T$_1$; T$_2$. *See also* Timothy H. Breen, *The Character of the Good Ruler* (1970), pp. 110-117; Richard S. Dunn, "Seventeenth-Century English Historians of America" in *Seventeenth-Century America*, ed. James Morton Smith (1959), pp. 211-215; Emory Elliott, *Power and the Pulpit in Puritan New England* (1973), pp. 149-154; David Hall, *The Faithful Shepherd* (1972), especially chs. 8-11 for background; Francis Jennings, *The Invasion of America* (1975), pp. 182-185, passim; Perry Miller, *The New England Mind: From Colony to Province* (1953), pp. 48-49, 135-136, 140-141; Kenneth B. Murdock, "William Hubbard and the Providential Interpretation of History," PAAS, 52 (1942), 15-37; Anne K. Nelsen, "King Philip's War and the Hubbard-Mather Rivalry," WMQ, 3rd ser., 27 (1970), 615-629; Cecelia Tichi, "Spiritual Biography and the 'Lord's Remembrancers,'" WMQ, 3rd ser., 28 (1971), 74-80.

Anne Kusener Nelsen
Washington, D.C.

EPHRAIM HUIT (fl. 1611-1644)

Works: *The Anatomy of Conscience* (1626); *The Whole Prophecie of Daniel Explained* (w. before 1639; pub. 1643).

Biography: Ephraim Huit (also spelled *Hewat*) matriculated sizar at St. Johns College, Cambridge, Eng., in 1611. He held positions as curate first in Cheshire and later at Knowle, Warwickshire, where he wrote his *Anatomy of Conscience*. Still later he preached at Wroxhall, Warwickshire, until silenced for nonconformity; Archbishop William Laud's papers for 1638 include a notation that "my Lord the bishop of Worcester proceeds against him [Huit], and intends either to reform or punish him." Huit completed *The Whole Prophecie of Daniel Explained* while at Wroxhall, but it could not be published until the overthrow of the Laudian party.

Along with several families from his congregation, Huit immigrated to New Eng. in 1639 and arrived at Windsor, Conn., that Aug. 17. On Dec. 10 he was called to office as teacher of the Windsor church; his colleague as pastor was John Warham. Outlines of forty-four of his sermons, which survive in the manuscript notebook of Henry Wolcott, reveal Huit's position on a number of contemporary issues. He upheld stringent requirements for church membership, preached strict predestinarianism including limited atonement, and urged all Christians to reflect upon their faith until they had achieved a "faith of assurance." Huit died in Windsor on Sept. 4, 1644, survived by his widow, Elizabeth, and four daughters. Windsor town records reveal that Elizabeth Huit received an annuity from the town at least until 1657.

Critical Appraisal: Huit directed his first book, *The Anatomy of Conscience or the Summe of Pauls Regeneracy*, particularly toward the "weake

Christian" who still doubted the sincerity of his faith. Because the truly justified person possessed "a faith that is lively and active in good works," Christians would naturally want to test the validity of their faith by the evidence of their works. Their consciences assisted them in this task by constructing practical syllogisms. Conscience's "speculative part, called *sunteresis*," supplied general principles as major premises; an example would be "there is no condemnation to them that are in Christ." Conscience's "practical part, called *suneidesis*," provided the concrete evidence "partly from its own acquaintance with our hearts, and lives, and partly from the evidence of Gods spirit in us [cf. Romans 8:16]"; this evidence generated the minor premise, in this example perhaps "but I am in Christ." The syllogism's conclusion,"ergo, there is no condemnation in me," followed logically.

Huit admitted that "so neare doth semblance represent substance, and so farre doth hypocrisie (sincerities Ape) proceede in way of religion" that even a hypocrite might perform works that appeared deceptively saintlike. Not only other Christians but also the hypocrite's own conscience might easily be deceived into assuming that he should actually be numbered among the true believers. Much of Huit's treatise therefore describes various techniques whereby hypocrisy could be exposed. For example, the conscience of a truly regenerate person would persist in requiring him to do good works, stir him to attend the means of grace faithfully, find that he acted from love of Christ rather than fear of hell, and be diligent in rooting out all sin. Little of this discussion is original; Huit's treatment of conscience largely follows that of the Cambridge Puritan William Perkins.

The Whole Prophecie of Daniel Explained, by a Paraphrase, Analysis and Briefe Comment: Wherein the Severall Visions Shewed to the Prophet, Are Clearly Interpreted, and the Application Thereof Vindicated Against Dissenting Opinions contains Huit's apocalyptic predictions. A Ramist chart or "analysis" precedes each chapter, followed by the running paraphrase of the scriptural text and accompanying commentary. Like most contemporary interpreters of Daniel and Revelation, Huit identified the Antichrist with the papacy. But he paid equal attention to the Turks, whom he identified as the little horn of Daniel 7:8. Huit interpreted the basic meaning of Daniel's visions as follows: God would first gather the Jews together "from the places of their dispersion" in the year 1650, and he would then convert them to Christ. The Turks would invade Palestine in anger, resulting in forty-five years of "most bitter wars," but in 1695 the Turks would be utterly overthrown. Both they and the papacy would then "be cast into the streams of fire and brimstone issuing from the ancient of days," and the victorious Jews would unite with the remaining faithful gentiles to compose "one glorious Christian church."

Such apocalyptic speculations, deriving from the work of Thomas Brightman, were common in midseventeenth-century Eng.; Huit's book breaks little new ground. Even his arguments against "dissenting opinions"—presumably those of Jesuits like Robert Bellarmine and Luis de Alcasar—are echoed in other contemporary sources. But his presence in New Eng. provides additional evidence that the eschatological fervor that permeated old Eng. in the first two-thirds of the seventeenth century had deep roots in New Eng. as well.

Suggested Readings: CCNE. *See also* Bryan Ball, *A Great Expectation: Eschatological Thought in English Protestantism to 1660* (1975); outlines of Huit's sermons in Douglas Shepard, "The Wolcott Shorthand Notebook, Transcribed" (Ph.D. diss., State Univ. of Ia., 1957); Henry Stiles, *The History of Ancient Windsor, Connecticut* (1859), pp. 46-51; John Venn and J. A. Venn, *Alumni Cantabrigienses* (1922-1927), I, 361.

Baird Tipson
Central Michigan University

JOHN HULL (1624-1683)

Works: "The Diaries of John Hull, Mint-master and Treasurer of the Colony of Massachusetts Bay," *Archaeologia Americana. Transactions and Collections of the American Antiquarian Society,* vol. III (1857).

Biography: The son of a Puritan blacksmith, John Hull was born in Leicestershire, Eng., on Dec. 18, 1624. At the age of 10, he immigrated with his parents to Boston, where, under the direction of his father and stepbrother, Hull trained as a goldsmith. The choice of this craft was well timed, for in the 1640s and thereafter, status-conscious New World Puritans were demanding elegant braziers, candelabras, and chalices to grace their tables and religious services. Hull's success as a craftsman came early and coincided with the growing material prosperity of the Bible Commonwealth.

In 1652, when the Bay Colony decided to produce its own silver currency, the Mass. General Court appointed Hull master of the mint. With his partner, Robert Sanderson, he coined what came to be known as "pine tree" shillings and continued to strike them off for the next three decades. Hull and Sanderson were well paid for their efforts (roughly one shilling for each twenty coined), and in succeeding years, Hull resisted the General Court's attempts to reduce their commission. His profits from this and other enterprises produced a personal fortune that became legendary, giving rise in later years to the tale that he provided his daughter Hannah, who married Samuel Sewall (q.v.) in 1676, with a dowry consisting of her weight in pine tree shillings. In fact, Hull's wealth was so great that he made substantial loans to the Bay Colony, at one time financing its military operations against hostile Indians during King Philip's War.

Throughout his forty years as one of America's most prosperous merchants, Hull engaged in many ventures. He had financial interest in a fleet of trading vessels, speculated in real estate, and bred horses. He also became selectman and treasurer of Boston, served as militia corporal, ensign, and captain, and was appointed treasurer of the Massachusetts Bay Colony in 1676. In his workshop with Robert Sanderson, Hull helped establish the silversmith's art in America and then trained a generation of craftsmen who later produced some of the finest examples of colonial silver. At the age of 59, Hull's health began to fail. He died on Oct. 1, 1683, and was buried in a tomb he had built in Boston's Granary Burying Ground.

Critical Appraisal: Despite the range of his activities, John Hull found time to record two diaries. The shorter work, known as the Private Diary, was not intended for public scrutiny and bears the title: "Some passages of God's providence about myself and in relation to myself; penned down that I may be the more mindful of, and thankful for, all God's dispensations towards me." Contained in this diary are brief accounts of his birth in 1624, his early childhood in Eng., his immigration to America, and his apprenticeship. The work also exhibits a miscellany of everyday activities and occurrences, as well as significant births, deaths, successes, and failures that Hull, in Puritan fashion, believed were Divine Providences, each containing a spiritual message directed to him from God. Additionally, the Private Diary demonstrates how thoroughly the life of one of America's most successful and most visible Puritans embraced the worlds of business and public affairs: nearly half of all entries from 1646 to 1682, the year before Hull's death, deal with the outcome of trading ventures and appointments to public offices. But perhaps more than anything else, the Private Diary reveals the underlying optimism that propelled Puritan theology. In the face of life's vicissitudes heaped upon man by an inscrutable Deity, there is always the belief that the final outcome will be glorious. "The Lord give me spiritual and heavenly treasure when he taketh from me earthly," wrote Hull after learning of the wreck of one of his ships, "and that will be a good exchange!"

Hull's longer diary is a chronicle of public rather than private events, written for his own benefit but also with an eye toward posterity. Known as the Public Diary, this work records the events, momentous and trivial, that bear upon the political, religious, and economic life of the Massachusetts Bay Colony from 1634 to 1682. Deaths of Puritan worthies, epidemics of disease and arson, hailstorms, earthquakes, and pestilences—both natural (caterpillars) and spiritual (Quakers)—appear with regularity. But the Public Diary also reveals the dilemma that confronted Hull and many of his New World compatriots when Charles II was restored to the English throne in 1660. Although disheartened by the king's anti-Puritan leanings, they remained Englishmen loyal to the crown. Hull's Public Diary indicates, however, that theirs was a grudging loyalty that would eventually give way to other allegiances. For better or worse, they began to see themselves as New Englishmen evolving a set of political values that gave no quarter to transoceanic dominance. When Charles II's representatives arrived in 1664, they were far from sympathetic to the needs of the colony, and Hull's sarcasm was barely masked when he wrote: "The honored commissioners seem to be elaborate in turning every stone to find the faults of this Colony and government, and to manage them to our disadvantage." Then, in coded shorthand, Hull asked rhetorically: "why are we imposed upon? Why do any, in his majesty's name, protest against us, discourage our magistrates, and sit, . . . without our consent, in our jurisdiction?" Finally, as the last of what he interjected as

"Some of my own meditations," Hull declared: "Strangers, though Englishmen, have no R[ight?] to think they may come hither, and seek the subversion of our civil and ecclesiastical politics." Such moments of pique are rare in the Public Diary, but they reveal the stirrings of provincial indignation more than a century before they became outwardly manifest as national rebellion.

Suggested Readings: DAB. *See also* Hermann F. Clarke, *John Hull, a Builder of the Bay Colony* (1940); Samuel S. Drake, *History and Antiquities of Boston* (1845); Martha G. Fales, *Early American Silver* (1973); Nathaniel Hawthorne, "Grandfather's Chair" (1854); Edmund S. Morgan, "Light on the Puritans from John Hull's Notebooks," NEQ, 15 (1942), 95-101; Samuel E. Morison, *Builders of the Bay Colony* (1930), pp. 135-182.

Carmine Andrew Prioli
North Carolina State University

DAVID HUMPHREYS (1752-1818)

Works: *A Poem Addressed to the Armies of the United States* (1780, 1784); *The Glory of America* (1783); *A Poem on the Happiness of America* (1786); *The Anarchiad* (in collaboration with Joel Barlow, John Trumbull, and Lemuel Hopkins; w. from Oct. 1786 to Sept. 1787; pub. in the *New Haven Gazette and Connecticut Magazine*); *The Life of Israel Putnam* (1788); *An Oration on the Political Situation* (1789); *Poems* (1789); *Miscellaneous Works* (1790); *The Widow of Malabar* (1790); *A Poem on Industry* (1794); *Miscellaneous Works* (1804); *A Poem on the Death of General Washington* (1804); *A Poem on the Love of Country* (1804); *The Yankey in England* (1815); *Letters to Sir Joseph Banks* (1817).

Biography: David Humphreys was born on Jul. 10, 1752, in Derby, Conn. At age 15, he was admitted to Yale, where he met Timothy Dwight (q.v.) and John Trumbull (q.v.) and organized the Brothers in Unity, a literary society. After tutoring in the early 1770s, Humphreys joined the Revolutionary army just after the Battle of Long Island in 1776. During the next four years, he rose to the rank of lieutenant colonel and was aide-de-camp to Gens. Israel Putnam and Nathanael Greene before being promoted to the military family of Gen. George Washington (q.v.). After the war, Humphreys was named secretary to a commerce commission in Europe and worked under Thomas Jefferson (q.v.), John Adams (q.v.), and Benjamin Franklin (q.v.). In 1787 Humphreys became a permanent member of Washington's household at Mount Vernon, where he remained until late 1790, when Washington sent him to Lisbon and Madrid. In 1791 Humphreys was named minister resident to the court at Lisbon, where he was instrumental in freeing the Algerine captives in 1796. Later that year, Humphreys was named minister plenipotentiary to the court at Madrid. By the time of Jefferson's election to the presidency, however, the formerly cordial relationship that had existed between them had cooled, and Humphreys was recalled to America in 1801. For the last sixteen years of his life, Humphreys gained considerable fame as the founder and proprietor of America's finest woolen industry. He died on Feb. 21, 1818, in New Haven, Conn.

Critical Appraisal: At the time of his death, David Humphreys was a remarkably successful woolen manufacturer, a member of the Royal Society, a distinguished American diplomat, an honored veteran of two wars, an elected politico, and a personal acquaintance of all five presidents. For George Washington, he had been aide-de-camp, secretary, trusted advisor, and close personal friend. He was as representative of the American Enlightenment as Jefferson or Franklin, although of course his accomplishments pale when compared to theirs.

It is all the more remarkable that this Enlightenment man should have been a prominent literary figure as well, but such, indeed, was the case, and David Humphreys became the fourth of the major Connecticut Wits. His fame was based primarily on the fact that he wrote openly patriotic verse, an attractive quality in the late eighteenth century. Humphreys's inspirational poetry reminded at least two generations of the peculiar blessings with which God had graced America. He found the seeds of American greatness in the past and urged new generations to replant those seeds to guarantee American greatness in the future. In this sense, Humphreys was a "conservative"; he viewed the possibilities of democratic and demagogic government with undisguised horror.

In both style and substance, Humphreys wrote what is known as epideictic poetry, a form adapted from Classical rhetoric and elocution. Epideictic oratory was occasional and more often than not written to praise someone; it was also a very ornamental form. By the late eighteenth century, the form included an exordium, an extended narration, and a peroration. Humphreys tried for the sublime style, because, as he had learned from John Ward's *A System of Oratory* (1759), dignified subjects demanded sublime language. To achieve this, Humphreys relied on standard formulas, including the use of earthquakes, stormy seas, thunder and lightning, roaring winds, cannon volleys, and so on. Anything grand and mighty was sufficient. Moreover, the proper method to attain heightened effects was through circumlocution, inversion, epithet, poetic diction, and strong figures: personification, apostrophe, exclamation, and interrogation. Epideictic oratory is at the heart of Humphreys's most important poems, from *Address to the Armies* in 1780 to *A Poem on the Death of General Washington* (1804).

Humphreys did write in other forms as well. He wrote satiric poetry in *The Anarchiad*, romantic biography in the *Life of Putnam*, original drama in *The Yankey in England*, and he even tried scientific narrative in *Letters to Sir Joseph Banks . . . Containing Some Account of the Serpent of the Ocean Frequently Seen in Gloucester Bay*. Although it does not include all of his work, Humphreys's most important single volume is the 1804 edition of *Miscellaneous Works*.

Humphreys's contribution to *The Anarchiad* was sizable. The collaborators chose not to sign their work, thus making attributions at this late date difficult at best. Evidence does exist, however, that argues that Humphreys originated the series and wrote at least five full numbers and parts of two others. Humphreys commented on the effect of the first two numbers of *The Anarchiad* in a letter to George Washington dated Nov. 16, 1786: "In some instances the force of ridicule has been found of more efficacy than the force of argument, against the Anti-federalists and Advocates for Mobs." In his *Life of Putnam*, Humphreys wrote what may be the prototype of romantic biographies that pursue a hagiographic purpose by creating a larger-than-life portrait of their subjects, of which Parson Mason Locke Weems's (q.v.) biography of Washington is probably the best known example. But despite its limitations as accurate biography, the *Life of Putnam* is both readable and entertaining, qualities that kept it in numerous editions throughout the nineteenth century. *The Yankey in England* (begun in 1792 and completed in 1815) contributed a character, Doolittle, whose Yankee nature was said by Humphreys to include simplicity, inquisitiveness, and credulity mixed with suspiciousness, prejudice, and obstinacy. Modeled on Tyler's Jonathan in *The Contrast*, Doolittle has taken a position in the history of the Yankee as a character in early American literature. One very interesting aspect of the play is Humphreys's effort to reproduce accurately the dialect of Doolittle; he even included a glossary of some 300 Yankee words and expressions.

Suggested Readings: DAB; Dexter (III, 414-420); LHUS; T$_2$. *See also* William K. Bottorff, ed., facsimile edition of *The Anarchiad* (1967); idem, ed., facsimile edition of the 1804 *Miscellaneous Works* (1968); Edward M. Cifelli, *David Humphreys* (1982); idem., "David Humphreys" (Ph.D. diss., N.Y. Univ., 1977); Leon Howard, *The Connecticut Wits* (1943); Frank Landon Humphreys, *Life and Times of David Humphreys* (1917); Vernon L. Parrington, *The Connecticut Wits* (1926).

Edward M. Cifelli
County College of Morris

ISAAC HUNT (c. 1742-1809)

Works: *A Letter from a Gentleman in Transilvania* (1764); *A Looking-Glass for Presbyterians* (1764); *A Humble Attempt at Scurrility* (1765); *The Substance of an Exercise . . . in Scurrility Hall* (continued under varying titles through eight numbers; 1765); *The Birth, Parentage, and Education of Praise-God Barebone* (1766); *The Political Family* (1775); *The Case of Isaac Hunt* (1776); *Faction, a Sketch* (1777); *Discourses on Public Occasions* (1786); *The Rights of Englishmen* (pt. I, 1791).

Biography: Isaac Hunt was born sometime around 1742 in Bridgetown, Barbados, W. Ind., to the Rev. Isaac Hunt, an Anglican clergyman of some local prominence, and Mary (Bryan) Hunt. In 1757 he was sent to the colony of Pa. to be educated. In 1763 Hunt graduated from the Philadelphia Academy, where he served for a short time as tutor. At this time, Hunt became deeply involved in Pa.

politics, and the satirical polemics he contributed to various public debates so angered the authorities that his M.A. (one of two he would earn) was withheld for five years. In 1766, after having read law in the informal style customary during the period, Hunt was admitted to the bar. In the following year, he married Mary Shewell, the daughter of a Philadelphia merchant. Their union produced eight children, five of whom lived beyond childhood. The youngest, Leigh Hunt, became a noted author. Hunt's efforts to establish himself in the legal profession, including an unsuccessful attempt to secure the patronage of Benjamin Franklin (q.v.), proved unavailing. To complicate matters, he found himself at odds with the Patriot movement, and his challenge of the legality of the local Committee of Safety earned him a carting through the streets of Philadelphia. Escaping imprisonment by bribing his guards, Hunt returned to Barbados and eventually rejoined his family in the expatriate community of London.

There the Hunts were taken in by Benjamin West, to whom the family was related through marriage. Still unsettled in his choice of careers, Hunt considered becoming an actor, dropped the idea, took orders in the Anglican Church (a way station, as it happened, on the road to Unitarianism), and was assigned to Bentinck Chapel. He sought to improve his position by tutoring the son of the duke of Chandos, an aristocrat whose political and social connections gave promise of rapid advancement in the church. But Hunt shattered those possibilities by championing the cause of the young artist John Trumbull, who was then imprisoned in London on spy charges. Hunt's tenacity in this affair, so puzzling to his contemporaries and still unexplained, alienated his patron. Hunt never secured another, living out the rest of his days in an ignominious struggle to avoid debtors' prison. He died in London in 1809.

Critical Appraisal: Isaac Hunt's literary output, while not large, does provide some interesting insights into the political, social, and religious conflicts within the colony of Pa. during the immediate pre-Revolutionary period. His first significant work, *A Looking-Glass for Presbyterians*, was a contribution to the "pamphlet war" that followed the Paxton Riots in Pa. during the winter of 1763-1764. At that time, a body of frontiersmen, some of whom faced prosecution for having murdered Indians living under the protection of the government, staged what proved to be an abortive march upon Philadelphia. The incident exploded into a more general struggle between the "Quaker" (or "Antiproprietary") and "Presbyterian" (or "Proprietary") political factions. As a member of the Anglican minority, Hunt appreciated the atmosphere of tolerance the Quakers had established, and he turned his critique of frontier lawlessness into a frontal assault upon Presbyterianism, a sect he considered to be inseparably tied to rebellion ("we shall find that in the Annals both of ancient and modern History, Presbyterianism and Rebellion, were twin-Sisters, sprung from Faction"). Hunt continued this attack in *A Humble Attempt at Scurrility* and in the eight numbers of the *Scurrility* series. The title of the first provides a perhaps too-accurate description of the contents of all. The works do, however, contain a noteworthy defense of Franklin, who was then under heavy fire from political opponents, and some clever jibes at New Light Presbyterians. As with all of Hunt's early writings, they also provide a healthy corrective to overly sanguine views of colonial America as a "melting pot." However, the unevenness of these pieces indicates that Hunt's temperament was not suited to the coarse demands of the genre.

As relations between G.B. and her North American colonies deteriorated, Hunt argued the Loyalist case in his pamphlet *The Political Family*, which was primarily a reminder to the mother country of the importance of the colonies. By 1775 that had become a very dated emphasis—a minor mystery since resolved: the essay had been prepared for a prize competition almost a decade earlier and was published with the hasty addition of a few topical footnotes. His poem *Faction, a Sketch*, provides a nearly exhaustive list of those whom the Loyalists saw as villains: Congregationalists and Presbyterians, smugglers masquerading as Sons of Liberty, rascals in Parliament, local demagogues, greedy merchants, debtors, an ignorant public, and apathetic "Men of Sense."

After settling into his new career in Eng., Hunt continued to be concerned with colonial matters. In his *Discourses on Public Occasions*, a volume of sermons preached after 1778, he often returned to the subject of the American Revolution. Contained in that volume is Hunt's fast-day sermon of 1781, his most detailed analysis of the causes of the rupture. Even at that late date, he remained fully committed to a vigorous prosecution of the war. He was equally concerned, however, that this be accompanied by a policy of toleration for the rebels, which is a reflection of his increasing tendency to perceive them as the unwitting tools of the ancient enemy, Fr.

Hunt's later publications are mostly sermons, none of them particularly striking in content, but each felicitously phrased and undoubtedly effective as originally delivered. His last publication, *The Rights of Englishmen*, was apparently conceived as an extended conservative rebuttal of the thoughts of Thomas Paine (q.v.). If so, the project was never completed.

Suggested Readings: DAB; T$_2$. *See also* Edmund Blunden, *Leigh Hunt and His Circle*, 2 vols. (1930); Leigh Hunt, *The Autobiography of Leigh Hunt* (1860); J. S. Littel, ed., *Graydon's Memoirs of His Own Time* (1969); Theodore Sizer, ed., *The Autobiography of John Trumbull* (1953).

David Sloan
University of Arkansas at Fayetteville

GEORGE HUNTER, S.J. (1713-1779)

Works: *A Short Account of the State and Condition of the Roman Catholics in the Province of Maryland, Collected from Authentic Copies of the Provincial Records and Other Undoubted Testimonies* (1756); unpublished sermons.

Biography: George Hunter was born in Northumberland, Eng., on Jul. 6, 1713, entered the Society of Jesus in 1730, and was ordained a priest. In 1747 he went to the Md. Mission of the English Province of the Jesuits and became the superior of the mission in 1756. That same year, he returned to Eng., perhaps in conjunction with the document analyzed below. In 1759, he was back in Md., where he was again a superior, a post he held until 1768. In 1769 he went first to Can. and then to Eng., but he returned to Md. He died at St. Thomas Manor, Charles Co., Md., on Aug. 1, 1779. The issue to which Hunter addressed himself in 1756 was an act of the colonial Assembly that would levy a double tax on Catholics, who had already been prohibited from bearing arms or serving in the militia and now were taxed because they did not serve in the militia. The disarming of Catholics and the introduction of new penal laws against them were part of the hysteria that swept Md. and Pa. during the French and Indian War and that resulted in one of the few arrests of a priest, James Beadhall, in colonial Md.

Critical Appraisal: George Hunter presented the second Catholic reflection on the Md. colonial tradition and, like his predecessor Peter Attwood, S.J. (q.v.), he used many of the same arguments. At the time of his writing, the double-tax bill was either pending before the upper house of the Assembly or awaiting the assent of the proprietor, Lord Baltimore. The special tax on Catholics, he argued, passed "a new law affecting the property of the subject," the sole basis of which was a particular religious persuasion. The double tax, he asserted, would depopulate the colony, as Catholics sought freedom elsewhere. He furthermore declared that English penal laws did not apply to Md. To justify his assertion, he summarized the history of freedom in Md. from its beginning and narrated the various acts of the Assembly in the eighteenth century. It had been mistakenly believed, he stated, that the Assembly had introduced the penal laws of William III in 1718, for if that were the case, the Assembly would not have sought since 1750 to introduce new bills, the effect of which was to impose the penal laws on Md. Catholics. Md., he concluded, was not subject to parliamentary statutes.

Hunter likewise argued that the double-tax bill was a breach of promise made to the ancestors of Md. Catholics, many of whom had originally left Eng. to gain freedom in Md. Although they had previously been subject to certain anti-Catholic laws, none of them had directly touched their property. He did not argue that there could be no taxation without representation, but rather that there should be no unequal taxation of Catholics.

Md. Catholics had traditionally appealed for protection to the upper house of the Assembly—the more aristocratic, propertied branch of the Assembly—the proprietor, or the crown. In this instance, their appeals were unsuccessful and Lord Baltimore approved the bill. The failure of the proprietor to protect the rights of those who had for so long defended his interests permanently alienated the Catholics from him. Two years later, the upper house moved to repeal the double-tax bill and thus restored its traditional alliance with the Catholics. The latter saw an essential relationship between property and civil rights. Betrayed, in their mind, by Lord Baltimore, they gradually became a conservative Revolutionary group, represented by Charles Carroll of Carrollton (q.v.) two decades later.

Hunter's treatise, which is not a work of literary merit, may have accompanied the Catholic petition to Lord Baltimore in Eng. It provides insight into the mentality of the Md. Catholic community on the eve of the Revolution with its arguments for the rights derived from the ownership of property, the civil basis for religious liberty, and the Md. Assembly's independence from Parliament.

Suggested Readings: CCMDG. *See also* Timothy W. Bosworth, "Anti-Catholicism as a Political Tool in Mid-Eighteenth-Century Maryland," CHR, 56 (1975), 539-563; George Hunter, "A Short Account of the State and Condition of the Roman Catholics in the Province of Maryland," WL, 10 (1881), 7-21; "Maryland Catholics in Penal Days (1759)," USCHM (1889-1890), 201-215.

Gerald P. Fogarty, S.J.
University of Virginia

ROBERT HUNTER (fl. 1714-1734)

Works: Wrote letters from America to English government and friends (including Jonathan Swift). May have contributed to *Tatler*. *Androborus, A Biographical Farce in Three Acts* (1714).

Biography: Born in Scot., Robert Hunter made his reputation as a soldier in the English army and fought in the Battle of Blenheim, where he served as lieutenant colonel until 1707. In 1707, after receiving an appointment as lieutenant governor of Va., he was captured en route and taken to France as a prisoner. After his release in 1709 he was appointed captain-general and governor-in-chief of N.Y. and N.J. When he arrived in N.Y. in 1710, he found political and religious intrigue the order of the day but over the years he managed to achieve amity among the various factions, and when he left for Eng. in 1719, he had achieved peace. In 1727 Hunter became governor of Jamaica, a position he held until his death on March 31, 1734.

Critical Appraisal: When he arrived as governor of N.Y. in 1710, Robert Hunter found himself at odds with all important members of the populace, from the clergy to the assembly. Upon the arrival of Gen. Francis Nicholson in N.Y. as the royal commissioner of accounts, all of Hunter's enemies rallied behind the general. Hunter, with something of a literary reputation already established, chose to satirize all of his enemies in a play, *Androborus*. Probably his friendship with Jonathan Swift was responsible for his choice of satire as a literary medium, although the success of George Villiers's satire *The Rehearsal* in 1671 may have influenced his choice of genre. It is not known whether *Androborus* was performed, but it was printed in 1714, and the resulting laughter seemed to prove the turning point in Hunter's fortunes.

The play is in three acts: The Senate, The Consistory, and The Apotheosis. The sole extant copy lists (probably in Hunter's own handwriting), next to the cast of characters, the actual person each stands for—Androborus, for example, was Gen. Francis Nicholson, and the Keeper was Hunter himself. The Keeper, his Deputy, and Tom of Bedlam conceal themselves while the Senate meets. The conversation in the play is adept; each member, with the exception of Aesop, who is constantly teaching moral lessons in verse, reveals his stupidity. Most of the first act is spent on procedural matters until Androborus (Man Eater) appears before the audience. He speaks, in almost totally garbled language, of future exploits, then struts off while the others agree to support him. The Keeper calls them hounds and sends them off to their kennels, assigning Tom to watch after them should they meet again. In the next act, the protagonists attempt to incorporate themselves into a Consistory in order to remove the Keeper. Fizle has a plan involving smearing his coat with excrement and claiming that the Keeper, in his hatred of long robes, has done it. Nothing comes of the plan. The third and final act finds the Keeper, his Deputy, and Tom preparing a scheme to convince Androborus that he is dead. The plan works until Androborus and several of the Keeper's enemies eventually drop into a vault which had been prepared for the Keeper, and the play ends.

Androborus has occasionally been listed as the first play written in America, but its value lies, rather, in other areas. As social history, it is biting, witty, and a thoroughly worthwhile literary contribution to early Americana.

Some of the letters Hunter exchanged with Jonathan Swift have been preserved. Evidently the relationship between them was fairly close, judging from such remarks as Swift's "I am now with Mr. *Addison*, with whom I have fifty times drunk your Health since you left us." Hunter's unhappiness with his situation in N.Y. is made quite clear: "Here is the finest air to live upon in the Universe and if our trees and birds could speake and our assembly men be silent the finest conversation too." Hunter was occasionally referred to in *The Tatler* and was especially praised in his role as governor, under the name Eboracensis.

Suggested Readings: DAB; DNB. *See also* Lawrence H. Leder, "Robert Hunter's *Androborus*," BNYPL, 58 (1964), 153-160; Montrose J. Moses, *The American Dramatist* (1925), p. 38; Arthur Hobson Quinn, *A History of the American Drama from the Beginning to the Civil War* (1951), p. 6; Jonathan Swift, *The Correspondence of*, ed. Harned Williams (1963), I (1690-1713), pp. 119, 132, 334, 363; George A. Aitken, ed., *The Tatler* (1898; rep. 1970), I, 68, II, 146.

Julian Mates
Long Island University

HERMAN HUSBAND (1724-1795)

Works: *Some Remarks on Religion, with the Author's Experience in Pursuit Thereof* (1761); *A Continuation of the Impartial Relation* (1770); *An Impartial Relation of the First Rise and Cause of the Recent Differences, in Publick Affairs, in the Province of North Carolina* (1770).

Biography: Herman Husband (also spelled *Husbands*) was born on Oct. 3, 1724, into the Anglican family of William and Mary Husband. Information relating to his early life is sparse and contradictory. He grew to maturity in East Nottingham, Md., but afterwards moved periodically to various places in both Md. and N.C. before settling in the latter colony in 1761. During that time, he was also engaged in a spiritual journey, first to Presbyterianism and eventually to the Society of Friends. Although Husband was "read out" of his Quaker meeting in 1764, apparently for marrying outside the faith, he continued to live by those tenets.

Having gained a reputation as an excellent farmer, a solid citizen, and an articulate advocate of human rights, Husband was drawn into the Regulator movement, one of the most serious reactions to arbitrary rule and political corruption of the entire colonial period. Although Husband never officially joined the movement, he became its spokesman, preparing lists of grievances and ultimately providing the most complete defense of its actions. He was arrested in 1768 for allegedly inciting a riot, but public opinion ran so strongly in his favor that an immediate trial was impossible. In the following year, he was acquitted and elected to the Assembly. After his reelection in 1770, Husband was expelled for promoting riots and publishing libels and was soon jailed on the same charges. There he remained until Feb. 1771, when he was freed after a grand jury refused to bring an indictment. Three months later, government troops crushed the Regulators at the Battle of Alamance. As a pacifist, Husband had refused to participate in this violent confrontation; nevertheless, the government outlawed him, destroyed his farm, and forced him to flee from the colony. After a brief stay in Md., Husband took up permanent residence in Pa. After the American Revolution, he came once again to public attention, this time as a leader of the Whiskey Rebellion of 1794. When the rebellion collapsed, Husband was captured, tried, and condemned to death, but President George Washington (q.v.), responding to the pleas of many prominent Pennsylvanians, issued him a pardon. Husband died in 1795 while returning to his home.

Critical Appraisal: Herman Husband's first-known published work, a short essay titled *Some Remarks on Religion*, describes his youthful conversion to Quakerism. Deep religious stirrings and a sense of personal inadequacy—an inability to control "excesses"—prompted the quest, but Husband was moved also by an interest in the broad theological question of "the Authority and Necessity of the inward and sensible Inspiration of the Holy Spirit" and more specifically by the Quaker rejection of the practice of christening children. The account is filled with references to the influence of New Light (or, in the author's description, "Whitefieldian") ministers, and the document is therefore of value not only to students of Husband but to those interested in the intellectual and emotional climate generated by the Great Awakening.

Husband's best-known work, however, is his anonymous contribution to the literature of the Regulator movement. In this two-part account of the activities of the Regulators, *An Impartial Relation. . . of the Recent Differences* and *A Con-*

tinuation of the Impartial Relation, Husband first established the Christian tradition and the British Constitution as the sources of legitimate authority, after which he presented a list of allegations against colonial officials that provided clear evidence, in his opinion, that the present government had forfeited any claim to legitimacy. Petty abuses of office—bloated fees, extraordinary expenditures, and the like—receive mention, but Husband concentrated upon crimes of a more fundamentally political nature: illegal taxation, denial of the principle of majority rule, and interference with "Meetings of Conference" called to preserve "the present Constitution. . . on its ancient foundation." All of this, according to Husband, made resistance inevitable, and when it was learned that 15,000 pounds was to be raised to construct a governor's mansion, there was born "what was commonly called the Mob; which was in a little Time altered to that of the Regulators." The strength of the movement increased when the government decided to equate legitimate protest with treason, and when it further threatened the rights of individuals by declaring "traditional" homesteading practices to be violations of the law. Widening the split were the clergy, who "instead of pointing out the way of righteousness, do treat their congregation like asses, and keep them in ignorance."

In *A Continuation*, Husband offered a sophisticated analysis of flaws within the legal system. He had already attacked the lawyers, whom he considered to be "the greatest Burden and Bane of Society" (a contemporary judgment certainly not unique to him); next he took up the matter of interference with and limitations upon the jury system. Arguing that "common Men could best understand the Meaning of common Men," he attacked the "mischevious and false Doctrine and Practice, that Juries are not Judges of Law, but of Facts only." If that were accepted, he noted, "arbitrary power" could create unjust laws and then bind a jury to an unjust decision on the facts. A case in point was the government's tactic of charging protestors with libel, and Husband here defended the relatively novel position that truth should be a defense in libel cases: "Now if publick Oppression cannot be removed without publick Complaining, and if such Complaints, tho' ever so just and true, should be deemed Libels against those who caused them, would not the Rights and Liberties of the Publick be in a fine situation?"

At the end of the second pamphlet, Husband moved briefly to a consideration of the general resistance movement then brewing against the mother country. Observing that anti-British groups in both Boston and Philadelphia had taken notice of the affair in N.C., he commented that "every one of our Enemies here are utter Enemies to WILKES, and the Cause of Liberty." This statement has sometimes been used to support the argument that the Regulators were part of the greater movement culminating in the War of Independence. The context of both pamphlets clearly indicates, however, that the anti-imperial theme is but an addendum to more decidedly localistic concerns.

Suggested Readings: DAB. *See also* John S. Bassett, "The Regulators of North Carolina," AHAAR (1894), 141-211; Archibald Henderson, ed., "Herman Husband's

Continuation of the Imperial Relation," NCHR, 34 (1941), 48-81; Marvin L. Michael
Kay, "The North Carolina Regulation" in *The American Revolution*, ed. Alfred F. Young
(1976), pp. 71-123; Mary E. Lazenby, *Herman Husband, A Story of His Life* (1940);
William S. Powell, James K. Huhta, and Thomas J. Farham, eds., *The Regulators in
North Carolina, A Documentary History* (1971).

David Sloan
University of Arkansas at Fayetteville

THOMAS HUTCHINSON (1711-1780)

Works: *A Letter to a Member of the Honourable House* (1736); historical
account of Massachusetts's currency, *Boston Evening-Post*, Jan. 4 and 11, 1762;
"Projection for Lowering the Value of Gold Coins, within the Province of the
Massachusetts-Bay" (rep. from *Boston Evening-Post*, Dec. 14, 1761, in [Oxenbridge
Thacher], *Considerations on Lowering the Value of Gold Coins within the Province of the Massachusetts-Bay*, pp. 3-8; 1762; *A Brief State of the Title of the
Province of Massachusetts-Bay to the Country Between the Rivers Kennebeck
and St. Croix* (pub. in appendix to the *Journals of the House of Representatives
of Massachusetts* for 1762; 1963); *The Case of the Provinces of Massachusetts-
Bay and New-York* (1764); *The History of the Colony of Massachussets-Bay*
[to]...*1691* (1764; 2nd ed., 1765; 3rd., 1795; L.S. Mayo, ed., 1936); [Essay on
the Stamp Act] (w. 1764; pub. 1948 by E. S. Morgan, NEQ, 21, 459-492); *The
History of the Province of Massachusetts-Bay*...*1691*...*Until 1750* (1767; 2nd
ed., 1768; L.S. Mayo, ed., 1936); *A Conference Between the Commissaries of
Massachusets-Bay and the Commissaries of New-York* (1768); [Essay on Taxa-
tion] (Ms. w. 1768, Mass. Archives, State House, Boston); dialogue between a
European and an American (w. 1768; pub. 1975 by B. Bailyn in *Perspectives in
American History*, IX, 343-410); *A Collection of Original Papers Relative to the
History of the Colony of Massachusetts-Bay* (editor; 1769); *Copy of Letters Sent
to Great-Britain* (1773); *The Speeches of His Excellency Governor Hutchinson*
(1773); "Vindication" or "Account and Defense of Conduct" (survives only in
ms., Chapin Library, Williams College, Williamstown, Mass. 1775-1776); *Strictures upon the Declaration of the Congress at Philadelphia* (1776; ed. M. Freiberg,
Old South Leaflets, 1958); *The History of the Province of Massachusetts Bay,
from 1749 to 1774* (w. 1776-1778; pub. by John Hutchinson 1828; L.S. Mayo,
ed., 1936; "Additions," ed. C.B. Mayo, 1949); "Hutchinson in America" (Ms.
w. 1778, The British Library, London; pub. in part by P. O. Hutchinson,
1883-1886).

Biography: Thomas Hutchinson, namesake of a prosperous merchant and
officeholder and great-great-grandson of Anne Hutchinson, was born in Boston,
Mass., on Sept. 9, 1711. Even before entering Harvard (A.B., 1727; A.M.,
1730), Hutchinson cultivated a lifelong interest in history. His participation in

public affairs began at age 24, when he wrote his first-known publication, an anonymous proposal to retire Mass.'s paper currency and introduce a medium backed by silver and gold. He ultimately achieved his goal in 1749, when as House speaker, he secured passage of legislation to put the province on the silver standard; Hutchinson considered this his greatest achievement and defended it in the decades that followed.

By 1740 Hutchinson was already established as a merchant in Boston and had begun his long public career, which would eventually embrace, often simultaneously, the province's most important legislative, judicial, and executive offices: member of the House (almost continuously, 1737-1749; speaker, 1746-1749); member of the Council (1749-1766); Suffolk county judge (of the inferior court, 1752-1758; of probate, 1752-1769); lieutenant governor (1758-1771); and chief justice of the Superior Court of Judicature (1760-1771; he did not sit after becoming acting governor in 1769). The appointment as chief justice evoked sustained criticism among various groups in the province of his thirst for office and made him a lightning rod for the opposition to British measures in Mass. after 1764.

Throughout the stormy years that followed, Hutchinson never wavered from his view that parliamentary sovereignty over the colonies was supreme and indivisible. Although he wrote to Eng. privately but effectively in opposition to the stamp duties, which he considered inexpedient, support of British measures in his official capacities brought him opprobrium. In the Aug. 1765 disturbances, a crowd demolished his splendid residence, destroyed part of his great collection of priceless historical documents, and trampled the manuscript of the second volume of his *History* in the mud, some said to prevent him from publishing any further. The Townshend duties he also regarded as ill-advised, but as nonimportation efforts continued and American opposition became increasingly violent, Hutchinson painstakingly formulated his views in two major but incomplete draft essays refuting the arguments in John Dickinson's (q.v.) *Letters from a Pennsylvania Farmer*: a straightforward treatise on taxation; and a unique, conversational dialog between a European (presumably Hutchinson) and an American that, according to Bernard Bailyn, "for lucidity and penetration must rank among the major writings of the Revolution." Reaching back to the history of ancient Rome, the "Dialogue" prophetically went beyond the issues at hand and the conventional parameters of political discourse to address universal questions of allegiance, civil disobedience, law, and morality.

Following Governor Francis Bernard's departure in 1769, Hutchinson became acting governor and played a crucial role in the aftermath of the Boston Massacre of 1770. After some hesitation, Hutchinson accepted the governorship for which he had spent over a quarter-century in preparation and was commissioned in 1771. His administration was marked by discordant battles with the legislature, in which Hutchinson kept the upper hand, assisted for a time by *The Censor* (Boston, 1771-1772), a newspaper he cofounded with his brother-in-law, Lieutenant Governor Andrew Oliver, until events in 1773 shattered his hold on the province. Following upon his officious Jan. debate with the General Court over the merits of parliamentary authority, the revelation that summer of earlier private correspondence with Thomas Whately, a former British undersecretary—which Benjamin Franklin (q.v.) had obtained and sent to Mass. and which the House of Representatives had published in pamphlet form—unleashed a storm of criticism throughout the colonies directed at Hutchinson's supposed central role in a conspiracy of royal officials to misrepresent American affairs to the British ministry. Widely reprinted in America and Eng., the letters formed Hutchinson's most notorious "publication," for in the volatile climate of 1769, he had somewhat loosely urged "an abridgment of what is called English liberty"; nevertheless, he repeated tirelessly but fruitlessly thereafter that his statement was consonant with his well-known views (including those in the *History*). In Dec. 1773 Hutchinson's refusal to allow the East India Company's tea ships to leave Boston harbor resulted in the celebrated Tea Party and brought on the Coercive Acts, which ultimately led to the hostilities at Lexington and Concord.

His usefulness in office at an end, Hutchinson sailed for Eng. in 1774. Received cordially by the king and administration, he acted for a time as an American advisor, adhering to a middle course between the need to subdue the colonies and his desire to mitigate British anger toward Mass. After attending the House of Commons as a spectator in Oct. 1775, where he heard himself accused of Machiavellian politics and held responsible for bringing on the rupture with the colonies, Hutchinson drafted a nineteen-page vindication of his official conduct in Mass.—a rehearsal for the concluding volume of his *History*—and had it presented to the king. In print, Hutchinson fulminated anonymously against the Declaration of Independence, subjecting it to a spirited, clause-by-clause analysis to show that the accusations against the king, and the reasons for the Revolution, were frivolous. It was the last work Hutchinson published during his lifetime. He also completed in manuscript the final volume of his *History*, which posthumously struck the last blow in the war of words with his adversaries. For his children and posterity, he composed a ninety-eight-page account of the Hutchinson family in America, a more personal, autobiographical document not intended for publication, in which he once again recounted, often with material not included in the *History*, his part in nearly forty years of public affairs in Mass. Steeped in bitterness and crushed by the death of his two youngest children, Hutchinson died an exile in London on Jun. 3, 1780, proscribed by the land of his birth and neglected by the empire he had so long faithfully served and defended.

Critical Appraisal: Thomas Hutchinson's most enduring work, his three-volume *History of Massachusetts Bay*, derived from his avocation as avid collector and conservator of public and private manuscript sources. Political and institutional in scope, it was written in his characteristically dry but convoluted style and resembled annals, particularly in volume I, where his portraits of individuals lacked the roundness and maturity they would later have. It was nevertheless a learned work distinguished, in volumes I and II especially, by professional detachment and a critical use of sources. Although the prewar volumes set a scholarly standard, they reflected a genteel mixture of Hutchinson's judicious political conservatism and Enlightenment rationalism. An abhorrence of fanaticism suffused his accounts of Puritan religious institutions, lawmaking, and the witchcraft trials and later surfaced in the treatment of his political adversaries in volume III. Hutchinson's cultural pluralism extended to the Indians, for although they frequently repelled him, he considered whites too quick to think them inferior and was sensitive enough to sympathize with the Indian's fate and to criticize the injustices of the white legal system.

Begun in the afterglow of Eng.'s victory over the French in North America, the *History* took for its central theme the birth and growth of Mass. within the British Empire. In volume I, which carried developments to the advent of the second charter in 1691, Hutchinson maintained that the first settlers had come to Mass. in quest of religious and civil liberty; having brought their charter, they stretched its authority until, during the Civil War and Commonwealth, the colony very nearly became an independent state. The compact theory that the colonists advanced to defend their privileges, Hutchinson endeavored to show, flowed from a misunderstanding of the relationship between colony and mother country. If colonists enjoyed British protection and claimed the liberties of British subjects, he argued, they also owed the inalienable and perpetual allegiance of English subjects to the supreme authority of king in Parliament. But he significantly prefaced volume I with a plea that "the privileges of free natural born English subjects" be preserved in perpetuity to Americans within the empire they had created with so little expense to the mother country.

Hutchinson divided volume II almost evenly between Mass.'s part in the first three intercolonial wars and the half-century of accompanying disputes between the governors and assemblies during which the latter came to tip the balance of power. His evaluation of the governors' problems was predictably sympathetic, and his assessment of the Assembly's claims surprisingly restrained; what he lamented most was the elected Council's lack of independence under the second charter. He devoted substantial attention to paper money and the land bank, but although he strove to explain all views, his contempt for both expedients was obvious. He registered his growing conservatism by closing the volume with a plea that Mass. submit to British trade regulations as a means of sharing the enormous debt Eng. had incurred in protecting her. Hutchinson had written for a local audience, but he had both volumes printed in 2nd editions at London and distributed among the British political establishment. He later gathered a substantial number of seventeenth-century documents in his *Collection of Original Papers*, a volume deservedly ranking him as the premier American historical editor of his day.

Although it would be another decade before Hutchinson would carry the *History* forward, as governor he frequently argued historical precedents with the General Court as he struggled to contain Mass.'s revolutionary impulses. In the ongoing political debate, the Patriots ransacked his *History* and used it alter-nately to support their arguments against British policy or to attack Hutchinson's interpretations. The most telling example came early in 1773, when Hutchinson, in an effort to halt the town meetings sparked by the Boston Committee of Correspondence to protest crown payment of judges' salaries, engaged the General Court in a wide-ranging debate to prove the authority of Parliament absolute and unlimited. "I know of no line that can be drawn between the supreme authority of Parliament and the total independence of the colonies," Hutchinson proclaimed in his opening address. The ensuing messages, in which the House quoted the *History* against its author, represented the boldest statement of arguments on both sides and earned Hutchinson a rebuke from the British colonial secretary for eliciting subversive doctrines from the legislature.

Volume III, begun and completed during Hutchinson's London exile, carried the narrative through his own administration as governor. Hutchinson ultimately revised the chapter on his own administration, which occupied nearly half the volume, deleting entire sections from his first draft to present the story more objectively. Although the volume as finally revised by Hutchinson and published nearly fifty years later by his grandson consequently lacked the emotional intensity of his original draft—it had never approached the hyperbole of his kinsman Peter Oliver's (q.v.) *Origin and Progress of the American Rebellion*—it still may be described as much justificatory memoir as history. Nevertheless, it shared with his *Strictures* and other autobiographical writings from this period, as well as with other Loyalist histories, the view that the Revolution was the result of a conspiracy for independence fomented by a small group of malcontents who led the opposition to British measures out of selfish motives and deceived the people into independence. Hutchinson attributed the first opposition to British authority in Massachusetts and ultimately the rebellion itself, to James Otis (q.v.), who carried out his threat to set the colony aflame after Hutchinson received the chief justiceship promised to Otis's father, James Otis, Sr. Otis's role was eventually assumed by Samuel Adams (q.v.), who, Hutchinson insisted, professed independence as his goal. The remainder of the volume unfolded this theme as Hutchinson described how the patriots by stages, almost imperceptibly over a decade, skillfully led the people to a complete denial of parliamentary sovereignty. Hutchinson also laid a significant share of the blame for the escalating conflict on the failure of the English government to maintain the authority of Parliament and support crown officials in the colony at crucial times. Hutchinson was at the vortex of the Revolution in Mass., the central figure in volume III of his *History*. Profoundest of the ironies of his long life was that this historian of his native colony and province so poorly understood the aspirations of Mass.'s people.

Suggested Readings: DAB; DNB; LHUS; Sibley-Shipton (VIII, 149-217); T$_2$. *See also* Bernard Bailyn, *The Ordeal of Thomas Hutchinson* (1974); Malcolm Freiberg, "Prelude to Purgatory: Thomas Hutchinson in Provincial Massachusetts Politics, 1760-1770" (Ph.D. diss., Brown Univ., 1950), pp. 23-30, 43-45, 69-81, 89-95, 166-169, 213-222; idem, "Thomas Hutchinson: The First Fifty Years (1711-1761)," WMQ, 3rd ser., 15 (1958), 35-55; idem, "Thomas Hutchinson and the Province Currency," NEQ, 30 (1957), 190-208.

Of the many studies in which Hutchinson figures prominently, space restricts mention to the following: Bernard Bailyn, *The Ideological Origins of the American Revolution* (1967); Richard D. Brown, *Revolutionary Politics in Massachusetts: The Boston Committee of Correspondence and the Towns, 1772-1774* (1970), pp. 31-37, 85-93, 119-120, 143-146; Gordon E. Kershaw, *The Kennebeck Proprietors, 1749-1775* (1975); Benjamin W. Labaree, *The Boston Tea Party* (1964), pp. 85-87, 104-150, passim; Edmund S. and Helen M. Morgan, *The Stamp Act Crisis: Prologue to Revolution*, rev. ed. (1962), pp. 53-54, 164-169, 184-186, 265-279, 374-375; Mary Beth Norton, *The British-Americans: The Loyalist Exiles in England, 1774-1789* (1972); Peter Shaw, *American Patriots and the Rituals of Revolution* (1981), pp. 24-47; John J. Waters, Jr., *The Otis Family in Provincial and Revolutionary Massachusetts* (1968), pp. 93-94, 118-125, 145-150, 166-167, 179-180; Hiller B. Zobel, *The Boston Massacre* (1970), pp. 9-11, 31-40, 155-163, 167-172, 202-209, 220-240 passim, 262-263.

A critical edition of the *History* has been edited by Lawrence Shaw Mayo, 3 vols. (1936), with passages Hutchinson deleted from the draft of the final chapter of vol. III presented in Catherine Barton Mayo, "Additions to Thomas Hutchinson's 'History of Massachusetts Bay,'" PAAS, New Series, 59 (1949), 11-74. An earlier draft of the section on the Salem witchcraft trials in vol. II and correspondence between Hutchinson and Ezra Stiles about the *History* are in the NEHGR, 24 (1870), 381-414; 26 (1872), 159-164, 230-233.

Critical editions of Hutchinson's other writings include: Bernard Bailyn, ed., "A Dialogue Between an American and a European Englishman by Thomas Hutchinson [1768]," *Perspectives in American History*, 9 (1975), 343-410; essay on the Stamp Act in Edmund S. Morgan, ed., "Thomas Hutchinson and the Stamp Act," NEQ, 21 (1948), 459-492, with corrections by Bernhard Knollenberg in vol. 22 (1949), 98; Peter Orlando Hutchinson, ed., *The Diary and Letters of Thomas Hutchinson*, 2 vols. (1883-1886), which includes fragments from "Hutchinson in America" in vol. I, 45-105, passim, and vol. II, 456-471, passim; Hutchinson's charges to the grand juries, 1765-1769, in Josiah Quincy, Jr., *Reports of Cases Argued and Adjudged in the Superior Court of Judicature of the Province of Massachusetts Bay, between 1761 and 1772*, ed. Samuel M. Quincy (1865), pp. 110-315, passim; Hutchinson's messages to the Mass. Assembly in *Journals of the House of Representatives of Massachusetts, 1769-1774*, vols. 46-50, ed. Malcolm Freiberg (Massachusetts Historical Society, 1977-1981), with selections in Alden Bradford, ed., *Speeches of the Governors of Massachusetts, 1765-1775* (1818), pp. 194-413; *Letter* (1736) in Andrew McFarland Davis, ed., *Colonial Currency Reprints, 1682-1751* (1910-1911), III, 152-162; Malcolm Freiberg, ed., *Strictures* (Old South Leaflets, no. 227, 1958).

John Catanzariti
Queens College of the City University of New York

I

GILBERT IMLAY (c. 1754-1828)

Works: *Topographical Description of the Western Territory of North America* (1792); *The Emigrants* (1793).

Biography: Gilbert Imlay was probably born in 1754 in Monmouth County, N.J., the date given in the parochial register; a later inscription found on his tombstone in 1833, however, gives Feb. 9, 1758, as his birth date. Imlay was a first lieutenant in the Revolutionary War, but he later referred to himself as "Captain." In 1784 Imlay was a "commissioner for laying out the back settlements" of Ky., where he was later engaged in land speculation, and in 1784 he was probably involved with Gen. James Wilkinson in a plot to separate Ky. and part of the Southwest from the federal government. Imlay had left America the year before, possibly as a result of bad debts, and in Europe he became active with the Girondists in their attempt to gain possession of La. His two works, the *Topographical Description* and *The Emigrants*, were published in Eng. in 1792 and 1793, respectively.

In 1793 Gilbert Imlay became acquainted with Mary Wollstonecraft, author of *Vindication of the Rights of the Woman*. Wollstonecraft had come to Fr. to get over her infatuation with the painter Henry Fuseli, and in 1793 she and Imlay lived together for about four months. Imlay left Wollstonecraft pregnant with Fanny, the future half-sister of Mary Shelley, her child from her subsequent marriage to William Godwin. Imlay lived for a time with an actress, and although Wollstonecraft, who considered her relationship with Imlay a true marriage, clung to the hope that they would be reconciled, such an event never took place. In despair over Imlay's treatment of her, Wollstonecraft attempted suicide by drowning.

Edith Franklin Wyatt described Imlay as "unscrupulous, independent, courageous, a dodger of debts to the poor, a deserter, a protector of the helpless, a revolutionist, a man of enlightenment beyond his age, a greedy and treacherous land booster," but in spite of the many character defects, his good qualities and personal charm and appeal obviously ingratiated him to many people. Little is known about the later years of Imlay's life. A tombstone bearing his name and the date 1828 was found on the Isle of Jersey, but there is no definitive evidence that this person was the same Gilbert Imlay.

Critical Appraisal: It is unfortunate that Gilbert Imlay's reputation as a writer is overshadowed by his flamboyant life and reputation in moral concerns. His two works—one a nonfictionalized account of the settlement of the Western Territory, the other a novel—reveal an interesting and lively style. Both works are filled with lavish praise for America, but both go beyond mere propaganda.

The *Topographical Description* consists of eleven letters written by Imlay to "a friend in England." The letters deal with matters such as a general history of America and early attempts at settlement, in particular the settlement of Ky., and the surveying of land west of the Ohio River for the government. The "western country" is described in detail in regard to its natural resources, climate, and flora and fauna. Imlay also told of making maple sugar, spoke of the rights of man and his abhorrence of slave trade, and gave an account of the defeat of Gen. Arthur St. Clair and the Indians in general. Also listed are some of the settlers of the territory. The contrast between the New and the Old World is obvious when Imlay expressed his pleasure in writing the *Topographical Description* "as it will afford me an opportunity of contrasting the simple and rational life of the American in these back settlements with the distorted and unnatural habits of the Europeans." Similarities have been noted between the *Topographical Description* and Michel Guillaume Jean de Crèvecoeur's (q.v.) *Letters from an American Farmer* (1782), an interesting observation, because the two writers were apparently well acquainted. Both works are letters addressed to a probably fictitious correspondent in Eng., both praise the country and represent it in the most favorable light, and letter IX of each work opposes slavery. In later editions, Imlay included George Washington's (q.v.) Treaty with Spain to open the Mississippi River to navigation, a record of the "Piankishaw Council and Treaty" with the Indians, and reprints of John Filson's (q.v.) "Discovery and Settlement of Kentucky" and "Adventures of Colonel Daniel Boone." The work is valuable as an aid to understanding the settlement of the frontier as well as being an engaging and at times folksy representation of customs and manners of the settlers.

Imlay's reputation as a serious writer is somewhat tarnished, however, by the question of his authorship of *The Emigrants*. The title page of the Dublin edition (1794) states that the work is "traditionally ascribed to Gilbert Imlay But, more probably By Mary Wollstonecraft." Most scholars, however, agree that the work was published, or at least written, before his relationship with Wollstonecraft. Like his nonfictionalized work, *The Emigrants* is highly propagandistic in its comparison of European and American cultures, but it also deals with the laws that make it virtually impossible for a woman to get out of an unhappy marriage by divorce. The technique is epistolary and the plot somewhat contrived and predictable. Briefly, the story concerns the T—n family, with their three marriageable daughters and a wayward son George. The family, having had financial problems, leaves London for Pittsburgh, leaving daughter Eliza in Eng. with her husband. Caroline is the beautiful heroine who often corresponds with Eliza, and Mary is the jealous sister who complicates the plot. Captain Arl—ton serves as the family's guide to its new home, and in the process, he and Caroline fall in love, although neither has expressed it to the other. Before Arl—ton can make any overtures, Mary creates a misunderstanding between him and Caroline resulting in Arl—ton's departure for Louisville. Later the T—n family follows him there, but Arl—ton has gone on another adventure, and it is not until much later that Caroline, kidnapped by Indians, is providentially rescued by Arl—ton, and the lovers are reunited. At the end of the story, Mary goes back to Eng., Eliza leaves her good-for-nothing husband and comes to America, and George reforms with the help of the mysterious Mr. P—P—, who turns out to be the long-lost brother of Mrs. T—n. The happy family proposes a utopian community on the Ohio near Louisville, and, one might assume, they lived happily ever after.

In spite of the obvious plot and fairy-tale ending and its propaganda, *The Emigrants* is an interesting and engaging story. It is written in traditional eighteenth-century style and has a modicum of the anticipation possible in the epistolary novel as earlier demonstrated by Samuel Richardson. Imlay shows a knowledge of literature with repeated allusions to writers such as Voltaire, Tomson, and La Rochefoucauld. As one of the earliest American novels to deal seriously with a social problem such as divorce laws and for its representation of life on the frontier, it anticipates writers such as James Fenimore Cooper. Imlay stated that his story is "founded upon facts" and that "in every particular I have a real character for my model." Edith Franklin Wyatt suggested models such as Daniel Boone, Richard Henderson, Sinclair, Gen. James Wilkinson, Crèvecoeur, and George Rogers Clark (q.v.). The use of such models would, in itself, recommend the novel for further consideration by the student of American literature.

That Imlay's literary reputation is tenuous seems fitting, given his unsettled, adventuresome way of life. It is unfortunate, however, that his works have been generally neglected. They provide some valuable insight into frontier life, deal with some important issues, and make for fascinating reading. The student of American letters would do well to give more careful consideration to Gilbert Imlay.

Suggested Readings: DAB; LHUS. *See also* Alexander Cowie, *The Rise of the American Novel* (1948), pp. 38-43; Oliver Farrar Emerson, "Notes on Gilbert Imlay, Early American Writer," PMLA, 39 (1924), 406-439; William Godwin, *Memoirs of Mary Wollstonecraft* (1930); Henri Petter, *The Early American Novel* (1971), pp. 216-219, 416-417; Arthur Hobson Quinn, *American Fiction: An Historical and Critical Survey* (1936), pp. 11-12; Ralph Leslie Rusk, "The Adventures of Gilbert Imlay," IUS, 10, no. 57 (1923); J. W. Townsend, *Kentuckians in History and Literature* (1907); Mary Wollstonecraft, *The Love Letters of Mary Wollstonecraft to Gilbert Imlay*, ed. Roger Ingpen (1980); Edith Franklin Wyatt, "The First American Novel," AM, 144 (1929), 466-475.

Robert L. Mc Carron
Bryan College

CHARLES INGLIS (c. 1734-1816)

Works: *An Essay on Infant Baptism* (1768); *A Vindication of the Bishop of Landaff's Sermon* (1768); *A Sermon on II Corinth. V. 6* (1774); *The Deceiver Unmasked* (1776); *The True Interest of America Impartially Stated* (1776); *The Christian Soldier's Duty* (1777); *A Sermon on Phillippians III, 20, 21* (1777); *The Letters of Papinian* (1779); *The Duty of Honouring the King* (1780); *A Sermon Preached Before the Grand Lodge* (1783); *Dr. Inglis's Defence of His Character* (1784); *A Farewell Sermon* (1784); *Remarks on a Late Pamphlet* (1784); *A Sermon Preached Before His Excellency* (1787); *Steadfastness in Religion and Loyalty Recommended* (1793); *A Sermon Preached. . .for a General Fast* (1794); *The Claim and Answer* (1799).

Biography: Charles Inglis was born at Glencolumbkille, County Donegal, Ire., sometime around 1734, the son of a long line of Anglican clergymen. His education was informal but thorough. In 1754 he immigrated to America and taught school at Lancaster, Pa., until 1758. He then returned to Eng. to be ordained and was put in charge of the mission parish at Dover, Pa. (now Del.). He remained there until late 1765, when be became assistant to Rev. Samuel Auchmuty (q.v.) at Trinity Church, N.Y. While he was an assistant to Auchmuty, Inglis's writings on theological subjects earned him an M.A. from Oxford in 1770, and he involved himself in efforts to establish an American episcopacy and a special mission to the Mohawks. Both schemes came to naught.

When the American colonists turned to armed rebellion, Inglis unhesitatingly supported the crown, yet, in spite of great personal risk, remained in N.Y. during George Washington's (q.v.) occupation of the city in the summer of 1776. During that time, he anonymously authored the "Letters of a New York Farmer" in the *New York Gazette*, as well as the pamphlet, *The Deceiver Unmasked*, which was burned in N.Y. by enraged rebels and reissued in Philadelphia as *The True Interest of America Impartially Stated*. When the British reoccupied N.Y., Inglis was able to demonstrate his support more freely and openly. After Auchmuty's death in 1777, he became rector of Trinity Church and remained so until the evacuation of 1783. He then returned to Eng. and in 1787 was selected to be the first bishop of Nova Scotia in charge of the Anglican Church in what remained of British North America. Through his efforts, the Diocese of Nova Scotia was established and the first university in Can. was built. He died on Feb. 24, 1816, and was buried at Halifax.

Critical Appraisal: Charles Inglis's works fall roughly into three categories: religious works (the largest category), political pamphlets, and defenses of his character. The latter is represented by two items published in 1784 in response to the Rev. Samuel Peters's (q.v.) attack on his character published in London during what developed into a "competition" for the bishopric of Nova Scotia. As defensive documents, they do not go far beyond the issue that necessitated them and are of little literary interest. Inglis's other polemic writings seem similarly restricted by their essentially defensive nature. His political pamphlets, *The True Interest of America Impartially Stated* and *The Letters of Papinian*, present competent, effective arguments articulating the Loyalist position and defending British policy, but, caught up in the strategies of argument, Inglis seemed unable to break out of the thrust-and-parry of political infighting to project a broad vision of human society that catches the imagination and that effectively counterbalances the democratic vision emerging from rebel literature. Inglis debated well, but the intensity of his efforts made it difficult to discern the concepts of reality that informed his perspective.

The complexity of his perspective and the scope of his vision of reality emerge most fully in his sermons. Because these works are essentially didactic rather than propagandistic in their intention, Inglis's approach generally operates to set specific occasions and occurrences in the prevailing universal, cosmic context (as he understands it) in which human reality unfolds and in which all human events find meaning. His cosmic perspective was basically that of an eighteenth-century rationalist. At its center lay a vision of order:

> Through all the works of God, we perceive a regular gradation—one part rising in perfection above another; which evinces him to be a God of order as well as love. Between the spiritual and material worlds, there would be an immense chasm, did not man fill it up: Man accordingly is the link which unites those worlds, and thereby preserves the due gradation which is everywhere observable. (*Sermon. . .Before the Grand Lodge*)

Church and state, the fundamental institutions of man, were bound together by the need to preserve order. They were "the pillars. . .on which society rests, and by which it is upheld; remove these, and the fabric sinks into ruin" (*Steadfastness in Religion*). Thus respect for authority and obedience become fundamental social and moral obligations in Inglis's view of man's individual responsibilities. His term for this central aspect of character was "loyalty," which manifested itself in spiritual righteousness and civil propriety. It was imperative that men recognize "how close a connection there is between Religion and Loyalty—between our religious and civil duties. He that sincerely serves God, will be loyal to his earthly Sovereign, from a principle of Conscience" (*Steadfastness in Religion*). In the British Constitution, it was the king who manifested this inseparable union of church and state:

> The Principles of our Church, founded on the Word of God, inculcate Loyalty in the strongest Manner, and teach us to consider our Sovereign as *supreme Head in Earth* of the Church of England: Our church also, which is modelled on the Plan of the pure, primitive Church of Christ, and according to his own instructions, is interwoven with the State; so that overturning the one, would be endangering, if not overturning the other. (*Sermon on Phillippians*)

It is from this perspective that Inglis viewed the lives of individual men and assessed the significance of the events of his time. As a result, throughout his sermons, there is a consistency of judgment and observation. His concept of what makes a good man remained firm and constant, and his abhorrence of the American Revolution and of the French Revolution (twenty years apart) was founded on the same set of principles. From this conceptual consistency, Inglis created an impressive sense of assurance that lent authority to his style and projected something of the strength of his conviction.

Suggested Readings: CCMC; DAB; DNB; Sprague (V, 186-191); T₂. *See also* A.W.H Eaton, *The Church in Nova Scotia and the Tory Clergy of the Revolution* (1891), pp. 109-134; J. Fingard, *The Anglican Design in Loyalist Nova Scotia* (1972); R.V. Harris, *Charles Inglis* (1937). J.W. Lydekker, *The Life and Letters of Charles Inglis* (1936).

Thomas B. Vincent
Royal Military College of Canada

JAMES IREDELL (1751-1799)

Works: *To the Inhabitants of Great Britain* (1774); *Answers to Mr. Mason's Objections to the New Constitution* (1788).

Biography: Born in Lewes in the county of Sussex, Eng., on Oct. 5, 1751, James Iredell was the son of the Bristol merchant Francis Iredell and his Irish wife, Margaret McCulloh. In 1766 Francis suffered a paralysis and subsequently was forced to give up his business. At that time, James, then 16 years of age, took over the support of the family. To do so, however, required the aid of influential relatives and friends, among them Henry McCulloh of N.C., who succeeded in obtaining for James the post of comptroller of customs at Edenton. To assume his new position, Iredell left Eng. for N.C. in 1768.

Iredell spent six years at the post in the custom house, in the meantime sending home to his invalid father his yearly income and studying law under the direction of Samuel Johnston, son of John Johnston, surveyor-general of N.C. and nephew of Governor Gabriel Johnston. Eventually, Iredell married Samuel's sister Hannah, and from their union came four children: Thomas, Annie, Helen, and James. A hard worker, Iredell gained his license as a lawyer in 1771 and shortly after plunged into the pre-Revolutionary War debates, penning the remarkable address *To the Inhabitants of Great Britain*, pointing out to the British their transgressions against the original colonial charters.

As his voice in support of the colonies became respected, numerous posts came his way, including the positions of state judge (1777), state attorney general (1779), and commissioner on the Council of State (1787). His work in support of the Constitution—as writer of the forceful *Answers to Mr. Mason's*

Objections to the New Constitution and as representative to the Constitutional Convention of 1788—attracted the attention of early notables, including George Washington (q.v.), who appointed Iredell associate justice of the Supreme Court in 1790. At the age of 38, Iredell began his illustrious, although brief, career in the Supreme Court. During this period, Iredell succeeded in enunciating the principles of states' rights. Important decisions in which he was instrumental include *Wilson* vs. *Daniel, Ware* vs. *Hylton, Chisholm* vs. *Georgia*, and *Hans* vs. *Louisiana*. After undergoing the rigors of the post of Supreme Court judge for ten years, Iredell died at home in Edenton on Oct. 20, 1799.

Critical Appraisal: As J.A. Leo Lemay pointed out, "Iredell's tastes were distinctly literary.... He was fond of the novels of Richardson, Fielding, and Sterne and of Dr. Fordyce's sermons.... In maturer years Iredell's favorite writer seems to have been Edmund Burke." His writings, though—with the exception of a few early verses, an anti-Deistic essay, and copious letters—are chiefly political.

His most famous political tract, *Answers to Mr. Mason's Objections to the New Constitution*, best demonstrates his staightforwardness and good sense. A point-by-point refutation of George Mason's (q.v.) *Objections to the New Constitution*, Iredell's *Answers* demonstrates his confidence in the government envisioned by the architects of the Constitution. Inclined to cite English precedent, Iredell appeared naive at certain points, as with the objection lodged by Mason that the president appears to have perhaps too much latitude with respect to his pardoning powers. Iredell's response demonstrates his confidence in the system, stating "The probability of the President of the United States committing an act of treason against his country is slight." Another occasion when he was somewhat limited in his vision was his assumption that freedom from tyranny automatically ensures a free press. At one point, Iredell departed from his role of defender of the Constitution to explainer of the circumstances surrounding adoption when he offered a reason (not an excuse) for the concessions made in the realm of slave trade to the southern states.

By and large, though, Iredell is right on the mark, assuring Mason and his readers of, for instance, the effectiveness of the system of checks and balances or the importance of trusting human nature, for one cannot, according to Iredell, guard against every abuse. What is most important to the N.C. lawyer and delegate is getting the ball rolling, for "if we continue as we now are, wrangling about every trifle [he concluded]... we shall probably present a spectacle for malicious exaltation to our enemies."

Suggested Readings: DAB; LHUS. *See also* Nettie Southworth Herndon, "James Iredell" (Ph.D. diss., Duke Univ., 1944); Griffith J. McRee, *Life and Correspondence of James Iredell*, 2 vols. (1857, rep. 1949); Stephen B. Weeks, "Judge Iredell and the Political Literature of the Revolution," AHAAR, (1895), pp. 244-247.

A. Franklin Parks
Frostburg State College

J

JOHN JAMES (c. 1633-1729)

Works: *Of John Bunyan's Life* (1702); *On...John Haynes* (1713); *To the Memory of Grace Nichols* (ms. in The John Hay Library, Brown Univ., w.c. 1702); "To the Memory of the Worthy and Much Bewail'd Mrs. Esther Buckinghame and Mrs. (Es)ther Beaumont" (c. 1702); *On the Death of...Gershom Bulkley* (1714).

Biography: The details of John James's early life remain uncertain. He was born sometime around 1633, probably in London, into a family of dissenting preachers. He received his education from a minister named Veal and began to preach in Eng. Some accounts assert that he arrived in Boston in 1681; others tell of his imprisonment for preaching in Eng. in 1682. By all accounts, however, James was in New Eng. in 1682, when the town of Haddam, Conn., invited him to preach. In 1686 James became the minister of Haddam, but within a few years, he was living in Wethersfield. In 1693 he took up the ministry in Derby, where he also served as town clerk and schoolmaster. During the time he spent in Derby, James suffered from a nervous disorder that prevented his remaining in the ministry. In 1706 he moved to New Haven, where he taught in a grammar school. He later taught in Guilford, Hadley, and Brookfield. In 1710 he was awarded the M.A. from Harvard, a degree conferred on ministers who had not attended a university. James died in Wethersfield on Aug. 10, 1729.

Critical Appraisal: John James's four published elegies are among the first verse printed in Conn. Fond of alchemical imagery, James incorporated such imagery into his poems. His elegy on John Bunyan, for example, compares God's saving grace with turning brass into gold. The elegy *On the Death of...Gershom Bulkley* compares the inefficacies of worldly cures with the glories of the heavenly cures of God, a theme he also took up in *To the Memory of Grace Nichols*. James's poetry, filled with puns, conceits, and word play, is more pious than polished, and it is representative of British metaphysical verse as it was practiced in New Eng. during the seventeenth and early eighteenth centuries.

Suggested Readings: CCNE; FCNEV; Sibley-Shipton (V, 13-17). *See also* Cotton Mather, *Magnalia Christi Americana* (1701), II, iv.

Cheryl Rivers
Manhattanville College

DEVEREUX JARRATT (1733-1801)

Works: *A Brief Narrative of the Revival of Religion in Virginia* (1778); *Thoughts on Some Capital Subjects in Divinity* (1791); *The Nature of Love to Christ* (1792); *A Sermon Preached Before the Convention of the Protestant Church in Virginia* (1792); *A Solemn Call to Sleeping Sinners* (1792); *Thoughts on Christian Holiness* (1792); *Sermons on Various and Important Subjects in Practical Divinity*, 3 vols. (1793-1794); *The Life of Devereux Jarratt* (1806).

Biography: Devereux Jarratt was born into a family of humble means in New Kent County, Va., on Jan. 17, 1733. Orphaned, he grew up under the influence of an older brother who was interested in the economic pursuits and worldly amusements of plantation society. While working as a tutor in the home of a family named John Cannon, Jarratt underwent a conversion experience to New Light Presbyterianism and remained an evangelical for the rest of his life. Nonetheless, Jarratt became an Anglican, in part, it is assumed, because of the Church of England's intrenched position in Va. society. After learning Latin and Greek, Jarratt sailed to Eng., where he was ordained in the Church of England. In 1763 Jarratt returned to Va. and became the rector of Bath Parish in Dinwiddie County.

As an evangelical clergyman in the Church of England, Jarratt was surrounded by controversy. Preaching extemporaneously, he attacked frivolity and emphasized the need for spiritual rebirth. Between 1763 and 1772, Jarratt's preaching, which took him to many parts of Va. and N.C., attracted large crowds and brought about numerous conversions. When he befriended the Methodists, however, other Anglican clergymen criticized his behavior, and the Baptists depleted his following.

Although Jarratt was a patriot, his ministry declined after the American Revolution. Disestablishment and a decline in religious interest hurt the Church of England as a whole, and when the Methodists broke with the Anglicans, Jarratt disapproved of their action and found himself criticized by both sides. During the 1780s and 1790s, his congregations were small and lacking in spirit, and although he continued to perform his parochial duties, he devoted more and more of his energy to scholarly pursuits. Jarratt died on Jan. 29, 1801. Francis Asbury (q.v.) preached his funeral sermon.

Critical Appraisal: Devereux Jarratt is best known for his autobiography, *The Life of Devereux Jarratt*, contained in a set of letters written during the 1790s. A literate man of the lower class, Jarratt gave convincing testimony to the strength of Va. class structure: as a youth he thought of *"gentle* folks as being of a superior order" and ran when he saw a rider wearing a wig. In addition to social commentary, the *Life* is valuable for its insights into the development of religion in revolutionary Va. Personal information, however, is curiously incomplete: Jarratt wrote at length about a tumor on his cheek that troubled his final years and barely mentioned his wife who worried about it with him. Essentially, Jarratt's *Life* is a spiritual autobiography in which the emphasis is on the author's religious awakening, his conversion, and his subsequent attempt to serve God.

The unorthodox nature of Jarratt's Anglicanism was evident in his publications. He wrote about the need to be "born again," explained his evangelical sermon style, and attacked "civil mirth" such as drinking, dancing, and gambling. He also criticized Anglican clergymen whose personal behavior fell short of his standards and those who were hostile to his ministry. Jarratt, however, was a staunch believer in the Church of England. Its worship was "beautiful and decent," its "doctrines, creeds, and articles" were sound, and its hierarchical organization was "truly primitive and apostolic."

In *Thoughts on Divinity*, Jarratt encapsulated his views on Christianity. The evangelical emphasis was apparent when he discussed salvation: "A Justifying faith comprehends these two particulars. First, a believing, with the heart, the truth of the gospel, and particularly the truth of that method of salvation, through Christ, which the gospel reveals. And, secondly, a hearty compliance with that method, and a full consent, and hearty approbation of that method of salvation." At the same time, Jarratt was no Antinomian. At the last judgment, Jarratt believed all men would be evaluated on the basis of their deeds, Christians according to biblical precepts, and heathens according to the law of nature.

It has been argued that Devereux Jarratt exaggerated his isolation from other Anglican clergymen, that he made clerical enemies by a self-righteous posture with respect to worldly pleasure, and that his origins and his demeanor were less humble than he affected. Despite these criticisms, one is struck with the difficult road that Jarratt traveled, choosing to join a church that would never fully accept him and cutting himself off from his natural allies. In a period when religion was divided between those individuals who sought to know God through reason and those who emphasized emotion, Devereux Jarratt sought the best of both approaches.

Suggested Readings: CCV; DAB; Sprague (I, 214-222). *See also* Douglas Adair, ed., "The Autobiography of the Reverend Devereux Jarratt, 1732-1763," WMQ, 3rd ser., 9 (1952), 346-393; Joan Rezner Gundersen, "The Anglican Ministry in Virginia, 1723-1776: A Study of Social Class" (Ph.D. diss., Univ. of Notre Dame, 1972); David L. Holmes, "Devereux Jarratt: A Letter and a Reevaluation," HMag PEC, 47 (1978), 37-49; Rhys Isaac, "Evangelical Revolt: The Nature of the Baptists' Challenge to the Traditional Order in Virginia, 1765 to 1775," WMQ, 3rd ser. (1974), 345-368; Harry G. Rabe, "The Reverend Devereux Jarratt and the Virginia Social Order," HMagPEC, 33 (1964), 229-336.

Sidney Charles Bolton
University of Arkansas at Little Rock

JOHN JAY (1745-1829)

Works: *The Address to the People of Great Britain* (1774); *New York, April 16, 1776. Extract of a Letter from John Jay* (1776); *The Charge Delivered by the Hon. John Jay. . .to the Grand Jury. . .at Kingston. . .September 9, 1777* (1777); *To the Inhabitants of the United States. . .the Present Situation Demands. . .Attention. . .John Jay, President. . .Annapolis* (1779); *The Diary of John Jay During the Peace Negotiations of 1782* (w. 1782; pub. 1934); *Letters, Being the Whole of the Correspondence Between. . .John Jay, Esq.; and Mr. Lewis Littlepage* (1786); *An Address to the People of the State of New-York, on the Subject of the Constitution* (1788); "Essays II, III, IV, V, and LXIV," *The Federalist* (1788); *The Charge of Chief Justice Jay...May, 1790* (1790); *A Charge Delivered by the Hon. John Jay. . .to the Grand Jury of the United States Court, Virginia* (1793); *Governor's Speech. Gentlemen of the Senate and Assembly, Perceiving the Various Objections* (1798); *By. . .John Jay. . .A Proclamation. Whereas It Is the Duty and the Interest* (1798); *Gentlemen of the Senate and Assembly* (1800); *Gentlemen, It Has Generally and Justly Been Considered as Highly Important to the Security and Duration of Free States* (1801); *Two Letters from the Hon. John Jay to the Rev. Cave Jones* (1812).

Biography: John Jay was born in New York City on Dec. 12, 1745. In keeping with his Huguenot heritage, the pious young boy began his formal education at a New Rochelle school run by Calvinist minister Peter Stouppe. After graduation from King's College in 1764, Jay studied law in Benjamin Kissam's N.Y. office and gained admission to the bar in 1768. The following year, he became chief clerk of the N.Y.-N.J. Boundary Commission. On Apr. 28, 1774, the young attorney married Sarah Van Brugh Livingston, youngest daughter of politically powerful William Livingston (q.v.).

Jay represented his colony in both the First and Second Continental Congresses. In 1777 he chaired the committee that drafted N.Y.'s constitution, and he became that state's first chief justice. Between Dec. 1778 and Sept. 1779, Jay served as president of the Continental Congress. He left that office to become minister plenipotentiary to Sp., but he departed Madrid in early 1782 to serve with Benjamin Franklin (q.v.) and John Adams (q.v.) in Paris, where Anglo-American peace was being negotiated. From Jul. 1784 until Mar. 1790, Jay served first as the Confederation government's secretary of foreign affairs and later as the new federal government's acting secretary of state (until Thomas Jefferson's [q.v.] return from Europe). Meanwhile, in 1785, he became first president of the New York Society for Promoting the Manumission of Slaves. From Mar. 1789 to Jun. 1795, he served as the U.S. Supreme Court's first chief justice. His decision with the majority in the case of *Chisholm* vs. *Georgia* (1793) led directly to adoption of the Eleventh Amendment. In 1794, while still chief justice, Jay traveled to Eng. to negotiate the controversial treaty bearing his name.

Upon his return in 1795, Jay learned of his election to N.Y.'s governorship. After retiring from that post in 1801, he devoted his energies to religious matters, becoming president of the Westchester Bible Society in 1818 and of the American Bible Society in 1821. Jay died at Bedford, N.Y., on May 17, 1829.

Critical Appraisal: John Jay's published writings reveal the growth of his calmly reasoned commitment to American union. His early reputation soared when the First Continental Congress adopted his draft of *The Address to the People of Great Britain* on Oct. 21, 1774. Thomas Jefferson admired the address as "a production certainly of the finest pen in America...the first composition in the English language." It appealed to the "people" of Eng. to prevent parliamentary ministers from forging additional links in a despotic chain, which Jay said threatened the liberties of all British citizens. He perceived the Quebec Act, with its provision for a Catholic bishop in Can., as a tyrannous indication that Parliament intended to encourage the "sanguinary and impious tenets" of a religion that fostered "bigotry, persecution, murder, and rebellion through every part of the world." He warned that a popular sense of justice ought to secure equal freedom for colonists and residents of Eng., because Americans would "never submit to be hewers of wood or drawers of water for any ministry or nation in the world." Should equal freedoms be secured, he believed they would promote an eternally glorious and happy union between the mother country and her colonies. His faith in this conciliatory, but uncompromising, stance manifested itself a year later in his initial draft of the "Olive Branch Petition," which in final form was authored by John Dickinson (q.v.).

In *The Charge Delivered by the Hon. John Jay...to the Grand Jury...at Kingston...September 9, 1777*, the author blamed King George's tyranny for the advent of Revolution, and he expressed abiding faith that Divine Providence would secure American victory. He cautioned the people to infuse their new Constitution with the "virtue, honour, the love of liberty and of science" that would be its soul. Warning that an educated vigilance furnished the best means of thwarting such villainous conspiracies and personal vices as threatened constitutional liberties, he exhorted every citizen "diligently to read and study the constitution of his country, and teach the rising generation to be free."

In Dec. 1785, when the flamboyant gadfly Lewis Littlepage accused him of personal treachery and conspiratorial villainy, Jay resorted to publication of his private correspondence to prove his faithful execution of public responsibilities while in Sp. and Fr. The 1st edition of *Letters, Being the Whole of the Correspondence Between...John Jay, Esq.; and Mr. Lewis Littlepage*, published by Francis Childs during the second week of Jan. 1786, contained so many errors that its author turned to printer Eleazer Oswald several months later with an expanded, revised edition. As promised in the introduction to the work, Jay calmly and methodically arranged the evidence to demonstrate that Littlepage's fulminations were "bare Assertions" unsupported by facts. Littlepage's response, *Answer to a Pamphlet* (1787), served only to weaken further the public reputation of Jay's detractor.

Using the pseudonym "Publius," Jay collaborated with Alexander Hamilton (q.v.) and James Madison (q.v.) to produce *The Federalist*, a series of eighty-five essays designed to promote ratification of the U.S. Constitution and destined to become a classic elaboration of the theory of American republican government. Jay authored "Essays II, III, IV, V, and LXIV," the first of which appeared originally in N.Y.'s *Independent Journal* on Oct. 31, 1787. In "Essay II" he candidly stated that the American states' strength and security in foreign affairs depended upon their achievement of stable union. He reasoned that common language, religious customs, and attachment to republican principles of government, as well as geographic circumstances, naturally established the advantage of union over independent regional confederacies or individual states. Warming to his theme in "Essay III," Jay argued that "a cordial union under an efficient national government" would most likely overcome the local "passions and interests" that provoke "direct and unlawful violence" and provide "just causes" for war against American states; he said the history of Indian-white relations proved that state-supported actions, unlike those of the national government, had frequently led to justifiable retaliation by Indians. In "Essay IV" he warned that disunity invited powerful, jealous nations like Eng., Sp., and Fr. to use the most fallacious pretexts for initiating "unjust" martial action against American states. Continuing his theme in "Essay V," Jay used Queen Anne's letter of Jul. 1, 1706, to the Scottish Parliament to support his contention that only union could furnish "a solid foundation of lasting peace." In a poignant, extended metaphor, he speculated that the "*Northern Hive*" would probably be strongest in a divided America, and not improbably, "its young swarms might often be tempted to gather honey in the more blooming fields and milder air of their luxurious and more delicate neighbors."

On Mar. 7, 1788, after a lengthy bout with crippling arthritis, Jay published "Essay LXIV," his final contribution to *The Federalist*. He defended the treaty-making provisions of the proposed Constitution on the grounds that they made national interest paramount, allowed the president the secrecy and dispatch to negotiate effectively, assured fairness to all states through Senate review, and guaranteed treaties the force of supreme law. In response to fear that corruption of unethical senators might result in unfair treaties, Jay reminded his readers that rules for election of senators, guarding as they did against unregulated democratic enthusiasm, promoted proven good character and sound reason over "those brilliant appearances of genius and patriotism, which like transient meteors, sometimes mislead as well as dazzle." He, like most of his contemporaries, staunchly defended republican government but regarded political democracy as anathema to its strength and stability.

An Address to the People of the State of New York, which the ailing Jay composed during the first months of 1788, furnished a more rousing appeal for adoption of the Constitution than had his *Federalist* essays. Reverting to the language of his religious heritage, he gave the Confederation government its due by saying, "Union was the child of wisdom—Heaven blessed it, and it wrought out our political salvation." But war's end "loosened the bonds of union," and "the spirit of private gain expelled the spirit of public good." The Confederation government, "destitute of power," could only preside over the economic and political collapse of the new nation, whose distresses were "accumulating like compound interest." Meanwhile, the American experiment in republican government had inspired people throughout the world, and Jay admonished Americans to remember that their failure might forever doom chances for freedom elsewhere. He wrote, "Experience is a severe preceptor, but it teaches useful truths, and however harsh, is always honest—Be calm and dispassionate, and listen to what it tells us." With those words, he pressed for immediate adoption of the Constitution as the most efficient means of salvaging America's providential political experiment.

Reaction to Jay's *Address* came swiftly. George Washington proclaimed, "The good sense, forcible observations, temper and moderation with which the pamphlet is written, cannot fail, I should think of making a serious impression upon the anti-federal mind." Noah Webster (q.v.), writing in the Apr. 1788 issue of *American Magazine*, echoed Washington's expressions and noted that several of Jay's observations were new. None of Jay's later writings would surpass the expository skill or republican fervor of his *Address*, which even today stands as a convincing monument to the literary abilities and national ardor of America's founding fathers.

Suggested Readings: DAB; LHUS; T₂. *See also* Gottfried Dietze, *The Federalist* (1960); Paul Leicester Ford, ed., *Pamphlets on the Constitution of the United States, Published During Its Discussion by the People, 1787-1788* (1888), pp. 67-86; Albert Furtwangler, "Strategies of Candor in *The Federalist*," EAL, 14 (1979), 91-109; William Jay, *Life of John Jay*, 2 vols. (1833); Henry P. Johnston, ed., *The Correspondence and Public Papers of John Jay*, 4 vols. (1890-1893); Frank Monaghan, *John Jay* (1935); Richard B. Morris, *John Jay: The Making of a Revolutionary* (1975); idem, *John Jay, the Nation, and the Court* (1967).

Rick W. Sturdevant
University of California, Santa Barbara

THOMAS JEFFERSON (1743-1826)

Works: *A Summary View of the Rights of British America* (1774); *Notes on the Establishment of a Money Unit* (1784); *Notes on the State of Virginia* (1788); *Observations on the Whale-Fishery* (1788); *Extract of a Letter...to George Wythe...Jan. 16* (1796); *Philadelphia, Dec. 31st* (1797); *A Supplementary Note on the Mould Board* (1798); *An Appendix to the Notes on Virginia* (1800); *A Test of the Religious Principles of Mr. Jefferson* (1800); *A Manual of Parliamentary Practice* (1801); *Republican Notes on Religion* (1803); *Leave and Permission Given to Samuel Grofton* (1808); *Address to the Citizens of Massachusetts* (1810);

The Proceedings of the Government of the United States in Maintaining the Public Right to the Beach of the Mississippi (1812); *Explanations of the Ground Plan of the University of Virginia* (1824); *Letter from Thomas Jefferson to Mr. Weightman, Late Mayor of Washington, Monticello, June 24th* (1826). For a complete bibliography of works by Thomas Jefferson, see Julian P. Boyd, ed., *The Papers of Thomas Jefferson*, 19 vols. (1950-1974), which contains all works written by Jefferson through 1791. See also Albert E. Bergh and Andrew A. Lipscomb, eds., *The Writings of Thomas Jefferson*, 20 vols. (1905), and Lester J. Cappon, ed., *The Adams-Jefferson Letters*, 2 vols. (1959).

Biography: Thomas Jefferson, the elder son of Jane Randolph and Peter Jefferson, was born Apr. 13, 1743, at Shadwell in Albemarle County, Va. His father was a surveyor who left him an estate of more than 2,700 acres and the slaves to tend it. In 1760 Jefferson went to William and Mary College and studied under Dr. William Small, who contributed much to developing his scientific and inductive mind. After finishing his schooling in 1762, he stayed on in Williamsburg for almost twenty years, studying the law for a time under George Wythe, who educated him to a sense of the social and humanizing force in law that guarantees liberties, and later serving as legislator and public figure.

From 1769 to 1776, Jefferson served in the House of Burgesses, developing his reputation for learning and for his ability to write. With the publication in 1774 of his *Summary View of the Rights of British America*, he began a series of significant public documents pushing for republican reform to counter any moves meant to further monarchical institutions. In 1776 Jefferson was asked to draft the Declaration of Independence. Thereafter, Jefferson worked on at least two drafts of a constitution for the state of Va. (1776-1783), a "Bill for the General Diffusion of Knowledge" (1779) and another for "Establishment of Religious Freedom" (1779). He was also responsible for the measures to abolish primogeniture and entailment in Va.

In the early 1780s, Jefferson began work on *Notes on the State of Virginia* (1785) as a response, in part, to queries and charges from Europe, especially the French, on life in the colonies. Jefferson may also have taken on answering these queries to ease his disappointments with political life and to distract himself from the pain and emotion surrounding his wife's final illness. In 1772 Jefferson married Martha Wayles Skelton, who gave him six children; only two daughters lived to maturity. When Martha died in Sept. 1782, Jefferson's grief was profound.

Jefferson's years as state legislator, as governor of Va., as a member of Congress, and as negotiator of treaties of foreign commerce all prepared him for his appointment to succeed Benjamin Franklin (q.v.) in Fr. and later for his appointment by George Washington (q.v.) as the nation's first secretary of state. In 1793 Jefferson resigned as secretary of state and retired to Monticello, and his political career of twenty-five years seemed to come to a halt. He had argued individual liberties and favored the new Constitution only while insisting on an addition of a Bill of Rights. He then backed away from the Federalists, in particular because of Alexander Hamilton's (q.v.) drive toward centralizing power, specifically through financial policies that Jefferson disapproved.

But public need would not let him retire. Three years later, he returned to serve as vice-president to John Adams (q.v.). Teaming with James Madison (q.v.), Jefferson fought the repressive Federalist measures contained in the Alien and Sedition Acts. When the Federalists were defeated in 1800, Jefferson found himself president only after action of the House of Representatives. His terms as president stand out for two reasons. He kept the nation out of war, allowing it to mature and strengthen under his direction, and he effected the Louisiana Purchase, bequeathing to the young nation vast quantities of land, which Jefferson considered vital to human happiness and liberty.

Retiring from the presidency, Jefferson returned to Monticello, where he planned and presided over the establishment of the University of Virginia. The university is the embodiment of his conviction that a people can hold neither land nor liberty unless educated to the task. Jefferson, as did John Adams, died on Jul. 4, 1826, fifty years after the signing of the Declaration of Independence.

Critical Appraisal: Since Thomas Jefferson published but one book in his lifetime, *Notes on the State of Virginia*, most of his collected works is made up of letters and public documents bearing designations such as bills, opinions, notes, resolutions, and reports. In his epitaph, Jefferson singled out two documents in which he took special pride: "Here was buried Thomas Jefferson / Author of the Declaration of Independance (sic) / of the Statute of Virginia for religious freedom / & Father of the University of Virginia." Jefferson's initial version of the Declaration would have, perhaps, undone slavery; but compromise needed for a successful vote struck his antislavery lines from the document. Jefferson's own holding of slaves throughout his life remains a paradox. Since Garry Wills has challenged earlier interpretations of the Declaration as typical Lockean fare, no longer can the work be called simplistically a general and summary statement of mideighteenth-century thought. The work now has to be studied in the light of additional sources not only as a Revolutionary document but also as a document making specific "scientific," "moral," and "sentimental" judgments about living as a nation of brothers. The national freedom and unity upheld in this document Jefferson later complemented by argument for religious freedom for the individual in the *Statute of Virginia for Religious Freedom* (1786). This two-page document states that opinion and belief depend not on will "but follow involuntarily on evidence" proposed to the mind. Since opinions and beliefs are not the object of civil government, as peace and good order are, Jefferson's document argues that no man shall be compelled to support or be hindered from supporting religious opinions, beliefs, or institutions. Religious freedom, said Jefferson, is a natural right outside the jurisdiction of civil government and subject only to truth, "the proper and sufficient antagonist to error."

Notes on the State of Virginia, Jefferson's sole book, has long provided a classic view of eighteenth-century scientific observation, regional self-appraisal, and factual response to European assumptions about life in colonial America.

Demeaned by Jefferson as "trifle," *Notes* is in fact a significant literary achievement. Because eighteenth-century conceptions of law encouraged "a particularistic methodology" and a "comprehensive view of subject matter," said Robert Ferguson, Jefferson's *Notes* emerges as a coherent text using the precision and consistency needed in law to present a sense of a particular geographic region and its specific human inhabitants—white, black, and red—struggling to galvanize into a state and ultimately a nation. Because Jefferson could answer the queries posed by Francois Marbois concerning matters such as boundaries, rivers, plants, climate, people, government, manufacture, and commerce, Jefferson not only presented Va. in literature but the whole of eighteenth-century America.

Two further areas of Jefferson's work deserve comment—his writing on education and his correspondence. Jefferson's writings on education, from his *Bill for the More General Diffusion of Knowledge* (1779) to *A Bill for the Establishment of District Colleges and Universities* (1817), insist on the necessity of education for having and maintaining liberty and a government of the people. Even his remarks on freedom of the press underscore this point. Education, as he envisioned it, proceeds in phases that are both practical and theoretical and permits authorities to select by regions the most capable students for continued study, allowing the development of those men of virtue and talents fit to direct the fortunes of the nation as he mentioned in an 1813 letter to John Adams. In 1811 Adams and Jefferson ended eleven years of silence between them and began a correspondence that lasted until their deaths. That correspondence provides a fine example of Jefferson's masterful epistolary skills. It is also the record of two great minds who presided at the birth of the American nation, participated in its expansion and formation, and were overseeing its development for fifty years. From beginning to end, Jefferson's life was directed by ties to the land and an enduring commitment to liberty. His services to public life and education were meant as a means by which to protect man's land and liberty. Jefferson's brilliance as a writer made him effective. His ideas had the range of libraries, his writings the concision of law, his arguments the cogency of briefs, and his evidence the facts and details supplied by a scientific mind.

Suggested Readings: BDAS; DAB; LHUS; T_1; T_2. *See also* Carl L. Becker, *The Declaration of Independence* (1922); Daniel J. Boorstin, *The Lost World of Thomas Jefferson* (1948); Robert A. Ferguson, "Mysterious Obligation: Jefferson's *Notes on the State of Virginia,"AL*, 52 (1980), 381-406; Adrienne Koch, *Jefferson and Madison: The Great Collaboration* (1950); idem, *The Philosophy of Thomas Jefferson* (1943); Dumas Malone, *Jefferson and his Times* (1948-1969): I. *Jefferson the Virginian*; II. *Jefferson and the Rights of Man*; III. *Jefferson and the Ordeal of Liberty*; IV. *Jefferson the President: First Term, 1801-1805*; V. *Jefferson the President, Second Term, 1805-1809*; Merrill D. Peterson, *Thomas Jefferson and the New Nation* (1970); Garry Wills, *Inventing America: Jefferson's Declaration of Independence* (1978).

John E. Kuhn
Northern Michigan University

JEDIDIAH JEWETT (c. 1705-1774)

Works: *The Necessity of Good Works as the Fruit and Evidence of Faith* (1742); *A Sermon Preached in the Audience of the First Church* (1760); *How the Ministers of the Gospel Are to Be Accounted of* (1774); *A Sermon Preached at Newbury* (1774). For the text of Jewett's exhortation at George Whitefield's (q.v.) grave, see Jonathan Parsons, *To Live Is Christ* (1770), pp. 40-44.

Biography: Jedidiah Jewett, son of Jonathan and Mary (Wicom) Jewett, was baptized on Jun. 3, 1705, at Rowley, Mass. His father was a farmer and tanner. After graduation from Harvard (B.A., M.A., 1726), Jewett was ordained on Nov. 19, 1729, as copastor of the First Congregational Church of Rowley, where he continued as pastor after his colleague's death in 1732. On Nov. 11, 1730, Jewett married Elizabeth Dummer, of Byfield, Mass.; they had five children of whom only two were alive when Elizabeth died on Apr. 14, 1764. On Oct. 29, 1765, Jewett married the thrice-widowed Elizabeth (Greenleaf, Bacon, Scott) Parsons. Although he opposed some of its excesses, Jewett was a moderate New Light and an early supporter of the Great Awakening.

The high point of Jewett's ministry was his delivery of an "Exhortation at the Grave of the Rev. Mr. [George] Whitefield" at the latter's funeral on Oct. 2, 1770. A number of factors brought this honor to Jewett: he had supported Whitefield, who had preached two sermons from Jewett's pulpit; Rowley was only seven miles from Newburyport, where the visiting Whitefield had died and was buried; and the Rev. Moses Parsons, in whose home at Newburyport Whitefield was a guest when he died, was Jewett's friend.

On Apr. 18, 1774, Jewett preached his last sermon, at an ordination at Newbury, after which, according to the sermon's preface, he "went home sick to his Bed, which proved a dying Bed to him." Jewett died at Rowley on May 8, 1774. The owner of a pair of female slaves inherited from his first wife's family, Jewett provided in his will for their support and eventual manumission.

Critical Appraisal: Although Jedidiah Jewett has been traditionally classified as "theologically ferocious" in his adherence to the teachings of Jonathan Edwards (q.v.), his published writings do not suggest an excessive adherence to the more "ferocious" aspects of Edwardsian thought. As evidence, for example, of Edwards's influence on Jewett's sermons, Clifford K. Shipton cited the following sentences from Jewett's *Sermon...in...First Church*: "Can you bear to dwell with devouring Fire, and to inhabit the ever-lasting Burnings? Have you either Strength or Patience enough to endure the Gnawings of the never-dying Worm, and the Tortures of the ever-living Flames?" Although these isolated sentences are certainly in the spirit of Edwards's *Sinners in the Hands of an Angry God* (1741), Edwards was not the only one from whom Jewett might have learned to preach about hell, and there is no evidence that Jewett ever preached about hell with the intense concentration that made Edwards's sermon so remarkable. In fact, Jewett's *Sermon...in...First Church* is a funeral sermon for a deceased schoolmaster, and in it Jewett said much more about the values of education than about the terrors of hell.

As further evidence of Jewett's Edwardsian leanings, Shipton noted that after Jewett's death, his congregation replaced him with a Princeton graduate instead of calling "a liberal young Harvard man who would preach less hell and more love." Edwards, of course, preached on many other topics besides hell, and he died in 1758. By the time of Jewett's death in 1774, Princeton (technically still called the College of New Jersey) was under the presidency of John Witherspoon (q.v.), who did not put excessive emphasis on hell.

In actuality, the theme that occurs most frequently in Jewett's published sermons is good works, not damnation. In his early sermon on *The Necessity of Good Works*, Jewett urged Christians to shun the solifidian view that makes justification and salvation by faith in Christ alone an excuse for licentious living and also to shun the pharisaical temper that hopes to earn justification and salvation through the works of the law, neglecting faith in Christ. Against such extremes, Jewett defended the doctrine *"That it greatly concerns those, who think, or say, that they have Faith in Jesus Christ, to shew the Reality and Truth of their Faith, by their practicing of good Works; this being the Way, to convince and satisfy Men, that their Faith is genuine."* In the improvement portion of the sermon, Jewett informed his hearers: "Indeed none of us, shall believe you have a genuine Faith, unless you do good Works....If you should say, (and say it again a Thousand Times) that you do believe in Christ; yet if your Actions don't vouch for your Profession, but notoriously contradict it; who will, who can believe you have Faith?" Thirty-three years later, in his last sermon, an ordination sermon preached at Newbury three weeks before his death, Jewett returned to the question of good works. Citing Titus 3:8 as his text, Jewett argued that it is not enough for ministers of the Gospel just to affirm the important doctrines of God's grace; they must do so with a view to making believers in God careful to practice the good works that God commands.

The fugitive poem "Our Family Pledge," attributed to Jewett in *The National Union Catalog Pre-1956 Imprints*, is not by him but by a later namesake who was living in Portland in 1855.

Suggested Readings: CCNE; Sibley-Shipton (VIII, 64-69). *See also* Emerson Davis, *Biographical Sketches of the Congregational Pastors of New England*, typescript, from a nineteenth-century ms., deposited in the Congregational Library, Boston, IV, 321-322; D. Hamilton Hurd, ed., *History of Essex County, Massachusetts* (1888), II, 1138; Harold Field Worthley, *An Inventory of the Records of the Particular (Congregational) Churches of Massachusetts Gathered 1620-1805*, HTS, 25 (1970), 527-529.

Richard Frothingham
University of Arkansas at Little Rock

EDWARD JOHNSON (1599-1672)

Works: "In peniles age I Woburne Towne began" (prefatory lines to *Records for the Towne of Woburne from the Year 1640; Good News from New-England: With an Exact Relation of the First Planting That Country*; [1648], attributed to Johnson by Harold Jantz in *The First Century of New England Verse* [1962]); *A History of New England from the English Planting in the Yeere 1628, untill the Yeere 1652*, better known for its running head titles, *Wonder-Working Providences of Sion's Savior in New England* (1653).

Biography: Edward Johnson was born in 1599 in the countryside not far from Canterbury, Eng. The record speaks next of his passage to America in 1630 on the *Arbella*, in the company of John Winthrop (q.v.). For unknown reasons, he returned to Eng. the next year only to return to America six years later with his family, declaring his occupation as "joiner." From 1637 until his death on Apr. 23, 1672, Johnson devotedly served the Mass. colony in many capacities: captain of the Charleston militia; town clerk of Woburne; deputy to the General Court; writer, editor, and printer of the 1648 Massachusetts Laws; surveyor; committee member of the task force that examined the affairs of Harvard College in 1653; historian; trusted cartographer and servant of the colony trusted to hide the "Patent" from the king's commissioners in 1664.

Critical Appraisal: Critical opinion differs sharply over the value of Edward Johnson's contribution to early American letters. For Perry Miller, Peter Gay, and his original editors, Johnson's style is ponderous and heavy, given to unpredictable rhetorical flights; and the polemical nature of *Wonder-Working Providences* obscures the personality of the writer and characterizes the Puritan mentality and religious orientation in its most primitive and unenlightened forms. On the other hand, numerous revisionist writers since the late sixties have looked to the work for glimpses into the Puritan mind that is frequently unrevealed in the works of more mature, more educated, and more self-conscious writers of the period.

As a historian, Johnson is not interested, as was William Bradford (q.v.), for example, in chronicling the daily affairs of his contemporary colonists. Rather, his was the self-appointed task of memorializing in prose and verse the triumph of God as God worked through his chosen few to create a new world where his will would be done. No small task, this; and owing to the cosmic dimensions of the drama Johnson chronicled, there is hardly reason to expect the prose medium to be other than a diffuse and extended analog to the sermon.

However, Johnson did provide the literary student with much that is valuable, specifically in the ways he used verse within the historical rubric. The assumption that permeates the historical text sounds something like this: the ways of God are as clear in the affairs of the collective endeavor of the colonists as they are in the lives of God's individual saints. Nowhere is this typical seventeenth-century

theory of correspondences so clearly enunciated as it is in the many verse enco-
miums that punctuate the historical text. The rationale that controls the transition
from macrocosmic view of God's providences as base chord of the history to the
microcosmic notelike poems addressed to the memory of specific servants of
God is nowhere spoken to in the *Wonder-Working Providences*. Yet the ubiqui-
tous presence of a rhetorical sensibility insists that such a transition be made and
made with the assumption that the presence of the verse serves some serious
purpose. No better purpose exists than documenting the presence of God in terms
of the whole as well as its parts. Clearly, God is the center and the circumference
for Johnson; the individual gives and takes equally to and from the experiment
known as New Eng. in ways usually reserved for members of ideal holy states,
where both state and individual are extensions of God's personal plan.

Of course, Johnson's work serves more specific purposes than the epistemological one just noted. His use of verse also adumbrates the theory of "kinds" that
operated in New Eng., just as it provides that useful function of personal enlightenment that characterized Puritan verse. One such example of the way in which
the Puritan engaged in redefining the "kinds" can be found in the poem addressed
to the Rev. Thomas Welde (q.v.). This is likely the earliest use of the sonnet in
America, and its use here documents the way in which a three-part structure
could, in the hands of a devout Puritan, be brought into harmony with Pauline
stages of Christian life: calling, sanctification, and glorification. The context for
the poetry, its form, the uses intended for the poetry, and the matching of form to
station in life all point to a well-defined theory of poetry, albeit a limited one.

Johnson will never emerge from the libraries as a major New Eng. historian,
regardless of how limited our past attentiveness to his style may have been. As a
representative of his period and its religious outlook, however, we are not likely
to encounter another writer of the period who so simplistically lays bare the
religious premises of Puritan intellect in seventeenth-century New Eng.

Suggested Readings: DAB; FCNEV; LHUS; T_1. *See also* Sacvan Bercovitch, "The
Historiography of Johnson's *Wonder-Working Providence*," EIHC, 104 (1968), 139-161;
Ursula Brumm, "Edward Johnson's *Wonder-Working Providence* and the Puritan Concep-
tion of History," JA, 14 (1969), 140-151; Edward V. Gallagher, "Critical Study of Edward
Johnson's *Wonder-Working Providences*" (Ph.D. diss., Univ. of Notre Dame, 1970);
idem, "Johnson's Wonder-Working Providence," EAL, 5 (1971), 40-49; idem, Introduc-
tion, *Wonder-Working Providences of Sion's Savior in New England* (1974); Kenneth B.
Murdock, "Clio in the Wilderness," CH, 24 (1955), 221-238; William Poole, ed., *Wonder-
Working Providence of Sion's Savior in New England* (1867), pp. i-iv; John E. Trimpey,
"The Poetry of Four American Puritans" (Ph.D. diss., Ohio Univ., 1970), pp. 1-36.

John E. Trimpey
University of Tennessee at Chattanooga

ROBERT JOHNSON (fl. 1600-1621)

Works: *Nova Brittania* (1609); *The New Life of Virginia* (1612; rep.,
1819).

Biography: Robert Johnson was a prosperous grocer who became an incor-porator of the East India Company in 1600 and was associated with the company for many years. He also served as deputy treasurer of the Virginia Company and was one of the purchasers of the Bermudas in 1612. By 1617 he was back in Eng., where he served as sheriff of London for a time. He remained a member of the Virginia Company for several more years, however, and was later thought to have initiated a campaign to withdraw its patents. In 1621 Johnson testified in Sir Francis Bacon's trial for taking bribes. Although there is some doubt about authorship, both *Nova Brittania* and *The New Life of Virginia* are traditionally attributed to Johnson.

Critical Appraisal: Robert Johnson's *Nova Brittania* (1609) is a serious defense of the Va. colony, which in recent years had become a joke in Eng. The work is addressed to Sir Thomas Smith, a member of the Council for Virginia and treasurer of the colony; it is cast in the form of an oration, delivered by the most voluble of a group of adventurers just returned from America. Revealing a very strong patriotic and anti-Catholic bent, the speaker argued "rudely" that, having sacrificed its men, money, printer's execution, and reputation in the colonies, Eng. had established its right to possess the New World. Offering no evidence, Johnson also suggested that the famous Lost Colony still flourished with its original inhabitants. Moreover, he cited a number of historical justifica-tions, ancient and modern, to support British expansionism, not the least of which was a God-given duty to usurp the pope's authority in the world and to prevent the spread of Catholicism.

Johnson's greatest obstacle, of course, was the then recent fate of Va. itself. What had become known as its "miseries"—poverty, crime, greed, dissension, disease, and bad weather—were natural deterrents to prospective settlers and investors. Yet these conditions, rightly seen, are but the crosses that accompany "all good Actions," including those of Alexander, Hannibal, Columbus, and most of the great men of the Old Testament. Once the crosses are borne in manly fashion, Englishmen of ambition will discover a paradise: "there are valleyes and plaines streaming with sweete Springs, like veynes in a naturall bodie: there are hills and mountaines making a sensible proffer of hidden treasure, never yet searched." The speaker admitted, as he must, that this Eden had been polluted by greedy factionalists and "lewd and naughtie practises," but these conditions made it even more imperative that men who honor God and the British king consider emigrating. If good men refuse this charge, the New World will be left to godless adventurere and papists. As a further challenge, Johnson tried to make all of the undone tasks in Va. seem like enchanting ventures; there are lands to clean and livestock to raise, and trade routes must be set up soon to ensure supplies for the colony. The oration ends with a guarantee of better days for Va.

In 1612 Johnson published another promotional piece, *A New Life for Vir-ginia*, also addressed to Sir Thomas Smith and meant as a supplement to the *Nova Brittania*. It sought to declare "the former success and present estate of that plantation." Its tone was shrill and earnest as it expanded on the themes of "crosses and disasters" as inevitable preludes to salvation. The work was an apology for Va., aiming to put into perspective what was then a subject for vulgar jesting. A learned man, Johnson wanted to appeal to the sort of reader who might, with either his money or his person, do Va. some good. Although the essay is divided into three parts, which cover the past, present, and desired future of the colony, its message was simply that, years ago, Queen Elizabeth I was appointed by God to remove "that mist of popish dimnes from our eyes" and to sponsor the salvation of primitive lands. No true Englishman could refuse to continue her good works.

Johnson's works in defense of Va. are comparatively long and certainly long-winded. Although he was a key member of the Virginia Company elite, he allowed few details of historical value to enter his argument. Nevertheless, he performed a useful service by shifting the promotional emphasis from the potential treasures to be found in America to the patriotic and religious obligations of Englishmen.

Suggested Readings: Alexander Brown, *The Genesis of the United States* (1890; rep., 1964), I, 242-243; II, 558-559, 932; Howard Mumford Jones, *O Strange New World: American Culture: The Formative Years* (1964), pp. 179-185; *Oxford Companion to American Literature* (1941), p. 377; David Beers Quinn, *England and the Discovery of America: 1481-1620* (1974), pp. 464-465.

James Stephens
Marquette University

SAMUEL JOHNSON (1696-1772)

Works: *An Introduction to the Study of Philosophy* (1731); *Eleutheria Enervatus* (1733); *A Letter...to Dissenting Parishioners* (1733); *A Second Letter...to Dissenting Parishioners* (1734); *A Third Letter...to Dissenting Parishioners* (1737); *A Letter from Aristocles to Authades* (1745); *Ethices Elementa* (1746); *A Sermon...Concerning Public Worship of God* (1746); *A Letter to Jonathan Dickinson* (1747); Preface, *A Second Vindication* by John Beach (1748); Preface, *A Calm and Dispassionate Vindication* by John Beach (1749); *Elementa Philosophica* (1752); *A Short Catechism* (1753); *A Demonstration of Prayer* (1760); *A Sermon on the Beauty of Holiness* (1761); *A Candid Examination* (1763); *First Easy Rudiments of Grammar* (1765); *English and Hebrew Grammar* (1767); *The Christian Indeed* (1768); *Autobiography* (1768-1770); *Raphael* (n.d.). These titles and many of Johnson's unpublished tracts and correspondence appear in Herbert Schneider and Carol Schneider, eds., *Samuel Johnson* (1929).

Biography: Perhaps the most intellectually distinguished of all colonial Anglicans, Samuel Johnson was born in Conn. in 1696. His life—at least the external portions of it—had the following pattern: initial obscurity during his early years in rural New Eng.; great notoriety following his open espousal of the Anglican Church at the Yale Commencement of 1722; again, a relative obscurity during a long Anglican ministry at Stratford; once more, notoriety as the first president of King's College (later Columbia); and, at last, a return to his Stratford pastorate until his death in 1772.

Educated at Saybrook's Collegiate School (later Yale College), Johnson became first a schoolmaster at nearby Guilford, then a tutor at the Collegiate School (already moved to New Haven), and finally—after taking an M.A.—a Puritan minister at West Haven. During this period, he and several friends read widely and eagerly in a collection of books sent back from abroad by Jeremiah Dummer (q.v.), the colony's agent. These books, which contained the best of what was then spoken of as the "New Learning," exposed Johnson to the ideas of Locke, Newton, and other "modern" thinkers and, in turn, forced him to question many of the assumptions on which his orthodox education had rested. This exposure also led him to read about the history and theology of the English church, which he found more in sympathy with the "New Learning" than those of his own.

Johnson's intellectual pilgrimage ended at the Yale Commencement of 1722, when he, as well as the rector of the college and several of its tutors, openly embraced the Church of England. As if this situation were not enough to shock and anger the Puritan establishment, Johnson sailed to Eng. to receive ordination in the Anglican Church.

For some thirty years, Johnson tended his Anglican flock at Stratford, participating now and then in pamphlet controversies with the Puritans, corresponding endlessly with his superiors in Eng., and leading many students and graduates of Yale toward the Church of England. From 1754 to 1763, he was the first president of King's College, a faction-ridden institution with a most troublesome set of trustees. After leaving the presidency, Johnson returned to his Stratford pastorate, from which he directed his remaining intellectual energies to the growing tensions, civil and religious, between Eng. and her American colonies. He died in 1772.

Critical Appraisal: Never a brilliant or profoundly original thinker, Samuel Johnson was intensely receptive to new currents of thought in the intellectual world about him, read actively all books he could get his hands on, took copious notes about them, and carried on a constant inner dialog with their ideas. In an important sense, the record of his own works is a most valuable template—a sensitive, receptive surface on which are displayed the critical movements of eighteenth-century thought as they affected the American mind.

For example, in a number of early manuscripts, among them "Logic" and "The Revised Encyclopedia," Johnson—recently converted to the New Learning— was at pains to reassess the value of his inherited universe of ideas. The major product of this reassessment, his *Elementa Philosophica*, did not appear until 1752. Still, early and late, on matters purely conceptual, theological, or ecclesiastical, Johnson's varied writings provide a clear index of what was in the air.

Paradoxes stand unresolved; divergent tendencies of thought, unreconciled. They register in a way unmatched by any other colonial writings the step-by-step intellectual evolution of a generation.

In Johnson's *Autobiography*, for example, there appears a deep attachment to dispassionate reason (a commitment weakened late in life by observing the irrational ravages of a smallpox epidemic) and to a well-ordered society that is expressed against the background of an unresponsive Puritan and rural culture. Even as a boy, Johnson admitted, he disliked all forms of enthusiasm in religion and all extemporaneity in prayer. He eventually found Puritan worship so much "Quakerish talk" and Puritan churches monuments to the ego of their clergy. Where else, he asked in retrospect, if not in the traditional forms of Anglican worship and the established church, can good sense and good order flourish?

Here we begin to grasp an essential fact about Johnson's cast of mind. Although his arguments are always given in the formal terms of learned debate, the genuine basis for much of the way he thought about things was purely aesthetic. Even when he was in Eng. to receive Anglican orders, what impressed him most—what stuck most firmly in his mind—was the glory of English church architecture, that outward and visible symbol of high culture, sound reason, and a stable, traditional social order. It may not be too extreme to suggest that much of the formal inconsistency in Johnson's thought was the result of just this doubleness of mind: a commitment to logical categories and the determinative power of reason, but a deeper allegiance to matters of taste and sensibility. As such, Johnson dramatized the inner difficulties of an entire generation.

Suggested Readings: CCMC; CCNE; DAB; Dexter (I, 123-128); LHUS; T$_2$. *See also* Carl Bridenbaugh, *Mitre and Sceptre* (1962); Arthur Lyon Cross, *The Anglican Episcopate and the American Colonies* (1902); Joseph J. Ellis, *The New England Mind in Transition* (1973); Richard Warch, *School of the Prophets* (1973).

Alan M. Kantrow
Harvard University

STEPHEN JOHNSON (1724-1786)

Works: Six letters in the *New London Gazette* (1765); *Some Important Observations* (1766); *Integrity and Piety the Best Principles of a Good Administration of Government* (1770); *The Everlasting Punishment of the Ungodly* (1786).

Biography: Stephen Johnson was born in Newark, N.J., on May 17, 1724. After graduating from Yale College (1742), he studied theology. In 1745 the New Haven Association licensed him to preach; in 1746 he became pastor of the Congregational Church in Old Lyme, Conn., where he remained until his death in 1786. In theological matters, Johnson was a strict Calvinist. An avid supporter of the American Revolution, he served as a regimental chaplain in 1775. Johnson was a fellow of Yale College from 1773. He died in Old Lyme, Conn., on Nov. 8, 1786, at age 62.

Critical Appraisal: Stephen Johnson was a competent theologian. In 1786 he published a lengthy discourse on *The Everlasting Punishment of the Ungodly*, in which he attacked the Universalist doctrine of unlimited salvation. But his major contribution to American letters was his political writings.

On the occasion of the Stamp Act in 1765, Johnson published a series of anonymous newspaper articles and a fast-day sermon (*Some Important Observations*). These works were among the best statements of the American position during the first major confrontation between G.B. and its colonies. As Bernard Bailyn has pointed out, the works are complementary. Although the articles are entirely secular in substance, the sermon overlays Johnson's tightly reasoned political arguments with "a variety of specific Protestant formulas." Johnson subjected recent parliamentary legislation on America to a searching political analysis. He attacked the Stamp Act as taxation without colonial consent, challenged the British theory of "virtual representation," cataloged the evil consequences of British tyranny, and called on the Americans to resist in a sober and orderly fashion. If they are forced by Br., however, they will "sacrifice their lives and fortunes before they will part with their invaluable freedom." In the sermon, Johnson paralleled the trials of the Jews in Egypt and the sufferings of the colonists under recent British rule. He then urged his countrymen to humble themselves before God to prepare for a similar deliverance. Like many other Calvinist preachers of the Revolutionary era, Johnson offered the hope that present tribulations are only a prelude to spiritual, moral, and political regeneration.

One of the most effective members of the "black regiment" of patriotic New Eng. clergy in 1765, Johnson never thereafter equaled his initial printed efforts. As Bernard Bailyn noted, his only other published work on politics, the 1770 election sermon, *Integrity and Piety*, is "an ordinary performance." But his vigorous synthesis of secular political arguments and traditional religious appeals played a part in rallying Conn. citizens to oppose British measures at a key moment in the imperial controversy.

Suggested Readings: CCNE; Dexter (I, 738-740); T₂. *See also* Bernard Bailyn, "Religion and Revolution: Three Biographical Studies," *Perspectives in American History* (1970), IV, 125-139, 144-169, which includes the texts of Johnson's newspaper articles; Alice M. Baldwin, *The New England Clergy and the American Revolution* (1928), pp. 63n, 99-102, 128, 130, 162n; Alan Heimert, *Religion and the American Mind from the Great Awakening to the Revolution* (1966), pp. 160-161; Oscar Zeichner, *Connecticut's Years of Controversy, 1750-1776* (1949).

Douglas M. Arnold
Yale University

SUSANNAH WILLARD JOHNSON (HASTINGS) (1730-1810)

Works: *A Narrative of the Captivity of Mrs. Johnson* (1796).

Biography: Susannah Johnson was born in 1730 in Mass. In 1747 she married James Johnson, an Irish orphan adopted by her great-uncle. In 1749 the

Johnsons moved from Lunenburgh, Mass., to Charlestown, N.H., where, five years later, renewed enmity between the Indians and the settlers led to the Johnsons' captivity on Aug. 30, 1754, by a raiding party of Abenaki Indians from Canada. At that time, Mrs. Johnson's son Sylvanus was 6; her daughter Susanna, 4; and her youngest daughter Polly, 2. Due to the trauma of being captured, Mrs. Johnson gave premature birth to a third daughter, whom she named Captive. Because they were probably intended for adoption rather than just ransom, the family was relatively well treated by the Indians. Once the Johnsons arrived in Canada, however, various bureaucratic and political difficulties caused them to be jailed by the French. In 1757 Susannah Johnson and two of her daughters boarded a ship bound first for Ire., then for N.Y. Although James Johnson was later released from jail, on the way to rejoin his wife he accepted a commission and died fighting. Susannah Johnson first published her narrative in 1796; her death in 1810 came shortly after she had finished revising the work for its 3rd edition (1814).

Critical Appraisal: Roy Harvey Pearce's classic article on the Indian captivity narrative identifies three important generic phases: religious document, political propaganda, and sentimentalized fiction. These stages, with their premise that Indians took white captives for ransom and mistreated them, are widely accepted. However, the phases blur somewhat when a narrative obviously shows—as Johnson's does—that the Indians were probably more interested in adopting their charges and, relatively speaking, did not mistreat them.

During her story, Johnson stressed that the Indians treated her well. She said, for instance, "In justice to the Indians, I ought to remark, that they never treated me with cruelty, to a wanton degree; few people have survived a situation like mine, and few have fallen into the hands of savages, disposed to more lenity and patience." Her captors built a separate lean-to where she gave birth to her daughter, allowed her to ride on horseback, and even carried her in a special litter for a while. Such treatment is in contrast to the bureaucratic bungling and unconcern the French displayed when the Johnsons arrived in Can. There they were imprisoned and contracted smallpox.

In her introduction, Johnson claimed, "simple facts, unadorned, is what the reader must expect." In other contemporary narratives, like Mary Kinnan's (q.v.), 1795, such a disclaimer is frequently irrelevant or untrue, but here it is not. An example of her precise detail occurs at the moment of capture, "my three little children were driven naked to the place where I stood. On viewing myself I found that I too was naked. An Indian had plundered three gowns, who, on seeing my situation, gave me the whole." Here is sensitive reportage rather than horrified sensibility. Johnson's use of detail reinforces her narrative skill as, for instance, when she mentioned early on that she lost a shoe, then later referred to her painful feet, and still further on described her legs and feet covered with blood.

A surprising element in the narrative is a certain lightness here and there. Just before being taken prisoner, the author described the celebrations on her husband's return from Conn.: "and time passed merrily off, by the aid of spirit and a ripe yard of melons." It is true that this description is in contrast to her later troubles, but even during captivity, she was capable of wry humor as when she recounted her unsuccessful attempt to squat, native style, and eat hasty pudding. Life with the Indians was not all bad.

In fact, Johnson's story anticipates those of white prisoners such as Mary Jemison and John Tanner who became thoroughly Indianized and no longer wished to return to "civilization." Like them, Johnson recognized the Indians' prudence, wisdom, and (at times) humanity. Despite the discomforts of wilderness living and the long-term effects of the experience, Johnson challenged her readers by insisting they reevaluate their prejudice toward Indians: "Can it be said of civilized conquerors, that they, in the main, are willing to share with their prisoners, the last ration of food, when famine stares them in the face? Do they ever adopt an enemy, and salute him by the tender name of brother?"

Suggested Readings: James Axtell, "Letters to the Editor," WMQ, 33 (1976), 148-153; idem, "The White Indians of Colonial America," WMQ, 32 (1975), 55-88; C. Marius Barbeau, "Indian Captivities," PAPS, 94 (1950), 522-548; Phillips D. Carleton, "The Indian Captivity," AL, 15 (1943), 169-180; J. Norman Heard, *White into Red: A Study of the Assimilation of White Persons Captured by Indians* (1973); Roy Harvey Pearce, *Savagism and Civilization* (1965); idem, "The Significances of the Captivity Narrative," AL, 19 (1947), 1-20, especially p. 12; Richard Slotkin, *Regeneration Through Violence: The Mythology of the American Frontier, 1600-1860* (1973); R.W.G. Vail, *The Voice of the Old Frontier* (1949).

Kathryn Zabelle Derounian
University of Arkansas at Little Rock

THOMAS JOHNSON (c. 1760-c. 1825)

Works: *The Kentucky Miscellany* (1789).

Biography: Very little biographical information is available about Thomas Johnson, except that he was a Virginian who moved to Ky. sometime around 1785, when he was approximately 25 years old. He was probably living in Ky. by at least 1786, for he wrote an epitaph on Col. William Christian, a former Virginian of the Revolutionary period who was killed fighting the Indians in Ky. in Apr. 1786. He was certainly living in Ky. by 1789, the year his volume of poems was advertised in the *Kentucky Gazette*.

According to one historian of Ky. literature, Johnson was known in Danville, at that time the capital of the state with a population of about 100, as being a drunkard. Since few records have survived the frontier conditions that existed in Danville at the time, there seems little hope of reconstructing many more details about Johnson's activities.

Critical Appraisal: The only extant copy of *The Kentucky Miscellany*, housed in the Durrett Collection at the University of Chicago, is a somewhat damaged copy of the 1821 edition. Published as a thirty-six-page pamphlet, the book was the 1st edition of poetry published and printed in the state of Ky. A collection of satiric verses upon people Johnson knew and general conditions that characterized the frontier life of the period, the work provided a refreshing contrast to much of the sentimental and generally inept epic verse published in America during the late eighteenth and early nineteenth centuries. As Ralph Rusk said of the work, "it is a much more faithful record than can be found in the abortive epics or in the flood of conventional sentimental poetry which came from the press before 1841." Writing in traditional couplet forms, Johnson possessed a sense of wit that could be pointed and acerbic. In one of his more memorable pieces, "Epigram on William Hudson who Murdered his Wife," Johnson wrote, "Strange things of Orpheus poets tell, / How for a wife he went to Hell, / Hudson, a wiser man no doubt, / Would go to Hell to be without."

Johnson detested what he regarded as religious hypocrisy, had a low opinion of many he encountered in Danville, and held a general aversion for all of Ky., an opinion he expressed in a poem titled "The Author's Hatred of Kentucky in General." Written in straightforward and unpretentious language, the poems are expressions of an honest, direct, and humorous appraisal of men and conditions during the rough and tumble days of the Ky. frontier. They reflect in tone and spirit a realistic outlook and a satiric bent that would not become very popular in American letters until the fictional treatment of the American frontier character and life-style by the southwestern humorists and realistic fictionalists such as Mark Twain.

Suggested Readings: Jay B. Hubbell, *The South in American Literature, 1607-1900* (1954), pp. 319-321; Willard R. Jillson, *Early Kentucky Literature: 1750-1840* (1931), p. 53; Ralph L. Rusk, *The Literature of the Middle Western Frontier* (1925; rep., 1975), I, 319-323; John W. Townsend, "The First Kentucky Poet," *Kentuckians in History and Literature* (1907), pp. 89-101.

Reed Sanderlin
University of Tennessee at Chattanooga

ABSALOM JONES (1746-1818)

Works: *Narrative of the Proceedings of the Black People, During the Late Awful Calamity in Philadelphia* (Richard Allen, co-author; 1794); *A Thanksgiving Sermon, Preached January 1, 1808* (1808).

Biography: Absalom Jones was born a slave in Sussex, Del., on Nov. 6, 1746. As a child, he learned to read and to save pennies, and as soon as he could, he purchased a speller and a Testament. When he was 16, his master took him to Philadelphia and put him to work in a shop, where a clerk taught him to write. In 1776 he was permitted to study in night school. In 1780 he married one of his master's slaves and bought her freedom with wages they earned in the evenings.

They continued to work hard, acquired a home, bought his freedom in 1794, and later built two houses for renting. He was already a leader among blacks in Philadelphia when Richard Allen (q.v.) arrived there in 1786. Jones and Allen were to collaborate as leaders in various projects for over three decades, usually for justice and equality for blacks in Philadelphia in religion and society or for the community's general welfare. In 1787 they organized the Free African Society in Philadelphia. After having been made unwelcome in the Methodist Church they attended, they moved to form a separate church for blacks, the African Church in Philadelphia, in 1791. In 1794 Jones led in forming the St. Thomas African Episcopal Church of Philadelphia, apparently the first Episcopal congregation for blacks, and became its rector. Ten years later, he was ordained the first black Episcopalian priest in this country, and he continued to serve until his death, also assisting in the organizing of other black Episcopal congregations. He also helped to found a school for black children, to found an anti-vice society, to create and direct an insurance company, and to organize protests and petition in behalf of black civil rights. With James Forten, he helped organize a Masonic Lodge for Pa. and became its first leader. With Allen, he was called on to organize blacks to assist Philadelphia in the yellow fever epidemic of 1793 and in 1814 during the war with the British. In 1810 Raphaelle Peale painted a very distinguished portrait of Jones.

Critical Appraisal: Not much of Absalom Jones's writing has survived, but what we do have (the *Narrative* and a few sermons and letters) shows a varied style that seems to have been adapted to the occasion at hand, becoming evangelical or reasoned in turn. (Information about and comment on the *Narrative* is given in the entry for its coauthor, Richard Allen.) The twenty-two-page *Thanksgiving Sermon* was preached to Jones's congregation, as its full title indicates, *On Account of the Abolition of the Slave Trade, on That Day, By the Congress of the United States*; and by request of the St. Thomas vestry on Feb. 11, it was published. Jones took as his text that section of Exodus that focuses on God's compassion for the Israelites in bondage in Egypt. He pointed to various parallels in the circumstances of the Israelites and those of American slaves, in an orderly and reasoned pattern, giving vivid details to heighten his audience's awareness, embellishing the biblical text as needed. Occasionally, he inserted a peroration of praise for emphasis. His style is easy and clear. The second part of the sermon is a call to remember to offer continuing thanks to God for the deliverance he has provided, both past and present, both physical and spiritual. In both parts, Jones also focused on the continuing plight of the brethren in Africa, with hope for its improvement. The sermon ends with a two-page prayer full of feeling, thanksgiving, praise, supplication, and hope.

Suggested Readings: George F. Bragg, Jr., *The Story of...Absalom Jones, 1746-1818* (1929); William Douglass, *Annals of...the African Episcopal Church of St. Thomas* (1862), passim; W.E.B. DuBois, *The Philadelphia Negro* (1899), passim; Philip S. Foner, *History of Black Americans from Africa to the ...Cotton Kingdom* (1975), passim; Carol V. R. George, *Segregated Sabbaths* (1973), passim; Sidney Kaplan, *The*

Black Presence in the Era of the American Revolution, 1770-1800 (1973), pp. 83-94; Vernon Loggins, *The Negro Author* (1931), passim; Ruth Miller, ed., *Blackamerican Literature, 1760-Present* (1971), pp. 63-81; Dorothy Porter, ed., *Early Negro Writing, 1760-1837* (1971), pp. 330-332, 335-342; Milton C. Sernett, *Black Religion and American Evangelism* (1975), passim; "Some Letters of Richard Allen and Absalom Jones to Dorothy Ripley," JNH, 1 (1916), pp. 436-443; Charles H. Wesley, *Richard Allen* (1935), passim.

Julian Mason
University of North Carolina at Charlotte

DAVID JONES (1736-1820)

Works: *A Journal of Two Visits* (1774); *Defensive War* (1775); *The Doctrine of "Laying on of Hands"* (1786); *Declaration of the Rev. Mr. David Jones...Sept. 26, 1799* (1799); *A Treatise on the Work of the Holy Ghost* (1804); *A True History of Laying on of Hands* (1805); *Peter Edwards's Candid Reasons, Examined, and Answered* (1811); *Review of Mr. John P. Campbell's Sermon* (1811).

Biography: David Jones was born at Welsh Tract, Del., on May 12, 1736. After completing his modest formal education at Isaac Eaton's Hopewell Baptist Academy, he continued his studies informally with Abel Morgan, the much-respected Baptist minister of Middleton, N.J., and he was subsequently ordained as pastor of the Crosswicks Baptist Church near Freehold, N.J., on Nov. 12, 1766.

In 1772-1773 Jones undertook a missionary effort among the Indians of the Ohio River Valley, an arduous journey reported in his first book, *A Journal of Two Visits* (1774). In 1775 his public career began in earnest when Tory opposition forced him from his pulpit because of his political views, and he became pastor in the more patriotic atmosphere of the Great Valley. On the Continental Fast Day in 1775, Jones preached his most famous sermon, *Defensive War in a Just Cause Sinless*, an impassioned defense of the escalating Revolution. Typically, Jones was not content with mere talk; he also joined the Continental Army, where he spent most of the war acting as chaplain (as well as surgeon and scout) under "Mad Anthony" Wayne.

After the war, Jones returned to the Great Valley, and except for six years as pastor of the Southampton Baptist Church in Southampton, Pa., he spent the rest of his life there. During his later life, he traveled widely and frequently, published several sermons defending Baptist positions, and (between 1811 and 1816) wrote newspaper articles in William Duane's (q.v.) *Philadelphia Aurora* counseling a hard line on Indian treaties and opposing the Second Bank of the U.S. He also returned as the only chaplain of the U.S. Army during the Indian Wars of

1790-1795 (again under Wayne) and once again served during the War of 1812. He died on Feb. 5, 1820, and was buried in the Great Valley.

   Critical Appraisal: During David Jones's 84 years, he published eight significant works, preached sermons on numerous important occasions (including one to the army of Col. Arthur St. Clair just before the fighting at Ticonderoga and one at the reinterment ceremony for Anthony Wayne), wrote newspaper articles on pressing political issues, and corresponded with the famous and near-famous. Still, although he was respected as a staunch patriot and leader in the Philadelphia Baptist Association, he made little lasting contribution to American letters.

   The one exception, and certainly Jones's most interesting piece, is his first work, *A Journal of Two Visits*. In it Jones described in detail his journey to the Ohio River Valley in the early 1770s and his efforts to convert the Indians. The drama of the piece comes not only from the great danger he faced—from harsh weather and recurring personal illness (and, on one occasion, from angry Indians)—but also from the repeated frustration of his designs. Forced to rely on an interpreter, he struggled to find a simple language in which to express his beliefs. Even when he thought he had succeeded, however, the Indians were generally unmoved. Among the Delawares, where he first traveled, he enjoyed minor successes, but when he reached the Shawnees, he met open skepticism and, finally, hostility. Yellow Hawk, a chief of the Shawnees, told him "that they had lived a long time as they now do, and liked it very well, and he and his people would live as they had done." Although modern readers may feel that Yellow Hawk calmly and effectively defended the integrity of his culture, Jones was understandably disappointed and even angered. He returned briefly to the more hospitable Delawares and then made his way back to the settlements.

   Jones's adventure makes good reading and offers abundant information about the Ohio River Valley in the 1770s. He described the topography, the white traders of the valley, the few scattered settlers, and his few fellow travelers, including George Rogers Clark (q.v.). To facilitate future missionary efforts, he described in some detail the Indians' way of life and even included the bits of vocabulary he acquired. He was finally incredulous that they would reject his efforts to improve them, even though, as he consoled himself, "it is common to judge of others by ourselves, so these Indians, from a consciousness of their own deceit, are very suspicious of us having some design to enslave them." After all, as he added in the next few sentences, "the *fear* of us is fallen on them, that they are almost in a similar case to the inhabitants of Jericho when besieged by the Israelites; and from hence we may judge as *Rahab* did, that the LORD is on our side, and will in his own time bring the heathens into subjection." Yellow Hawk may have seen all too well what the final effect of such missionary efforts would be. It is not surprising that later in Jones's life, embittered by his abortive efforts to save their souls, as well as his first-hand experience of the savagery of Indian wars, he recommended crushing the Indians and forcing them to adopt a life of small-scale farming—to "civilize" them with Christianity and Freeholder political principles.

Most of Jones's later published writings were sermons, and most offered derivative, if vehement, defenses of Baptist doctrine. In some pieces, he provided a matter-of-fact explanation of his beliefs. But more often, he was hurried into print by his anger, as when he assailed the ignorance and apostasy of those like Samuel Jones (himself a prominent Baptist) who questioned the Welsh Baptist practice of "laying on of hands." Not only is David Jones's argument in such pieces unoriginal, but his characteristic truculence is far from charming. In a sermon like *Defensive War in a Just Cause Sinless*, his opponents could be reduced to caricature and attacked with vigor without offending his patriot audience (or his modern readers); the result is a spirited example of the fusion of Real Whig and evangelical ideologies offered by the patriot clergy. In too many of Jones's other efforts, however, including his shorter newspaper pieces on the secular issues of the day, he was merely irascible and pedantic.

Suggested Readings: CCMC; DAB; Sprague (VI, 85-89). *See also* David Jones, *A Journal of Two Visits* (for the "Biographical Notice of the Author" by Horatio Gates Jones, Jr. 1865); Benson J. Lossing, *Pictorial Field Book of the Revolution* (1860), II, 165-166; George Truett Rogers, "A Biography of David Jones, 1736-1820" (Ph.D. diss., Univ. of Colo., 1976); Charles J. Stille, *Major-General Anthony Wayne and the Pennsylvania Line* (1893), pp. 350-351.

Barry R. Bell
Washington State University

HUGH JONES (1671-1760)

Works: *An Accidence to the English Tongue* (1724); *The Present State of Virginia* (1724); *The Panchrometer or Universal Georgian Calendar* (1753).

Biography: Hugh Jones—clergyman, mathematician, historian, and educator—was born in Eng. in 1671 and was educated at Oxford (B.A., 1712; M.A., 1716). After ordination in the Church of England, Jones immigrated to Va., where in 1717, on the recommendation of the bishop of London, he was appointed to the chair of mathematics and natural philosophy at the College of William and Mary. As chaplain of the House of Burgesses and assistant rector of Bruton Church in Williamsburg, Jones soon became a friend and ally of Governor Alexander Spotswood (q.v.) and an active opponent of Commissary James Blair (q.v.), a founder of William and Mary, whom he opposed over a number of ecclesiastical privileges and academic matters.

Against Blair's opposition, Jones held his post at the college until 1721, when he returned to Eng. for a period of three years. In 1724 he returned to Va., but he soon settled at a parish in Md. In 1731 he moved again to a parish in Cecil County, along the Eastern Shore, and remained rector there until shortly before his death in 1760. A supporter of and scientific adviser to Lord Baltimore, Jones made frequent excursions from Md. to Philadelphia, where he associated with notables such as Benjamin Franklin (q.v.), James Logan (q.v.), William Smith (q.v.), and Francis Alison (q.v.). In Md. Jones continued his vigorous intellectual life, publishing several scientific and mathematical papers in British journals as well as polemics against Roman Catholicism.

Critical Appraisal: An active intellectual force and public figure in the colonies of Va. and Md. for more than four decades, Hugh Jones has three noteworthy literary works: *An Accidence to the English Tongue* (1724), a grammatical treatise; *The Present State of Virginia* (1724), an invaluable survey of contemporary conditions in early eighteenth-century Va.; and *A Protest Against Popery* (1745), a widely read sermon.

Jones stated that he had worked on three textbooks or manuals for students while teaching at William and Mary: "An Accidence to Christianity," "An Accidence to the Mathematicks," and *An Accidence to the English Tongue*. Only the third of them is known to have been published. Printed in London in 1724, Jones's *Accidence* is the first grammar written by an American. It breaks no new ground in the study of grammar, but it represents part of a then expanding movement away from studying Latin grammar and toward studying English grammar. In sixty-nine pages, Jones presented the alphabet, the construction of syllables, parts of speech and etymology, syntax, and discourse or speech, which includes a rudimentary rhetoric, discussion of figures of speech, and techniques of argumentation. This arrangement follows that of seventeenth-century Latin grammars. Jones's grammar is simple, direct, and reasoned, sometimes fresh with a bit of etymological speculation, and sometimes parsonic with advice or admonition to the reader.

In many ways, Jones was an educational reformer. He advocated, for example, a chair of history and a school of administration at William and Mary, and his grammar apparently represents his desire to give colonial students study in the vernacular language so they would neither continue to study Latin nor have to travel to Eng. to study English. Unfortunately, however, there is no evidence that Jones's grammar was ever imported to the colonies or used in colonial classrooms.

In 1724 Jones also published in London *The Present State of Virginia*, intended to supplement existing histories of the colony such as those by Robert Beverley (q.v.), John Clayton (q.v.), and Capt. John Smith (q.v.). This volume is now recognized as the most thorough survey of education and of the affairs of the Church of England available for early eighteenth-century Va. The main text of this volume is an account, primarily firsthand, of contemporary social, economic, and ecclesiastical conditions of Va. written to defend and promote the colony and to counter any mistaken impressions of it in Eng. In four lengthy appendixes, Jones offered his proposals or practical "schemes" for developing and reforming the schools, the religious structure, manufacturing, and trade in Va. For someone personally embroiled in the educational and ecclesiastical disputes in Va. with Commissary Blair, Jones presented an account that is conspicuously detached and unbiased.

After three short chapters discussing the settlement of Va. and describing the habits and life of the Indians of the colony, Jones presented a vivid picture of metropolitan Williamsburg, showing the layout of the town and its principal buildings. Next he discussed the colony as a whole, mentioning the woods and crops of Va. and portraying the colony as an idyllic haven. Virginians are justly known for their hospitality. The life of the Negroes "is not very laborious," and they are learning many skills. Although the climate often makes Virginians lazy, it also effects natural cures. Va. is free of religious extremism and is blessed in having a staunch Anglican clergy. Jones ended the main text by listing Virginian authors and public officials and by concluding that both neighboring colonies of Md. and N.C. are "inferior" to Va.

Jones's forward-looking "scheme" for education in Va. included the development of a grammar school in every parish and the supplanting of Latin and Greek, for which he thought the colonists had no use, by English without delay. He urged the improvement of the College of William and Mary's physical plant and the reform of its curriculum, including introducing the study of public administration, so that Virginians would no longer have to travel to Eng. for their education and so that the college could train the colony's clergymen and leaders. In addition, he advocated that clerical salaries be equalized throughout Va., and he concluded that the colony needed a dean, a stronger authority than its commissary, to run its religious affairs.

Jones's *The Panchrometer or Universal Georgian Calendar* (1753) is a series of essays offering his plan for regularizing the length of the year. The plan offers a "natural calendar" based in part on Scripture, but it was not taken seriously even in Jones's day.

Suggested Readings: BDAS; CCMD; CCV; DAB; LHUS; Sprague (V, 9-13); T_1. *See also* R. B. Davis, *Intellectual Life in the Colonial South, 1585-1763* (1978); Grace Warren Landrum, "The First Colonial Grammar in English," WMQ, 2nd ser., 19 (1939), 272-285; Rollo LaVerne Lyman, *English Grammar in American Schools Before 1850* (1922); Colyer Meriwether, *Our Colonial Curriculum, 1607-1776* (1907).

Michael Montgomery
University of South Carolina

JOHN JOSSELYN (c. 1608-1675)

Works: *New England's Rarities Discovered: In Birds, Beasts, Fishes, Serpents, and Plants of That Country. Together with the Physical and Chyrurgical Remedies Wherewith the Natives Constantly Use to Cure Their Distempers, Wounds and Sores* (1672); *An Account of Two Voyages to New England* (1674).

Biography: John Josselyn, naturalist and traveler par excellence of the American seventeenth century, was born sometime around 1608, the second son of Sir Thomas Josselyn of Willingale Doe in Essex, Eng. Josselyn first visited America at the home of his brother Henry at Black Point, near Scarborough, Maine, in 1639, after a two months' voyage aboard the *New Supply* from Gravesend. Soon after his arrival, according to Josselyn's own account, he visited John Winthrop (q.v.) and John Cotton (q.v.) in Boston, presenting the latter with certain sample translations of the Psalms by the poet Francis Quarles. Recent scholarship indicates that the efforts of the Anglican Quarles were not thought appropriate for the *Bay Psalm Book* by the New Eng. Puritans.

Josselyn returned to Eng. in Oct. of 1639. His activities from that time until his second visit to America (Jul. 1663, to Aug. 1671) are unknown. During his later stay, he evidently traveled extensively in New Eng., although he appears also to have resided principally with his brother in Maine. A Royalist by tradition and temperament, Josselyn easily found things to criticize in the Puritans of New Eng. (He was himself presented to the grand jury for nonattendance at church). His brother, moreover, was allied with the interests of the Mason and Sir Ferdinando Gorges (q.v.) families of Maine, rivals of the Bay Colony. In Eng. again after 1671, Josselyn set himself to the writing of his two books, *New England's Rarities Discovered* and *An Account of Two Voyages to New England*. Nothing more of Josselyn's whereabouts or activities after 1675 is known.

Critical Appraisal: A man of considerable learning and abundant wit, John Josselyn in his works is congenial company. Although both of his books contain much that was fabulous, they nonetheless constitute the most complete natural history of New Eng. in the seventeenth century. They are also of considerable literary and historical merit. Although Josselyn's prose has usually been ranked below that of William Wood (q.v.), whose *New England's Prospect* (1634) Josselyn undoubtedly read, both *New England's Rarities* and *An Account of Two Voyages* bear the marks of a conscientious stylist, and each has moments of wit and drama. The latter, in addition to many lively prose passages, contains one of the finest short poems of early American literature, the ten-line "And the Bitter Storm Augments; the Wild Winds Rage," a tightly constructed, sharply etched description of a storm at sea. Carefully controlled and developed, the rendering is wholly satisfying and aesthetically correct, a truly fine work. Josselyn's observations of personalities and events during his years in New Eng. have proven valuable (and intriguing) to historians of the period, and his *Chronological Observations of America...[to] 1673* contain some useful early data. As a whole, Josselyn's work belongs to the canon of promotional and travel literature of early America, and he himself ranks well among writers whose numbers include in addition to Wood, Capt. John Smith (q.v.), and Thomas Morton (q.v.). Although his scientific efforts were superior to these latter two, his literary accomplishment is less, although not inconsiderable when viewed in the context of his time and locale.

Suggested Readings: BDAS; DAB; DNB; FCNEV; LHUS; T$_1$. *See also* Karl J. Höltgen, "Francis Quarles, John Josselyn, and the *Bay Psalm Book*," SCN, 34 (1976), 42-46; Raymond P. Stearns, *Science in the British Colonies of America* (1970), pp. 139-150.

Donald P. Wharton
Castleton State University

K

SAMUEL KEIMER (1688-1742)

Works: *A Brand Pluck'd from the Burning* (1718); *The Platonick Courtship* (1718); *A Search After Religion* (1718); *Universal Instructor in All Arts and Sciences; and Pennsylvania Gazette* (1728-1729); *Caribbeana* (1741).

Biography: Samuel Keimer was born in 1688 in the parish of St. Thomas, Southwark, Eng. In 1699 he entered the Merchant Taylors' School, and eight years later he was apprenticed to Robert Tookey, a London printer. That same year (1707), Keimer and his sister Mary joined the French Prophets, or Camisards, "a small, noisy set of cataleptics, exhibitionists, and their dupes," according to George Genzmer. Keimer married in 1713, and his printing shop briefly prospered, but he was soon imprisoned for debts, first in Ludgate and then in Fleet, where in 1715 he still managed to publish *The London Post*. After a brief period of freedom, Keimer was again imprisoned, for sedition; yet here he wrote his major works—the autobiographical *A Brand Pluck'd from the Burning* and his several long religious poems. In 1722 he left his wife and home for Philadelphia, Pa., where he proposed a plan for the Bible education of male Negroes, published spurious editions of Jacob Taylor's (q.v.) and Titan Leeds's (q.v.) almanacs, and, in 1723, met Benjamin Franklin (q.v.). Despite various business schemes (including a lottery) and printings (the N.J. currency, the *Universal Instructor*—an unsuccessful precursor to Benjamin Franklin's *Pennsylvania Gazette*, and several more notable publications), by 1729 Keimer was forced to sell his press to his apprentice, David Harry, and sail for Barbados. There he published the island's first newspaper (1731-1738) and became entangled in a libel suit. Keimer died in Bridgetown, Barbados, apparently in 1742.

Critical Appraisal: Samuel Keimer's full and controversial life makes an evaluation of his literary significance difficult. Franklin's characterization of Keimer has long dominated historical judgment: "In truth, he was an odd fish; ignorant of common life, fond of rudely opposing receiv'd opinions, slovenly to extream dirtiness, enthusiastic in some points of religion and a little knavish withal." George Genzmer told us that "Keimer was a negligible person, maundering, frowzy, and incompetent, half-fool, half-knave, and wholly pitiable," and Stephen Bloore added that "A charitable estimate of his character might be that he was harmlessly crazy. Otherwise he must be adjudged a fool." Although these personal evaluations may be at least partially correct, they should not blind us to Keimer's real contributions to American literary history.

Without a doubt, Keimer was a significant force in early American printing. As Anna Janney DeArmond reminded us in her study of Andrew Bradford (q.v.), Keimer "distinguished himself by reprinting Steele's *The Crisis*; William Penn's (q.v.) Charter of Privileges of 1701; an English dictionary; and two histories, one of Diodorius Siculus, and the other of the wars of Charles XII of Sweden." In addition, Keimer issued the first translation of a Latin or Greek Classic in America, Epictetus's *Morals*, with Franklin's assistance printed Willem Sewel's *History of the Quakers*, was largely responsible for introducing Defoe's work to Pa., and started the *Barbadoes Gazette*—apparently the first twice weekly newspaper in the Americas.

Much of Keimer's own work, unfortunately, was not of such value. *The Universal Instructor*, Keimer's response to Andrew Bradford's *American Weekly Mercury* and to Franklin's plans for a similar weekly, was a plodding reprint of Ephraim Chambers's encyclopedia, with an occasional poem added by Keimer. He was only able to issue the paper from Dec. 1728 to Oct. 1729, when he relinquished control to Franklin.

Keimer's major literary work was completed before he arrived in Pa. *A Brand Pluck'd from the Burning* (1718), an often self-pitying account of his religious trials and experiments in Eng., is, as C. Lennart Carlson stated, "repetitious and badly proportioned"; yet it retains some interest as the most thorough first-hand report of the French prophets in London. *The Platonick Courtship* (1718), redolent of the Bible, and particularly the Song of Solomon, offers "decidedly vulgar" comments, as Stephen Bloore noted, "added to the horrors of the doggerel verse."

Of Keimer's poetic work in Pa., surely the most notorious is his elegy to Aquila Rose (q.v.), best remembered for Franklin's account of its composition. The poem has also been judged by the *Cambridge History of American Literature* to be "perhaps the worst elegy ever written," "illustrating," added James Onderdonk in *The History of American Verse* (1901), "how close seriously intended panegyric may come to the burlesque and even the idiotic":

> In Sable CHARACTERS the News is Read,
> Our Rose is wither'd and our Eagle's fled.
> In that our dear Aquila Rose is dead,
> Cropt in the Blooming of his precious Youth!
> Who can forbear to weep at such a Truth!

Keimer printed several other of his pieces in the *Universal Instructor*, including a four-line poem against drinking rum, an "Epitaph" for Franklin's Busy-

Body (a source of rather virulent attack on Keimer's paper), and an earlier "Answer to the BUSY BODY":
> You think there's no one smarter,
> But now you'll find you've caught a Tartar.

Keimer's wrath is directed both at Franklin's pose (which Franklin wittily, although perhaps not wholly honestly, later recorded in the *Autobiography*) and at Franklin's unacknowledged use of Addison and Steele:
> But prithee tell me, art thou mad,
> To mix good writing with the bad?
> Fie, Sir let all be of a Piece
> *Spectator, Swans,* or *Joseph's Geese* [Joseph Breintnall (q.v.)].

When Keimer arrived in Barbados, his anger did not subside. "The Sorrowful Lamentation of Samuel Keimer," first published in his *Barbadoes Gazette* and reprinted in the *Pennsylvania Gazette* of Sept. 25, 1734, shows that he had not forgotten prior injustices:
> In Penn's wooded country, type feels no disaster,
> Their printer is rich and is made their Post Master [Andrew Bradford]
> His father [William], a printer, is paid for his work,
> And wallows in plenty just now at New York,
> Tho' quite past his labour, and old as my grannum,
> The government pays him pounds sixty per annum.

Although certainly not memorable lines, the "Lamentation" at least reveals Keimer's energy and wit, if not his poetic talent.

Keimer remains an intriguing, if minor, character on the fringe of literary history. C. Lennart Carlson supplied perhaps the fairest evaluation of his significance:
> When he died in 1742, there passed from the colonial scene one of its most baffled and curious figures, a man whose eccentricities have almost overwhelmed his accomplishments, whose concern for others gained him only their ridicule, and whose constant self-pity drove him to fail in all his own affairs. Surely none but the self-assured can condemn him, and even he ought temper his contempt with pity.

Suggested Readings: DAB; T₁. *See also* Stephen Bloore, "Samuel Keimer: A Footnote to the Life of Franklin," PMHB, 54 (1930), 255-287; C. Lennart Carlson, "Samuel Keimer: A Study in the Transit of English Culture to Colonial Pennsylvania," PMHB, 61 (1937), 357-386; Benjamin Franklin, *The Autobiography*, ed. Leonard Labaree et al. (1964); Chester Jorgenson, "A Brand Flung at Colonial Orthodoxy: Samuel J. Keimer's 'Universal Instructor in All Arts and Sciences,'" JQ, 12 (1935), 272-277; James Sappenfield, *A Sweet Instruction: Franklin's Journalism as a Literary Apprenticeship* (1973).

Timothy K. Conley
Bradley University

GEORGE KEITH (c. 1638-1716)

Works: The following include jointly authored works: *Help in Time of Need* (1665); *A Salutation of Dear and Tender Love* (1665); *Immediate Revelation* (1668); *The Benefit. . . of Silent Meetings* (1670); *The Light of Truth* (1670); *The Vail Rent* (1670); "An Additional Postscript" (pub. in George Whitehead, *Nature of Christianity*; 1671); *A General Epistle to Friends* (1671); *Universall Free Grace* (1671); *An Account of the Oriental Philosophy* (1674); *George Keith's Vindication* (1674); *A Looking-Glass for Protestants* (1674); *The Woman-Preacher of Samaria* (1674); *Quakerism No Popery* (1675); *Quakerism Confirmed* (1676); *The Way Cast Up* (1677); *The Way to the City of God* (1678); *The True Christ Owned* (1679); *The Rector Corrected* (1680); *Truth's Defence* (1682); *Divine Immediate Revelation* (1684); *The Fundamental Truths of Christianity* (1688); *The Presbyterian and Independent Visible Churches in New England* (1689); *A Plain Short Catechism* (1690); *The Pretended Antidote* (1690); *A Refutation of Three Opposers of Truth* (1690); *An Appeal from the Twenty Eight Judges* (1692); *The Christian Faith* (1692); *A Counter Testimonial* (1692); *False Judgments Reprehended* (1692); *The Plea of the Innocent* (1692); *A Serious Appeal* (1692); *Some Reasons and Causes* (1692); *A Testimony* (1692); *Truth and Innocency* (1692); *The Christian Quaker* (1693); *Exhortation and Caution to Friends* (1693); *The False Judgment of a Yearly Meeting* (1693); *Heresie and Hatred* (1693); *New England's Spirit of Persecution* (1693); *The Arraignment of Worldly Philosophy* (1694); *The Causeless Ground of Surmises* (1694); *A Chronological Account of the Several Ages of the World* (1694); *A Further Discovery* (1694); *A Seasonable Information* (1694); *Truth Advanced* (1694); *Gross Error and Hypocrisie* (1695); *The Pretended Yearly Meeting of the Quakers* (1695); *The Anti-Christs and Sadduces* (1696); *An Exact Narrative* (1696); *A Seasonable Testimony* (1696); *A Sermon Preached. . . in Turner's Hall* (1696); *A Second Narrative* (1697); *Some New Geometrical Problems* (1697); *The Arguments of the Quakers* (1698); *A Christian Catechism* (1698); *A Short Catechism* (1698); *A Third Narrative* (1698); *An Abstract* (1699); *The Deism of William Penn* (1699); *A True Relation* (1699); *An Account of the Quakers Politicks* (1700); *Bristol Quakerism Expos'd* (1700); *George Keith's Fourth Narrative* (1700); *A Narrative of. . . George Keith* (1700); *A Serious Call* (1700); *A Sermon Preach'd at. . . St. Helen's* (1700); *A Sermon Preached at Turners Hall* (1700); *Two Sermons* (1700); *An Answer to 17 Queries* (1701); *George Keith's Fifth Narrative* (1701); *An Occasional Conference* (1701); *A Plain Discovery* (1701); *The Doctrine of the Holy Apostles* (1702); *A Refutation of a Dangerous. . . Opinion* (1702); *A Reply to Mr. Increase Mather* (1702); *The Standard of Quakers* (1702); *The Power of the Gospel* (1703); *Some of the Many False. . . Assertions* (1703); *The Spirit of Railing Shimei* (1703); *An Answer to Mr. Samuel Willard* (1704); *The Great Necessity. . . of Baptism and the Lord's Supper* (1704); *The Notes of the True Church* (1704); *Some Brief Remarks* (1704); *Two Sermons* (1705); *A Journal of Travels* (1706);

The Magick of Quakerism (1707); *The Necessity of Faith* (1707); *News out of Sussex* (c. 1707); *Geography and Navigation Compleated* (1709); *The Magick of Quakerism Confirmed* (1711); *The Will of George Keith* (1716); *A Reply to . . . Usher* (n.d.).

Biography: Born about 1638 in Aberdeenshire, Scot., George Keith proceeded with an M.A. from Marischal University in 1658 well regarded as a mathematician and Orientalist. Inclined first toward the Presbyterian ministry, he soon became a dedicated convert to the principles of Quakerism (principles for which he was several times imprisoned), helping spread them throughout Scot., Eng., Hol., and Ger. In person and through his writings, he exercised a major influence on other Quakers, among them Robert Barclay, the great early apologist.

After immigrating to Philadelphia in 1689 to become a schoolmaster, Keith aspired to a central position among Pa. Quakers but ran head-on into determined opposition from the colony's religious and lay establishment. This opposition arose in no small part because of heretical tendencies in Keith's own thought, including an interest in the transmigration of souls, a concern for the sacraments, and a growing belief in the historical and dogmatic basis of Christianity. Tensions erupted at last into an open split known as the "Keithian schism," in which Keith and his "Christian Quaker" followers separated from the main body of Quakers. More convinced than ever of the objective historical dimension of the church and disowned finally even by the London Yearly Meeting, Keith took Anglican orders in 1700. After returning to America in 1702, he traveled widely as a missionary for the SPG, proving especially effective in winning Quakers over to the Church of England. He returned to Eng. in 1704, where he died on Mar. 27, 1716, some twelve years later.

Critical Appraisal: George Keith was often charged by his opponents with an irascible temper and an inconstancy of mind. The former charge was certainly merited; the latter, not. During his long and varied career, Keith returned again and again in his writings to a distinct set of intellectual concerns. Although his audience and antagonist often changed, the central direction of his thought did not. At the heart of that thought lay an evolving understanding of the objective historical basis of Christianity in general and of the institutions of the True Church in particular.

To be sure, much in an intransigently independent mind like Keith's responded early on to the Quaker doctrine of "inner light," but Keith gradually came to see the inadequacy of resting the church on so precarious a foundation. In his *Farewel Sermon* to English Quakers before taking Anglican orders, Keith at last explicitly condemned the Quakers' reliance on "fickle Fancies and vain imaginations" —that is, on the "mere testimony of a private spirit." By contrast, he found the Church of England adamant in its refusal to base doctrine or practice on any individual's "private strains," or so Keith argued in *The Doctrine of the Holy Apostles*. Instead, the church was constituted by the presence of a legitimate ministry and a legitimate administration of the sacraments—in short, by external, not spiritual, criteria whose bona fides could be established by appeal to the historical record. Lacking such outward forms of authority or such outward means of conveying grace, no church could long resist the disciplinary chaos with which Keith had been only too familiar among the Quakers.

Keith's analyses of the shortcomings of Quaker belief are, on balance, a more impressive intellectual production than his defense of the Anglican Church. Nevertheless, his Anglican writings transcend rote citation from Scripture. Especially in his tract on *The Great Necessity. . .of Baptism and the Lord's Supper*, Keith ventured well beyond the commonplace by offering a rationale for the sacraments based on the human mind's susceptibility to external sensory evidence.

Keith was, all of his life, an intellectual Seeker, a Roger Williams (q.v.) in reverse, moving ever farther away from an unreliable inner light. His voluminous writings provide a clear and appealing transcript of that constant search for objective religious truth.

Suggested Readings: CCMC; CCNE; CCV; DAB; DARB; DNB; Sprague (V, 25-30). *See also* Gerald Goodwin, "The Anglican Middle Way in Early Eighteenth Century America" (Ph.D. diss., Univ. of Wis., 1965); Ethlyn W. Kirby, *George Keith* (1942).

Alan M. Kantrow
Harvard University

JAMES KIL(L)PATRICK (c. 1700-1770)

Works: "To the Reverend and Learned Doct. Neal" (1734); *A Full and Clear Reply to Doctor T. Dale* (1739); *An Essay on Inoculation* (1743); *A Letter to the Real and Genuine Pierce Dod* (1746); *The Sea-Piece* (1750); *Some Reflections* (1751); "An Epistle (in Verse) to Alexander Pope Esq. from South Carolina" (n.d.); *The Case of Miss Mary Roche* (n.d.).

Biography: Although little is known about the early life of James Killpatrick (later *Kirkpatrick*), he attended Edinburgh in the first decade of the eighteenth century and journeyed to S.C. in 1717 or 1718, and in 1724 he showed up as administrator of the estate of David Kilpatrick of Charleston. In 1725 the young Killpatrick married Elizabeth Hepworth, daughter of the secretary of the province. From this union came three children—William, Anne, and Thomas—the last of which died in the smallpox epidemic of 1738. Although not yet a degreed physician, Killpatrick performed the services of a "practitioner of physic" through the 1730s and early 1740s, at which time he rendered medical aid to patients of St. Philip's Church Hospital and dispensed drugs. Furthermore, he received a royal grant of land—230 acres in Ganville County—in 1733.

In 1738 an unfortunate event occurred that brought Killpatrick into the limelight. A smallpox epidemic, stemming from a slave ship, afflicted Charleston, leaving more than 2,000 people dead in its wake. Out of this tragedy emerged a renewal of interest in inoculation. Spearheading the movement to inoculate the populace were the slave ship's physician, a Mr. Mowbray, and James Killpatrick. Of course, on the other side of the issue was stubborn resistance, comparable to what Cotton Mather (q.v.) confronted in New Eng. and headed by Thomas Dale (q.v.)—an influential physician. So although Killpatrick was successful in proving the value of inoculation, he could not totally convince South Carolineans to submit to the treatment, popular sentiment against it being too strong to overthrow. He did, however, make good use of his experience with smallpox treatment and subsequent findings. Upon journeying to Eng. in 1742, he changed his name to *Kirkpatrick*, attained the M.D. degree, revived flagging interest in inoculation there, and subsequently gained wide recognition and respect. He died in 1770.

Critical Appraisal: James Killpatrick's publications, while in America, include both prose and poetic productions. As a prose writer, Killpatrick tended, as Austen Warren pointed out, to produce pamphlets that were "full of literary references, loaded with quotations from the works of physicians of current and earlier fame, and heavily documented." His *Full and Clear Reply to Doctor Thomas Dale*—inspired by Dale's splenetic reaction to Killpatrick's case study of the treatment of a smallpox patient, one Mary Roche, shows Killpatrick's range as a writer: his chattiness, ire, and breadth of knowledge. In general, this medical pamphlet focuses on his defense against Dale's objections to his procedures. Establishing first the facts of the case, Killpatrick proceeded to refute the objections historically; for instance, Killpatrick defended his having moved the patient during a critical stage and his not employing the "fly-blistering" method for combating fever, arguing in reference to the latter that "Blistering here cou'd do nothing, but aggravate the Phrenzy and Ebullition, which it was the proper Indication to allay." In opposition to Dale's objections to the inoculation of Roche, Killpatrick took a swipe at the wealthy Dale when he stated, "As an early Consideration of this important Subject of Inoculation, encourag'd me to be perhaps one of the very earliest Approvers of it here; so I am truly conscious, that a Reflection of the lives it would save, not the Patients it would make, was my first and greatest Inducement to it."

Killpatrick very often abandoned the medical issues at hand to attack Dale personally, commenting at one point that "he has not only discover'd, that (a) very little Creature can throw Dirt, and give abusive Language, but afforded us the clearest Demonstration of it in himself." Perhaps Dale's boorishness was most offensive to Killpatrick when he introduced into the conflict the name of the English poet Alexander Pope (for whom Killpatrick had great admiration). Killpatrick's reaction was swift and biting: "I am seriously ashamed for Mr. Dale's gross Rudeness and Impropriety, in naming the finest Genius of the Age, in a Controversy so very remote, and so meanly conducted." It was no mean sin, to Killpatrick's mind, to defame Pope, for as the practitioner of medicine revealed in his poetic exercises dedicated to the beleaguered Augustan, Killpatrick thought they had at least one thing in common: enemies. In his "Epistle to Mr. Pope from South Carolina," after praising Pope's skill as a poet and translator of the *Iliad*, Killpatrick proceeded to assure Pope that his detractors gained whatever recognition they possessed by being connected with their victim: "Themselves, their Being, but for thee forgot; / We own a Maevius, when a Maro wrote." His "Epistle" displays other affinities with the neo-Classicist, as well, as he proceeded to attack Puritans and contrast the life of the American planter to that of the poet in London. He made allusion to Classical myth and balanced his lines in couplets that could display a certain amount of epigrammatic wit. His verse, though, was necessarily unskilled, and his heavy reliance on the hiatus midline for abrupt parallelism gave his verse a sing-songy quality.

Suggested Readings: Joseph Ioor Waring, M.D., "James Killpatrick and Small-pox Inoculation in Charlestown," AMH, 10, (1938), 301-308; Austen Warren, "To Mr. Pope: Epistles from America," PMLA, 49 (1933), 61-73.

A. Franklin Parks
Frostburg State College

MARY KINNAN (1763-1848)

Works: *A True Narrative of the Sufferings of Mary Kinnan* (1795).

Biography: Mary Lewis Kinnan was born in Va. on Aug. 22, 1763. Only 15 when she married Joseph Kinnan, she bore three children. On May 13, 1791, during a period of increased Indian raids into Pa., Ky., and Va., the Shawnees took her captive, after shooting her husband and tomahawking her daughter. The Shawnees then sold her to the Delawares, who kept her prisoner for three years. In Oct. 1794 her brother Jacob Lewis rescued her near Detroit and took her to N.J., where she stayed with relatives. Mary Kinnan continued to live in N.J. until her death on Mar. 12, 1848; she never returned to her previous home in Va. *A True Narrative of the Sufferings of Mary Kinnan* forms her only literary work. According to her grandniece, it was transcribed and edited by Shepard Kollock, the printer of the 1st edition.

Critical Appraisal: In his classic article on the Indian captivity narrative, Roy Harvey Pearce traced the genre's development from religious document to anti-Catholic and anti-Indian propaganda to sentimentalized romance. Published in 1795, Mary Kinnan's narrative falls into the third phase. Lacking the realism and religion of early captivities like Mary Rowlandson's (q.v.), Kinnan's story displays fictionalization and secularism. One reason for this change may be that the Puritan documents were written by the author-participants, whereas later narratives were sometimes euphemistically "improved" by others. The title of Kinnan's work, *A True Narrative...*, is ironic, for nonrealistic elements abound.

The story's opening immediately distances and romanticizes Kinnan's experience as she (or her editor-printer Kollock) consciously made herself the heroine of her story: "Whilst the tear of sensibility so often flows at the unreal tale of woe, which glows under the pen of the poet and the novelist, shall our hearts refuse to be melted with sorrow at the unaffected and unvarnished tale of a female, who has surmounted difficulties and dangers, which on a review appear romantic, even to herself." This passage also hints at the heightened melodrama in a story that—again, ironically—intrinsically possesses ample dramatic potential. Even the style here is "literary" and stilted compared to the force and directness of earlier captivity narratives. Kinnan's sensationalism excluded precise details, as she preferred to generalize and judge rather than to specify and observe: "I lived during four days with the sister of the savage who bore me from my peaceful home, and often contemplated with a sigh the depth of degradation, of which the human character is capable." Like many captivities, this one gains special emphasis because the captive is female and her suffering and victimization can therefore be exaggerated.

Richard VanDerBeets, in his anthology of captivity narratives, summed up the significance of Kinnan's work: "it stands as a forerunner of later whole-cloth sentimental fiction and novels of sensibility that employ the context of Indian captivity solely as a fictive device for narrative arrangement."

Suggested Readings: C. Marius Barbeau, "Indian Captivities," PAPS, 94 (1950), 522-548; Phillips D. Carleton, "The Indian Captivity," AL, 15 (1943), 169-180; Roy Harvey Pearce, "The Significances of the Captivity Narrative," AL, 19 (1947), 1-20; Richard Slotkin, *Regeneration Through Violence: The Mythology of the American Frontier, 1600-1860* (1973); Boyd B. Stutler, *The Kinnan Massacre* (1969); Richard VanDerBeets, "'A Thirst for Empire': The Indian Captivity Narrative as Propaganda," RS, 40 (1972), 207-215; Oscar M. Voorhees, "A New Jersey Woman's Captivity Among the Indians," NJHSP, 13 (1928), 152-165. *A True Narrative* is reprinted in Richard VanDerBeets, ed., *Held Captive by Indians: Selected Narratives, 1642-1836* (1973), pp. 319-332.

Kathryn Zabelle Derounian
University of Arkansas at Little Rock

FRANCIS KNAPP (1671-1717)

Works: "An Epistle to Mr. B—" (pub. in John Dryden, *The Annual Miscellany*; 1694); "Tauris in Circo" (pub. in *Examen Poeticum Duplex*; 1698); "To Mr. Pope, on His Windsor-Forest" (pub. in Alexander Pope, *Windsor Forest*; 1720).

Biography: Although Francis Knapp is cited in numerous sources as an American poet, scholar, and musical composer who lived in Watertown, Mass., in fact he never set foot on American soil. Born in Chilton, Compton Hundred, Berkshire, Eng., and baptized on May 28, 1671, Knapp matriculated at St. John's College, Oxford, on Dec. 16, 1688, and received a B.A. on Jun. 6, 1692, and an M.A. on Apr. 30, 1695. By 1697 he was the vicar of Ballysakeery and Kilmoremog in Ire. On Jan. 31, 1701/2, he was instituted as the dean of Killala, in which role he continued until his death. He was buried on Jun. 1, 1717, in Chilton, Compton Hundred, Berkshire.

Critical Appraisal: Only three of the six poems commonly attributed to Knapp were actually written by him. As J. A. Leo Lemay has shown, *Gloria Brittanorum* (1723) was written after Knapp's death, probably by "a young boy who looked forward to going to Harvard." "A New England Pond" (1731) was written by the Md. writer Richard Lewis (q.v.). Similarly, "A Pastoral" (1758), a poem lamenting the death of Alexander Pope, was written by another Md. author, the Rev. James Sterling (q.v.).

Except for "Tauris in Circo," a minor poem in Latin, the poems Knapp wrote are skillful examples of familiar late seventeenth- and early eighteenth-century poetic forms. The first, "The Epistle to Mr. B.—," is a humorous satire on the Grub Street hacks of the day. Like many of the satirical poems of that period, Knapp's "Epistle" vacillates between ironic praise and straightforward criticism of his subjects. Knapp's only other poem in English, his "To Mr. Pope, on His Windsor-Forest," is also in heroic couplets, but instead of satirizing the bad writers of the day, it lauds Alexander Pope. According to J. A. Leo Lemay, it is this poem, with its allusions to "Atlantic shores" and "wilds remote from public view," that led Samuel L. Knapp to identify Knapp as an American author, an error repeated in numerous works on American literature.

Suggested Readings: T₁. *See also* Evert A. Duyckinck and George L. Duyckinck, *Cyclopaedia of American Literature* (1875), I, 77; J. F. Hunnewell, *Early American Poetry* (1894), pp. 22-23; Samuel L. Knapp, *Biographical Sketches of Eminent Lawyers, Statesmen, and Men of Letters* (1821), p. 140; idem, *Lectures on American Literature* (1829), pp. 143, 153; J. A. Leo Lemay, "Francis Knapp: A Red Herring in Colonial Poetry," NEQ, 39 (1966), 233-237; John Nichols, *A Select Collection of Poems* (1780-1782), IV, 289; Agnes Marie Sibley, *Alexander Pope's Prestige in America, 1725-1835* (1949), pp. 85, 131; Oscar Wegelin, *Early American Poetry* (1903), p. 34.

David Jauss
University of Arkansas at Little Rock

SARAH KEMBLE KNIGHT (1666-1727)

Works: *The Journal of Madam Knight and the Reverend Mr. Buckingham* (1825).

Biography: Born in Boston on Mar. 19, 1666, to Thomas and Elizabeth (Trerice) Kemble, Sarah Kemble married Capt. Richard Knight, who was many years her senior, and when he died sometime around 1706 inherited his property and business responsibilities. Even earlier, however, perhaps because of his failing health, she had already assumed much of the management of the family's finances; indeed, her one piece of writing, the *Journal*, is the product of one such business trip she undertook alone from Oct. 1704 through Mar. 1705. While in Boston, Knight also ran the writing school that Benjamin Franklin (q.v.) is thought to have attended; when her daughter married in 1714, Knight moved to

Conn. and operated property in Norwich and New London until her death on
Sept. 25, 1727. Her *Journal* was first published in 1825 and again in 1847 and
1858; the most readily available modern edition is to be found in the second
volume of *The Puritans: A Sourcebook of Their Writings*, edited by Perry Miller
and Thomas H. Johnson in 1938.

Critical Appraisal: Critical discussion of Madame Knight's *Journal* has
been scant and, until recently, almost entirely concerned with providing biographical and historical information about the author and her times. In the last
several decades, commentators have attempted to connect the *Journal* with both
picaresque and mock-epic literary traditions, but although there may seem to be
elements of each tradition in the work, it is clear that neither one gave shape or
final imaginative definition to Knight's journey. Indeed, Knight is in no sense a
picaro, that is, a rogue on the road, so that similarities between the *Journal* and
picaresque fiction—*Lazarillo de Tormes* is, of course, the *locus classicus*—is
incidental rather than essential. In the same way, mock-romantic, mock-epic,
and mock-heroic elements play a significant role in only a few brief episodes and
are important chiefly in that they provide a stylistic and linguistic ideal against
which the racy idiom of Yankee dialect (including Knight's own language on
occasion) may reverberate. Even the descent into the underworld at "mr. Devills,"
for example, seems to have been inspired as much by an obvious play on words
as by any awareness of epic and mock-epic conventions. It seems, in short, far
more fruitful to regard the *Journal* as having originated in folk traditions, which
even this early had created a gallery of Yankee character types—the shrewd and
not entirely honest man of business balanced by the country bumpkin, the loquacious guesser and questioner matched against the taciturn master of understatement and total silence—which she was able to employ for comic purposes. One
is struck by a general formal (which in this case is to say formless) resemblance
to William Byrd of Westover's (q.v.) *Secret History* and *History of the Dividing
Line* (1728) and to Dr. Alexander Hamilton's (q.v.) *Itinerarium* (1750), for like
these works, the *Journal* gropes tentatively but creatively toward an open-ended
and hybrid literary vehicle appropriate to the American experience.

Perhaps the most striking feature of the *Journal* is the rich mix of dialect,
colloquial speech, foreign and Indian phrases, professional terminology, and (for
want of a better term) the high style: biblical and other literary allusions, Latinate
diction, and the like. Language, in fact, becomes almost a standing metaphor for
the apparent disorganization of the narrative, which is held loosely together only
by the general direction of the journey but in other ways does not lead from one
episode to another, and displays both the delights and the dangers of American
eclecticism, the potpourri of speech, religion, terrain, and character type that
already at the outset of the eighteenth century and even in so limited a space as
the distance between Boston and N.Y. were hallmarks of America. In the absence of any visible trappings of cultural and social order, language alone is left
to bear the burden of civilizing the frontier but frequently betrays its own hol-
lowness in the process, establishing a verbal process of reciprocal definition,

culture versus nature, that is integral to American humor at its finest. Here also one will find nearly all of the familiar stylistic techniques—understatement, comic circumlocution, outrageous similes—employed by later American humorists, as when Madame Knight described an especially awful dish she was served as "contrary to my notion of Cookery" or one of her guides on horseback as looking like "a Globe on a Gate post."

Suggested Readings: DAB; FCNEV; LHUS; NAW; T₁. *See also* Alan Margolis, "The Editing and Publication of the Journal of Madam Knight," PBSA, 58 (1964), 25-32; R. O. Stephens, "The Odyssey of Sarah Kemble Knight," CLAJ, 7 (1964), 247-255; Peter Thorpe, "Sarah Kemble Knight and the Picaresque Tradition," CLAJ, 10 (1966), 114-121; Anson Titus, "Madam Sarah Knight, Her Diary and Her Times," BSP, 9 (1912), 99-126; Faye Nell Vowell, "A Commentary on the Journal of Sarah Kemble Knight," ESRS, 24, iii (1974), 27-37.

Robert D. Arner
University of Cincinnati

EDWARD KNOTT, S.J. (1582-1656)

Works: *Charity Mistaken* (1630); *A Modest Briefe Discussion of Some Points Taught by M. Doctour Kellison in His Treatise of the Ecclesiastical Hierarchy* (1630); *Mercy and Truth, or Charity Maintayned by Catholykes* (1633); *A Direction to Be Observed by N. N. if Hee Meane to Proceade in Answering the Booke Intitled Mercy and Truth* (1636); *Christianity Maintained, or A Discovery of Sundry Doctrines Tending to the Overthrow of Christian Religion, Contained in the Answer to a Book Intitled Mercy and Truth* (1638); *Infidelity Unmasked, or The Confutation of a Booke, Published by M. William Chillingworth* (1652); *Protestancy Condamned by the Expressive Sentence and Verdict of Protestants* (1654); letters.

Biography: Edward Knott was the pseudonymn assumed by Matthew Wilson—a practice common among English Catholic priests to protect their relatives. Born in Catchburne, Northumberland, Eng., he studied at the English College in Rome and was ordained a priest on Mar. 27, 1606. Later that year, he entered the Jesuits. In 1633 he became vice-provincial under Richard Blount, S.J., the provincial of the English Jesuits, and continued in that post under Henry More, S.J. In 1639 he became provincial, but at that time, he was involved in the controversy between the English secular and religious clergy. He, therefore, took up residence on the Continent and left the province's administration in Eng. to More. In 1643 he returned to Eng., where he remained as provincial until 1647. In 1653 he was again named provincial and died in office in London on Jan. 11, 1656.

Critical Appraisal: Edward Knott's accession to office in 1639 occurred not only on the eve of the English civil war but also during a period of controversy between the English Jesuits in Md. and Lord Baltimore. The occasion for the controversy was the Jesuits' acceptance of land from the Indians for support of their missionary work. Baltimore reacted by confiscating the land. This issue in turn gave rise to a series of colonial legislative proposals that would have severely restricted Jesuit activity in Md. To this controversy, Knott contributed three documents: a letter to Monsignor Rosetti, the papal nuncio to Belgium; his notations on Lord Baltimore's points to settle the dispute in his own favor; and a memorial to the Holy Office or the Inquisition. Each of the documents was written in Nov. 1641.

Knott presented the Jesuit case before ecclesiastical authority, his arguments falling into two categories. First, he asserted the right of the Indians to convey land to the Jesuits to support their missionary work. In this, he was going counter to the charter for Md., which gave Lord Baltimore the exclusive right to grant land to settlers. In addition, he asserted the right of the missionaries to church property such as they would have had in a Catholic country. For him, it was unjust that the Jesuits should be treated like the other settlers, which had been part of the original agreement with Lord Baltimore. The second category of his arguments was more complex and involved more doctrinal issues. John Lewger, the secretary to the governor of Md., asserted that the pope had only internal jurisdiction over matters of conscience. He furthermore had the Assembly introduce bills stating that a young woman who took a vow of virginity would forfeit her property if she did not marry, that clerics were to be tried in secular courts, and that priests needed the civil authority's permission to work with the Indians—a work that had been one of the original motivations for the Jesuits to accompany the settlers. Knott saw Lewger's proposals against the background of English laws that gave the civil government jurisdiction over ecclesiastical affairs. The importance of Knott's tedious arguments in Latin, however, is to provide a glimpse into the way in which Md. was putting into practice its theory of religious liberty. The Jesuits ultimately acknowledged that none of their property could be properly considered church property; they were to remain in the colony as self-supporting settlers. Baltimore and Lewger, for their part, had to acknowledge the Jesuits' legitimate jurisdiction over ecclesiastical affairs.

Suggested Readings: Thomas Hughes, S.J., *History of the Society of Jesus in North America, Text*, vol. I (1908); *Documents* (1908), I, pt. I, 165-172, 178-181 (for Knott's letters).

Gerald P. Fogarty, S.J.
University of Virginia

L

JOSEPH BROWN LADD (1764-1786)

Works: *The Poems of Arouet* (1786); *The Literary Remains of Joseph Brown Ladd* (1832).

Biography: Joseph Brown Ladd was born in Newport, R.I., in 1764. Tiring of farm labor at which his father had set him at the age of 11, he found a more congenial occupation at 14 as an apprentice to the printer of the *Newport Mercury*. His quick satirical pen getting him into trouble as he wrote squibs directed at prominent citizens, he was at 15 placed with a local physician for the study of medicine. At 20 he set out for S.C., in search of fame and fortune. There, as Dr. Ladd, he lectured on scientific subjects and, for want of better practice, offered his services as a physician without pay to the needy poor of Charleston. As "Arouet" he contributed popular poems to the *Columbian Herald*, advertised a "New American Version" of the Book of Psalms, and set in motion a drive for subscribers for a collection of his own verse. When the volume appeared in 1786, it was warmly received, not only in Charleston, but in N.Y. and Philadelphia. Hardly more than a month later, its author died at the age of 22 as the result of wounds received in a duel with a person who apparently had questioned both his morals and his qualifications as a physician. Almost half a century later, his *Literary Remains* were published by his sister, after she had apparently offered the opportunity more than twenty years earlier to her brother-in-law William Emerson (q.v.), who seems to have been dissuaded by other members of the Anthology Club in Boston from undertaking the task.

Critical Appraisal: Ladd was a chameleon versifier. He wrote in the manner of Ossian, Thomas Chatterton, William Collins, John Milton, and the Old Testament prophets. He seemed at ease with Fénelon and Voltaire; he knew Thomas Paine (q.v.) and Socrates; he bandied about the names of Locke, Blair, Newton, Bacon, and Statius. His readers were led to understand that he translated with equal ease from Hebrew, Greek, Latin, German, and French. Readers responded by finding Ladd the American successor to Virgil, Voltaire, Pope, and Dryden, as heir to the mantle of Homer. His voice was so like the voice of so many others that people responded to it as comfortably familiar. It used language certified by long usage as poetical. It sometimes swelled to bombast. Ladd himself once wrote that "every writer who is deficient in real genius, will affect pomposity, and magnificence in language. It gives him popularity; and popularity is the food of authors." Ladd was well fed, during the two years of his popularity in Charleston and for a few years after his death, so young. But his fame was brief. Samuel L. Knapp in his pioneer *Lectures on American Literaure* called him Josiah Ladd. Samuel Kettell in his *Specimens of American Poetry* called him William. Few anthologists remember him today.

Suggested Readings: LHUS. *See also* Elizabeth Haskins, ed., *The Literary Remains of Joseph Brown Ladd* (1832); Lewis Leary, "Joseph Brown Ladd of Charleston" in *Soundings: Some Early American Writers* (1975), pp. 112-130.

Lewis Leary

The University of North Carolina at Chapel Hill

RALPH LANE (1530-1603)

Works: *A Dissertation on Military Affairs* (1576); letters to Walter Raleigh, Philip Sidney, Richard Hakluyt (1585-1586); entries in Richard Hakluyt, *Principall Navigations, Voiages, and Discoveries of the English Nation* (1589, 1598-1600).

Biography: Ralph Lane was born in Northampton, Eng., in 1530. As the second son of Sir Ralph Lane of Orlingbury and Maud Parre, cousin to Katherine Parre, queen of Eng., Lane saw the family inheritance go to his older brother Robert upon the death of his father in 1540. Forced to fend for himself, Lane served first as Northamptonshire representative to the Parliaments of Queens Mary and Elizabeth, next as soldier in the queen's service to Fr., and then against the "rebel Earls" of Northumberland and Westmoreland. Despite loyal service, Lane rose not even to the rank of captain and was appointed one of the queen's equerries. Desperate for a position in 1573, he preferred his military skills to Philip of Sp. and to the kings of Fez and Algiers. In 1576 he was made a customs agent and was beaten by smugglers and thrown overboard, causing him to lament he was "more fit for a camp than for a court." In 1583 he complained of penury, claiming he had not received "one groat, by her majesty's gift, towards a living" and was made governor of Kerry, Clanmorris, and Limerick counties in Ire. from Jan. 1584 to Feb. 1585.

On this date, Lane sailed to the New World under the captaincy of Sir Richard Greenville and under the aegis of Sir Walter Raleigh to become the first full-year governor of a British colony in America. The previous year a camp that lasted a bare three months had existed, but Lane's colony of 108 men at Roanoke lasted from around Jul. 1585 to Jun. 18 or 19, 1586. It was at this time that John White made twenty-one drawings of Indians and landscapes and drew the first map of the entrance to Chesapeake Bay that made later colonies possible. Thomas Hariot (q.v.), whom Lane recommended for his honesty and truthfulness in

1588, made many scientific studies of America's flora and fauna. Lane himself, besides governing the colony, studied Indian methods of planting, arranged for the exploration of the Pimlico River to Albemarle Sound, searched for mines, saved his men from poisoning, and was the first English commander to massacre Indians who apparently intended to massacre him. Lane is important for having written the first complete official dispatches from America to Eng. even though a storm in Jun. 1586 forced Lane and his men to cast many of their "cards, books and writing...overboard." The colony abandoned America because of food shortages, Indian hostility, Lane's distrust of being supplied by Raleigh or Green-ville, and the timely arrival of Francis Drake. A subject of controversy in late nineteenth-century America, Lane was praised by I. N. Tarbox (1884)—"for clearness of judgment, for manly integrity, for breadth and comprehension, he stands out prominently in this effort to plant a colony in America" —but Edward Everett Hale complained (1860) that he "failed so lamentably to accomplish the wishes of those who sent him....He seems to have been an eager courtier, a bold soldier, a good disciplinarian, an incompetent governor, a credulous adven-turer, and on the whole, though not a worthless, an unsuccessful man."

After returning to Eng., Lane was made muster master of Ire. in 1591, which post he held until his death. Dangerously wounded, he was knighted and made his final will in 1594. In Feb. 1601 he complained he was too weak to work, and he died in Oct., 1603, apparently never marrying.

Critical Appraisal: Ralph Lane's non-American writings, even *A Disserta-tion on Military Affairs*, which shows his expertise on fortifications, are habitu-ally wordy, argumentative, officious and arrogant. Their main purpose appears to be to put Lane forward. As his superior in Ire. complained, "he wanted to rule everything and have the disposal of all the land himself." Although his writings from or about the newly found land are more taut, Lane's essays are important more for historical reasons than for style. Besides being responsible for introduc-ing tobacco to Eng., Lane learned from the Indians how to plant maize and to catch fish with weirs, oversaw scientific and topographical studies of the region, and praised the new land for being "the most pleasing territory of the world" with "the goodliest soil under the cope of heaven" so that "no realm in Christendom were comparable to it." Three events are particularly important: his confrontation with Indians who at first welcomed the English and then turned on them, causing the earliest example of Anglo-Indian guerrilla warfare, to which Lane devoted half of his personal report; his brief expedition up the Roanoke River in search of fabled copper mines, the British equivalent of the quest for El Dorado; his memoir to Raleigh, found in Hakluyt (vol. III), describing what he would have done had he sufficient supplies, especially his advice that Chesapeake Bay, where James-town was subsequently established, would be more hospitable to colonization.

Suggested Readings: DAB; DNB. *See also* E. E. Hale, "Life of Sir Ralph Lane," TAAS, 4 (1860), 317-344; D. B. Quinn, *Raleigh and the British Empire* (1962); I. N. Tarbox, *Sir Walter Raleigh and His Colony in America* (1884).

Henry L. Golemba
Wayne State University

THOMAS PIKE LATHY (1771-c. 1821)

Works: *Reparation* (1800); *Paraclete*, 5 vols. (1805); *Usurpation*, 3 vols. (1805); *The Invisible Enemy*, 4 vols. (1806); *Gabriel Forrester*, 4 vols. (1807); *Memoirs of the Court of Louis XIV*, 3 vols. (1819). Credited with *The Misled General* (1807); *Love, Hatred, and Revenge, A Swiss Romance*, 3 vols. (1809); *The Angler* (1820).

Biography: Both *The Dictionary of National Biography* and *A Biographical Dictionary of the Living Authors of Great Britain and Ireland* recorded that Thomas Pike Lathy, born in Exeter, Eng., in 1771, was "bred to trade." His professional activity, however, at least between 1799 and 1821, emphasized the arts. Eventually somewhat infamous, but generally undistinguished, Lathy evolved from actor to novelist, from playwright to plagiarist. Although the British seem to claim him, Lathy achieved some minor recognition in America primarily, and presumably only, in the Boston area, where he worked as an actor. He belonged for a time to the reputable Federal Street Theatre—perhaps his main reason for immigrating to America. Still struggling under the harsh "Act to Prevent Stage-Plays and Other Theatrical Entertainments" passed by the General Court of Mass. in 1750, the Boston theater actively recruited British actors to help give life to the cause of theater in the North. From Mar. through Apr. 1799, Lathy performed in several plays: as a shepherd in *Cymon and Sylvia*; as a robber in *The Haunted Castle*; as one of the "Officers and Soldiers" in *Major André*; as Antonio in *The Tempest*. That season, however, was not particularly good for the Federal Street Theatre, and available histories of the Boston stage provide no substantive mention of the plays or actors. Also in 1799, Lathy married Miss Sally K. Johns of Boston, whose ancestors had emigrated from Cornwall to the Mass. colony in 1703. After 1799, Lathy's activity seems to have been confined to literary production. He wrote one play, *Reparation*, published "for the benefit of the author" and performed "at the Boston theatre, with great applause," and at least five multivolume novels, all of them published in Br. In 1819 he apparently "perpetrated a successful plagiaristic fraud." Taking advantage of the popularity of "angling literature" in Eng., he convinced a "sporting bookseller" and publisher named Gosden to buy for thirty pounds an "original" poem, "The Angler." Later, the poem was discovered to be a copy of Dr. Thomas Scott's "The Anglers," first published in 1758 and reprinted in 1773 in Ruddiman's *Scarce, Curious, and Valuable Pieces*.

Critical Appraisal: That Thomas Pike Lathy ended his career as an accused plagiarist may have been the fitting, if unfortunate, conclusion of his erratic literary habits in general. According to early reviewers of his fiction, Lathy's prolix, often tedious novels are little more than confused imitations and combinations of popular forms and tales of the day. Lathy revealed, for example, a fondness for the "exotic" and historical romance, in terms of setting and situation; and he was obviously enamored of elaborate plots and subplots that parlay disguise and deceit mostly into lovers' reunions and moral lessons. *Usurpation* was described by a contemporary as "a series of unexpected adventures drily told; half-finished characters, and love stories." In a review of *Paraclete*, an unhappy critic admonished the publisher: "Twenty shillings! This is, indeed...rather better than your usual productions, but consider, good Sir, consider, twenty shillings! A man might buy a *good book* for that sum." Of *The Invisible Enemy*, a "Polish Legendary Romance," another critic judged that "Everything is trite and trumpery." Perhaps the best of Lathy's novels—if early reviewers are to be heeded—is *Gabriel Forrester*. Although it exhibits Lathy's tendency to lapse into "inelegance of language" and "indelicacy of description," the novel did strike at least one critic as having merit, especially for its characterization and its *Tom Jones*-like plot, and its author as being "above the generality of modern writers."

Reparation; Or, The School for Libertines, a three-act play set in Switz., is apparently Lathy's only substantial literary venture in America. If indeed the play was performed to great applause, *Reparation* earned that applause for its sheer entertainment value, including its foreign setting, much music and singing, fighting, and characters in disguise. Moreover, in its effort to teach two or three obvious moral lessons and to avoid direct political controversy (there are no American characters, and the penitent English lord and his poor, courageous French comrade negotiate non-political business), the play did not risk seriously offending either the adamant antitheater faction in Boston or the city's American theatergoers. Bringing an aristocratic Englishman to his knees in reparation and in thanksgiving to a plebian benefactor may have, in fact, been a mild attempt to appease democracy-minded Americans who were beginning to demonstrate a resurgence of anti-British feeling during the decade before the War of 1812.

Loosely combining the stories of Samuel Richardson's *Pamela* and *Clarissa Harlowe* with the parable of the Prodigal Son and William Shakespeare's *Romeo and Juliet*, *Reparation* has two main plot lines. In the first, Lord Staunton returns, after eight years of libertinism, to the site of his treachery—the seduction and desertion of a young virgin—to make amends. Staunton is wretched with grief and remorse over the misery he has caused not only the maiden Julietta but also her father and brother. Old Latouche himself is greatly tormented by his own heartless abandonment of his daughter, whom he evicted from his house when she told him of her ignominy. Julietta and the child she bore as a result of the illicit liaison have been living incognito with the Pastor and his wife.

Young Latouche, who has been Staunton's friend since he rescued the aristocrat from ambushers, does not know that his companion is the man responsible for his family's distress. But Young Latouche has other problems as well. He had left home in rage, sorrow, and humiliation because greedy Palaco, the father of his beloved Valence, refused to allow his daughter to marry a man of lowly means, a "Mr. six-pence-a day." Now Young Latouche returns to make reparation to the family he deserted and to renew his courtship of Valence. To his aggravation, he finds that Palaco is scheming to marry Valence off to one "Don

Chicano, Estrapada, De Olla Podrida, Grandee of Spain, Knight of La Mancha, and Viceroy of Barataria." Don Chicano, coincidentally, turns out to be the charlatan Chapone, the man who had ambushed Lord Staunton and who was once that lord's untrustworthy servant.

Perhaps the characters who finally put life into the play are Blanco and the Pastor. A Falstaff-like old servant, Blanco claims that, for the right price or its equivalent in alcohol, he would "'go to the Devil'. . . if I could but find the way." Although tempted to stray and betray, Blanco remains true to the cause of honesty. His repossession of his self-respect parallels the restoration to virtue of Lord Staunton and Young Latouche. If Blanco redeems the major portion of the play, the Pastor saves the final scenes from banality. Although the Pastor is obviously mimicking the action of Friar Laurence in *Romeo and Juliet* as he engineers a melodramatic meeting between Julietta and Staunton in what Staunton believes to be Julietta's tomb, the occasion seems as deliberately humorous as solemn. Not only is there the loud Shakespearean echo, there is also the hopefully comic note provided by Julietta and her child, who are dressed in white as the Pastor has suggested and whom Staunton at first perceives to be ghosts!

There are some distinct—even praiseworthy—literary touches in *Reparation*. The first words that Lord Staunton and Young Latouche speak, for example, are an apology for arriving so late at the inn. As Staunton explains, they had taken "the wrong road" in "the darkness." No mere incident of plot, the apology actually rehearses the major posture of both young men: they have for the past eight years been on the "wrong road" that they had taken in "the darkness" of their youthful passion. Sorrowful, both men have returned to atone for their sins and their libertinism. Julietta's "tomb" becomes symbolic of the moral and spiritual darkness in which especially Staunton has lived, as it becomes the symbol also of Julietta's social imprisonment that has been the result of Staunton's crime against her.

From a literary and certainly thematic standpoint, the parent-child issue is a significant dimension of *Reparation*. Within each of the two main plot lines, a father has been harsh and unfeeling in his treatment of a daughter. Old Latouche has disowned Julietta for bringing disgrace upon the family, and Palaco wants Valence to marry someone she does not love. Both Old Latouche and Palaco are, in this respect, libertines in their own right; they have selfishly violated their moral obligations as parents. Hence they, too, must make reparation for their eight years of wrongdoing. *Reparation* throughout emphasizes the necessity of family unity and compassion. That its final words are "My father," spoken by Young Latouche, and that the last major scene presents a portraitlike study of Staunton, Julietta, and their child as a Holy Family of sorts reflects that emphasis.

Suggested Readings: DNB. See also T. W. William Ball, "The Old Federal Street Theatre," BSP, 8 (1911), 41-92; *A Biographical Dictionary of the Living Authors of Great Britain and Ireland* (1816), p. 196; William W. Clapp, Jr. , *A Record of the Boston Stage* (Rep., 1968); Arthur Hornblow, *A History of The Theatre in America* (1919);

William S. Ward, comp., *Literary Reviews in British Periodicals: A Bibliography* (1972), II, 364-365.

Patricia Lee Yongue
University of Houston

DEODAT(E) LAWSON (fl. 1660-1715)

Works: *A Brief and True Narative* (1692); *Christ's Fidelity the Only Shield Against Satan's Malignity* (1693, 1704); *The Duty and Property of a Religious Householder* (1693); *Threnodia, or A Mournful Remembrance, of...Anthony Collamore...Dec. 16, 1693* (1694).

Biography: Deodat Lawson was born in Eng., probably in the late 1640s, son of the Rev. Thomas Lawson (c. 1620-1695), a Puritan minister who received an M.A. from the University of Cambridge in 1640 and became a fellow of St. John's College on Jun. 11, 1644. Deodat's father served as rector of Langenhoe, Essex, 1645-1646; vicar of Fingringhoe, Essex, 1646-1654; rector of East Donyland, Essex, 1647-1654; and rector of Denton, Norfolk, c. 1654-1660. In 1649, while still holding his preferments, Thomas Lawson joined an Independent Church at Norwich, Norfolk; in 1661, he was a member of an Independent Church at Market Weston, Suffolk. Deodat's mother, who died a few weeks after his birth, joined with his father in dedicating him to the Gospel ministry and in choosing for him a name that means "given to God," and Deodat probably grew up under heavy pressure to become a minister. After the Restoration, Thomas Lawson was ejected from his living at Denton by the Act of Uniformity of 1659. Deodat, following a reference in *Christ's Fidelity* to his "Education (both in Schoole and Colledge learneing)," went on to state: "And whereas by my Fathers being silenced, and his Estate much weakened, I was hindered of some Academical Preferments, and after Six Years Standing at Colledg, necessitated to make digression to secular affaires." Because Deodat is probably using the term *Colledg* in the sense of an English "public school" (he would hardly have attended a university for six years without earning a degree), this passage helps us to approximate how old he was around 1660.

It is not known when Deodat immigrated to America, but a letter that his father directed to him at Martha's Vineyard, Mass., Jan. 20, 1676-1677, suggests that by 1676 Deodat was living there, that he was married, and that he had informed his father that he felt a calling to the ministry. Writing about the same time to Thomas Mayhew then governor of Martha's Vineyard, Thomas Lawson cited several letters from Boston ministers commending Deodat and his yokefellow. If Deodat Lawson was seeking Mayhew's help in being settled as a minister at Martha's Vineyard, that did not work out. By 1680 Lawson was living in Boston, where he took the freeman's oath and joined the Old South Congregational Church that year. He was settled as an unordained minister at the First Parish (Congregational) of Edgartown, Mass., 1681-1682.

In 1682 Lawson's wife, Jane, gave birth to a son, Deodat, at Boston. Still unordained, Lawson served from 1683 to 1688 as minister of the First Parish (Congregational) of Salem Village, Mass. (since 1752 called Danvers), where his wife and his daughter Ann died. Lawson's lack of an academic degree may have been one reason—but probably not the only one—why he was expected to serve a long probationary period before ordination. The refusal of the church at Salem Village to ordain Lawson—just one of the things about which the people there were divided—led him to resign in 1688 and return to Boston. James Savage suggested that leaving Salem Village was lucky for him: if he had remained, he might well have suffered the fate of the Rev. George Burroughs who, serving terms as minister there both before and after Lawson, was convicted of witchcraft in 1692 and hanged. On May 6, 1690, Lawson married Deborah Allen at Boston. In Nov. 1694 Lawson was finally ordained at the Second Congregational Church of Scituate, Mass. (since 1888, the First Parish [Unitarian] of Norwell). He probably started preaching at Scituate around 1693: in an inscription, dated Aug. 6, 1693, in a book, Lawson is addressed as "pastor of the church of Scituate," and his broadside *Threnodia* deals with the deaths by drowning of six persons from Scituate, Dec. 16, 1693. A daughter, Deborah, was born at Scituate in 1694, and a son Richard, in 1696. Following the death of his father in 1695, Lawson returned to Eng. in 1696. He did not resign and his parishioners apparently thought that he had gone to Eng. just for a visit.

Over the next two years, Lawson failed to explain to his congregation why he was staying away so long or when he would return. On Sept. 26, 1698, the congregation voted to seek the advice of an ecclesiastical council on what to do about their pulpit. Two days later, the Council, meeting at Weymouth, Mass., concluded that Lawson had desisted from his pastoral duties "merely for secular advantages" and authorized the congregation "to settle themselves with another Pastor, more spiritually and more fixedly disposed." No pastoral records from Lawson's ministry at Scituate have survived, and Samuel Deane suggested that Lawson took all of these records to Eng. with him. Under censure in Eng. for some misconduct, he was restored to the ministry at London in 1712, according to a printed sheet that he circulated in 1715.

Critical Appraisal: Deodat Lawson returned to Salem Village for a visit, Mar. 19-Apr. 5, 1692, when the witchcraft excitement was in full swing. *A Brief and True Narrative* is his day-by-day account of that visit. Lawson witnessed some examinations of accused persons by the magistrates of Salem, and several of the afflicted persons interrupted him when he preached at the village on the Lord's day, Mar. 20, 1692. In his *True Narrative*, Lawson confined himself to reporting "what I either saw my self, or did receive Information from persons of undoubted Reputation and Credit." Robbins called Lawson's book "the first published account of the Salem troubles"; and although it covers only three weeks of the many months of agitation over witches, it remains an absorbing eyewitness account.

No copy of Lawson's Lord's day sermon at Salem Village has survived, but he preached there again on lecture day, Mar. 24, 1692, and this sermon was published as *Christ's Fidelity*. Here Lawson surveyed the major biblical teachings about Satan, and he maintained that when God's covenant people are subject to Satan's rage and malice, Jesus Christ is their only source of relief. In a 2nd edition (1704), Lawson added an appendix, organized as a systematic account of witchcraft phenomena observed at Salem Village, in contrast to the chronological arrangement of his *True Narrative*. In the appendix, Lawson revealed that he returned to Salem Village to witness for himself the complete trial of at least one of the accused (the Rev. George Burroughs, tried and condemned on Aug. 5, 1692, after being charged, among other offenses, with killing Jane and Ann Lawson by witchcraft).

There has been a great deal of controversy about *Christ's Fidelity*. Charles Upham held that Lawson's sermon was preached to stir up the people's emotions, so that they would maintain the high fever of their excitement about witchcraft. "It justified and commended every thing that had been done, and every thing that remained to be done." On the other hand, Chadwick Hansen argued that Lawson actually cautioned against rashness and credulity in the witchcraft investigations; he held that Lawson, far from seeking to make the persecutions of persons accused as witches more intense, actually sought to calm people's passions by warning them that there was no satisfactory secular defense against witchcraft and that, in the words of his sermon title, *Christ's Fidelity* was indeed *the Only Shield Against Satan's Malignity*. Charles Upham suggested that Lawson's zeal was motivated by his credulity in accepting the truth of intimations that his wife and daughter had died as victims of witchcraft. Here Upham overlooked the fact that these reports originated after Lawson's Mar.-Apr. 1692 visit to Salem Village, so that he could not have known about them when he preached on lecture day. Indeed Lawson mentioned these reports only in his appendix (1704) to *Christ's Fidelity*, not in *True Narrative*.

The Duty and Property is a sermon on Christian family duties. Although Lawson delivered this sermon on Dec. 25, 1692, he did not refer to Christmas, which Puritans did not observe. In view of the subject of Lawson's only other published sermon, it is interesting that he made a passing reference to the saying that "some men are *Saints abroad and Devils at home*."

The latter part of Lawson's *Threnodia* is a conventional lament on the drowned Capt. Collamore, who is eulogized as a model of virtue and piety, but the beginning of this broadside poem is a narrative, sometimes stirring, about a voyage from Scituate Harbor, a sudden storm at sea, a shipwreck, six drownings, and the eventual recovery of only two bodies, including Collamore's. Harold Jantz ranked stanzas 3-6 of this poem as "among the finest ballad verse of early New England," the promise of which is not carried out in the other twenty-three stanzas, which "become lost in weak narrative, lament, and eulogy." Perhaps a case can be made for regarding several other passages in *Threnodia* as narrative poetry of merit, including stanza 9, in which Lawson speculated about the cause of the shipwreck: "Or whether *Loaden* over deep with *Wood*, / The Swelling

Waves did fill her by degrees; / If then their Frozen *Pump* would do no good, / They soon became a Prey unto the *Seas*: / Which Violently over them did go, / And bore them down, into the deeps below."

In writing about Thomas Lawson, Edmund Calamy noted that he was "the Father of the unhappy Mr. *Deodate Lawson*, who came hither from *New England*." Calamy's choice of an epithet for Deodat may be significant: since Calamy was an English biographer of persecuted and impoverished Puritan ministers, none of whom had much reason to be happy after the Restoration, there must have been something extraordinary about Deodat Lawson's unhappiness for Calamy to single it out for special comment. Of Lawson's return to Eng., Upham wrote: "A cloud of impenetrable darkness envelopes his name at that point. Of his fate nothing is known, except that it was an 'unhappy' one." Some light on that darkness may be shed by Lawson's own words, in *Duty and Property*: "And I, may well from my own Experience, Declare as *Jacob* did, Gen. 47. 9—*Few* and Evil, *have the dayes of the Years, of my life been*; In respect of those many Afflictive *Changes*, which have gone over my head; by which I have been *Emptyed, from Vessel to Vessel*." One of Lawson's troubles may have been a proneness to feel sorry for himself, which kept him from being content anywhere, in either Old or New Eng. Lawson's short pastorate at Edgartown, his failure to get ordained at Salem Village, and his irregular behavior in absenting himself from his congregation at Scituate—in an era when Puritans normally expected an ordained pastor to serve for a lifetime where God had called him— are suggestive, when they are all considered together, and although Lawson made conventional statements to the effect that he was confident that God was guiding him through all of the adversities of his life, he may have been protesting too much. Perhaps Lawson would have been happier and more successful in the ministry if his parents had not put him under the heavy pressure that was inevitable when they dedicated him to this vocation at his birth, but rather had merely prayed privately for him to have a sense of this calling as something growing out of his own personal spiritual experience.

Suggested Readings: CCNE; FCNEV. Lawson's *True Narrative* (rep. in Cotton Mather, *The Wonders of the Invisible World*; 1693), is easily available in reprints of Mather's book. It is also reprinted in numerous other collections, including George Lincoln Burr, *Narratives of the Witchcraft Cases* (1914). For selections from *Christ's Fidelity*, see Charles W. Upham, *Salem Witchcraft* (1867), II, 78-87, 90-92, 525-537; and *Salem-Village Witchcraft*, ed. Paul Boyer and Stephen Nissenbaum (1972), pp. 124-128. For a reprint of *Threnodia*, with a facsimile of the original broadside, see *The Mayflower Descendant*, 11 (1909), 65-69. A facsimile is also printed in Ola Elizabeth Winslow, *American Broadside Verse* (1930), p. 19. Significant biographical details can be gleaned from incidental references in Lawson's writings, including quotations from his father's letters in his preface to *Christ's Fidelity*. See also Samuel Deane, *History of Scituate* (1831), pp. 195-197; Emerson Davis, *Biographical Sketches of the Congregational Pastors of New England*, typescript, from a nineteenth-century ms., deposited in the Congregational Library, Boston, V, 83; Samuel Gardner Drake, *The Witchcraft Delusion in New England* (1866), I, vi-vii, 156, 186, 205; II, 154-155; III, 7-9, 12, 13,

63, 64, 68, 113; Chadwick Hansen, *Witchcraft at Salem* (1969), pp. 2, 44-51, 186; Perry Miller, *The New England Mind: From Colony to Province* (1953), pp. 191-208; Russell Hope Robbins, *The Encyclopedia of Witchcraft and Demonology* (1959), p. 430; James Savage, *Genealogical Dictionary of the First Settlers of New England*, III (1861), 63-64, 646; IV (1862), 688; Samuel Sewall, *Diary* (1973), I, 47, 167, 170, 285, 291, 302; Charles W. Upham, *Salem Witchcraft* (1867), I, 268-284; II, 7-9, 70-93, 450-452, 513-516; Harold Field Worthley, "An Inventory of the Records of the Particular (Congregational) Churches of Massachusetts Gathered 1620-1805," HTS, 25 (1970), 171-173, 204-206. On Thomas Lawson, see Edmund Calamy, *Account* (1713), 357, 483; idem, *Continuation* (1727), II, 629; Alexander Gordon, in DNB; John and J. A. Venn, eds., *Alumni Cantabrigienses*, pt. I (1924), III, 56; A. G. Matthews, *Calamy Revised* (1934), p. 319.

Richard Frothingham
University of Arkansas at Little Rock

JOHN LAWSON (d. 1711)

Works: *A New Voyage to Carolina* (1709).

Biography: Nothing positive is known about John Lawson's life before his sailing for North America. Although formerly he was said to be from Yorkshire or Scot., recent findings point more directly to London. His winsome travel book evinces an education in the natural sciences, his cultured background, and sophisticated wit. He signed himself "Gent." and obviously had sufficient means to wander afar when the notion struck him. In late Dec. 1700, at Charleston, he began a thirty-nine-day, 550-mile (not, as he wrote, "a Thousand Miles") exploration into the Carolina hinterlands. The daily record he kept of the trip later was the primary source for his *New Voyage*. He settled in eastern N.C., purchased land, became a surveyor (eventually, he was appointed "Surveyor-General of North-Carolina"), participated in an abortive attempt to resolve the boundary-line dispute with Va., and was cofounder of both Bath, oldest N.C. town (1705), and New Bern. His common-law wife, Hannah Smyth, and daughter Isabella lived in Bath. The year 1709 was spent in Eng. planning the publication of his book. In London he met Baron Christopher von Graffenried, a Swiss colonizer who, with Lawson's aid, arranged for 650 German and Swiss Protestants to settle in N.C. Meanwhile, encroachments by the Europeans had disquieted the neighboring Tuscarora and Coree Indians. Previously friendly with Lawson, they now misunderstood his surveying as somehow responsible for the settlers' inroads on tribal lands. In Sept. 1711 Lawson and von Graffenried were surrounded and captured on a short trip upcountry. Accounts of what then happened vary, but certain it is that von Graffenried managed to return to New Bern and that Lawson was killed, probably in a manner he had described in *A New Voyage*: the Indians stuck pine splinters "into the prisoners Body yet alive," then lighted them "like so many Torches" and made the victim "dance round a great Fire, every one buffeting and deriding him" until he fell dead.

Critical Appraisal: With its folk yarns, anecdotal humor, comic exaggeration, salty style, and jaunty narrative skill, John Lawson's *New Voyage* is one of the delights of early American travel literature. On "natural history" and the Indians, it is unsurpassed among the promotional tracts of its period. Lawson's meticulous notations on flora and fauna apparently were due to an agreement with James Petiver, London apothecary and collector, to gather botanical and zoological specimens.

The first of its five sections deals with the journey itself. Accompanied by Indian guides and several Englishmen, Lawson undertook a semicircular course up the S.C. rivers into the Piedmont, then moved to the northeast along the Indian Trading Path, and finally made a direct swoop to coastal N.C. Whenever possible, he stayed in Indian villages, compiling a vocabulary of their various dialects and observing their day-to-day activities. For Lawson, the handsome, ingenuous native was a Noble Savage who had "learnt several Vices of the Europeans," he opined, "but not one Vertue as I know of." Lawson wrote on the geography of the land, its rivers and inlets, and followed this with a section on its government, remarking that the "Inhabitants of *Carolina*, thro' the Richness of the Soil, live an easy and pleasant Life. . . under one of the mildest Governments in the World." Furthermore, in Carolina, "The Women are very fruitful," and "Women long marry'd, and without Children, in other Places, have remov'd to *Carolina*, and become joyful Mothers." After a full account of the trees, fruits, animals, insects, and reptiles, Lawson wrote more fully of the Indians: their food, shelter, religion, government, customs, and morals. The most joyous passages are those, amply sprinkled throughout his work, in which Lawson's sense of humor simply bubbled over. For example, in his catalog of animals, he listed the "Bat or Rearmouse," then commented: "The Indian Children are much addicted to eat Dirt, and so are some of the Christians. But roast a Bat on a Skewer, then pull the Skin off, and make the Child that eats Dirt, eat the roasted Rearmouse; and he will never eat Dirt again. This is held as an infallible Remedy."

A New Voyage was justifiably popular, was reprinted a number of times, and was translated into German. In 1714 it appeared as *The History of Carolina*, a misleading title that persisted until the 1960s. The most notable among the numerous plagiarisms of Lawson was *The Natural History of North Carolina* (1737) by Edenton's Dr. John Brickell (q.v.), who, when not purloining paragraphs of pure Lawson, managed to insert some beguiling observations of his own.

Suggested Readings: BDAS; DAB; DNB; LHUS; T₂. *See also* A. L. Diket, "The Noble Savage Convention as Epitomized in John Lawson's *A New Voyage to Carolina*," NCHR, 43 (1966), 413-429; E. Bruce Kirkham, "The First English Editions of John Lawson's 'Voyage to Carolina': A Bibliographical Study," PBSA, 61 (1967), 258-265; Hugh Talmage Lefler, ed., *A New Voyage to Carolina* (1967), with introduction, notes, and appendixes; J. Ralph Randolph, *British Travelers Among the Southern Indians, 1660-1763* (1973), pp. 78-88.

Richard Walser
North Carolina State University at Raleigh

JOHN LEACOCK (fl. 1776)

Works: *The Fall of British Tyranny* (1776).

Biography: Little is known about the author of *The Fall of British Tyranny*, who is identified variously as John (Joseph?) Leacock (also spelled *Laycock* or *Lacock*). John F. Watson cited a note by a former Philadelphia resident during the Revolution that "Joseph Lacock, Coroner wrote a play, with good humour, called 'British Tyranny.'" Subsequent scholars have attributed the play to John Leacock, and a recent study identified Leacock as a Philadelphia gold- and silversmith who in 1767 moved to the countryside, becoming a wine maker. He had been one of the Sons of Liberty and knew John Dickinson (q.v.), Benjamin Rush (q.v.), Benjamin Franklin (q.v.), and James Franklin (q.v.).

Critical Appraisal: *The Fall of British Tyranny*, one of the first American chronicle plays, if not the first, is a propaganda play termed by Moses Coit Tyler as "simply a tremendous Whig satire." Focusing on the nefarious schemes of the British politicians to bring about the Revolution in order to restore the Stuarts to power and the subsequent ridiculous, cowardly actions of the British and their military blunders, the play is notable for its well-delineated characters, distinct and vivid dialog, rapid-fire scenes, and Juvenalian satire. Its characters include British politicians and military men, frontiersmen, sailors, shepherds, American military leaders and heroes, common folk, and blacks, and the dialog ranges from the heroic and pompous to the ribald, colloquial, and dialectical. Among the scope of settings extending from Eng. and Mass. to Va. and Can. are long speeches, vivid battle descriptions, and intense pathos, all directed toward revealing the British arch-villainy. The play is also notable in being one of the first to use blacks as dramatic characters and the first to represent George Washington (q.v.).

Suggested Readings: T$_2$. See also *The Fall of British Tyranny* (rep. in Montrose J. Moses, ed., *Representative Plays by American Dramatists* [1946], pp. 279-350; and Norman Philbrick, ed., *Trumpets Sounding: Progaganda Plays of the American Revolution* [1972], pp. 18-19, 41-134); Arthur Hobson Quinn, *A History of the American Drama from its Beginning to the Civil War*, 2nd ed. (1943), pp. 48-50; Kenneth Silverman, *A Cultural History of the American Revolution* (1976), pp. 310-312; John F. Watson, *Annals of Philadelphia and Pennsylvania* (1850).

Dennis Gartner
Frostburg State College

THOMAS LECHFORD (c. 1590-c. 1644)

Works: *Notebook Kept by Thomas Lechford* (w. 1638-1641; pub. 1885); *Plain Dealing, or News from New England* (1642).

Biography: No information exists about when or where Thomas Lechford was born or whom his parents were. His life is documented fully only for the difficult years, 1638-1641, which he spent in Mass. A "Student or Practiser" of the law in Eng., Lechford became the only qualified attorney in the Mass. of 1638. He turned up first in the 1630s as a resident of one of the Inns of Court, and when last we hear of him, he had returned to the Inns to write *Plain Dealing* (appropriately retitled in 1644 as *New England's Advice to Old England*). It is for this straightforward, if polemical, critique of the New England Church that Lechford is best known, although social historians have found his *Notebook* invaluable as well.

Clearly, Lechford left Eng. in disgust. The religious atmosphere of those immediate pre-Revolutionary years had forced him to face an unpleasant truth: reform of both the English church and the monarchy along Puritan lines would come but only through violence and forced compromise. Already, Lechford had been involved in the defense of his friend William Prynne, the notorious Puritan pamphleteer. In 1637 Prynne lost his fortune and both his ears after his second trial for sedition. Although Lechford was to become the most fractious member of Boston society, then, there is no doubt that he arrived in Mass. in 1638 confident of finding his spiritual home.

Within weeks of setting himself up as an attorney and solicitor, however, Lechford had offended most of the powerful figures in the colony, largely because of his lawyer's propensity for objective questioning and argument, which failed to charm the civil and ecclesiastical authorities. Lechford often advised farmers, for example, about their legal rights, which legislators resented. His particular offense was to question obsessively, and in detail, the strict rules of church government, and he wondered—out loud—about why such a small proportion of the public was allowed to join the congregation and why so little was done to convert the native Indians. Even his friends were stung by his candid questions, and it is not surprising that the General Court ignored his petition in 1639 for a full hearing of his ideas on church government or that he was finally barred from practicing law before New Eng. tribunals. In 1640 Lechford was indicted by a grand jury for offenses against doctrine and, willingly or otherwise, professed himself a shameful meddler in affairs he was ill-equipped to understand. Having lost his right to work, and thus most of his income, he left Mass. in 1641. The Eng. he returned to was in turmoil. *Plain Dealing* was written to warn that country of what it faced if it went the way of Mass., abandoning the episcopacy and turning to a Congregational structure of church government. Even Prynne, who was now out of prison, had changed his views on civil and church authority. But the damage had been done.

Critical Appraisal: Thomas Lechford's readers always acknowledged his objectivity and sincerity, while also speaking of his dryness, stiffness, and lack of charm or style. His self-effacement and boyish humility tired the reader nearly as much as the shallow scriptural exegesis that is a common quality of the prose of his time. Yet, historically, *Plain Dealing* is of great interest and deserves to be compared favorably with those writings of John Winthrop (q.v.) that treat the same material with the same innocence but from an insider's point of view. Moreover, Lechford was a genuinely prophetic writer who argued, in an age that admired authority, that his experience deserved a hearing.

Essentially, *Plain Dealing* is a polemic against both church and state government in New Eng., but it is addressed to Old Eng., for its benefit. The method was simply to compare traditional English government, blemishes and all, with something newer but less effective, in the hope that British authorities and rebels alike would give the "gravest consideration" to the risks they ran (all of this is said on Lechford's title page). The questions to be answered are posed in the preface: "Whether the Episcopall Government by Provincial and Diocesan Bishops. . .in England, being, if not of absolute Divine authority, yet nearest, and most like thereunto, and most anciently here embraced, is still safest to be continued?" Or whether a congregation of some 40,000 should be divided into separate groups, each of which is allowed to rule itself, a form of government "whereof we have no experience, and which moderate wise men think to be lesse consonant to the Divine patterne?" Lechford, sincerely repenting youthful errors and hoping to purge himself of "so great a scandall," thus urged Eng. to retain its present forms of political and ecclesiastical hierarchy.

Rhetorically, *Plain Dealing* is a success. On every page, the author reminded readers of his sad initiation in New Eng., where an ill-conceived, idealistic civil and church government forced him to come to terms with himself. Relying as he did on the ethos of a mature man willing to bare his youthful sins for his readers' good, Lechford convinced them that he had no special pleading in mind. He would speak plainly, that is, of what he knew. *Plain Dealing* treats objectively (thus often inconclusively) the varieties of worship, sermons and the conduct of church services, democracy in the congregations, church-state relationships, missionary work, and other difficult subjects. He ended the work shrewdly by appending letters he wrote to Eng. during his stay in Mass.; they tend to document his growth as a thinker and his consequent change of opinion.

Lechford's other work, the *Notebook*, although of less literary merit than *Plain Dealing*, is of equal historical interest. It speaks in detail of several years of domestic life and daily routine during the early days of the Massachusetts Bay Colony, documenting economic, meteorological, and political conditions with his characteristic blend of accuracy and objectivity.

Suggested Readings: DAB; T₁. *See also* James Truslow Adams, *The Founding of New England* (1921); Everett Emerson, ed., *Letters from New England: The Massachusetts Bay Colony, 1629-1638* (1976); John Graham Palfrey, *History of New England* (1890), I, 553-559; *Records of the Governor and Company of the Massachusetts Bay in*

New England, 2 vols. (1853); William B. Weedon, *Economic and Social History of New England* (1891), I, 106-120; John Winthrop, *The History of New England from 1630 to 1649*, ed. James Savage (1825; rep., 1972).

James Stephens
Marquette University

JOHN LEDERER (b. c. 1644)

Works: *The Discoveries of John Lederer, in Three Several Marches from Virginia, to the West of Carolina* (1672); "Extrait d'une Lettre" (1681); "Le Medecine des Ameriquains" (1681).

Biography: Born in Ger. about 1644, Lederer spent his youth in Hamburg, where his father Johann Lederer had moved. At the Hamburg Academic Gymnasium, his presumed specialization was medicine and, although never receiving a degree, he later was frequently referred to as "doctor." Although he was fluent in Italian and French as well as German and could write in Latin, his English at first was indifferent. Sometime after 1665, Lederer was in Va. Governor Sir William Berkeley (q.v.), scheming to profit on trade with the Indians, became his patron and in 1670 used government funds to underwrite Lederer's three fact-finding explorations into the interior. His connection with the unpopular Berkeley soon made enemies for Lederer, and he fled to Md. There he quickly became acquainted with Sir William Talbot, secretary of the province and cousin of Deputy Governor Charles Calvert. Talbot not only provided him with a commission to trade in furs but also undertook to translate his travel account from Latin into English. Talbot's departure for Ire. caused Lederer to move on to Conn., where by 1674, under the auspices of Governor John Winthrop (q.v.), he had established a large and lucrative practice of medicine. In 1675, after a ten-year sojourn in the colonies, he sailed via Barbados for Europe and thereupon vanished from the records, except for some brief notes published in a French periodical in 1681. Talbot called Lederer "a modest ingenious person, & a pretty Scholar."

Critical Appraisal: John Lederer's *Discoveries*, translated gracefully by Talbot (the original Latin has been lost) and containing a fascinating map based on one drawn by Lederer, is an important scientific and ethnological treatise. Lederer was the first explorer to write up an excursion to the Blue Ridge Mountains, and the first to describe the valley of Va. and the Carolina Piedmont. His immediate purpose was to mark out gainful fur-trading routes, but his ultimate objective, he wrote, was to find a passage through the mountains to the western ocean. Thus the *Discoveries* is not so much a promotional tract as a document on the region's geography and on its Indians, their religion and customs, their manners and medical practices, and their various languages and tribal divisions. He reported observations such as that the Indians never disciplined their much indulged, much loved children, and that he encountered only one tribe that had a truly democratic government.

On the first journey in Mar. 1670, cold weather turned him back after reaching the top of the Blue Ridge, whence he said he could see the Atlantic Ocean— impossible, of course. (Was it a mirage, or perhaps a fog bank?) The longest and most important expedition came in May, when he started out with twenty-one horsemen and five Indians, all of whom except for his Susquehanna guide Jackzetavon left him after fifteen days. The two continued southwest along the Indian Trading Path. Lederer wrote that they crossed an extensive grassland in midstate N.C., arrived at a vast brackish lake, and returned to the James River after traversing the waterless, sandy "Arenosa desert" on the coastal Carolina plain. These three geographical untruths have called Lederer's veracity into question, although apologists have countered that Lederer was merely exaggerating to impress his patron, or accepting hearsay as fact, or repeating errors of earlier cartographers. On the third expedition in Aug. he turned back after seeing only more mountains blocking his way. Appended to *Discoveries* are three short essays, one speculating on a possible passage to the "Indian Ocean," a second containing advice to future travelers headed toward the backcountry, and a final one concerning trade with the Indians. Take along, he wrote, "small Looking-glasses, Pictures, Beads and Bracelets of glass, Knives, Sizars, and all manner of gaudy toys and knacks for children, which are light and portable."

Lederer's two French extracts of 1681 deal with Indian medicine and with mnemonic devices used by the American aborigines, in their lack of a written language, to record their history.

Suggested Readings: DAB; LHUS. *See also* Percy G. Adams, *Travelers and Travel Liars, 1660-1800* (1962), pp. 203-210, 266-267; William P. Cumming, ed., *The Discoveries of John Lederer* (with notes by Cumming; 1958); Christian F. Feest, ed., "Another French Account of Virginia Indians by John Lederer," VMHB, 83 (1975), 150-159.

Richard Walser

North Carolina State University at Raleigh

JOHN LEDYARD (1751-1789)

Works: *A Journal of Captain Cook's Last Voyage to the Pacific Ocean* (1783); *The Siberian Journal* (w. 1787-1788; pub. 1966).

Biography: John Ledyard was born in Groton, Conn., in 1751. At age 11, Ledyard lost his father, a sea captain. Failure to receive an expected inheritance early threw him on his own resources. After a year at Dartmouth College, Ledyard went to sea on a merchantman commanded by a friend of his father's. Upon learning that Capt. Cook was planning a third voyage, Ledyard sought out the great explorer, who assigned him to his own *H.M.S. Resolution* as corporal of marines. Back in New Eng. after four years of adventure, which included the death of Cook in Hawaii, Ledyard wrote the book that gave him instant fame as an author and world traveler.

In 1784, in Fr. to seek help in mounting a fur-trade expedition to the Pacific Northwest, he met Thomas Jefferson (q.v.), minister to Fr., who became Ledyard's "friend, brother, father." Undiscouraged despite failure to get financial backing for his venture, Ledyard proposed—with Jefferson's support—exploring the Pacific Northwest via Siberia. With few material possessions besides his greatcoat, Ledyard, in 1787, left St. Petersburg (which he had reached circuitously), to travel halfway across Siberia before being arrested upon orders of Empress Catherine and sent posthaste to Pol.

From London, in 1788, he was engaged to explore the sources of the Niger in Africa. He died suddenly in Cairo while organizing the expedition. Cause of death was a hemorrhage induced by a too-strong emetic, but anger, arising from frustrations over delays to his expedition, and a weakened constitution, greatly contributed to his untimely demise.

Critical Appraisal: Like Herman Melville, with whom he invites comparison, John Ledyard early gained a reputation as an intelligent observer who had lived among cannibals. Both New Englanders sought to delay career decisions made difficult by economic hardships through escape to the sea, and both found a focus for their restless imaginations in the pristine beauty and primitive naturalness of the South Sea Islands. Unlike Melville, however, who returned home to marry, settle down, and assimilate his experiences, Ledyard restlessly sought new images with which to satisfy basic needs and unarticulated yearnings.

Ledyard's one book—*A Journal of Captain Cook's Last Voyage* (1783)—was published three years after his return from a voyage of discovery of great significance, its principal purpose being to look for the Northwest Passage from the Pacific side. Although only a huge ice field lay northeast of the Bering Strait, the expedition succeeded in discovering Christmas Island and the Hawaiian Islands, and they returned the "Noble Savage" Omai to his home in Polynesia. Ledyard was the first American to see Haw. and Alas. (and later the first to visit Sib.). Ledyard's unauthorized account beat the huge Admiralty edition into print by a year, was eagerly read, and helped promote American interest in Alas. It is not truly a *journal*—that is, a logbook or diary composed while the events occur— and it is not completely original, as Ledyard's biographer Jared Sparks maintained. Its sources include John Hawkesworth's official account of Cook's first voyage (1773) and John Rickman's unsigned and unauthorized account of the third voyage (1781). But Ledyard's keen powers of observation and his ability to look objectively at foreign cultures made his work distinctive. He contributed to anthropology by inferring, from cultural similarities, that North American Indians came from Asia, and his geological speculations anticipated later discoveries. Ledyard's style is perspicuous in factual narration but often tortuously circumlocutory in abstracting social customs from direct observation, such as his comments on the "enamouratoes" of the crew with the Polynesian girls and the practice of sodomy among the Hawaiian chiefs. Ledyard's most noteworthy accomplishment on the voyage was being selected by Capt. Cook for a two-day trip, alone and unarmed, to investigate the presence of white men (who proved to be Russians) on Unalaska Island in the Aleutians. This trip by Indian canoe was a test of Ledyard's intrepidity and cool judgment, which he admirably passed.

Ten years later, the journal of his trip to Siberia—from Jun. 1787 to Apr. 1788—reveals that time and fate had not been kind to him. After his arrest in Irkutsk in 1788, where he had repaired from Yakutsk to spend the winter, he was spirited out of Russia by sled and pony carriage at the killing rate of 1,000 miles a week for a month. From Nizhni-Novgorod, he dejectedly wrote: "I am emaciated. It is more than twenty days since I have eat and in that time have been dragged in some miserable open Kabitka 5,000 Versts." The original of Ledyard's journal through Catherine's empire has been lost, but two important transcriptions survive, which along with twenty letters related to the journey were published in 1966.

Among Ledyard's correspondence, his letters to Thomas Jefferson are the most interesting, for they evidence a close affinity between the urbane statesman and the intense young man with the tatoos. Ledyard's tragedy is that he rightfully should have done for American continental development what Lewis and Clark were to do under the aegis of President Jefferson only two decades after Ledyard first met him.

Suggested Readings: DAB; DNB; LHUS. *See also* Helen Augur, *Passage to Glory: John Ledyard's America* (1946); Henry Beston, *Book of Gallant Vagabonds* (1925), pp. 19-56; E. M. Halliday, "Captain Cook's American," AH, 13 (1961), 60-72; Donald Jackson, "Ledyard and Lapérouse: A Contrast in Northwestern Exploration," WHQ, 9 (1978), 495-508; James K. Munford, ed., *John Ledyard's Journal of Captain Cook's Last Voyage* (1963); Stephen D. Watrous, ed., *John Ledyard's Journey Through Russia and Siberia, 1787-1788: The Journal and Selected Letters* (1966).

Eugene L. Huddleston
Michigan State University

ARTHUR LEE (1740-1792)

Works: *Essay in Vindication* (1764); *Extracts from an Address* (1767); *Farmer's and Monitor's Letters* (1769); *Political Detection* (1770); *Answer to Considerations* (1774); *Appeal to the Justice* (1774); *True State of the Proceedings* (1774); *Rise, Progress, and Present State* (1775); *Second Appeal to the Justice* (1775); *A Speech Intended* (1775); *Extracts from a Letter* (1779); *Observations* (1780).

Biography: Born Dec. 20, 1740, Arthur Lee was the youngest of nine children of Councilor Thomas Lee and Hannah Ludwell of Stratford Hall, Westmoreland County, Va. When his parents died in 1750, his father, a substantial planter, was acting governor. Arthur's oldest brother Phillip directed his impressive education: six years at Eng.'s Eton College and five years at the University of Edinburgh, Scot., where he studied medicine and won a gold medal in botany. Dr. Lee, M.D. and F.R.S., returned home in 1766 after some additional study at Leyden.

Lee left Va. in 1768 to crusade against British taxes in America. In London he engaged in city politics, wrote to American leaders, lobbied at Parliament, placed his controversial message in pamphlets and in scores of essays for British and American newspapers, became secretary for John Wilkes's radical Bill of Rights Society, and studied law for four years at the Inns of Court.

By 1775 Lee was a practicing attorney in London with close ties to the lord mayor and to opposition leaders, including the earl of Shelburne. A lobbyist since 1770 for the Mass. Assembly, he became a secret agent for the Continental Congress and secured the first French aid for American Revolutionaries. In Dec. 1776 he joined Silas Deane (q.v.) and Benjamin Franklin (q.v.) in Paris as a diplomat. The three commissioners completed an important treaty of alliance with Fr. in 1778, but Lee was already involved in an acrimonious dispute with his colleagues over Deane's conduct that split Congress into factions and led to his recall in 1780. Elected to the Va. House of Delegates and to Congress, where he served from 1781 to 1785, he was also a head of the U.S. Board of the Treasury from 1785 to 1789. Lee opposed the Constitution in 1787, and he retired in 1789 to Lansdowne, his plantation near Urbanna, Va. He died there, unmarried, on Dec. 12, 1792.

Critical Appraisal: In the decade that preceded their Revolution, Americans produced a remarkable body of political literature that placed the institutions of representative government under intensive scrutiny. Some of it dealt with sophisticated theory, much of it pilloried the British government, and most of it appeared in tracts, broadsides, pamphlets, and newspaper essays. Arthur Lee's contribution to this "war of words" on British colonial policy was voluminous. He published at least ten pamphlets from 1764 to 1776. Another specialty was the newspaper essay, generally of 700 to 800 words, in the open forum newspaper of the day. A striking essay on the front page of a London paper was often picked up and published verbatim by editors on both sides of the Atlantic. After 1768, when he moved his base from the colonies to London, Lee wrote mainly for the two great English dailies, the *Gazetteer* and the *Public Advertiser*.

Like other Americans of his genre, Lee got his training in political journalism through experience. His first pamphlet, *An Essay in Vindication of the Continental Colonies of America* (1764), was written during his student days and succeeded in doing little more than establishing his antislavery credentials and his strident opposition to British policy in America. Two bitter essays on slavery for William Rind's *Virginia Gazette* followed in 1767. They stressed British guilt for encouraging the slave trade, the danger of a slave revolt, and the urgent need for an end to the institution. Rind refused to print the second essay, but both appeared in the *Pennsylvania Chronicle*, and they were later published together in tracts that were useful to Quaker abolitionists.

Even the ten famous essays signed "Monitor" that Lee prepared in 1768 for Rind's newspaper (Feb. 25 to Apr. 28) exposed the author as an unpolished amateur. They gained him a measure of fame, mainly because they captured the angry public mood that Parliament's Townshend taxes of 1767 had generated. They also enhanced Lee's reputation because they were included in a pamphlet, *The Farmer's and Monitor's Letters* (1769), that featured the work of John Dickinson (q.v.) of Philadelphia. During the next eight years, Lee, with greater skill, wrote at least thirty-one additional "Monitors" for British and American newspapers.

After Lee went to London, he invented "Junius Americanus," his most popular pen name. The first essay was featured on the front page of the *Gazetteer* on Jul. 17, 1769. Seventy-six known essays appeared over that signature by 1776, and the Mass. Assembly financed the publication of twenty-four of them in a pamphlet titled *The Political Detection, or The Treachery and Tyranny of Administration, Both at Home and Abroad* (1770).

Lee's daring message as "Junius Americanus" was the one that often appeared over his other pen names: "An American," "Raleigh," "A Bostonian," "A.L.," "C.L.," "C.O.," "Vespucius," "Memento," and "An Old Member of Parliament." Since 1763 successive ministries in Eng. had engaged in a "settled conspiracy" to enslave the people and fasten arbitrary power upon the American colonies. The instruments of this plot were corruption and taxation without representation, and the crown officials in America, particularly in Mass., were said to be eager participants. Lee solicited his material about events in America from patriots who believed in what he did. His favorite informant was Samuel Adams (q.v.) of Boston.

From 1774 to 1776, Lee concentrated on pamphlets to spread his message. Six of them with an aggregate total of 440 pages appeared, the best-known of which was *An Appeal to the Justice and Interests of the People of Great Britain* (1774). It went through four editions in Eng. and one in America, and it was serialized by Alexander Purdie's *Virginia Gazette* in Apr. 1775. The pamphlet was well argued and well written, a reasonable and calm appeal to the sense of fair play in the English nation. Lee opposed British taxation in the colonies on the basis of constitutional right and on grounds of expediency. On both counts, he could discover no case for the parliamentary position. This striking demonstration of Lee's maturity as a writer was repeated in both *A Speech Intended to Have Been Delivered in the House of Commons* (1775) and his *A Second Appeal to the Justice and Interests of the People* (1775), a 90-page pamphlet that was designed especially to support the so-called Olive Branch Petition, which arrived in London from the Continental Congress in 1775. *A Second Appeal* was the last pamphlet Lee wrote before he joined the Revolutionaries as a member of the American diplomatic mission that successfully negotiated a treaty of alliance with Fr. in 1778.

Arthur Lee's works, whether polemical or filled with sweet reason, are significant in the light of what is known about the causes of the American Revolution. His essays and pamphlets helped create a sense of outrage among Americans. Thus the conspiracy theory he spread through his writings—for him the only cause—became itself a reason for rebellion.

Suggested Readings: DAB; Sibley-Shipton (XIII, 245-260); T$_2$. *See also* Burton J. Hendrick, *The Lees of Virginia* (1935); Marguerite Du Pont Lee, *Arthur Lee, Diplomat* (1936); R. H. Lee, *Life of Arthur Lee*, 2 vols. (1829); Richard K. MacMaster, "Arthur Lee's Address on Slavery," VMHB, 80 (1972), 141-157; A. R. Riggs, *The Nine Lives of Arthur Lee* (1976); idem, "Penman of the Revolution: A Case for Arthur Lee," in *Essays in Early Virginia Literature*, ed. J. A. Leo Lemay (1977), pp. 203-219.

A. R. Riggs
McGill University

CHARLES LEE (1758-1815)

Works: *Defense of the Alien and Sedition Laws* (1798).

Biography: Charles Lee, of the "Leesylvania Lees" of Va., was born in 1758. Potent lineage, eminent training at the College of New Jersey (A.B., 1773) which became Princeton Univer., service as a naval officer on the Potomac during the War for Independence, and abiding friendships with George Washington (q.v.) and John Marshall all propelled him to high stature in the early American Republic. Yet despite attaining a position as U.S. attorney general (1795-1801), he never realized all of his opportunities. Youthful exuberance and precocity gave way to staunch Federalism, which culminated in extreme Francophobia. After 1802 he retired from public service to focus on private practice as a lawyer. He gained some celebrity in thwarting the Jeffersonians in cases such as *Marbury* vs. *Madison*, the impeachment of Justice Samuel Chase (q.v.), and the treason trial of Aaron Burr. Lee died near Warrenton, Va., on June 24, 1815.

Critical Appraisal: The Leesylvania Lees were ardent Federalists, both in defending the Constitution and in later partisan battles over the powers of the central government. A lawyer by training and a loyal standard-bearer in the administrations of Washington and John Adams (q.v.), Charles Lee was taciturn. Yet in 1798 in the midst of the uproar over the Alien and Sedition Acts, even he was moved to enter into the public debate. As "Virginiensis," Lee sought to defend the recent Federalist legislation and to cool the ardor of some "few restless, unhappy, disappointed, and mischievous individuals" in his native state. Most dispassionately, he outlined the constitutionality of the controversial acts, pointed out that the Sedition Act was in fact more liberal than prior law, and lectured Virginians to consider the Constitution as "the sacred palladium of their and their children's rights." In this brief series of eight letters, Lee's straightforward analysis, call for reason, and trust in the government placed him apart from the alarm and vituperation echoing through the press.

Suggested Readings: DAB; P; T_2. *See also* Burton J. Hendrick, *The Lees of Virginia* (1935); Stephen G. Kurtz, *The Presidency of John Adams* (1957); Edmund J. Lee, *Lee of Virginia, 1642-1892* (1895).

Louis W. Potts
University of Missouri at Kansas City

HENRY LEE (1756-1818)

Works: *To the Inhabitants of Certain Counties* (1794); *Plain Truth: Addressed to the People of Virginia* (1799); *A Funeral Oration in Honour of the Memory of George Washington* (1800); *The National Eulogy of the Illustrious George Washington* (1800); *Memoirs of the War in the Southern Department*, 2 vols. (1812).

Biography: Henry Lee of Va., born on Jan. 29, 1756, bequeathed three legacies to America. His exploits as a dashing cavalry leader during the Revolutionary War led to various myths about "Light-Horse Harry" and "Lee's Legion" in the partisan strife through the Carolinas. His youngest son, Robert Edward (Gen. Robert E. Lee), surpassed the father not only as a tactician and strategist but also as the most chivalric officer in American military annals. Finally, Henry Lee was provided by fate to offer the national eulogy for his personal benefactor and the nation's father, George Washington (q.v.).

Beneath a veneer of glory and prominence lurked disillusionment and tragedy for Lee. Possessed of an extravagant sense of self-importance, he resigned from Washington's army when he felt his heroics were overlooked. In politics, he served as delegate to the Continental Congress, 1785-1788, as the most potent oratorical advocate of ratification of the Constitution in Va., and as governor, 1792-1795. But he was increasingly troubled by partisan criticisms of his Federalism. Harassed by creditors, crippled by an injury from a riot in Baltimore, and increasingly separated from his family, he sought refuge in the W. Ind. After a number of years, he attempted to return home but died, pathetically, at the plantation of his late commander, Nathanael Greene, on March 25, 1818.

Critical Appraisal: Henry Lee's military valor and political popularity were well balanced by literary craftsmanship. Training at Princeton (A.B., 1773) stood him in good stead. Furthermore, his career in the Continental Army deeply etched Federalism into his perspective. He was quick to enlist his pen in any cause that would enhance the prestige of the national government. In 1794, as head of combined state militias, Lee was empowered to quell the Whiskey Rebellion in western Pa. His proclamation did much to secure peaceful acquiescence by the populace. When tempers boiled up over the Alien and Sedition Acts in 1798-1799, Lee, as "Plain Truth," called for peace with European nations and union among the American states. Plain Truth had a penchant for imagery: he cast America as a youthful athlete and spoke of the development of a "national identity." He castigated the Virginia Resolves as authored by James Madison (q.v.) and other inflammatory statements of the states rights camp. Partisanship and sectionalism were equally flayed. To Lee, both the Constitution and the separate state governments derived powers from the people. As Federalism evolved, he recognized that conflicts would occur, but he believed self-government, the mission of the Republic, was best entrusted to a strong central government.

Washington's death soon after Lee took office in the House of Representatives provided Lee with the opportunity to deliver the national eulogy. In a frequently reprinted oration, Lee spoke of the edifying example set by his esteemed commander: "First in war-first in peace-and first in the hearts of his countrymen." In flashbacks, prophecies, and other literary conceits, Lee proudly proclaimed that in Washington, America had produced a virtuous hero who eclipsed both Classical and European statesmen or soldiers. Speaking through Washington's "august image," Lee exhorted the mourning nation to "let Liberty and Order be inseparable companions. Be American in thought, word, and deed—Thus will you give immortality to that union." This effective oratory proved popular literature, as did Lee's memoirs. Therein he produced a model analysis of the strategy, tactics, and heroics of both sides in battles that raged through Ga., the Carolinas, and Va. Lively narration was complemented by didactic digressions in military science. These writings served a later generation, such as Lee's sons, as a textbook. Unfortunately, the lessons were used in a Civil War that sought to cut asunder the Union Light-Horse Harry labored to cement.

Suggested Readings: DAB; P. *See also* Richard M. Beeman, *Old Dominion and New Nation* (1972); Noel B. Gerson, *Light-Horse Harry* (1966); Burton J. Hendrick, *The Lees of Virginia* (1935); Edmund J. Lee, *Lee of Virginia, 1642-1892* (1895).

Louis W. Potts
University of Missouri at Kansas City

RICHARD HENRY LEE (1732-1794)

Works: *Observations Leading to a Fair Examination* (attrib. 1787); *An Additional Number of Letters from the Federal Farmer* (attrib. 1788).

Biography: Richard Henry Lee, born in 1732 in Va., was foremost among the "Stratford Lees," a band of brothers in the vanguard of the American Revolution. Following private tutoring and schooling in Br., he returned to Westmoreland County to assume prominent political and social roles accorded his baronial family. At the age of 26, he entered the House of Burgesses. A gifted orator—known as Cicero by his contemporaries—Lee was early linked with the insurgence of Patrick Henry in fights versus the Tidewater faction of Speaker John Robinson. An unquenchable thirst for praiseworthiness plus a tremendous appetite for work drove him repeatedly to leadership roles. Some of his colleagues believed Lee a self-seeker and untrustworthy. Nevertheless, he was a most vigilant and visible patriot: a strenuous advocate of American liberties in quarrels with the mother country, 1765-1783, as well as an avid defender of basic democratic values in the building of the Republic, 1775-1792.

Lee was the archetypical legislator rather than political theorist. Service in the Burgesses stretched from 1758 to 1775 and in the Va. House of Delegates from 1779 to 1784. At other times, 1774-1779 and 1784-1788, he served his state in the Continental Congress. There in the first period, he joined radicals such as Thomas Jefferson (q.v.), John Adams (q.v.), and Samuel Adams (q.v.) to seek independence from Br., to ally on equal footing with other European powers, and to develop a confederation of American states. In 1784-1785 he was president of Congress. He often supported causes unpopular in his native Va., yet he was one of the state's first two senators to sit in the new federal government in 1789. Chronically ridden by gout and periodically afflicted by other ailments and accidents, Lee was forced to retire from public service in 1792. He died two years later at Chantilly, his unpretentious home on the Potomac.

Critical Appraisal: Although Richard Henry Lee had his hand in much of the politics of Va. and America in the Revolutionary era, his personal contributions to the period's literature are difficult to ascertain. He chose to refine his powers of persuasion within the aural-oral context of his culture and had few peers within legislative assemblies or in electioneering. Although learned in the ideology of his era, Lee was not prone to write extensively. Private correspondence and committee reports rather than the extended public piece were customary outlets for his views. Jefferson, among others of the Revolutionary generation, considered Lee an inferior penman. Subsequently, Americans have come to idolize Jefferson's Declaration but have forgotten that it was Lee who initiated in Congress the tripartite motion to declare independence, seek foreign alliances, and develop an interstate government.

It is increasingly doubtful that scholars should continue to attribute the letters from a "Federal Farmer" to Richard Henry Lee. This series of eighteen pieces (published in two separate pamphlets) was produced between Oct. 8, 1787, and Jan. 25, 1788. It was rated by contemporaries and historians alike as the most articulate anti-Constitutional argument in print. Although Lee never claimed authorship, his personal views were congruent with those of the farmer, and he was the acknowledged congressional critic of the Constitution. Both sought a true federation of American states and were fearful of consolidation; both believed that aristocrats sought to gain at the expense of the demos; both requested a bill of rights be amended to the Constitution before its ratification. Yet in emphasis and tone, the farmer and Lee differ dramatically. Ever the orator, Lee used the hyperbolism of the ideologue. The farmer, in contrast, wrote with measured candor and fairness. Lee's writings were charged with emotion, of a reformer in quest of the millennium; the farmer presented objective analysis of the ways and means of constructing governments. In the essays of the federal farmer, there are glimmers of the self-righteous democracy of the coming era. In the writings of Richard Henry Lee, in contrast, are the shrill and suspicious prophecies of the eternal radical.

Suggested Readings: DAB; LHUS; T_2. *See also* James C. Ballagh, ed., *The Letters of Richard Henry Lee*, 2 vols. (1911-1914); Walter H. Bennett, ed., *Letters from the Federal Farmer to the Republican* (1978); Oliver P. Chitwood, *Richard Henry Lee: Statesman of the Revolution* (1967); Jack P. Greene, "Character, Persona, and Authority" in *The South During the American Revolution*, ed. W. Robert Higgins (1979), pp. 3-42; Burton J. Hendrick, *The Lees of Virginia: Biography of a Family* (1935); Edmund Jennings Lee, *Lee of Virginia, 1642-1892* (1895); Gordon S. Wood, "The Authorship of the Letters from the Federal Farmer," WMQ, 31 (1974), 299-308.

Louis W. Potts
University of Missouri at Kansas City

DANIEL LEEDS (1652-1720)

Works: *An Almanack* for 1687-1704 (all except those for 1687, 1693-1694, 1696-1700, and 1704 were published the year before the date in the title); *The American Almanack* for 1705-1713 (1705-1713); *The Temple of Wisdom* (1688); *The Innocent Vindicated* (1695); *News of a Trumpet* (1697); *The Case Put & Decided* (1699); *A Trumpet Sounded* (1699); *A Challenge to Caleb Pusey* (c. 1701); *News of a Strumpet* (1701); *A [Second] Challenge to Caleb Pusey* (listed by Hildeburn, no copy seen; 1701); *The Rebuker Rebuked* (1703); *The Great Mystery of Fox-craft Discovered* (1705); *The Second Part of the Mystry of Fox-craft* (1705).

Biography: Born in Eng., probably in Nottinghamshire, Daniel Leeds and his two brothers came to America with their father, Thomas, the founder of the N.J. branch of the Leeds family. They eventually settled in Shrewsbury, N.J., where the East Jersey proprietors had allotted Thomas, Sr., and his wife 240 acres of land for themselves and 120 acres for each of their three sons. Daniel Leeds moved to Burlington in 1677, was elected in 1682 to the Assembly and appointed surveyor-general of the province of West Jersey, and made the first official map of Burlington in 1696. He served on Lord Cornbury's Council from 1702 until 1708.

Leeds was married once in Eng. and again in 1681 to Ann Stacy, daughter of Robert Stacy, a Burlington tanner. Ann died shortly after the birth of their daughter, who died in infancy. In 1682 Leeds married Dorothy Young, daughter of Robert Young of Burlington. She bore him eight children. Between 1700 and 1705, he was married for the fourth time, to Jane Revell, daughter of Anthony Elton and Elizabeth Revell and widow of Samuel Abbott and Edward Smout. Leeds lived most of his life in Burlington, N.J., and was buried there in St. Mary's Church. The Leeds family originally were Quakers but left the Society of

Friends before the end of the seventeenth century. Daniel Leeds turned Episcopalian and became an avid critic of Quakerism and an associate of its leading enemies, resulting in a highly publicized pamphlet attack by Caleb Pusey to which Leeds retaliated in kind.

Critical Appraisal: As an almanac maker, Daniel Leeds was chiefly responsible for adding the practical information for farmers that resulted in a farmer's almanac different from the philomath (or pedantic) Cambridge almanac prepared by Harvard postgraduates since 1639. The Harvard almanac makers, who generally styled themselves "philomaths" on their title pages, specifically designed their almanacs to educate the public in science and to edify them in theology. Leeds, however, referred to himself on his title pages as "a Student of Agriculture." His was technically the first farmer's almanac in America. Imitating the kinds of almanacs that had long been popular in Eng., he included humor, astrology, weather predictions, cures for diseases, tips on husbandry, and proverbs similar to those inserted later by almanac makers such as Benjamin Franklin (q.v.) and Nathaniel Ames (q.v.). Leeds's principal contribution to the basic format of the American almanac was the first description of highways in his 1695 edition, when he gave the route from N.Y. to Philadelphia. The description of roads was a popular feature of almanacs thereafter.

Although Daniel Leeds was not the first to publish an almanac for Pa., he was preceded only by Samuel Atkins in 1685 (for 1686). The Leeds almanacs, printed by William Bradford (q.v.) at first and later by Andrew Bradford (q.v.), William's son, dominated the market in Philadelphia for many years, particularly from 1712 to 1723, when Andrew Bradford was the only printer in the city, his father having moved to N.Y. to begin a printing press there. The 2nd edition of Leeds's almanac (for 1688) got him into trouble with the Quakers, who were offended by his flippancy. The Friends bought up all copies of this edition, causing Leeds to renounce his Quakerism, turn Episcopalian, and engage in a feud with a Quaker almanac maker, Jacob Taylor (q.v.), whose attacks and rebuttals were communicated to the public in their respective almanac prefaces.

Leeds's first publication was neither almanac nor attack on Quakers—nor was it original. *The Temple of Wisdom for the Little World* (1688), a miscellany, included in its 126 pages "a postscript 'To all Students in Arts and Sciences; and to Astrologers in particular'" (by Jacob Böhme), essays from Sir Francis Bacon and poems by Fr. Quarles and George Wither. His second work, *The Innocent Vindicated* (1695) was a personal vindication of Samuel Jennings whose case had involved Leeds, who also had been slandered by implication.

Leeds and his friends William Bradford and George Keith (q.v.) accused George Fox, the founder of the Society of Friends, of forgeries. Furthermore, Leeds accused William Penn (q.v.) of knowing about the forgeries and covering them up. Bradford printed the anti-Quaker pamphlets in Pa. and, after 1693, in N.Y. The first of the anti-Quaker pamphlets was *News of a Trumpet* (1697) in 151 pages, a warning to Eng. to beware of Quakerism. Leeds pointed out specific errors and contradictions, as well as examples of hypocrisy. Published by Bradford and shipped to a London bookseller, the same work was reprinted in 1699 as *A Trumpet Sounded Out of the Wilderness of America*. Leeds claimed that his *News* was reprinted in Eng. and translated and printed in Dutch. More anti-Quaker literature followed in the next two years: *The Case Put & Decided, A Challange to Caleb Pusey*, and *A [Second] Challenge to Caleb Pusey*. Co-authored with John Talbot, *The Great Mistery of Fox-craft Discovered* (1705) included two letters of George Fox purported to be in his own handwriting, primarily ridiculing Fox's illiteracy, but also sarcastically referring to Quaker plainness and sincerity. Leeds added comments on the 1705 "Quaker Almanack," an almanac by Jacob Taylor with some remarks appended by Caleb Pusey about Leeds's almanac attacks on Quakerism. *The Second Part of the Mystry of Fox-craft* (1705) dealt with further discrepancies in Quaker logic and was directed against Caleb Pusey in particular. Pusey countered these attacks on his religion and himself with "Satan's Harbinger Encountered" (1700), "His False News of a Trumpet Detected" (1700), "Daniel Leeds Justly Rebuked" (1702), and "Remarks on Daniel Leeds Abusive Almanack for 1703" in *Proteus Ecclesiasticus* (1704).

A provocative title appeared in 1701: *News of a Strumpet Co-habiting in the Wilderness, or A Brief Abstract of the Spiritual & Carnal Whoredoms & Adulteries of the QUAKERS in America. Delinated in a Cage of Twenty Unclean Birds*. Although there is no author on the title page, Daniel Leeds signed his name to the only extant copy just above the printed "J.B. a Protestant." Spotlighting the injustices of the Quakers, he commented that some people were punished for the same crime that those who were Quakers freely committed. He presented, for example, the names of the Quaker preachers who were involved with other people's wives in sundry cornfields. The number one unclean bird in the cage was Samuel Jennings, who remained unpunished for cheating the Indians (the same Jennings that Leeds had "vindicated" in 1695?).

Leeds's style in his anti-Quaker pamphlets is personal, caustic, and rationalistic. His sarcasm is sometimes amusingly clever, notably in *News of a Strumpet Co-habiting in the Wilderness*, which is perhaps his most readable work other than his almanacs, although all of his anti-Quaker pamphlets are important to students of religion.

Suggested Readings: DAB; T_1. *See also* Clara Louise Humeston, *Leeds: A New Jersey Family* (1905), pp. 1, 3-4; Marion Barber Stowell, "American Almanacs and Feuds," EAL, 4 (1975), 278-281; idem, *Early American Almanacs* (1977), pp. 56-58, 66-67, 156-158.

Marion Barber Stowell
Milledgeville, Georgia

FELIX LEEDS (1687-1744)

Works: *The American Almanack* for 1727 (1726), 1728 (1727), 1729 (1729), 1730 (1729), 1731 (1730).

Biography: Son of Daniel Leeds (q.v.) and Dorothy (Young) Leeds of Burlington, N.J., Felix Leeds was never really a professional almanac maker, as were his father and his brother Titan Leeds (q.v.). Felix married Hannah Hewlings, daughter of William and Dorothy (Eves) Hewlings, and they had six children: Isaac, Abraham, Titan, Sarah, Mary, and Rebecca. Felix's wealthy wife contributed to the family estate a prosperous farm, Hog Ponds, in Burlington County between Marlton and Medford, and a 500-acre farm northeast of Marlton. Felix had also inherited land from his father.

Critical Appraisal: Felix Leeds supposedly prepared five almanacs. These productions may actually have been the work of printers eager to capitalize on the Leeds name. Felix Leeds's father, Daniel, and Titan Leeds were genuine almanac makers, who consistently produced superior almanacs. Felix, Titan's older brother, may have indeed (as Titan publicly claimed in an almanac in 1729) signed his name to an almanac he neither calculated nor wrote. Either Felix's first work—published by the Leeds family printer, Andrew Bradford (q.v.)—caused brother Titan to choose another printer, or the fact that Titan chose another printer (as Felix claimed) caused his brother to publish the "Leeds" almanac. The mystery remains unsolved.

The Felix Leeds almanacs were so similar to those of Titan Leeds that no distinguishing characteristics are evident. The most interesting aspect of Felix's entry into the almanac market is the mystery that surrounded the publications. Felix had one story; Titan, another. The Bradfords themselves may have been the culprits, for they were skilled, ambitious, and clever. The conflict seems to have been among the printers rather than the brothers, and the Leeds brothers may have been duped.

Felix Leeds explained in his first preface that his father and brother had for many years written successful almanacs and that the Bradfords (Andrew in Philadelphia and William Bradford [q.v.] in N.Y.) had always printed them. But "my Brother was prevailed upon by *Sam. Keimer* (q.v.), to let him have his Copy." Felix felt an obligation to William Bradford and to his own friends who had requested that he publish an almanac. He described his "Method" as "entirely the same as my Father and Brother all along used" and promised a "larger" almanac for the following year. Beneath the name of Felix Leeds was added a blasting personal attack on Keimer and an expression of surprise "that any Artist should be of so mean a Spirit as to let the aforesaid *Keimer* have their Copies upon any Terms." The following year, Felix Leeds gallantly refused to "say something in Answer to some Reflections publish'd against" him the year before, since he knew the "Reflections" were "False." Again, he reminded his readers that his "Method" was the same as his father's and brother's. This year (1728) his almanac carried the same ornate title page in use since 1726 by Titan—the word *LEEDS* in large Old English script on a banner borne by two cherubs against a background of sun and stars. In 1730 William Bradford in N.Y. was printing both Titan's and Felix's almanacs. The Felix Leeds version was similar to the Nearegress and Arnot edition of Titan's work. Several pages were identical, indicating that the printers could have actually exchanged typeset pages.

Suggested Readings: Clara Louise Humeston, *Leeds: A New Jersey Family* (1905), p. 4; Marion Barber Stowell, "American Almanacs and Feuds," EAL, 4 (1975), 281; idem, *Early American Almanacs* (1977), pp. 69-72.

Marion Barber Stowell
Milledgeville, Georgia

TITAN LEEDS (1699-1738)

Works: *The American Almanack* for 1714-1739, as well as a second title in 1730, *The Genuine Leeds Almanack* (1730), continued by the printers William and Andrew Bradford with the Leeds pseudonym from 1740 to 1746, including *The Dead Man's Almanack* for 1744. Almanacs for 1714-1715, 1735-1737, were published the year stated in title; those for 1716-1720, 1723, 1725, 1727-1728, published the year before the date in the title. All others were published both the year before as well as the date in the title.

Biography: Titan Leeds was the son of Daniel Leeds (q.v.) and Dorothy (Young) Leeds of Burlington, N.J. He married May Newbold, daughter of Joshua and Hannah Newbold. He probably remained in Springfield on the farm he had inherited from his father, for he was listed as "yeoman" in the guardianship papers in 1724 for Mary Peeps. Between 1725 and 1730, he may have been sheriff of the county of Burlington. When he was only 15 years old, Leeds took over his father's almanac series and continued it for twenty-five years.

Critical Appraisal: Titan Leeds believed in a utilitarian almanac and even apologized in 1718 for putting "Verses at the top of the Months," because "People expect it; yet if I knew whether the Major number of Votes would be against it, I would Insert other things more useful to some." He was also humorous, one of his favorite targets being the printer whom he occasionally blamed (in rhyme) for errors in his publication.

Although spurious editions of almanacs were not uncommon and business practices in general were frequently unscrupulous, "pirates" within the family were rare. In 1728, however, Felix Leeds (q.v.) entered the competition with an almanac bearing the same title as his brother's. Samuel Keimer (q.v.), Titan's publisher in Philadelphia, appended a note, "Beware of the Counterfeit One." Titan added a note to his chronology table in 1729: "*Felix Leeds* was hir'd to sign his Name to an Almanack he never wrote one Page of, and has contin'd that base Practice." In 1730 the Titan and Felix editions (both published by William Bradford [q.v.] in N.Y.) were alike except for the verse and the courts sections. Pirating became more plausible this year as the plot thickened: Titan also had two printers in Philadelphia, Nearegress and Arnot, and D. Harry, who had titled his version *The Genuine Leeds Almanack*. William Bradford in N.Y. and Andrew Bradford (q.v.) in Philadelphia had always printed the Leeds almanacs, but during the few years of the Felix Leeds conflict and confusion, Titan changed printers occasionally and apologized to his readers in doggerel. By 1731 the Bradfords and Titan Leeds were apparently reconciled.

Titan Leeds was shrewdly equivocal toward astrology. In 1725 he conscientiously predicted the effects of the moon's eclipse and concluded with "the generality of the World are made sensible that Eclipses proceed from natural causes."

Titan's topical verse for Aug. 1714 (at age 15) was in the tradition of John Tulley (q.v.): "The Weather's hot, days burning eye / Doth make the earth in favour frye, / Dick on the Hay doth tumble Nell, / Whereby her Belly comes to swell." A lame Ogden Nashian couplet appeared in 1720: "Some write so humerous Dogmaticall, / To please great Sir and Madam What de call."

Titan Leeds is probably most famous for his unwitting participation in the launching of Benjamin Franklin's (q.v.) *Poor Richard* in 1733. In his first preface, Franklin as Richard Saunders explained that he had delayed issuing an almanac because of his good friend Titan Leeds. In imitation of Swift's prediction of the death of the British almanac maker John Partridge, Franklin then stated with assurance that since Titan Leeds would "surely expire" on Oct. 17, 1733, the occasion to publish was justifiable. Titan, unamused, played into Franklin's hands by reporting in his 1734 almanac that he was alive and Franklin was "a Fool and a Lyar." Leeds insisted he was not dead, despite Franklin's contention in 1734 that the sharpness of Leeds's preface in 1734 proved that his good friend Titan Leeds would not have written it, that the stars were infallible, that Leeds in fact must die for the honor of astrology as traditionally upheld in the Leeds family, and that the contents of the alleged Leeds almanac were of abysmally low quality— especially the verse that no "living" astrologer could have composed. He eulogized Leeds and mourned his death. The nonplussed Titan retorted in 1735. In their 1739 Leeds edition, the Bradfords announced that Titan was indeed officially dead. The game, however, had not ended. Poor Richard in 1740 wrote of a letter received from Titan's ghost, and the Bradfords's Leeds almanac for the same year published an amusing "bona fide" letter from the ghost, contradicting Franklin.

The Leeds (Daniel and Titan) series of almanacs is one of America's best. Its popularity was based not only on its being a real farmer's almanac but also on the lively feuds in its prefaces and the humor (both conscious and unconscious) scattered throughout its pages.

Suggested Readings: Clara Louise Humeston, *Leeds: A New Jersey Family* (1905), p. 5; Marion Barber Stowell, "American Almanacs and Feuds," EAL, 4 (1975), 281-282; idem, *Early American Almanacs* (1977), pp. 25, 29-30, 66, 67-72, 158-161, 163, 240, 264, 266.

Marion Barber Stowell
Milledgeville, Georgia

JOHN LELAND (1754-1841)

Works: *The Bible-Baptist* (1789); *The Virginia Chronicle* (1790); *The Rights of Conscience Inalienable* (1791); *The History of Jack Nips* (1792); *A True*

Account (1793); *An Oration, Delivered at the Internment of Mrs. Lydia Northrop* (1794); *The Yankee Spy* (1794); *A Blow at the Root* (1801); *A Storke at the Branch* (1801); *Strictures on the Consecration of Christ* (1801); *An Oration Delivered at Cheshire* (1802); *Two Short Discourses* (1804); *An Elective Judiciary* (1805); *An Examination of Infant-rantism* (1806); *The Flying Seraphim* (1806); *Politics Sermonized* (1806); *An Oration Delivered at Bennington* (1808); *The Jarring Interests of Heaven* (1810); *Remarks on Holy Time* (1815); *Free Thoughts on War* (1816); *The Advantage and Necessity of the Christian Revelation* (1818); *A Summary Account of the Evidence and Nature of Revealed Religion* (1820); *Part of a Speech Delivered at Suffield* (1826); *Short Sayings on Times, Men, Measures and Religion* (1830).

Biography: Born in Grafton, Mass., on May 14, 1754, to Congregationalist parents, John Leland received only a common school education. He lacked religious conviction and a settled career until the age of 18, when he came under the guidance of the Baptist (later Universalist) preacher Elhanan Winchester. Leland was baptized in 1774 and that same year began his lifelong career as an itinerant Baptist preacher. In Oct. of 1775 he made his first journey to Va. He returned to Mass. in Sept. 1776 to marry Sally Devine and then returned to Va. There he was formally licensed to preach and engaged in extensive preaching trips throughout Va. for the next fourteen years. He was nominated as an anti-Federalist delegate to the Va. convention called to consider ratification of the federal Constitution but after a private conversation withdrew and threw his support to the Federalist candidate James Madison (q.v.).

In 1791 Leland returned to New Eng. and in 1792 settled in Cheshire, Mass., which remained his home parish for the rest of his life, although he frequently left on preaching incursions into Conn., R.I., and N.Y., as well as several brief returns to Va. He achieved his greatest public attention in 1801 when he journeyed to Washington, D.C., to present President Thomas Jefferson (q.v.) with a "mammoth cheese." Weighing 1,235 pounds, the cheese had been made by Leland's congregation as a token of their support for Jefferson's politics. Leland publicly presented the cheese to Jefferson and afterwards preached to members of Congress and the president, as well as to curious crowds that assembled along his route to hear the "mammoth priest." Leland served in the Mass. legislature from 1811 to 1813, where he criticized the "standing order" of the established church. In 1824, when the Republican party split into factions, he supported Andrew Jackson and remained a Jacksonian Democrat from that time on. He died in Cheshire on Jan. 14, 1841, at the age of 86.

Critical Appraisal: Two aspects of John Leland's worldview are constantly evident in his published writings. The first was what one contemporary referred to as Leland's "almost mad devotion to politics." Leland frequently delivered Fourth of July orations and other speeches to the Republican citizens of Cheshire and other communities, and even in his sermons, the political themes were never absent. In a fast sermon in 1801, for example, Leland told his audience that "America's God" had raised up Jefferson "in righteousness" and would "strengthen his hands, to be a guide and father to you," and thirty years later, he characterized Andrew Jackson as one of those "men of singular qualities" raised up by "the Almighty Being, who seems to have a peculiar regard for the United States." Although his own audiences fully concurred, Leland's critics portrayed him (with some justice) as "eccentric" in his political expressions. Another aspect of Leland's politics reflected in his writings was his total commitment to the separation of church and state. This belief was most forcefully stated in *The Rights of Conscience Inalienable*, which put him far in advance of most coreligionists and contemporaries in his call for Jefferson's "wall of separation" between church and state. Many of Leland's writings were aimed at overthrowing the "standing order" in Mass. and Conn., both of which he lived to see.

Leland's religious sermons and tracts reveal a colorful, forceful style, frequently characterized by wit and biting ridicule. They show, however, that he was no systematic theologian. His sermons were mostly calls for salvation and attacks on those who distort the simple gospel message with dogma and cant. Leland was never able to reconcile predestination and free will, both of which he preached, and once advised a listener who also had difficulty reconciling these concepts simply to "skip it." Despite his lack of higher education, Leland's writings generally were well-composed and showed some familiarity with contemporary religious writers as well as major American and British poets. He occasionally cast some of his religious writings in the form of short poems.

Suggested Readings: CCNE; CCV; DAB; Sprague (VI, 174-188). *See also* L. H. Butterfield, "Elder John Leland, Jeffersonian Itinerant," PAAS, 62 (1953), 155-242; L. F. Greene, *The Writings of the Late Elder John Leland* (contains Leland's autobiography and most of his published and a sampling of his unpublished writings; 1845); Dumas Malone, *Jefferson the President: First Term, 1801-1805* (1970), pp. 106-108; William G. McLoughlin, *New England Dissent: The Baptists and the Separation of Church and State, 1630-1833* (1971), II, 915-938.

John F. Berens
Northern Michigan University

DANIEL LEONARD (1740-1829)

Works: *Massachusettensis* (1775); *The Origin of the American Contest with Great Britain* (reprints several of the early "Massachusettensis" letters; 1775).

Biography: The only son in a wealthy and prominent family, Daniel Leonard was born in 1740, in Norton, Mass. After graduation from Harvard in 1760, he studied law and was admitted to the bar in 1766. Settling in Taunton, Mass., he was appointed king's attorney for Bristol County in 1769 and was elected to the General Court in the same year. In this assembly, Leonard was one of the most vehement speakers against G.B. and the royal governor during the early 1770s, even serving on the Committee of Correspondence in 1773. By the next year, however, distressed by mob outrages, especially the Boston Tea Party, and courted by Governor Thomas Hutchinson (q.v.), whom he had earlier opposed, Leonard became a strong Tory Loyalist. When he was appointed to the Mandamus Council in 1774, the public had proof of his political shift, and an angry mob marched on his Taunton house, even firing bullets into it. He soon removed himself and his family to Boston to be protected by British troops. To defend his actions and to arouse Tory supporters, Leonard wrote a series of seventeen letters in late 1774 and early 1775 under the pseudonym of "Massachusettensis." Partly as a reward for writing these strong defenses of British authority, Leonard was soon appointed solicitor general for customs. Forced to leave Boston in Mar. 1776, when the British troops retreated to Halifax, he reached London by Aug.

Before he left Mass., Leonard gained a widespread reputation for his ornate dress, expensive tastes, and gambling. Mercy Otis Warren (q.v.) in *The Group*, a play ridiculing the leading Tories, satirized Leonard as "Beau Trumps," and John Trumbull (q.v.) in *M'Fingal* wrote of him: "Did not our Massachusettensis / For grave conviction strain his senses? / Scrawl ev'ry moment he could spare, / From cards and barbers and the fair."

In London, unlike most American exiles there, Leonard quickly established himself and his family. He apparently enjoyed British society and was admitted to the Middle Temple in 1777. He was appointed chief justice of Bermuda in 1781, a post he retained until 1815. He had been proscribed from Mass. in 1778, but he visited there in 1799 and 1808. After his retirement in Bermuda, he settled in London, where he became the dean of the Inner Temple. In 1829, at the age of 89, he died from a self-inflicted gunshot, his family claiming that he had not realized the gun was loaded.

Critical Appraisal: As the writer of the *Massachusettensis* letters, Daniel Leonard was one of the most talented Loyalist writers in the Revolutionary period. After first appearing weekly in the *Massachusetts Gazette and Post Boy*, these letters were immediately reprinted in N.Y. and Boston, and appeared in London in 1776 as "the best Tory argument written in America." Even John Adams (q.v.), who countered these letters under the pseudonym of "Novanglus" and who until late in life thought Jonathan Sewall (q.v.) was "Massachusettensis," admitted their brilliance:

> These papers were well written, abounded with wit, discovered good information, and were conducted with a subtlety of art and address wonderfully calculated to keep up the spirits of their party, to depress ours, to spread intimidation, and to make proselytes among those whose principles and judgment give way to their fears—and these compose at least one-third of mankind.

Although the seventeen letters are somewhat repetitious, they build on one another and cumulatively provide a full delineation of Loyalist thought. The first few are especially vehement, yet logically sound, and the middle ones are more theoretical and, at times, strained. In the last few, Leonard responded directly to

Adams's counterarguments, but without descending to personal abuse. Overall, Leonard relied heavily on a historical perspective to attack the claims of the colonial rebels and to justify British imperial policy. Throughout, he had two central emphases: the colonists had no substantial grievances, and it was in their own interest to remain a part of the British realm: "Allegiance and protection are reciprocal. It is our highest interest to continue a part of the British empire, and equally our duty to remain subject to the authority of parliament." He reiterated that because the colonies enjoyed many economic and political benefits through their relationship with Br., they had no substantial cause to rebel (from Letter V: "Perhaps the whole story of empire does not furnish another instance of a forcible opposition to government with so much apparent and little real cause"). Several of the letters asserted that historical precedents and colonial charters justified current British policies and that British authority had not been questioned by colonists earlier, not even by James Otis (q.v.) and Benjamin Franklin (q.v.) as recently as the 1760s. His stress was on colonial obligations, not colonial rights, and on existing colonial benefits, not British abuses, but equally emphatically, he argued that the colonists had been misled and misinformed by many of their own leaders and by the press.

While denying colonial grievances, Leonard demonstrated the folly of thinking that a Revolution could succeed. In his first letter, he argued that British military power was too great, that the colonies could not unite themselves, that they lacked arms, that a war would cut them off from the rest of the world, and that in a war they would be attacked by Indians and Canadians, as well as by the British. After discounting the possibility of independence for these reasons, he asserted in the eighth letter that independence would produce harmful effects even if it were attainable, claiming that it would harm Br. much less than it would the colonies.

Besides his persuasive application of historical precedent and political theory, Leonard also exhibited keen psychological insights. He recognized that the rebels' arguments were inherently more appealing to the public than his, for they "flattered the people with the idea of independence," while his belief in their need to be subordinated was comparatively humiliating. "Besides," he added, "there is a propensity in men to believe themselves injured and oppressed when they are told so." More generally, his psychological perspicacity is demonstrated by his ability to play upon the fears of the colonists, while creating a believable persona for himself. In the opening letter, for instance, he compared himself to a courageous physician who prescribes a needed medicine even though he knows that the patient considers it unpalatable. His use of imagery and epigrammatic syntax also increased the force of his rhetoric (for instance: "contradiction and disputation, like the collision of flint and steel, often strike out new light"). Taken as a whole, Leonard's combination of logical, ethical, and emotional appeals made his letters, in Adams's words, shine among the Tory writings "like the moon among the lesser stars." Had Leonard devoted his talents to the eventual winning side, his literary fame today would probably rival that of Adams, for his writings certainly match Adams's in eloquence, psychological perceptivity, historical and legal understanding, and argumentative ability. As shrewd and forceful statements of political conservatism, Leonard's *Massachusettensis* letters illuminate a side of Revolutionary America that has been often overlooked.

Suggested Readings: DAB; Sibley-Shipton (XIV, 640-648); T_2. *See also* North Callahan, *Flight from the Republic* (1967), pp. 174-176; idem, *Royal Raiders* (1963), pp. 48-49, 56-57, 264; Ralph Davol, *Two Men of Taunton* (1912); Bernard Mason, ed., *The American Colonial Crisis* (prints Leonard's letters and Adams's replies; 1972); Charles E. Modlin, "The Loyalists' Reply" in *American Literature, 1764-1789*, ed. Everett Emerson (1977), pp. 59-71; Lorenzo Sabine, *Biographical Sketches of Loyalists of the American Revolution* (1864), II, 10-12.

John S. Hardt
Ferrum College

RICHARD LEWIS (c. 1700-1734)

Works: *Muscipula: The Mouse-Trap, or The Battle of the Cambrians and Mice* (1728); "To Mr. Samuel Hastings" (1729); "A Journey from Patapsco in Maryland to Annapolis, April 4th, 1730" (1730); "Food for Criticks" (1731); *Carmen Seculare, for the Year MDCCXXXII* (1732); "Congratulatory Verses" (1732); *March 1, 1731/2. A Rhapsody* (1732); "Verses: To the Memory of His Excellency Benedict Leonard Calvert" (1732); "Verses, to Mr. Ross" (1732); "Elegy on the Much Lamented Death of the Honourable Charles Calvert" (1734); "Upon Prince Madoc's Expedition" (1734).

Biography: Little is known about Richard Lewis's life. He was probably of Welsh ancestry, a student at Eton and perhaps at Balliol College, Oxford, in Apr. 1718 (see letter from Benedict Leonard Calvert to Thomas Hearne, dated Mar. 18, 1729, in *Remarks and Collections of Thomas Hearne* [1915], X, 109n.). If the latter, he was the son of Richard Lewis of Llanfair, County Montgomery, Wales. He immigrated to Md. by 1719, succeeding Michael Piper as schoolmaster at King William's School, Annapolis, and becoming clerk in the Md. General Assembly, May 27-Jun. 16, 1732, during which time revision of the tobacco laws was investigated. Although he may have owned property in Baltimore County, he seems to have lived in Annapolis, Anne Arundel County. He was interested in education and improvement of the cultural life of Md. and thus may have been the author of "Proposals. . .for founding an Academy at Annapolis" (*Archives of Maryland*, XXXVIII, 456-461), submitted to the governor and the General Assembly sometime before Jan. 1733. The "Proposals" envision an institution not only rivaling the intellectual skills developed at Eton and Westminster School, but one engaged in practical skills (trade, husbandry) while preparing students for holy orders. Two revolutionary educational concepts are the admission of adults and the welcoming of dissenters. He was informed in areas of scientific knowledge and observation, communicating in letters to Peter Collinson of the Royal Society of London essays on the Aurora Borealis (sighted in Annapolis on Dec. 10, 1730), earthquake (at Patapsco on Oct. 22, 1725), and insects; see *Philosophical Transactions of the Royal Society*, XXXVII, No. 418 (1732), 55-69, 69-70; XXXVIII, No. 429 (1733), 119-121; and an unpublished letter of August 10, 1733. He married Elizabeth Batee at All Hallows Parish, Anne Arundel County, in Jan. 1719; their son Richard was apprenticed by Daniel Dulaney (q.v.) to a saddler Richard Tootel in Mar. 1735. Lewis died in late Mar. 1734, his estate being administered on Apr. 10, 1734, by John and Benjamin Howard (see documents in the Maryland Hall of Records, Anne Arundel County). An elegy and epitaph by W. Byfield appeared in the *Pennsylvania Gazette* on Dec. 5, 1734. Imitating Lewis's own "Upon Prince Madoc's Expedition," an "Elegy on the Much to Be Lamented Death of Mr. Richard Lewis, Late Master of the Free-School of the City of Annapolis" compared him to Virgil, Cicero, and Milton. An accompanying anonymous letter offered praise of Lewis as poet; the author may have been Joseph Breintnall (q.v.).

Critical Appraisal: The canon of Richard Lewis's poetry is most uncertain. The works listed above have not always been assigned to him, and other poems have been suggested as his. *Muscipula* was printed by William Parks (q.v.) in Annapolis in 1728, the first literary production in the southern colonies. A translation of Edward Holdsworth's *Muscipula, Sive Kambromyomaxia* (1709), a Latin burlesque satirizing the Welsh in imitation of the Homeric "Battle of the Frogs and Mice," the poem is given in facing Latin and English texts. The title page is *rubricated* (that is, printed in red and black, the first such production in the colonies). Numerous other translations of this popular work were produced in Eng.; see Richmond Pugh Bond, *English Burlesque Poetry, 1700-1750* (1932), pp. 215-223. Dedicated to Governor Benedict Calvert in a poem concerned with the state of the arts in the colony, Lewis's version perhaps came into being because of his Welsh ancestry, for one of his aims was to celebrate the Welsh, reversing some of Holdsworth's effect. Furthermore, he hoped to encourage the cultivation of polite literature in Md., and his preface and notes give clear indication, as his later work would also, that Lewis was a scholar, a student of the Classics, and one concerned with the literary theory of his day. The translation is a "*Mock Heroic*, or *Burlesque* kind," that describing "a *ludicrous Action*, in *Heroic Verse*." The preface discusses poetic genres, the usefulness of translation, and literary theories and attitudes.

"To Mr. Samuel Hastings (Ship-wright of Philadelphia) on His Launching the Maryland-Merchant" was apparently printed in the *Maryland Gazette*, Dec. 30, 1729 (no copy exists), and reprinted in Benjamin Franklin's (q.v.) *Pennsylvania Gazette*, Jan. 13, 1730, and the *American Weekly Mercury*, Jan. 14, 1730. "A Journey from Patapsco" probably first appeared in the *Maryland Gazette* in 1730 (now lost) and then in the *Pennsylvania Gazette*, May 21, 1731, being reprinted in the *New York Gazette*, Jun. 21, 1731; the London *Weekly Register*, Jan. 1,

1732 (anonymous and revised, but with a biographical note; titled "Description of Spring"), and Apr. 7, 1733 (author identified and preceded by a letter of praise from "Philalethes"); *Gentleman's Magazine*, Mar. 1732 (II, 669-671); Eustace Budgell's *The Bee*, April 7-14, 1733 (I, 393-404, with discussion praising the poem); *London Magazine*, Apr. 1733 (II, 204-207); and *American Museum*, 1791 (IX, 9-16), Appendix I. Both the journey theme and a time scheme order the poem, which offers striking pictures of local nature, both flora and fauna, and optical images of sky, light, color. Occurring in but a single day, the journey has the feeling of a real experience because of its descriptive powers. "Food for Criticks," formerly attributed to Francis Knapp (q.v.), was perhaps printed in the *Maryland Gazette* in 1731 (no copy known); it was reprinted in variant form, adapted to the respective locales, in the *New England Weekly Journal*, Jun. 28, 1731, and the *Pennsylvania Gazette*, Jul. 17, 1732. The latter version is probably closer to the original. Perhaps the earliest nature poem in America, it is structured as an allegorical journey, lamenting the passing of the American wilderness, a theme that has come to dominate American literature.

A Rhapsody (Bristol 875), a single folio of two pages, was printed on Mar. 1, 1732, undoubtedly by William Parks at Annapolis, although there is no colophon. It reappeared in the *Maryland Gazette*, Feb. 9, 1733, and *Gentleman's Magazine*, Jul. 1734 (IV, 385). It depicts the ramble through a woods of a meditative shepherd, who thanks God for his providential care. "Verses, to Mr. Ross on Mr. Calvert's Departure from Maryland, May 10th 1732" and "Verses. To the Memory of His Excelly, Benedict Leonard Calvert; Late Governour of the Province of Maryland Who Died at Sea, June—1732" (signed "Richd Lewis") were discovered in a manuscript notebook in the U.S. Naval Academy Library. Both were first published by Norris. The elegiac poem—an informal verse epistle— narrates Calvert's many accomplishments with admiration and a sense of loss. The *Pennsylvania Gazette*, Aug. 21, 1732, printed "Congratulatory Verses, Wrote at the Arrival of our Honourable Proprietory" (Thomas Penn's arrival in Pa.); the attribution is not certain. *Carmen Seculare, for the Year MDCCXXXII* (Bristol 874) also came from the press of William Parks in Annapolis in 1732, although again there is no colophon. It is a folio in two leaves, dated Nov. 25, 1732, and was reprinted in *Gentleman's Magazine* in both Apr. and May 1733 (III, 209-210, 264) and in *American Museum* in Nov. 1789 (IV, 413-415) under the title "A Description of Maryland." The poem, celebrating the arrival of Lord Baltimore, is built on the structure of a progress, praising the colony, its people, and its luxuriant countryside and covering its history and present plight. Lewis prophesied that Baltimore's presence would effect the remedy, religious and cultural, proposed. "Upon Prince Madoc's Expedition to the Country Now Called America in the 12th Century Humbly Inscrib'd to the Worthy Society of Ancient Britons, Meeting at Philadelphia, March the 1st, 1733-4" is dated "Jun. 29, 1733-4" (an error for "Jan." and note the error of the century) in *American Weekly Mercury*, Feb. 26, 1734, signed by "Philo Cambrensis" (that is, lover of the Welsh). "An Elegy on the Much Lamented Death of the Honourable Charles

Calvert, Esq;...Who Departed This Life, February 2, 1733-4," *Maryland Gazette*, Mar. 15, 1734, is undoubtedly Lewis's. Of the few additional items that have been suggested as Lewis's, mention should be made of "An Address to James Oglethorpe, Esq; in His Settling the Colony in Georgia"; it appeared in *South Carolina Gazette*, Feb. 10, 1733; *Gentleman's Magazine*, Apr. 1733; and *New England Weekly Journal*, Jul. 16, 1733.

Lewis exhibited a good knowledge of various Classical and recent authors, among them Homer, Virgil, Tacitus, Ovid, Cicero, Quintilian, Spenser, Shakespeare, Bacon, Milton, Butler, Dryden, Pope, Addison, Eachard, Parnell, and Robert Beverley (q.v.—*The History and Present State of Virginia*). His poetry is influenced by the work of Shakespeare (for example, "The Tempest" in "A Rhapsody"), Milton ("Lycidas" in "Verses, to the Memory of Calvert"), Pope ("Windsor Forest" in "Food for Criticks"), Thomson ("Summer" in "A Journey"), as well as others. Philosophically, he was influenced by Newton, Shaftesbury, and Deism. Although he is a neo-Classical poet in his use of the heroic couplet and treatment of nature, Lewis varied his meters by spondaic and trochaic effects (as in the elegy on Charles Calvert), emphasized an emblematic and symbolic use of words (as in "A Journey"), and developed structures (particularly the mythic and allegoric journey and balanced patterns). He is an important nature poet, whose imagery and its treatment are not always conventional. Meager though the poetic canon is, Lewis wrote the pastoral, elegy, verse epistle, occasional poem, mock-heroic, and topographical poem. As J. A. Leo Lemay wrote, "Richard Lewis was the first important American nature poet, and the finest Augustan poet in the new world."

Suggested Readings: LHUS. *See also* Robert A. Aubin, *Topographical Poetry in XVIII-Century England* (1936), pp. 245-247, 366, 386; Robert Bain, Joseph M. Flora, and Louis D. Rubin, Jr., eds., *Southern Writers: A Biographical Dictionary* (entry by Richard E. Amacher; 1979); Percy H. Boynton, ed., *American Poetry* (1921), with a "Critical Note," pp. 600-602, by George W. Sherburn; C. Lennart Carlson, "Richard Lewis and the Reception of His Work in England," AL, 9 (1937), 301-316; Richard Beale Davis, *Intellectual Life in the Colonial South, 1585-1763* (1978), passim; Jay B. Hubbell, *The South in American Literature, 1607-1900* (1954), pp. 65-67, 947; Edward Kimber, "Itinerant Observations in America," *London Magazine*, 15 (Jul. 1746), 327-328; J. A. Leo Lemay, *Men of Letters in Colonial Maryland* (1972), pp. 126-184, 362-368; Walter B. Norris, "Some Recently-Found Poems of the Calverts," MdHM, 32 (1937), 112-135; Kenneth Silverman, ed., *Colonial American Poetry* (1969), pp. 301-313; Bernard C. Steiner, ed., *Early Maryland Poetry* (1900, 1959).

John T. Shawcross
University of Kentucky

JOHN BLAIR LINN (1777-1804)

Works: *Miscellaneous Works, Prose and Poetical* (1795); *The Poetical Wanderer* (1796); *The Death of Washington* (1800); *The Powers of Genius*

(1801); *A Discourse...on the Death of the Reverend John Ewing* (1803); *A Letter to Joseph Priestley* (1803); *A* [Second] *Letter to Joseph Priestley* (1803); *Valerian* (1805).

Biography: Born in Big Spring (later Newville), Pa., John Blair Linn grew up in Md., N.J., and finally N.Y., where in 1786 his father, William Linn, was appointed a pastor of the Collegiate Dutch Reformed Church. After graduation at the age of 18 from Columbia College, Linn briefly studied law, but his interests were literary. While he was still a collegian, his verse and prose had appeared with some regularity in the *New-York Magazine*, and before his 17th birthday, he had been distributing proposals for the publication of his *Miscellaneous Works*, which would appear just before he left college. Two months before his 20th birthday, his play *Bourville Castle; Or, The Gallic Orphans* was presented, although without great success, at the John Street Theatre. Meanwhile, wearied of what he called the "tricks and artifices" of law, he studied divinity at Union College in Schenectady, and in 1799, at 22, accepted a call from the First Presbyterian Church in Philadelphia. There he found congenial and encouraging literary companions in Joseph Dennie (q.v.) and Charles Brockden Brown (q.v.), who after Linn's death was to marry the deceased young man's sister and who would later write a biographical memoir of the person who became posthumously his brother-in-law. By the summer of 1802, Linn's health, never robust, had begun to decline seriously, although not enough to prevent him from a spirited exchange with Joseph Priestley on the humanity of Jesus. Linn died on Aug. 30, 1804, at the age of 27.

Critical Appraisal: A minor, but not necessarily an unimportant, transitional poet, whose literary activities are suggested only by a listing of his published works, John Blair Linn's range was large, including verse, drama, prose fiction, and both literary and biblical criticism. As a very young man, poetry was to him "the language of passion and fancy," the product of solitude in which the poet might indulge his "bosom's secret thought." His early taste was catholic, more enthusiastic than critical. He admired Ossian, Chatterton, William Shakespeare, and Robert Merry, whose Della Cruscan sentimentalities were popular among people of feeling. He found Joel Barlow's (q.v.) *Vision of Columbia* among "the first productions of the age" and admired John Trumbull (q.v.) as "unsurpassed in wit." Timothy Dwight (q.v.), he thought, was sometimes sublime, although wordy to excess, but Philip Freneau (q.v.), seeking simplicity, produced lines that seemed to "flow without labor." In his own writing, Linn imitated, but imitated well. But growing up or illness or Presbyterianism roiled his early, perhaps courageous, literary explorations. Poetry became sublime divination, which perhaps it is, through which earth-bound mortals briefly glimpse God-given truths. Its language must avoid the commonplace—Wordsworth's "pretended simplicity" seemed to him pathetically ludicrous. The poet must deal in superlatives and sweeping generalities that can startle and inspire.

Linn never did articulate a complete or consistent aesthetic theory. His poetics was a scramble of other people's thought and his own vague vacillations. In the history of literature in the U.S., perhaps more than any other writer, he represents the tug between a nascent Romanticism and a desire for regularized certainty in which, in his opinion, religion must be allowed to replace poetry. But he never was completely on one side or the other. His posthumous *Valerian* was intended as a poem "suitable to the profession of a minister of God," but rises toward impressive excellence only in a few rhapsodic passages in which theme is forgotten and a young poet soars without fetters. However much in some of his attitudes Linn may seem to have anticipated, although faintly, attitudes of the future, it does not seem likely that he would have developed further as a man of letters. His youthful verve seems to have been increasingly submerged in dedication to what he thought to be better things.

Suggested Readings: DAB; Sprague (IV, 210-215). *See also* Lewis Leary, "John Blair Linn" in *Soundings: Some Early American Writers* (1975), pp. 175-207.

Lewis Leary
The University of North Carolina at Chapel Hill

ANNE HOME LIVINGSTON (1763-1841)

Works: *Nancy Shippen, Her Journal Book, 1783-1791*, ed. Ethel Armes (1935).

Biography: Born in Philadelphia, Pa., on Feb. 24, 1763, Anne (Nancy) Shippen seemed, at 18, unusually fortunate; her family had wealth and social position, and she was being courted by several distinguished young men, each of whom claimed to be devoted to her. However, instead of following her own heart and judgment by marrying Louis Otto, a French attaché, she acceded to her father's will and married Col. Henry Beekman Livingston, a member of one of the richest and influential families in N.Y. All too soon, her husband's unfounded jealousy and the mistreatment that resulted from it led to an estrangement. Livingston sought a reconciliation and even sent her beloved baby daughter to live with her husband's mother in a futile hope of saving her marriage and her child's prospects. Later a new future seemed possible when Otto, who had gone back to Fr., returned to America, but her husband's price for a divorce was her permanent separation from their daughter. Choosing her child over the man she loved, Livingston took her daughter and increasingly withdrew from the world. The two lived as recluses, devoting themselves to religion.

Critical Appraisal: It is appropriate that Anne Home Livingston's diary was published under a title that uses the author's maiden name, even though the material was written after her marriage. The feminist implications of the use of the maiden name here are significant, even though Livingston would probably not have considered herself a feminist. Modern readers and critics will find much in the work that suggests feminist arguments and the beginning of a feminist awareness. Certainly, the life described in the diary is tragic not only because of the actions of men, but also because of male oriented sets of values imposed on the society. Moreover, the distinct heroism that Livingston demonstrated came from her decisions finally to reject domination by either individuals or society.

Livingston did initially accept patriarchal standards and Romantic values, as can be seen in her early use of fictional code names: Lord Worthy for her father and Leander for Louis Otto. However, after learning the danger of sacrificing one's own judgment to that of even a loving father, she rejected the belief that women should "suffer and obey" their husbands, endorsing instead a marriage of equals. Her eventual isolation from society was not a totally free choice, but rather it was the only one that the laws and customs of the time provided. The situations developed in the work make the diary an important document in the social history of America, and the effective presentation of a human tragedy make it one of the best American diaries.

Suggested Readings: Steven E. Kagle, *American Diary Literature* (1979), pp. 92-97; Randolph Shipley Klein, *Portrait of an Early American Family: The Shippens of Pennsylvania* (1975).

Steven E. Kagle
Illinois State University

(HENRY) BROCKHOLST LIVINGSTON (1757-1823)

Works: "Decius" letter, New York *Journal* (Feb. 15, 1792); *Democracy: An Epic Poem* (authorship doubtful; 1794); "Cinna" letters, New York *Journal* (Aug. 1, 12, 15, 19, 1795); "Decius" letters, New York *Argus* (Jul. 10, 11, 13, 14, 1795); "Camillus Junius" letter, New York *Argus* (Mar. 15, 1796); legal opinions: *New York Common Law Reports*, Books 1-3 (1883); *United States Reports*, 4 *Cranch* to 8 *Wheaton* (1809-1828); *Paine's Circuit Court Reports*, 2 vols. (1810-1823).

Biography: Henry Brockholst Livingston was born in New York City on Nov. 26, 1757, to William Livingston (q.v.) and Sara (French) Livingston and grew to maturity in the colony of N.J. as a member of colonial America's informal aristocracy. The Livingston family was extensive and powerful, and both its influence and its factionalism figured prominently in Livingston's career. He graduated from the College of New Jersey (later Princeton) in 1774, as the colonies moved toward an open break with Eng. Upon joining the Revolutionary army, he advanced rapidly to the rank of lieutenant colonel (aided, perhaps, by his father, who was governor of N.J. at the time). In 1779 he accompanied his brother-in-law John Jay (q.v.) on the abortive diplomatic mission to Sp. and was captured by the British on the return trip. Upon his release, he took up the study of law and was admitted to the N.Y. bar in 1783.

A politically oriented lawyer, Livingston (now having dropped his first name) plunged into the volatile political atmosphere of N.Y. in early support of the

Democratic-Republican organization led nationally by Thomas Jefferson (q.v.) and James Madison (q.v.). He served three terms in the State Assembly, helped to organize the pro-French Democratic Society of New York City, bitterly attacked Jay's Treaty with Eng. (even attending a rally at which brother-in-law Jay was burned in effigy), and shared in orchestrating the N.Y. electoral swing to Jefferson in the national election of 1800.

Livingston was appointed to the State Supreme Court in 1802, serving there until his elevation to the U.S. Supreme Court four years later. On that bench, he proved to be a skilled and innovative jurist; his most important contributions to the American legal tradition can be traced to this period. President Jefferson seems to have selected Livingston to create a counterforce to Chief Justice John Marshall, but Livingston proved no less vulnerable to the force of that powerful personality than other Jefferson appointees. He served on the Court until his death in Washington, D.C., on March 18, 1823, at the age of 66. Although his expertise in maritime and commercial law proved valuable, he wrote few opinions and none of constitutional significance.

Livingston was married, successively, to Catharine Keteltas (five children), Ann Ludlow (three children), and Catharine Kortright (three children).

Critical Appraisal: Henry Brockholst Livingston has long been accepted as the anonymous author of *Democracy: An Epic Poem*, published in N.Y. in 1794. But his authorship has never been verified, and there is good reason not to attribute the poem to him. *Democracy* is a twenty-page satirical attack upon both the political pretensions of the lower classes in New York City and the hypocrisy of their upper-class champions. Livingston certainly had sufficient talent to write the poem, but hardly, one would think, the inclination, for he was an organizer of the very coalition it villified. To have written such a piece at that time would have been a remarkable and politically disastrous exercise in self-deprecation. Quite likely the mystery of his ever having been connected to the poem may be resolved as follows: the pseudonym used in *Democracy* is "Acquiline Nimble-Chops, Democrat"; since observers of Brockholst Livingston always noted his most Roman of noses and his quick wit, it seems probable that the pseudonym was at some time correctly identified as a jibe at him, and that some time thereafter this identification was mistakenly thought to have indicated his authorship.

There remain, however, numerous interesting newspaper pieces of which Livingston was most probably the author. As "Decius" in 1792, he attacked Alexander Hamilton (q.v.) as the chief conspirator in a plot to block a banking venture in N.Y. The argument effectively illustrates the paranoiac, byzantine nature of N.Y. politics during that decade. Again as "Decius," and also as "Cinna," Livingston outlined at least his public reasons for opposing the Jay Treaty; the series of essays provides insights into the question of why that issue was central to the formation of political attitudes in the early national period. Finally, as "Camillus Junius," Livingston presented a bold argument against legislative interference with freedom of expression.

Most of Livingston's legal writings are distinguished only for their elegance of style and also for a wit not often seen in that context. His State Supreme Court decisions, however, have recently been appreciated as catalytic to the development of the "productive use" doctrine of property and to the redefinition of the concept of contract, both of which were parts of a fundamental alteration of American legal principles under way at the time.

Suggested Readings: DAB; P. *See also* Alden Chester, *Courts and Lawyers of New York* (1925); George Dangerfield, *Chancellor Robert R. Livingston of New York, 1746-1803* (1960); Gerald T. Dunne, "Brockholst Livingston" in *The Justices of the United States Supreme Court, 1789-1969*, vol. I, ed. Leon Friedman and Fred Israel (1969); Morton J. Horwitz, *The Transformation of American Law, 1780-1860* (1977); E. B. Livingston, *The Livingstons of Livingston Manor* (1910); Alfred F. Young, *The Democratic Republicans of New York: The Origins, 1763-1797* (1967).

David Sloan
University of Arkansas at Fayeteville

WILLIAM LIVINGSTON (1723-1790)

Works: *Philosophic Solitude* (1747); *Some Serious Thoughts on the Design of Erecting a College* (1749); *Letter to the Freemen* (1750); *The Art of Pleading* (1751); *Address to Sir Charles Hardy* (1755); *A Funeral Eulogium on the Reverend Mr. Aaron Burr* (1757); *A Letter to...John, Lord Bishop of Landaff* (1768); *A Soliloquy* (1770); *America: Or, A Poem* (1770).

Biography: William Livingston was born in Albany, N.Y., in 1723, the fourth son of Philip and Catherine Livingston and the grandson of Robert Livingston, the founder of the wealthy and powerful N.Y. landowning family. He graduated from Yale in 1741 and then studied law in New York City with James Alexander and William Smith, Sr., being admitted to the bar in 1748, the year after he published his poem *Philosophic Solitude*. He and his friends, William Smith, Jr. (q.v.) and John Morin Scott, collaborated on *The Art of Pleading*, a poem satirizing ignorant lawyers, and he and Smith codified N.Y.'s laws in 1752. He maintained an interest in establishing professional standards for lawyers and in 1770 became the first president of the New York Moot. He, Scott, and Smith began *The Independent Reflector* in 1752 as a series of weekly philosophical and political essays intended to reform "public Abuses." In the *Reflector* and in a continuing stream of satirical and polemic letters and essays to the press, he attacked the efforts of the De Lancey party and the Anglican establishment to control the new Kings College and supported the Whig policies of the Livingston faction in the N.Y. Assembly. In 1770 he retired to N.J., erected a mansion he named Liberty Hall, and supposedly left politics. But his retirement was short; he became a member of the Essex County Committee of Correspondence, a delegate to both the First and Second Continental Congresses, commander of the N.J. militia, and in 1776 became the state's first governor under its Revolutionary constitution, a position to which he was reelected nearly unanimously every year until his death. He continued his occasional writings with sharply satirical attacks on the Tories during the Revolution and "hints and observations... salutary to the cause of liberty and virtue" thereafter. He died in 1790 at Elizabethtown, N.J.

Critical Appraisal: In his own lifetime, William Livingston's most popular work was *Philosophic Solitude*, his pastoral poem—a reprint in 1790 claimed to be the 13th edition—but in the twentieth century, he is best remembered for his share in *The Independent Reflector*. Subtitled "The Choice of a Rural Life," *Philosophic Solitude* reveals itself as one of the many offspring of John Pomfret's "The Choice," but Livingston's strong moral sensibility and his ultimate commitment to human social responsibilities distinguish his point of view from Pomfret's rather insipid Epicureanism. His expressed desire to leave behind the corrupt city led him to idealize a scene enlivened by converse with virtuous and amiable friends, by scientific observations of nature that can lead to knowledge of the "Architect divine," by reading from a list of profitable authors, and, finally, by a reasonable and loving marriage to "the Lass that shou'd my joys improve." Written in heroic couplets and in the standard diction of so much eighteenth-century poetry, the poem is stylistically competent but highly conventional, although its moral vision, well-chosen imagery, and informing intelligence gave it a deserved popularity in its time.

Livingston's real talent was not for pastoral poetry, however, but for polemic prose, and here he was most effective in the essays he wrote for *The Independent Reflector*. For this series of weekly essays carried on with William Smith, Jr., and John Morin Scott, Livingston wrote thirty-three of the fifty-four published numbers and coauthored four more. The title of the series calls attention to its English models, *The Spectator* and John Trenchard and Thomas Gordon's *The Independent Whig*, particularly the latter. Intended as "a Reformer of public Abuses," the *Reflector* covered a great deal of ground, from the extravagance of funerals to passive obedience and nonresistance, but the hottest public issue of 1752-1753 was whether or not the new college in N.Y. would be set up on an Anglican foundation, and at least seven of the essays take up the question of the college. In confronting the Anglican establishment, Livingston came to argue lucidly and forcefully for a separation of church and state, and he vigorously attacked all forms of intellectual coercion and political oppression. Various *Independent Reflector* essays were reprinted in American newspapers and magazines both before and after the Revolution, and the lively and pungent prose of the *Reflector* still offers an attractive introduction to the Whig ideology of the founding fathers.

Suggested Readings: DAB; Dexter (I, 682-686); LHUS; T$_1$; T$_2$. *See also* Dorothy R. Dillon, *The New York Triumvirate* (1949); Milton M. Klein, Introduction, *The Independent Reflector* (1963); idem, "The Rise of the New York Bar: The Legal Career of William Livingston," WMQ, 15 (1958), 334-358; Theodore Sedgwick, *A Memoir of the Life of William Livingston* (1833).

Frank Shuffleton
University of Rochester

JAMES LOGAN (1674-1751)

Works: *The Charge Delivered from the Bench to the Grand Jury* (1723); *The Latter Part of the Charge Delivered from the Bench to the Grand Inquest* (1733); *Cato's Moral Distichs Englished in Couplets* (1735); *The Charge Delivered from the Bench to the Grand Inquest* (1736); *Experimenta et Meletemata de Plantarum Generatione* (1739); *Demonstrationes de Radiorum Lucis in Superficies Sphaericas* (1741); *M. T. Cicero's Cato Major, or His Discourse of Old Age* (1744).

Biography: James Logan was born in Lurgan, Ire., in 1674, the son of a Scots Quaker schoolmaster. After a brief career as the master of his father's school in Bristol and an unsuccessful attempt to establish himself there in the linen trade, he accompanied William Penn (q.v.) as his secretary to Philadelphia in 1699. He soon became indispensable as Penn's personal agent—and later that of his widow and heirs—handling the complicated land sales on the proprietary's behalf and his other financial affairs in Pa. He treated with the Indians peacefully, although he has been accused of overshrewd dealing in the Walking Purchase of 1737. Nonetheless, as a British imperialist he stressed friendship with the Indians to prevent French expansion in North America. He was one of the very few Quakers who believed in self-defense and in 1747 contributed toward Benjamin Franklin's (q.v.) project of fortifying Philadelphia against incursion by sea.

Logan was extensively and lucratively engaged in the fur trade, developing for the shipment of the goods the Conestoga, or covered, wagon based on the standard army supply vehicle. As the chief representative of the proprietary party in provincial politics, first secretary and later member of the governor's Council, judge of various city and county courts, mayor of Philadelphia, chief justice of the Supreme Court of Pa., and briefly acting governor of the province, Logan was in the first half of the eighteenth century the most influential man in the colony. But he was much more; fluent in Latin and Greek, competent in French, and with a smattering of Hebrew from his schooldays, he taught himself languages from Italian to Arabic. With polymathic curiosity, the Philadelphia merchant familiarized himself with the new mathematics and physics of the age of Newton, made astronomical observations with a telescope, and—his most celebrated scientific venture—experimented with the sexual fertilization of corn.

In 1735 he began to compose a major philosophical treatise, "The Duties of Man Deduced from Nature," which, incomplete, survives unpublished. In spite of Logan's autocratic and pedantic manner, he instructed and was the advocate of Thomas Godfrey, glazier and inventor of an improved mariner's quadrant; John Bartram (q.v.), the "natural" naturalist; and Benjamin Franklin, printer, founder of a subscription library, and experimenter in electricity. His manifold interests

Logan buttressed with relevant books, gathering what was qualitatively the finest library in colonial America. He intended to found an American Bodleian Library by leaving it for the benefit of Philadelphians, an intention his heirs fulfilled. After suffering several strokes, James Logan died in 1751. In 1792 the Loganian Library was placed in the care of the Library Company of Philadelphia where it still is.

Critical Appraisal: Stylistically, in Latin and English, Logan suffered from an inability to end a sentence. He linked one thought after another with conjunctions and extended his sentences with modifying relative clauses that went on and on. In addition to his not very voluminous printed pieces, Logan's very voluminous letterbooks and prose writings—from scraps to finished essays—survive to form a *corpus operum* of massive size, most of which has never been published. From a literary point of view, his two translations stand out. Logan was constrained in versifying the moral maxims of *Cato's Distichs* to a precise and limiting form: rhyming iambic pentameters. In the better known *Cato Major*, Cicero's own clear style exerted a beneficial influence on his translator. Logan's version has an easy grace, as Frederick B. Tolles put it, "far removed from the crabbed and tortuous syntax" of his usual prose. His speeches to the grand jury were essentially homilies. From the judge's bench, the stern and earnest Quaker set forth standards of behavior that were reflections of his belief in the Inner Light and his respect for Classical philosophers and moralists. He longed for a Pa. aristocracy, not of birth but of merit and moral fibre. He saw the role of people as that of undertaking and fulfilling duties. His unfinished philosophical treatise, "The Duties of Man Deduced from Nature," was his attempt to syncretize nonconformist religion, Classical philosophy, and Newtonian science. There is much to be said for his erudite presentation, an erudition unmatched in colonial America, but Logan's inability to be direct, concise, and lucid enveloped his thoughts in a fog of prolixity.

Several of his scientific observations were published in brief form in the *Transactions* of the Royal Society. The most important of them, expanded and written in Latin (later translated back into English by Dr. John Fothergill), was the *Experimenta et Meletemata* in which Logan described in detail how kernels of corn were fertilized up the silk by pollen from the tassels. It was the first fully explicit account of that sexual process. This received high praise on the Continent; the great Linnaeus among others acknowledged its importance. Other scientific papers, also published at Leyden, dealt with optics. *Canonum pro Inveniendis Refractionum*, printed irrelevantly as the second part of the *Experimenta*, is a geometrical demonstration of a method for finding the foci of lenses, an attempt to simplify propositions propounded by the Dutch physicist Huygens. The *Demonstrationes* was Logan's effort to improve on Huygens's and Newton's solutions of the problem of spherical aberration. Although both of these brief monographs were exceptional as productions of an American amateur, "a bearskin merchant" as he described himself, they were of no lasting importance in the study of optics.

Logan's competence as a Classicist was never demonstrated in a published recension of a Greek or Latin Classic, but it is evidenced by his critical annotations in the books he owned. Although other colonial Americans wrote works of scientific import, he was the only one who contributed an article on Latin textual criticism to a scholarly journal. Such was the learned Philadelphian's essay on the life of Pythagoras by Iamblichus that appeared in 1740 in the Amsterdam periodical *Miscellaneae Observationes Criticae Novae*. The Dutch scholar Johann Friedrich Gronovius, who was Logan's scholarly intermediary on the Continent, compared him to Scaliger, Casaubon, and Saumaise.

Logan was not a stylist. He was more at home in science and pedantic textual criticism than in the literature of his native tongue. His knowledge of many disciplines, however, was remarkable.

Suggested Readings: BDAS; DAB; LHUS; T_1. *See also* Edward Armstrong, ed., *The Correspondence of William Penn and James Logan*, MHSP, 9-10 (1870-1872), dealing almost entirely with financial and political matters and inaccurately transcribed; Roy N. Lokken, ed., "The Scientific Papers of James Logan," TAPS, New Series, 62 (1972); Frederick B. Tolles, *James Logan and the Culture of Provincial America* (the only complete, although brief biography of Logan; 1957); idem, "Philadelphia's First Scientist: James Logan," *Isis*, 47 (1956); idem, "Quaker Humanist: James Logan as a Classical Scholar," PMHB, 79 (1955) 415-438; Edwin Wolf 2nd, *The Library of James Logan of Philadelphia* (1974).

Edwin Wolf 2nd
Library Company of Philadelphia

JOHN LONG (fl. 1768-1791)

Works: *Voyages and Travels of an Indian Interpreter and Trader* (1791).

Biography: Little is known of John Long's life other than what is related in his *Voyages and Travels*. There he described how he sailed from Eng., landing at Montreal in 1768. In Can. he was at first an articled clerk to a fur merchant, under whose direction he was to learn the Indian trade. An apt pupil, he soon became proficient in the Iroquois and French languages and was sent to Caughnawaga, a village near Montreal on the St. Lawrence, where he remained for seven years. There Long learned much about the customs and habits of the Indians. During the American Revolution, he fought with the Indians against the invading Americans in several actions around Montreal.

After learning the Ojibway language, Long led a party of voyageurs on a trading party to the Nipigon district north and northeast of Lake Superior in 1777. After a successful two years, during which time he was adopted by the noted Chippewa chief Madjeckewiss, he left the interior for the relative comfort of Michilimackinac, an outpost at the tip of the lower peninsula of Mich.

In 1780 Long led a party of Canadians, Foxes, and Sioux to Green Bay, up the Fox River to the Wisconsin, and from there to Prairie du Chien, Wis., on the

Mississippi. There he retrieved a cache of furs, preventing their capture by George Rogers Clark (q.v.). He then traded on the Saguenay River in Can., covering the territory east of Hudson's Bay. After this tour he traveled to Quebec, where he embarked for Eng. in 1783, only to come back to North America the following year. He spent some time in N.Y., stayed with some Loyalist friends near Kingston, Ont., and engaged in an abortive trading venture with the Iroquois. In Oct. 1787, he left Can. and returned to Eng. for good. His book was published there in 1791.

Critical Appraisal: John Long's *Voyages and Travels* was popular in Eng., as were many travel books during this period. The *Monthly Review* published a favorable review, and the volume was translated into French and German. The French translation, issued by J.B.L.J. Billecocq in 1794 and 1810, is marred by the absence of the Indian-language vocabularies. The two German translations, B. Gottlob Hoffmann's and G. Forster's, were published in 1791 and 1792, respectively.

In his preface, Long stated that he was not a *"Tourist,"* but a "commercial man" whose observations might appeal especially to "the merchant and the philosopher." In many ways, the volume can be described as a primer for fur traders, containing accounts of the customs and practices of many of the northern Indian groups along with vocabulary tables for the Inuit, Algonquin, Chippewa, Iroquois, Mohegan, and Shawnee tongues. The selection of words—the lists of names of animals, furs and skins, and trading merchandise, for example—indicate Long's intended audience. Although the book is interesting for its philological content, dedicating in the original edition 113 of its 295 pages to Indian languages, it is far more important for Long's candid observations of the Native Americans he encountered, lived with, and worked with. He included descriptions of Indian dances and song, marriage ceremonies, religious beliefs and superstitions, tactics and practices in battle, sports, and other information. He described geographical areas and settlements and depicted historical events to which he was an eyewitness, such as clashes with enemy raiding parties during the American Revolution.

Long proved himself an astute political and social commentator. A good example of his political sense is his compelling argument for Br.'s development of the former French outposts and settlements in Western Ont. Similarly revealing of his social awareness are his statements on the corrupting influence of European—especially English—civilization on the Indian cultures. His anthropological observations are valuable as well: Long was the first to use the term *totamism* [sic] to indicate the importance of the totem to the cultural system that underpins many primitive societies. *Voyages and Travels* is an important document in the study of North American history.

Suggested Readings: *Dictionary of Canadian Biography*, IV, 486. Editions of *Voyages and Travels* include M. M. Quaife (1922); reprints of the original (1968, 1971); R. G. Thwaites, *Early Western Travels, 1748-1846*, vol. II (1904-1966).

James W. Parins
Little Rock, Arkansas

BENJAMIN LORD (1694-1784)

Works: *The Faithful and Approved Minister* (1727); *True Christianity Explained* (1727); *The Necessity of Regeneration* (1738); *Believers in Christ* (1742); *God Glorified* (1743); *Humble Importunity* (1743); *Heaven, a Glorious Retreat* (1751); *Religion and Government* (1752); *The Great Importance* (1759); *Love to Jesus Christ* (1761); *Christ's Embassadors* (1763); *Great Preparations* (1763); *Ministers of the Gospel* (1763); *Sober-Mindedness* (1763); *Jubilee* (1768); *The Important Connection* (1769); *Civil Rulers* (1773); *The Parable of the Merchant-man* (1773); *The Christian's Comfort* (1774); *The Aged Minister's Solemn Appeal* (1783).

Biography: Benjamin Lord was for ninety years a citizen of some prominence in the colony, province, and state of Conn. He was born in Saybrook in 1694, educated at Yale College (A.B., 1714; M.A., 1719), and was called to a sixty-seven-year ministry in Norwich (1717-1784). He was a respected intellectual and served as a trustee for his college from 1740 to 1772. In 1774 he was named a doctor of sacred theology by Yale. But the dignity and rewards appropriate to his long tenure as a minister were denied him as a result of the intrusion of the Great Awakening into his already disturbed congregation. Although in 1774 he declared his adherence to the Saybrook Platform, and although he continued to admit Half-Way Covenanters to the sacraments of his church, he sympathized with the Awakening and made a serious effort to cooperate with the revivalists. Nevertheless, the New Lights separated, formed a new church, and refused to pay the taxes that went to his support. After 1747 Lord seldom received more than a small portion of his salary. An attempt in 1752 to enforce his claims resulted in the imprisonment of more than forty of the Separatists but failed to profit Lord. In 1748 his first wife, Anne, died painfully after a long illness. Lord remarried twice but spent his last years in poverty and infirmity. Although suffering from blindness and senility, he made a last appearance in his pulpit to celebrate the end of the war in 1783, the year before his death. James Cogswell, in his funeral sermon for Lord, noted that the "spirit of enthusiasm" had disrupted his ministry, but added that "few, I believe, very few, dared to censure him as an unconverted, unfaithful or unskilful minister."

Critical Appraisal: Benjamin Lord's long list of publications is relatively undistinguished, consisting largely of sermons that are notable neither for doctrine nor style. They are, nonetheless, often interesting for their revelation of the character of this long lived but unappreciated minister. Particularly revealing are those sermons on occasions of personal involvement. *Heaven, a Glorious Retreat*, taking as its text a line from *Job*, is Lord's moving farewell to his wife, Anne (daughter of the poet Edward Taylor [q.v.]). Mrs. Lord had been an invalid for sixteen years, immobile for twelve, and unable even to feed herself for eight. Her pious endurance is evoked; Lord calculated that he had spent 4,000 nights beside her bed, at considerable "disadvantage to me in my Publick Work."

Lord's late sermons—for example, *Great Preparations, Jubilee, The Aged Minister's Solemn Appeal*—also often took on a personal significance as he accumulated evidence of mortality: he referred to the eighty area ministers who had died since his ordination (or the five or six who had died in the past weeks); sometimes he appended tabulations of the baptisms and deaths in his congregation (averaging twenty deaths a year for fifty years). These charts and footnotes invoke the special dignity of mere longevity.

Unquestionably, Lord's most important and popular work was the pamphlet *God Glorified in His Works*, an account of the "marvellous" recovery of Mrs. Mercy Wheeler (1706-1796). (The event is also treated in his sermon *Humble Importunity*.) At the age of 20, Mercy Wheeler contracted a nervous fever that prostrated her for a period of five years, during which she ate no solid food. On the anniversary fast day in 1732 she recovered her voice; on May 25, 1743, she asked to be carried to hear the preaching of Rev. Hezakiah Lord (a cousin of Benjamin). Following the sermon, she was inspired and enabled to walk some sixteen feet. Lord's narration is convincingly circumstantial: he included notarized statements from neighbors and doctors, and he quoted at length Mercy Wheeler's own statements concerning her spiritual condition throughout her long ordeal. Lord was clearly impressed by the significance of this special providence, but because he did not enthusiastically overdramatize or overinterpret it, he managed to produce a persuasive testimony. The work was published five times before 1800 in New London, Boston, and Hartford. The "third," New London edition contains an interesting series of postscripts by Lord and Rev. Joel Benedict, which trace the continuing life—marriage, widowhood, and destitution—of the woman who experienced a "signal Deliverance."

Suggested Readings: CCNE; Dexter (I, 129-133); Sprague (I, 297-300). *See also* William G. McLoughlin, *New England Dissent, 1630-1833* (1971).

J. Kenneth Van Dover
Lincoln University

ISRAEL LORING (1682-1772)

Works: *The Duty and Interest of Young Persons* (1718); *Two Sermons Preached at Rutland* (1724); The *Nature and Necessity of the New Birth* (1728, 1740); *Ministers Must Die* (1731); *Three Discourses* (1731); *It Is Good to Bear the Yoke* (1732); *Serious Thoughts on the Miseries of Hell* (1732); *Private Christians* (1735); *The Duty of an Apostatizing People* (1737); *The Service of the Lord*, with *False Hopes Discover'd* and *Spiritual Light* (1738); *Ministers Insufficient* (1742); *Justification Not by Works* (1749); *The Duty Which Ministers* (1754).

Biography: Israel Loring was born in Hull, Mass., on Apr. 6, 1682, the son of John and Rachel (Wheatley) Loring. He died in Sudbury, Mass., on Mar. 9,

1772, at the age of 89. He was the minister in Sudbury for sixty-six years; for later generations, according to Ezra Stiles (q.v.), he became the type of the Puritan divine. Loring received a B.A. from Harvard in 1701, and an M.A. in 1704. Within two years, he was settled as minister in Sudbury. When the town was divided into two precincts, Loring was chosen pastor by both sides. He accepted the call from the West Precinct, moving there on Jul. 25, 1723.

Loring combined theological rigor and liberalism in eccentric ways. During his long tenure as minister, he baptized 1,400 children. But as a young minister, he adamantly refused to baptize children born on a Sunday. He believed that a child born on the Sabbath had been conceived on the Sabbath, and he would not countenance such profanation. Fortunately for the parents of Sudbury, Loring's own daughter Elizabeth was born on a Sunday (Nov. 16, 1712); Loring changed his opinion. Loring supported John Leverett, a layman, for the presidency of Harvard. He was tolerant of other Protestant sects and spoke well of the Great Awakening. Yet he attacked illiterate preachers, opposed George Whitefield (q.v.), and suppressed minority dissent in his church.

Loring's long life was not especially eventful. He never had an assistant but dedicated himself to the ministry without stint or complaint about low and erratic salary. One biographer observed that Loring never became involved in outside business, but Alfred Hudson's *History of Sudbury* shows that he did have land-holdings in Rutland, Mass., which was settled by Sudbury people.

Loring appears to have looked favorably upon movements toward liberty. He recorded in his diary "the horrible slaughter of the Men at Boston by regular soldiers." On Jun. 4, 1770, he was honored at Faneuil Hall by the Sons of Liberty as the oldest minister in America.

Critical Appraisal: Israel Loring was a popular preacher, as evidenced by his many published sermons. He kept to the usual themes, especially the declension of the third generation. *The Duty and Interest of Young Persons* (1718), *Three Discourses* (1731), and *It Is Good to Bear the Yoke* (1732) combine lamentations about declension with promises of rewards in this life as well as in the next for those who accept grace. Declension was also the theme of his election sermon of 1737, *The Duty of an Apostatizing People*, but by then Loring had been heartened by the revival of religion. Six years earlier, in one of his *Three Discourses*, "The Great Duty of Self-Examination," he had warned: "When the Gospel and the Means of Grace have been for some considerable Time in a Place, it is much to be feared, that those who have not in that Time felt the saving Power and Effect of it upon their Hearts, never shall." But by 1737 he welcomed the "Out-pouring of the Spirit of God for the reviving of Religion among us" and referred favorably to Jonathan Edwards (q.v.). The election sermon is also notable for Loring's recommendation that the confiscated estates of those condemned in the witchcraft trials be returned to their posterity. The General Court soon approved his recommendation.

Loring's reaction against the excesses of the Great Awakening was made clear in *Ministers Insufficient* (1742), which was given at the Massachusetts Bay

Ministerial Convention in Boston. He accused the revivalist preachers of presuming on their own strength, of failing to acknowledge the external power of divine grace. His attack on the revivalists was not simply the irritation of a settled, conservative minister. His understanding of the role of the minister was complex. In the second of *Two Sermons Preached at Rutland* (1724), Loring suggested that the presence of a duly ordained minister might, providentially, protect a settlement from Indian attack, although it evidently did not at Rutland. Although Perry Miller dismissed these sermons for their conventionality, Loring did make the point even then that ministers only prepare souls for harvest, whereas God brings them to maturity.

Loring's evaluation of the role of the minister derived from his understanding of the act of conversion. In *The Nature and Necessity* (1728) and in *False Hopes Discover'd* (1738), he argued that grace operated gradually and progressively, through the understanding to the will. In the later sermon, he warned against "the natural illumination very similar to Grace," which may be stimulated by preaching. In the earlier sermon, which Samuel Sewall (q.v.) valued, Loring explained the epistemology of grace, citing both Thomas Shepard (q.v.) and Jonathan Edwards. Loring always retained a pure Calvinist strain: there was no sure guarantee of the presence of grace; one simply must persevere. But if Loring's doctrine harked back to the Calvinism of Shepard, his psychology owed something to Edwards. In *Serious Thoughts on the Miseries of Hell* (1732), he took up the ancient problem of the justice of eternal punishment. After a cursory rehearsal of the idea of retributive justice—that is, the gravity of the crime is determined by the dignity of the one offended—Loring turned to a more psychological defense: "Every Sinner hath sinned in *Suo Infinito*, to the utmost line of his time, and wanted nothing but more time to have sinned more, for he had a will to have sinned *infinitely*."

Loring's interest in psychology bore major fruit in *Justification Not by Works* (1749). After a thorough review of the controversy between faith and works, he turned to the distinction of justification and sanctification. Justification is "*a Change of State*," from spiritual death to life. Sanctification is "*a Change of Nature*, he that was unholy, is now made holy, his Heart is changed." The distinction is a compromise: justification occurs instantaneously; sanctification, by degrees. But it is more than a compromise; Loring introduced a psychological element to clarify the objective power of grace. If grace is really a power from God, outside of man, then both faith and works are subjective, arising within man, and both are distinct from grace. Justification cannot truly be by faith, Loring observed, because faith cannot be a material cause of grace. Loring took the next step: faith is actually a kind of work, in that both are responses to the objective power of grace. Loring's turn to psychology allowed him to reestablish the Calvinist emphasis on the otherness of God's power and grace.

Loring was a strong thinker, but not a great theologian or a preacher who revealed himself in his sermons. Yet in one sermon, *Serious Thoughts*, he dilated on the miseries of "the illusions of black and sooty Melancholy." In his diary, he complained of his own melancholy disposition. In the sermon, there is a note of personal truth when he confessed that melancholy is "so terrible as to make men weary of their Lives and sometimes persuade them to be their own Executioners." Loring's diaries, which extend from 1748 to 1772, are divided among the Goodnow Library, Sudbury, the Massachusetts Historical Society, and the Connecticut Historical Society.

Suggested Readings: CCNE; Sibley-Shipton (V, 75-83); Sprague (I, 257-260). *See also* Alfred Sereno Hudson, *The History of Sudbury, Massachusetts* (1889), pp. 169, 290; Perry Miller, *The New England Mind: From Colony to Province* (1953); NEHGR, VII, 326-328; Samuel Sewall, *The Diary* (1973); Ezra Stiles, *The Literary Diary of Ezra Stiles* (1901), I, 218.

William J. Irvin
New York, New York

SAMUEL LOUDON (1727-1813)

Works: Editor and principal writer, pamphlets and broadsides (1776-1796); *New York Packet and The American Advertiser* (1776-1783); *The New-York Packet* (1783-1792); *The Diary and Universal Daily Advertiser* (1792-1796).

Biography: Born in Ire. of "Scotch-Irish stock" in 1727, Samuel Loudon immigrated to N.Y. shortly before 1753 and was a merchant, ship chandler, printer, and editor until his retirement in 1796. He was engaged in land-promotion schemes in upstate N.Y. with Philip Schuyler in the 1760s and had one of the city's most popular bookstores by 1771—when he also established one of the colony's first "circulating libraries." *The Packet* was the last weekly established in the city before the Declaration of Independence, first appearing Jan. 4, 1776. After briefly resuming his career as a merchant in Norwich, Conn., he moved his shop and paper to Fishkill (just ahead of the occupation of N.Y. by the British), reopening *The Packet* on Jan. 16, 1777, and continuing it—as paper supplies allowed—until Aug. 28, 1783. He returned to his Water Street shop two months later and continued *The Packet*—with several name changes—until Jun. 26, 1792, with his son John as a partner for most of the time. A month later, he began publishing a daily, *The Diary, or Loudon's Register*, which continued— again with several name changes—until his "retirement," Feb. 1, 1796. He had outlived both John and another partner-son—Samuel, Jr.—and continued to serve as one of the city's finest printers and most successful booksellers until shortly before his death in 1813.

Critical Appraisal: As seems to have been the case with so many of his contemporary printer-editors, Samuel Loudon presented much of his literary output either anonymously or simply as a part of his paper. An avowed Whig, he nevertheless reflected an independence of thought that was not appreciated by the radical Revolutionaries, although it is as a "patriot editor" that he is best remembered. Shortly before he fled N.Y. for Fishkill, a committee of extremists looted his shop after he had begun printing "The Deceiver Unmasked," a not-too-gentle serialized reply to Thomas Paine's (q.v.) *Common Sense*. Despite this incident, he was regarded as one of the period's finest patriot printers; he served as the colony's most consistent spokesman for the young nation's cause during the British occupation, served as state printer for N.Y. while in Fishkill, and printed the new state's first paper currency and its first compilation of statutes. After his return to N.Y. in 1783, he had such lucrative printing contracts as that for Noah Webster's (q.v.) *American Magazine*, as well as several tracts for the Scotch Presbyterian Church (of which he was an elder) and for his beloved St. Andrews Society.

Suggested Readings: DAB. *See also* Charles R. Hildeburn, *Sketches of Printers and Printing in Colonial New York* (1895), pp. 146, 241; "Loudon's Diary" in *Old New York*, by W. W. Pasko (1889); M. E. Perkins, *Old Houses of the Ancient Town of Norwich, 1660-1800* (1895); Isaiah Thomas, *The History of Printing in America* (1810).

Donovan H. Bond

West Virginia University

SAMUEL LOW (1765-c. 1810)

Works: *The Glory of America; Or, Peace Triumphant Over War* (1783); *Winter Displayed* (1784); *The Politician Outwitted* (1798); *Poems* (1800).

Biography: Little is known of Samuel Low's early life and education. Born in New York City on Dec. 12, 1765, he is presumed to have grown up in that city, his family remaining there during its occupation by British troops. His *The Glory of America*, published in Philadelphia when he was 18, may suggest, however, that he and his family had, at least briefly, left New York City for refuge in the patriot capital in Pa. The war over, Low lived and wrote in New York City for some sixteen years, active in Masonic affairs and employed first as a clerk in the Treasury Office and then as a bookkeeper in the Bank of New York. During these years, he seems to have been the city's "official poet," preparing verse, often circulated as broadsides, for almost every civic or Masonic occasion. In 1788 he wrote a five-act comedy that, when it was rejected by the managers of the New York theater, he published the next year at his own expense to prove, it has been said, the managers wrong. Low married twice and had four children, three by his first wife who died in her mid-20s, and one by his second who is presumed to have outlived him. In 1800 his *Poems* were collected in two splendid volumes, supported by subscriptions from many of N.Y.'s most prominent citizens, John Jacob Astor, William Irving, James Cooper, and William Dunlap (q.v.) among them. Shortly thereafter, Low disappeared, remembered only as a person who had once been a poet, although not consistently a good one, who had "become a drunkard, abandon'd his wife," and fled somewhere— it was thought to the South. Nothing was heard of him again.

Critical Appraisal: Little distinction can be claimed for Samuel Low, as person or poet. He was simply there. His *The Glory of America* was the first volume of verse to celebrate America's victory over G.B. His *Winter Displayed* has been called the first long poem to attempt a picture, other than political, of life in the U.S. It considers winter pleasures such as skating, sledding, and snug fireside companionship and winter perils such as snow and storm and numbing cold, and it finally concludes that "when the howling blast is o'er," then "Spring vouchsafes to visit us once more." His *The Politician Outwitted* is the first play, intended for the stage, to be published by a citizen of the new nation. As a poet, Low was often fluid, although almost always imitative. He seems to have been most comfortable with odes and elegies that could be recited with effective rhetorical fervor, but his collected *Poems* reveal him an experimenter in various stanzaic forms, including sonnets on disparate subjects such as the violet ("Emblem of innocence"), wine ("that makes the heart of men rejoice"), and tobacco ("Sweet antidote of Sorrow, Toil, and Strife"). Except for Philip Freneau's (q.v.) *Poems* (1786), no previous gathering of verse in the U.S. is more interesting or various. Low's failure may be thought to have been personal as well as literary. He was unable in his 30s to fulfill the promise of earlier verse written in his late teens. His literary life, apparently filled with alternate periods of enthusiasm and despair, may be thought of as an exemplar of the struggles of other young men of his time to present by well-intentioned imitation the new nation with a literature of its own.

Suggested Readings: Lewis Leary, "Samuel Low, New York's First Poet" in *Soundings: Some Early American Writers* (1975), pp. 67-82.

Lewis Leary
The University of North Carolina at Chapel Hill

PERCIVAL LOWELL (1571-1664)

Works: *A Funeral Elegie on the Death of John Winthrope* (1676).

Biography: Born in North Somerset County, Eng., in 1571, Percival Lowell founded a long line of illustrious Lowells in America, including the renowned poets James Russell Lowell, Amy Lowell, and Robert Lowell. Little is known about Lowell's education and training in Eng. He was probably born at Kingston-Seymore, where he was appointed "Assessor" at the age of 26. The position was held by his father before him. Early in the 1600s, he moved his family to Bristol to establish a wholesale business in exports and imports, recorded as "Percival Lowle & Co." Shortly after 1613, Lady Elizabeth Berkeley named Lowell Landlord of the Berkeley Arms Inn, six miles from Bristol. But in 1639 inordinate export taxes and strict supervision of the shipping industry caused Lowell at the ripe age of 68 to sail for New Eng. Lowell and his family settled in Newbury, Mass., where he received 100 acres of land after contributing fifty pounds to the commonstock. In the remaining years, he was involved with community affairs and wrote an elegy on the death of John Winthrop (q.v.), probably in 1649. Living to be 93 years old, Lowell died Jan. 8, 1664.

Critical Appraisal: Within the tradition of seventeenth-century elegies in New Eng., Percival Lowell's *A Funeral Elegie on the Death of John Winthrope* follows the Classical model in form but goes beyond being simply a *memento mori* precipitated by the death of a famous person. Published as a broadside in 1676, the elegy is an early example of poetic hagiography in which the New Eng. Puritans are reminded of their "errand into the wilderness" through the elegiac praise of a saint. Since subsequent generations would need to be reminded of that original errand, Lowell addressed his elegy not to the deceased Winthrop but directly to "You English Mattachusians all." The narrator urged them to "Forbear sometime from sleeping"—that state of forgetfulness—and to "Prepare themselves for weeping"—an act presupposing remembrance. At the outset, the special purpose of the elegy is made clear.

Although it is clearly directed at its New Eng. audience, the elegy also adheres to the traditional three divisions of praise, lament, and consolation prescribed by ancient Greek rhetoricians and freely employs both Classical and biblical comparisons and models. After asking his audience to weep as the "Jews did for their Moses," Lowell invoked the "Muses every one" to "extol his Fame, / Exceeding far those ancient Sages / That ruled *Greeks* in former Ages." The customary review of the governor's reputation reveals him as "an Israelite full true" who gave his goods to "Church and Commonwealth."

At this point, Lowell brought a strategic halt to a pedestrian mode of praise by professing that "My tongue, my pen, my rustick art / Cannot express his true desert." This not uncommon ploy of protesting inadequacy not only points to the greatness of the late governor but allows the speaker to shift to a quick paced list of biblical figures to whom Winthrop is compared. Following these typological parallels is the recognition of the ruin wrought by "Grim Death," the lament. Except for the eye-opening simile, "Death like a murth'ring Jesuite / Hath rob'd us of our hearts delight," the lament is composed of several hyperboles: eyes are fountains, heads are springs, and sighs tear clouds to "make an eccho ring." Nature in the guise of Classical deities is called upon to participate emotionally in the lamentation. Hyperboles and pathetic fallacy were commonplace literary techniques of the Renaissance, and Lowell's unoriginal dependence on them no doubt contributed to Harold Jantz's remark that the poem is "hardly of high poetic excellence." Yet the lamentation culminates in two lines that bring the reader back to a specific time, place, and vision in an original and capsulizing descriptive phrase, "O weep with us for *Joshua* / The Loadstone of *America*." In this elegy of highs and lows of rhetorical effects, the lament concludes with the anticlimactic lines, "My sences they are all too weak / His praises due to write or speak." The consolation, coming next, acts as a synthesis to the first two sections and does not deviate from the standard assumption that grief should not be immoderate and go unanswered: "They yet survive who may renew / Decay'd and dying hopes in you." This is the raison d'etre for the elegy. A resurrection of hope and purpose for those remaining Israelites, by remembering "*New-Englands Conservator*," is a resurrection of Winthrop himself. In a sense, Winthrop and hope for the Puritans become synonymous and are both resurrected in the course of the poem. The elegy ends with a separate stanza in which Lowell remarks on his poetic ability, asking the critics not to view his lines with "Mommus eye."

Although little critical attention has been paid to Lowell's elegy, he was perhaps the oldest English-born American poet, and his posthumously published elegy demonstrates how remembered saints represented renewed hope for the Puritans in their endeavor to make a millennial paradise out of an ungodly wilderness, a recurring central theme throughout Puritan poetry and prose.

Suggested Readings: FCNEV. *See also* Ferris Greenslet, *The Lowells and Their Seven Worlds* (1946); Ola Elizabeth Winslow, *American Broadside Verse* (1930, rev. 1974), pp. 2-3.

L. A. Norman
University of Cincinnati

BENJAMIN LYNDE (1666-1745)

Works: Fitch Edwards Oliver, ed., *The Diaries of Benjamin Lynde and of Benjamin Lynde, Jr. with an Appendix* [*Containing the Thomson's Island Poem*] (w.1690-1742; pub. 1880).

Biography: Benjamin Lynde was born in Salem, Mass., in 1666 and graduated from Harvard at the age of 20. In 1692 he went to Eng. to study law in the Middle Temple, London, and became a barrister. Returning to New Eng. in 1697, he settled again in Salem, served several terms as a representative to the General Court of Mass., and in 1712 became the first professionally trained lawyer appointed to the bench of the Superior Court. Following Samuel Sewall's (q.v.) resignation in 1728, he advanced to chief justice. Lynde held this post until his death and was a member of the Council from 1713 to 1737. His son Benjamin also became a prominent jurist. Lynde died in Salem in 1745, leaving behind extensive landholdings and a diary subsequently published by one of his descendants.

Critical Appraisal: As with Thomas Tillam (q.v.) and Thomas Dudley (q.v.), Benjamin Lynde's slender repute as a poet depends on a single poem. From Sewall's *Letter Book*, we know that Lynde wrote two broadside verses, now apparently lost; and F. E. Oliver specified in 1880 that a few other descriptive poems survived among Lynde's privately held papers. Yet the one poem now available, the judge's "Lines Descriptive of Thomson's Island," has provoked critical admiration from Harold Jantz as "one of the most readable and enjoyable descriptive poems of the period."

Starting off in the manner of Horace's epistle describing his Sabine Farm,

Lynde's poem unfolds a vivid, detailed panorama of the island's setting in Massachusetts Bay. So fully do these lines recreate both the visual and historical backdrop of each scene, regarded from diverse vantage points on Thomson's Island, that Lynde playfully imagines the reader usurping his legal ownership of the place: "Nay, if thro' Fancy strong one claim the soil / At sight, without possession right or toil, / I'll not mind such whimseys of ye brain." On its one face, the island provides a gracious pastoral retreat, the pleasures of which Lynde described more literally in his diary. But this natural jewel is only set off the more by its civilized setting. Lynde also enjoyed hearing villagers gossip toward the island's "hamlet side"; and the poem builds toward a climactic prospect of the spires, streets, and piers of flourishing "Bostonia" to the northwest. In the end, Lynde celebrated a vista that finds the blending of land and sea, town and nature, crowned by the institutional presence of "pure religion."

Lynde's published diary, which gives fragmentary coverage over the years 1690-1742, is worth examining for its record of customs and leading personalities of the day. Although sprinkled with pious expressions, it is even less introspective than Sewall's comparable diary and perhaps less colorful. Lynde refers to spiritual anxieties endured by his wife and elder son, but never to his own. Sometimes outlining the content of sermons, he seems more compulsively concerned with the amount of his contribution. Yet the diary includes revealing remarks about church conflicts in Salem, modes of criminal punishment, and a comfortable New Englander's experience of travel, food, and clothing in the earlier eighteenth century.

Suggested Readings: FCNEV; Sibley-Shipton (III, 356-357). *See also* Harrison T. Meserole, ed., *Seventeenth-Century American Poetry* (1968), which reprints the Thomson's Island poem on pp. 491-494.

John J. Gatta, Jr.
University of Connecticut

RICHARD LYON (fl. 1620-1651)

Works: *The Psalms Hymns and Spiritual Songs of the Old and New Testament Faithfully Translated into English Metre* (1651; trans., rev., and expanded by Henry Dunster and Richard Lyon).

Biography: Almost all that is known about Richard Lyon (also spelled *Lion, Lions,* and *Lyons*) is the result of research conducted by Zoltán Haraszti during his investigation of the composition of the Bay Psalm Book. Lyon was born in Eng., probably in Lancashire. In 1645 he may have been a student at Emmanuel College, but sometime between 1644 and 1646 he is known to have come to Mass. as the "Tutor or Attendant" of William Mildmay, a 1647 graduate of Harvard College and the oldest son of Henry Mildmay, a British knight.

Lyon's age at that time is estimated to have been approximately 25, making his year of birth sometime around 1620.

In New Eng., Lyon lodged in the home of President Henry Dunster (q.v.) of Harvard, whom he assisted in revising and expanding the famous *Whole Book of Psalmes*, commonly known as the "Bay Psalm Book." In 1651, after his work on the Psalm Book was completed, Lyon sold his possessions in New Eng. and returned to his homeland. Records of his subsequent activities in Eng. are sketchy, but he is believed to have been the same "Richard Lyons" who served as "minister" or "master" of the *Resolution* at the Battle of the Gabbard during the Dutch wars and later as captain of the *Taunton*. The rest of Lyon's life remains a mystery.

Critical Appraisal: Displeased with the Sternhold-Hopkins version of the psalms, which they felt was more "a paraphrase than the words of David," the founders of the Bay Colony set as one of their first priorities the writing of "a plain and familiar translation" of the psalms, one closer to the original meaning of the Bible than they believed was currently available elsewhere. To accomplish this momentous task, a group of ministers, among whom were John Eliot (q.v.), Richard Mather (q.v.), and Thomas Welde (q.v.), began work on the project. The result of the combined efforts of this group of men was *The Whole Book of Psalmes*, published in 1640 as one of the first books from the press of Stephen Day at Cambridge. Steadfast in their opinion that "Gods Altar needs not our polishings," the compilers of the Bay Psalm Book "attended Conscience rather then Elegance, fidelity rather than poetry, in translating the hebrew words into english language, and Davids poetry into english meetre." In the words of the preface to the Psalm Book, "a plaine translation" was far preferable, in the minds of the translators, to one which was "smooth" and "sweet" but which corrupted the meaning of the original text.

As a consequence of this decision to sacrifice, when necessary, art for meaning, *The Whole Book of Psalmes* proved unpopular among the churches of New Eng., where it was found difficult, if not almost impossible, to sing. As Moses Coit Tyler explains, the Bay Psalm Book is replete with "sentences wrenched about end for end, clauses heaved up and abandoned in chaos, words disembowelled or split quite in two in the middle, and dissonant combinations of sound that are the despair of such poor vocal organs as are granted to human beings." "Everywhere in the book," he continues, "is manifest the agony it cost the writers to find two words that would rhyme—more or less; and so often as this arduous feat is achieved, the poetic athlete appears to pause awhile from sheer exhaustion, panting heavily for breath."

Aware that, in the words of Cotton Mather (q.v.), *The Whole Book of Psalmes* was in need of "a little more Art," Henry Dunster, with "some Assistance" from Richard Lyon, set upon providing a "Revised and Refined" edition. Subsequently called the "New England Psalm Book," this project was begun in 1747, while Dunster was still president at Harvard, and published in 1651 under the title *The Psalms Hymns and Spiritual Songs of the Old and New Testament Faithfully*

Translated into English Metre, for the Use, Edification, and Comfort, of the Saints, in Publick & Private, Especially in New-England. Celebrated for his skill as an accomplished "Hebrician," Dunster is credited with having performed whatever translations were needed. Lyon is thought to have provided the versification, which consisted primarily of regularizing the rhymes and meters of the earlier edition and composing the lines for the not insubstantial number of "Hymns and Spiritual Songs" added to the text of the earlier edition. As Zoltán Haraszti has indicated, these latter works included "the Songs of Moses, of Deborah and Barak, of Hannah, David's Elegy, the whole Song of Songs, the Songs of Isaiah, the Lamentations of Jeremiah, the Prayer of Habakkuk, and the Song of the Virgin." In addition, Lyon is credited with having supplied one of the versions for Psalm 112. Followed by Lyon's initials, this psalm is, according to Haraszti, "the only psalm whose authorship can be authenticated by external evidence."

Although Cotton Mather later lamented that the text of the New England Psalm Book was still in need of "mending," the work was a popular success. More accessible to the ordinary audience than its predecessor, Dunster and Lyon's *Psalms Hymns and Spiritual Songs* was widely adopted as the standard psalter and hymnal for Protestant churches both in New Eng. and Europe, where it was published in more than fifty editions and remained in use until well into the eighteenth century. Lyon, however, has never received full recognition for his contribution to American letters, possibly because the Bay Psalm Book has become synonymous, in the opinion of many literary historians, with the aesthetic shortcomings of early American poetry in general. In any event, Lyon deserves recognition for writing the first hymnal published in America and, as Haraszti has pointed out, for composing and printing, next to Anne Bradstreet (q.v.), "more verse in America than any of the early Colonists."

Suggested Readings: FCNEV; T$_1$. *See also* Norman S. Grabo, "How Bad Is the *Bay Psalm Book?*", PMichA, 46 (1961), 605-615; Zoltán Haraszti, *The Enigma of the Bay Psalm Book* (1956).

James A. Levernier
University of Arkansas at Little Rock

_ M _

JAMES McCLURG (1746-1823)

Works: *Tentamen Medicum Inaugurale, de Calore* (1770); *Experiments upon the Human Bile* (1772); "The Belles of Williamsburg" (coauthor; 1788).

Biography: James McClurg was born near Hampton, Va., the son of a prominent physician, Walter McClurg. He graduated from the College of William and Mary and went to Edinburgh, where he studied medicine under some of the eminent teachers of the day and obtained his degree in 1770. He conducted further study and research in Paris and London, publishing his research on the human bile in 1772. In 1773 McClurg returned to Williamsburg, where he practiced medicine, mainly as a consulting physician, until 1783 when he moved to Richmond. During the Revolutionary War, he served as a surgeon in the Va. militia, and in 1779 he was elected to a professorship of anatomy at William and Mary. McClurg was esteemed as a physician, was popular in social circles, and took an active interest in politics. His popularity and his acquaintance and friendship with men such as George Washington (q.v.), Thomas Jefferson (q.v.), and James Madison (q.v.) were instrumental in his election to the Constitutional Convention and later to the Executive Council of the state. After 1797 he served at least three terms as mayor of Richmond. He was a member of the American Philosophical Society (from 1774), a counselor of the proposed Quesnay Academy (1783), a subscriber for Mathew Carey's (q.v.) *American Museum* (1787-1792), and the first president of the Virginia Medical Society (1820-1821). He was sought out by polite company, was considered an excellent conversationalist, and dabbled in *vers de société*. McClurg died on Jul. 23, 1823.

Critical Appraisal: James McClurg's first published work was his inaugural essay, *Tentamen Medicum Inaugurale, de Calore* (1770). This work in Latin was well received and was generally considered by his contemporaries and scientists of the following generation to have introduced original concepts later confirmed by the French school of chemistry. Before returning to Va., McClurg published *Experiments upon the Human Bile* (1772). The report of experiments is introduced by an essay "On Reasoning in Medicine." This piece, although readable, is hardly an eighteenth-century scientific tract. It is an argument for the cessation of antagonism between the empiricists and the dogmatists in the medical field and for the integration of other sciences into the study of medicine. The language is almost excessive at times, liberally sprinkled with metaphors that are sometimes strained, literary allusions, Classical quotations, and elaborate parallels between the schools of medical thought and social, political, or religious institutions. The report on McClurg's thirty-eight experiments upon the human bile is clearly and precisely presented and is followed by McClurg's conclusions or "reflections" that, like the introduction, suffer from excesses in the language. This work, like his first, was well received. He published nothing else in the medical field, although he maintained an active interest in science and medicine. Apparently, he had so great an interest in polite literature and other matters that he failed to fulfill his potential as a medical scientist. Yet his contribution to medicine in America was recognized by his contemporaries. In 1820 the first volume of Nathaniel Chapman's *Philadelphia Journal of the Medical and Physical Sciences* was dedicated to him, and the same journal, revived in 1828, reprinted his essay "On Reasoning in Medicine" in the first volume.

McClurg's most generally known work is "The Belles of Williamsburg," a conventional poem he wrote with St. George Tucker (q.v.) in 1777. McClurg wrote nine of the twenty stanzas that delineate the charm, grace, and character of various young ladies of Williamsburg. The poem was published in the *Richmond Standard* on Jul. 16, 1788, and was reprinted in an anthology by Margaret Lowther (later Mrs. Page) in 1790. Parts of the poem also found their way into one of the parlor scenes in John Esten Cooke's novel *The Virginia Comedians* (1854).

Suggested Readings: DAB; T_2. *See also* Wyndham B. Blanton, *Medicine in Virginia in the Eighteenth Century* (1931), pp. 328-334; Richard Beale Davis, *Intellectual Life in Jefferson's Virginia, 1790-1830* (1964); Howard A. Kelly and Walter L. Burrage, eds., *American Medical Biographies* (1920), pp. 731-732; James Brown McCaw, *A Memoir of James McClurg, M.D.* (1854); James Thacher, *American Medical Biography* (1828; rep., 1967), I, 379-383.

Daniel F. Littlefield, Jr.
Little Rock, Arkansas

SAMUEL EUSEBIUS McCORKLE (1746-1811)

Works: *A Sermon on. . .Sacrificing* (1794); *A Charity Sermon* (1795); *A Sermon on the Comparative Happiness and Duty of the United States* (1795); *Four Discourses on. . .Deism* (1797,1798); *A Discourse on. . .Keeping the Sabbath* (1798); *Three Discourses on the Terms of Christian Communion* (1798); *The Work of God for the French Republic* (1798); *True Greatness* (1800).

Biography: Samuel Eusebius McCorkle was born in Lancaster County, Pa., on Aug. 23, 1746. When he was 9 years old, his family moved to N.C. and settled near Salisbury on the lands of the earl of Granville. In 1772 McCorkle graduated from the College of New Jersey (later Princeton University) in the same class as Aaron Burr and immediately began the study of theology. He was licensed to preach by the Presbytery of New York and, at the direction of the Synod, spent the following two years preaching in Va. In 1776 he accepted an invitation to become pastor of the Presbyterian congregation at Thyatira, N.C., where his parents resided, and in Aug. 1777 was ordained and installed there. During the Revolution, McCorkle preached ardently on moral and doctrinal topics, both at Thyatira and at Salisbury. He opened a Classical school in 1785, which he called Zion-Parnassus to reflect its admixture of Christianity and Classicism. The school lasted about ten years, during which time McCorkle trained forty-five future ministers, including six of the University of North Carolina's first seven graduates. In 1792 he was awarded a doctor of divinity from Dickinson College, Carlisle. He remained at his post at Thyatira until his death on June 21, 1811.

Critical Appraisal: During the early national period in N.C., Samuel Eusebius McCorkle was an important educator, a learned and prolific preacher, and a literary figure of some significance. McCorkle's forte was the doctrinal sermon, but his published works are much more than academic exercises or sectarian squabblings, for McCorkle was above all a moralist, and the relationship of Christian doctrine and Christian duty was his great subject. The chief purposes of his lengthy but forceful sermons were to inculcate morality in the young members of his backwoods congregation and to convince wayward adults that Christianity provides the only means to a secure and virtuous community. In his *Charity Sermon*, he appealed to the doctrine of Christian love to solicit funds for the newly founded University of North Carolina. The Christian's duty to love his neighbor as himself, McCorkle suggested, bids him to build a moral society, the basis of which is the early education of the young. The same notion appears in *Three Discourses on the Terms of Christian Communion* and receives some emphasis in *A Sermon on. . .Sacrificing*, one of McCorkle's strongest statements on the necessity of good works in a Christian's life.

McCorkle seemed to fear that Christianity might lose its force as a dominant institution in the New World democracy, just as it had in the French Republic, whose faults McCorkle blamed on Deism. In *The Work of God for the French Republic. . .or the Novel and Useful Experiment of National Deism* (1798), he painted a lurid picture of the atrocities of the French government and appealed to his audience's worst fears. But he concluded optimistically that God's cause is furthered by these great evils, because they demonstrate for the Christian world the inadequacy of Deistic moral doctrine, which can only lead to libertinism and moral chaos. The same sentiments without the prophetic tone appear in the blandly patriotic *Sermon on the Comparative Happiness and Duty of the United States*, in which he urged his countrymen to follow the twin "lights of revelation and reason." McCorkle's strongest attack on Deism and some of his best writing are found in *Four Discourses on. . .Deism* (1797). Here he abandoned politics and, as "a friend of revelation," attacked the Deists on philosophical grounds. Most of his remarks are directed against Thomas Paine (q.v.), whose *Age of Reason* had just been published, but McCorkle quoted and jousted with a number of authors thought to be Deists, most of them English or French. Paine's work is full of inconsistencies, he argued, and Deism in general full of contradictions. Human reason is insufficient for human needs; revelation is necessary to fill the gaps. Reason is useful only to the wise, McCorkle suggested, and not everyone is wise: "if human reason be a sufficient and universal principle why have not all ages been *ages of reason*?" McCorkle seemed to reject the historical theory of progress in his insistence that people in Christ's time were not abject, ignorant, and superstitious. They were the mental and spiritual equals (perhaps the superiors) of modern man, and they were thus reliable witnesses to revelation.

McCorkle's sermons have a significant place in N.C.'s intellectual and literary history. They demonstrate that knowledge of Classical, Christian, and modern literature was not absent in the growing frontier towns, although learning and intellectual energy such as McCorkle's must have established him as something of a prodigy among his congregations in remote towns like Thyatira and Salisbury.

Suggested Readings: CCV; P; Sprague (III, 346-349). *See also* Walter Clark, ed., *State Records of North Carolina* (1905), XXIV, 30, 690; XXV, 22; James Franklin Hurley and Julia Goode Eagan, *The Prophet of Zion-Parnassus, Samuel Eusebius McCorkle* (c. 1934); William L. Saunders, ed., *Colonial Records of North Carolina* (1887), V. 1193-1194, 1217-1220; Ernest Trice Thompson, *Presbyterians in the South, Volume One: 1607-1861* (1963), 82-83, 224, 245, 261.

M. Jimmie Killingsworth
New Mexico Institute of Mining and Technology

DAVID McGREGORE (1710-1777)

Works: *Professors Warn'd* (1742); *The Spirits of the Present Day* (1742); *The Spirits of the Present Day*, 2nd ed. (1742); *The True Believer's All Secured* (1747); *The Christian Soldier* (1755); *A Rejoinder to the Reverend Mr. Robert Abercrombie's late Remarks* (with Jonathan Parsons; 1758); *Christian Unity* (1765); *An Israelite Indeed* (1774); *The Voice of the Prophets* (1776).

Biography: The third son of James McGregore (1677-1729), a Scotch-Irish religious leader who became pastor of the first Presbyterian church in New Eng. about 1719, David McGregore was born in Londonderry, Ire., and immigrated to New Eng. with his family and a number of Protestants from northern Ire. in 1718. McGregore was educated at home, principally by the Rev. Matthew Clark, his father's successor both in the Londonderry, N.H., pulpit and in marriage to the widow McGregore. Keeping in the homely way, David McGregore subsequently married Mary Boyd, twenty-three years his junior, a foster child who lived in his parents' home, by whom he fathered nine children. Ordained in

1737, McGregore was chosen to minister to the West parish of Londonderry, N.H., although the society was not actually incorporated until 1739. There he endured the controversies between the old and new parishes that continued for forty years. More significantly, he took an active part in the Great Awakening of the 1740s, traveling about to see the Awakening for himself and preaching a series of awakening sermons to his own congregation to good effect. He also defended the fruits of the Awakening through a letter of attestation published in *The Christian History, 1743*. McGregore had a fine mind, and he became a popular preacher whose congregation regularly included persons from neighboring towns; moreover, he proved a stable and effective pastor. In 1755 a Presbyterian congregation of New York City called him, but he declined to leave his flock, and in 1764 the College of New Jersey (later Princeton Univ.) granted him an honorary M.A. degree. McGregore served to the end, preaching and serving communion in a state of extreme debility only five days before his death, May 30, 1777.

Critical Appraisal: Despite his not having a formal collegiate training, David McGregore's sermons attest to his genuine learning and reveal an unpretentious eloquence rare in any age. In sermons with relatively long doctrines and brief but pungent applications, McGregore invariably stressed balance: between reason and emotion, between loyalty to perceived orthodoxy and the necessity of unity among Christians, and between a Calvinistic sense of sin and a recognition of man's potential through Christ.

Although he published several sermons, McGregore is probably best known for an exchange of sermons with the pastor of the older congregation in Londonderry, the Rev. John Caldwell, over the merits of the Great Awakening. Both preachers published, in 1742, sermons with titles including "trial" and "spirit[s]" in such a way as to make clear their polemic engagement. McGregore's *The Spirits of the Present Day Tried*, preached in Boston's Brattle-Street Church, is a learned and remarkably fair-minded statement of the conflict between the theologically liberal and conservative factions, particularly with respect to the central issue of justification, and the many often paradoxical attending conflicts between the Old Lights and the New Lights. Although clearly taking up the cause of the New Lights, McGregore maintained eminent civility, reason, and poise. In the appendix to the 2nd edition of his sermon later the same year, McGregore displayed a ready wit in a humorous account of his personal confrontation with Caldwell in McGregore's meetinghouse, and in the rejoinder to Caldwell's published polemics.

Apparent in his first published sermon, *Professors Warn'd of Their Danger*, are McGregore's preoccupation with the inner life, his practical piety, and his rejection of mere convention and external decorum as significant spiritual signs. In later years, he was equally insistent upon the element of struggle and even turbulence as concomitants of the true Christian life; however, with the passage of time, he became increasingly weary of the ecclesiastical bickering that followed upon the Great Awakening, and in *Christian Unity* (1765), he inveighed against "party names, such as new lights, old lights. . .a separating spirit," the prevalence of ignorant ministers who stress emotion and neglect the intellectual rigor of "human learning," and in general "the ecclesiastical anarchy of this day." A later sermon, *An Israelite Indeed* (1774), more positively argues for the mere knowledge of Christ's teachings, as opposed to the concern with orthodoxy or "politeness." Here McGregore indentifed the "genius of the christian religion; which is *to hide pride from man; to humble the vain creature, while it saves him; to empty him of himself; to exalt God; to promote universal holiness.* When he has found this, he will adhere to it with an unshaken stability." It is the stability and sense of proportion that seem never to have left McGregore.

In his last publication, *The Voice of the Prophets*, printed the year before his death, McGregore seems to have addressed both the incipient American Revolution and the eternal quest for salvation in an unsigned publication of remarkable subtlety. The clear implication of the heavily scriptural argument is that the people must remove unjust rulers; yet the thesis is elaborated in such a way that the dominant impression is of the inevitable checks and balances in society, ancient and modern.

All in all, this remarkable preacher's sermons are heavily scriptural, but with a seasoning of carefully selected secular images, the whole expressed in disciplined rhetoric: smooth without seeming facile, strong without being labored.

Suggested Readings: CCNE; Sprague (III, 28-30). *See also* William Allen, *The American Biographical Dictionary*, 3rd ed. (1857), p. 567; Alan Heimert and Perry Miller, eds., *The Great Awakening* (1967), pp. 214-227; Thomas Prince, ed., *The Christian History* (1744-1745), I, 193-195.

Wilson H. Kimnach
University of Bridgeport

JOHN MACPHERSON (c. 1726-1792)

Works: *Mount-Pleasant, May 5, 1766. . .That Duty Incumbent on Every Honest Man to Vindicate His Character* (1766); *Letter to John Dickinson, Esq.* (Nov. 13, 1770); *Macpherson's Letters, &c.* (1770); *A Pennsylvania Sailor's Letters, Alias the Farmer's Fall; with Extracts from a Tragic Comedy, Called Hodge Podge Improved* (1771); *To Be Published. . .Every Saturday, until a Pamphlet Is Complete, a Pennsylvania Sailor's Letters, Alias the Farmer's Fall* (1771); *An Introduction to the Study of Natural Philosophy* (1782); *A History of the Life, Very Strange Adventures, and Works of Captain John Macpherson* (1789); *Lectures on Moral Philosophy* (1791, 1798); *McPherson's Vorlesungen Über Philosophische Sittenlehre* (1792).

Biography: John Macpherson was born at the head of Skinner's Close in Edinburgh, Scot. His father was second son to Lord Cluney, one of the most powerful chieftains in the Highlands of Scot., and his mother was a great-granddaughter of Mr. Heriot who built the hospital for the education of poor boys called Heriot's Works. He mentioned two brothers in his letters, Angus and Robert or "Roby," who became deputy secretary to the trustees for improvements in Edinburgh. Their father, a lawyer, "fell into hard times" and became a supervisor in the revenue service. When John was 4 years old, his father was attacked by three men in the Links of Aberdeen and lost his life while wounding two of his assailants and killing the third.

His mother sent John to school to study Latin for the clergy, but he proved a better student of math. To his displeasure, his mother apprenticed him to his uncle Mr. Akenhead the apothecary. He observed and probably aided his uncle's apprentices in stealing corpses for dissection.

His first attempt to sail from Edinburgh was thwarted when Capt. William Jones of the *St. David* returned the runaway youngster to his mother and uncle. They relented and apprenticed him for five years to Capt. Jones, with whom he sailed to Hol., Nor., and the W. Ind. But his service ended when Jones fled the ship, which he had stolen from Boston harbor for his smuggling trade. Other adventures saw young Macpherson sail to Leith with James Mason; to New Castle with Capt. John Jervis, returning to Edinburgh almost naked after the ship wrecked between Stockton and Hartlepool near Durham; and from Goteberg, Swed., with Capt. David Drybrogh on *The Old Christy*. He reached London from Yarmouth on the *Cat, John, and Hannah*. Macpherson was later to boast of his sailing prowess, although he had never formally studied navigation.

A privateer in the French war of 1757 and the Spanish war of 1762, Macpherson lost his right arm in action and was made a burgess of the city of Edinburgh on Jul. 6, 1764, for his gallantry as commander of the British ship *Britannia* in the West Indies. In 1761, he bought land at Mt. Pleasant near Philadelphia, Pa. (today, Fairmount Park) and built a celebrated stone mansion. His first wife, Margaret Rodgers, was sister to the Rev. Dr. John Rodgers of N.Y. She bore him sons John Jr. and William and two daughters, Peggy and Polly. In 1769 William was commissioned as ensign of the British Sixteenth Regiment of Foot in America, but in 1779 he was appointed a major in the Revolutionary army. While serving as an aide-de-camp to General Richard Montgomery, John, Jr., was killed at the age of 21 in the assault on Quebec. In 1769, John, Jr., had been indentured to the lawyer John Dickinson (q.v.), famed author of *Letters from a Farmer in Pennsylvania to the Inhabitants of the British Colonies (1767-1768)*, an agreement Macpherson had cause to regret. Macpherson's wife Margaret died on Jun. 4, 1770; by 1772, he had married again on a trip to Edinburgh.

For his wife, Macpherson declared himself a Presbyterian, although his mother had been of the Church of England. In his *Lectures on Moral Philosophy* (1791), he "professes having long been a Deist" who was "brought to Christianity" by the Rev. Dr. Samuel Magaw of St. Paul's in Philadelphia.

For 108 days beginning May 10, 1769, Macpherson was confined in chains for mental illness, an action that caught him by surprise. He never forgave his wife her participation in his confinement and spent considerable effort the remainder of his life explaining how he was wronged by family and friends. In his *Life* and published letters, he attacked John Dickinson, whom he accused of perpetrating the plot, calling him "Oliver Cromwell Jr."; his wife; his wife's brother Dr. Rodgers whom he called "Bishop Laud the Second"; Dr. Cadwalader, Dickinson's uncle; and Mr. Bayard, former apprentice to Cadwalader. He also accused the doctors of deluding John, Jr., into believing his father's illness incurable, whereby they could manipulate his estate and holdings. In Dec. 1769 Macpherson appointed attorneys Blathwaite Jones and Robert Smith to protect his interests.

In the year of his death, the *Gazette of the United States* (May 26, 1792) reported Capt. Macpherson's recommendation to prevent fire by soaking shingles in a trough of strong pickle for fourteen days before nailing them to the roofs of Philadelphia homes. Macpherson died on Sept. 6, 1792.

Critical Appraisal: Capt. Macpherson's writing is characterized by the narration of his youthful misadventures and his later alienation from his wife and John Dickinson, while maintaining governance over his family and his business interests. The tone of his later writing is compulsive. He sought to vindicate himself of charges of madness by conducting an unrelenting attack upon his enemies. Details are told in *Macpherson's Letters* (1770), the *Pennsylvania Sailor's Letters* (1771), and the *Life* (1789), which are, for the most part, reproaches for the insults he was forced to bear those 108 days.

Macpherson laid claim to seventeen separate publications, some of which were possibly confiscated and destroyed during his confinement. Among the missing titles listed in the *Life* are *Plain Truth Addressed to All Freemen of Pennsylvania*; the *Quaker Unmasked, Written for Quaker Friend Israel Pemberton; John Macpherson's Last Legacy, or A Treatise upon Religion, Friendship, Love, and Marriage; Captain Roderick Random, Junior; Conversation Between Jack Ratling and Tom Bowling About the Captain's Method of Fighting a Ship;* and *The Account of My Jaunt Through the British Army, by Permission of George Washington, and the Plan I Laid to Take the Hessians at Trenton.* Macpherson trifled with the reader by claiming he had "mixed the works of other men with my own very often," acknowledging his eclectic borrowing from Pope, Swift, Gay, Bolingbroke, Voltaire, Rousseau, the Rev. Dr. Magaw, and others. In his *Letter to John Dickinson, Esq.* (Nov. 13, 1770), he claimed authorship of a patriotic song written by Dickinson, doubtless alluding to the "song for American freedom," a copy of which Dickinson mailed to James Otis (q.v.) on Jul. 4, 1768, with a letter attributing eight lines to Dr. Arthur Lee (q.v.) of Va.

In the *Life*, his youthful escapades recount the restive nature of a Scottish lad who, on one occasion, accidentally shot a cow belonging to a local minister and, on another occasion, purposely set fire to grain fields to discover how Samson burned the Philistine's corn. The cow episode he shared with his boyhood friend Marquis Car, later a general in Fr. But it was not until 30 years after the episode that he admitted to an uncle his complicity in the disastrous fire. He and a friend set a cat on fire through the fields, burning two and a half acres of oats, causing the death of one rider, and wounding others in the melee. Young Macpherson proved himself resourceful when he saved his uncle the apothecary from a mob angered over the theft of the body of a child by hiding the corpse in his coat as the citizens searched his uncle's home. He ended his apprenticeship when he fought with his uncle and knocked him to the ground.

Details of his confinement consume a large part of his writings. Letter 65 of *Macpherson's Letters* provides a detailed account of his incarceration. On May 10, 1769, four men seized him in his Mount-Pleasant home and restricted him to a small hut on his estate once meant to accommodate his shepherd. He escaped twice, once by slipping his leg out of his chains, a second time by breaking apart the bedstead to which he was chained. At one period, he was taken from Mount-Pleasant to Mrs. Bell's on Society Hill. During his confinement, his business affairs were handled by his wife and son through Dickinson and others. Macpherson was irate over the sale of 140 head of cattle and other attempts to deal with his property and real estate holdings. Letter 7 he sent to John Dickinson with a sixty-four-line poem originally scratched with a nail on a white wall: "Must my flocks from pastures be sold, / Whilst I am confin'd and can't see; / My pen too denied, I am told, / For fear I diverted should be....O Woman, you swore to obey, / To love and stick close to my side. / Your children of late were so blest; / Your husband was happy and gay; / But now he's in prison distress'd, / By you or the *auto da' fe*."

When his wife sought a divorce after his release, Macpherson refused her conveniences, limiting her resources to a single room at Mrs. Orrick's in Philadelphia. Letter 63 tells of his anger: "When I was master of a house, you was always called mistress; yet you chose to be master and mistress too, to obtain which end, you kept me chained in a hut, for one hundred and odd days." He ordered his son John, Jr., to cancel his indentures to John Dickinson, but Dickinson denied the request, initiating a series of letters between John and his father in which the son sought dutifully to obey his father's wishes. The letters are of topical interest, but they lack the fictive structure of a planned narrative. Narration lacks Defoe's tautness; epistolary art lacks Richardson's psychology. A commercial sailor protecting his private interests, Macpherson offered neither the sonorous rhythms of a Chesterton nor the cosmopolitan breadth of a Walpole.

John Dickinson wrote Macpherson on Aug. 13, 1769, expressing his belief that his friend's "reason is injured" and offering to help Macpherson regain his strength. A man of aggressive disposition, Macpherson may have given his family and friends cause to suspect his judgment on several occasions. Two events in his later life possibly precipitated his confinement, his altercation over a lost horse, and his stubborn intent to race his sloop in competition.

In his letter of May 5, 1766, Macpherson defended himself against the charges of Samuel Garrick, who laid claim to a horse in Macpherson's possession. Garrick complained that Macpherson found the horse but misrepresented its appearance in advertisements to prevent its being restored to its rightful owner. Macpherson was compelled to defend his actions, detailing how his servants found the horse in Nov. 1775 and his subsequent efforts to advertise the animal in the Robin Head Tavern, on trees at the Wissahickan Road, and in the *Pennsylvania Gazette* and the *Journal*. Seeking to redeem his reputation, Macpherson agreed to return the horse upon the owner's paying expenses for the keep of the animal, the cost of advertising, and payment of one pistole for the benefit of the Pennsylvania Hospital. Macpherson wrote, "If McPherson [sic] meddles with Filth, he will bedaub himself."

Not long before he was seized, Macpherson offered to race his sloop the *Felis* on the Delaware River for a wager of 10,000 pounds. His rents from fourteen tenants in Dec. 1769 amounted to about 239 pounds, and we might surmise that his family thought he was risking too much in the race.

While Macpherson was confined, Dickinson leased Mount-Pleasant to a tenant under John, Jr.'s name and sold part of Macpherson's effects. Macpherson attacked Dickinson in his fragmentary tragicomedy *Hodge Podge*, where he depicted a farmer soliloquizing about his deception of a friend and laying plans to have the doctors declare his friend mad.

Suggested Readings: T. W. Glenn, *Some Colonial Mansions* (1900), pp. 445-483; William Macpherson Hornor, *Extracts from the Letters of John Macpherson, Jr., to William Paterson, 1766-1773* (1899), rept. from PMHB, 23 (1899). The principal source of information on Macpherson is his own works. For information about the song without mention of Macpherson, see Paul Leicester Ford, ed., *The Life and Writings of John Dickinson: 1764-1774* (1895; 1970), II, 419-432.

Irving N. Rothman
University of Houston

JAMES MACSPARRAN (1693-1757)

Works: *A Sermon Preached at Naraganset* (1741); *Dr. MacSparran's Sermon Preached at the Convocation of the Episcopal Clergy* (1747); *The Sacred Dignity of the Christian Priesthood* (1752); *America Dissected* (1753); *A Letter Book and Abstract of Our Services (1743-1751)* (1899). *An Answer to a Printed Letter* (1739) was written by an opponent of MacSparran.

Biography: James MacSparran probably was born in Dugiven, Ire. He received an M.A. from the Univ. of Glasgow in 1709 with the intention of becoming a Presbyterian minister. He arrived in Mass. in search of a church in 1718, and the congregation at Bristol, now in R.I., nearly accepted him. But dissension in that church caused him to return to the British Isles, where he was ordained a clergyman in the Church of England the following year. In 1721 the Society for the Propagation of the Gospel sent him to St. Paul's Parish in North Kingstown, R.I., which was his base while he preached in R.I., Mass., and Conn.

With a few interruptions, such as his return to Eng. in 1736-1737 to earn a doctor of divinity from Oxford, he served as a missionary until his death in

North Kingstown. Concerned with the spiritual welfare of the church, MacSparran rejected the introduction of lay readers into the church. This response to the scarcity of ordained ministers and the influence of the Great Awakening, he thought, deprecated the historic responsibilities of the priesthood. As a missionary, he was successful; his own congregation, made up of whites, Indians, and Negroes, expanded severalfold. This achievement was in part due to MacSparran's ability to fit into the plantation society of southern R.I. He frequently socialized with the planters and became a slaveowner, as his diary entries in the *Letter Book* indicate. Yet he refused to identify himself as a member of colonial society; rather, he viewed himself as a loyal son of Britain on a mission in a foreign land.

Critical Appraisal: Adherents of the Great Awakening could approve of MacSparran's style of preaching even if they rejected parts of his message. He spoke without pretense, refusing to quote texts in foreign languages and rarely referring to the Classics. He avoided metaphysical discussions. Rather than speak in abstract terms, MacSparran used examples from history or employed similes and metaphors from everyday experience to make his meaning clear. His sermon of 1741 was a model of simple but eloquent prose devised to cause his listeners to repent before God punished the wicked.

The graceful style of the 1741 work was not as evident in his later sermons, which defended the Church of England. Like the Old Lights, MacSparran feared that the enthused ministry of the Great Awakening did spiritual harm: self-proclaimed ministers whose spiritual authority was based merely on having experienced religious conversion could have deceived themselves. They might actually spread heresy and social disorder rather than truth. For him, the priesthood and ecclesiastical organization of the Church of England provided a bulwark against religious error. He supported this thesis in the *Sacred Dignity* by tracing the history of the Primitive Church, which he documented with citations from Scripture. The ministry, he found, was a distinct vocation whose members received the grace of the Holy Spirit to administer the sacraments and preach from ordination by the bishops. Through the apostolic succession, the bishops had the authority to evaluate the spiritual credentials of ministerial candidates to ensure that the rites and doctrines of the church would not be defiled. By virtue of the apostalic succession, MacSparran found that the Church of England was an heir of the true church.

MacSparran's sermons lacked the invective that frequently colored the discourses of the Great Awakening era. He emphasized the positive aspects of the Church of England rather than the failings of the sects. He did not exclusively identify the Church of England with the true church and specifically denied that his church had the power to impose religious conformity. Nevertheless *Sacred Dignity* was controversial, and it was rebutted by John Aplin, in *An Address to the People of New England* (1753), for MacSparran was the agent of the church that had persecuted the Puritan founders of New Eng., and their descendants feared that if that church became more powerful its supporters would become oppressive once again.

America Dissected indicates that MacSparran was more hostile to New Eng. than his sermons suggested. In this work, a series of letters written to friends in Ire. that portrayed an unflattering portrait of the geography and culture of British America, he wrote that "Vagrant, illiterate Preachers sworm where I am." America was a "Field full of Briars and Thorns and Noxious Weeds, that were all to be eradicated, before I could implant in them the Simplicity of Truth." He wrote as a sojourner among a provincial people: "As the Shadow lengthens as the Sun grows low, so, as Years increase, my longings after *Europe* Increase also."

In *Dr. MacSparran's Sermon. . .to the Clergy*, he commended the "Majestic simplicity" of the Apostle Paul's language. It was the Anglican missionary's self-appointed task to apply Paul's literary style to defend the Church of England from American innovations.

Suggested Readings: CCNE; DAB; DNB; Sprague (V, 44-47). *See also* Calvin R. Batchelder, *A History of the Eastern Diocese* (1910), II, 241-259; Carl Bridenbaugh, *Mitre and Sceptre: Transatlantic Faiths, Ideas, Personalities, and Politics, 1689-1775* (1962), pp. 23-115, 314-341; Wilkins Updike, *A History of the Episcopal Church in Narragansett, Rhode Island*, 2nd ed., 3 vols., ed. Daniel Goodwin (1907), vols. I (text) and III (documents).

Robert Brunkow
Santa Barbara, California

JAMES MADISON (1751-1836)

Works: *The Federalist* (1788); William T. Hutchinson and W.M.E. Rachal, eds., *The Papers of James Madison* (1962-).

Biography: James Madison was born at Port Conway, Va., in Mar. 1751. At age 12, Madison began formal schooling under Donald Robinson in King and Queen County, studying the Classics, French, and Spanish. In 1769 he entered the College of New Jersey (Princeton), where he was a student of history and government and a founder of the American Whig Society, a college debating club. Following his graduation in 1771, Madison spent another year at Princeton studying Hebrew and ethics under President John Witherspoon (q.v.).

After returning to Va., he was elected in 1776 to the Va. convention, where he was a member of the committee that framed the Constitution and Declaration of Rights. He served as a member of the First Assembly to the governor's Council in 1778, and in 1780 he was made a delegate to the Continental Congress, where he served until Dec. 1783. His notes on the debates are a useful supplement to the official journal of the Congress. Madison suffered from Va.'s failure to pay his salary and relied at times on loans to survive financially. In Dec. 1783 he returned to Va., where he was able to take up a number of intellectual pursuits including the study of law. He corresponded with Thomas Jefferson (q.v.), then in Philadelphia and later in Paris, asking him for books that aided Madison's studies of natural history and chemistry. Such diversions, however, were merely an adjunct to his public life. Shortly after his return to Va., he was elected to the House of Delegates from Orange County, an office he retained until the end of 1786. Madison emerged as a leader in the Assembly and showed a continuing interest in the importance of trade and commerce. He came to see that only by the adoption of a united commercial policy could the states effectively regulate commerce, and toward that end, he urged the Assembly to grant Congress necessary powers. He also helped instigate a series of interstate conferences commencing with the commercial convention of 1786 through the Federal Convention at Philadelphia in 1787.

Madison's role in the Constitutional Convention is reflected particularly in the resolutions drawn up by the Va. delegates and submitted as the Va. or Randolph plan. Madison served as the chief recorder of the convention's proceedings, resulting in his "Journal of the Federal Convention," first published in 1840. Providing valuable assistance in securing the passage of the new Constitution by the states, he cooperated with Alexander Hamilton (q.v.) and John Jay (q.v.) in a series of essays published in several N.Y. newspapers over the collective pseudonym "Publius." These essays were later collected and published in 1788 as *The Federalist*. In Va. Madison was elected to the ratifying convention that met in Jun. 1788 and was instrumental in securing a vote for ratification. Although blocked by Patrick Henry in his bid for election to the new U.S. Senate, he was elected to a seat in the House of Representatives. As a Congressman, he took a leading part in the passage of revenue legislation, the creation of the executive departments, and the framing of the first ten amendments to the Constitution, the Bill of Rights. Madison was married to Dolly Payne Todd, a young Philadelphia widow, in 1794.

Following the election of 1800 and Jefferson's inauguration as president, Madison again came into a permanent position in public life as the president's secretary of state and chief advisor. Since both the president and vice-president were widowers, Mrs. Madison became the capital's leading lady, known for her personal charm and great popularity. While Madison was secretary of state, the Louisiana Purchase was concluded in 1803. Madison became Jefferson's successor and entered upon his new duties on Mar. 4, 1809. He was to serve two terms as president. Under Madison, the Congress declared war against G.B. in 1812. Despite a number of early reverses including the capture of the city of Washington that forced the president and his family to flee to Va., the war was seen as an American triumph by the time the treaty was concluded on Christmas Eve of 1814. Madison left the presidency in 1817 to be followed by Monroe. He later served in the Va. Constitutional Convention of 1829. He supported Jefferson in the founding of the University of Virginia and became rector after Jefferson's death in 1826. Madison spent the end of his life quietly at his home in Montpelier, where he arranged for the publication of his notes on the federal Constitutional Convention. He died at the age of 87.

Critical Appraisal: James Madison is perhaps best known for his contribution to the *Federalist* essays. Although not so numerous as those of Hamilton, who had enlisted Madison's assistance in this project to promote acceptance of the new Constitution, Madison's contributions reflect a balanced emphasis on the role of government as a control over the influence of competing rivals: "Among the numerous advantages promised by a well-constructed Union, none deserves to be more accurately developed than its tendency to break and control the violence of faction." This concern reflects a departure from emphasis on radical democratic philosophy characterizing the literature of the Revolution. Madison combined faith in popular government (a view that coauthor Hamilton did not share) with an appreciation for the restraining role of government. His "rounded urbane prose line" aided in his forceful exposition of the Constitution.

Suggested Readings: DAB; LHUS; P; T_2. *See also* Irving N. Brant, *James Madison*, 6 vols. (1941-1961); Adrienne Koch, *Jefferson and Madison: The Great Collaboration* (1964); Louis C. Schaedler, "James Madison, Literary Craftsman," WMQ, 3 (1946), 515-533.

L. Lynn Hogue
George State University, Atlanta

FRANCIS MAKEMIE (1658-1708)

Works: *A Catechism* (1691); *An Answer to George Keith's Libel on a Catechism* (1694); *Truths in a True Light* (1699); *A Plain and Friendly Perswasive to the Inhabitants of Virginia and Maryland for Towns and Cohabitation* (1705); *A Good Conversation: A Sermon Preached at the City of New York* (1707); *A Narrative of a New and Unusual American Imprisonment* (1707). Evans's *Bibliography of American Imprints* lists another work by Makemie titled *Letter to Lord Cornbury*; however, there is no other source for this. The letter in question is included in Makemie's *Narrative*.

Biography: The "Father of American Presbyterianism" was born of Scottish parentage in Ramelton, County Donegal, Ire., in 1658. In 1675 he was enrolled as a student at the University of Glasgow. Makemie was licensed by the Presbytery of Laggen, St. Johnstown, Ire., in 1681 and ordained in 1682 when he was sent to America. He reached America in 1683, after stopping off at Barbados. For the next fifteen years, Makemie traveled and preached from S.C. to Philadelphia, where he preached the first Presbyterian sermon in that city in 1692. He also made another trip to Barbados. At this time, Makemie began to publish his writings, beginning with his *A Catechism* in 1691. When this work was attacked by the Quaker George Keith (q.v.), Makemie wrote *An Answer to George Keith's Libel on a Catechism* in 1694.

Makemie married Naomie Anderson, daughter of a prominent Va. planter, sometime during 1697 or 1698 and settled in Accomack County, Va. He continued to travel as far north as Boston and conducted a regular correspondence with Increase Mather (q.v.). Also during this period, Makemie was involved in trading activities with Barbados. In 1707 Makemie and a companion, the Rev. John Hampton, were arrested and imprisoned by Lord Cornbury, governor of N.Y. and N.J., for preaching in New York City without the permission of the governor. Cornbury's actions were illegal, since they were contrary to the Act of Toleration, under which both Makemie and Hampton were licensed to preach, in Va. and Md., respectively. Although they refused the governor's demand that they promise never to preach in N.Y. again, both men were finally released, Hampton's name being dropped from the charges. Makemie returned to N.Y. to stand trial and was acquitted by a jury. Further details of this affair can be found in his *A Narrative of a New and Unusual American Imprisonment*. Makemie then resumed his normal activities and continued them until his death, which probably occurred in Jul. of 1708. The exact circumstances of his death are unknown.

Critical Appraisal: Francis Makemie was one of the earliest strong voices of Presbyterianism in America. Most of his works deal with his religion, expounding its tenets and showing the value of Christianity to everyday life. As a spokesman for his faith, Makemie involved himself in one of the fundamental areas of early American life, that of religion and religious freedom.

No known copies of *A Catechism* have survived, but certain statements in *An Answer to George Keith's Libel on a Catechism* offer a general picture of Makemie's first published work. *A Catechism* was at least forty-one pages and was designed to instruct young people in the Presbyterian faith. It dealt with central issues, such as the keeping of the Sabbath, the maintenance and government of the church, and Christian virtues. Keith attacked Makemie on many points in a letter to another minister, pointing out where, in light of Keith's Quaker views, Makemie had erred. In *An Answer*, Makemie reprinted Keith's "Libel" and answered the objections point by point. The points over which these two men argued show the basic differences between the two faiths they represented and largely concern the spiritual nature of man and interpretation of the Bible. Makemie's method of refuting Keith in *An Answer* was to refer to Scripture passages that support the Presbyterian view or to show how Keith's views were not consistent with Scripture. Makemie also included a brief section on differences of opinion among the Quakers.

In *Truths in a True Light*, Makemie turned to the relationship between Presbyterianism and the Church of England. He contended that the Presbyterian Church was the dissenting church that was closest to the Church of England and that the differences between them were only in matters of ceremony, government, and discipline. Addressed to the Protestants of Barbados, *Truths in a True Light* calls for unity among Protestants against the Catholic Church. Makemie also condemned terms such as *Puritan* and *Calvinist* as being tools of the Catholic Church designed to divide the Protestant faiths.

Makemie's *A Good Conversation* is a thorough and well-ordered sermon on salvation. Employing a logical approach and many Scripture passages to develop his points, Makemie discussed the way to salvation, the necessity of salvation, and the reasons why some people fail to find it. This was the sermon Makemie preached in N.Y., for which he was arrested.

A Narrative of a New and Unusual American Imprisonment is Makemie's account of the affair with Lord Cornbury. It contains transcripts, written from the author's memory, of conversations between Makemie and Lord Cornbury, statutes regarding religious freedom, and letters and other documents relating to the case. Makemie's knowledge of the law is evident in *A Narrative*.

A Plain and Friendly Perswasive, Makemie's only published work dealing entirely with secular matters, shows us something of Makemie's secondary occupation as a trader. He pointed out the advantages of forming towns with respect to commerce, education, and religion. Makemie addressed this work to the new governor of Va., Edward Nott.

Makemie's style is in some ways typical of his day. He was occasionally verbose, but no more so than other religious writers of the period. His arguments were always clear, however, due to their well-ordered and logical presentation and adequate supporting material.

Suggested Readings: CCMDG; DAB; DARB; DNB; Sprague (III, 1-4). *See also* Littleton Purnell Bowen, *The Days of Makemie: Or, The Vine Planted* (c. 1885); Richard Beale Davis, *Intellectual Life in the Colonial South* (1978); William Henry Foote, *Sketches of Virginia: Historical and Biographical* (1850-1855); Henry Pringle Ford, "Chronological Outline of the Life of Francis Makemie," JPHS, 4 (1907-1908); I. Marshall Page, *The Life Story of Reverend Francis Makemie* (1938); Boyd S. Schlenther, *The Life and Writings of Francis Makemie* (1971); Henry Alexander White, *Southern Presbyterian Leaders* (1911). See also numerous JPHS articles.

Frank Crotzer
University of Delaware

THOMAS MAKIN (1665-1733)

Works: *Encomium Pennsylvaniae* (1728); *In Laudes Pensilvaniae Poema, Seu, Descriptio Pensilvaniae* (1729).

Biography: Thomas Makin was born in Eng. in 1665. We know nothing of his early life until 1689, when he was listed as an usher in George Keith's (q.v.) Friends' Grammar School. In 1697 Makin and Francis Daniel Pastorius (q.v.) were directed by the Friends' Monthly Meeting of Philadelphia to organize a public school, which they began early the following year. Makin directed the arithmetic curriculum (aimed primarily at preparing students for business); Pastorius supervised Latin instruction and, apparently, school discipline. (In at least one instance, Makin escaped the censure of a parent angry at the whipping his son had received from Pastorius.) In 1700 Makin shared the position of schoolmaster with John Cadwallader, who succeeded Pastorius. In 1706 Makin retired as schoolmaster to become clerk of the Provincial Assembly, a position he held until 1709. He is then said to have left Philadelphia for the interior of the colony. We know nothing further of his life until Benjamin Franklin (q.v.) in his *Pennsylvania Gazette* recorded that this "ancient man," now reduced to extreme poverty, "fell of[f] a wharff into the Delaware, and before he could be taken out again, was drowned."

Critical Appraisal: Like most of his contemporaries, Thomas Makin was not a literary stylist or a poet of the first rank. His two long Latin poems, both inscribed to James Logan (q.v.), in whose papers they survive, are not memorable for their literary craftsmanship. They are, however, interesting examples of early colonial Latin poetry and, more significantly, specimens of descriptive poetry in the tradition of Richard Frame's (q.v.) *Short Description of Pennsylvania* (1692) and John Holme's (q.v.) *True Relation of the Flourishing State of Pennsylvania* (1696).

Certainly, Makin's poems have received little critical acclaim. The *Descriptio Pensilvaniae* reminded Francis H. Williams of "one of those adolescent excursions into the realms of the muses, wherein we are taught the order of the alphabet through the medium of a jingle." According to E. Gordon Alderfer, James Logan himself "must have been pained by their mediocrity." What praise Makin's work has been accorded is, at best, qualified. Thomas Wharton admitted that Makin's Latin hexameters were "probably the first attempt to describe the institutions and scenery of the province in the lofty language of Rome," but they remain nonetheless "uncouth." Joshua Fisher believed that the poems "deserve praise for metrical correctness and descriptive fidelity," but they are "rude."

Despite this tepid response, we should not overlook the poems' virtues. In the *Descriptio*, Makin provided a lengthy account of William Penn (q.v.), the origins of his province, and the climate, natives, flora, fauna, agriculture, and administration of Pa. He took pains as well to emphasize three essential traits of life in the province: peace, prosperity, and liberty. Of the Indians, Makin wrote: "O gens Indorum, vos terque quaterque beati! / Nulla quibus requiem follicitudo vetat!" [O happy Indians! bless'd with joy and peace; / No future cares of life disturb your ease]. This tranquility is a product of their inherited life-styles and, significantly, the just treatment they received from Penn and the Quakers—a policy that Makin sharply contrasted to that of New Eng.'s colonists.

Makin likewise contrasted the liberty and opportunities of Pa. to those of Europe: "Qualis in Europa concessa licentia non est, / Commoda ubi curat quisque tenere sua." [Such privilege in Europe is unknown; / Where ev'ry man is bounded with his own]. Makin thus belongs among the earliest advocates of the American Adam. Although his verse may be crude, his sentiments remain in the mainstream of much of the best American literature.

Makin also wrote at least two poems in English. One honored the arrival of Thomas Penn at Philadelphia, and the second Franklin included in his obituary notice. Although the latter is admittedly slight, it does repeat Makin's affection for Pa. and offers in its opening lines the promise, however unfulfilled, of some poetic gift: "Some purchase land, some stately buildings raise." Makin was an able schoolmaster, not an accomplished poet. We would be negligent, however, wholly to ignore his contributions to colonial descriptive literature.

Suggested Readings: Joshua Fisher, "Some Account of the Early Poets and Poetry of Pennsylvania," MHSP, 2, ii (1830), 78-79; Robert Proud, *History of Pennsylvania* (1797-1798), II, 360-373 (reprints the "Descriptio Pensilvaniae"). "Thomas Makin," PMHB, 37 (1913), 368-374. See Leo M. Kaiser, "Lost Early American Latin Poems," SCN, 40 (1982), 34-35, for a translation of a previously unpublished poem by Makin.

Timothy K. Conley
Bradley University

HERMAN MANN (1771-1833)

Works: *The Female Review; Or, Memoirs of an American Young Lady* (1797); *The Minerva* (editor; 1797-1804).

Biography: Herman Mann was born on Nov. 10, 1771, in Walpole, Mass. He married in 1792 and had eleven children. Before 1797 he was a teacher, but in that year he moved to Dedham, Mass., where he engaged in printing and started a newspaper called *The Minerva* (later the *Columbian Minerva*), which he published until Sept. 4, 1804. In 1812 Mann moved to Providence, R.I., but returned to Dedham the following year to become a book binder and seller. According to his own "Catalogue of the Principal Works Published and Unpublished, of Herman Mann: Arranged in 1827," he wrote a moral and philosophical essay, *The Memento Mori*, in addition to the works previously mentioned. He died Sept. 25, 1833, in Dedham.

Critical Appraisal: *The Female Review* is a novel based on the actual career of Deborah Sampson, who served in the Continental Army in 1782-1783. Herman Mann appended a series of documents as evidence of his heroine's historical existence and assumed the role of an editor. Disclaimers throughout the text state that he was not a novelist embellishing for poetic effect. Despite its factual basis, however, the book is shaped by Mann's didactic and sensational purposes and self-consciously directed to a feminine audience. As the editor, Mann assured readers that he had ameliorated anything in the account that might offend feminine sensibility and stated that he had "taken liberty to intersperse, through the whole, a series of moral reflections and...attempted some literary and historical information."

The book begins with long sections advocating the education of women, summarizing British injustices against the colonies, and presenting maxims of feminine manners and human wisdom (William Kendrick's *The Whole Duty of Women* [1761] is specifically recommended). Once Deborah has disguised herself as a man and enlisted in the army, however, the text is primarily concerned with a description of her exploits during and just after the Revolutionary War. Her misfortunes include a series of illnesses and wounds, seemingly as serious in their threat to her disguise as to her health. Ultimately, an illness results in the discovery of her sex and a recuperative journey during which she is captured by cannibalistic Indians. When her wit and courage enable her to escape, she is honorably discharged and resumes her private life.

The Female Review presents a series of contradictions, not always successfully treated by Mann. First, between praise of Deborah's virtues and condemnation of her duplicity: she is both a model for emulation and an example of "a breach in feminine delicacy." Second, between homo- and heterosexual love: she experiences love for both women and men. As a man, Deborah makes a series of conquests. Even after the revelation of her sex, she continues a relationship with a lady from Baltimore. Mann wrote, "The passion entertained by the sexes towards each other. . . will always be laudable when managed with prudence." Heterosexual love is, of course, never seriously questioned, and the appendix reveals that Deborah marries and has three children. The cardinal sin is flirtation—whether homosexual or heterosexual—as for example Deborah's behavior after her discharge when she reassumes her disguise and must be reprimanded by her uncle for "her freedom with the girls." Mann sternly counseled prudence, warning especially those readers who may have been conquered by Robert Shurtlieff (Deborah's alias). Third, between the cause of feminism and subservience of women to men: Deborah is an example of both. While lamenting that opportunities for women are seldom commensurate with their abilities, Mann agreed with Deborah that a woman's place is to be found in "amiable acquiescence" to her husband. Fourth, between the expressed didacticism and the latent sensationalism of the text: the moral objective of imparting practical advice and wisdom is not always well served by the titillating descriptions of near discoveries of Deborah's sex. She does represent, however, a kind of American Moll Flanders, and Mann's novel deserves a place in the emergence of a national literature.

Suggested Readings: Herbert Ross Brown, *The Sentimental Novel in America: 1789-1860* (1940), pp. 10, 92, 105; DedHR, 7 (1896), 60-63 (prints "Catalogue of the Principal Works"); Elizabeth Evans, *Weathering the Storm: Women of the American Revolution* (1975), pp. 303-334; Tremaine McDowell, "Sensibility in the Eighteenth-Century Novel," SP, 24 (1927), 383-402; Henri Petter, *The Early American Novel* (1971), pp. 381-383; Arthur Hobson Quinn, *American Fiction: An Historical and Critical Survey* (1936), p. 23; John Adams Vinton, ed., *The Female Review: Life of Deborah Sampson with Notes and Introduction* (1866).

Randall Craig
State University of New York at Albany

JOHN MARKLAND (fl. 1721-1735)

Works: *Three New Poems* (editor; 1721); "To the Countess of Warwick, in Defense of Mr. Addison, Against the Satire of Mr. Pope" (1723); "An Ode on the Happy Birth of the Young Princess" (1723); *Typographia: An Ode on Printing* (1730); "To the Right Honourable Charles, Lord Baron of Baltimore" (1733).

Biography: Of John Markland, the author of *Typographia*, little is known. Apparently he was the New Kent, Va., attorney of that name, although this identification has never been established conclusively. J. A. Leo Lemay has argued convincingly that Markland was a son of an English clergyman, the Rev. Ralph Markland, and a brother of Jeremiah Markland, a "well-known scholar" to whom at least two of John Markland's works have been attributed erroneously. In 1718/1719 Markland matriculated as a pensioner in St. Peter's College, Cambridge. During the early 1720s, he was an established if minor English poet of occasional verse. By 1730, the year *Typographia* was published, he was in Va., where he published a second poem in 1733. References to him appear in Va. records in 1734 and 1735, and then nothing is heard of him in America or Eng. Lemay speculated that he died shortly after 1735.

Critical Appraisal: Of the poems that John Markland wrote before leaving Eng., the best, "To the Countess of Warwick," had appeared in *Cytheria, or New Poems upon Love and Intrigue* (1723). Lemay credited Markland with having edited this collection and believed that he wrote "nearly all" of its poems. Earlier, Markland had brought out *Three New Poems* (1721), which included a piece by himself, and in 1723 his ode on the birth of the princess had appeared. These poems, along with his two Va. pieces, demonstrate his ability as a versifier as well as his intimate acquaintance with the Classics and the English poets.

Typographia ostensibly celebrated William Parks's (q.v.) establishment of the first permanent printing press in Va. It may have been the first issue of that press. An ode in the neo-Classical tradition, it relies heavily upon Classical allusions to tell how "Mournful Virginia" had asked the kind "sun" of Br. to dispense on it "a nearer Ray of his mild Influence," and in response King George had sent as his viceroy to Va. William Gooch, whose arrival brought happiness and prosperity to the colony. Gooch, by filling Va.'s need for a printing press, enabled the colonists to become well informed and thus "eschew" the errors of their fathers. Although its twelve stanzas do not offer regular patterns of rhyme and line length, the ode has a graceful lyricism. Despite its flattery of Gooch and George— "too effusive for the modern taste," according to Jay B. Hubbell—it nevertheless is a laudable performance for its time and place.

Markland's other known American poem also fawns upon its subject, Lord Baltimore, "A *Calvert* can his People's Good prefer, / And his own Safety to their Weal postpone!" The poem sees James Edward Oglethorpe's (q.v.) settlement of Ga. as having been inspired by Baltimore's "brave Example" and generally implies approval of the proprietors' conduct in America. This seven-stanza untitled poem contains eighty-four workmanlike iambic pentameters, including a number of closed couplets. Like its predecessor, it must be regarded as a very good colonial poem, and as in *Typographia*, its many Classical allusions testify to Markland's rich background. These two poems have prompted Lemay to rank Markland with Henry Potter (1700-1752), author of *The Decoy*, and William Dawson (q.v.), a president of the College of William and Mary and author of the first collection of poems to be published in America, "among the prominent literary men of Virginia in the 1730s." Certainly, the two Va. poems, each intended to win the goodwill of a powerful dignitary and thus enhance the position of the colony in Eng., suggest that Markland stood high in Williamsburg's literary circles.

Suggested Readings: LHUS. *See also* Richard Beale Davis, *Intellectual Life in the Colonial South, 1585-1763* (1978), III, 1488-1489; Jay B. Hubbell, *The South in American Literature* (1954), pp. 36-37; J. A. Leo Lemay, ed., *A Poem by John Markland of Virginia* (with introduction by Lemay; 1965); John Markland, *Typographia: An Ode on Printing* (with introduction by Earl G. Swem; 1927). Markland's second American poem, first printed in a now lost copy of the *Maryland Gazette*, was reprinted in *The American Weekly Mercury* of Aug. 9, 1733. David Foxon of Oxford University is preparing a *Calendar* that will list Markland's English poems.

Joseph H. Harkey
Virginia Wesleyan College

PETER MARKOE (c. 1752-1792)

Works: *The Patriot Chief: A Tragedy* (1784); *The Algerine Spy in Pennsylvania* (1787); "An Epistle to Mr. Oswald," *Pennsylvania Journal* (Feb. 21, 1787); *Miscellaneous Poems* (1787); *The Storm; A Poem* (1788); *The Times; A Poem* (1788); *The Reconciliation; Or, The Triumph of Nature: A Comic Opera* (1790).

Biography: Peter Markoe was born around 1752 in St. Croix, in the W.Ind. He entered Pembroke College, Oxford, in 1767 and was admitted to Lincoln's Inn in 1775. That same year, he came to America and joined the Philadelphia Light Horse. After visiting St. Croix, he returned to Pa. in 1784, serving in the militia between 1785 and 1789. Lewis Leary wrote that Markoe, a friend of Philip Freneau (q.v.), "divided his time among law, poetry and conviviality"; however, there is no evidence of a legal practice. When combined with Markoe's relatively small literary output, this suggests that much time was devoted to conviviality. While living in Philadelphia, Markoe achieved a limited reputation for poetry and was sometimes referred to as "the city poet." He died in Philadelphia in 1792.

Critical Appraisal: Peter Markoe's writing must be understood against the political background of the 1780s. Several works were dedicated to political figures, and all of his writing implicitly or explicitly expresses his faith in Jeffersonian democracy, Christian ethics, and neo-Classical rationalism.

Markoe's epistolary novel, *The Algerine Spy in Pennsylvania*, purports to be the translation of twenty-one letters from Mehemet to a friend in Algeria. Three additional letters are used solely to advance the plot near the end of the book. Markoe exploited the innocent perspective of the non-Christian foreigner for comic and satirical purposes. Dances and religious meetings, experiences new to Mehemet, were described in a humorously objective manner. In other cases, his observations were more analytical: "In most nations there are three forms of tyranny; the first civil; the second ecclesiastical; the third I shall call the tyranny of *fashions*.... The Pennsylvanians have known but a little of the first, and nothing of the second; but the greater part of them is grievously oppressed by the last." Although he suggested taking advantage of national disunity to establish an Ottoman kingdom in Mass. and R.I., Mehemet became a citizen and a Christian when he learned that he had been discredited at home. The change in allegiance was sudden and arbitrary, but it serves to emphasize the advantage of life in America and to lessen, while not ignoring, Markoe's social criticisms. He adapted the epistolary technique and thin story line to political rather than fictional purposes.

Neither of Markoe's plays has ever been produced. *The Patriot Chief* relies on the conventions of Classical tragedy. The plot involves a conspiracy against King Dorus of Lydia organized by friends of the king and supported by the Persians. The insurrection is defeated and Olinthus, the king's son, succeeds his father to the throne. The play is dedicated to Gen. George Washington (q.v.), and its message to a country divided against itself and threatened by foreign powers is clear. Although its form is clearly imitative, *The Patriot Chief* expresses themes that demonstrate Markoe's use of native materials. *The Reconciliation* is an adaptation of a one-act play, *Erast* (1788), by Solomon Gessner. Markoe expanded the play to two acts, changed the names, and added a character but is otherwise faithful to the original pastoral idyll. When Wilson is disinherited for marrying the virtuous but impoverished Amelia, the couple lives in the country with the rustics Simon and Debby. Wilson's honesty leads to a reconciliation with his father and to the comic resolution. The play's literary significance resides in its use of a number of songs, making it one of the first operas written in America.

In his own day, Markoe was known primarily as a poet. The poetical works include a short volume of occasional, lyric, and comic poems and adaptations written early in his life. "An Epistle to Mr. Oswald" and *The Times* are social and political satires. Much of the point of the latter is lost as the figures who are given Classical and mythological names cannot be identified. But Markoe's criticism of economic and political policies is clear. *The Storm* was written "to express my ideas of a late event, which, whilst it awakened poetical feelings, must have excited national ideas." He interpreted the tempest as a warning to those who had abandoned the principles of freedom and industry. Markoe used conventional stanzaic forms and meters, most frequently relying on the heroic couplet. As in the plays, he employed inherited forms to comment upon the political and social situation of the U.S. in the 1780s. The body of his work reflects the political confusion and literary contradictions that accompanied the emergence of the new nation.

Suggested Readings: DAB. *See also* William Alfred Bryan, *George Washington in American Literature: 1786-1860* (1940), p. 175; Sister Mary Chrysostom Diebels,

Peter Markoe (1752-?1792): A Philadelphia Writer (1944); Lewis Leary, *That Rascal Freneau* (1964), pp. 121-122; Walter J. Meserve, *An Emerging Entertainment* (1977), pp. 151-152; Henri Petter, *The Early American Novel* (1971), pp. 107-108; Arthur Hobson Quinn, *A History of the American Drama* (1946), pp. 62-63; Oscar G. Sonneck, "Early American Operas," QMIMS, 6 (1904-1905), 428-495.

Randall Craig
State University of New York at Albany

JOHN MARRANT (1755-1791)

Works: *A Narrative of the Lord's Wonderful Dealings with John Marrant, a Black* (1785); *A Sermon Preached...at the Request of...the African Lodge of...Masons* (1789); *A Journal of the Rev. John Marrant* (1790).

Biography: In his *Narrative*, John Marrant gave a full, if at times incredible, account of his life before 1785. This early black American minister of the Gospel was born on Jun. 15, 1755, in N.Y. After several years of moving about, the family settled in Ga. Marrant learned to read and spell by his 11th birthday but apparently did not learn to write until the period of the *Journal* (1790), which Marrant claimed to have written himself. The Rev. William Aldridge recorded the earlier *Narrative*. Rather than choosing a trade, Marrant preferred learning to play the violin and the French horn, mastering both in eighteen months. One of Marrant's "friends" later challenged him to use his musical abilities to break up a revival meeting of the Rev. George Whitefield (q.v.), the voice of the Great Awakening. Before Marrant could play, however, Whitefield "looked around, and, as I thought, directly upon me, and pointing with his finger, he uttered these words, 'Prepare to meet thy God, O Israel' "—whereupon Marrant fell to the ground. He then experienced his conversion, but his family reacted by shunning him and acting as if he had lost his mind. So Marrant ran away from home, taking with him "a small pocket Bible and one of Dr. Watts's hymbooks." After wandering several days in the wilderness, he was seized by Cherokee Indians, who intended to put him to death. But at the point of death, Marrant began praying in their own language (which he had learned in ten weeks of travel with "an Indian hunter"), eventually converting the king of the Cherokee nation.

Thus began Marrant's career in the ministry, which later took him to London where he came under the auspices of the generous Selina Hastings, Countess of Huntingdon, who had also been the patroness of Phillis Wheatley (q.v.). The countess encouraged Marrant to return to the New World and carry his gospel message to blacks, whites, and Indians. Marrant's *Journal* narrates his many perils and spiritual backslides between 1785, when he arrived in Nova Scotia, and 1790, when he lived in Boston. About this time Marrant was asked to serve Boston's African Lodge of the Honorable Society of Free and Accepted Masons as its chaplain and to preach his *Sermon* of 1789. According to Sidney Kaplan, the Rev. John Marrant died in 1791 in Islington, a borough of London.

Critical Appraisal: John Marrant's short but eventful life provides the basis for two of his known works, *A Narrative of the Lord's Wonderful Dealings with John Marrant, a black* and *A Journal of the Rev. John Marrant*. While the *Narrative* tells of his early life, his conversion to Christianity, and his early career as a minister, the *Journal* records the trials and successes of his later ministry. The *Narrative* was immensely popular, having been reprinted nineteen times before 1825. Perhaps its popularity, as Dorothy Porter suggests, lies in its close ties with the Indian captivity narrative. But the work certainly shows considerable action and imagination. For example, after being nearly roasted alive by the Cherokees, Marrant again escaped almost certain death during the Revolutionary War, having been pressed into service on board the *Scorpion*, a British sloop of war. This ship was "overtaken by a violent storm," and Marrant was washed overboard three times. After the second such event, he tried to secure himself to the ship: "I now fastened a rope around my middle, as a security against being thrown into the sea again; but, alas! forgot to fasten it to any part of the ship." On the third occasion, he was attacked by sharks, "one of enormous size, that could easily have taken me into his mouth at once." But as providence would have it, "he who heard Jonah's prayer, did not shut out mine, for I was thrown aboard again." Marrant took this trial as a certain sign that God wanted him to return to his ministry.

The *Journal*, which continues the *Narrative*, has a more restrained tone. At one point, Dr. Samuel Stillman, a liberal Baptist minister, rescued Marrant from an angry Boston mob that had come "prepared that evening with swords and clubs." With Stillman's approval, however, Marrant answered the mob by establishing a school and expanding his ministry in the area. The *Journal* also described Marrant's friendship with Prince Hall (q.v.), a founder of the lodge for black Masons in Boston, the first in America. It was Hall who asked him to become chaplain to the lodge and to preach his only published sermon.

In his *Sermon Preached...at the Request of...the African Lodge*, Marrant intended to prove that the members of the lodge had "a just right as Masons to claim" the titles of "honourable, free, and accepted." The *Sermon* is a fairly sophisticated performance for a man whose formal schooling had terminated at age 11. While explicating the biblical text, Marrant alluded to Seneca and his observations on God's most splendid workman. Then he supplied a learned geography lesson about the probable location of paradise that gradually evolved into a biblical history of African Masons. The point of Marrant's *Sermon* appears to have been to establish among the lodge a sense of identification in the face of the oppressive threat of slavery (despite the title "Free" held by these Masons). He made the fine point that all races of men have histories of enslavement, "which is not just cause of our being despised." He cited, for example, Gregory the Great's story of the fair-complexioned Angles (whom Gregory had called angels) who were being sold as slaves in Rome. In his "Application," Marrant exhorted his hearers to "let the characters of our enemies be. . .to blow the coals of contention and sow the seeds of strife among men—but ours to compose their differences and heal up their breaches." Assuming such a posture of returning love for evil will ensure the attainment of "the great and glorious Lodge in heaven."

Marrant's determined pacifism prefigures that of Dr. Martin Luther King. By acknowledging the gravity of the racial problem (as his contemporary Jupiter Hammon [q.v.] seemed unable or unwilling to do) and at the same time refusing to recommend violence for violence, Marrant gave sensible, sane advice applicable to all seasons. The *Narrative* and the *Journal* are not really slave narratives or Indian captivities. Each is finally a spiritual confessional, relating the vicissitudes of a lost soul's discovery of Christianity and following a great tradition from St. Augustine's *Confessions* to Jonathan Edwards's (q.v.) "Personal Narrative." But Vernon Loggins gave an unfair assessment of Marrant's achievement when he wrote "neither the *Journal* nor the *Sermon* contains the slightest allusion to the pitiable condition of his people in American life." Marrant's known works reveal the mind of a man concerned for the future of all men, regardless of color, while acknowledging the black's undeniable difficulties in a white world.

Suggested Readings: Sidney Kaplan, *The Black Presence in the Era of the American Revolution: 1770-1800* (1973), pp. 95-99; Vernon Loggins, *The Negro Author: His Development in America* (1931), pp. 31-34, 95, 374, 411; Dorothy Porter, *Early Negro Writing: 1760-1837* (for a modern reprint of *Narrative*; 1971), pp. 402-403, 427-447; Theressa G. Rush, Carol F. Myers, and Esther S. Arata, *Black American Writers, Past and Present* (1975), II, 527; Roger Whitlow, *Black American Literature: A Critical History* (1973), p. 24.

John C. Shields
Illinois State University

JONATHAN MARSH (1685-1747)

Works: *An Essay, to Prove the Thorough Reformation of a Sinning People Is Not to Be Expected* (1721); *The Great Care & Concern of Men under Gospel Light* (1721); *God's Fatherly Care of His Covenant Children* (1737).

Biography: For nearly forty years, Jonathan Marsh was Congregational minister of the First Church of Christ at Windsor, Conn. Born in Hadley, Mass., he received a B.A. from Harvard College in 1705 and returned to Hadley as teacher at the grammar school from 1706 to 1707. In Dec. 1707 he was called to assist at the First Church in Windsor. He qualified for an M.A. from Harvard in 1708, when he also became colleague minister at the Windsor church because of the failing health of the regular minister, Samuel Mather. He was probably ordained in 1710, the same year he married Margaret Whiting of Westfield and

Hartford, Conn. They had two sons—Jonathan and Joseph—and five daughters—
Margaret, Mary, Dorcas, Hannah, and Ann.

Known as a "two-hour preacher," Marsh published one of his Windsor church
sermons and an election sermon in 1721. When the First Church in Guilford
became embroiled in controversy over the appointment of a minister whom a
large minority rejected, Marsh was one of the clergymen the General Assembly
named to the peacemaking commissions of 1729 and 1732. However, both the
Assembly and the commission were unsuccessful in averting a separation, and
after five years of contention, the dissenters won approval to form their own
church. Marsh led a revival at his Windsor church in 1735, but when some
members of the church were touched by the "fanatical spirit" of the Great
Awakening, he rejected its excesses. He was again invited to preach the election
sermon at Hartford in 1736. Conn. records also indicate his involvement in civic
affairs and his work in executing several estates for parishioners. Marsh became
trustee of Yale College in 1732 and served in that capacity until 1745, the year
Yale was incorporated. He died two years later on Sept. 7, 1747, leaving to his
wife and children a sizable estate. His elder son, Jonathan, followed him into the
ministry.

Critical Appraisal: Traditional Puritan form and style dominate Jonathan
Marsh's three published sermons. His first, *The Great Care & Concern of Men*,
was preached in Dec. 1720. The text, Hebrews 2:1-3, offers imagery of the
hunt, which Marsh used to show the need for Christians to "look diligently" lest
they "fail of the Grace of God." Parents, ministers, and private Christians are
likened to archers, their mark being heaven. If they come "short" of the grace of
God, they miss the mark of salvation. If they are alert to temptation and attentive
to duty, they attain saving grace and reach the heavenly mark. To the hunt
metaphor are added more original figures of sinners like fencers who "ward off
the sword of the word" and men who are grown "sermon-proof."

Marsh's first election sermon, *An Essay to Prove the Thorough Reformation*,
was delivered before the General Assembly at Hartford, May 1721. Marsh
examined the roles of both the ruler and citizens in reformation, chiding those
who absolve themselves of responsibility and blame rulers for the sins of the
times. Scriptural and historic models are presented as leaders worthy of emulation. Proposals for reformation offer unambiguous directions to the assembled
leaders of Conn. to legislate for the "Public Good."

In the election sermon of 1736, *God's Fatherly Care*, Marsh took his theme
from Psalm 102, "Like as a Father pitieth his Children, so the Lord pitieth them
that fear Him." Conventional father and child imagery carries the message of
God's compassion and concern for his children, correcting them when necessary,
as a father, not as "an incensed Judge." Marsh emphasized the need for reverence
for "Superiors in every Order," but nevertheless cautioned against trusting men
and worldly means rather than God. Marsh treated at length the obligation of the
civil rulers to imitate God's "tender concern" for the welfare of the people. The
solution of political problems implies understanding of human "privileges" and

protection "under the Umbrage and Protection of our most gracious Sovereign." All leaders—rulers, judges, ministers, and heads of families—should care for their people yet look to the higher authority of Christ. The father-child motif continues to the end where Marsh returned to God's covenant with his children.

The three sermons show Marsh's command of Puritan plainstyle: prose that is simple, clear, restrained, yet lively and effectual. They ring with conviction and zeal, tempered with compassion and understanding.

Suggested Readings: CCNE; Sibley-Shipton (V, 279-280). *See also* Charles J. Hoadly, ed., *The Public Records of the Colony of Connecticut*, vols. 6 (1872); 7 (1873); 8 (1874); Henry R. Stiles, *The History of Ancient Windsor* (1859); Benjamin Trumbull, *A Complete History of Connecticut* (1818).

Mary S. Bond
University of Houston

HUMPHREY MARSHALL (1760-1841)

Works: *A Reply to the Address of . . . George Muter* (1795); *An Address to the People of Kentucky* (1796); *The Aliens: A Patriotic Poem* (1798); *The American Republic* (editor; 1810); *History of Kentucky* (1812, 1824).

Biography: Close friends with Davy Crockett, John Jay (q.v.), and his cousin Chief Justice John Marshall and firm enemy of Aaron Burr, Henry Clay (with whom he fought a duel), and Charles Scott (the governor of Ky. who promised full executive clemency to anyone who murdered "Old Humphrey"), Humphrey Marshall was known as the "best hated man of his day" partly for his published atheism but mostly for being an ultra-Federalist in Ky. when that state fought over whether to join the Union or become allied to the French, Spanish, or British empires. He was born in 1760 in Fauquier County, Va., the great-grandson of Thomas Marshall who had settled in Westmoreland County as a planter in 1649. His mother, Mary Quisenberry, who had married John Marshall in 1758 or 1759, came as did her husband from solid yeoman stock. Humphrey did not attend school but studied under Scottish tutors with his cousin Mary (1759-1824) whom he married in Sept. 1784. When Mary's father, a friend of George Washington (q.v.), joined the American Revolution as colonel of a Virginia State Regiment of Artillery, Humphrey enlisted as a cadet at the age of 18 and in three years rose to the rank of captain. He was rewarded for his service with 4,000 acres of land in "Western Virginia," or present-day Ky. Following his father and uncle to Ky. in 1782 as surveyor and then lawyer, Humphrey prospered through land investments principally near Lexington and Frankfort. With wealth and family connections came power, which Marshall chose to direct at political ends marked by three major events—the Constitution's ratification, the Jay Treaty, and the Burr Conspiracy.

In 1787 Marshall attended the Va. State Convention as a delegate from Ky.

and, against orders, voted to ratify the U.S. Constitution, which carried by only ten votes. This disobedience riled many, including one who tried to murder him on Main Street in broad daylight in 1788 (Marshall beat him off with a long staff he had taken from the assassin's uncle, who earlier had tried to thrash Marshall). But Marshall managed to be elected twice as state representative in 1793 and 1794 and as U.S. senator from 1795 to 1801, supporting the Alien and Sedition Laws and the Jay Treaty. Over the latter issue, he was burned in effigy at home, denounced as a traitor in public meetings, and referred to the House of Representatives for perjury. Once he was taken out by a mob to be ducked but dissuaded the mob and then eloquently denounced them from a stump.

Marshall lived quietly as a farmer the next five years, but in 1806 he used the pages of the *Western World* to expose the Burr Conspiracy, attacking Burr and his lawyer Henry Clay and inaugurating what was known as the Ky. newspaper wars, climaxing in the 1809 duel with Clay in which Marshall was shot in the stomach, Clay in the thigh. After three more years in the state legislature, Marshall founded *The American Republic* on Jun. 26, 1810, the state's only Federalist paper. When opponents dubbed this newspaper "the snake," Marshall adopted the emblem of a rattlesnake, added the motto "Don't Tread on Me," and wrote a fairly good poem explaining their significance. The paper was renamed the *Harbinger* in 1812 and claimed 800 subscribers but was sold in 1825 after Marshall had suffered a stroke paralyzing him on one side. He remained a staunch advocate of "Old Court" and "Anti-Relief" parties and strongly favored the self-colonization of slaves. A slaveholder himself, he held slavery to be morally repulsive, freed some of his slaves while he was alive, and released all at his death on Jul. 3, 1841. In 1888 the Ky. Senate forgave its strong-willed son and voted 300 dollars to remove his remains to the State Cemetery and to erect a stone.

Critical Appraisal: Humphrey Marshall published in four genres—tracts, poetry, newspaper articles, and history. His "Atheistic tracts," self-published in the 1780s and quoted at length by A. C. Quisenberry, are marked by a cantankerous tone and an earnest plea to persuade readers away from emotionalism to reason. Deistically inspired, they argue for a devotion to an ultimate public good based upon active individual commitment as opposed to passive obedience to an abstract Supreme Being. They represent what Marshall called his main goal of "Public Utility," although he despised the masses at the "nether end of society." Purportedly religious tracts, these essays are more properly sociopolitical writings. Of his poetry, little survives except *The Aliens* and a few newspaper poems that seem competent but not creative, as conservative in style as Marshall was in mood. Even *The Aliens*, a long poem that Marshall published in 1798 and later suppressed, suffers from this slant. His journalism is his second-best effort, important for historical reasons, as in the exposé of the Burr Conspiracy and, as William H. Perrin's *Pioneer Press of Kentucky* puts it, for having "had no equal in the period in which he lived." Marshall used an elevated diction, terse sentences, and frequent exclamation points; he specialized in sarcastic understatement to accent political ideas. Even at the age of 72, Marshall could rise to the occasion and employ a vigorous gentlemanly style: reviewing G. D. Prentice's *Biography of Henry Clay* in 1832, he lamented its "sycophantic unction."

Marshall's greatest achievement is his *The History of Kentucky, Including an Account of the Discovery, Settlement, Progressive Improvement, Political and Military Events and Present State of the Country*, published first by Henry Gore in 1812 (407 pages) and then in 1824 by George Adams in Frankfort in two volumes (522 and 524 pages). Previously, the only "real" history was that by John Filson (q.v.) (1784), containing his important biography of Daniel Boone, but otherwise consisting mostly of "railroad ads." Marshall's history, as R. D. Collins's *History of Kentucky* claimed, became more prominent at least until 1834. Although often partisan, bitter, and prejudiced, the *History* is important for its philosophy that even great individuals are "governed by circumstances" and its contemporary views of leaders who have since been mythologized. A caveat to scholars is that the 1st edition is far more vitriolic than the 2nd. For example, Benjamin Franklin (q.v.) is called a "singular composition of formal gaiety, of sprightly gravity, of grave wit, of borrowed learning, of vicious morality, of patriotic treachery, of political folly, of casuistical sagacity and republican voluptuousness—Dr. Franklin!" In the 2nd edition, this pasage is greatly modified, tamed in the face of mythology. Also the 2nd edition generally lacks the footnotes, references, and superior proofreading of the first. In short, Marshall's writings mirror the man—elevated diction from this six-foot two-inch Kentuckian, independent views from one dressed eccentrically in French brocade vests over homespun shirts, always sporting a long staff of belligerence to defend his idiosyncratic convictions, and polite to the point of seeming to be patronizing.

Suggested Readings: DAB. *See also* R. D. Collins, *The History of Kentucky*, 2 vols. (1891); A. C. Quisenberry, *The Life and Times of the Honorable Humphrey Marshall* (1892); William H. Perrin, *Pioneer Press of Kentucky* (1888).

Henry L. Golemba
Wayne State University

HUMPHRY MARSHALL (1722-1801)

Works: *Arbustrum Americanum, or The American Grove* (1785).

Biography: Abraham Marshall was born in Derbyshire, Eng., became a Quaker and a minister in the Society of Friends, and immigrated to Pa. around 1697, settling on the west branch of the Brandywine River. He married Mary Hunt whose father had been a companion of William Penn (q.v.), and they had nine children, the eighth being a robust boy born Oct. 10, 1722, whom they named Humphry. Humphry attended school until the age of 12 and, as he claimed, "was instructed only in the rudiments of the plainest English education." When a teenager, he was apprenticed to a stone mason and became proficient at the trade, erecting his own two-story house, mill, and astronomical observatory. He was elected local tax assessor from 1757 to 1761, served as Pa. treasurer (1762-1767), and was a trustee of the Provincial Loan Office from 1773 until 1778, when he felt compelled to resign because of American animosity toward antiwar Quakers. His later public services include erecting the County Almshouse and organizing the Westtown Boarding School.

Marshall had married Sarah Pennock in 1748, and when his father died in 1767 leaving him a large inheritance, he started the scientific work that made him famous. It began with an essay on "Observations upon the Spots on the Sun's Disk from November 15, 1770, to December 25, 1771," which helped elect him to the American Philosophical Society and was followed by an address called "Observations on the Utility of Botanical Knowledge in Agriculture," which was offered to the Royal Society by Benjamin Franklin (q.v.), where, said Franklin, it was "well received." But Marshall's greatest work, *Arbustrum Americanum* (1785), grew from his botanical garden at West Bradford, which, established in 1773, was second in American history only to that of his cousin John Bartram (q.v.). Marshall collected plants from various parts of America and propagated and then sold the plants or their seeds at modest prices and in good condition. Starting in 1767, he sent specimens, seeds, plants, and bird eggs to professors, scientists, and nurserymen all over Europe, but most importantly to John Fothergill in Eng. who reciprocated in trade with letters, books, a reflecting telescope, and, on Franklin's recommendation, a microscope and thermometer. *Arbustrum Americanum* was "the first truly indigenous botanical essay published in the Western Hemisphere" and was immensely popular in Europe (being translated into French within three years) but was ignored in America, selling only two copies in N.Y. the first two years.

Marshall's other major contribution began in 1785 when he appealed for a nationally sponsored natural-history exploring expedition to the West with William Bartram (q.v.) and his nephew and chief assistant, Dr. Moses Marshall. He declined an invitation to venture west of the Mississippi in May 1792, probably because of failing eyesight (a cataract operation the following year was only partially successful). It is possible that he discussed the need for an exploring expedition with Thomas Jefferson (q.v.) in mid-1792. At any rate, as one historian has asserted, the Lewis and Clark expedition of 1803-1804 was "almost in direct response to the Marshall proposal."

His first wife died in 1786, and Marshall married Margaret Minshall in 1788. He died on Nov. 5, 1801, and left no children. A West Chester park was established in his name in 1848, and a marker was erected at his home and arboretum by the Chester County Historical Society in 1913.

Critical Appraisal: Humphry Marshall's duodecimo volume of 174 pages— containing about 300 entries, a dedication to Benjamin Franklin, an index of Latin and popular names, and many blank double pages for notes, drawings, and leaf specimens—was the first botanical book on American trees and shrubs published in America (1785). Its purpose can best be ascertained from its full title: *Arbustrum Americanum: The American Grove, or An Alphabetical Catalogue of Forest Trees and Shrubs, Natives of the American United States, Arranged According to the Linaan System; Containing, the Particular Distinguishing Characters of Each Genus, with Plain, Simple and Familiar Descriptions of the Manner of Growth, Appearance, and c. of Their Several Species and Varieties; Also, Some Hints of Their Uses in Medicine, Dyes, and Domestic Oeconomy; Compiled from Actual Knowledge and Observation, and the Assistance of Botanical Authors.*

Marshall's equal emphasis on business, medicine, and science fulfilled the Quaker ideal of "useful knowledge." He often signed his name "Botanist and Seedsman," and the profitability of his science may be suggested by the fact that when the scarlet azalea was first introduced into London a single plant sold for forty pounds sterling. *Arbustrum* (more correctly, "arbustum") covers only trees and shrubs, but some evidence indicates he wrote a similar treatise no longer extant, on native herbaceous plants. All Marshall's writings, even his letters, show the traits of the technical writer—terseness, directness, exactness, and detail.

Besides this one book, Marshall was influential in five ways. His arboretum as a site for scientific study and practical application has been seen as the precursor of the land-grant college of a century later. His proposal for scientifically exploring the West gave impetus to the Lewis and Clark expedition. In 1851 one writer claimed that "no two men in this country ever contributed so much to the botanical treasures of England, nor anything like so much to the chief ornaments of her grounds" as did Marshall and his cousin John Bartram. These two men have also been perceived as progenitors of a direct two-century lineage of Pa. botanists as witnessed by the William Darlington biography of 1849 and the memorial exercises of 1913. Finally, his arboretum germinated others, perhaps most notably Longwood Gardens near the Brandywine Battlefield, which was founded in 1800 on Marshall's plan, renewed in the 1920s by Pierre S. Dupont, and remains open to the public today.

Suggested Readings: BDAS; DAB. *See also* W. Darlington, *Memorials of John Bartram and Humphry Marshall* (1849; prints Marshall's letters); Joseph Ewan, Introduction, *Arbustrum Americanum* (1967); *Exercises in Memory of Humphry Marshall and William Darlington* (1913); F. W. Pennell, "Humphry Marshall, Botanist," BFHA, 24 (Autumn 1935), 479-585.

Henry L. Golemba
Wayne State University

ALEXANDER MARTIN (1740-1807)

Works: *America, a Poem* (c. 1769); "An Inscription, Proposed for the Monument of General Wolfe, in Westminster Abbey" (1774); "Tribute to Gen.

Francis Nash" (1778); "On the Death of Governor Caswell" (w. 1789; pub. 1844); *A New Scene Interesting to the Citizens of the United States of America, Additional to the Historical Play of Columbus* (1798).

Biography: Eldest of five sons and two daughters of Hugh Martin, a Presbyterian minister who immigrated to America in 1721 from County Tyrone, Ire., Alexander Martin was born in Hunterdon County, N.J., and at age 16 graduated from the college at Princeton. Eventually, all five brothers moved south and achieved prominence. By 1771 Martin, a merchant and lawyer, was active in military and political affairs in the colony of N.C. He was a member of the Colonial Assembly in 1774 and 1775, at which time he was appointed an officer in the Continental Line. In 1777 at the Battle of Brandywine, he was colonel of a regiment when Francis Nash, its general, was killed. For six times beginning in 1779, Martin was elected to represent his county in the N.C. Senate. When Governor Thomas Burke (q.v.) was captured by the Tories in 1781, Martin, then speaker of the Senate, became acting governor, and the following year was elected to succeed Burke, the first of his five terms as governor of the state. In 1793-1799 he was a U.S. senator in Philadelphia, where he was a strong Federalist. Once more in 1804 and 1805, he served his county in the state Senate. About 1789 Martin moved to his Dan River plantation near the Va. line and there, affluent and hospitable, he entertained his long-time friend George Washington (q.v.) in 1791, and there he died Nov. 10, 1807. He was never married.

Critical Appraisal: Alexander Martin's verses doubtless are, as a historian wrote in 1851, "more patriotic than poetic." Yet to a dynamic, many-talented, deep-feeling man like Martin, the writing of poetry was no less instinctive than the planting of fields, the fighting of battles, and the governing of a state. He sang the praises of his country and eulogized his heroes in the manner acceptable during the male-dominated last decades of the eighteenth century.

His long poem *America*, considered by one authority to be his major work, is introduced by an Argument and embellished in the approved style of the period with "notes giving identifications and imitations." Martin's panegyric on Gen. James Wolfe was followed several years later by his lines on Francis Nash, with their opening couplet: "Genius of Freedom! Whither art thou fled? / While fields of Death thy sons undaunted tread." (The poem was included in the popular anthology *Wood-Notes; or, Carolina Carols: A Collection of North Carolina Poetry*, compiled in 1854 by Mary Bayard Clarke, and thus it became his best-known poem. Clarke wrote that Martin's lines were "copied from the original draft," which had been turned over to her by a friend.) When Governor Richard Caswell of N.C. died in 1789, the ever-ready Martin dashed off six eight-line stanzas and had them "transmitted to the family of the deceased." That his effusions were less highly regarded by others than by Martin himself may at least partially be due to lines such as the following on Caswell: "Let Carolina dales, / Her mountains and her vales / On Caswell's name reflect; / His memory respect." Martin's final attempt at poetry was written in Philadelphia during his residence in the city as a U.S. senator. A triumph of the 1797-1798 theater season was *Columbus: Or, A World Discovered* by the English dramatist Thomas Morton. So appealing was the play to Martin's patriotic sensibilities that he provided for it *A New Scene*. For the most part, it was a static declamation by "The Genius of America," who in over 200 lines of iambic pentameter prophesied those glories that would come to the continent Columbus had discovered: Freedom from "despotic Rule," heroes like Benjamin Franklin (q.v.) and Washington, and a District of Columbia honoring the discoverer.

Martin "was quite vain of his accomplishments" in poetry; this vanity, rather than an objective assessment of his work, can probably be blamed for the low status to which he has been assigned. One critic wrote that Martin, "eminent as soldier, patriot, statesman and scholar, thought that he was a poet. I regret to say that the deliberate judgment of posterity is that in this view he was mistaken." A more seasoned estimate would be that Martin was simply a politically active man who, like others of his age, took pride and pleasure in writing patriotic and occasional poems.

Suggested Readings: DAB; P. *See also* Beth G. Crabtree, *North Carolina Governors, 1585-1974, Brief Sketches* (1974), pp. 49-50; J. A. Leo Lemay, "A Note on the Canon of Alexander Martin," EAL, 7 (1972), 92; Robert Sobel and John Raimo, eds., *Biographical Directory of the Governors of the United States, 1789-1978*, 4 vols. (1978), III, 1111-1112; Richard Walser, "Alexander Martin, Poet," EAL, 6 (1971), 55-61 (reprints "Tribute... Nash").

Richard Walser
North Carolina State University at Raleigh

LUTHER MARTIN (1748-1826)

Works: *To the People of Maryland* (1779); *To the Public...Aug. 19, 1779* (1779); *To Robert Lemmon...Oct. 2, 1779* (1779); *Queries Addressed to Robert Lemmon...Oct. 22, 1779* (1779); *An Address to Robert Lemmon* (1779); *The Genuine Information* (1788); *Modern Gratitude* (1801; 1802).

Biography: Few leaders during the formative years of the U.S. had a more humble beginning and a more destitute end than Luther Martin, long-time attorney general of Md. A descendant of early New Eng. settlers who had moved south in 1666 for greater freedom, Martin was born near New Brunswick, N.J., in 1748, the third of nine children in a farming family. Through family sacrifices, especially by his two older brothers, Martin attended the College of New Jersey (now Princeton Univ.) from which he was graduated at the head of his class in 1766. He then studied law while teaching school in small communities on the Md. Eastern Shore. In 1772 he began to practice law in both Md. and Va., particularly in the counties of the Eastern Shore, where he was one of the first to advocate independence from G. B. With a rapidly growing legal practice, he was appointed attorney general of Md. in 1778, largely through the influence of Samuel Chase (q.v.).

Without giving up his private practice, Martin remained attorney general until 1805 and held the position again from 1818 to 1822. In his early years in this post, he was noted especially for his vigorous prosecutions of British sympathizers and abettors and soon became the best-known lawyer in the state. A relatively unimportant delegate to the Continental Congress in 1784, he became extremely significant as a delegate to the Constitutional Convention of 1787, where he was a leading advocate of small-states' rights. Away on business during the last weeks of the convention, he worked diligently, although unsuccessfully, against the ratification of the constitution in Md., fearing the rapid growth of the national government at the expense of state governments.

Although a vehement opponent of the Federalists at the convention, Martin later became a strong supporter of the Federalist administrations of George Washington (q.v.) and John Adams (q.v.), at least partially because of his long-standing political and personal feud with Thomas Jefferson (q.v.), who once called Martin "an unprincipled & impudent federal bull-dog." As a result of this feud and his reputation as the nation's most effective defense advocate, he was defense attorney in two of the nation's most famous political trials, successfully defending both Supreme Court Justice Samuel Chase against impeachment charges before the Senate in 1805 and Aaron Burr against treason charges in 1807. As Md.'s attorney general, he unsuccessfully argued the state's position in the famous *McCulloch* vs. *Maryland* case in 1819.

Throughout his career Martin had been noted for his profligate spending and his excessive drinking, but it was a paralytic stroke late in 1819, not profligacy or alcoholism, that ended his legal effectiveness. The stroke made him a mindless derelict until his death in 1826 in N.Y., where he had moved to be cared for in the house of Aaron Burr. Before this move, the Md. legislature, recognizing his past accomplishments and present poverty, enacted an annual license fee on all lawyers in the state to fund a personal pension for Martin, an act unparalleled in American history.

Critical Appraisal: Luther Martin entertained few serious literary pretensions; instead, his writings grew directly out of his many personal and political conflicts. Almost invariably, his writings were extremely partisan and vehement, sometimes even petty and vindictive. Many of his contemporaries complained of his prolixity, especially in his speeches, but this prolixity was often a by-product of his extraordinary thoroughness, his unusual memory for legal precedents, his ability to accumulate facts, and his keen understanding of legal theory and its application. Famous for his speeches (especially for one at Chase's trial) and often a writer of brief pamphlets and newspaper letters, he published only two book-length works, *The Genuine Information* and *Modern Gratitude*.

Martin's most significant writings appeared when he attempted to prevent Md. from ratifying the Constitution. Having been a delegate to the Constitutional Convention, he was called to give a report of the convention to the Md. General Assembly. This speech on Nov. 29, 1787, soon appeared serially in the *Maryland Gazette* and was expanded and printed separately early the next year as *The*

Genuine Information. Characterizing the convention as "a violent struggle," Martin meticulously reconstructed its rules, procedures, and arguments, even though he was violating the convention members' pledge of secrecy in doing so. From this basic information, he built his argument against ratification, appealing to diverse authorities such as moral principle, historical precedent, and the political theories of Montesquieu. He was especially thorough in describing the debates on proportional representation, which he strongly opposed. In his view, the national government should be a union of equal states, with the states retaining full jurisdiction over individuals. His greatest fear was that the proposed Constitution would produce "the utter extinction and abolition of all State governments." He also objected to a standing army, the great powers of the president, and the increase in the number and value of government offices. Not only a forceful statement against ratification—a kind of counterpoint to the famous writings of James Madison (q.v.), Alexander Hamilton (q.v.), and John Jay (q.v.)—*The Genuine Information* contains details about the convention that are found nowhere else and is the fullest account of the convention from the perspective of an opponent of ratification. In the separate publication of this work in 1788, Martin appended two other important and influential writings: an argument against a standing army and an argument on the necessity of a Bill of Rights. Although *The Genuine Information* did not prevent Md. from ratifying the Constitution, it remained an important minority report from the convention, a strong statement for states' rights that John C. Calhoun would later cite in his arguments for nullification.

During his career, Martin became involved in several heated exchanges of newspaper letters and pamphlets. The earliest of these controversies, with Robert Lemmon in 1779, was extremely petty, personal, and vindictive, but in 1788 Martin wrote a series of six letters in the *Maryland Journal* in which he stated his objections to the Constitution as forcefully as he had in *The Genuine Information* and more succinctly. These letters began as a personal defense of Elbridge Gerry (q.v.) and himself from the attacks of "The Landholder" (Oliver Ellsworth) in the *Connecticut Courant*, but in the last three letters, with appeals to logic, history, analogy, the Deity, Aesop, and his own character, Martin produced some of his most effective and eloquent, and least personal, writing. His main point was again that the proposed central government would be too powerful at the expense of states and individuals.

Although a vehement opponent of the Constitution, Martin admitted the weaknesses of the Articles of Confederation, which he had strongly supported a decade earlier in his pamphlet, *To the People of Maryland*. This early pamphlet shows a different side of Martin's argumentative abilities, for it is one of his few writings to advocate, rather than oppose. Emphasizing the compromises that had produced the proposed articles, he demonstrated the legal and logical benefits to Md. of joining the confederation and the dangers of not joining. He argued that failure to join would increase the probability of external violence and internal dissension. The ending of this pamphlet exhibits Martin's rhetorical eloquence, a quality his contemporaries often failed to recognize because of his reputed prolixity:

> Let us, then, my countrymen, hesitate not a moment longer to place ourselves as a link in the grand and golden chain of the continent. Let us put an end to every expectation of our enemies. Let us relieve the fears, and gratify the wishes of our friends, by immediately acceding to the confederacy, and thereby erect an empire, for the security of our liberty, freedom, and independence.

Martin's longest publication, *Modern Gratitude*, shows his most vindictive and petty side. Written in five parts, it is an extremely detailed condemnation of his son-in-law Richard Raynall Keene. After Martin had taken Keene into his family and office, Keene used the position to gain surreptitiously the affections of 14-year-old Eleonora Martin, against the expressed wishes of her father. Martin emphasized the rascality of Keene and the infancy of his daughter for over 100 pages, carefully detailing each step in his relations with Keene. Although clearly an insignificant work, *Modern Gratitude* demonstrates Martin's satiric abilities as well as his wide learning (he included, for example, references to Shakespeare, Milton, the Bible, Horace, Juvenal, Sterne, and Rousseau). The primary present value of this work is as a biographical source, for the fifth installment contains an extended autobiographical account of Martin's family background and early life up to 1778, an account he included to build his own credibility.

Taken as a whole, Martin's writings are as uneven and stormy as his life. At his best, however, he was a dedicated, forceful, learned, and eloquent writer. Particularly, as one of the earliest to call for a Bill of Rights to protect individual freedoms, he deserves a place in the roll of American political writers.

Suggested Readings: DAB; P. *See also* James M. Beck, *The Constitution of the United States* (1924), pp. 81-90, 186; Paul S. Clarkson and R. Samuel Jett, *Luther Martin of Maryland* (1970); Max Farrand, ed., *The Records of the Federal Convention of 1787*, 3 vols. (prints *The Genuine Information*, III, 172-232, and other pertinent records and letters; 1911); Paul Leicester Ford, ed., *Essays on the Constitution of the United States* (prints series of six letters from the *Maryland Journal* of 1788 in which Martin responded to attacks by Oliver Ellsworth; 1892); Hastings Lyon, *The Constitution and the Men Who Made It* (1936), pp. 71-72, 282; Clinton Rossiter, *1787: The Grand Convention* (1966), pp. 49, 115-116, 250, 326; Robert Allen Rutland, *The Ordeal of the Constitution* (1965), pp. 28-29, 149-158.

John S. Hardt
Ferrum College

BENJAMIN MARTYN (1699-1763)

Works: *Timoleon: A Tragedy* (1730); *Some Account of the Designs of the Trustees for Establishing the Colony of Georgia in America* and *A New and*

Accurate Account of the Provinces of South Carolina and Georgia (both sometimes attributed to James Oglethorpe; both 1732); *Reasons for Establishing the
Colony of Georgia* (two editions, the second including correspondence of Oglethorpe; both 1733); *The Life of A. A. Cooper, First Earl of Shaftesbury* (w. c.
1734; pub. 1836 as revised by A. Kippis and edited by G. W. Cooke); *An
Account Shewing the Progress of the Colony of Georgia* (1741); *An Impartial
Enquiry into the State and Utility of the Province of Georgia* (1741).

Biography: Born in Wiltshire, Eng., in 1699, Benjamin Martyn was the son
of a South Sea Company agent. The father died in Buenos Aires, in the New
World about which his son Benjamin would write but would never himself visit.
Educated at the Charterhouse, a famous "public school," Martyn found employ-
ment as an export examiner, but his real business with the world across the
Atlantic began in 1732 with his appointment as secretary to the Trustees for
Establishing the Colony of Ga. in America. During the next nine years, he
produced promotional tracts for the colony project.

Martyn, a bachelor who supported his mother and sisters lifelong, was a man
of considerable culture. A charter member of the Society for the Encouragement
of Learning, he counted Alexander Pope as his friend. Pope may even have had a
hand in *Timoleon*, a tragedy Martyn published in 1730. He also collaborated with
Pope and others to fund a Shakespeare monument in Westminster Abbey. Martyn
died in Kent, in 1763.

Critical Appraisal: Despite his belletristic aspirations, Benjamin Martyn
would be remembered today, if at all, as a poor playwright and a failed hack
were it not for his Ga. writings. *Timoleon* did please Martyn's friends, but it is
partly plagiarized and partly obscene, yet surprisingly dull. The plot, elaborated
from Plutarch, relates the adventures of Timoleon, who, while fighting to liber-
ate Syracuse from tyranny, saves his brother Timophanes in battle. The victory
won, however, Timophanes makes himself a tyrant and is assassinated by Timoleon's
cohorts as Timoleon helplessly looks on.

Martyn also wrote a prologue for a performance of *Julius Caesar* staged in
1738 to raise money for the Shakespeare monument. A biography of the first earl
of Shaftesbury, commissioned in 1734, was so botched that it was printed only
after many revisions by other hands long after Martyn's death.

In 1732 King George II chartered the trustees to plant the colony of Ga.
Almost immediately, the trustees began a vigorous promotional campaign aimed
at Parliament and private investors. Secretary Martyn wrote probably five excellent pamphlets, which may be divided into two groups: the three promotion tracts
of 1732-1733 and the two defensive tracts written in 1741, when the trustees
came under fire for mismanagement of the project.

The works of the first group propose six basic reasons for establishing the
colony. Georgia will act as a buffer between British S.C. and the French and
Spanish settlements to the south and west; produce valuable exports, especially
silk; be a market for English exports; provide insolvent Britons with work and
land; be a haven for persecuted Continental Protestants; and furnish Indians ripe

for conversion to Christianity. *Some Account of the Designs of the Trustees*, sumptuously printed in 1732, is a brief and stirring advertisement. *A New and Accurate Account of the Provinces of South Carolina and Georgia*, published later the same year, develops the six arguments mentioned above, rehearses the history of Carolina colonization, and provides an unabashedly Edenic vision of Ga. drawn mainly from John Archdale's *New Description of That Fertile and Pleasant Province of Carolina* (1707) and from *Description Abregee de l'Etat Present Caroline Meridionale* (c. 1730) by Jean Pierre Purry. The *Account* is seductive rather than "accurate," describing, for example, the fruit of Ga. as "so delicious, that whoever tastes [it] will despise the insipid watry Taste of [what] we have in *England*." The climate, neither too hot nor too cold, is "Antedeluvian"; indeed, Martyn implied that the lifespan of a Georgian might approach that of an Old Testament patriarch, perhaps 300 years. Dysentery, to which newcomers are subject, is a mere "Seasoning" process. Indians, although inconvenient, war among themselves and lack husbandry, so may be expected to die off within a century—especially under the additional influence of two European imports, rum and smallpox.

These two pamphlets, sometimes attributed to James Edward Oglethorpe (q.v.), are almost certainly the work of Martyn. The pamphlet of the following year, *Reasons for Establishing the Colony of Georgia*, went through two editions and bears Martyn's name on the 2nd. Although the argument is identical to that of the first two pamphlets, the rhetoric is far less fanciful. With an eye toward Parliament, the 1733 work is a painstaking exercise in persuasion. Martyn played upon joint motives of profit and philanthropy with a virtuosity anticipating Benjamin Franklin (q.v.), uniting commerce and conscience in a peroration hailing the impending "Perfection of Man's Happiness." Venturing into utopianism, but never quite leaving the realm of quotidian possibility, *Reasons* is colonial promotion at its most persuasive and eloquent.

Within two years after the first of the trustees' ships landed in Ga., dissatisfaction with the conduct of the colony was becoming increasingly evident. By 1739 Ga. was the butt of almost casual ridicule, and in 1741 Patrick Tailfer (q.v.), a Savannah physician, and others published *A True and Historical Narrative of the Colony of Georgia in America*, a savage, distressingly influential satire. Tailfer's chief complaints concerned unhealthy climate and barren soil, the difficulty of raising and transporting produce, restrictive land-grant and tenure policies, and the prohibition of black slavery. Martyn immediately answered these complaints in two pieces of what might be called defensive promotion, *An Impartial Enquiry into the State and Utility of the Province of Georgia* and *An Account Shewing the Progress of the Colony of Georgia*. The first concentrates on present conditions, explaining that difficulties must be expected in establishing a colony of "low and necessitous people." If Georgia is unhealthy, it is chiefly because of the illegal importation of rum, which threatens to poison an Eden capable of producing "a beautiful large Grape, as big as a Man's Thumb." The pamphlet also contains an illuminating discussion of slavery. The second work, the bitter tone of which

eclipses Tailfer's sarcasm, is a detailed and convincing historical vindication of
the Ga. project, a useful narrative of the colony from inception to the time of
trouble. It is replete with first-hand accounts of commercial, social, and political
conditions. Both of these defensive pamphlets, written in Eng., should be compared with the journal William Stephens (q.v.) wrote in Ga. as an investigative
agent for the trustees.

   Suggested Readings: DNB. *See also* Verner W. Crane, "The Promotion Literature of Georgia" in *Bibliographical Essays: A Tribute to Wilberforce Eames* (1924), pp.
281-298; Richard Beale Davis, *Intellectual Life in the Colonial South, 1585-1763* (1978),
I, 59-65; *A General Dictionary, Historical and Critical* (prints Martyn's prologue to
Julius Caesar; 1739), IX, 189; John Genest, *Some Account of the English Stage* (1832),
III, 252-254; Hugh T. Lefler, "Promotional Literature of the Southern Colonies," JSH, 33
(1967), 3-25; Trevor R. Reese, "Benjamin Martyn, Secretary to the Georgia Trustees,"
GHQ, 38 (1954), 142-147; idem, *The Clamorous Malcontents* (1973); idem, *The Most
Delightful Country of the Universe*. (The last two volumes reprint the five pamphlets and
provide valuable introductions; 1972.)

Alan Axelrod
Furman University

GEORGE MASON (1725-1792)

   Works: Robert A. Rutland, ed., *The Papers of George Mason, 1725-1792*,
3 vols. (1971).

   Biography: George Mason, fourth of the name and line to live along the
Upper Potomac shores, was descended from Cavalier immigrants of the 1650s.
With the single exception of his journey to Philadelphia in the summer of 1787, a
triangle with points on Washington (the ferry that connected Georgetown with
Va. via the island that now memorializes Theodore Roosevelt was Mason property), Williamsburg, and Richmond marks the boundaries of his life. An intensely private person, he was active manager of his 5,000-acre plantation Gunston
Hall, nine miles below Mount Vernon, and the responsible parent of the nine
children left motherless on the death of his wife, Ann Eilbeck Mason, in 1773.
(Contrary to the custom of the period, he did not remarry promptly; Sarah Brent
became his second wife in 1780.) Yet from the beginning of the Stamp Act
controversy in the mid-1760s to the ratification of the first amendments to the
U.S. Constitution, Mason was a continual contributor to the development of
American political ideas until his death in 1792.

   Critical Appraisal: George Mason's writings do not appear under his
own name. They were prepared for consideration by political bodies ranging
from his county Committee of Safety to the colonial and later the state legislature
to the Philadelphia convention of 1787. Correspondence and notes of his colleagues indicate his vigorous participation as a draftsman of documents adopted
by these bodies, particularly the Va. Declaration of Rights of 1776, but his

authorship is always obscured by appearing as the work of a deliberative group. His own signature is confined to his considerable correspondence and his statement of objections to the Constitution. For that reason, it is necessary to turn to the events of his active years, rather than to publications, to understand his thought.

Many of the principles later enlarged in documents of state and nation were foreshadowed in the Fairfax Resolves, drafted by Mason and adopted by citizens of his home county under the chairmanship of George Washington (q.v.) in mid-summer 1774. The two men were constant collaborators from the opening of the crisis until Aug. 1775, when Mason declined membership in the Va. delegation to the Continental Congress on the grounds of his family responsibilities, and Washington set forth for Philadelphia, there to be named commander of the American forces and to be absent from Mount Vernon for the next six years.

As the break with Eng. became imminent, Mason served in the colonial legislature and then on the Revolutionary Committee of Safety. In 1776, as a member of the state convention in Williamsburg, he drafted the first Declaration of Rights to be published on the American continent, a document adopted with minimum change and thereafter widely copied by other states up and down the coast. He was likewise active in the making of the Va. Constitution, inaugurating the sequence of written constitutions that was a new feature of the political structure of the Western world.

Although not an attorney, he served as an initial member of the Committee of Law Revisors that under Thomas Jefferson's (q.v.) chairmanship proposed a wide range of innovations for the state; his expertise in land law had been especially desired because of his lifelong interest in Va.'s western lands reaching to the Mississippi. When George Rogers Clark (q.v.) undertook the conquest of the Northwest Territory in 1778, Mason was one of the three legislators—George Wythe, the current speaker, and Jefferson were the others—to whom the project was confided.

Through the Revolution, he struggled with the difficulties of obtaining men and supplies for the army and with the chaos of the Confederation's finances. By the time the war ended, he was acutely aware of the insufficiencies of the central government: he became a participant in the Mount Vernon Convention of 1785 from which grew the Annapolis meeting of the next year and the full-scale Constitutional Convention of 1787.

Mason went to Philadelphia as a member of the seven-man delegation whose "Virginia Plan" became the convention's agenda. James Madison's (q.v.) notes demonstrate the frequency with which he spoke in debates; he was the Va. member of the special committee that broke the deadlock between the large and the small states by recognizing the former in the composition of the House of Representatives and the latter in that of the Senate. Not only his ideas but some of the language that he offered became part of the final document—his wording on the impeachment of the president among them.

But the compromise by which the New Eng. states and the Deep South traded recognition of a special interest in slavery for recognition of a special interest in trade regulations revolted Mason—his first public paper had begun with a castigation of the slave trade. When he proved unable to secure the inclusion of a bill of rights in the proposed Constitution, he declined to sign the document.

During the ratification process, his "Objections" were cited by the opposition up and down the coast; with Patrick Henry, he led the proponents of further revision of the document at the Va. ratifying convention of 1788. Va. was among the states that appended to their ratifications a list of proposals for revision by the first Congress under the new government; accordingly, in 1778 Congressman Madison drafted a declaration of rights for circulation to the states, and Va.'s ratification in 1791 put the first eight amendments to the Constitution into force. So before his death the next year, Mason had seen the ideas of his major state paper included in the nation's basic document.

Suggested Readings: DAB. *See also* Pamela C. Copeland and Richard K. MacMaster, *The Five George Masons, Patriots and Planters of Virginia and Maryland* (1975); *Debates and Other Proceedings of the* [1788] *Convention in Virginia* (1805); Max Farrand, ed., *The Records of the Federal Convention of 1787*, 4 vols. (1911-1937); Hugh Blair Grigsby, *The Virginia Convention of 1776* (1855); idem, *The Virginia Ratifying Convention of 1788*, 2 vols. (1890-1891); Jay B. Hubbell, *The South in American Literature, 1607-1900* (1954); Helen Hill Miller, *George Mason, Gentleman Revolutionary* (1975); Kate Mason Rowland, *The Life of George Mason, 1735-1792, Including His Speeches, Public Papers and Correspondence; with an introduction by General Fitzhugh Lee*, 2 vols. (1892); Robert A. Rutland, *The Birth of the Bill of Rights, 1776-1791* (1955); idem, *George Mason, Reluctant Statesman, with a foreword by Dumas Malone* (1961).

Helen Hill Miller
College of William and Mary

JOHN MASON (c. 1600-1672)

Works: *A Brief History of the Pequot War* (1736)—first published by Increase Mather in *A Relation of the Troubles Which Have Hapned in New-England by Reason of the Indians There* (1677), pp. 24-43.

Biography: Not to be confused with the more famous John Mason who colonized N.H. and may have been his relation, John Mason was born in Eng. sometime around 1600. An experienced soldier who had trained in the Netherlands under the celebrated Sir Thomas Fairfax during the Dutch conflicts, Mason had, by early 1633, immigrated to Mass., where he served for a time as captain of the Dorchester militia. In 1635 Mason left Mass. to become one of the founders of Windsor, Conn. After John Endecott's unsuccessful attempt to crush the Pequot Indians provoked that tribe into attacking English settlements along the Connecticut River, the General Court of Connecticut placed Mason in command of some eighty English soldiers with orders to destroy the Pequot strongholds on the Mystic and Pequot Rivers.

Joining forces at Saybrook Fort with Capt. John Underhill (q.v.) from Mass., Mason decided to disobey his instructions to attack the main Pequot fort on the Pequot River by sea and instead chose to lead an overland assault on a lesser Pequot fort at Mystic, where several hundred Indians were encamped. Advancing toward the fort, Mason's troops, along with a large contingent of Narragansett and Mohegan allies, attacked the Pequots shortly before dawn on May 26, 1637. Shouting that "We must burn them," Mason personally threw a firebrand into the Pequot encampment and thus forced the frightened Indians, totally surprised by the assault, to flee for safety. As they ran through the doors of their fort, all but a handful of the Pequots, women and children included, were mercilessly slaughtered by Mason's troops, who had formed a circle around the fort through which the Indians could not escape. In little more than thirty minutes, the ground was covered with corpses. It has been estimated that as many as seven hundred Pequots perished during the massacre. Only twenty-two Englishmen were killed or wounded. Their confidence broken, the remaining Pequots were soon tracked down and either murdered or sold into bondage. As a result of Mason's military maneuvering, the Pequot tribe in effect ceased to exist.

Despite the fact that he had quite consciously disobeyed orders by making an overland attack on the lesser of the Pequot forts, Mason was celebrated as a hero. Putting aside their differences of opinion with Conn., William Bradford (q.v.), John Winthrop (q.v.), and even Roger Williams (q.v.) applauded his actions, and he was later promoted to the rank of a major. For much of the remainder of his life, Mason served as head of military affairs for Conn., and between 1637 and his death on Jan. 30, 1672, he held high offices in the state's government, including those of magistrate and deputy governor. During the final years of his life, Mason lived in Norwich, which, like Windsor, he had helped to found. He was twice married, and he was the father of many children, seven of whom survived him.

Critical Appraisal: John Mason's *A Brief History of the Pequot War* is generally considered the most reliable and most readable of the four contemporary accounts of the conflict. Written some nineteen years after the events it describes, Mason's *Brief History* was recorded at the request of the General Court of Connecticut, which felt that "History *most properly is a Declaration of Things that are done by those that were present at the doing of them.*" After Mason's death in 1672, the manuscript of the *Brief History* came into the possession of John Allyn, the *"Secretary of Connecticut Colony,"* who in turn gave it to Increase Mather (q.v.), that indefatigable collector of "special providences" relating to the history of New Eng. It was not until 1677, however, when Mather included an abridged version of the narrative, which he mistakenly attributed to Allyn, in his *Relation of the Troubles Which Have Hapned in New-England by Reason of the Indians There*, that Mason's story was finally published, and it was not until 1736, when Thomas Prince (q.v.) published the narrative separately under the title *A Brief History of the Pequot War*, that Mason's authorship was fully established and his narrative published in its entirety. The other three seventeenth-century accounts of the war were John Underhill's *Newes from America* (1638), Philip Vincent's (q.v.) *A True Relation of the Late Battell Fought in New-England* (1638), and Lion Gardiner's (q.v.) "Relation of the Pequot Warres," which remained unpublished until the early nineteenth century, when it was printed by the Massachusetts Historical Society.

At the time when Mason wrote his *Brief History*, he probably did not intend it for publication, and it was very likely at his insistence that it remained in manuscript until well after his death. In a note "to the Judicious Reader," Mason comments that if he "*had thought that this* [his narrative] *should have come to the Press*," he would "*have endeavoured to have put a little more Varnish upon it.*" His intention in writing his *Brief History*, Mason states, was a simple one:

> *that so at least some small Glimmering may be left to* Posterity *what Difficulties and Obstructions their* Forefathers *met within their first settling these desart Parts of* America; *how* God *was pleased to prove them, and how by his wise Providence he ordered and disposed all their Occasions and Affairs for them in regard to both their* Civils *and* Ecclesiasticals.

It is precisely, however, because Mason wrote his *History* without excessive rhetorical "*Varnish*," leaving it, as he claimed, "*rude and impolish'd*," that it has for more than two centuries remained one of the most popular and influential examples of Puritan historiography relating to the Indian wars of the seventeenth century. Intending for his "*Discourse*" to be "*both Plain and Easy*," Mason wrote his *History* less "*to stir up the Affections of Men*" than "*to declare in Truth and Plainness the Actions and Doings of Men.*" Accordingly, Mason's method of organizing his recollections was clear and direct: "*I shall therefore set down Matters in order as they Began and were carried on and Issued; that I may not deceive the Reader in confounding of Things.*" "*When the Bones are separated from a living Creature*," explains Mason, "*it becomes unserviceable: So a History, if you take away Order and Truth, the rest will prove to be but a vain Narration.*" Adhering to these principles of organization and rhetoric, Mason begins his *History* with an account of the events leading up to the Pequot War, proceeds to a narration of the war itself, and concludes wih a discussion of the return of the soldiers to the safety of their homes.

Like many of his Puritan contemporaries, Mason viewed the war with the Pequots in providential terms. Within the context of Mason's cosmology, the war "*was the* Lord's Doings." Because the Pequots had, in Mason's opinion, grown "cruel," "warlike," and "malicious" in their dealings with the English, whom Mason erroneously insisted "had never offered them the least Wrong," God "*was pleased to smite*" the Indians "*in the hinder Parts, and to give us* [the English] *their Land for an Inheritance.*" Combining the bluntness of a soldier with the zeal of a Puritan, Mason is perhaps most successful as a writer when he dramatizes for his readers the climactic moment of the war, the point at which the Indians fled from their fort only to be butchered at the hands of the British: "And indeed such a dreadful Terror did the Almighty let fall upon their Spirits, that they would fly from us and run into the very Flames, where many of them perished." Those Indians who escaped the flames, states Mason, "perished by the Sword," and the Lord thereby brought *"the Mischief they plotted, and the Violence they offered and exercised, upon their own Heads in a Moment; burning them up in the Fire of his Wrath, and dunging the Ground with their Flesh."* It was, continues Mason, a *"wonderful"* moment, *"marvellous in our Eyes,"* and worthy *"to be remembred "* as an example of *"How the Face of God is set against them that do Evil."*

Although subsequent Puritan historians such as William Hubbard (q.v.) and Cotton Mather (q.v.) turned to Mason's *History* as an important source of information about the Pequot War, it should be noted that during the twentieth century Mason's motives for writing have become suspect. Disturbed by the excessive glee with which Mason gloats over the annihilation of his "Enemies," modern historians have called into question the accuracy of the *History*. It has been suggested, for example, that there were far fewer Indians at the "Mistick-Fight" than the *"six* or *seven Hundred "* that Mason would have us believe there were, that the majority of the Indians in the fort were old men, women, and children who were unable to defend themselves, and, perhaps most damagingly, that Mason decided to attack the lesser encampment, rather than the greater one, because he feared open confrontation with an enemy stronger and superior to himself. Whatever the facts might be, Mason's *Brief History* remains a major document in the history of the Pequot War and the literature of seventeenth-century New England. As Moses Coit Tyler has pointed out, it possesses "all the charm of authenticity and strength" and is "a plain but vigorous narrative of a very plain and very vigorous campaign."

Suggested Readings: DAB; DNB; T$_1$. *See also* George D. Ellis, "Life of John Mason," in *The Library of American Biography*, ed. by Jared Sparks, 2nd ser. (1855), III, 204-428; Francis Jennings, *The Invasion of America: Indians, Colonialism, and the Cant of Conquest* (1975), pp. 186-227; Louis Bond Mason, *The Life of Major John Mason of Connecticut* (1935); Richard Slotkin, *Regeneration Through Violence: The Mythology of the American Frontier, 1600-1860* (1973), pp. 92, 184-188, 208-209, 221, 279, 295; Alden T. Vaughan, "From White Man to Redskin: Changing Anglo-American Perceptions of the American Indians," AHR, 87 (1982), 917-953; idem, *The New England Frontier: Puritans and Indians, 1620-1675* (1965), pp. 138-154; idem, "Pequots and Puritans: The Causes of the War of 1637," WMQ, 3rd ser., 21 (1964), 256-269; idem, "A Test of Puritan Justice," NEQ, 38 (1965), 331-339; Wilcomb E. Washburn, "The Moral and Legal Justifications for Dispossessing the Indians," in *Seventeenth-Century America: Essays in Colonial History*, ed. by James Morton Smith, (1959) pp. 15-32.

James A. Levernier
University of Arkansas at Little Rock

AZARIAH MATHER (1685-1737)

Works: *Wo to Sleepy Sinners* (1720); *None but Christ* (1722); *Good Rulers a Choice Blessing* (1725); *The Gospel-Minister Described* (1725); *The Sabbath-*

Day's Rest Asserted, Explained, Proved, and Applied (1725); *A Gospel Star, or Faithful Minister* (1730); *A Discourse Concerning...Rev. Moses Noyes* (1731).

Biography: Azariah Mather was born on Aug. 29, 1685, at Windsor, Conn. His father was the Rev. Samuel Mather, an original trustee of Yale College, minister of Windsor, and first cousin of Cotton Mather (q.v.), and his mother was Hannah Treat, daughter of Governor Robert and Jane (Tapp) Treat. He received an A.B. from Yale College in 1705 and afterwards studied divinity under his father. In 1709 he accepted a tutorship in the College at Saybrook (now Old Saybrook), which led to an invitation to succeed the recently deceased Thomas Buckingham (q.v.) as pastor of the First Church there. Mather accepted the invitation on Jun. 13, 1710, and was ordained at the church on Nov. 22, 1710. For the next two decades, he served his congregation and community with distinction as indicated by the request of the Conn. General Assembly that he preach the election sermon for 1725 and by one account of his career that claimed, "As a linguist he greatly excelled, and was an able preacher." A charge of irregular conduct was raised against Mather in 1732, and he was dismissed from his pulpit by a council in Jun. of that year. Survived by Martha Taylor to whom he was married in 1710, Mather died at Saybrook on Feb. 11, 1737. His tombstone inscription describes him as "a faithfull minister, a generall scholar, an eminent Christian, a very great sufferer, but now in glory a triumpher."

Critical Appraisal: In 1783 a successor to Azariah Mather described him as "a very pungent preacher, and fearless reprover." The validity of that characterization is easily established by a review of Mather's printed works, all of which are sermons. Although few, Mather's sermons were preached on a variety of occasions. There are two lecture sermons, two ordination sermons, one sermon preached to a religious society, one funeral sermon, and one election sermon. In all we find repeated the sermonic themes and subjects typically developed by the leading defenders of New Eng. orthodoxy during the late seventeenth and early eighteenth centuries, and we also find the Jeremiah persona through which these defenders of orthodoxy harangued against New Eng.'s backsliding during that time. Thus, in *The Gospel-Minister Described* and *A Gospel Star*, the two ordination sermons, Mather restated an old theme when he argued that ministers are, really, God's "watchmen," guiding the remnants of his chosen people. In *The Sabbath-Day's Rest Asserted*, which was preached, appropriately, out of Exodus 35:2, Mather denounced the abuse under which Sabbath rites had fallen, and he provided, as some have said, a local tinge to his thoughts by speaking against "Unnecessary Sailing" and "Unnecessary Folding...of Sheep" on the Sabbath. Supporting Mather's defense of traditional New Eng. ways was "An Attestation" by Cotton Mather that prefaced the printed version of the sermon.

However, for both its occasion and its style, *Good Rulers a Choice Blessing* is the most noteworthy of Mather's works. Preached during election-day observances on May 13, 1725, the sermon, as its title suggests, develops a favorite theme among New Eng. election preachers of this period. Mather's tone toward his subject and his audience is calm, in fact, fatherly, during the text and doctrine sections of the sermon. There he outlined the qualities of the good ruler, and he took notice of the privilege enjoyed "where People have the Liberty of Choosing their Rulers...as this Colony is Favoured with" and of the calamity caused a people by either bad rulers or the loss by death of good rulers. Then as he moved to the applications, Mather dramatically shifted in both his tone and his point of view. In the applications, his tone is that of Jeremiah warning the rulers against the ignorance and sinfulness of those they rule. For instance, Mather said to the officials gathered before him: "The People over whom you Rule are...Giddy and Head-strong, and a levelling Spirit prevails [among them]." What is needed now, he told them, is "Reformation-work." "Oh! that it might ly with due weight upon you," he exclaimed. Along with instigating reform, Mather challenged the officials to "Sharpen the Sword of Justice" and to establish a better-than-present rapport between themselves and the ministry, a rapport typified by that "between *Moses* and *Aaron*." In a jeremiad voice reminiscent of that used by Increase Mather (q.v.), the younger Thomas Shepard (q.v.), Samuel Torrey (q.v.), and others during the 1670s and 1680s, Mather addressed the people of Conn. thus at the end of the sermon: "*Be much upon your Knees, Seeking to that God by whom Princes Rule, and Plead hard for our Rulers, that God would set up and Continue such to Rule...that shall be rich Blessing to our Land,*" and, he added, "Obey CHRIST in the Government of His Grace, or you'll be found at Last among the Number...in that Awful Place." Mather's only significant departures from these subjects in this portion of the sermon are a lengthy tribute to Governor Saltonstall, who had died during the previous year, and a bid for higher salaries for ministers.

History records that as New Eng. moved on into the eighteenth century, the warnings of Mather and his ministerial colleagues were increasingly ignored as the old New Eng. way merged almost imperceptibly with the ways of worldly cosmopolitanism. But that fact does not diminish the historical significance of figures such as Azariah Mather or the quality of sermons such as *Good Rulers a Choice Blessing*.

Suggested Readings: CCNE; Dexter (I, 33-35).

Ronald A. Bosco
State University of New York at Albany

COTTON MATHER (1663-1728)

Works: *Memorable Providences Relating to Witchcrafts and Possessions* (1689); *The Wonderful Works of God Commemorated* (1690); *The Wonders of the Invisible World* (1693); *Magnalia Christi Americana* (1701); *The Negro Christianized* (1706); *Bonifacius: An Essay upon the Good* (1710); *Psalterium Americanum: The Book of Psalms, in a Translation Exactly Conformed unto the Original, but All in Blank Verse* (1718); *The Christian Philosopher* (1721); *The*

Angel of Bethesda (1724); *Parentator. Memoirs of Remarkables in the Life and the Death of the Ever-Memorable Dr. Increase Mather* (1724); *Manuductio ad Ministerium* (1726); *Agricola, or The Religious Husbandman* (1727); *Diary of Cotton Mather* (1911-1912). See also Thomas J. Holmes, *Cotton Mather: A Bibliography of His Works*, 3 vols. (1940).

Biography: Cotton Mather was born in Boston on Feb. 12, 1663, the eldest child of Increase Mather (q.v.) and Maria Mather, who was also the daughter of John Cotton (q.v.). He graduated from Harvard College and lived out his life in the Boston area, always in the shadow of his then more illustrious father, with whom he shared the pulpit of the Old North Church. Unlike his father, he was never to be chosen president of Harvard, a post he would have liked, but his reputation today exceeds that of his father, perhaps because he wrote voluminously, completing some 445 printed works during his lifetime, and leaving large volumes of extensive work in manuscript, such as the "Biblia Americana." Although all of the Mathers are unfortunately identified with a false image of New Eng. Puritanism and its harsher doctrines, Increase and Cotton Mather were unusually enlightened colonists and were responsible for the acceptance of smallpox vaccination in New Eng. when it was introduced in the early eighteenth century. Moreover, Cotton Mather was married three times, like John Milton, and was the father of a large family of children, most of whom he buried as a result of loss to disease or tragedy. He was visited during his life by Benjamin Franklin (q.v.) and was considered a leading intellectual in New Eng., Old Eng., and on the Continent. The year 1713 offers a microcosm of his varied and strained existence. In that year alone, he was elected a fellow of the Royal Society of London and became father to his tenth and eleventh children, the twins Martha and Eleazar, who were born on Oct. 30. However, his losses were equally great. During an epidemic of measles his second wife, Elizabeth, died Nov. 9; the twin Eleazar died at midnight, Nov. 18; Martha followed on Nov. 20; and another child, Jerusha, died on Nov. 21. The extraordinary strength of character required to sustain such losses is reflected in Mather's *Diary*, where the details of his daily life are less important than the faith and purpose that sustained him throughout his life of hard work, spiritual leadership, and dedication to the sense that he was predestined for an important role in the evolution of the New English Israel. In 1702 he had the pleasure of seeing his *Magnalia Christi Americana* published in London. This ecclesiastical history of the New Eng. settlements contained not only accounts of Harvard College and of the settlements, but also presented biographies of the leading personages so that now the settlers had a comprehensive guide to their enterprise viewed retrospectively. His *Pietas in Patrem: The Life of His Excellency Sir William Phips*, originally published in 1697, was reprinted in this volume with many others.

Mather's life may be measured in authorship and published works, as the day-to-day political life of the Massachusetts Bay Colony was more effectively in the hands of his father, who predeceased him by only five years. For example, when William Phips and Increase Mather were brought into the Salem witchcraft controversy in 1692, Cotton Mather engaged the situation more intellectually than politically, publishing *Wonders of the Invisible World* in 1693 and *Cases of Conscience*, which while warning the world of the dangers of judging too hastily and condemning witches without sufficient evidence nevertheless reflected Mather's consistent belief that the authorities should be allowed to deal with the very real presence of witchcraft.

In some respects, Cotton Mather's life may be viewed as tragic. He never achieved the personal satisfaction of rising to the political and social positions held by his father. His *Diary* is a record of the anguish he felt because he was insecure in his religious commitment and tormented by temptation; the record of his marriages and the deaths of his children show a pattern of testing known only to the biblical Job. Through his writings, he preserved the record of a strong, central faith and the chronicle of his earthly pilgrimage. In 1727 he became seriously ill toward the end of the year, and he died on Feb. 13, 1728. He is buried in the family tomb at Copps' Hill, Boston.

Critical Appraisal: Cotton Mather's writing is so varied and extensive that a brief summary hardly does it justice. He wrote and analyzed poetry (*Psalterium Americanum*); developed new methods for writing history and biography (*Magnalia Christi Americana* and *Parentator*); he was at the forefront of some of the important scientific movements of his time and was elected a fellow of the Royal Society of London, primarily for these achievements (*The Angel of Bethesda*); he authored numerous pieces reflecting the developments in the moral theology of his time (*Bonifacius*); and he was actively attempting to reconcile the theological structures inherited from the seventeenth century with the discoveries of nature embraced by new thinkers in the eighteenth century (*The Christian Philosopher: A Collection of the Best Discoveries in Nature, with Religious Improvements*). Some of his unpublished writing, such as the monumental "Biblia Americana," which is a manuscript translation of the entire Bible with extensive annotations and other exegetical apparatus, shows the deep commitment he had to discovering truth in whatever form he found it, whether it be in the revelation of God through the natural world or in the obvious and complex manifestations revealed in Scripture. Cotton Mather was a man of enormous intellectual power; his association with the rigid and harsh doctrines of Puritanism often obscures the sheer strength of his mind and the range of his intellectual capabilities. But his writings reveal both. Modern students neglect Cotton Mather's writing because his style is often wooden and his approach to matters humorless and directed. But his analytical skills were keen, and his contributions to literature, theology, history, and the writing of the age in a variety of genres is unquestioned. The essays recommended below make clear these achievements.

Suggested Readings: BDAS; CCNE; DAB; DARB; DNB; FCNEV; LHUS; Sibley-Shipton (III, 6-158); Sprague (I, 189-195); T_1. *See also* Otho T. Beall and Richard Shryock, *Cotton Mather, First Significant Figure in American Medicine* (1954); Sacvan Bercovitch, "Cotton Mather" in *Major Writers of Early American Literature*, ed. Everett Emerson (1972), pp. 93-149; Peter Gay, *A Loss of Mastery: Puritan Historians in Colo-*

nial America (1966); Babette Levy, *Cotton Mather* (1979); Mason I. Lowance, "Cotton Mather's *Magnalia* and the Metaphors of Biblical History" in *The Language of Canaan: Metaphor and Symbol in New England Writing from the Puritans to the Transcendentalists* (1980); Robert Middlekauf, *The Mathers: Three Generations of Puritan Intellectuals, 1596-1728* (1971); Perry Miller, *The New England Mind: From Colony to Province* (1953); Larzer Ziff, *Puritanism in America: New Culture in a New World* (1973).

Mason I. Lowance
University of Massachusetts, Amherst

ELEAZER MATHER (1637-1669)

Works: *A Serious Exhortation* (1671).

Biography: Eleazer Mather is one of the least known members of seventeenth-century New Eng.'s most distinguished ministerial family. Born in Dorchester, Mass., in 1637 where his father Richard Mather (q.v.) served as pastor, Eleazer entered Harvard College with his younger brother Increase Mather (q.v.), graduating in 1656. Two years later, Eleazer agreed to go to the small frontier settlement of Northampton, Mass., where he would spend the rest of his life in a sometimes stormy ministry. Mather moved to the town in 1658 only after the residents agreed to allow him to bring some families from Dorchester and to give him a grant of good land. In 1661 he formally organized a church drawn largely from the Dorchester group. Opposition to Mather always existed in the town and grew when he opposed the Half-Way Covenant in the 1660s. When he died in 1669, Mather left a church and town divided on the question of church membership and the handling of the young. These questions were the subjects of his last sermons and only printed work.

Critical Appraisal: Eleazer Mather's *A Serious Exhortation* is an excellent example of what became a common type of sermon in the latter half of the seventeenth century in New Eng. Mather's subject was the apparent decline in piety from one generation to another, a charge that was often made by second-generation ministers. The Northampton pastor perceived God leaving his people and prayed that the people would come to their senses and ask the Lord to pour his grace on New Eng.'s children as he had on their fathers. The signs of the Lord's forsaking the colonists enumerated by Mather were typical of those listed by others: the colonists seem to be little interested in searching their souls for God's grace; the leading men of New Eng. are dying off; men are more concerned with material gain than religion; divisions plague the churches; and people appear unaffected by sermons and other religious exercises.

Significantly, Mather directed most of the sermon at the older generation; that group needed to understand its responsibilities and failings. The minister reminded the older generation that God had often aided them and that he gave them a special opportunity to raise a holy people to live after them. In noting that the younger generation had not had to suffer the persecution and afflictions of the founders of New Eng., Mather made those sufferings appear as blessings. Members of the founding generation had had opportunities to search their hearts such as their children did not enjoy. In rather blunt language, Mather blamed the sins of the young on the bad example set by the elders. There was little hope for the rising generation until the fathers reformed themselves and performed the duties required of them as loving patriarchs.

A *Serious Exhortation* is a composite of several of Mather's sermons and was edited by his brother. In this process, some of the literary refinements may have been deleted. What remains is a tract structured in the usual Puritan form of text, doctrine, reasons, and uses. Mather's use of direct language makes it a readable sermon but one without striking metaphors, except for his comparing the younger generation to a ship in distress.

Suggested Readings: CCNE; Sibley-Shipton (I, 405-409); Sprague (I, 159-160). *See also* Emory Elliott, *Power and the Pulpit in Puritan New England* (1975), pp. 103-105, 138-140; Paul R. Lucas, *Valley of Discord* (1976), pp. 83-85, 112-114; Robert Pope, *The Half-Way Covenant* (1969), pp. 51-52, 147-150.

Timothy J. Sehr
Indiana University Archives

INCREASE MATHER (1639-1723)

Works: *The Mystery of Israel's Salvation* (1669); *The Life and Death of...Richard Mather* (1670); *Wo to Drunkards. Two Sermons...Against... Drunkenness* (1673); *The Day of Trouble Is Near. Two Sermons* (1674); *Some Important Truths About Conversion, Delivered in Sundry Sermons* (1674); *A Discourse Concerning the Subject of Baptisme* (1675); *The First Principles of New-England, Concerning...Baptisme & Communion of Churches* (1675); *The Times of Men Are in the Hand of God* (1675); *The Wicked Mans Portion* (1675); *A Brief History of the Warr with the Indians in New-England* (1676); *An Earnest Exhortation to the Inhabitants of New-England* (1676); *A Discourse Concerning the Danger of Apostasy* (preached 1677; pub. 1679); *An Historical Discourse Concerning...Prayer* (1677); *A Relation of the Troubles Which Have Hapned in New-England, by Reason of the Indians There* (1677); *Renewal of Covenant the Great Duty* (1677); *Pray for the Rising Generation* (1678); *A Call from Heaven to the Present and Succeeding Generations* (in three sermons; 1679); *The Necessity of Reformation* (1679); *The Divine Right of Infant-Baptisme* (1680); *Returning unto God, the Great Concernment of a Covenant People* (1680); *Heavens Alarm to the World* (1681); *Cometographia, or A Discourse Concerning Comets* (1682); *Diatriba de Signo Filii Hominis, et de Secundo Messiae Adventu* (1682); *The Latter-Sign Discoursed of* (1682); *Practical Truths Tending to Promote the Power of Godliness...Delivered in Sundry Sermons* (1682); *A Sermon Wherein*

Is Shewed That the Church of God Is Sometimes a Subject of Great Persecution (1682); *An Arrow Against Profane and Promiscuous Dancing* (1684); *The Doctrine of Divine Providence, Opened and Applyed: Also Sundry Sermons on*...*Other Subjects* (1684); *An Essay for the Recording of Illustrious Providences* (1684); *The Greatest Sinners Exhorted*...*to Come to Christ* (1686); *The Mystery of Christ Opened and Applyed. In Several Sermons* (1686); *A Sermon Occasioned by* [an] *Execution* (1686); *A Testimony Against*...*Prophane and Superstitious Customs* (1686); *A Narrative of the Miseries of New-England* (1688); *New-England Vindicated* (1688); *De Successu Evangelij Apud Indos in Nova-Anglia* (1688); *A Vindication of New-England* (c. 1688); *A Brief Discourse Concerning*...*Common Prayer Worship* (1689); *A Brief Relation of the State of New-England* (1689); *Reasons for the Confirmation of the Charters Belonging to*...*New-England* (c. 1689); *A Brief Account Concerning*...*the Agents of New-England* (1691); *Cases of Conscience Concerning Evil Spirits* (1692); *The Great Blessing of Primitive Counsellours* (1693); *The Judgment of*...*Eminent Divines of the Congregational Way* (1693); *The Answer of Several Ministers to That Case*...*Whether It Is Lawful for a Man to Marry His Wives*...*Sister* (1695); *Solemn Advice to Young Men* (1695); *Angelographia, or A Discourse Concerning*...*Angels* (1696); *A Case of Conscience Concerning Eating of Blood* (1697); *David Serving His Generation* (1697); *A Discourse Concerning the Uncertainty of the Times of Men* (1697); *Masukkenukeeg Matcheseaenvog Wequetoog kah Wuttooanatoog Uppevaonont Christoh* (five sermons of Increase Mather translated into the Indian language by Samuel Danforth; 1699); *The Surest Way to the Greatest Honour* (1699); *Two*...*Discourses Concerning Hardness of Heart* (1699); *The Blessed Hope*...[of] *Jesus Christ*...*in* [Six] *Sermons* (1700); *The Order of the Gospel, Professed and Practised by the Churches* ...*in New-England* (1700); *A Discourse Proving*...*the Christian Religion, Is the Only True Religion* (1702); *The Excellency of a Publick Spirit* (1702); *The Glorious Throne* (1702); *Ichabod*...*A Discourse, Shewing What Cause There Is to Fear That the Glory of the Lord, Is Departing from New-England* (1702); *The Righteous Man a Blessing*...*Two Sermons* (1702); *Some Remarks on a*...*Sermon*...*by George Keith* (1702); *The Duty of Parents to Pray for Their Children* (1703); *Soul-Saving Gospel Truths*...*Several Sermons* (c. 1703); *A*...*Discourse Concerning the Prayse Due to God* (1704); *Practical Truth's Tending to Promote Holiness*...*Delivered in Several Sermons* (1704); *The Voice of God, in Stormy Winds*...*Two Sermons* (1704); *A Letter, About the Present State of Christianity, Among*...*Indians* (1705); *Meditations on the Glory of the Lord*...*Delivered in Several Sermons* (1705); *A Discourse Concerning Earthquakes*...*Also, Two Sermons* (1706); *A Discourse Concerning the Maintenance Due to Those That Preach* (1706); *A Plea for the Ministers of the Gospel* (1706); *A Disquisition on the State of the Souls of Men* (1707); *The Doctrine of Singular Obedience* (1707); *Meditations on Death. Delivered in Several Sermons* (1707); *A Dissertation, Wherein the*...*Doctrine*...*to Encourage Unsanctified Persons*...*to Approach the Holy Table*...[Is] *Confuted* (1708); *A Dissertation Concerning the Future Conversion of the Jewish Nation* (1709); *Awakening Truths Tending to Conversion...in Several Sermons* (1710); *A Discourse Concerning Faith and Fervency in Prayer...Delivered in Several Sermons* (1710); *A Discourse Concerning the Grace of Courage* (1710); *An...Exhortation to the Children of New-England* (1710); *Burnings Bewailed* (1711); *A Discourse...Occasioned by the Death of...John Foster* (1711); *Meditations on the Glory of the Heavenly World* (1712); *Meditations on the Sanctification of the Lord's Day* (1712); *Seasonable Meditations...for Winter & Summer. Two Sermons* (1712); *Some Remarks, on...Common-Prayer Worship* (1712); *The Believers Gain by Death* (1713); *Now or Never Is the Time for Men to Make Sure of Their Eternal Salvation. Several Sermons* (1713); *A Plain Discourse, Shewing Who Shall, & Who Shall Not, Enter...Heaven* (1713); *A Sermon Wherein Is Declared That the Blessed God Is Willing to Be Reconciled to the Sinful Children of Men* (1713); *A Sermon Concerning Obedience & Resignation to the Will of God* (1714); *Several Sermons* (on Christ and death; 1715); *A Discourse Concerning the Existence... of God* (1716); *A Disquisition Concerning Ecclesiastical Councils* (1716); *Two Discourses...That the Lord's Ears Are Open to...Prayers...The Dignity & Duty of Aged Servants of the Lord* (1716); *Practical Truths, Plainly Delivered* (in several sermons; 1717); *A Sermon* [at the Ordination of] *Thomas Walter* (1718); *Sermons Wherein...the Beatitudes, Are Opened & Applyed in Fifteen Discourses* (1718); *Five Sermons on Several Subjects* (1719); *Awakening Soul-Saving Truths Plainly Delivered in Several Sermons* (1720); *A Seasonable Testimony to Good Order in the Churches of the Faithful* (1720); *Advice to the Children of Godly Ancestors* (pub. in Cotton Mather, *A Course of Sermons on Early Piety*; 1721); *Some Further Account...of the Small-Pox Inoculated* (1721); *A Dying Legacy of a Minister to His...People* (Mather's last three sermons; 1722); *The Original Rights of Mankind* (Mather's authorship is doubtful; 1722); *A Call to the Tempted* (preached 1682; pub. 1724).

Biography: Born on Jun. 21, 1639, in Dorchester, Mass., Increase Mather was the long-lived teacher and pastor of the Second Church of Boston, the founder of the first intellectual society in America, the sixth president of Harvard College, an emissary and, later, official agent for colonial and Congregational interests at the courts of James II and William III, the recipient of the first doctor of divinity degree offered in the New World, and throughout his life, a singularly vigorous, insightful, and eloquent defender of the old New Eng. way. The son of the Rev. Richard Mather (q.v.), pastor of the church at Dorchester, and Katherine Holt (or *Hoult*) Mather, Increase was prepared for college in the strict religious environment of his father's home and at the free school in Boston. At the age of 12, he entered Harvard College, receiving most of his education under the tutorship of the eldest Rev. John Norton (q.v.) and completing an A.B. in 1656. On Jun. 21, 1657, he preached his first sermon in his father's pulpit; then on Jul. 3 of that year, he set sail for Eng. and Ire., where he visited his brother Samuel, who was a Puritan minister in Dublin. In Ire. he entered Trinity College, Dublin, and obtained an A.M. there in 1658. Between 1658 and 1660,

Mather held ministerial posts at Great Torrington (Devonshire), Guernsey, and Gloucester. Just before the Restoration, he returned to Guernsey because of the anti-Puritan sentiment then current in Eng., but after Charles II was proclaimed king in May 1660, it became apparent to Mather that if he wanted to live in peace abroad, he would have to subscribe to the Church of England, which, of course, he declined to do. After brief stays in Weymouth and Dorchester in Dorset, Eng., he sailed for Boston, where he arrived in Sept. 1661.

Although several churches immediately called him to settle, Mather remained in Dorchester with his father. In 1662 he was elected a delegate from Dorchester to the ecclesiastical Synod during which the Half-Way Covenant was adopted. Initially opposed to the Half-Way measure because he believed it would weaken New Eng. Congregationalism, by 1670 he accepted the measure's necessity, and in 1675 he published two books in defense of it. On May 27, 1664, he was ordained over the Second Church, beginning a career of distinguished service to its congregation that would last for more than a half-century. Upon his father's death in 1669, he quickly rose to the position of prominence and power that the elder Mather had once occupied among New Eng.'s Congregational churchmen. In sermons such as *The Day of Trouble Is Near*, two fast-humiliation sermons preached in 1673, and *A Discourse Concerning the Danger of Apostasy*, the Mass. election sermon for 1677, Mather demonstrated his mastery of the psychological and spiritual possibilities of the sermon as he argued against declension and for a return to the ideals of New Eng.'s founders. By the time of the Reforming Synod of 1679, the results of which he published under the title *The Necessity of Reformation*, Mather had become the leading spokesman for the orthodox position on such issues in New Eng. Additionally, during the 1670s, he was appointed licenser of the Cambridge press and fellow of Harvard College (in 1674), and he began in earnest his lifelong interest in Puritan history and in Indian affairs with the publication of a volume on King Philip's War in 1676 and a volume on Indian and white relations in 1677.

His interest in the significant issues and his participation in the important events and decisions of the 1680s and 1690s represent the high point of Mather's political, ministerial, and literary career. In 1681 he declined election to the Harvard presidency because the congregation at the Second Church demanded most of his time and attention. In 1685, however, he became acting president of Harvard, and although the position required that he split his time between Cambridge and Boston, he assumed full responsibility for the college in 1686 under the title of rector. Responding to the need for the organization and exchange of scientific information locally, Mather formed the Philosophical Society of Boston in 1683. Modeled after the Royal Society of London, the Boston group was the first of its kind to form anywhere in the world after the founding of the parent society in 1662. This effort, which was a reflection of Mather's personal interest in science, anticipated his support of the introduction of science courses into the Harvard curriculum. In 1688 he was chosen to argue for the interests of the Congregational Churches of Massachusetts Bay before James II, who had revoked the colony's original charter in 1684. Later appointed one of four official colonial agents to the court, Mather impressed James and, after him, William III with the reasonableness of the colony's claims, and largely through his expertise in diplomacy, a new, although somewhat weakened, charter was secured for Massachusetts Bay. Although Mather won a number of major concessions for the new charter, among them the right of the people to elect a representative assembly, the fact that the charter prevented the colonists from electing their own governor was seen in some circles as overshadowing Mather's success. Nevertheless, obtaining the new charter was a significant accomplishment for Mather as was his orchestration of the selection of William Phips, who was sympathetic to the Congregational cause, as the first royal governor under it. In addition, during his stay in Eng., Mather participated in drawing up the plan for the union of Presbyterians and Congregationalists, made the acquaintance of leading scientists and theologians, including Robert Boyle and Richard Baxter, and developed a framework through which Harvard College later enjoyed various grants and endowments from wealthy Englishmen, especially from Thomas Hollis.

On his return to Boston in 1692, Mather was faced with a series of challenges to his authority and prestige. The witchcraft phenomenon was fairly advanced by the time of his return, and Mather was immediately lured into the fray because of the role played in it by his son and colleague at the Second Church, Cotton Mather (q.v.). Although he was more skeptical of the validity of spectral evidence than was his son and although he had reservations about the legitimacy of the witchcraft trials, the fact that neither he nor Cotton spoke out to question either at the time endured to haunt both men in later years. To Increase's credit stands the report of both his son and Phips that it was his course of moderation, urged upon them privately, that prevented the trials and executions from going any further than they did. Yet neither that report nor Mather's publication of *Cases of Conscience Concerning Evil Spirits* in 1693 in which he openly questioned the evidence used to convict most of the "witches" was sufficient to save him from the abuse (albeit mild abuse in comparison to that directed against Cotton) of Robert Calef (q.v.) and others at the turn of the century. At this same time, Mather was confronted by hostile elements on two other fronts. First, there was the resistance of political and theological foes who objected to his defense of Harvard as a stronghold for Congregationalism. Largely through their influence, Mather was prevented from going to Eng. to secure a charter specifically for the college, and, finally, in 1701 Mather was forced into deciding between the presidency of Harvard and his ministry. Much as he loved the college, with which by that time he had been associated in various capacities for nearly fifty years, he was unwilling to give up his position at Second Church. Second, Mather and his son became unpopular as the champions of an increasingly unpopular religious and political persuasion. As the most forceful spokesmen for the conservative brand of Puritanism typified by earlier New Eng. generations, the Mathers were out of step with the rising secular values and cosmopolitan taste of late seventeenth- and early eighteenth-century New Eng. Their opposition to the polity of the Brattle Street Church, for instance, signaled their support of the old New Eng. way, but at the expense, as they soon understood, of their position in the "new" New Eng.

After he resigned the Harvard presidency, Mather occupied himself principally with his pastoral responsibilities. As his publication record indicates, he continued to write on his favorite subjects, with pieces on theological, historical, or scientific matters appearing regularly. Although he generally avoided political controversy in his later years, he joined with Cotton in an unsuccessful bid to undermine the power of Governor Joseph Dudley (q.v.), and he was an early supporter of Yale College, hoping that it might succeed Harvard as orthodoxy's stronghold against the rising Anglican influence. A startling measure of the vitality of his mind is that he continued to preach until the last year of his life. In all such appearances, he voiced his sorrow at New Eng.'s loss of a sense of its "original purpose" and his hope that that purpose would be recovered in a rediscovery of religion. In his preface to his son's *Course of Sermons on Early Piety* (1721), Mather, then in his 81st year and speaking as New Eng.'s spiritual grandfather, raised his familiar theme:

> In our time, *there is a Grievous* Decay of Piety...*and a* Leaving of [our fathers'] first Love: *And...the* Beauties of Holiness *are not to be seen as once they were: A* Fruitful Christian, [has] *grown too Rare a Spectacle...*[as] *too many are* Given to Change, *and Leave that* Order of the Gospel, *to Sett up and uphold which, was the very Design of these Colonies.*

Mather's death on Aug. 23, 1723, was lamented by friend and foe alike. In *The Prophet's Death Lamented and Improved*, Benjamin Colman (q.v.), whose liberal theology and politics Mather once found distasteful, summarized the prevailing opinion of Mather thus:

> He was the *Patriarch* and *Prophet* among us, if any one might be so called: a holy Man, and *a Man of God*....He had read and searched...far into the *Prophecies* of Scripture...and had formed...many just and clear *Conceptions* of, and *Conclusions* from, those abstruse and mysterious revelations....The *Prophets* of old were sober, grave, wise, virtuous, thoughtful, solid and judicious Men; as well as devout and gracious; delighting in retirement, study, contemplation, and secret communion with Heaven. In these respects truly the *signs* of a Prophet of God were upon him. He had...the courage, zeal, and boldness of a Prophet in what he...esteemed to be the Cause of God, his Truth, his Worship and his Holiness.

Mather was married twice, first in 1662 to Maria Cotton, his stepsister and the daughter of the Rev. John Cotton (q.v.), by whom he had ten children, the most notable of which was the aforementioned Cotton, and then in 1715 to Ann (Lake) Cotton, the widow of his nephew John.

Critical Appraisal: During this century, two major biographies of Increase Mather have appeared, and both assert the justice of highly positive estimates of Mather by his contemporaries, including appraisals by one-time adversaries such as Benjamin Colman and those by naturally biased observers such as son Cotton in *Parentator* (1724). In his *Increase Mather* (1925), Kenneth B. Murdock developed his subject as "the greatest of the native Puritans," and in *Increase Mather* (1974), Mason I. Lowance, Jr., after agreeing with Murdock, stated, "[Increase Mather] is the most representative man of his time and place in the history of human thought....He was a 'Puritan's Puritan'" noteworthy for "the magnitude of his intellect and achievement." Indeed, more than any public figure of his time, Mather achieved an honorable personal balance between the practical necessities of this world and the ideals of the next. As preacher, political strategist, diplomat, pastor, teacher, and scientist, he demonstrated that there was a place for a Puritan conscience in a world then becoming increasingly inclined to the terms of a rational, republican temperament. As it happens, his only significant "competitor" for the praise and interest so often lavished upon him is his son Cotton, but although Cotton may have surpassed his father in print, the consensus is that he did not surpass him in point of public service or, probably, in depth of critical capacity.

Mather's publication record is the most tangible index of his wisdom and measure of both his contribution to his time and his influence on American culture. John Sibley, Kenneth Murdock, and others provided various estimates of the number of Mather's published works, but the total of 102 discrete titles offered by Mather's bibliographer Thomas James Holmes is acceptable. It should be noticed, however, that Holmes's estimate includes pieces that in fact incorporate several additional discrete titles. In addition, Mather signed prefaces, notes, and letters of support for works by others that Murdock estimated to number in excess of 65. Certainly, this represents no mean accomplishment for a writer of the late seventeenth and early eighteenth centuries, particularly if one bears in mind the writer's religious association and if one acknowledges the variety of places in which the works were printed, the variety of languages in which they were written or into which they were translated, and the number of reprints or new editions that some titles went through. Although the body of Mather's printed work is divisible into the categories of political and historical writings, scientific writings, and sermonic writings, there is considerable overlapping of content, theme, and intellectual "approach" between these categories, so that no one group of writings is absolutely separable from the other two.

Mather's political and historical writings constitute what was probably the most controversial group of his writings during his own time. Most of his political writings were the result of his representation of colonial interests at home and abroad during the 1680s and 1690s. In *A Narrative of the Miseries of New-England* (1688), *New-England Vindicated* (1688), and *A Brief Account Concerning...the Agents of New-England* (1691), Mather demonstrated a command of the legal and moral issues involved in the revocation of the original charter, in the imposition of royal authorities (particularly those with strong Church of England sympathies) at the head of colonial offices, and in the possible undermining of the civil rights of the Puritan colonists, especially in the areas of worship and education. Although in the final analysis Mather's personal position in both these works and the deliberations abroad in which they played some part has to be called "Loyalist," there is a strong "patriot" sentiment throughout. Except for his acceptance of the governor's role as established by the new charter, Mather would likely have been an agreeable companion to the generation of popular political thinkers in America at the end of the eighteenth century.

The connection between Mather's political and historical writings is such that the two are in fact complements to each other. Often Mather uses historical precedents (some of which date from the earliest days of New Eng. settlement) to substantiate his position in the political tracts. Additionally, the historical works tend to support the authority of the Puritan leadership by developing instances of the power of the principals over all adversaries, either because of the direct intervention of God on the side of the principals or because of the reserve of moral strength that the righteous eventually draw upon to conquer their foes. It is out of such perspectives that Mather writes of Puritan fortunes during King Philip's War in *A Brief History of the Warr* (1676) or of the relations between Puritans and Indians in *A Relation of the Troubles. . .in New-England* (1677).

Mather's view of Puritan history, particularly his acceptance of the doctrine of providential intervention in the affairs of man and his belief that the will of God is discernible in secondary causes or events, has significance for both his historical and scientific writings. In many ways, but especially through the influence of these two assumptions about history, the scientific writings have their origins in Mather's historical sensibility. This is true of major treatises such as *An Essay for the Recording of Illustrious Providences* (1684) and sermonic pieces such as *The Doctrine of Divine Providence* (1684) and *The Voice of God in Stormy Winds* (1704). In these works, Mather uses science and natural phenomena variously to defend or "objectively" authenticate Puritan theology and to instruct New Eng.'s people on their temporal and spiritual conditions. Although Mather's most recent biographer has accused his subject of being, like many of his day, a "pseudoscientific" rationalizer of natural phenomena, the editor of a recent reprint of *An Essay* argued convincingly that Mather was "a skilled scientific inquirer who. . .kept abreast of significant new advances." Indeed, in *An Essay* and in his pieces on comets (*Cometographia* [1683]), angels (*Angelographia* [1696]), and earthquakes (*A Discourse* [1706]), for instance, Mather employed an acceptable scientific method of the time, made no unsupported claims, and typically cited as his authorities men of scientific learning and reputation such as Johannes Kepler, Tycho Brahe, and Robert Boyle.

Yet without doubt, Mather's third category of writings was the most accessible and influential category during his life and exerted a direct influence upon the writers and thinkers of the following generation. As a writer and preacher of sermons, Mather had few equals in Puritan New Eng. Every legitimate Puritan occasion for a sermon is represented in his printed sermons. For instance, there are sermons for fast, prayer, or humiliation days, Sabbath days, lecture days, executions, funerals, and ordinations. In all instances, Mather's sermons display his erudition, his command of language and the means of persuasion, and his ability to relate and apply biblical doctrines to the precise condition of his audience. Mather's contemporaries recognized his pulpit talent; on four occasions, he was invited to preach the Mass. election sermon (in 1677, 1693, 1699, and 1702), and on two occasions, he was invited to preach the annual Artillery Election Sermon (in 1665 and 1710). In *The Prophet's Death*, Colman singled out Mather's ability to preach for special remembrance: "As the sacred study was his element, so his excellency was in the pulpit; and God gave his Ministrations an abundant success as well as acceptance. I trust there are many living. . . witnesses of what I say. . . and there are many. . . already in Heaven who have been converted by his Ministry."

It would be unfair to Mather's talent and the extent of his sermonic invention to cite one sermon as his best or most typical. Instead, one might consider *A Discourse Concerning the Danger of Apostasy, The Doctrine of Divine Providence*, and *Ichabod*, the published title given to two humiliation sermons preached in 1702, as a collective representation of Mather's sermons. The first and last of these works are jeremiads in which Mather, who did much to advance the popularity of that sermonic genre in the 1670s and later, addressed the issues usually associated with that form, namely, New Eng.'s declension, God's anger toward and judgments against his people for their decline, and the need for New Eng.'s reform. In all, there is a common theme of trust in the will of God and a common lament for the passing of New Eng.'s glory. Speaking at times as a spiritual father, at times as a latter-day Jeremiah, and yet at other times as a gentlemanly observer upon whom the significance of events has not been lost, Mather appealed to his audience to keep alive New Eng.'s "errand" and original ideals. The matter receives its most succinct treatment in *Ichabod*, in which Mather stated,

> We are the Posterity of the *Good, Old Puritan Nonconformists* . . . a Strict and Holy People. Such were our Fathers who followed the Lord into this Wilderness. . . . Oh! That the present and succeeding Generations in *New-England* might be like the *First Generation* of Christians, who transplanted themselves in this part of the world.

At the time Mather began his career, these issues and themes were receiving their first formal statement. By the end of his career, Mather had become the unquestioned authority on the orthodox position regarding such matters. In his public ministry, he exerted an immediate influence in support of orthodoxy, and in his writings, he exerted an influence that was felt at the time and remains today as a measure of his literary talent and worth. With Mather's death in 1723 and that of son Cotton in 1728, New Eng. orthodoxy entered a revisionist phase during which many of the principles for which the Mathers fought were challenged and, in some cases, discarded. Yet to Increase Mather's credit must stand the admission of so many writers of that revisionist generation that in all of their dealings, they realized that the force and weight of Mather's opinion and reputation were such that revision could not be undertaken lightly.

Suggested Readings: BDAS; CCNE; DAB; DARB; DNB; FCNEV; LHUS; Sibley-Shipton (I, 410-470); Sprague (I, 151-159); T₁. *See also* Benjamin Colman, *The Prophet's Death Lamented and Improved* (1723); Thomas James Holmes, *Increase Mather: A Bibliography of His Works*, 2 vols. (1931); James A. Levernier, Introduction, *An Essay for the Recording of Illustrious Providences* by Increase Mather (1684; rep., 1977); Mason I. Lowance, Jr., *Increase Mather* (1974); Cotton Mather, *Parentator: Memoirs of Remarkables in the Life and Death of. . .Increase Mather* (1724); Increase Mather, *The Autobiography of Increase Mather*, ed. M. G. Hall (1962); Robert Middlekauff, *The Mathers: Three Generations of Puritan Intellectuals, 1596-1726* (1971); Perry Miller, *The New England Mind: From Colony to Province* (1953); idem, *The New England Mind: The Seventeenth Century* (1961); Kenneth B. Murdock, *Increase Mather: The Foremost American Puritan* (1925); Vernon L. Parrington, "The Mather Dynasty" in *Main Currents in American Thought* (1927), I, 98-117; Williston Walker, "Increase Mather" in *Ten New-England Leaders* (1901).

Ronald A. Bosco
State University of New York at Albany

NATHANIEL MATHER (1630-1697)

Works: To the Reader, *A Disputation Concerning Church-Members and Their Children* (by R. Mather; 1659); To the Reader, *The Power of Congregational Churches* (by J. Davenport; 1672); To the Reader, *Figures or Types of the Old Testament* (by S. Mather; 1683); *A Sermon Wherein Is Shewed* (1684); To the Reader, πηαωνηια (by J. Flavel; 1691); *Righteousness of God Through Faith* (1694); Preface, *The Conquests and Triumphs of Greece* (by M. Mayhew; 1695); To the Reader and Epistle Dedicatory, *Batteries upon the Kingdom of the Devil* (by C. Mather; 1695); [Attestation] and Epistle Dedicatory, *Pietas in Patriam* (by C. Mather; 1697); *A Discussion of the Lawfulness of a Pastor's Acting* (1698); *Twenty-Three Select Sermons* (1701); *A Sermon Preach'd from 1 Corinthians 11, 30* (1711).

Biography: Nathaniel Mather, son of the Rev. Richard Mather (q.v.), was born in Lancashire, Eng., where he lived until the age of 5. In Aug. 1635 his father took him to live in Boston, Mass., where he later earned a Harvard B.A. in 1647 and an M.A. in 1650. Oliver Cromwell's appeal for ministers willing to serve in Eng. and Ire. prompted his return to his native land. From London he wrote in 1651, "Tis incredible what an advantage to preferm[en]t it is to have been a New English man." Cromwell's appointments sent him first to Harberton and later to Barnstable, Devonshire. A 1662 parliamentary act forbidding nonconformists to preach ended his ministry at Barnstable. The Bishops' Courts, he wrote in describing persecution of dissidents like himself, "make the Sheriff the Devill." To escape harassment, Mather transferred to Hol., where he served as minister to the English congregation at Rotterdam. Upon the death of his brother Samuel in 1671, he went to Dublin, succeeding Samuel as pastor of the Congregational Church in New Row. There increased persecutions eventually necessitated his holding services in private dwellings. Mather demonstrated his own more liberal attitudes when he required that relief funds he helped to gather for the victims of King Philip's War be distributed to all of the needy, regardless of sect. In 1688 he moved to London to succeed John Collins as the head of a thriving congregation in Lime Street. Before his death in 1697, Mather was selected to be merchants' lecturer at Pinners-Hall, and he was one of the founders of the Congregational Fund Board. Survived by his wife, Mary (Benn) Mather, he was buried at Bunhill. His monument bears a Latin inscription believed to be the work of Isaac Watts.

Critical Appraisal: Relatively, the number of Nathaniel Mather's sermons ever to appear in print is small, for which there may be several explanations. The printed correspondence covering the years 1650 through 1687 reveals three dominant concerns: the growing power of the papists and consequent increased persecution of the Puritans, the problems of preparing his brother's typological study for the press, and the remote possibility of having some of his own sermons published anonymously in New Eng. The historical circumstances surrounding his career, other preoccupations, and his self-confessed "backwardness to appear in Print" may share accountability. Nonetheless, Mather's conviction that reputation is valuable only insofar as it advances his church prompted him to engage many of the vital questions of his day. His foreword to his father's thoughts on the Half-Way Covenant, for example, not only presents the synodical context of the ensuing debate over whether, and to what age, children can covenant in their parents, whether parents need necessarily covenant before the child's birth, and whether, indeed, bond servants and adopted children are "Covenant-seed," but also addresses the audience polemically in this manner: This present discussion of God's truths, it is to be hoped, will lead to a new reformation "in such of our Parishes as retain any thing of the essence of a Church in them. . . to such a measure of purity, as may take off the just distaste and dissatisfactions of such, as are conscientiously tender of their Church-Communion." Thus did Mather indicate that the debate to follow was no mere distant and parochial one. In *The Righteousness of God Through Faith*, he announced his own stand on the thorny issue of justification, publishing his two sermons only because persons not present at the preaching had confused and condemned his position. Placing himself in the company of Luther, Calvin, Zwingli, Peter Martyr, and others, Mather concluded with a postscript that "in such a subject we should not. . . be mealy-mouthed" lest God's truths be shrouded in darkness. The sermons he so defended are cast in catechetical form with the emphasis resting throughout on what he termed the "Suretiship-righteousness of Christ." The careful distinction he wanted to make is between "Vital Union" ("reciprocal or mutual, in it not only are we in Christ, but he is also in us") and a necessarily preceding "Union in Law" ("the cause of the latter...the rule and measure of the latter...extending to all those only who are comprised within the former"). Such insistence on precise understanding and the rigorous, aggressive analyses that understanding requires are typical of Mather's sermon style. It is a style revelatory of Mather's reported amiability, piety, learned judiciousness, his nice balance of oratory and plainness of speech, the "awfulness" of his manner "greatly calculated to strike the arrows of conviction."

Suggested Readings: DNB; Sibley-Shipton (I, 157-161). *See also* Joseph B. Felt, *The Ecclesiastical History of New England* (1855), I, 598; II, 496; Thomas James Holmes, *The Minor Mathers: A List of Their Works* (1940), pp. xxv-xxvi, 37-50; *Letters of Nathaniel Mather*, CMHS, 4th ser., 8 (1868); A. G. Matthews, *Calamy Revised* (1934), p. 344.

Cheryl Z. Oreovicz
Purdue University

RICHARD MATHER (1596-1669)

Works: *The Whole Booke of Psalmes* (1640), called *The Bay Psalm Book* and, in later editions, *The New-England Psalm Book; An Apologie for Church Covenant* (1643); *Church-Government and Church-Covenant Discussed* (1643); *A Modest and Brotherly Answer* (1646); *A Reply to Mr. Rutherfurd* (1647); *A Platform of Church Discipline* (1649); *A Catechism, or The Grounds and Principles of Christian Religion* (1650); *An Heart-Melting Exhortation* (1650); *The Summe of Certain Sermons* (1652); *A Farewel Exhortation to the Church and People of Dorchester in New-England* (1657); *A Disputation Concerning Church-Members and Their Children* (1659); *A Defence of the Answer and Arguments of the Synod Met in Boston in the Year 1662* (1664); *An Answer to Two Questions* [concerning the power of the people in church government], "Published by His Son, Increase Mather, D.D." (1712).

Biography: Richard Mather, Puritan clergyman, was born at Lowton, Lancashire, Eng., the son of Thomas and Margrett (Abrams) Mather. After a grammar school education, he became master of a school at Toxteth Park, near Liverpool, read divinity and heard Puritan sermons, and under the influence of Edward Aspinwall, a landowner with whom he lived, experienced a conversion. His stay at Brasenose College, Oxford, which he entered to improve his qualifications for the pulpit, lasted but six months; at that time, he returned to Toxteth, in answer to a call to preach, and the next year was ordained. His independence of mind is seen in his favoring a congregational polity, in tearing up the certificate of Episcopal ordination, which he regarded as "superstition," and in departing from accepted practices—neglecting the ceremonies and refusing to wear a surplice. Twice suspended for such conduct, Mather became receptive to suggestions of John Cotton (q.v.) and Thomas Hooker (q.v.) that he cast his lot with the Puritan community in New Eng. Accordingly, on Apr. 16, 1635, with his family, he left Warrington for Bristol, set sail Jun. 4, narrowly escaped shipwreck, and reached Boston Aug. 17. A year later, he became teacher in the newly organized church at nearby Dorchester, where he remained the rest of his life.

He contributed to the composition of the *Bay Psalm Book* (1640), wrote its preface, and became respected for his powerful and influential preaching. Mather's chief contribution to the Puritan experiment was serving in the councils of church governance. He was the principal architect of both the "Cambridge Platform" (1649), the basic statement of New Eng. Congregationalism, and the "Half-Way Covenant," the compromise settlement of the debate over admitting children of believers to church membership. He married twice: in Lancashire, Katherine Holt (1624), who bore six sons, including Samuel Mather, Nathaniel Mather (q.v.), Eleazer Mather (q.v.), and Increase Mather (q.v.), all clergymen; in New Eng., Sarah Cotton, widow of John Cotton. Healthy all of his life, Mather died of a severe attack of the stone.

Critical Appraisal: If the niche in the pantheon of Puritan worthies accorded Richard Mather is less conspicuous than the most prominent, it is so for three reasons. His jingly renditions in the *Bay Psalm Book*, notwithstanding his disclaimer of aesthetic intent, have worked to his disadvantage. Also, founding in the New World what Moses Coit Tyler first called the Mather Dynasty has kept his name alive, although partly this is owing to the prominence of his descendants Increase Mather and Cotton Mather (q.v.). That the judgment of Richard Mather is based, in the minds of all but close students of the period, on little more than these two accomplishments results from the third reason for his shadowy position: he wrote little that can be expected to interest later readers, which probably is why his writings are virtually inaccessible. Yet Mather perhaps deserves more recognition than he has received. This was his own opinion, not unnaturally, and it may well be just. For one thing, he was an impressive presence, a fine preacher in the generation of Thomas Shepard (q.v.), John Cotton, and Thomas Hooker. Even more important was his contribution of the voice of moderation in the disputes of the first Puritan generation. On several important occasions, he was selected to draft a document that would reconcile differences and summarize a compromise position. Although he has been called a "trimmer," sacrificing principle to expediency, it is perhaps preferable to think of him as a master of the art of the possible, which is politics. Antinomian dissent was more heroic to later generations. Mather's service to the ecclesiastical and social community, always threatened by disruption in the early colonies, was to keep it intact. Long before his more renowned descendants had begun to distinguish themselves, Richard Mather was lending his judicious character to the threatening debates of his day, earning from a contemporary an epitaph that recognized his principal talent: "Vixerat in synodis, moritur moderator in illis."

Suggested Readings: CCNE; DAB; DNB; FCNEV; LHUS; Sprague (I, 75-80);
T$_1$. *See also* B. R. Burg, *Richard Mather of Dorchester* (1970); Thomas M. Davis,
"Edward Taylor's Elegies on the Mathers," EAL, 11 (1976), 231-244; Benjamin Franklin
V and William K. Bottorff, *Life and Death of Richard Mather (1670) by Increase Mather*
(a facsimile reprint with an introduction; 1966); Thomas J. Holmes, *The Minor Mathers,
A List of Their Works* (1940); Cotton Mather, "The Life of Mr. Richard Mather," Book III
of *Magnalia Christi Americana* (1702); Horace E. Mather, *Lineage of Rev. Richard
Mather* (1890); Robert Middlekauff, *The Mathers* (1971); Edmund S. Morgan, *Visible
Saints* (1963); Robert G. Pope, *The Half-Way Covenant: Church Membership in Puritan
New England* (1969); Williston Walker, *Ten New England Leaders* (1901); Alexander
Young, *Chronicles of the First Planters of the Colony of Massachusetts Bay from 1623 to
1636* (includes Mather's journal of his Atlantic crossing; 1846).

Leon T. Dickinson
University of Missouri-Columbia

SAMUEL MATHER (1706-1785)

Works: *The Departure and Character of Elijah* (1728); *The Life of the Very
Reverend and Learned Cotton Mather* (1729); *A Country Treat* (1730); *A Letter
to Doctor Zabdiel Boylston* (1730); *An Essay Concerning Gratitude* (1732); *Vita
B. Augusti Hermanni Franckii* (1733); *An Apology for the Liberties of the Churches*
(1738); *The Fall of the Mighty* (1738); *War Is Lawful* (1739); *The Faithful Man*
(1740); *A Funeral Discourse...Prince Frederick* (1751); *The Walk of the Up-
right* (1753); *A Dissertation Concerning the...Name of Jehovah* (1760); *Of the
Pastoral Care* (1762); *The Lord's Prayer* (1766); *A Modest Account Concerning
the Salutations* (1768); *An Attempt to Shew* (1773); *Christ Sent to Heal the
Broken Hearted* (1773); *The Sacred Minister: A New Poem* (1773); *All Men Will
Not Be Saved Forever* (1782); *To the Author of a Letter to Doctor Mather* (1783);
The Dying Legacy of an Aged Minister of the Everlasting Gospel (1783); *A
Serious Letter to the Young People of Boston* (1783).

Biography: Born in 1706 of Cotton Mather's (q.v.) second marriage, to
Elizabeth Clark, Samuel Mather was the fourth generation of a dynasty of New
Eng. ministers. His great-grandfather Richard Mather (q.v.) had been an influential leader in the Congregational Church, a joint author of *The Bay Psalm Book*,
and author of the *Platform of Church Discipline*. His grandfather Increase Mather
(q.v.) was president of Harvard, minister at the Old North Church in Boston, and
author of some 175 publications. His father, Cotton, was a learned minister and
author of more than 450 works. Under the burden of family tradition and expectation, Samuel Mather labored to make his own contribution. A precocious
learner, he studied Latin at 6 and entered Harvard at 12, graduating in 1724.
Exposed to smallpox while a student, he urged his father to inoculate him, and
later wrote several pamphlets in defense of this controversial method of preven-
tion. He was granted an honorary M.A. from Yale in 1724 but went on to earn

the M.A. at Harvard two years later. He began his ministerial career as chaplain for soldiers at Castle William. Cotton's death in 1728 occasioned the book that earned his literary reputation, *The Life of the Very Reverend and Learned Cotton Mather*. Three years later, Samuel was asked to assist his father's successor, Rev. Joshua Gee (q.v.), at the Old North Church. In 1732 he became pastor and the following year married Hannah Hutchinson, Governor Thomas Hutchinson's (q.v.) daughter. During the next decade, criticism by the congregation and differences with Gee forced his withdrawal. Followed by ninety-three church members, he formed the Tenth Congregational Church of Boston, where he preached for the next forty-three years.

Critical Appraisal: Although Samuel Mather published three books, a number of sermons and pamphlets, and a poem, his single lasting contribution is his first long work, *The Life of the Very Reverend and Learned Cotton Mather*. Despite the highly selective nature of the biography, it presents not only a portrait of Cotton Mather but, indirectly, one of his scholarly and devoted son. A brief account of Cotton's early life is followed by a valuable commentary on his enlightened methods of childrearing, his obsessive efforts to do good each day, his forbearance in the face of repeated losses (only two of his fifteen children survived him), and descriptions of his works and correspondence. The book is a useful introduction to the study of Cotton Mather, although it lacks the objectivity modern readers have come to expect. As Babette Levy noted, Samuel glosses over Mather's disappointment in his favored son "Cressy," who drowned at sea; the insanity of Cotton's third wife, Lydia; and the morbid doubts that prompted Mather's vigils and fasts and the "confessions" recorded in his diaries. In fact, large sections of the diaries are presented verbatim or loosely paraphrased in the *Life*. Like the tributes to Richard Mather and Increase Mather, *The Life and Death of That Reverend Man of God, Mr. Richard Mather* (1670) and *Parentator. Memoirs of Remarkables in the Life and the Death of the Ever-Memorable Dr. Increase Mather* (1724), by their sons, Samuel Mather's book presents an exemplary, if idealized, portrait of a godly and learned man, illustrating and extending the tradition of filiopietism in early American literature. As such, it may interest students considering the claims of Quentin Anderson, R.W.B. Lewis, and others that, by the nineteenth century, American writers like Ralph Waldo Emerson, Walt Whitman, and Henry James had lost their sense of origins, of fathers. In 1755 Mather's *Life* was abridged and published in London; by 1835 it had been reprinted five times in Eng., Scot., and America.

Of minor interest are the *Apology for the Liberties of the Churches in New England* and *A Dissertation Concerning the Most Venerable Name of Jehovah*. The former identifies and defends the distinguishing features of Congregational Churches in New Eng. against would-be detractors from abroad. The defense includes the right to choose officers, ordain ministers, have delegates, withdraw from the elders, refuse communion to the disqualified, judge brethren in public, and have councils and synods. The *Dissertation* considers the history and etymology of various forms of the name Jehovah: El, Eloah, Elohim, Adonai,

Shaddai, Tzebaoth, Elion, Ehjeh, and Jah. Mather's pamphlet *All Men Will Not Be Saved Forever*, an attack upon a Universalist pamphlet, *Salvation for All Men*, attracted sufficient interest for a 2nd edition in 1783. It is evidence of his orthodox convictions despite charges by some of his contemporaries that he lacked firmness and was sliding into Arminianism.

Suggested Readings: CCNE; DAB; Sibley-Shipton (I, 216-238); Sprague (I, 371-374); T₁. *See also* Thomas J. Holmes, *The Minor Mathers: A List of Their Works* (1940); Babette M. Levy, Foreword, *The Life of Cotton Mather*, by Samuel Mather (1729; rep., 1970).

Lynn M. Haims
Westfield, New Jersey

THOMAS MATHEW (c. 1650-c. 1706)

Works: "The Beginning, Progress, and Conclusion of Bacon's Rebellion in Virginia" (w. 1705; pub. 1804).

Biography: Thomas Mathew was most likely one of that large number of Englishmen who came to Va. with money to invest, stayed awhile, then returned across the Atlantic to spend their final years (as Mathew apparently had done by 1690). The owner of tobacco plantations in Stafford and Northumberland Counties, he lived a life in the New World that was more eventful than he may have wished. By his own account, at least, he was highly reluctant to become embroiled in Nathaniel Bacon's (q.v.) armed challenge to the administration of Governor Sir William Berkeley (q.v.) (1676-1677); yet he was elected to the "reforming" Assembly swept into office in 1676 by the Baconian ferment and was sufficiently identified with the rebel party to be excepted by name from Berkeley's general pardon of Feb. 10, 1677. Mathew's account of the uprising discreetly fails to mention that he himself was involved in trade disputes with the Indians that cost him a son and indirectly led to the civil conflict. He died in Westminster about 1706, soon after completing his memoir.

Critical Appraisal: Thomas Mathew's chronicle is less than wholly reliable as history, partly because of his personal reticence but mostly as a result of the intervening thirty years between the rebellion and his formal recording of it. It is obvious, however, that he was working from notes or a diary kept during his Va. sojourn, and his pictures of scenes he had personally witnessed (such as Bacon's tumultuous entry into Jamestown to demand a commission from Berkeley) are thus far more lively and accurate than those parts of the narrative for which he had to depend on secondhand information. Mathew's account is basically a series of episodic vignettes, often fascinating in themselves although not always selected on the most rational principles: he provided, for example, an elaborate description of an Indian queen's costume but left Nathaniel Bacon's physical appearance to the reader's imagination. With the native caution of a businessman, he refused to endorse either the loyalist or the rebel faction whole-heartedly. Although he clearly had supported Bacon's aggressive policy toward the Indians and shared the popular suspicion that the governor was scheming to maintain economic advantages for himself, the circumspect Mathew was horrified by the insurgent leader's intentions to oppose any British troops sent to quell his movement, and he ascribed Bacon's death to "God's exceeding Mercy."

Even had he not been writing at the request of so eminent a statesman as Secretary Robert Harley, Mathew no doubt would have written a prose style more serviceable than flamboyant. In many respects, however, with its sharply etched images and stretches of dialog that still ring true to the ear, his is the most evocative and lifelike of the early accounts of Bacon's Rebellion.

Suggested Readings: Charles M. Andrews, *Narratives of the Insurrections, 1675-1690* (includes the most recent edition of Mathew's text; 1915), pp. 11-41; Jane Carson, *Bacon's Rebellion, 1676-1976* (1976), pp. 22-24; Richard Beale Davis, *Intellectual Life in the Colonial South, 1585-1763* (1978), I, 78-80; Howard Mumford Jones, *The Literature of Virginia in the Seventeenth Century*, 2nd ed. (1968), pp. 110-111.

W. H. Ward
Appalachian State University

THOMAS MAULE (c. 1645-1724)

Works: *Truth Held Forth and Maintained* (1695); *New-England Persecutors Mauled with Their Own Weapons* (1697); *An Abstract of a Letter to Cotton Mather* (1701); *For the Service of Truth, Against George Keith* (1703).

Biography: The life of the Quaker merchant Thomas Maule provides an insight into the boundaries of dissent in colonial Mass. After leaving Eng. at 12 and learning the tailor's craft in Barbados, Maule settled in Salem in 1688 and soon became one of the town's most prosperous merchants. He also became a Quaker and one of the community's leading troublemakers. Between 1688 and 1695, he was frequently in court, was jailed five times, and was publicly whipped twice. Maule had a quick temper and was incapable of remaining silent in the face of any insult to himself or his sect. In 1696 he gained wide notoriety by publishing *Truth Held Forth and Maintained*, a vitriolic attack on the colony's ministers and civil authorities, which brought an immediate indictment for slander. His trial became the first test of freedom of the press in colonial America. Despite pressure from both ministers and magistrates, a jury acquitted Maule, and he revelled in his victory by publishing more diatribes against the ministry. Maule's acquittal illustrated not only the declining power of the Congregational ministry, but also the growing tolerance of his fellow laymen. Despite his quarrelsome disposition and unorthodox religious views, Maule was held in high esteem by his community. He held minor political offices throughout his life, won accolades for his scrupulous business practices, and died rich. Maule's success revealed that by 1700 commercial towns like Salem were no longer pristine Puritan cities on a hill; it also suggested the course that their development would take in the decades to come.

Critical Appraisal: Thomas Maule's polemical pamphlets were among the earliest public attacks on the Congregational ministry, but they are even more notable for the specific criticisms they leveled at Cotton Mather (q.v.) and his clerical colleagues. When earlier writers like Thomas Morton (q.v.) and Robert Child had bewailed their persecution at the hands of New Eng.'s Congregational establishment, their complaints were primarily against the religious bigotry of their persecutors. But Maule saw an even more insidious reason for the oppression of himself and his fellow Quakers—the established clergy's love of money. Maule was the first New Englander to suggest that ministers were more concerned with their own pocketbooks than with their parishioners' souls. In the following years, this theme became increasingly important in the relationship of church and society.

After working for two years on the long and rambling treatise that became *Truth Held Forth and Maintained*, Maule was spurred to seek a publisher by the conduct of the clergy during the witchcraft trials of 1692-1693. Although he believed in witchcraft, Maule was genuinely appalled by the clergy's management of the crisis. To him, the execution of innocent people demonstrated the clerical tyranny under which his sect suffered. The real agents of Satan in Mass., he asserted, were not the pathetic individuals tried as witches, but their judges, who were not Christ's ministers, but "the World's teachers, set up and upheld by the World." Maule had enough experience with the Mass. judicial system to know that these bold remarks would probably result in his arrest. Yet he also knew, as his acquittal proved, that the witchcraft crisis had damaged the clergy's credibility. His timing of the publication of *Truth Held Forth and Maintained* reflected the good judgment that had made him a successful businessman.

Maule was even less restrained after his acquittal. *New England Persecutors Mauled with Their Own Weapons* and *An Abstract of a Letter to Cotton Mather* are filled with jibes, unflattering metaphors, and insults to the clergy and Cotton Mather, his chief accuser. In these pamphlets, he developed further his case against the greedy ministers, asserting that "The Love of Money leads thee for to preach." Maule correctly believed that his opponents would not risk the embarrassment of trying him again. Cotton Mather could only list Maule's writings as one of the many sins that plagued New Eng. and pray for the Quaker's retribution in hell.

Maule stated in the preface to *Truth Held Forth and Maintained* that "Humane Learning I have not," and little in any of his writings refutes this self-assessment. His arguments are incredibly convoluted; his logic is often impossible to follow; and he frequently employed some of the worst doggerel verse and most strained punning in all of colonial American literature. Records of his trial suggest that one reason for his acquittal was that the jury was unable to follow much of what his pamphlet said.

Yet despite their style, Maule's works are important, not only because they demonstrated that New Englanders were willing to allow at least some freedom of expression, but also because they introduced a new perspective to discussions of religion and politics in Mass. Maule's assessments of the clergy's nefarious activities were all colored by his experience as a merchant. Maule was known for his honesty in business, and his career had no doubt taught him much about the evils of greed and dishonesty. When he criticized Cotton Mather and the other ministers, he did so as much from the perspective of an honest merchant as from that of a Quaker. Maule himself may not have had great impact, but as more New Englanders busied themselves in commerce, many made similar observations about the clergy's role in society, especially when Cotton Mather's successors continually demanded higher salaries in the 1720s and 1730s.

Suggested Readings: Chadwick Hansen, *Witchcraft at Salem* (1969), pp. 249-251; Matt Bushnell Jones, "Thomas Maule, the Salem Quaker, and Free Speech in Massachusetts Bay, with Bibliographical Notes," EIHC, 72 (1936), 1-42.

James W. Schmotter
Cornell University

JAMES MAURY (1718-1769)

Works: "Dissertation on Education" (James Maury to Robert Jackson, Jul. 17, 1762; pub. 1941-1942); *An Address Enforcing an Inquiry into . . .Anabaptists* (w. c. 1763; pub. 1771).

Biography: James Maury—preacher, educator, essayist—was born in Dublin, Ire., on Apr. 18, 1718, into the French Huguenot family of Matthew and Mary Ann (Fontaine) Maury. In 1719 Matthew Maury settled in Va., where three of his Fontaine brothers-in-law were to live and raise families. Young James Maury received a good secondary education, for both sides of the family were well educated and deeply committed to education. Maury entered the College of William and Mary probably around 1738, was made an usher in the grammar school there in Jul. 1741, was ordained by the bishop of London in Eng. in 1742, received the king's bounty for Va. in 1742, and returned home to be rector of King William Parish. On Nov. 11, 1743, he married Mary Walker, niece of Dr. Thomas Walker, and thus connected himself to an influential family. In 1752 Maury assumed the rectorship of the frontier Fredericksville Parish in a part of Louisa County, which later became Albemarle County.

James Maury's name is best known in histories in connection with the Parsons' Cause. It was at Maury's Dec. 1, 1763, trial for damages resulting from the 1758 Two-Penny Act that Patrick Henry made the impassioned speech that brought about his election soon afterwards to the House of Burgesses. Although he was a close associate and friend of John Camm (q.v.) and other Tory clergymen involved in the Parsons' Cause, Maury's letters concerning the Stamp Act and his other writings indicate that he would have sided with the patriots had he lived to see the Revolution.

Before his death on Jun. 9, 1769, Maury had established a wide reputation as an exceptionally able, hardworking minister, a thorough and inspiring teacher, a competent essayist, and a deeply spiritual man. In addition, he was the patriarch of a great American family that included his son James who was U.S. consul to Liverpool for many years and his grandson Matthew Fontaine Maury, the well-known nineteenth-century naval leader and oceanographer.

Critical Appraisal: Although he did not publish a great many works, James Maury was one of the ablest Anglican clergymen in Va. in both theology and literature. His former pupil Thomas Jefferson (q.v.) remembered Maury respectfully as a "correct classical scholar" and his close friend the Rev. Jonathan Boucher (q.v.) praised his "fine style." Maury's letters are as valuable as his other writings; most of them are well-written epistolary essays that reveal a man well informed and perceptive about public affairs who had a wide knowledge of American geography and a profound concern about western lands and commerce. Maury has been seriously considered, along with the Rev. Samuel Davies (q.v.), as a possible author of the 1756-1757 Va. "Centinel" essay series—one of the best written of Va. essay series. This series dealt with the French and Indian War, a subject on which Maury was well informed, as his letters indicate. One letter to an uncle in Wales indicates that Maury may have written one or more pamphlets on the subject and another letter includes a detailed plan for a system of forts on the frontier. When Maury's letters, sermons, and essays are edited and published, he will be recognized as a highly significant literary figure of his age in Va.

Maury conducted one of the best private schools in Va., a boarding school that provided for many sons of the Va. gentry their preparation for college or university. Among Maury's many pupils were Thomas Jefferson, James Madison (Va.'s first bishop and president of the College of William and Mary), James Monroe, Dabney Carr the elder, and Maury's son James. Maury was one of the most learned Classical scholars of his day and at his death left a major colonial Va. library of some 400 titles and 44 pamphlets (probably more than 500 volumes).

On Jul. 17, 1762, Maury wrote a pioneer treatise on education in a letter to his friend Robert Jackson. Jackson had given him an essay on education by Jonathan Boucher (whom Maury did not as yet know) in which Boucher insisted on a thorough grounding in Greek and Latin as the foundation for all further intellectual acquirements. Maury considered the whole question of what is "useful, practical Knowledge" for a young Virginian and advocated the anti-Classical, pragmatic view of education that was to gain ascendency in America. He expressed a great admiration for the Classics and cited their necessity to the learned professions of divinity, medicine, and law; he noted, however, that very few persons in Va. enter these underpaid professions. Because gaining a knowledge of the Classical languages is a long, laborious, all-consuming task, Maury believed that the knowledge might be "bought too dear" for a Virginian if it left no time for boys to learn the basics for a successful and useful life in Va. He indicated that even the very wealthy gentry in Va. lead busy lives managing their plantations, with inadequate leisure to pursue Classical studies in later life. Certainly, gentlemen of the second rank must engage in business to earn a living. Maury believed that those preciously few years of boyhood education should be spent acquiring basics such as English grammar, reading, writing, arithmetic, history, geology, eloquence, and a taste for the best literature in the student's native language. They are the studies that would enable a Va. gentleman to live a satisfying private life, perform as a useful citizen, and serve well in public office. The essay is well written and employs the elements of Classical rhetoric in an effective and polished manner. This epistolary dissertation on education is indeed an interesting document when one considers that Maury was an avid Classical scholar and that his pupil Thomas Jefferson, who learned his Classics from Maury and found enjoyment in them all of his life, also opposed the requirement of the Classical languages as basic to learning.

Maury's sermons reveal him to be as able a preacher as any colonial Anglican clergyman of his day. He was a deeply spiritual but thoroughly rational theologian who abhorred the excessive enthusiasm of the Great Awakening. In Maury's sermons, Christianity appears above all else as a rational religion and God's dealings with man are seen to be on the rational level. Maury's arguments on topics such as prayer are based on both reason and the Bible, and one sermon on the Ascension goes so far as to say that the Ascension is "undoubtedly figurative," for God is spirit and consequently has no bodily parts. Although from a Huguenot background, Maury, like his uncle the Rev. Peter Fontaine, appears in his sermons as an anti-Calvinist theologian.

A sermon tract entitled *An Address Enforcing an Inquiry into . . . Anabaptists*, published posthumously in 1771 but probably written a year or two after 1763, takes to task the itinerant Baptist enthusiast preachers for claiming to be "sent from God" and for intolerantly insisting that those who did not follow them were going to hell. The dominant emphasis in the sermon is on man's reason and man's duty to use that reason to test the credentials of preachers. Maury masterfully employed the plain style with its clear, logical organization and displayed his skill in suasory discourse. He made a sophisticated and effective use of the schemes and tropes of Classical oratory to establish his persona and to impress his arguments upon the audience.

Suggested Readings: CCV. *See also* Helen Duprey Bullock, ed., "A Dissertation on Education in the Form of a Letter from James Maury to Robert Jackson, July 17, 1762," PAHS, 2 (1941-1942), 36-60; Richard Beale Davis, *Intellectual Life in the Colonial South, 1585-1763*, 3 vols. (1978); J. A. Leo Lemay, "The Rev. Samuel Davies' Essay Series: The Virginia Centinel, 1756-1757" in *Essays in Early Virginia Literature Honoring Richard Beale Davis* (1977), pp. 121-163; Dumas Malone, *Jefferson the Virginian* (1948), pp. 40-46, for a discussion of Maury's school; Anne Maury, ed., *Memoirs of a Huguenot Family* (1853; rep., 1967), for several of Maury's letters; William Meade, *Old*

Churches, Ministers and Families of Virginia (1857; rep., 1966); Richard L. Morton, *Colonial Virginia* (1960).

Homer D. Kemp
Tennessee Technological University

SAMUEL MAVERICK (c. 1602-c. 1676)

Works: *A Briefe Discription of New England and the Severall Townes Therein* (w. 1660; pub. 1885).

Biography: Apparently associated with Sir Ferdinando Gorges's (q.v.) colonizing ventures, Samuel Maverick came from Eng. to America about 1624. When John Winthrop's (q.v.) group arrived in 1630, they found Maverick and his wife, Amias, living in a fortified house at Winnisimmet (Chelsea) on Noddle's Island in Boston Bay. Maverick soon clashed with Puritan authorities on civil as well as religious issues. In 1641, when they fined him for harboring two fugitives, he accused the authorities of pursuing "an inquisition-like course." Five years later, he was fined and jailed for signing Robert Child's petition requesting establishment of English common law within Mass., admission of non-Puritans to full civil rights or exemption from taxation and military service, and freedom to choose one's place of worship. Maverick seems to have left the Massachusetts Bay colony about 1650 and traveled to Eng. following the Stuart restoration. While there he wrote *A Briefe Discription of New England*, which called for more rigid supervision of New Eng.'s affairs by English authorities. He returned to New Eng. in 1664 as one of four royal commissioners appointed to settle intercolonial territorial disputes as well as to encourage more vigorous compliance with the Navigation Acts. When the duke of York granted him a house on Broadway in 1669, Maverick moved to New York City and remained there until his death.

Critical Appraisal: After it had lain undetected for approximately 220 years amidst the British Museum's Egerton papers, the unsigned, undated manuscript titled "A Briefe Discription of New England" was discovered by researcher Henry F. Waters. Internal evidence indicated Samuel Maverick composed the work in 1660. The loosely written lines on thirty foolscap pages originally served to further the author's private real estate interests in New Eng. as well as the mother country's imperial interests by calling for tighter English supervision of colonial affairs. The work first appeared in print in the Oct. 1884 issue of *The Proceedings of the Massachusetts Historical Society* and quickly reappeared in the Jan. 1885 issue of *The New England Historical and Genealogical Register*.

Maverick provided a surprisingly thorough verbal atlas of New Eng.'s communities. His presentation of distances between towns, historical details of settlement, and major economic activities in each population center evidence keen observational abilities. He argued that extraordinary population growth and naval strength testified to New Eng.'s rich exploitable resources. Approaching his opening thrust against the government of Massachusetts Bay Colony, Maverick cataloged each area's activities, from Maine's profitable fishing and fur-trading industries to southern New Eng.'s bountiful production of cattle, fruits, and Indian corn. Finishing the thrust, he asserted that Eng. might derive great benefits from the successful diversity of the colonial economy "if well managed." Obviously, proper management included restriction of the powers of the colonial governments, especially Mass.

With seething, but controlled, hostility, Maverick attacked the government of Massachusetts Bay Colony for incursions upon towns and territories beyond its chartered limits. He perceived such incursions as detrimental to the interests of both those territories and Eng., because they were perpetrated by men chosen without the knowledge or consent of prior inhabitants who held older patents. The Winthrops and the General Council had, in Maverick's opinion, deprived "many thousands" of civil and religious rights guaranteed under royal charter provisions. In a series of pointed charges, he outlined what he thought constituted treasonous disloyalty on the part of Mass. authorities: in the early 1630s, they had defaced the English flag and had flown to arms upon hearing a rumor that an approaching ship carried a royal governor; in about 1636 they had tolerated vilification of Eng.'s civil and ecclesiastical government; in 1646 and 1647, they had supported the authority of Parliament over the king and had forced all men over age 16 to subscribe to an "oath of fidelity" to the colonial government rather than to the crown; they had melted down English money to coin their own; and they had in several specific cases denied others the very liberty of conscience that they had sought for themselves. Finally, he accused them of misusing funds supplied by the Society for the Propagation of the Gospel. Although he mentioned the number of meetinghouses in various towns, the avowedly Episcopalian, secularly oriented Maverick did not find that enumeration indicative of what the staunch Puritan Edward Johnson (q.v.) had termed *God's Wonder-Working Providence.*

Maverick's indictment of colonial government and his pressure for reassertion of royal prerogatives stands as more than an eloquent monument to the effects of the Stuart Restoration in New Eng. It serves as striking evidence of the longstanding conflict between New Eng.'s "saints" and "strangers," and it serves as a literary signpost in the developing struggle over who should rule the colonies. The document captures with clarity the crux of a complex problem that one day would have revolutionary consequences.

Suggested Readings: DAB. *See also* Charles Francis Adams, *Three Episodes in Massachusetts History* (1892), I, 328-335; Mellen Chamberlain, "Samuel Maverick's Palisade House of 1630," PMHS, 2nd ser., 1 (1885), 366-373; Benjamin W. Labaree, *Colonial Massachusetts* (1979), p. 111; William H. Sumner, *History of East Boston* (1858), pp. 60-177. The text of "A Briefe Discription of New England" appears in PMHS, 2nd ser., 1 (1884), 231-249.

Rick W. Sturdevant
University of California, Santa Barbara

EXPERIENCE MAYHEW (1673-1758)

Works: *The Massachusee Psalter* (1709); *A Brief Journal* (w. 1713-1714; pub. 1896); *A Discourse* (1720); *Observations on the Indian Language* (w. 1722; pub. 1884); *All Mankind* (1725); *Indian Converts* (1727); *A Right to the Lord's Supper* (1741); *Grace Defended* (1744); *A Letter to a Gentleman* (1747).

Biography: Born on Jan. 27, 1673, at Chilmark on Martha's Vineyard, Mass., Experience Mayhew was a great-grandson of Thomas Mayhew, Sr., the founder of English settlements on the island. Since its arrival on the island in 1641, the Mayhew family had devoted itself to missionary work among the Indians, a tradition continued by Experience. After his father's death prevented him from attending Harvard, Experience, with little formal education but with a thorough knowledge of the native language, began preaching to Indian congregations by 1694. Under the aegis of the Society for Propagation of the Gospel in New England and Parts Adjacent (SPGNE), Mayhew spent his entire adulthood ministering to the Indians, supporting himself, like most Congregational ministers, largely from his own farm. His missionary work led him to the related field of translating religious texts into the Indian language. In recognition of his work with the Indians, Harvard awarded Mayhew an honorary M.A. in 1723. In later years, Mayhew also became known for his relatively liberal theological writings. Although he considered his views orthodox, they planted the seeds of liberalism and rationalism that sprang up in the next generation, even in his own famous son Jonathan Mayhew (q.v.). Still teaching and preaching among the Indians of Martha's Vineyard, he died on Nov. 20, 1758, at the age of 85.

Critical Appraisal: Experience Mayhew's writings fall into two distinct categories: his writings about his work with the Indians (and his translations and language guides to facilitate this work) and his expositions on theological doctrine. In both categories, his prose often lacks smoothness and economy; yet his writings demonstrate him to be a perceptive observer and a knowledgeable scholar. These strengths enabled him to produce works in both categories that continue to have historical importance and interest.

Mayhew's earliest publications, translations of three Cotton Mather (q.v.) sermons (1705, 1707, 1714), grew directly out of his needs as a missionary to the Indians on Martha's Vineyard. These early translations of *The Hatchets to Hew Down the Tree of Sin, The Day which the Lord Hath Made,* and *Family Religion Excited* led the SPGNE to commission and support his translation of the Psalms and the Gospel of John (*The Massachusee Psalter*), printed in parallel columns of Massachusee and English. He probably also played a major role in the revised edition of the *Indian Primer* in 1720 that, like the *New England Primer*, sought to combine instruction in reading and writing with instruction in theological dogma. Mayhew's familiarity with the Massachusee language and his work on the translations made his brief *Observations on the Indian Language* one of the earliest authoritative discussions of the language.

Mayhew also wrote observations on other aspects of Indian culture and his work in it. His journal of 1713 and 1714 (not published until 1896-1897 in *Some Correspondence Between the Governors and Treasurers of the New England Company*), describing his brief unsuccessful attempts in Conn. to convert the Narragansetts, Pequots, and Mohegans, is a detailed source of Indian attitudes in New Eng. during the early eighteenth century. Among these particular tribes, Mayhew, for one, realized the immense cultural conflict being waged between red and white groups. Among the natives of Martha's Vineyard, however, he did not see such a great conflict. His "Brief Account of the State of the Indians on Martha's Vineyard" (printed with his 1720 *Discourse*) emphasizes this group's religious piety, but also describes the Indian society becoming more British-like in other areas besides religion. He provided a fuller account of this society in *Indian Converts*, perhaps his most famous work, an unabashed justification of his missionary work in which he claimed to have won many Indian souls to Christ. Despite its possibly exaggerated claims and its obviously narrow viewpoint, this work remains a useful record of the confrontation between the British colonists and the native New Eng. culture.

Well known for his missionary work, Mayhew became even more widely known through his theological publications during the last half of his life. Although not numerous or smooth, his theological writings occupy an interesting position in the history of New Eng. Calvinism. His earliest original theological publications were two sermons he preached in Boston. In their biblical catalogs and their text-doctrine-application divisions, these two sermons use rhetoric typical of eighteenth-century New Eng. sermons, although they are perhaps even more repetitious than usual. In dogma, however, the sermons, especially the first one, *A Discourse Shewing That God Dealeth with Men as with Reasonable Creatures*, are not as typical. As the title suggests, the first sermon, pointing to the covenant, stresses the rationality of man and the benevolence of God. Although granting the doctrine of original sin and the need for conversion, Mayhew viewed both God and man favorably. In its basic theology, this sermon was a conventional argument for the covenant theology, but its implications elevated man above where orthodoxy usually placed him. Mayhew's second published sermon, *All Mankind, by Nature, Equally Under Sin*, does not view man as hopefully. It emphasizes man's inherent wickedness and his need for conversion. Although the earlier sermon calls for rationality and obedience, this one calls for humility and self-abasement. Because this second sermon is more orthodox than *A Discourse*, it is less revealing of Mayhew's distinct theological position.

Besides these two sermons, Mayhew published three other significant theological works. The most ambitious of the three, *Grace Defended*, a work of more than 200 pages, synthesizes his relatively liberal views. Although he still accepted the original-sin doctrine and the need for repentance, Mayhew here tried to define the salvation process and to prove that salvation is in the grasp of all. Unable to accept the doctrine of total depravity, he granted a measure of free will and also strongly defended his view of a merciful and just God. In the preface, Mayhew admitted that these views separate him from the strict Calvinists, but contended that he is closer to them than he is to the Arminians. His other two publications, both in letter form, expand parts of his liberal dogma. In *A Right to the Lord's Supper*, he argued that regeneration is not necessary for one to partake of the sacrament. Among his many supporting reasons is the argument that because men cannot adequately determine who has been regenerated, they might mistakenly bar someone from the sacrament. He also contended that the unregenerate are not necessarily wicked. These arguments make this work a rather explicit statement of the liberal position on the importance of regeneration. His other publication, *A Letter to a Gentleman*, is a relatively unimportant exposition on the distinctions between saving grace and common grace.

Taken as a whole, Mayhew's theological writings are often an unpolished mixture of logical analysis, scriptural citation, and almost endless repetition. Although not works of a first-rate, well-educated mind, they are, nonetheless, historically important for their delineation of the middle ground between the more famous theologies of Jonathan Edwards (q.v.) and Mayhew's son Jonathan.

Suggested Readings: CCNE; DAB; Sibley-Shipton (VII, 626, 632-639); Sprague (I, 131-133). *See also* Cedric B. Cowing, *The Great Awakening and the Revolution* (1971), p. 80; Perry Miller, *The New England Mind: From Colony to Province* (1953), p. 430; Charles M. Segal and David C. Stineback, *Puritans, Indians, and Manifest Destiny* (1977), pp. 217-218.

John S. Hardt
Ferrum College

JONATHAN MAYHEW (1720-1766)

Works: *Seven Sermons* (1749); *A Discourse Concerning Unlimited Submission* (1750); *A Sermon Preached at Boston. May 26, 1751* (1751); *A Sermon Preach'd in the Audience of His Excellency* (1754); *A Discourse on Rev. XV. 3d, 4th* (1755); *The Expected Dissolution of All Things* (1755); *Sermons upon the Following Subjects* (1755); *Two Discourses Delivered November 23d. 1758* (1758); *Two Discourses Delivered Oct. 25th, 1759* (1759); *A Discourse Occasioned by the Death of...Stephen Sewall* (1760); *God's Hand and Providence* (1760); *Practical Discourses Delivered on Occasion of the Earthquakes* (1760); *Two Discourses Delivered October 9th, 1760* (1760); *A Discourse Occasioned by the Death of George II* (1761); *Striving to Enter in at the Strait Gate* (1761); *Christian Sobriety* (1763); *A Defence of the Observations* (1763); *Observations on the Charter* (1763); *Two Sermons on the Nature* (1763); *A Letter of Reproof*

(1764); *Remarks on an Anonymous Tract* (1764); *Popish Idolatry* (1765); *The Snare Broken* (1766).

Biography: Jonathan Mayhew was born in Chilmark, on Martha's Vineyard, Mass., the son of Experience Mayhew (q.v.) who, along with John Eliot (q.v.), was one of the most dedicated missionaries to the New Eng. Indian tribes. Jonathan graduated from Harvard College in 1744, and in 1747 was called to the pastorate of Boston's new West Church, one of the most affluent and liberal churches in the city. Unlike some of his colleagues who after the violent disruptions of the Great Awakening attempted to minimize their differences in theology, Mayhew quickly emerged as one of the most outspoken advocates of a liberalized, rational Christianity that stressed the power of man's free will in moral judgment. Furthermore, as early as 1750 in his *Discourse Concerning Unlimited Submission*, Mayhew attacked the tyranny of rulers whose laws proved contrary to those established by God; and, later, in other political sermons like *The Snare Broken* (1766), he continued to alert his countrymen to the British threat to their natural rights.

Because of such politically explosive sermons, Mayhew became known as one of the leaders of the resistance to British encroachments on American rights until his premature death due to a "violent nervous disorder." He attacked organizations such as the Society for the Propagation of the Gospel in Foreign Parts, as well as coercive actions such as the imposition of the Stamp Act, and he cultivated friendships with men who later would lead the call for American independence. Although never interested in writing systematic divinity per se, Mayhew, along with Charles Chauncy (q.v.), clearly enunciated doctrines that in the nineteenth century served as the cornerstone of the Unitarian faith. Mayhew did not live to see the results of America's increasingly severe difficulties with Eng., but during the Revolutionary years, his sermons were pointed to as among the first rigorous challenges to the increasingly intolerable exercise of British prerogatives.

Critical Appraisal: Jonathan Mayhew's writings fall into two broad categories: those dealing with his conception of rational Christianity and moral responsibility under such a faith and those that focus on more overtly political matters. The two works that best illustrate his liberal theological views are *Seven Sermons* (1749), a volume reprinted in London and for which Mayhew received an honorary doctorate from Aberdeen, and *Christian Sobriety* (1763), addressed explicitly to young men in his parish and offering instruction in proper moral behavior under rational and enlightened views of Christianity. Both books consist of sermons preached either to his own parish or at Thursday lectures Mayhew gave in Boston and evidence a concern with the application of his liberal views to the development of a strong moral character. Also noteworthy for their doctrinal interest are *Striving to Enter in at the Strait Gate* (1761) and *Two Sermons on the Nature, Extent and Perfection of Divine Goodness* (1763), in which Mayhew elaborated his notion of a divinity that has allowed men a significant amount of free will and moral responsibility.

His political writings, particularly polemical works such as *Observations on the Charter*, display a boldness of rhetoric not found in the work of many clergymen among his contemporaries. While appealing to New Eng.'s ingrained loyalty to Congregational Church government, he also couched more general attacks on Eng.'s cultural and political institutions and their destructive influence on New Eng.'s church and political government. In the years following Mayhew's death, his *Discourse Concerning Unlimited Submission* became a rallying point for those clergy and their supporters who found in that work a premonition of the arguments they themselves would have to muster in their escalated opposition to the crown. In such sermons, Mayhew's style, although more polished than Chauncy's, displays a straightforwardness and rhetorical power that betrayed the genteel intentions behind most of his pastoral sermons. Although the brevity of his career precluded his exercising the kind of doctrinal and stylistic influence over Unitarianism that his friend and colleague Charles Chauncy did, in the nineteenth century he, along with Chauncy and Ebenezer Gay (q.v.), often was pointed to as one of the spiritual midwives of the American Unitarian movement.

Suggested Readings: CCNE; DAB; DARB; LHUS; Sibley-Shipton (XI, 440-472); Sprague (VIII 22-29); T$_1$; T$_2$. *See also* Charles W. Akers, *Called unto Liberty: A Life of Jonathan Mayhew* (1964); Alden Bradford, *Memoir of the Life and Writings of Rev. Jonathan Mayhew, D.D.* (1838); Richard J. Hooker, "The Mayhew Controversy," CH, 5 (1936), 239-255; Clinton Rossiter, "The Life and Mind of Jonathan Mayhew," WMQ, 7 (1950), 531-558; Conrad Wright, *The Beginnings of Unitarianism in America* (1955).

Philip F. Gura
University of Colorado, Boulder

MATTHEW MAYHEW (1648-1710)

Works: *A Brief Narrative of the Success Which the Gospel Hath Had, Among the Indians, of Martha's Vineyard* (1694), reprinted in London as *The Conquest and Triumphs of Grace* (1695).

Biography: Born on Martha's Vineyard, Mass., in 1648, Matthew Mayhew was the most influential political figure on the island other than his grandfather, Governor Thomas Mayhew, Sr., who had bought the island in 1641. After the death of his missionary father Thomas Mayhew, Jr. (q.v.), in 1657, Matthew and his younger brother John were sent to school in Cambridge. It was assumed Matthew would continue the work of Christianizing the Indians begun by his father; however, it was John who received the religious calling. Matthew was destined to devote nearly forty years to public service.

Matthew Mayhew's political life began in 1670 when he served as an envoy for his aging grandfather. In 1671 he was commissioned collector of customs for Martha's Vineyard. At the same time, Governor Francis Lovelace, a representative of the duke of York, cemented the Mayhew family's rule of Martha's

Vineyard by granting virtual manorial rights to Governor Mayhew and his grandson Matthew. After the governor's death in 1683, Matthew assumed all of the duties and responsibilities of governor without the title. He became chief magistrate while continuing to hold numerous other public offices such as sheriff (1683), clerk of the court (1685), register of deeds (1685), and chief justice of the peace (1683).

The relative isolation of the island enabled the affairs of government to proceed without major interference from the mainland, and the successful missionary efforts of the Mayhews protected the island during King Philip's War. The autocratic rule of the Mayhews was periodically challenged, but rarely with any impact. The greatest threat came in 1692 when the Massachusetts Bay Colony absorbed the islands. When it became apparent that ignoring the new rulers would not change anything, Matthew Mayhew yielded to the inevitable without forfeiting the authority he would continue to wield until his death in 1710.

Critical Appraisal: The format of Matthew Mayhew's narrative follows that of Daniel Gookin's (q.v.) 1674 *Historical Collections of the Indians in New England*, a "progress report" for the Society for the Propagation of the Gospel [SPG] in New England. Mayhew's account deleted the frequent Bible verses quoted by Gookin, giving Mayhew's text a slightly more secular tone. Both his father and his brother received financial assistance from the SPG, and the untimely death of his brother in 1688 left the Vineyard without an English missionary. Without directly mentioning the society, Mayhew's dedication suggests his association with it: "I shall only desire of You, that incouragement might be given to some *English*, or *Indian*, Spirited for such Service...to visit the Indians, bordering on *New England*; who might carry to them the glad Tydings of the Gospel."

An intimate knowledge of the family's missionary work and proficiency in the Indian language enabled Mayhew to write a creditable account of the Indians of Martha's Vineyard. The narrative begins with a discourse on the Indian language and its various dialects with linguistically sound explanations of variations in pronunciation and spelling. Mayhew next provided a detailed description of the hierarchy of the government of the Indians, using English nomenclature to identify Indian princes, nobles, and yeomen. His discussion of the Indians' religion begins with an objective account of the powers Powwows were believed to possess. His description of the selection of a Powwow resembled the nurturing of young boys for the priesthood. Mayhew related several incidents to illustrate the relative importance and power of the Powwows among the Indians while indicating the concurrent progress of the Christian Gospel.

After the preamble, Mayhew related the history of the conversions accomplished on the island, especially by his father. He told the story of I a-coomes [Hiacoomes], the first convert who became an Indian minister and assistant, working among the Indians until his death. Mayhew provided an accounting of the Praying Indians, calculating the total number of adult Indians on all islands to be 3,000 at their peak. Mayhew pointed out that there were enough Praying

Indians to establish an Indian church on Martha's Vineyard (Aug. 22, 1670). He was slightly defensive in reporting that the number of proselytes on all islands had decreased, and he cited death as the main reason for the decline on Martha's Vineyard. Mayhew took pains to emphasize the fidelity of Indians, who seemed to be more strict in the observance of their religious duties than many English who felt superior to the Indians. Mayhew solicited specific information concerning the Christian state of the Indians on neighboring islands. He concluded his narrative by quoting the letters he received in response to his inquiries.

Mayhew's prose is concise, his argument direct and unembroidered—a fairly unemotional description of the Indian culture and religion. His subject is religious, but he did not belabor the theological aspects. As the "governor" of an area recently incorporated by the Massachusetts Bay Colony, Mayhew appeared to be justifying the governing of the islands in general and the Christianizing of the Indians in particular.

Suggested Readings: Charles Edward Banks, *The History of Martha's Vineyard* (1911-1925; rep., 1966); Daniel Gookin, *Historical Collections of the Indians in New England* (1792).

Ann Mahan
University of Houston

THOMAS MAYHEW, JR. (c. 1621-1657)

Works: Letters in *The Glorious Progress of the Gospel, Amongst the Indians in New England* (1649); *The Light Appearing More and More Towards the Perfect Day* (1651); *Strength Out of Weakness* (1652); *Tears of Repentance* (1653).

Biography: Born in Eng. about 1621, Thomas Mayhew, Jr., probably came to Medford, Mass., in 1631 with his father Thomas Mayhew, Sr., who worked as factor for London merchant Matthew Cradock. In 1641 father and son became patentees of Martha's Vineyard, Nantucket, and the Elizabeth Islands. The following year, young Thomas led a small band of colonists from Watertown on the mainland to Great Harbor (now Edgartown) on Martha's Vineyard, and the group selected him as their pastor. In 1643 Hiacoomes, a Wampanoag Indian, requested Christian instruction from Mayhew, thereby initiating a lengthy process that culminated in the conversion of most of the island's 3,000 Indians. Described by Rev. Henry Whitfield as cheerful, uncomplaining, and exceedingly modest, the younger Mayhew conducted his mission to the Indians without resort to coercion or offers of material reward. His work entitled him to share with John Eliot (q.v.) the distinction of being the earliest Protestant missionaries in New Eng. Thomas Mayhew, Jr., disappeared in 1657 on a voyage to Eng., where he hoped to secure title to the estate of his deceased father-in-law, as well as report on his missionary activities.

Critical Appraisal: Promoters of missionary ventures have long used collections of published letters to garner support and solicit charitable contributions. Thomas Mayhew's four printed letters appeared in such early collections. The first letter, addressed to Edward Winslow (q.v.) on Nov. 18, 1647, appeared with correspondence from John Eliot in Winslow's *The Glorious Progress of the Gospel, Amongst the Indians in New England*. Mayhew ascribed the Indians' voluntary acceptance of Christianity to their "notable reason, judgement, and capacitie." He attributed further conversions to three striking "providences," each involving miraculous recovery of an Indian whom the powwows had pronounced incurable. The tract containing Mayhew's letter, published in May 1649, was intended to muster parliamentary support for a public corporation to finance Indian missions. The Long Parliament responded on Jul. 27, 1649, by establishing the Society for the Propagation of the Gospel.

Mayhew's second published letter was written to Henry Whitfield on Sept. 7, 1650, at the latter's request. Having observed Mayhew's financial distress during a ten-day visit to the island, Whitfield decided to publish *The Light Appearing More and More Towards the Perfect Day*, a collection of letters designed to elicit contributions from wealthy English patrons. The tract included Mayhew's letter, which offered a well-organized history of the Martha's Vineyard mission from Hiacoomes's conversion in 1643 to the crisis surrounding the death of the first "meeting Indian," Hiacoomes's 5-day-old child, in 1650. Mayhew emphasized that conversion was due to the Indians' volition and God's will; it was not due to his efforts. He attributed many Indians' rejection of Christianity to desire for earthly riches, opposition of tribal leaders, and fear of the powwows' devilish powers. In a detailed relation of sagamore Towanquatick's conversion, which he had mentioned briefly in the 1647 Winslow letter, Mayhew demonstrated adeptness at catching and retaining his reader's attention. Stylistically, he captured for each reader the vitality of the Indians' conversion experiences, thereby structuring an empathic bridge that now spans three centuries.

A third Mayhew letter, written to Whitfield on Oct. 16, 1651, appeared in *Strength Out of Weakness*, the first tract actually published by the Society for the Propagation of the Gospel. Mayhew continued his historical relation of God's testing of the Indians' faith. His letter contained a colorful description of the powwows' witchcraft. It detailed the conversion of the "notorious" powwow Tequanonim, Hiacommes's preaching at Sabbath meetings, and Mayhew's intention to establish a school and town for the "meeting Indians." The most poignant theme in the six-page letter is the severity of the communal rift that the conversion process sparked among the Wampanoags. Demand for copies of *Strength Out of Weakness* sent the tract through four printings and reissuance in 1657 under a new title, *The Banners of Grace and Love Displayed in the Farther Conversion of the Indians in New-England*.

Mayhew's fourth letter, originally written to the society on Oct. 22, 1652, was printed in John Eliot's tract *Tears of Repentance*. Good news abounded, because the Indian school had opened its doors to thirty eager pupils on Nov. 11, 1651, and in the spring of 1652 the Praying Indians had taken the unprecedented step of adopting a written covenant. As in prior letters, Mayhew inspired readers with terse yet fervid testimony to the earnestness and strength of the Christian Indians' faith.

Suggested Readings: CCNE; DAB; Sprague (I, 131-132). *See also* Charles Edward Banks, *The History of Martha's Vineyard*, vol. I (1966); Lloyd Custer Mayhew Hare, *Thomas Mayhew, Patriarch to the Indians* (1932), pp. 84-116; William Kellaway, *The New England Company, 1649-1776* (1962), pp. 13-14, 22-23, 96-99; Francis Jennings, *The Invasion of America: Indians, Colonialism, and the Cant of Conquest* (1975), pp. 230-232, 245-247. All tracts containing letters from Thomas Mayhew, Jr., are printed in CMHS, 3rd ser., 4 (1834).

Rick W. Sturdevant

University of California, Santa Barbara

JOHN MAYLEM (1739-c. 1762)

Works: *The Conquest of Louisbourg* (1758); *Gallic Perfidy* (1758); Du Simitière Papers (a collection of thirteen pieces: nine poems and four letters, in the Library Company of Philadelphia).

Biography: Thanks to the research of Lawrence C. Wroth, many of the details of Maylem's short life have been gathered and, in some cases, corrected. Born in Boston on Apr. 30, 1739, he was the youngest of nine children of John, Sr., and Ann (Dehane) Maylem. A graduate of Harvard College, his father was a restless, unsuccessful man who changed occupations and locations frequently. The poet was raised in Newport, R.I., and although the details of his education are nonexistent, we do know that he enlisted in the British army in 1756, at the age of 17, describing himself as a "farmer" for the registration records.

By 1758 he had been promoted to the rank of captain and had published his first known work, *Gallic Perfidy*, recounting his capture in 1757 by Indian forces, incarceration in Montreal, and eventual freedom. After the publication of *The Conquest of Louisbourg*, Maylem moved to N.Y., where he lived from Jun. 1759 until Oct. 1760 and wrote three unpublished poems. A letter to a friend recounted his journey, after a drunken spree, to Philadelphia. Penniless and ashamed, he attempted and failed at suicide and then moved to R.I. In the May 19, 1761, edition of the *Newport Mercury*, there appeared the anonymous satire, "The Boston Sabbath," which is attributed to Maylem. His name appears for the last time in 1762 on a roster of soldiers headed for the battle in Havana. Because there were heavy casualties in this incursion and because his name vanished from further official records, scholars believe that Maylem probably died there.

Critical Appraisal: John Maylem's literary reputation rests primarily on his two long poems, *Gallic Perfidy* and *The Conquest of Louisbourg*, both published in 1758. Written in bombastic, fiery couplets, the first of them opens with a reference to an earlier, and now lost, poem, *The Conquest of Beausejour*, composed sometime between 1755 and 1758. In *Gallic Perfidy*, the poet warned us that he would write "in rougher Strain, for softer Rhyme / Seems not adapt to this my solemn Theme." He then invoked the aid of the Furies, rather than the Muses, to recount the unprovoked French and Indian attack on Fort William Henry, an attack that broke a treaty. He described the horror of the eight-day siege and his escape into the woods and ensuing capture by "Three brawny Savages." He and other captives were taken to a desolate area and eight days later to Montreal, where he was eventually "redeemed" by Monsieur Vaudreil. During this captivity, he described the fate of one whose heart was torn out and eaten and whose blood was drunk by the Indians. In the closing lines, Maylem vowed to avenge himself and those killed by pursuing "the wily Savage from his secret Haunts."

Also written in heroic couplets that abound in mythological allusions, *The Conquest of Louisbourg* is a far more conventional, less impassioned, and less effective account of a British victory in the French and Indian War. The poem begins with the traditional invocation of the Muses and describes early French and Indian victories over the British. Next, the scene shifts to a worried King George who calls his advisers, and Mr. Secretary Pitt suggests a landing on the Island of Cape-Breton under the direction of Adm. Edward Boscawen and Gen. Jeffery Amherst. The piece then extols the heroics of leaders such as James Wolfe, Simon Fraser, Thomas Scott, and, of course, Gen. Amherst, who at one point is compared to Achilles. It details the British victory and praises these forces for the pity they take on the vanquished. The poem then concludes with a tranquil image of smooth waters and rolling lands now under British domination.

The Du Simitière Papers contain nine other poems, seven of which are reprinted in Lawrence Wroth's seminal article. Two are youthful acrostics that playfully extol the virtues of two girls to whom the poet was attracted. Four others ("Description of Newport," "Satire on Halifax," "The Boston Sabbath," and "The Birdiad"), although of negligible literary value, are interesting for the angry, bitter, satirical visions they present of people and places. As Wroth pointed out, "none of the towns in which he lived gave him happiness." Although his reputation is now obscure, Maylem was definitely popular in his day. A generation later, Joseph Brown Ladd (q.v.) hyperbolically praised him as "a poet of genius...[whose] genius rose superior to every inconvenience, and he remains a shining example of the maxim, that 'Poeta nascitur non fit.' "

Suggested Readings: T₁. *See also* Evert A. Duyckinck and George L. Duyckinck, *Cyclopedia of American Literature*, vol. I (1866); Lawrence C. Wroth, "John Maylem: Poet and Warrior," PCSM, 32 (1937), 87-120.

David W. Madden
University of California, Davis

JOSIAH MEIGS (1757-1822)

Works: *An Oration Pronounced Before a Public Assembly* (1782); *New-Haven Gazette* (co-owner and editor; 1784-1786); *To the Public, and Particu-*

larly to the Readers of the New-Haven Gazette (with Eleutheros Dana; 1786); *The New-Haven Gazette, and the Connecticut Magazine* (owner and editor; 1786-1789); *Statement of the Causes of the Removal from Office* (1811); *Memorial. . .for an Act of Incorporation of a National Vaccine Institute* (with others; 1820).

Biography: Josiah Meigs was born on Aug. 21, 1757, at Middletown, Conn., a brother of the Revolutionary War officer Return Jonathan Meigs (q.v.). After graduation from Yale in 1778, he taught in N.Y., in 1781 became a tutor at Yale, and in 1783 was admitted to the bar. A year later, Meigs resigned from Yale and with Daniel Bowen and Eleutheros Dana established a weekly, *The New-Haven Gazette*. After his partners withdrew in 1786 and 1787, he continued with *The New-Haven Gazette, and the Connecticut Magazine* until 1789. From 1789 to 1794, he practiced law in Bermuda and then became professor of mathematics and natural philosophy at Yale. In 1800 he was elected professor of mathematics at the University of Georgia and in 1801 was named president. He remained president until 1810, taught one more year, but left Ga. in 1812 to become surveyor general of the U.S. In 1814 he was appointed commissioner of the General Land Office and remained at that post until he died on Sept. 4, 1822.

Critical Appraisal: *An Oration*, which was delivered in 1781 to celebrate the victory over Cornwallis, is a celebration of the triumph of liberty, which, according to Meigs, had always been "the darling object of mankind." This work praises the vitality of the American continent that in a short century and a half rose from wilderness to "a powerful and polished empire." In reviewing the war, Meigs quoted liberally from the Classical epics, suggesting that the war of liberty assumed epic stature in history. Its hero was George Washington (q.v.), a neo-Classical man, capable of forming and executing great designs and possessed of the virtues of regularity, discipline, and temperance. The glory of Washington, Meigs said, would attend the prosperity and progress of the states to their manifest destiny at the "western ocean." Education is a source of America's progress, for like Thomas Jefferson (q.v.), whom he admired, Meigs believed that political prosperity was founded in private virtue.

Meigs's most significant contribution to American literature came from the editorial policy begun with the change from *The New-Haven Gazette* to *The New-Haven Gazette, and the Connecticut Magazine*. In their notice *To the Public*, Meigs and Dana acknowledged complaints that advertisements had crowded out "those amusing or constructive articles" in the *Gazette*, and they promised to expand the paper and print the advertisements in a supplement, hoping that the format would encourage "men of genius" to submit their works. Meigs published large quantities of poetry, tales, and essays, including works by Benjamin Franklin (q.v.), Thomas Paine (q.v.), Joel Barlow (q.v.), David Humphreys (q.v.), and others. "The Anarchiad" by Barlow, Humphreys, John Trumbull (q.v.), and Lemuel Hopkins (q.v.) appeared in the *Magazine* in 1786-1787, and when the Constitution was written, the *Magazine* supported its adoption.

Meigs's *Statement of the Causes*, concerning his dismissal as professor of mathematics and natural philosophy at the University of Georgia, reflects the high level of political passions of his day. His strong attachment to Jeffersonian Republican principles had caused him to run afoul of the strongly Federalist Timothy Dwight (q.v.), who replaced Ezra Stiles (q.v.) at Yale. Those same principles, his strong sectional bias against Ga., and his sense of exile contributed to his dismissal. Despite his dislike for Ga., Meigs contributed significantly to the university's development. When he assumed the presidency, only wilderness existed where Athens now stands, and Meigs oversaw the erection of the first buildings there.

As commissioner of the General Land Office, Meigs instituted a system of daily meteorological observations at the land offices throughout the country and reports of information to Washington. As his *Memorial* shows, he also took an active part in promoting the widespread use of inoculation. As these activities indicate, Meigs maintained a lifelong interest in scientific work beyond his teaching, an interest due, in general, to having been trained during an age of rapidly expanding scientific knowledge and, in particular, to his close association with Stiles and the scientific curriculum he instituted at Yale.

Suggested Readings: DAB; Dexter (IV, 43-47); T_2. *See also* O. Burton Adams, "Yale Influence on the Formation of the University of Georgia," GHR, 51 (1967), 175-185; *Appleton's Cyclopaedia of American Biography*, IV, 288-289; E. Merton Coulter, *College Life in the Old South* (1973), pp. 17-18; G. H. Hollister, *The History of Connecticut* (1855), II, 648-649; Augustus Longstreet Hull, *A Historical Sketch of the University of Georgia* (1894), pp. 12-16, 22-25; Charles Edgeworth Jones, *Education in Georgia* (1889), pp. 44-46; William M. Meigs, *Life of Josiah Meigs* (1887).

Daniel F. Littlefield, Jr.
Little Rock, Arkansas

RETURN JONATHAN MEIGS (1740-1823)

Works: *A Journal* (1776).

Biography: Return Jonathan Meigs was born at Middletown, Conn., on Dec. 17, 1740. During the Revolutionary War, he quickly rose in the ranks. As a major, he served in Benedict Arnold's (q.v.) expedition to join Gen. Montgomery's army at Montreal. At Quebec, he was among those captured but was exchanged in 1776. Eventually made colonel, he led the successful attack on the British at Sag Harbor and in 1779 served under Anthony Wayne at the capture of Stony Point. In 1788 Meigs was appointed one of the surveyors of the Ohio Company, and at Marietta, he drafted a code of conduct by which the settlers lived until the appointed judges arrived. He later served as a judge of the Court of Quarter Sessions, clerk of the Court of Common Pleas, and surveyor. At the Treaty of Greenville in 1795, he worked for the return of white captives among the Indians. In 1801 he became agent to the Cherokees and as U.S. commissioner negotiated several treaties with that tribe. He lived among the Cherokees until his death on Jan. 28, 1823.

Critical Appraisal: *A Journal* is a daily record of events during Benedict Arnold's march up the Kennebec and then to Montreal and Quebec, from Sept. 9, 1775, to Jan. 1, 1776. Although written in the sometimes abbreviated style of a journal or diary, it offers vivid accounts of the daily routine of camp life during the war, the hardships of travel in the wilderness, abandoned native fields, smallpox among the troops, battle scenes, and tactics. It also offers brief insights into the character of historical figures such as Arnold. *A Journal* was published in pamphlet form in 1776, excerpted in the *London Magazine*, and published in John Almon's *American Remembrancer* that same year. It has been reprinted since in the Massachusetts Historical Society *Collections* (1846) as *Journal of the Expedition Against Quebec* (1864), and in the Winchester, Va., *Annual Papers* (1931) as *Journal of Major Return Johnathan* [sic] *Meigs*.

Suggested Readings: DAB; T_2. See also *Allibone's Dictionary of American Authors*, II, 1261; *Appleton's Cyclopaedia of American Biography*, IV, 288; Samuel Prescott Hildreth, *Biographical and Historical Memoirs of the Early Pioneer Settlers of Ohio* (1852), pp. 258-278; National Archives, *Letters Received Relating to Indian Affairs, 1800-1823* and *Records of the Cherokee Agency in Tennessee, 1801-1835*; Thomas J. Summers, *History of Marietta* (1903), pp. 47, 62, 69, 115, 147, 160, 164-165.

Daniel F. Littlefield, Jr.

Little Rock, Arkansas

RETURN JONATHAN MEIGS (1764-1825)

Works: *A Poem Spoken in the Chapel of Yale-College* (1784); "A Prophecy" (1789).

Biography: Return Jonathan Meigs was born at Middletown, Conn., on Nov. 17, 1764, and graduated from Yale in 1785. He studied law before moving to Ohio in 1788, where he and his father, Return Jonathan Meigs (q.v.), were among the first settlers at Marietta. In 1798 he became a territorial judge, and in 1799 he was elected to the first territorial legislature. Upon statehood, he became chief justice of the Ohio Supreme Court. In 1805 he served as a judge in Louisiana Territory and in 1807 and 1808 served briefly as district judge in Michigan Territory before being elected to the U.S. Senate. In 1810 he was elected governor of Ohio, a position he held until 1814. During the War of 1812, Meigs raised militia to protect the exposed frontier. For his efforts, he was appointed postmaster general of the U.S. in 1814, serving in this capacity until 1823, when he returned to Ohio, where he died on Mar. 29, 1825.

Critical Appraisal: As a youth, Meigs apparently aspired to be a poet before he devoted himself to a career in public life. Two works, highly patriotic in theme, survive. The first, *A Poem Spoken in the Chapel of Yale-College*, is a long poem in heroic couplets and is in many ways typical of the neo-Classical poetic tradition. Fancy allowed the poet to visit Europe and reflect on her history. In Greece, the glory and culture that inspired Homer are in ruins as is the Rome that inspired Cato. Russia is rising from darkness, but her people are only polished barbarians. France's Louis, seeing Columbia's struggle for liberty, sent aid: "Blest are the realms where monarchs fill the throne, / Who make their subjects' happiness their own." Albion, whose glory of 1588 is gone, is falling into ruin. The poet contrasted these scenes to the "Goddess Columbia, " with her great towns, her heroes such as George Washington (q.v.), and her centers of education that would foster scientific discovery and eventually give rise to a new and great tradition of philosophers, thinkers, and writers. Finally, Meigs prophesied that Columbia's empire would rise until the last trumpet and until the earth spun from its orbit and the laws of nature broke down. The patriotism and national self-consciousness displayed in the poem place Meigs squarely in the tradition of poets such as Timothy Dwight (q.v.), Philip Freneau (q.v.), Joel Barlow (q.v.), and others.

This vision of America is further developed in "A Prophecy," which Meigs delivered at the Fourth of July celebration at Marietta in 1789. In this work, Meigs noted how, in Ohio, the savage lately hid in ambush and how the wilderness prevailed. Now, however, nature, instead of brooding, repays the industry of the settler. The forests yield to the axes, "domes and temples" rise, and justice reigns. According to Meigs, "villas" would spring up along the Ohio and Mississippi Valleys. Everywhere would be flocks, fertile fields, and vineyards; religion, charity, and social virtues would spread over the land. Unlike his earlier poem, the emphasis here is less on the intellectual seats of America than on the opinion that the destiny of America rests in the hands of the industrious, hardworking frontiersman who would subdue the wilderness and make the land ready for the town builders and the yeoman farmers. This is clearly an early statement of manifest destiny, much akin to Michel Guillaŭme Jean de Crèvecoeur's (q.v.) theory of social development in America, anticipating by a number of decades the basic theme of works such as James Fenimore Cooper's *The Pioneers* and some stories in Washington Irving's *The Sketch-Book*.

Besides these poems, *A Brief Sketch of the State of Ohio* (1822) has been ascribed to Meigs. Published under the name of Naham Ward of Marietta, this propaganda piece encourages immigration to Ohio.

Suggested Readings: DAB; Dexter (IV, 428-430). *See also Appleton's Cyclopaedia of American Biography*, IV, 288; [William Hart], *An Appeal to the People* (1822); G. H. Hollister, *The History of Connecticut* (1855), II, 648; *Ohio Archaeological and Historical Publications* (1911), 20, 251-252; Thomas J. Summers, *History of Marietta* (1903), pp. 75-76, 308-309.

Daniel F. Littlefield, Jr.
Little Rock, Arkansas

JOHN MERCER (1704-1768)

Works: Mss. Account Book and Diary (w. 1725-1768); *An Exact Abridgment of the Public Acts of the Assembly of Virginia* (1737), and its *Continuation* (1739); *An Exact Abridgment. . .in Force and Use January 1, 1758* (1759); "To the Worshipful. . .the House of Burgesses, the Case and Petition of John Mercer" (w. 1747); possible author, Major "Dinwiddianae" poems and letters (1754-1757), Henry E. Huntington Library (manuscript BR 74); other Mercer papers and poems in manuscript at the Virginia Historical Society, and the Virginia State Library.

Biography: A political and legal theorist, John Mercer was born in Dublin, Ire., and educated at Trinity College. In 1720 he came to Va., settling in Stafford County in 1726. There he built Marlborough, one of the most elaborate and original houses in colonial America. The extensive archaeological work done by the Smithsonian in 1957 reveals that Mercer's household contained the best equipment available in eighteenth-century Va. Mercer also owned one of the largest and finest colonial libraries, including at least 1,500 volumes. A prominent and vocal attorney for more than forty years, Mercer sustained a series of reprimands and reinstatements, particularly in Prince William County. In 1741 he was admitted to practice in Williamsburg, and in 1748 he was appointed presiding justice of the Stafford County Court. Also a man of business, Mercer served as secretary and general counsel of the Ohio Company of Va., speculating in western lands. Less successfully, he attempted to recoup his fortune by establishing a brewery at Marlborough, where he died in debt on Oct. 14, 1768.

Critical Appraisal: John Mercer's abridgment of Va. laws is known to every legal historian and was indispensable to court justices soon after its publication in 1737. The first digested code printed in Va., the work was, in fact, purchased in 1759 for all Va.'s court justices. Encouraged by subscriptions, Mercer felt obliged to make the laws as intelligible as possible, and he modeled his work after Edmund Wingate's *Abridgment of English Statutes*. He provided several tables listing the acts alphabetically, giving different titles for the same acts and supplying the years, numbers of chapters, and pages of the laws to facilitate use. The work covers laws, punishments, and fines for public and private acts from stealing hogs to standardizing weights and measures to describing the architecture for towns and buildings such as the capitol in Williamsburg. Indicative of the ties between church and state are laws that impose fines for refusing to baptize children and for denying the existence of God. An invaluable resource, the *Abridgment* clarifies laws, indicating which are obsolete, expired, repealed, or annulled. Mercer added to and altered the work in 1739 and 1759, always with the chief intention to make the laws understandable.

Also among Mercer's works are his manuscript Account Book (1725-1732), which concerns his private expenses and legal fees, and his manuscript Diary (Jan. 1, 1740-Mar. 31, 1768), which covers his activities at Marlborough, Stafford County. Compressing much information into a small space, Mercer recorded in the Diary the number of miles he traveled annually, the number of days he was home, the kind of native and imported flowers he planted, and the temperature and the weather. Although more a ledger than a diary since it contains no reflections, the work's entries provide information about the law practice of the times. Mercer, for example, traveled on legal business 3,880 miles in 1731; he was home only 137 days that year. The Diary records some details about the county courts and the General Court in Williamsburg and is indicative of the wide acquaintances of colonial lawyers.

Not only a legal scholar, Mercer was also a belletristic writer. Known as a literary man among his contemporaries, Mercer is described in his *Virginia Gazette* obituary as "a gentleman of great natural abilities improved by extensive knowledge not only in his profession, but in several other branches of polite literature." He is the most probable candidate for the *Dinwiddianae*, a series of poems and letters dated between Nov. 4, 1754 - May 3, 1757, satirizing Governor Robert Dinwiddie, Gen. Edward Braddock, and other favorites of the governor. The documents contain poems, prose glossaries, and quasi-dialectal letters attacking matters such as taxation, settlement of western lands, and the Jacobites.

As a whole, the work documents the widespread literary opposition to the Royalist policies. The satirist at work was clearly conscious of popular forms of satire, including the works of Pope and the Hudibrastic verse of Samuel Butler. In the *Dinwiddianae*, the author employed mock heroic, burlesque, pun, and direct invective. The roughness in rhyme and meter may be intentional, and the marginal annotations a device to enhance the satire.

Although several candidates for authorship have been suggested, most of the evidence points to Mercer as author of the three major "Dinwiddianae" poems and the letters following them. He would have been familiar with the activities of Dinwiddie, since he was frequently in Williamsburg. Mercer is known to have been a writer, and his papers contain poems similar to those in the *Dinwiddianae*. Furthermore, although primarily devoted to law books, Mercer's library contained works on the arts and sciences, the Classics, divinity, history, and gardening— books the satirist used extensively. Perhaps exhibiting more political than literary merit, the *Dinwiddianae* is representative of the early political resentment of British authority. Parts of the poems compare favorably with British counterparts, and the *Dinwiddianae* reveals the wit, creativity, and artistic and intellectual pursuits of our colonial ancestors.

Suggested Readings: Richard Beale Davis, *The Colonial Virginia Satirist* (1967), prints "Dinwiddianae" poems and prose; J. A. Leo Lemay, Review of *The Colonial Virginia Satirist*, VMHB, 75 (1967), 492; Helen Hill Miller, "A Portrait of an Irascible Gentleman: John Mercer of Marlborough," VC, 26 (1976) 74-85; Lois Mulkearn, *George Mercer Papers Relating to the Ohio Company of Virginia* (1954); Sarah P. Stetson, "John Mercer's Notes on Plants," VMHB, 61 (1953), 34-44; C. Malcolm Watkins, *The Cultural History of Marlborough* (1968).

Meta R. Braymer
Virginia Commonwealth University

GEORGE MICKLEJOHN (d. 1817)

Works: *On the Important Duty of Subjection to the Civil Powers: A Sermon Preached Before His Excellency William Tryon, Governor, and the Troops Raised to Quell the Latest Insurrection* (1768).

Biography: Relatively little is known of George Micklejohn's life until the preaching and publication of his sermon supporting the rule of Governor William Tryon in 1768. He apparently arrived in N.C. in 1766, made an excellent impression on Tryon, and soon became the rector of St. Matthew's Church in Orange County. He acted as mediator between the Regulators and county officials in early 1768, but sided with the governor when the Regulators' attempts at governmental reform failed and they resorted to open rebellion. Micklejohn probably supported Tryon more out of friendship than out of political temperament, for he also came to the protection of Thomas Person, a patriot and Regulator, sought by British soldiers in 1771, the year of the Regulators' defeat by Tryon's militia at Alamance. Person, who became a brigadier general during the Revolutionary War and afterwards served in the N.C. legislature, bequeathed his house "Goshen Place" in Granville County to Micklejohn.

A reluctant rebel, Micklejohn swore an oath of allegiance to the patriots only as a means of obtaining his release after his capture at Moore's Creek in 1775. He did not return to Orange County but remained in Granville and soon became rector of St. John's Church. He was named one of the trustees of Granville Hall Academy in 1779, and in 1790 he became president of the first Convention of the Clergy and Laity of N.C. In the early nineteenth century, he apparently moved to Mecklenburg County, Va., where he frequently preached but was not officially connected with any particular church or parish. He died in 1817.

Critical Appraisal: Although later a supporter of the Revolution, George Micklejohn clearly supported William Tryon's government of N.C. province when he published *On the Important Duty of Subjection* in 1768. The sermon was preached on the text of St. Paul's Epistle to the Romans 8:1-2, "Let every soul be subject unto the higher Powers; for there is no Power but of God; the powers that be, are ordained of God. Whosoever therefore resisteth the Power, resisteth the Ordinance of God; and they that resist, shall receive to themselves Damnation." In this occasional sermon, the text calling for obedience to God is interpreted also as a call for obedience to the "Guardians of the public and general welfare" upon which "God has been pleased to confer a divine authority." Micklejohn's sermon, then, is a reiteration of the concept of divine rule passed down, in this instance, to Governor Tryon and his Assembly.

Micklejohn cited as examples of obedience Christ's deference to God's will and Christ's avoidance of conflict by paying taxation imposed by the civil powers of Capernam, although he had to perform a miracle to do so. Even if, Micklejohn argued, one feels no love of God and reverence for his commands, one should at least have a regard for his own personal salvation. As Micklejohn emphasized, those who resist authority "shall receive to themselves DAMNA-TION." If Christian example and the threat of damnation are not enough, Micklejohn also made a plea to nationalism: "for an *Englishman* to oppose the laws of his country, is an instance of the highest folly and contradiction." Micklejohn's loyalties were divided, of course, since he was close friends with both the governor and Person. Obviously, he wanted merely to avoid open conflict between the two factions and believed that a suitable solution could be arrived at by working with the established governmental system.

Micklejohn's sermon is important because it is a fine example of the plain style so often attributed to Puritan writers. That style was not confined to New Eng. and, in fact, existed in even "plainer" form in the southern colonies. Micklejohn, an Anglican, not only avoided the flowery language associated with Anglican sermon writers but also the metaphorical language of "plain stylists" such as Jonathan Edwards (q.v.). The sermon follows a straightforward, logical argument, a form influenced by scientific writing of the period. Using only examples from the Bible and from common experience to convince his listeners and readers, Micklejohn thoroughly explained and supported the biblical text; the points of contention are elaborated upon and the proof is carefully numbered. Like Benjamin Franklin (q.v.), Micklejohn apparently enjoyed the status quo of English rule, and his sermon can be read as a plea to return to unity with God and with the crown and as one of the few attempts devoid of political motive to put off the bloodshed that was to come in the 1770s.

Suggested Readings: CCMC. *See also* William Kenneth Boyd, ed., *Some Eighteenth Century Tracts Concerning North Carolina* (1927), reprints *On the Important Duty* (1768). Richard Beale Davis, *Intellectual Life in the Colonial South, 1585-1763*, vol. II, (1978); Rolf P. Lessenich, *Elements of Pulpit Oratory in Eighteenth Century England, 1660-1800* (1972); Tom D. Kilton, "Post-Restoration English Commemorative Sermons," JLH, 14 (1979), 297-318; William L. Saunders, ed., *The Colonial Records of North Carolina* (1886).

Leonard C. Butts
Florida Southern College

GEORGE RICHARDS MINOT (1758-1802)

Works: *An Oration Delivered March 2, 1782* (1782); *The History of the Insurrections in Massachusetts* (1788); *Thoughts upon the Political Situation of the United States of America* (attributed author; 1788); *An Address to the Members of the Massachusetts Charitable Fire Society* (1795); *Continuation of the History of the Province of Massachusetts Bay*, 2 vols. (1798-1803); *An Eulogy on George Washington* (1800).

Biography: George Richards Minot was born in 1758, the son of a Boston merchant. He graduated from Harvard in 1778, studied law with William Tudor of Boston, and received a masters degree from Harvard in 1781. Appointed clerk of the Mass. House of Representatives in 1782, he served for a decade in that position. In 1787 Minot was secretary of the Mass. convention to ratify the federal Constitution, and in 1792 he was appointed judge of probate in Suffolk County, Mass.; he held this position and several other judicial offices until his death. Minot was a member of the American Academy of Arts and Sciences, the president of the Mass. Charitable Fire Society, and one of the founders of the Massachusetts Historical Society. He died in Boston in 1802.

   Critical Appraisal: Although Minot was an accomplished orator, as indicated by the examples of his public addresses that survive, his major contribution to American letters was as a historian.

   His most ambitious project was the *Continuation of the History of the Province of Massachusetts Bay.* Intended to extend Governor Thomas Hutchinson's (q.v.) *History of the Province,* Minot's two volumes (the second posthumous and incomplete) carried the story from 1748 to 1765. That Hutchinson was loyal to Br. and that Minot was a conservative supporter of the Revolution account for both their differences and their similarities in emphasis. Hutchinson opposed the Revolutionary movement and defended British authority. Minot approved of orderly resistance to Br. but, like Hutchinson, decried the excesses of the Boston "mobs" during the Stamp Act controversy. Although the *Continuation* was largely supplanted by the posthumous publication of the final volume of Hutchinson's *History* in 1828 (carrying the governor's narrative to 1774), Minot's account still provides insight into the mentality of the moderate New Eng. Revolutionaries who became Federalists and highlights many of the author's particular concerns: his hope for the success of popular government in America, his fear of unrestrained crowd action, and his sophisticated understanding of financial and monetary issues.

   The History of the Insurrections in Massachusetts is Minot's major contribution to American historiography. It is still an indispensable source for the history of Shays's Rebellion, the 1786 revolt of farmers and debtors against the fiscal policies of the Mass. government. Minot believed that the Revolution had established a legitimate popular polity in the state. Also, as Robert Feer has proved conclusively, he hoped to ingratiate himself with the established ruling circles of eastern Mass. But it is unfair to describe him, as Michael Kraus once did, as "giving only the Federalist side" of the controversy over Shays's Rebellion: his personal sympathies were certainly with the established government, but his temperament was conciliatory. He was also concerned with demonstrating to Europeans that the American Revolution was not a prelude to anarchy. Robert Feer has shown the care with which Minot revised the *History* to satisfy all interested parties. Although he castigated the rebels' actions, he explained their grievances and offered the hope that the state government had relieved their distresses.

   Particularly noteworthy is Minot's emphasis on impersonal economic forces. He tried to show how postwar disruption, debt, and inflation created a situation in which rebellion, if not justified, was at least understandable. His interpretation still offers major insights into the perennial question of how authority based on revolution can legitimize itself.

Suggested Readings: DAB. *See also* Richard F. Amacher, *American Political Writers, 1588-1800* (1979), pp. 180, 232n; Bernard Bailyn, *The Ordeal of Thomas Hutchinson* (1974), pp. 19-20, 360-361, 367-368, 384-385; Robert A. Feer, "George Richard Minot's *History of the Insurrections*," NEQ, 35 (1962), 203-228; Michael Kraus, *The Writing of American History* (1953), pp. 76-77; Arthur H. Shaffer, *The Politics of History* (1975), pp. 3, 18, 27, 127-129, 165; Daniel F. Szatmary, *Shays's Rebellion: The Making of an Agrarian Insurrection* (1980), pp. xi-xii; David D. Van Tassel, *Recording America's Past* (1960), p. 51.

Douglas M. Arnold
Yale University

JONATHAN MITCHEL (1624-1668)

Works: "On the Following Work, and Its Author," prefatory poem to Michael Wigglesworth, *The Day of Doom* (1662); "The Great End and Interest of New-England" (w. 1662; pub. in William Cooper, ed., *Elijah's Mantle*, 1722); *A Defence of the Answer and Arguments of the Synod Met at Boston in the Year 1662* (with Richard Mather, 1664); "Upon the Death of That Reverend, Aged, Ever-Honoured, and Gracious Servant of Christ, Mr. John Wilson" (pub. in Nathaniel Morton, *New-Englands Memorial*; 1669); *Nehemiah on the Wall in Troublesome Times* (1671); "A Letter Concerning the Subject of Baptisme" (pub. in Increase Mather, *The First Principles of New-England*; 1675); *A Discourse of the Glory to Which God Hath Called Believers by Jesus Christ* (1677); Elegy on Henry Dunster (pub. in Cotton Mather, *Ecclesiastes: The Life of the Reverend and Excellent Jonathan Mitchel* [1697], and in Cotton Mather, *Magnalia Christi Americana* [1702; rep. 1820, II, 80]); *The New-Birth, Assisted* (1719); *The Reverend Mr. Jonathan Mitchel's Letter to His Friend* (1741); *Mr. Mitchel's Letter to His Brother* (1750).

Biography: Jonathan Mitchel was born in Halifax, Yorkshire, Eng., in 1624, into a family of property and piety. In 1635, after considerable trouble with the government and Church of Eng., Mitchel's family immigrated to Mass. and settled in Cambridge. Under the tutelage of Richard Mather (q.v.) and Thomas Shepard (q.v.), Mitchel soon began to show promise of becoming both a pious believer and a gifted student. In 1645 he entered Harvard College, where he continued to manifest a seriousness beyond his years: *"they that knew him from a child,"* Cotton Mather (q.v.) wrote, *"never knew him other than a man."* Combining rigorous study and intense self-examination with fasting, meditating, and praying, Mitchel soon acquired a reputation for learning and piety that his later life confirmed. Having taken a B.A. in 1647, he remained at Harvard as a tutor. A year later, having taken an M.A., he was elected a fellow, a position he retained until his death in 1668.

In 1649 Mitchel received a call from the church in Hartford inviting him to become successor to "their ever famous Thomas Hooker" (q.v.). Having delivered his first sermon in Hartford, however, he decided to return to Cambridge, in part to be near the village and school he had come to love and in part to be near Sarah Cotton, a daughter of the ever famous John Cotton (q.v.). There, in Aug. 1650, Mitchel was ordained by Cotton as successor to another of New Eng.'s most honored ministers, Thomas Shepard; and there, in Nov. 1650, following the untimely death of Sarah Cotton, he was married to Margaret Shepard, the young widow of his distinguished predecessor.

During his eighteen years as pastor of the church in Cambridge, Mitchel became one of the most respected and influential leaders of New Eng. Working in a period of rapid change, he sought to defend the Congregational Way as God's gift to the people who had followed him into the wilderness. So eloquent was he in this work, Cotton Mather reported, that "vast assemblies of people from all the neighboring towns" came to hear him preach and lecture. In 1662 he played a crucial role in the Synod, where the compromise known as the Half-Way Covenant was adopted. Two years later, he joined Richard Mather in writing a formal defense of the Synod's proposals. When he died Jul. 9, 1668, at age 44, leaving his wife, two sons, and one daughter, he was mourned, Mather told us, "throughout all the churches."

Critical Appraisal: For Jonathan Mitchel as for many Puritan ministers, writing was an adjunct to his ministry, and we must examine his writings carefully if we are to gain a sense of their role in making him one of the shapers of New Eng. thought in the seventeenth century. As *Nehemiah on the Wall* plainly shows, Mitchel recognized that as one generation gave way to the next, it was becoming more and more difficult for the people of New Eng. to continue to "Work with *Courage*, and *Constancy*, and *Confidence*" toward the great end to which their ancestors had pledged them. Unlike some ministers working in this troubled context, however, Mitchel was not content merely to decry and resist change. He wanted to conserve what seemed to him essential, but he was willing to compromise. In his letter on baptism (1675), in his definition of New Eng.'s "great end," and especially in his *Defence of the Answer*, his purpose was "to finde and keep the right middle way of Truth." To him this meant finding ways of adjusting the framework imported from Eng. to the exigencies of the American wilderness; and it meant developing a tone that combined lamentation and celebration.

Like his prose, Mitchel's poetry came after some things and in addition to others, and it too served what he thought of as a larger cause. Only two of his poems—his elegy on John Wilson (q.v.) and his prefatory piece to Michael Wigglesworth's (q.v.) *Day of Doom*—survive intact, although five four-line stanzas of his elegy on Henry Dunster (q.v.) are also extant. In each of these pieces, Mitchel showed modest skill and wide learning. He echoed and alluded to ancients as well as moderns, pagans as well as Christians, but he did so always to serve and honor God and always in the hope of reaching those whom his sermons had missed.

Suggested Readings: CCNE; DAB; FCNEV; Sibley-Shipton (I, 141-157); Sprague (I, 135-137); T₁. *See also* Cotton Mather, *Ecclesiastes: The Life of the Reverend and Excellent Jonathan Mitchel* (1697) in *Magnalia Christi Americana* (1702), II, Book IV; Harrison T. Meserole, ed., *Seventeenth-Century American Poetry* (1968), pp. 412-413, 457-459; Perry Miller, *The New England Mind: From Colony to Province* (1953), pp. 93-104; Samuel E. Morison, *Harvard College in the Seventeenth Century* (1936), pp. 16-17, 143-144, 370-372, 542-543.

David Minter
Emory University

JOHN MITCHELL (1711-1768)

Works: *Dissertatio Brevis de Principiis Botanicorum et Zoologorum* (1738); *Nova Plantarum Genera* (1741); "An Essay upon the Different Colours of People in Different Climates," *Philosophical Transactions of the Royal Society*, 43 (1744), 102-150; "An Account of the Various Kinds of Pot-ash," *Transactions*, 45 (1748), 541-563; *A Map of the British and French Dominions in North America* (1755); "Yellow Fever in Virginia, 1737-1742," *American Medical and Philosophical Register*, 4 (1755); *The Contest in America Between Great Britain and France* (1757); "A Letter Concerning Electrical Cohesion," *Transactions*, 51, pt. 1 (1759), 390-393; *The Present State of Great Britain and North America* (1767); letters to Cadwallader Colden and Benjamin Franklin, *Philadelphia Medical Museum*, 1 (1805).

Biography: The son of a merchant-planter, John Mitchell was born in 1711 in Lancaster County, Va. After completing his scientific training at Edinburgh University, Mitchell settled near the Rappahannock River in Urbanna, Va., where John Clayton (q.v.), William Byrd of Westover (q.v.), and John Custis also lived. During the yellow fever epidemics of the early 1730s, Mitchell conducted a private medical practice in Va.; after 1735 he also served as physician for the poor of Christ Church parish in Middlesex County. In addition, Mitchell studied botany, zoology, climatology, agriculture, chemistry, and medical theory. His efforts at collecting, classifying, and dispatching countless specimens of colonial plant life to Europe resulted in the discovery of several new plants, one of which—the Va. partridge berry—was labeled "Mitchella repens" by Linnaeus. In 1737 a manuscript Mitchell wrote on yellow fever was given to Benjamin Franklin (q.v.), who copied the work and transmitted it to Benjamin Rush (q.v.), who credited it with helping him save over a thousand lives during the 1793 Philadelphia epidemic.

Forced by poor health to leave America, Mitchell sailed to Eng. in 1745-1746.

En route, he lost both his personal possessions and more than a thousand colonial plant specimens when a Spanish raider captured his ship. In Eng. Mitchell remained active in scientific pursuits. He aided the Earl of Bute in establishing the Royal Botanical Garden and in 1747 was elected a fellow of the Royal Society. Although he briefly wanted the office of colonial postmaster general, Mitchell remained in Eng. for the rest of his life. Aided by the Earl of Halifax, who owned extensive archives of North American maps, Mitchell spent five years constructing a map of North America. In his later years, Mitchell wrote about colonial agriculture and argued for the maintenance of the colonial system. John Mitchell died in 1768, shortly before the American Revolution was to disprove his beliefs that the colonies did not truly want independence and that the repeal of oppressive tax legislation would sustain the British empire in North America.

   Critical Appraisal: There is substantial agreement that John Mitchell was—along with John Clayton and Alexander Garden (q.v.)—one of the most important scientific figures in colonial America. His early botanical work in the colonies resulted, for example, in the first taxonomic system of American plants, supplementing and in some instances modifying Carl Linnaeus's more celebrated classification. Although Mitchell's argument that skin color is determined by climate has, of course, been discredited, his descriptive essays on the opossum and his report on Robert Symmer's experiments in electricity helped dislodge previous errors on these subjects. Besides his scientific investigations, Mitchell's activities in Eng. and America linked discoveries in the New World to Europe's Enlightenment. During his career, he was acquainted not only with Clayton, John Bartram (q.v.), Cadwallader Colden (q.v.), and Franklin, but he knew or corresponded with European scientific luminaries such as Carl Linnaeus, Peter Collinson, John Gronovius, Charles Alston, and John James Dillenius. In addition, Mitchell presented Franklin's 1749 essay on electricity to the Royal Society.

   Although Mitchell's medical and scientific contributions alone merit attention, his most enduring contribution to American culture is his 1755 map of North America. Frequently reprinted and translated, this map details both the colonial coastline from Labrador toTexas and the Ohio and Mississippi Valley land grants. Of monumental geopolitical importance at a time when Br., Fr., and Sp. were wrangling over the boundaries of their North American claims, Mitchell's map was used during the peace negotiations at the close of the Revolutionary War, was displayed in the halls of Congress, and has since been influential in settling boundary disputes ranging from the 1842 Webster-Ashburton treaty to a 1932 court dispute between Del. and N.J. An ardent Anglophile, Mitchell believed that advancing the human condition in his native colonies would best occur under British rule, and toward this end, he published his map and argued the immediate necessity of G.B. recognizing the full economic and strategic importance of the colonies to prevent the French from dominating the interior river valleys of North America. As late as 1767, while contrasting the differences of British and American agriculture, trade, manufactures, and population, Mitchell mounted a skillful argument for sustaining the colonial relationship between North America and G.B.

Although often verbose and arrogant, Mitchell's prose reveals intelligent humor, powerful intelligence, and deft observation—qualities that support the judgment that the work of this intensely inquisitive and productive person is unwarrantedly among the more neglected in colonial letters.

Suggested Readings: BDAS; DAB; DNB; T₁. *See also* Edmund Berkeley and Dorothy Berkeley, *Dr. John Mitchell, the Man Who Made the Map of North America* (1974); Lyman Carrier, "Dr. John Mitchell, Naturalist, Cartographer, and Historian," AHAAR, 1 (1918), 201-209; Richard Beale Davis, *Intellectual Life in the Colonial South, 1585-1763* (1978), II, 855-858, passim; John F. Dorman and James F. Lewis, "Dr. John Mitchell, F.R.S., Native Virginian," VMHB, 76 (1968), 437-440; Gordon W. Jones, "The Library of Dr. John Mitchell of Urbanna," VMHB, 76 (1978), 441-443; Theodore Hornberger, "The Scientific Ideas of John Mitchell," HLQ, 1 (1946-1947), 277-296; Raymond P. Stearns, *Science in the British Colonies of North America* (1970); Herbert Thatcher, "Dr. Mitchell," VMHB, 39 (1931), 126-135, 206-220; 40 (1932), 48-62, 97-110, 268-279; 41 (1933), 59-70, 144-156.

Stephen Tatum
University of Utah

ELIZABETH MIXER (fl. 1707-1720)

Works: *An Account of Some Spiritual Experiences and Raptures* (1736).

Biography: The scant remains of Elizabeth Mixer's life can be pieced together from her spiritual autobiography. Mixer was a native of Ashford, Mass., born early in the eighteenth century, probably as early as 1707. (Her *Account* suggests that she was at least 13 in 1720 when she experienced the visions recorded there.) Her parents provided her with a basic education concentrating on religious training. Elizabeth Mixer was received into full communion with the congregation at Ashford on Nov. 6, 1720. Little else is known of her, although a few other biographical details may be contained in parts of the *Account*, some of which is damaged in the American Antiquarian Society copy used for Charles Evans's Early American Imprint Series.

Critical Appraisal: *An Account of Some Spiritual Experiences and Raptures* is a gathering by the Rev. James Hale of Elizabeth Mixer's sayings, visions, advice to young people, and spiritual autobiography. The *Account* opens with reports of three visions Mixer experienced in 1720, the first on Jun. 28 during a serious illness. Mixer spoke "after a Rapturous manner" of seeing Christ in the Heavenly City of "pure transparent Gold." Christ appeared to her later in her bedroom, assuring her of his assistance as she "passed thro' the valley of *the shadow of Death.*" The third and apparently final vision, on Jul. 1, led Mixer to describe the Last Judgment. As she noted in her spiritual autobiography, these visions, combined with her religious training and her experience of watching by the deathbed of her sister Rebecca, triggered a desire for full communion in the Ashford congregation: "And I saw that I must first shine in Grace, before I could shine in Glory." She began to speak of the state of others' souls, anxious at one point *"That any of the Indians Souls should go to Hell"* and at other times concerned for the young people in her community: *"Young People take care to prink and fine up their Bodies, but they have more need to take care of their Souls, to get Christ to stand their Friend. O that any should put a dust of Powder upon their Hair, or a Ribbon on their Caps, that have more need to put on Sackcloth."*

James Hale's preface to the *Account* reveals his purpose in compiling Mixer's work: to add to the testimony lending credibility to the revivalism of the Great Awakening. The *Account* is a conventional, almost formulaic, record of Mixer's conversion experience. It is neither so personal as earlier such accounts nor so full of doubt and individual anguish. Mixer alluded to her struggles with Satan but did not detail them; instead she emphasized the scriptural passages by which she overcame temptation. Mixer's advice to the unregenerate around her was simple to the point of matter-of-factness: *"They should keep Christ nearest their hearts, the World under their feet, and Eternity in their eye."* Students of American religious history and of spiritual autobiography will find Mixer's *Account* useful for its lucid if impersonal "Relation" of her conversion and for the calculated use James Hale made of her experiences "to Excite and stir up People to seek the LORD."

Suggested Readings: Jacqueline Hornstein, "Elizabeth Mixer" in *American Women Writers*, ed. Lina Mainiero (1979-1981), III, 197-198; idem, "Literary History of New England Women Writers: 1630-1800" (Ph.D. diss., N.Y. Univ., 1978), pp. 183-184.

Pattie Cowell
Colorado State University

JUDAH MONIS (1683-1764)

Works: *The Truth; The Whole Truth; Nothing but the Truth* (1722); *Proposals for a Hebrew Grammar* (1734); *A Grammar of the Hebrew Tongue* (1735); *Dissertation on Genesis* (1735).

Biography: Little is known of the early life of Judah Monis, except that he was born in Venice (or Algiers) in 1683, probably studied in rabbinical schools in Leghorn and Amsterdam, came to America via Jamaica (which had a significant Sephardic population at the time), and first settled in New York City where the mayor's court for Feb. 28, 1715, recorded him as a freeman and "merchant." It was not as a merchant or in N.Y., however, that Judah Monis made his fame, but as an academician in Cambridge, Mass. There, on Jun. 29, 1720, Monis submitted to the Harvard Corporation a draft proposal for a Hebrew grammar for which he was awarded the first academic degree conferred upon a Jew in North

America, an honorary M.A. This award was followed in 1722 by his appointment as the first instructor of Hebrew at Harvard College, a position he was to hold until his retirement in 1760. Although his scholarly credentials for such a position have been questioned, he did acquire one mandatory qualification. Before his appointment, Monis converted to Christianity. His public baptism took place in College Hall on Mar. 27, 1722, when he was sponsored by no less than John Leverett, president of Harvard College, and Increase Mather (q.v.). Thereafter, Monis's tenure at Harvard was without either difficulty or distinction. He married a Christian woman, bought land near Harvard, kept a shop in addition to his teaching, published his Hebrew grammar in 1735, reliquished his instructorship on the death of his wife, and died a short time later.

Critical Appraisal: Although not a prolific writer, Judah Monis is assured a place in American letters for his defense of New Eng. Puritanism from a Jewish perspective. The three tracts he published when he was baptized are "dedicated to the Jewish nation," but propound the legitimacy of Protestant Christianity. In both content and method, these works are unique. The amalgamation of prosaic Hebrew defenses of Christ with Puritan apologetics is as novel as the synthesis of traditional Hebraic hermeneutics and Hellenic rhetoric. The resulting syncretism is unparalleled in colonial American literature. The arguments Monis offered to validate Christianity are conventional and employ the analytical and inductive text-centered methods of Talmudic and Midrashic literature with added substantiation from a wide range of readings: the Bible, medieval Jewish commentators, Maimonides, the cabalistic writers, and even some more recent anti-Christian polemicists. But these standard proofs incorporate Protestant dogmatics and Puritan rhetoric in a distinctive way. The ultimate synthesis of the European Hebraic and New Eng. Protestant traditions is one that awaits closer scholarly scrutiny.

Monis's first discourse, titled *The Truth*, offers individual refutations for the nine traditional Jewish denials of Christ's Messianic identity. The overall structure of the tract owes much to Classic rhetoric, but each objection is confuted by various text and word-oriented ratiocinations that depend upon traditional Jewish methods: minute distinctions and subtle exegesis. *The Whole Truth*, written later but published with the first tract, offers an apparently original compilation of eight reasons why Jews fail to convert to Christianity, including the "idolatrous Worship of the Roman Church," Jewish "stubbornness," and the fragmentation of Protestant sects. Following this catalog, Monis proceeded to his central objective, proving the divinity of Christ. Once again, he accomplished this proof by resorting to conventional Jewish dialectic, abstruse analogies, and secondary authority. The last of the three tracts, "Nothing but the Truth," begins with a conventional Protestant attack upon the "Papists," but the focus of the work soon shifts to a contemporary New Eng. phenomenon, the schismatic "Aryans." This piece of Puritan invective against growing heterodoxy (in tone and content similar to observations made by Increase Mather) leads into Monis's explanation of the Trinity. Monis discloses that the Trinitarian concept, rather than being a major stumbling block for Jews, is actually a corroboration of the traditional Jewish injunction that "The Lord our God is one Lord." In proving this, Monis again resorts to subtle interpretations.

Of purely historic rather than literary interest is the other contribution Monis made to American letters. *A Grammar of the Hebrew Tongue* was the first book printed in Hebrew in North America from a specially imported font of type; this grammar (which was retired with Monis) was published with help from Harvard College provided for its publication, help that became the forerunner of the Harvard University Press.

Suggested Readings: DAB; Sibley-Shipton (VII, 639-646). *See also* Arthur H. Chiel, "Judah Monis, the Harvard Convert," *Judaism*, 23 (1974), 228-232; Lee M. Friedman, "Some Further Notes on Judah Monis," PAJHS, 37 (1947), 121-134; Jacob R. Marcus, *The Colonial American Jew, 1492-1776* (1970); George F. Moore, "Judah Monis," PMHS, 52 (1919), 285-312.

John F. Schell
University of Arkansas at Little Rock

JOHN MONTRÉSOR (1736-1799)

Works: Journal of expedition in 1761 from Quebec through Maine (1831, 1938); journal of expedition in 1760 across Maine from Quebec (1882); journal of expedition in 1763 to Detroit (1928); journals, 1757-1778, 1785-1786 (1882).

Biography: The son of British military engineer James Gabriel Montrésor, John Montrésor was born in Gibraltar on Apr. 6, 1736. He came to America with his father in 1754 and served as ensign, engineer, and lieutenant under Gen. Braddock. Wounded at Monongahela, he was also present during the Seven Years' War at the siege of Louisbourg (1758) and Gen. Wolfe's capture of Quebec (1759). In 1760 he led a rugged winter scouting expedition from Quebec to Topsham, Me. In the summer of 1761, he led another party to chart the Chaudiere and Kennebec River route through Quebec and Maine, writing a journal used to guide Benedict Arnold's (q.v.) ill-fated American invasion of Quebec (1775).

Montrésor saw action in Pontiac's War (1763) and later supervised improvements of British fortifications at Boston, New York City, and Philadelphia. Appointed chief engineer of America by King George III in 1775, he played roles at Lexington, Bunker Hill, the capture of Long Island, and Brandywine and served as an aide to Gen. Howe. Yet he returned to Eng. in 1778 a bitter man. Montrésor believed that despite his outstanding service and thorough knowledge of America, he never received the acknowledgment he deserved from the British government. Promoted at last to colonel, he traveled with his family in Europe (1785-1786). He lived out his life at Belmont, Kent, and Portland Place, London, where he died on Jun. 26, 1799.

Critical Appraisal: From the French and Indian War through the early years of the Revolution, John Montrésor witnessed an extraordinary number of major events. A disciplined and concise writer, he offered the historian invaluable observations of social conditions and descriptions and opinions of British strategy.

Two separately published Montrésor journals are important in regard to Benedict Arnold's American invasion of Quebec (1775). The first records Montrésor's 1760 winter scouting expedition. Leaving Quebec on Jan. 26, his party suffered terribly from severe cold and hunger and were reduced to "eating their Moccassins and Bullet Pouches, snow-shoe Netting and strings" and "raw Woodpeckers" before reaching Topsham, Maine, on Feb. 20. The second journal, used by Arnold to plan and guide his march to Quebec, records Montrésor's expedition from Quebec to Fort Halifax in Maine and back to Quebec in Jun. and Jul. 1761. Montrésor carefully observed the topography and sources of game, assessed Fort Halifax, and noted canoeing conditions. Kenneth Roberts pointed out that the usually reliable "Montrésor's failure to mention the swamps at the mouth of Seven Mile Stream. . .nearly resulted in the death, fourteen years later, of a large part of Arnold's detachment." Also separately published is the journal of Montrésor's 1763 expedition to relieve Pontiac's siege of Detroit. Montrésor detailed several skirmishes and negotiations with the Indians before his departure on Nov. 20 with Maj. Robert Rogers (q.v.).

The extensive Montrésor journals (1757-1778), edited by G. D. Scull, reveal the crisp vigor and occasional acid judgments of a professional military engineer as Montrésor described the sieges of Louisbourg (1758) and Quebec (1759); the Stamp Act disturbances in Albany and New York City (1765), Fort Castle William, and Boston (1770); battles such as Brandywine (1777); and other notable events and expeditions. Montrésor matter of factly detailed engineering plans, the weather, and troop movements, but he also assessed the rebel army, criticized the actions of British officers, and described American attitudes and local events.

Montrésor's notes written on his return to Eng. in 1778 recorded the pathetic end of a brilliant career. Convinced that he had been ill-used by his own government, he obsessively listed his achievements and took credit for several successful tactics. He declared that "During the 24 years I acted as Engineer in America, I was so fortunate as never once to have had a work carried of my Construction," a sentence echoed later. He recited his family's long history of military service and in a bitter litany described how he had been "*reduced*" by service in America: his wounds, ailments, loss of property and money, and, worst of all, "The cruelty of my extensive Command as Chief Engineer in America, without a proper rank to honour it." He cited British blunders in America and lamented that engineers, well educated and playing an increasingly crucial role in modern warfare, were accorded such a lowly status in the British army. Montrésor's valuable journals prove that he deserved better.

Suggested Readings: DAB; DNB. *See also* Kenneth Roberts, comp., *March to*

Quebec (Montrésor's journal for 1761; 1938), pp. 1-24; Gideon Delaplaine Scull, ed., "Lt. John Montrésor's Journal of an Expedition in 1760 across Maine from Quebec," NEHGR, 36 (1882), 29-36; idem, ed., *The Montrésor Journals*, CNYHS, 14 (1882), 1-542 ("Journals of Capt. John Montrésor, 1757-1778," 115-520); John Clarence Webster, "Life of John Montrésor," TRSC, 3rd ser., 22, sec. 2 (1928), 1-31 ("Journal of John Montrésor's Expedition to Detroit in 1763").

Wesley T. Mott
University of Wisconsin

JOSHUA MOODEY (1633-1697)

Works: *Souldiery Spiritualized* (1674); *Lamentations upon the Never Enough Bewailed Death of the Rev. Mr. John Reiner* (1676); *A Practical Discourse Concerning the Choice Benefit of Communion with God* (1685); *An Exhortation to a Condemned Malefactor* (1686); *The Great Sin of Formality in God's Worship* (1691); *Believers Happy Change by Death* (1697).

Biography: Born in Ipswich, Eng., sometime in 1633, Joshua Moodey (also spelled *Moody*) arrived in Mass. during the Great Migration of the 1630s and settled with his parents in Newbury, outside of Boston. After graduation from Harvard College (A.B., A.M., 1653), Moodey moved to the frontier settlement of Portsmouth, N.H., where in 1671 he established a church and was ordained a Congregational minister. A man of strong convictions, Moodey voiced his opinions on colonial affairs, and these opinions often clashed with those of the governor of N.H., Thomas Hinckley Cranfield. In 1684 Cranfield could tolerate Moodey no more, and he ordered the clergyman arrested for refusing to administer the sacraments according to the rites of the Church of England. After thirteen weeks of imprisonment, Moodey was released under the injunction "to preach no more in the Province." As a result, he took up residence in Boston, where the congregation of the First Church appointed him its minister.

During the witchcraft hysteria of the 1690s, Moodey again exercised his convictions by using the pulpit to urge Philip English, a former parishioner whose wife had been imprisoned on charges of witchcraft, to take his wife and escape from the province. The text for his sermon was the following: "If they persecute you in one city, flee to another." When English hesitated to take Moodey's advice, Moodey told his parishioner that if he didn't see to his wife's escape then he himself would do so for her.

In July of 1684, after the sudden death of John Rogers (q.v.), Moodey was offered the presidency of Harvard College, but he declined the position. In 1693, after Governor Cranfield was dismissed from N.H., Moodey returned to his former congregation at Portsmouth. He died on Jul. 4, 1697, while on a visit to Boston and was buried in King's Chapel Burial Ground. About Moodey's many accomplishments as a religious leader and as a preacher, Cotton Mather (q.v.)

wrote, "He had the honour to be the First, that *suffered*...for the cause of religion in these parts of the World." Despite their frequent differences of opinion, it was Mather who preached Moodey's funeral sermon.

Critical Appraisal: As a literary figure Joshua Moodey is best remembered for the unusually high quality of his sermons, many of which are preserved in the manuscript collections of the Massachusetts Historical Society. Although he often disagreed with the leading religious figures of the day on matters of doctrine and church discipline, Moodey's skillful preaching won the respect of even his sternest opponents. Perhaps the best testimony of Moodey's skill as a preacher was the fact that he was frequently selected by the ministers and leaders of New Eng. to deliver sermons of great political import during times of domestic crisis.

In 1675, for example, at the onset of King Philip's War, Moodey delivered the General Election Sermon. In 1674 and again in 1685, he gave the Artillery Election Sermons, and in 1692, at the beginning of the Salem proceedings, he was honored with a second invitation to speak at the General Election. Few other New Eng. ministers were so honored. Regrettably, no copy of this last sermon, *The People of New England Reasoned With*, seems to have survived, but the title of this document suggests the tantalizing possibility that Moodey may in fact have used the occasion to denounce, or at least question, the events at Salem.

Like many early New Eng. preachers, Moodey excelled at the plainstyle of writing and preaching. His most famous sermon, *Souldiery Spiritualized*, aptly reveals Moodey's skill as both a stylist and a thinker. Preached before the soldiers of New Eng. on the day when they elected their officers, *Souldiery Spiritualized* was written, as Moodey put it, in "blunt *and* homely" language to which his audience could readily relate. Throughout the sermon Moodey likens the occupation of the soldier to that of the Christian, and to drive home his point, he develops the analogy by means of military terminology, which is appropriate both to the text and to the situation of the sermon. The result is a carefully articulated statement of seventeenth-century Puritan cosmology and the role of the individual soldier within it. The Artillery Company must have been pleased indeed with its choice of a speaker, for *Souldiery Spiritualized* was one of the first Artillery Election Sermons published in New Eng.

The verse inscriptions which Moodey wrote for the tombstones in the Watertown graveyard of Thomas and Lydia Bailey have the distinction, according to Harold Jantz, of being "perhaps the only examples of conscious free verse in English in seventeenth-century New England." Moodey's only other surviving poem is titled *Lamentations* and was published as a broadside elegy on the death of John Rayner, who Jantz tells us was the Dover, N.H., pastor who died of a "cold and fever" he received as a result of his service as a chaplain during King Philip's War. While no complete copy of the original broadside has survived, Samuel Sewall (q.v.) copied large portions of the poem into his commonplace book, and by comparing Sewall's copy with a fragment of the broadside, Jantz has compiled a relatively complete reconstruction of what must have been the original text. Replete with references to the recent battles with the "Heathen," *Lamentations* is a moving tribute to the "faithful friend" whose death was a grievous loss to "Immanuels Land" and a seeming victory to its "treach'rous Foes."

Suggested Readings: CCNE; FCNEV; Sibley-Shipton (I, 367-380); Sprague (I, 160-163). *See also* Emory Elliott, "The Development of the Puritan Funeral Sermon and Elegy: 1660-1750," EAL, 15 (1980), 151-164; Robert Henson, "Form and Content of the Puritan Funeral Elegy," AL, 32 (1960), 11-27. For the text of *Lamentations*, see Harold Jantz, *The First Century of New England Verse* (1944), pp. 151-154.

James A. Levernier
University of Arkansas at Little Rock

JAMES MOODY (1744-1809)

Works: *Lieutenant James Moody's Narrative of His Exertions and Sufferings in the Cause of the Government, Since the Year 1776* (1783).

Biography: Born in 1744, James Moody was a prosperous N.J. farmer at the outbreak of the American Revolution. He described his prewar life as being "contented...settled on a large, fertile, pleasant, and well improved farm of his own, in the best climate and happiest country in the world." This contentment did not last long. Although he denied any early political involvement and expressed only a desire to live at peace with his wife and three children, his Tory sympathies were well enough known to make him despised by his rebellious neighbors. Moody, a proud and conservative man, was "perpetually harassed" by the area's different committees and associations. After being shot at and chased from his farm in Apr. 1777, he led a band of seventy-three men to the safety of British lines, where they enlisted in Gen. Skinner's famous Tory Brigade.

Moody's participation in the war lasted nearly five years. His first adventures involved creating a network of Loyalists to gather information and recruiting for military service. After a year's service as a volunteer, he received an ensign's commission and was sent back into "Rebel country." Moody scouted the armies of George Washington (q.v.), John Sullivan, Horatio Gates, and Anthony Wayne while destroying supplies, taking numerous captives, and freeing British prisoners of war. On Jul. 21, 1780, he and his band were captured by Wayne's army. He was imprisoned at West Point, where he received particularly cruel treatment from the post's commander, Benedict Arnold (q.v.). Early in 1781 he received a lieutenant's commission after successfully completing several more missions. His last adventure, a bold attempt to steal the important papers of Congress, resulted in tragedy. His party was betrayed, and his younger brother was captured and executed. Soon afterwards, due to poor health and enormous debts, he sailed for Eng., hoping to restore health, wealth, and spirits. There he wrote his adventures and received a pension and small tract of land in Weymouth, Nova Scotia, where he retired in 1786. He died in 1809, a colonel in the local militia.

Critical Appraisal: Before the Revolution, James Moody never suspected that he would soon "beat his plough share into a sword," nor later his sword into a pen. Yet in a short period, he became both soldier and writer. Although these changes were forced on him, and he suffered great loss and disappointment, Moody was well suited for both. Consequently, *Lieutenant James Moody's Narrative* is one of the best accounts of the Revolution from the Tory point of view.

The narrative's greatest contribution to American culture is its unique perspective on the war, one that is usually overlooked. The war, at least that part of it Moody observed, is not a crusade of individuals unanimously joined in ideological commitment. It is a war of neighbors. Many in pre-Revolutionary America shared Moody's belief that political rebellion was the "foulest of all crimes," that no matter how great the grievances were, rebellion was not the way to redress them. The struggle between loyalties was bitter, often violent. Different levels of sympathies were not tolerated. According to Moody, the choice to those caught in this struggle was either "Join or Die." Those unable to decide were harassed and pressured until they were pushed in one direction or the other. For those who remained loyal to the crown, there was little alternative but to abandon everything, sometimes even family, and seek refuge behind the British lines. Paradoxically, in a country where freedom and tolerance were taken for granted, it is somewhat surprising to discover how little political freedom there actually was during the first precarious years.

Moody's claim that most Americans remained loyal but refused to express their loyalties in order to save their property and lives should not, however, be accepted as fact, although he stated that "he speaks the sentiments of a great majority of the peasantry of America." His intention in writing the narrative must be considered. By the time he had reached Eng., he was a bitter man, having lost his property, his wealth, and even his younger brother. In return, he had received almost nothing. He wrote the narrative to publicize his exploits, hoping to receive some compensation for his losses. As a result, his self-descriptions are too heroic and too grand. Writing in the third person, Moody continually referred to his courage and dedication, and his comments on the conflict's political issues are both brief and biased.

His descriptions of the military engagements, however, are good. His war is not a war of battles, but of guerilla excursions—not of armies, but of individuals. Gathering prisoners, destroying enemy supplies, and intercepting military dispatches are more important than meeting the enemy in open conflict. The war is described in terms of small towns and local militias. The style is lively and, in spite of the self-aggrandizement, moves well. Moody's sense of pace and suspense was keen, especially when describing his raids and the inevitable pursuit that followed.

Moody's final passages offer one last paradox for American readers. By the end of 1782, the military issues had nearly been decided. Both sides continued fighting, but only to gain a better bargaining position. Moody concluded that although the "Rebels" had won the war, they had defeated themselves. Instead of gaining freedom, they had placed themselves "under the tyranny of present rulers." Americans, he believed, would "continue to feel the worst punishment their worst enemies can wish them—nominal independency, but real slavery."

Suggested Readings: DAB. *See also* Charles I. Bushnell, ed., *Narrative of the Exertions and Sufferings of Lieutenant James Moody, with an Introduction and Notes* (1865); Evert Duyckinck and George Duyckinck, *Cyclopaedia of American Literature* (1881), I, 259-261; Lorenzo Sabine, *Biographical Sketches of Loyalists of the American Revolution* (1864), pp. 90-97.

Daniel E. Williams
Abteilung für Amerikanistik
Universität Tübingen

SARAH PARSONS MOORHEAD (fl. 1741-1742)

Works: "Lines...Dedicated to the Rev. Mr. Gilbert Tennent," *New England Weekly Journal* (Mar. 17, 1741), p. 1, reprinted in *General Magazine and Historical Chronicle*, 1 (Apr. 1741), 281-282; *To the Reverend Mr. James Davenport on His Departure from Boston* (1742).

Biography: Few materials are available for detailing the life of Sarah Parsons Moorhead. Joseph Sabin's *Bibliotheca Americana* mentioned in passing that she was the wife of the Rev. John Moorhead. Her extant poems reveal that she lived and wrote in Boston during the 1740s. Her competence with heroic couplet and her willingness to address complex theological issues (as well as the political disputes surrounding them) suggest that she obtained a substantial religious and literary education. She used the tools that education provided to become an outspoken critic of the excesses of the Great Awakening. Whether she wrote additional verse or explored other issues remains a mystery.

Critical Appraisal: Sarah Moorhead's poems were published during the controversies surrounding the Great Awakening in New Eng. Itinerant ministers, Gilbert Tennent (q.v.) and James Davenport among them, traveled from pulpit to pulpit seeking to revitalize religious zeal in local congregations and (occasionally) criticizing the methods and sincerity of local ministers. In the midst of the resulting turmoil, Moorhead's three extant poems sound a note of caution. All three poems speak directly to the New Light or evangelical clergy, two in the slim volume addressed *To the Reverend Mr. James Davenport on His Departure from Boston* and one "Dedicated to the Rev. Mr. Gilbert Tennent" in the *New England Weekly Journal*. The poem for Gilbert Tennent is unsigned, but when it was reprinted in Benjamin Franklin's (q.v.) *General Magazine and Historical Chronicle*, it was attributed to "Mrs. S. M." The attribution is further supported by the author's critical attitude toward Tennent's revivalism, a milder version of her later warnings to James Davenport.

Although Moorhead balanced her poems with respect for the motives of the evangelical clergy, her verse is sharply critical of their methods. She warned of the dangers of their preoccupation with divine law to the exclusion of free grace, a preoccupation that Moorhead argued would lose more souls than it saved: "Yet, O dear sacred TENNENT, pray beware, / Least too much Terror, prove to some a Snare." For Moorhead, the hysteria provoked by revivalist preaching worked to trivialize the conversion experience: "Conversion is become the Drunkard's song; / GOD's glorious Work, which sweetly did arise, / By this unguarded sad Imprudence dies."

In addition to criticizing the doctrinal emphasis of New Light clergy, Moorhead questioned the political wisdom of dividing congregations by criticizing local ministers. Noting that "Contention spreads her Harpy Claws around," she warned of the consequences: in "A POSTSCRIPT, to the Rev. Mr. [Andrew Croswell], On his writing against some of the worthy Ministers of the Gospel," she pointed out that "Each have their different Talents from the Lord, / And each to Wandring Souls their help afford."

Ironically, Moorhead added to the boldness of her critique by making the personal attacks she deplored in others. Her poem to Davenport, for example, a dream vision featuring his entrance into heaven, pointedly censured him for his pride: "'Favourite of Heaven! How came it in thy Mind / That Grace was so much to thy self confin'd. . . . Success is not confin'd, dear Man, to you.'" In the dream, Davenport recanted his errors, turned his "Praise to Free Grace," and pleaded for pardon from the churches he had "rashly rent." Moorhead's severe criticisms—doctrinal, political, and personal—make her a rare figure for an eighteenth-century woman writer: not only did she set herself the task of social criticism, but her work was published contemporaneously with the events it details.

Suggested Readings: Pattie Cowell, *Women Poets in Pre-Revolutionary America* (reprints selections from the verse; 1981), pp. 269-272; Jacqueline Hornstein, "Literary History of New England Women Writers: 1630-1800" (Ph.D. diss., N.Y. Univ., 1978), pp. 127-131; idem, "Sarah Parsons Moorhead" in *American Women Writers*, ed. Lina Mainiero, (1981), III, 218-219; Joseph Sabin, *Bibliotheca Americana* (1868-1936), XXV, 261.

Pattie Cowell
Colorado State University

ABEL MORGAN (1673-1722)

Works: *Cyd-Gordiad Egwyddorawl o'r Scrythurau [A Concordance of the Sacred Scriptures]* (1730).

Biography: Baptist clergyman and biblical scholar Abel Morgan was born to Morgan ap Rhydderch ap Dafydd ap Grufydd (minister of the Rhydwilym

Baptist Church) in Alltgoch, Llanwenog, Cardiganshire, S. Wales, in 1673. Following contemporary Welsh custom, Abel took his father's Christian name as his surname. Among the generations of scholars in his family was Abel's uncle, Sion Rhydderch ("John Roderick"), who was not only a painter, antiquary, and poet, but also the compiler of both the first English-Welsh dictionary and one of the first Welsh grammars, as well as the translator of many religious works into Welsh.

Morgan grew up in Abergavenny and began his preaching career before the age of 18. In 1692 he moved to Llanwenarth, a nearby town in Monmouthshire, to minister to a congregation there. Four years later, he followed a group that had split off from his congregation to Blaenegwent and became its pastor. He rose to prominence among the Baptists of Wales but in 1711 decided to join his brother Enoch and other members of his family in the growing Welsh Baptist community in Pa. He set out from Bristol on Sept. 28, 1711, for Philadelphia with his wife (Priscilla [Powell] Morgan), infant son, daughter, and mother-in-law. His wife and son did not survive what was a long voyage even for the time.

Upon his arrival in Philadelphia on Feb. 14, 1712, Morgan became minister of the Pennepek Baptist Church, where he served until his death. He soon became a leader among Baptists in Pa. and helped to set up new congregations in N.J. and Del. as well. He took Martha Burrows as his second wife and, after her death, married Judith (Griffiths) Gooding. Judith and their four children survived Abel Morgan on his death on Dec. 16, 1722.

Critical Appraisal: Abel Morgan is said to have translated the Century (Baptist) Confession of Faith into Welsh, adding two articles he authored on hymn singing and the laying on of hands. He edited a catechism as well, but his major work remains his *Cyd-Gordiad*, published after his death by his brother Enoch and half-brother Benjamin Griffiths in Philadelphia in 1730. It is a significant book in many ways, being the earliest complete concordance to the Bible printed in the Welsh language (and for many years the only one) as well as the second book in Welsh published in America.

Morgan composed his concordance while still a minister in Monmouthshire and brought it with him to America. Why it remained unpublished until eight years after his death remains unknown. Its 232 pages begin with a dedication to David Lloyd, Welsh-born chief justice of Pa.; an introduction by the Rev. Enoch Morgan; and notes by John Cadwalader. There follows the concordance itself, from "Aaron" through "Zidon," closing with "Trinitati Gloria Sempiterna" ("For the Everlasting Glory of the Trinity").

The *Cyd-Gordiad* served as a basis for Peter Williams's concordance, printed in Carmarthen, Wales, in 1773 and, according to David Jones, in the *Cambrian*, made Morgan's name "a household word in Wales and America among the Welsh people," both Baptist and Quaker. The book survives to document the Welsh migration to Pa. (and the rest of America) and the highly religious and literary nature of the Welsh people; yet it survives almost alone due to the rapid assimilation of the Welsh community into the general English-speaking population.

Suggested Readings: CCMC; DAB; DNB. *See also* J. Davis, *History of the Welsh Baptists* (1835); Morgan Edwards, *Materials Towards a History of the Baptists in Pennsylvania* (1770); Horatio Gates Jones, "The Rev. Abel Morgan," PMHB, 6 (1882), 300-310; articles in the *Cambrian*, 13 (1893).

Randal A. Owen
St. Mary's Dominican College

JOSEPH MORGAN (1671-after 1745)

Works: *The Great Concernment of Gospel Ordinances* (1712); *The Portsmouth Disputation Examined* (1713); *The History of the Kingdom of Basaruah* (1715); *A Letter to the Authors of a Discourse* (1724); *The Duty, and a Mark of Zion's Children* (1725); *The Only Effectual Remedy Against Mortal Errors* (1725); *Love to Our Neighbours* (1727); *The Nature and Origin of Sin* (1727); *Brief History of the Country of Humanity* (1728); *Sin Its Own Punishment* (1728); *The Nature of Riches* (1732); *The Temporal Interest of North America* (1733); *The General Cause of All Hurtful Mistakes* (1741).

Biography: The grandson of the Welch immigrant, Morgan was born in Preston, Conn., on Nov. 6, 1671. Apparently without formal éducation, he learned some Greek and Hebrew and enough Latin to write an amateurish, unpublished treatise on physics. Ordained in 1696, he served Congregational and Presbyterian Churches in Conn., N.Y., and N.J. until 1740. Morgan gained sufficient distinction to be awarded an honorary M.A. by Yale in 1719, but his career was dotted with controversy. He left a congregation in N.Y. after quarreling with Anglican officials. A congregation in Greenwich, Conn., dismissed him for refusing to abandon the grist mill he operated. He was charged with immoral conduct by congregations in Freehold and Hopewell, N.J., once suffering a three-year Synod suspension. Throughout his career, Morgan staunchly defended the minister's need for full financial maintenance from his congregation, claiming that his own ministry was most effective when he had such support. He lived until at least 1745, but his death is not recorded.

Critical Appraisal: Joseph Morgan viewed writing as an extension of his parish ministry. "I never seek to put any thing in print," he said in the preface to *Sin Its Own Punishment*, "except I think that God has given me something new to suggest, which...may...help blinded mankind out of the misery fallen upon us." His theology embraced the New Eng. convenant tradition. His logic was Classically sound and sometimes ingenious. He valued language as both an exegetical tool and as a literary device. Occasionally raising plain-style prose to rhapsodic heights, he could sustain complexly extended metaphors like the image of Aaron's rod in *The Only Effectual Remedy*. But the artistic quality of his writing was always subservient to its didactic function.

The Portsmouth Disputation and *Letter to the Authors of a Discourse* refute

Quaker objections to Calvinism with a logic built of biblical exegesis, the authority of church fathers, and intricate linguistic propositions. Labeling Quakers
Pelagians, Morgan contended that any rational Christian, provided with accurate
evidence, must accept the doctrines of election, infant baptism, and a professional clergy. His sermons and *discourses*—Morgan used the latter term to
indicate significant revision before publication—instructed members of his own
denomination about the nature of sin, the need to rely on the Holy Spirit, the role
of the ministry in the church, and the mandate to love one's neighbor. Morgan
seldom achieved the power of the best eighteenth-century preaching. But his
sermons illustrate the manner in which major doctrinal themes were treated in
middle-class Presbyterian and Congregational pulpits throughout colonial America.

Although claiming to be another religious discourse, *The Nature of Riches*
moves toward social analysis. In a perfect world, Morgan argued, material goods
would be held in common, men contributing to and drawing from the common
store as their abilities and their needs dictate. But a fallen world requires private
property to stimulate productivity. Profit gained through honest toil is morally
good, because it also provides commodities needed by other men. A farmer's
extra crops, for example, feed his neighbors. But entirely selfish motives bring
evil riches such as the interest on inherited money. Perhaps influenced by Benjamin Franklin (q.v.), the book's publisher, Morgan praised the public-spirited
rich man and proposed revisions in statutes governing civil law suits.

From a literary perspective, Morgan's major work is *The History of the Kingdom of Basaruah*, an allegory presenting the Calvinist view of man's fall and
redemption. More like John Bunyan's *Holy War* (mentioned in Chapter 9) than
Pilgrim's Progress, the history traces the life of a covenant nation, not the
progress of an individual soul. Morgan replaced personal drama with a theological scope that is intellectually impressive but emotionally stagnant. He wove
almost all of Calvinism's major tenets into *Basaruah*. Yet the allegory is clear
and consistent throughout, and Morgan never lost control of the fictional mode
embodying his theology.

Although no summary can do justice to the book's pervasive complexity, the
surface allegory is easily decoded. Located somewhere in North America,
Basaruah—the name combines Hebrew roots to mean "flesh-spirit"—lives happily under a benevolent charter from its king, Pantocrator (Almighty), until the
rebellious destruction of a levee redirects the River of Turbulent Waters, cutting
Basaruah off from the beautiful land of Shamajim and rendering the people
unable to pay the tax imposed by the charter. Failure to pay is punishable by
slavery in the sulfurous country of Gehenna. But Pantocrator is merciful as well
as just. His son, Prince Theos ho Logos, becomes a citizen of Basaruah, earns
the revenue required of the kingdom, establishes a ford across the river, and
offers a home in Shamajim to any citizen willing to follow his appointed path. A
new charter replaces the old without negating it. Pantocrator issues a proclamation defining the new charter and ordains native Basaruahans "Publishers of the
Proclamation." He also sends his lord high secretary, Ruah Kadosh (Holy Spirit),

into Basaruah to lead believers across the river. But stumbling blocks remain. Some citizens mistake islands such as "Being Thought Well of by Others" for the Happy Land adjoining Shamajim. Some, like the residents of the county of Morality, refuse to leave their homes. Others quibble about the proclamation's meaning. Still others reject the Publishers' authority. The history concludes with "the last Great and General Court in Basaruah," an account of the final judgment akin to Michael Wigglesworth's (q.v.) *Day of Doom*.

Suggested Readings: CCMC; CCNE. *See also* Richard Schlatter, ed., *The History of the Kingdom of Basaruah and Three Letters*, by Joseph Morgan (1946); Henri Petter, *The Early American Novel* (1971), pp. 65-66.

Kennedy Williams, Jr.
Bentley College

WILLIAM MORRELL (fl. 1623-1625)

Works: *Nova Anglia* or *New England* (1625).

Biography: Little is known of William Morrell's life apart from his brief excursion to the New World from Sept. 1623 to 1625, when this Anglican clergyman went to Mass. with the [Sir Ferdinando] Gorges (q.v.) company sent out by the Plymouth Council to establish a feudal colony. However, the surprising success of the middle-class settlements of the Pilgrims and of the Massachusetts Bay Company prevented its taking root. The ecclesiastical court in Eng. had commissioned Morrell to superintend all New Eng. churches, but the failure of the Gorges colony effectively eliminated his authority. Wisely, he chose not to exercise his commission, apparently not even mentioning it until shortly before his return to his native Eng. There he published *Nova Anglia*, probably the first poetic treatment of New World experience. Although his postscript mentions a subsequent book, it never appeared.

Critical Appraisal: William Morrell's book consists of two parts, *Nova Anglia* in elegant Latin hexameters and its translation into English heroic couplets. Conscious of his literary precedence but unaware of the major tradition he was inaugurating, Morrell opened his poem with profuse apologies that, although traditional, seem especially sincere. Despite his understandable timidity, Morrell's long poem adumbrated significant themes and treatments of the New World experience that were later amplified and refined by the major figures of our literature. Prominent if contradictory concerns of *Nova Anglia* include the New World as Eden; the secular possibilities for the self-reliant, well-prepared entrepreneur; the character of the Native American; and Christianity's place in the New World. Although the secular opportunities were a continuing theme of writers of promotion tracts, Morrell had no such vested interest, so that his celebration of "a Grand-childe to earths Paradize" predominates, and his catalogs anticipate later writers' identification of the correspondence between natural and divine benediction: "There Natures bounties though not planted are, / Great store and sorts of berries great and faire: / The Filberd, Cherry, and the fruitfull Vine, / Which cheares the heart and makes it more divine."

Although he introduced his treatment of the natives as if they were some satanic threat to this new Eden, clearly they fascinated more than terrified him. Again resorting to systematic cataloging, he detailed the Indians' dress, social structure, religion (with a provocative early description of the medicine men and "their curst Magicke"), notion of heaven, and their women, closing with the Indians' amusing observation that the Englishmen were fools for doing all of the work while their "women live / In that content which God to man did give."

Morrell concluded by calling for Christian assistance to the colonies and initiating the traditional lament that the homeland ignores its colonies. A postscript offers some hardheaded advice that somewhat undercuts his earlier description of the place as Edenic.

Although not a major work of American literature, *Nova Anglia*'s sympathetic speaker, cataloged observation of detail, and prophetic treatment of themes make it lamentable that Morrell's projected later book was never published.

Suggested Readings: CCNE; DNB; FCNEV; T_1. *See also* Charles Francis Adams, *Three Episodes of Massachusetts History*, rev. ed. (1892), I, 105-129; Charles M. Andrews, *The Colonial Period of American History: The Settlements* (1934), I, 338-340; William Bradford, *History of Plymouth Plantation, 1606-1646*, ed. William T. Davis (1908), p. 163; John A. Goodwin, *The Pilgrim Republic* (1895), pp. 168, 239; Leo M. Kaiser, "On Morrell's *Nov-Anglia*," SCN, 28, no. 1 (1970), 20; *National Cyclopaedia of American Biography*, 8 (1924), 365.

Mark A. Johnson
Central Missouri State University

GOUVERNEUR MORRIS (1752-1816)

Works: *Our Admonishment* (1778); *Observations on the American Revolution* (1779); *Diary of the French Revolution* (w. 1789-1793; pub. 1888, 1939); *Letters on Appreciation* (1780); *An Oration, upon the Death of...Washington* (1800); *Speech on the Free Navigation of the Mississippi* (1803); *Funeral Oration on Alexander Hamilton* (1804); *An Answer to War in Disguise* (1806); *Notes on the United States of America* (1806); *To the People of the United States* (1810); *An Oration, in Honor of the Memory of George Clinton* (1812); *Discourse...Before the New York Historical Society...December 6, 1812* (1813); *An Oration...in Commemoration of American Independence* (1813); *The Advantages of a Proposed Canal from Lake Erie, to Hudson's River* (1814); *An Oration...in Celebration of the Recent Deliverance of Europe* (1814); *Salem, Mass.* (1814); *An Inaugural Discourse* (1816).

Biography: Gouverneur Morris, the son of Lewis Morris and Sarah Gouverneur, was born on Jan. 31, 1752, into a cosmopolitan niche of colonial American society. His grandfather Lewis Morris (q.v.) and his father, the first and second lords of the manor of Morrisania, N.Y., were prominent figures in the political and legal circles of that colony. His mother's family had been part of the Huguenot emigration from Fr. that followed the revocation of the Edict of Nantes. Educated first at New Rochelle, N.Y., and then at King's College, Morris graduated at age 16 with a reputation for intellect, wit, and social grace, as well as a certain worldliness not typical of his classmates. Having read law under the direction of William Smith (q.v.) (later to be chief justice of the province), Morris was admitted to the bar in 1771. He opposed the resistance movement against G.B.—less from love of the mother country, it would seem, than from fear and hatred of the "mob"—but joined the patriot cause when conflict became inevitable. He served in the N.Y. provincial Congress in 1775 and played a major role in the state's Constitutional Convention of 1776. As a delegate to the Continental Congress in 1778-1779, Morris drafted numerous state papers, willingly participated in committee work, and established valuable contacts with the political and military leaders of the period. Defeated for reelection because of his refusal to support N.Y.'s claim to Vt., Morris moved to Philadelphia. From 1781 to 1785, he served as assistant superintendent of finance under Robert Morris. As a member of the Pa. delegation to the Constitutional Convention, Morris actively (if ineffectively) stated the case for a conservative, highly centralized system. He gradually tempered his views, however, and eventually promoted the spirit of compromise that produced the Constitution. As chairman of the Committee of Style, but working virtually alone, he prepared the final draft of that document.

By this time, the business affairs of Morris and his associates required his services abroad. The trip evolved into a busy decade of business dealings, touring, and political intrigue. Morris gained diplomatic status in 1792 when George Washington (q.v.) appointed him minister to Fr., where he served with distinction and no little courage through the Terror. He lost the position in 1794 amidst the furor of the Genêt affair, but stayed on in Europe for four more years. After his return to America, he filled an unexpired term in the U.S. Senate, but soon found his brand of Federalism to be out of fashion. He lost the seat in 1802 and retired to his estate at Morrisania. In 1809 he married Anne Carey Randolph of Va., and in 1813 their only child, Gouverneur, Jr., was born. Through these years, his distaste for the policies of the Democratic-Republicans gradually soured into a contempt for the Union. During the War of 1812, he came to the brink of advocating secession. The war's outcome failed to convince him that the nation of the Revolution had survived, and he died in 1816 with his pessimism unrelieved.

Critical Appraisal: For one whose literary style was so admired by his contemporaries, the volume of Gouverneur Morris's printed writings is surprisingly small. His most carefully read work, the *Constitution of the United States*, was officially a committee product, and his *Diary of the French Revolution*, now considered to be a historically invaluable record of that turbulent period in French history, remained in manuscript form until long after his death.

Morris's first published work, a rousing denunciation of both the terms and the motives of the Carlisle armistice delegation of 1778, appeared as *An Admonishment* in the *Pennsylvania Gazette*. Morris had already authored the formal rejection, a terse and restrained statement; under the pseudonym *An American*, however, he was able to display the talent for civilized invective so familiar to his private correspondents. In the following year, the Congress published his white paper, *Observations on the American Revolution*, a document of great interest to students of the emerging American sense of "mission." Morris's diatribe against G.B. is predictable enough, but his characterization of America as a country under "providential favor" to be a "Temple...to Freedom" and an "Asylum to Mankind" shows how rapidly the messianic tenor first introduced by Thomas Paine (q.v.) had superceded the generally conservative cast of the resistance movement.

Morris next turned his attention to the complex problem of financing the War of Independence. In his *Letters on Appreciation* (1780), Morris rejected the proposed methods of recreating an equilibrium between the quantity of money and the quantity of goods: raising taxes was politically impossible; borrowing, he argued, had wrecked Eng. and would have the same effect upon America; stabilization through legislative fiat had already been tried without success. Since depreciation worked as a gradual and reasonably equitable tax, he suggested letting it continue until the conclusion of the war, when steps could be taken to pay off the remaining debt at its market value.

For some years after the Revolution, Morris's works did not appear in print, excepting the publication of a few of the public eulogies that he, as a master of those orotund rejections of the plain republican style, was often called upon to deliver. He published again in 1806, when British restrictions upon American neutral trade raised the serious probability of war. Unlike most of his fellow conservatives, Morris's position on domestic issues had never inclined him toward a favorable view of the British. His animosity surfaced here in a brilliantly argued polemic against that country's unilateral efforts to determine the rules of war at sea. Morris advanced the argument, later used by President James Madison (q.v.) in his war message to Congress, that Br.'s real aim was to use the Napoleonic Wars to drive trade competitors out of business. In the same year, Morris, having by this time acquired a solid reputation as a business expert, responded to requests that he appraise the climate of economic opportunity in America by publishing *Notes on the United States*. Although his correspondence clearly indicates that he was sinking into the deep private disillusionment that would soon dominate his thinking, in this work he still spoke highly of his country and its people. He did discourage preachers, lawyers, "physiks," and anyone wanting to follow a career in the fine arts (and all Englishmen—these people defined a temperate climate as rain four days out of five and would find

Nootka Sound more to their taste), but he encouraged those "sober, industrious, and honest" people who would welcome the opportunity to be judged by talent rather than title. His counsel against investing in southern land contains an early hint of the embryonic sectionalism that was to divide the country. Nothing in the South would increase in value, according to Morris, until slavery was abolished.

This public optimism did not last. In his *Discourse...Before the New York Historical Society*, the disenchanted Federalist employed a review of N.Y.'s history (with remarks upon the relationship of the environment to "American" traits that are strikingly similar to those later advanced by Frederick Jackson Turner) to suggest that the state could support a population of 4 million people— implying that, if necessary, New Yorkers could join with their "Eastern brethren" in the creation of a new polity. His *Oration...in Commemoration of American Independence* (1813) openly attacked the administration for promoting an unjust war. He denied charges that he was promoting secession, but implicitly reversed the denial by dismissing the charges as the cheap canards of those whose policies could produce no other result. These late works provide an interesting measure of the deteriorating concensus over the meaning of the American Revolution in the early national period.

Suggested Readings: DAB; LHUS; T_2. *See also* Mary-Jo Kline, *Gouverneur Morris and the New Nation, 1775-1788* (1978); Max M. Mintz, *Gouverneur Morris and the American Revolution* (1970); Theodore Roosevelt, *Gouverneur Morris* (1888); Jared Sparks, *The Life of Gouverneur Morris, with Selections from His Correspondence and Miscellaneous Papers*, 3 vols. (1832); Daniel Walther, *Gouverneur Morris, Witness of Two Revolutions* (1934). For Morris's diaries, see: Beatrice C. Davenport, *A Diary of the French Revolution by Gouverneur Morris*, 2 vols. (1939), and Anne Carey Morris, *Diary and Letters of Gouverneur Morris*, 2 vols. (1888).

David Sloan
University of Arkansas at Fayetteville

LEWIS MORRIS (1671-1746)

Works: *The Chief Justice's Speech to the General Assembly* (1726); *The Opinion and Argument of the Chief Justice* (1733); *Some Observations on the Charge Given by the Honourable James De Lancey* (1734); *The Case of Lewis Morris, Esq.* (1735); *Observations on the Reasons Given by Mr. Hamilton's Advisers* (1736); "The Papers of Lewis Morris, Governor of the Province of New Jersey, from 1738 to 1746," NJHSC, 4 (1852); *Documents Relating to the Colonial History of the State of New Jersey*, vols. IV-VII (1854-1855); *Archives of the State of New Jersey*, vol. I, series IV-VII (1882-1883); Manuscript Poems, The Morris Papers, Rutgers University Library Special Collections.

Biography: Lewis Morris, son of a Cromwellian officer who had settled in what is now the Bronx, N.Y., was born there in 1671 at Morrisania, the family estate. Left parentless in infancy, he was raised by his uncle and namesake, whose supervision he found so onerous that, according to family tradition, he left home as an adolescent, wandering as far as Jamaica and supporting himself as a legal scrivener. His education seems to have been self-acquired, for the records list no formal schooling. By 1691 Morris had returned from his travels and taken up residence in N.J., where a year later he was appointed a judge of the Common Court and a member of the governor's Council.

In the contentious politics of the time, Morris allied himself with those who opposed the system of proprietary government and who hoped to see N.J. politically severed from N.Y. and assigned its own governor. Because of his stormy opposition to Proprietary Governor Jeremiah Basse, Morris was in 1698 discharged from the Council. In 1702 he traveled to London to urge the transfer of governance from the proprietors to the crown. These efforts were successful, and Morris was reassigned his old post on the Council of the new governor, Lord Cornbury. However, his tenure in that job proved intermittent, as he found himself repeatedly dismissed and reinstated when he charged Cornbury and successive governors with exceeding their authority. In 1710, after the appointment of Col. Robert Hunter (q.v.) as governor, Morris's political fortunes improved. Under Hunter and his successor, William Burnett, Morris played a prominent role in the Council, the Assembly, and the courts, where after 1715 he served as chief justice of N.Y. and N.J..

In 1732, however, when William Cosby became governor, Morris led the opposition to his highly unpopular administration. Dismissed as chief justice, Morris was selected by his fellow assemblymen to go to Eng. (as he had thirty-three years earlier) to urge Cosby's removal and the establishment of a separate government for the province of N.J. In London both of Morris's petitions were rejected, but in 1736, when Cosby died, the crown at last agreed to divide the governing structures of the two colonies. In light of his long experience in N.J. politics and his prominence as the people's champion against oppressive rulers, Morris was selected to become N.J.'s first separate governor. His appointment was initially very popular, but—ironically—Morris soon found himself under bitter attack, and his administration was characterized by repeated accusations of arbitrary rule. On May 21, 1746, after eight years of jealously defending his gubernatorial prerogatives, Morris died at the age of 77 and was buried at Morrisania.

Critical Appraisal: Although his crowded and argumentative political career left him relatively little time to pursue wider literary concerns, Lewis Morris was an exceptionally cultivated man. His private library of some 2,500 volumes was, according to Ezra Stiles (q.v.), "replete with learned Works in Law, Politics, Hist^y, Phil^o, the Sciences, and Theol^y." Likewise, Stiles reported that "the Gov, understood Heb., Arabic & the Oriental Languages, as well as Gr. & Lat. And . . . he got it all himself, . . . by his own Pliability." Moreover, through his visits to Eng. and his close friendship with Robert Hunter (himself the friend and correspondent of Swift and Addison), Morris gained a more than merely bookish knowledge of the world of London wit and sophistication.

As might be expected, the majority of Morris's writings are the documentary by-products of his political and legal battles. The importance of these speeches, memoranda, and petitions is primarily historical, although they are not without literary graces. Morris commands a lucid, vigorous, and occasionally eloquent prose style, which becomes especially effective when he is polemicizing (as he so often is) against tyrannical royal governors. Less praiseworthy is his notable tendency toward prolixity—a quality that elicited Cadwallader Colden's (q.v.) remark (after reading one of Morris's extended legal opinions) that "it is the fault of the Morris family that they exhaust the subject they treat on."

Of wider interest are Morris's poems, evidently written for private amusement, since none were published. Eighteen of them—mostly political satires in the Hudibrastic manner—have survived. Morris's verse, although lacking in polish, nonetheless generates considerable comic energy. Thus in "The Mock Monarchy or the Kingdom of Apes: A Poem by a Gentleman of New Jersey in America," Morris gave an amusingly cynical account of how the American colonies (settled, in his jaundiced view, by the dregs of Europe) had spinelessly yielded up their liberty to greedy politicians ("and tis but Just, that any man / who won't take freedom when he can / should remain a Slave"). Similarly concerned with power-hungry politicians is Morris's longest poem, the 668-line "Dream & Riddle," which offers a parable of a colonial emissary who visits the mother country to petition for recall of a corrupt governor. There he meets a "Councilor" who, in the course of explaining how hopeless such a mission is, delivers a lengthy indictment of the moral and social decadence that (aside from the brief interludes of Cromwell and William of Orange) has permeated the last century of English history. In a mellower vein is "Upon the Assembly Desireing Him to Fix His Own Seat," in which Morris pondered the choice of locales for his official residence as the newly appointed governor. The 190-line poem takes the form of an ironic catalog listing the various attractions and drawbacks of N.J.'s principal towns. In general, if no great claims can be made for the artistry of Morris's verse, it is nevertheless well worth reading for the entertainingly sardonic perspective from which its knowledgeable author views the colonial scene.

Suggested Readings: DAB; T_1. *See also* Richard Cook, "Lewis Morris—New Jersey's Colonial Poet-Governor," JRUL, 24 (1961), 100-113; Robert Davidson, "Memoir of Lewis Morris," NJHSP, 4 (1849), 19-32; Stanley Katz, "A New York Mission to England: The London Letters of Lewis Morris to James Alexander, 1735-1736," WMQ, 28 (1971), 438-489; E. Lefferts, *Descendants of Lewis Morris of Morrisania* (1907); Maureen McGuire, "Struggle over the Purse: Governor Morris versus the New Jersey Assembly," NJHSP, 82 (1964); Charles Parker, "Lewis Morris, First Colonial Governor of New Jersey," NJHSP, 13 (1928), 273-282; Gordon Turner, "Governor Lewis Morris and the Colonial Government Conflict," NJHSP, 67 (1949), 260-304.

Richard I. Cooke
Kent State University

THOMAS MORRIS (c. 1732-c. 1802)

Works: *The Bee: A Collection of Songs* (1790); *Miscellanies in Prose and Verse* (includes *Journal*; 1791); *A Life of Rev. David Williams* (1792); *Quashy, or The Coal-Black Maid* (1796); *Songs, Political and Convivial* (1802).

Biography: Not a great deal is known about Thomas Morris's life, and much that we do know stems from his *Journal* and the "Preamble" in *Miscellanies in Prose and Verse*. He was born into an English family of soldiers, both his grandfather and father (also Thomas Morris) being captains in the Seventeenth Regiment, the same unit that Morris joined. Morris enrolled in Winchester College in 1741 and in 1748 entered the army while in Ire. He also studied for fifteen months in Paris, which gave him an understanding and appreciation of the French.

Morris came to America in 1758 as a lieutenant and saw action at Louisbourg. In 1759 he joined Lord Jeffrey Amherst in the campaign around Lake Champlain. Promoted to a captain in 1761, he was stationed at the garrison of Fort Hendrick in the Mohawk Valley. He is also believed to have accompanied Gen. Monckton on an expedition to Martinique in the W.Ind. in 1762, which undoubtedly promoted the writing of *Quashy*.

On Aug. 26, 1764, Morris set out on his most famous adventure, an expedition from Cedar Point, Ohio, to Detroit in the hope of winning over the support of Midwest Indians from the French. His journal recounts his often dangerous and frustrating fortunes. He remained in Detroit for some time, eventually returning to Eng. in 1767.

Two years later, he married Miss Chubb, sired six children, retired from the army in 1775, and subsequently lost much of his property through speculation. With the publication of *Songs, Political and Convivial* in 1802, Morris passed from sight.

Critical Appraisal: Although he wrote a number of poems, translated many of them into French, and translated Roman verse from Latin into English, Thomas Morris is not remembered as an accomplished poet. Certainly, his most important work is his *Journal of Captain Thomas Morris of His Majesty's XVII Regiment of Infantry*, actually written to win him a pension after his financial collapse and printed in *Miscellanies in Prose and Verse*. Morris began his expedition to Detroit at the request of Gen. Bradstreet, who was himself traveling to aid the beleaguered Detroit garrison. Morris was accompanied by Jacques Godefroi, a traitor, pardoned when he agreed to aid Morris in winning Indians over to British sovereignty. Morris related his perilous adventures with great dramatic flair and considerable attention to minute details. The climax of his travels occurred with his imprisonment by 500 of Pontiac's warriors, threats of torture and death, reprieve by Pontiac himself, and eventual escape. Although the *Journal* abounds in anecdotes and descriptions of unique Indian customs and traditions, the scene of Morris leisurely reading *Antony and Cleopatra* (in an edition of Shakespeare that he acquired in a trade with an Indian for some gunpowder) while his companions are taken captive is utterly amazing and amusing. Throughout his journal, Morris exhibited an incredibly objective understanding of the Indians whom he regarded, despite his captivity and threats of torture, as "an innocent, much-abused, and once happy people."

His compassion for the victims of British colonialism further extends into his longest and most important poem, *Quashy, or The Coal-Black Maid*. In recounting the life of a black field slave in the city of St. Pierre on the island of Martinique, Morris condemned the institution of British and French slavery. The poem details the humiliating and cruel treatment Quashy, her lover Quaco, and the other slaves receive at the hands of a master who refuses to accept an edict freeing all slaves. When the British attack Martinique, the slaves riot, Quaco is killed, and a despairing Quashy commits suicide. At various moments, Morris interrupted his narrative to question the existence of a God who would allow such barbarity, to rebuke Hume for regarding blacks as an inferior race, and to rail against ports such as Bristol and Liverpool that trafficked in slave trading. Shocked by the enormity of these injustices, Morris at one point questioned, "Was man alone to toil for man design'd; / And tribes, distinguish'd by a sable face, / To pine in bondage to a paler race?"

Like many of his day, Morris was a noble warrior, concerned as much with literature as with warfare. He was, however, unique in the magnanimity he showed for his tormentors and enemies and for his keen and astute powers of observation.

Suggested Readings: DNB. *See also* Allan W. Eckert, *The Conquerors* (1970); Francis Parkman, *The Conspiracy of Pontiac* (1870); Howard H. Peckham, *Pontiac and the Indian Uprising* (1947); Milo Milton Quaife, ed., *The Siege of Detroit in 1763* (1958); Reuben G. Thwaites, ed., *Early Western Travels, 1748-1846*, vol. I (contains Morris's *Journal*; 1904).

David W. Madden
University of California, Davis

JEDIDIAH MORSE (1761-1826)

Works: *Geography Made Easy* (1784, 1790, 1794, 1809, 1820); *To the Friends of Science* (1787); *New-York, June 23d, 1788, Sir, Whoever* (1788); *The American Geography* (1789, 1794); *The History of America* (1790, 1795, 1808); *A Sermon Preached Lord's Day, February 28, 1790* (1790); *A True and Authentic History of His Excellency George Washington* (1790); *The American Universal Geography* (1793); *Tegenwoordige staat der Vereenigde Staaten van Amerika* (1793-1796); *The Life of General Washington, Commander in Chief* (1794); *Elements of Geography* (1795, 1825); *A New and Correct Edition of the American Geography* (1795); *The Present Situation of the Other Nations* (1795); *The*

Duty of Resignation (1796); *The American Gazetteer* (1797, 1798, 1804, 1810); *A Description of the . . . Georgia Western Territory* (1797); *Proposals, for Printing by Subscription, a Gazetteer of America* (1797); *An Abridgement of the American Gazetteer* (1798); *The Character and Reward* (1798); *A Sermon, Delivered at the New North* (1798); *A Sermon Delivered Before the Grand Lodge* (1798); *A Sermon, Preached at Charlestown, November 29, 1798* (1798); *An Address, to the Students* (1799); *A Sermon, Exhibiting the Present Dangers* (1799); *The Two Following Documents* (1799); *A Prayer and Sermon Delivered at Charlestown* (1800); *Bijdraagen ter Gedachtenis van G. Washington* (1801); *Elements of Polite Education* (editor; by Philip Dormer Stanhope, fourth earl of Chesterfield; 1801); *A Sermon Preached Before the Humane Society* (1801); *A New Gazetteer of the Eastern Continent* (with Elijah Parish; 1802); *A Sermon, Delivered Before the Ancient & Honorable Artillery Company* (1803); *A Sermon, Preached at the Ordination of the Rev. Hezekiah May* (1803); *A Compendious History of New England* (with Elijah Parish; 1804, 1808, 1809); *Signs of the Times. A Sermon* (1805); *The True Reasons* (1805); *A Sermon, Delivered at Charlestown* (1806); *A Sermon, Preached in Brattle-Street Church* (1807); *A Discourse, Delivered at the African Meeting-House in Boston* (1808); *A Sermon, Delivered, May 18th, 1808* (1808); *A Sermon Delivered Before the Convention* (1812); *A Sermon, Delivered at Charlestown, July 23, 1812* (1812); *An Appeal to the Public* (1814); *A Compendious and Complete System of Modern Geography* (1814); notes for *Letters on the Study and Use of Ancient and Modern History* (by John Bigland; 1814); *The Gospel Harvest, Illustrated in a Sermon* (1815); *Review of American Unitarianism* (1815); *Sermon Before Society for Foreign Missions, January 2, 1815* (1815); *The General Gazetter* (revisor and editor; by Richard Brookes; 1816); "Report to the General Association of Massachusetts" and "Report of the Committee" (pub. in John Lowell, *An Inquiry into the Right to Change the Ecclesiastical Constitution*; 1816); *Review of the Unitarian Controversy* (1816); *The Christian Ambassador* (1817); *A New Universal Gazetteer* (with Richard C. Morse; 1821); *A Sermon, Delivered Before the American Board of Commissioners for Foreign Missions* (1821); *Ancient Atlas Adapted to Morse's New School Geography* (1822); *Modern Atlas Adapted to Morse's New School Geography* (1822); *A New Universal Atlas of the World* (with Sidney Edwards Morse; 1822); *Proposals . . . for Publishing, by Subscription, A Report to the Secretary of War of the United States* (1822); *A Report to the Secretary of War of the United States* (1822); *The Traveller's Guide* (with Richard C. Morse; 1823); *Annals of the American Revolution* (1824); *Report on the Oneida, Stockbridge, and Brotherton Indians, 1796* (with Jeremy Belknap; 1955).

Biography: Jedidiah Morse was born at Woodstock, Conn., on Aug. 23, 1761. He graduated from Yale in 1783 and was licensed to preach in 1785. He was installed as pastor of the First Congregational Church at Charlestown, Mass., in 1789, a position he held for thirty years. In 1816 Morse's church split over Unitarianism but was saved by a revival in 1816-1817. He was removed from his post in 1819 and moved to New Haven, where he wrote and took a new interest in Indian affairs. In 1820 he was appointed by the government to visit the Indians and report on their condition.

Morse often involved himself in both political and religious controversies. A staunch Federalist, he was concerned, almost paranoid, about attempts by the French in general and the Illuminati in particular to subvert American freedom. Orthodox in his Calvinism, he strongly opposed the Unitarians, became embroiled in the Harvard controversy in 1804, established *The Panoplist* in 1805, and was instrumental in the union of Congregational and Presbyterian clergy into the General Association of Massachusetts in 1802 and the founding of Andover Theological Seminary in 1807. He was also a founder of the New England Tract Society in 1814 and of the American Bible Society in 1816 and was active in the American Board of Commissioners for Foreign Missions and the Society for Propagating the Gospel.

Shortly after graduation from Yale, Morse began his study of geography that earned him the title of Father of American Geography. He published his first geographical study in 1784 and worked steadily in that field until his death in New Haven on Jun. 9, 1826.

Critical Appraisal: Morse's first significant work was done as a geographer. His *Geography Made Easy* (1784) was the first geography printed in America. Seeking information from men such as Ebenezer Hazard (q.v.) and Thomas Hutchins, he worked for utility rather than originality. He wanted Americans to break the old pre-Revolutionary War habits of relying on Europeans for information and, by thinking for themselves, to develop a literary and national character. Because Morse believed that European literature did not reflect republicanism and that it would imbibe American youth with monarchial ideas, he wanted to make his geography accessible to the public. Consequently, he abridged it into less expensive volumes, but more significantly, he aimed most of his geographical writing specifically at schoolchildren. According to Morse, civil liberty depended on the population's being enlightened by true and useful knowledge, the groundwork for which was laid in the schools. No science like geography gratified the "rational curiosity," and Morse tried to blend entertainment with improvement, instructing students to be grateful and respectful to the government, the leaders, and the country. Realizing that geography was a growing science, Morse continuously revised and updated his works throughout his life, assisted in the later years by Sereno Dwight and his sons Sidney and Richard Morse. Unlike many of his day, Morse was conscious of his sources and freely acknowledged them.

Much of the patriotic flavor of his geographic work resulted from his ardent Federalism. Morse tried to instill patriotism as well in his historical works and his life of George Washington (q.v.). He strongly supported Washington and John Adams (q.v.) and was sympathetic to the views of Alexander Hamilton (q.v.) and John Jay (q.v.). In fact, his printed sermons before 1800 were more political than religious, "exposing" French intrigue in America, condemning the

French Revolution as the work of the Illuminati, and charging that a general conspiracy was under way to destroy liberty in America. In 1801 he was instrumental in planning the Federalist paper *The Mercury and New England Palladium* at Boston.

Morse's belief in political conspiracy was no doubt bolstered by Unitarian inroads on orthodox Calvinism. He had spoken out occasionally on the divinity of Christ, but his main public involvement came with the election of Henry Ware to the divinity chair at Harvard. Believing that only a Calvinist should hold that honor, Morse unsuccessfully fought Ware's election. In response to this controversy, he published *The True Reasons* (1805) and established *The Panoplist*, which he edited until 1808, after which it was edited by Jeremiah Evarts as the Mass. *Missionary Magazine*.

The rise of Calvinist fervor that resulted from the stand Morse and others took against the tide of Unitarianism had lasting effects on American society. Throughout the latter part of his life, Morse labored strenuously in support of religious-oriented philanthropic causes. From 1792 he was active in the Society for Propagating the Gospel among the Indians and Others in North America, serving for several years as secretary. Morse was particularly interested in the Indian missions established by the society, visiting the Oneidas in 1796 and the Stockbridges in 1810. He worked tirelessly for improvement of the condition of the Indians in Mass. and in 1819 undertook to report to the federal government on the condition of the Indians in the U.S. His report still stands as a valuable source for historians. Morse also worked for blacks, preaching to them, helping to establish a school for them, opposing the slave trade, and encouraging the colonization efforts of Paul Cuffee, which eventually led to the American Colonization Society. From 1803 Morse was a member and officer of the Massachusetts Society for Promoting Christian Knowledge, and under his direction thousands of religious tracts were distributed. When the American Tract Society was established, Morse was chairman of the Executive Committee. He also helped draft the constitution of the American Bible Society and was active in the American Board of Commissioners for Foreign Missions, established in 1810, under whose auspices a number of Indian missions were established.

As has been noted, Morse was identified with every great movement of the period. The controversies in which he engaged and the organizations that he helped found or to which he devoted his efforts gave direction to much of America's social, political, intellectual, religious, and racial history of the nineteenth century.

Suggested Readings: DAB; DARB; Dexter (IV, 295-304); LHUS; Sprague (II, 247-256). *See also* Madison Kuhn, "Tiffin, Morse, and The Reluctant Pioneer," MichH, 50 (1966), 111-138; Gary B. Nash, "The American Clergy and the French Revolution," WMQ, 22 (1965), 392-412; Joseph W. Phillips, "Jedidiah Morse: An Intellectual Biography" (Ph.D. diss., Univ. of Calif., 1978); Samuel I. Prime, *The Life of Samuel F. B. Morse* (rep., 1974), pp. 1-171; William Buell Sprague, *The Life of Jedidiah Morse, D.D.* (1874); Vernon Stauffer, *New England and the Bavarian Illuminati* (1918).

Daniel F. Littlefield, Jr.
Little Rock, Arkansas

CHARLES MORTON (c. 1627-1698)

Works: *The Little Peace-Maker* (1674); "Eutasia, A Discourse of the Improvement of the County of Cornwall," *Philosophical Transactions of the Royal Society* (1676), X, 293-296; *The Way of Good Men* (1681); *Debts Discharge* (1684); *The Gaming-Humour Considered* (1684); *The Spirit of Man* (1693); *Some Meditations on . . . "Exodus," in Meeter* (16—); "Advice to Candidates for the Ministry" (pub. in Edmund Calamy, *A Continuation of the Account*, I, 198-210; 1727); "A Vindication of Himself and His Brethren" (pub. in Edmund Calamy, *A Continuation of the Account*, I, 177-197; 1727); "An Enquiry into the Physical and Literal Sense of That Scripture, Jeremiah VIII, 7," *The Harleian Miscellany*, vol. II (1744); (1809), II, 578-588; *Compendium Physicae*, PCSM, 33 (1940).

Biography: Charles Morton was born in Cornwall, Eng., about 1627, the son and grandson of ministers. Although his father, Nicholas Morton, had been ejected for nonconformity during the reign of Charles I, Charles Morton followed his grandfather, Rev. Kestle, in upholding the ceremonies of the Church of England. Morton entered Wadham College, Oxford, and received the B.A. in 1649 and the M.A. in 1652. In 1653 he was awarded the same degrees from Cambridge. While at Oxford, Morton became associated with Dr. John Wilkins, who was instrumental in the founding of the Royal Society. During this time, Morton also shifted his allegiance to the Puritan party. At the Restoration, Morton was forced out of his position as rector of Bliswell, Cornwall, and eventually, in 1666, founded a dissenters' academy at Newington Green. There he achieved substantial success as an educator, earning praise from two of his most famous students, Daniel Defoe and Samuel Wesley. In 1685 the authorities at Oxford forced the closing of his academy. Morton abandoned Eng. for New Eng., invited by Increase Mather (q.v.) to become pastor at Charlestown, with a suggestion that he might become president of Harvard College. But before Morton arrived in Boston on Jun. 1, 1686, the colonial charter had been revoked and the college charter cast in doubt. Morton's unpopularity with the royal party in Eng. made it impolitic to appoint him president of Harvard. He was installed as pastor at Charlestown on Nov. 5, 1686. At the ceremony, he refused the "laying on of hands," because, he contended, his original ordination in Eng. was still valid. In spite of the harassment by the authorities in Eng., Morton always emphasized that Puritans were part of the Church of England.

Morton soon found himself at odds with both the colonial government and Harvard College. The Andros government charged him with sedition for a sermon that suggested that the old charter was still valid. Popular support, however, forced his acquittal. His difficulty with Harvard arose over his practice of tutoring some of its students, especially one, John Emerson, whose father believed that the preparation by the college instructors was inadequate. Morton ended his tutorials in 1687, but remained connected with Harvard. According to Samuel

Morison, Morton's *Compendium Physicae* was introduced at Harvard during 1687 and continued in use there for forty years. In 1692 Morton was elected a fellow at Harvard and in 1697 he became its vice-president. After 1687 he was an established member of Boston's intellectual and ministerial community. He supported the Mather party wholeheartedly, subscribing to its handling of the witchcraft trials and the charter negotiations. In 1690 he founded the Cambridge Association, which provided for regular meetings of the Boston area ministers; this association helped to consolidate ministerial power.

Morton received accolades from his contemporaries for his "sweet natural temper" and "pleasant" manners. He was most successful as a teacher; as Edmund Calamy recounted, he "had indeed a peculiar talent of winning youth to the love of virtue and learning both by pleasant conversation, and by a familiar way of making difficult subjects easily intelligible." Perhaps the best evidence of the affection in which Morton was held are the many references to him in Samuel Sewall's (q.v.) diary. Sewall even hazarded the ice of the Charles River to hear one of Morton's sermons, and he was in attendance at Morton's death on Apr. 8, 1698.

Critical Appraisal: Charles Morton's writings are not remarkable for originality of thought or style. His sermons and his one attempt at verse are, in fact, pedestrian. The verse *Meditations on... "Exodus"* initially implied a connection between the plight of the Jews in Egypt and the Puritans in Eng. Morton asked why the Egyptians suspected the Jews: "Would *they* betray the Land where they were bred, / Where their *foreFathers* more than once were fed / In their distress?" But the poem quickly drops the analogy to rehearse the biblical events in detail. *The Little Peace-Maker* attempted to construct a dialog on the vices of contention and pride, but resolved itself into a standard sermon form.

Morton's most important writing in the sermon form is the series titled *The Spirit of Man*. Perry Miller criticized this work for its reference to the four humors, obsolete even then. Furthermore, it sidesteps terminological difficulties and shifts from its psychological theme to become a handbook on political power. Nevertheless, Morton has made a powerful attempt to overcome the duality so often found in Christian moral theology by asserting a cohesive unity of the individual. "Spirit is... taken for some *Qualifications*, or *Inclinations* of the mind as *United* to the Body.... Each man hath something peculiar to himself in this Respect, as he has in the Features of his Countenance, Stature, Shape, Mean, or Carriage of his Body, whereby he is Distinguished from any other." The theological issue is how to account for the salvation of this individual by the universal or generic grace of Christ. Morton argued that whereas the individual spirit joins the soul and the body, the soul itself is not individual because *"Souls in themselves are all Equal."* The soul, therefore, is the organ through which grace enters the individual. Nevertheless, this grace does not overpower the individuality of the spirit; rather, it *"Uses* the Parts, Humours, and Members, as its *Instruments* or *Organs*, in all its Operations." *The Spirit of Man* can be seen as a document in the Mather camp because it stresses self-knowledge as the means to do good. But the theoretical ground that Morton provided for the sanctified spirit looks forward, unintentionally to be sure, to a radical individuality and to a detachment of the soul from the self. This soul, created innately good by God, has power of its own. Morton's attempt to account for the Calvinist scheme of saving grace acting upon the individual has almost created an Over-Soul.

Morton's literary strengths are more evident in his polemical and pedagogical works. His "Vindication of Himself" and "Advice to Candidates," both written in Eng. and published by Calamy, are lively arguments, addressed more to goodwill and understanding than to a disputatious victory. Their language is more colorful, even conversational, than that of the sermons. For example, Morton advised young ministers that the use of notes for sermons was "an affected Curiosity, to scratch itching ears." He warned that notes are used "least (forsooth) the startch'd Oration should be ruffled by a rough Expression." The familiar tone in these writings explains Morton's success as a teacher. His pedagogical writings always addressed the student as one struggling through the material, who could use whatever help Morton had to offer.

The sermons and the verse give evidence that Morton had difficulty keeping to a stated theme or method. Perhaps that is why he so emphasized method in his pedagogical works. Both Miller and Morison have criticized Morton's reliance on Aristotle in his science text, *Compendium Physicae*. But Morton made clear that his choice of an Aristotelian scheme was more pedagogical than philosophical: "Because the former Philosophers had their Method more Systematical, than the latter; I have therefore chosen their Method, and noted the Other Matter by the Way in those places where I observe a discrepance." Although such an approach may not elicit praise from the historian of ideas, it must have been deeply appreciated by the harried undergraduate.

Morison has pointed out that the *Compendium Physicae* changed the nature of Harvard theses in science by establishing the importance of empirical observation. Morton introduced the theories of Descartes and Boyle, and presented material from the Royal Society, but never forgot that his main purpose was to teach a general course in natural science to nonscientists. Thus he warned his students not to "be dishartened when you meat with diversities of opinions."

Much of Morton's work remains in manuscript, primarily at Harvard University and the Massachusetts Historical Society. His pedagogical methods warrant their study.

Suggested Readings: CCNE; DAB; DNB; FCNEV; Sprague (I, 211-213). *See also* Bernard Bailyn, *Education in the Forming of American Society* (1960); Edmund Calamy, *A Continuation of the Account of Ministers...Ejected and Silenced After the Restoration* (1727), I, 177-210; idem, *The Noncomformist's Memorial* (1775), I, 273-274; CMHS, 1st ser., 8; 2nd ser., 1 and 2; 4th ser., 8; Theodore Hornberger, "An Introduction" in *Compendium Physicae*, by Charles Morton, PCSM, 33 (1940); Perry Miller, *The New England Mind: The Seventeenth Century* (1954); Samuel Eliot Morison, "Charles Morton" in *Compendium Physicae*, by Charles Morton, PCSM, 33 (1940); idem, *Harvard College in the Seventeenth Century* (1936), I, 236-251; idem, *The Intellectual Life of Colonial New England* (1956); PMHS, 17 (1880), 262-280; Josiah Quincy, *The History of*

Harvard University (1860), I, 69-84; Samuel Sewall, *The Diary* (1973); Larzer Ziff, *Puritanism in America* (1973), pp. 212-216.

William J. Irvin
New York, New York

GEORGE MORTON (1585-1624)

Works: *A Relation or Iournall of the Beginning and Proceedings of the English Plantation Setled at Plimouth in New England* (possibly editor; 1622), commonly referred to as *Mourt's Relation*.

Biography: George Morton was born into a wealthy Roman Catholic family residing in Harworth, Nottinghamshire, Eng. At a youthful age, he joined the Separatist congregation led by William Brewster and John Robinson in nearby Scrooby. For a time, he was occupied as a merchant in York, but later rejoined the Scrooby congregation in Hol., whither it had fled in 1608. In Leyden in 1612, Morton married Juliana Carpenter. In 1619 he journeyed to London to seek financial backing for the Pilgrim Separatists' proposed immigration to North America. Not one of the *Mayflower* passengers, he remained in London for several years representing the interests of Plymouth Plantation, but in the summer of 1623, he sailed to the colony on the *Anne* with his wife, his children (one was born on the voyage), his brother Thomas, and his sister-in-law the widow Alice Southworth, who married Governor William Bradford (q.v.) the next year. Morton was allotted a parcel of land; but he did not enjoy it for long, for he was dead within a year of his arrival. He was one of the three original members of the old Scrooby congregation to reach Plymouth, the other two being William Bradford and William Brewster. One of his sons, Nathaniel Morton (q.v.), became a leader in the colony and the author of *New Englands Memoriall* (1669).

Critical Appraisal: George Morton's literary accomplishments, so far as can be conjectured, were limited to the assembling and probably the editing of the material contained in a volume titled *A Relation or Iournall*, generally known as *Mourt's Relation*, because its address "To the Reader" is signed G. Mourt. Although most scholars believe that G. Mourt was actually George Morton, there is no definite proof of Mourt's identity. Various explanations have been put forth about why Morton's correct name might not have appeared in the book. For example, some scholars believe that he did not wish to embarrass his Catholic family by identifying himself with a Separatist venture. Others assume that Mourt is a typographical error for Mourton, an acceptable alternate spelling. A few, like Samuel Eliot Morison, flatly state that thus far no one can be sure who Mourt was.

Whoever compiled the *Relation*—and the evidence remains strong that it *was* George Morton—the book is of major historical importance and is not without literary merit. In the preface, "To the Reader," G. Mourt stated that most of the material in the volume was taken from writings by Plymouth colonists well known to him. It is believed almost beyond question that the chief contributors were William Bradford and Edward Winslow (q.v.), the manuscripts of whose journals were carried to Eng. by Robert Cushman (q.v.) on the *Fortune* in 1622. George Morton would, of course, have been well acquainted with these two (and it should be added that no other person closely involved in the Pilgrim enterprise had a name even remotely resembling Mourt).

The narrative portion of the *Relation* consists of five sections. The first, the style and content of which strongly suggest Bradford's authorship, deals with the Pilgrims' "difficult passage, their safe arivall, their ioyfull building of, and comfortable planting themselves in the now well defended Towne of New Plimoth." The writing in this lengthy account is vivid, concrete, fast-paced—a style analogous to the most memorable passages in Bradford's *Of Plimmoth Plantation*, but less freighted with references to God's providence and the religious implications of the venture. The remaining four narrative sections of the *Relation*, attributed to Edward Winslow, are highly readable accounts of dealings with various Indian tribes in the area. In addition, the volume includes a letter from the Rev. John Robinson counseling and blessing those members of his congregation who were undertaking the voyage to the New World; a promotional "Letter," signed E. W. (Edward Winslow, undoubtedly), setting forth in glowing, if not entirely candid, terms the supposed attractions awaiting any new colonist; and a statement, signed R. C. (Robert Cushman), demonstrating with copious biblical references the "lawfulnesse" as well as the advantages of "removing out of England into the parts of America." Indeed, the overall purpose and tone of *Mourt's Relation* is that of a promotional tract, giving in informal, almost confidentially conversational, language the information and the encouragement needed in reassuring prospective colonists.

Suggested Readings: DAB; LHUS; T₁. *See also* J. K. Allen, *George Morton of Plymouth Colony and Some of His Descendants* (1908); Henry M. Dexter, ed., *Mourt's Relation* (1865), Introduction and notes, passim; Dwight B. Heath, ed., *A Journal of the Pilgrims at Plymouth: Mourt's Relation* (1963), Editor's Introduction; Perry D. Westbrook, *William Bradford* (1978), pp. 90-93; George F. Willison, *Saints and Strangers* (1945), pp. 196-198, 235-236.

Perry D. Westbrook
State University of New York at Albany

NATHANIEL MORTON (1613-1685)

Works: *New Englands Memoriall* (1669).

Biography: Born into the Pilgrim community at Leyden, Hol., Nathaniel Morton was the eldest son of George (q.v.) and Juliana (Carpenter) Morton (or *Mourt*). Nathaniel journeyed to Plymouth with his father's family aboard the

Anne in 1623. Upon the death of his father the following year, he was taken into the family of Governor William Bradford (q.v.), an uncle through marriage. Morton was very much influenced by Bradford, with whom he developed a close personal and working relationship that continued until the governor's death in 1657. From Dec. 1647 until his death, Morton was secretary of Plymouth colony and official keeper of the records. In this connection, he became involved in the daily operations of government as well as in drafting laws. Other official functions included being town clerk and in 1671 becoming secretary of the Council of War to conduct campaigns against King Philip. He married Lydia Cooper in 1635 and then a year after her death took as his second wife Ann (Pritchard) Templar (Apr. 29, 1674). Morton died in 1685, having made a significant contribution to the legislative and civil affairs of Plymouth colony.

Critical Appraisal: Nathaniel Morton acknowledged in his "Epistle Dedicatory" the indebtedness of his history to Bradford, the man who has been both creator and destroyer of Morton's reputation as historian. At Bradford's death, Morton became curator of Bradford's papers, and gradually he came to be recognized as the man most knowledgeable about Plymouth history. Sensing "the weight of duty that lies upon us to commemorize to future generations the memorable passages of God's providence to us and our predecessors, in the beginning of this plantation," Morton prepared *New Englands Memoriall: or, A Brief Relation of the Most Memorable and Remarkable Passages of the Providence of God, Manifested to the Planters of New England, in America: With Special Reference to the First Colony Thereof, Called New Plymouth*. The history is largely based on Bradford's *Of Plymouth Plantation*, but until the rediscovery of that document in 1855, Morton's history was considered the most authoritative source on Plymouth. It is still considered especially useful for providing certain historical details absent from Bradford and information on the years 1647-1668.

Although Bradford's history has largely overshadowed Morton's, a comparison of the two documents reveals a good deal about the changing flavor of the times. Perhaps the most obvious difference appears in the tone of each history. Morton is less moving and dramatic than Bradford. Bradford is given to emotional outbursts; for example, when relating how the Indians came into possession of firearms, he exclaimed, "O, the horribleness of this villainy!" Morton, on the other hand, restrained himself from such outbursts. The Indian threat becomes a fact of life rather than something that triggers an emotional response. Morton's tone is consistently more professional, public, and impersonal than Bradford's. In reading Bradford, one is aware of the human dimensions and the personality of the author, but Morton attempted to efface himself and to present a more "objective" history. In this way, the two documents reveal the decline of spontaneity and loss of spirit and vision associated with the succeeding generations of New Englanders.

Several elements of style and substance contribute to the more restrained tone of Morton's history. Morton sometimes adopted Bradford's phrasing, but often he paraphrased in general terms. When he omitted Bradford's details, they were frequently those that evoked emotion or formed a vivid picture. One example is the description of the smallpox epidemic that afflicted the Indians in 1634. Morton eliminated details of their dire straits, how "some would crawl out on all fours to get a little water, and sometimes die by the way and not be able to get in again." He recorded Bradford's description only up to a point and then almost arbitrarily stopped, as if impatient with Bradford's sensuous indulgence.

When Morton embellished the Bradford text, it was to be more didactic or more informative. In one representative instance, he applied the lesson of Thomas Morton (q.v.) to his own times. Bradford explained Morton's success in a parenthetical, absolute clause, "base covetousness prevailing in men that should know better," but Nathaniel Morton urged the point more strongly upon the present time: "that so far base covetousness prevailed, and doth still prevail, as that the savages become amply furnished with guns, powder, shot," the altered syntax making the lesson about covetousness equal in importance to the historical narrative. Morton did more than Bradford in the way of framing events to point a lesson. Morton almost formally introduced the Pequot War ("Now followeth the tragedy of the war that fell betwixt the English and the Pequots"), boldly proclaiming his reasons for describing the war: "that by discerning the whole matter in the several parts and circumstances, the more of the mercy and goodness of God may be taken notice of to his praise, for destroying so proud and blasphemous an enemy." Although Bradford, too, pointed morals and messages, the effect in the Bradford text frequently is that the man himself is recognizing the lesson in the process of recording it in the history. The effect in Morton is that the author has known it all along and is now framing his understanding in order to teach others. For this reason, perhaps, Morton is more prone than Bradford to designate an event as providential or to see the yearly chronicle as providential, as when he terminated the account of 1622 with the sentence: "And herewith I end the relation of the most remarkable passages of God's providence towards the first planters, which fell out in this year."

In addition to his embellishing with frames and his insistence that we understand events as providential, Morton also added to the essential content of the history. His major inclusions tend to be the more official kinds of information available to him as keeper of records. Whereas Bradford characteristically recorded at the beginning of his account of the year only the name of the man chosen governor of the colony, Morton listed in addition all assistants. Although he omitted some of the letters that Bradford copied out, he included other documents that probably interested him in his official capacity, such as the document signed by John Cotton (q.v.), Thomas Oliver, and Thomas Leverett titled "Errors in Doctrine Mentioned by Some of the Brethren of the Church of Salem, Tending to the Disturbance of Religion and Peace in Family, Church, and Commonwealth."

This particular document also indicates another difference between the Bradford history and Morton's. Nathaniel Morton was more concerned with the other colonies, more aware of the congruency of Plymouth's interests with those of the other colonies, than Bradford seems to have been. The document mentioned above, for example, which does little more than relate the "errors" attributed to Roger Williams (q.v.), was sent from the Boston church to the Salem church and, in a narrow sense, has nothing to do with Plymouth. Indeed, not only with the Roger Williams case but with others as well, such as the Pequot War, Bradford was willing to leave the topic to others, but Morton, seeing the broader historical implications, included them.

Despite its loss of prominence in the late nineteenth and twentieth centuries, *New Englands Memoriall* is an important document not only in its overt function as a repository for source material on the period, but also in its more subtle service as an indicator of the interests and concerns of a later generation. In many ways, *New Englands Memoriall* appears to be the work of a man confident about what a history should be—its function and its purpose—and of a man who envisioned himself as "official Pilgrim." As such, the history goes far beyond its usefulness in providing insights into the social, political, and economic tides of the period it describes and points to a developing aesthetic as well as a "national" character and the party line. Morton, in fact, has probably been more influential than most historians would initially guess, for because of *New Englands Memoriall*, Morton, not Bradford, formulated the historical consciousness of men like Hawthorne, whose views in turn have prevailed in the American consciousness to the present.

Suggested Readings: DAB; FCNEV; LHUS; T₁. *See also* Peter Gay, *A Loss of Mastery: Puritan Historians in Colonial America* (1966), pp. 54-56; Samuel Eliot Morison, *The Puritan Pronaos: Studies in the Intellectual Life of New England in the Seventeenth Century* (1936), pp. 174-176; Kenneth B. Murdock, *Literature and Theology in Colonial New England* (1949), pp. 92-94; *National Cyclopedia of American Biography* (1897), VIII, 38-39.

Paula K. White
Upsala College

PEREZ MORTON (1751-1837)

Works: *An Oration; Delivered at King's Chapel* (1776).

Biography: Perez Morton was born in Plymouth, Mass., Nov. 2, 1751, son of Joseph and Anna Bullock Morton. He attended the Boston Latin School and Harvard College, graduating in 1771. After Harvard he read law with Josiah Quincy, Jr. (q.v.), and was recommended to practice before the Court of Common Pleas in Jul. 1774. A year later, he was named province secretary by the Council. Morton became an intimate of the patriot leaders meeting regularly at the White Horse Tavern in Boston, owned by his father. An active Mason and popular orator, he was asked by the Masons to give the funeral oration for Dr. Joseph Warren (q.v.), killed at Bunker Hill.

Morton seems to have been a passionate man in both his public and private life. In 1789 he married Sarah Wentworth Apthorp (Morton [q.v.]), by whom he had five children. But he also fathered a child of his wife's sister Frances (Fanny). An investigation following Frances's suicide cleared Morton, but the incident was immortalized in William Hill Brown's (q.v.) *The Power of Sympathy* and two other works. Sarah, in the meantime, began a literary career and was soon known as "the American Sappho." In 1794 Morton was elected to the House of Representatives from Boston and, after moving to Dorchester, was elected to the House of Representatives from that town in 1803. In 1811 he was appointed attorney general of Mass., an office he held for twenty years. He died Oct. 14, 1837.

Critical Appraisal: Perez Morton's one published work is *An Oration; Delivered at King's Chapel April Eighth, 1776*, delivered on the occasion of the reinterment of the late Joseph Warren, killed at Bunker Hill on Jun. 17, 1775. Morton, a Mason, was asked by that organization to give the memorial oration for Warren, who had been a grand master of the Masons. The *Oration* is an excellent example of the inflammatory rhetoric characteristic of many writings of the period from the Boston Massacre to the end of the war. (Indeed, Warren himself was author of a fiery speech commemorating the Boston Massacre.)

The *Oration* begins with an impassioned apostrophe to the remains of Warren: "Illustrious Relicks! What tidings from the grave! Why hast thou left the peaceful mansions of the tomb, to visit again this troubled earth!" The occasion is used to praise the life of Warren; he possessed sensibility to the suffering of others, never was self-serving, and helped the indigent as well as the wealthy. For the most part, however, Morton stirred the emotions of the Americans against the British. He asked his audience:

> Have we not proofs, wrote in blood, that the corrupted nation from whence we sprang . . . are stubbornly fixed on our destruction! . . . O shameless Britain! . . . when thy glory shall have faded like the western sunbeam—the name and virtues of Warren shall remain immortal.

With these and other inflammatory rhetorical statements, Morton was no doubt successful in his purpose.

Suggested Readings: Sibley-Shipton (XVII, 555-561). *See also* Philip Davidson, *Propaganda and the American Revolution* (1941); Everett Emerson, ed., *American Literature, 1764-1789* (1977), pp. 19-38.

Elaine K. Ginsberg
West Virginia University

SARAH WENTWORTH MORTON (1759-1846)

Works: *Ouâbi* (1790); *Reanimation* (1791); *Beacon Hill* (1797); *The Virtues of Society* (1799); *Dedicatory Hymn* (1806); *My Mind and Its Thoughts* (1823).

Biography: Sarah Apthorp was born in Boston in 1759. Proud of her Welsh heritage, she adopted her mother's maiden name, Wentworth, and remained devoutly Anglican throughout her life. After the Apthorps moved to Braintree, she read extensively, met diversely notable men such as John Adams (q.v.) and John Trumbull (q.v.), and studied architecture with her cousin Charles Bullfinch. In 1789 she married Perez Morton (q.v.), an active patriot who would become speaker of Mass.'s House of Representatives and the state's attorney general. The couple's engaging personalities led them into fashionable and intellectual company in Boston and, later, in Dorchester. Perez's sexual liaison with his sister-in-law Frances during 1786-1787 shook the family but caused no lasting rifts in the marriage. (The incident is fictionalized in William Hill Brown's [q.v.] *The Power of Sympathy*, a novel once attributed to Mrs. Morton.) Surviving her husband and their five children, Morton died in Quincy in 1846.

Critical Appraisal: Prepared by her unusual education and encouraged by younger Boston writers such as Robert Treat Paine, Jr. (q.v.), Sarah Wentworth Morton used the time allowed by "the appropriate occupations of [her] sex and station" to write poetry. The Jul. 1789 issue of the *Massachusetts Magazine* included "Invocation to Hope," probably her first published poem. Through 1807 her verse appeared frequently in Boston periodicals under the pseudonyms of Constantia, which she gave up in deference to Judith Sargent Murray's (q.v.) prior claim, and Philenia. Her work was reprinted in N.Y. and Philadelphia journals as well as in Elihu Hubbard Smith's (q.v.) anthology of American verse (1793). She wrote most often in heroic couplets or ballad stanzas, applying conventional imagery to local material. But unlike her neo-Classical predecessors, Morton's verse is neither humorous nor satiric. Her favorite themes are patriotism ("Philadelphia"), sentimental morality ("Prayer to Patience"), and personal reflection ("Lines to the Mansion of My Ancestors, on Seeing It Occupied as a Banking Establishment"). Readers in 1791 seemed particularly taken by Philenia's poetic exchange with an unidentified Alfred in the *Columbian Centinel*.

The productive decade before the turn of the century also issued three long poems. *Ouâbi, or The Virtues of Nature* recounts a love triangle between Ouâbi, an Illinois chief; his wife, Azakia; and an European named Celario, whom Ouâbi rescues from a Huron warrior and nurtures as an adopted brother. Humiliated as a prisoner of war and recognizing Celario's love for Azakia, Ouâbi dissolves the marriage, gives Azakia to Celario as a reward for his heroism, and dies. In spite of the author's claim that the work is "wholly American," the poem is national in location alone. The plot flavors sentimental tragedy with documented but secondhand Indian lore, while noble savages demonstrate the superiority of natural moral instinct over the corruptions of society. Read widely, the poem inspired at least one play, and Ouâbi's "Death Song" was set to music by Hans Gram (1793).

Beacon Hill, published as the first book in an uncompleted longer work, is Morton's most ambitious poem and one of her best. Reflecting on the view from the title location, the speaker is led to consider the end of the Battle of Bunker

Hill, the character of each American colony and the strengths of its leaders, the personal and professional superiority of George Washington (q.v.), the siege of Boston, and the Declaration of Independence. The work ends with "The Poet's prophetic apostrophe to the progress of freedom throughout the world." Although in a mode foreign to later tastes, *Beacon Hill* illustrates both the depth of national pride at the close of the eighteenth century and the ability of neo-Classical verse to convey such feelings.

The Virtues of Society includes some of the material intended for the extension of *Beacon Hill*, but was conceived as a companion to *Ouâbi*. The poem records the story of Harriet Ackland, a British officer's wife who accompanies her husband to America during the Revolution and saves his life by crossing colonial lines to nurse his wounds. The poem's theme and characterization are saccharinely sentimental, and its rhymed couplets lapse into sing-song repetition. Its failure may have influenced Morton's decision to give up lengthy composition.

Even beyond *Beacon Hill*, Morton's writing was more than the avocation of a society lady with time on her hands. The longer poems drew on extensive historical research and broad reading. She occasionally expressed enlightened social concern, especially against slavery, a conviction voiced in the portions of *Beacon Hill* devoted to the Carolinas and in "The African Chief" (1792). Her collected short poems demonstrate a mature understanding of the complex demands of her chosen poetic forms. *My Mind and Its Thoughts, in Sketches, Fragments, and Essays*, the only publication bearing her name, gathers work from throughout her life, interspersing poems among prose pieces considering topics such as fortune, hasty opinion, and civility. Much of the early poetry has been carefully revised to polish metrical patterns and to clarify meaning. "Ode to the President," for example, becomes "Ode to Music" by deleting eight lines (the equivalent of a full stanza), rephrasing seventeen passages (usually making them more concrete), and changing spelling or punctuation in numerous instances. These alterations, strengthening the poem while retaining its original vitality, reveal the hand of a skillful poetic craftsman.

Suggested Readings: DAB; LHUS; NAW. *See also* Pattie Cowell, *Women Poets in Pre-Revolutionary America, 1650-1775* (1981); Roy Harvey Pearce, *The Savages of America* (1965), pp. 185-188; Emily Pendleton and Milton Ellis, *Philenia: The Life and Works of Sarah Wentworth Morton, 1759-1846* (includes a number of the short poems; 1931); Emily Stipes Watts, *The Poetry of American Women from 1632 to 1945* (1977), pp. 54-56.

Kennedy Williams, Jr.
Bentley College

THOMAS MORTON (c. 1579-1647)

Works: *New English Canaan* (1637).

Biography: One of seventeenth-century New Eng.'s earliest reprobates and the subject of several novels, short stories, and poems, Thomas Morton was born in Eng. sometime around 1579, probably in the West Country. While his parentage is unknown, the history of Morton's early life suggests that he was born into a family of means. Respected as a "gentleman," Morton studied law at Clifford's Inn in London, eventually becoming a lawyer by profession.

Married to a prosperous widow in Nov. of 1621, Morton became involved in a series of disputes and rumors that included suggestions that he may have mistreated his wife and perhaps even murdered a business associate. Possibly to escape such entanglements, Morton invested in Captain Wollaston's plan to establish a commercial venture in Mass., and during the spring of 1642 he arrived in New Eng. and helped to set up a fur-trading post near the present location of Quincy, which he named "Ma-re-Mount" ("Merry Mount"), probably in mock defiance of the more sober lifestyle practiced by the Pilgrims in neighboring Plymouth.

Through adept trading with the natives, Morton and his band of followers prospered, but Morton's fondness for merriment, his setting up of a maypole on the hillside overlooking the Atlantic, his relaxed business and personal relationships with the Indians, and most of all the possibility that he was selling the Indians guns and ammunition in return for pelts resulted in his arrest by Miles Standish in 1628, his subsequent trial at Plymouth, and his deportation, after a month spent in exile on the Isle of the Shoals, to Eng. By Aug. of the following year, however, Morton returned to Plymouth and to his settlement at Mount Wollaston, much to the displeasure of the Pilgrims. While in Eng., Morton had managed to befriend the colonial adventurer, Sir Ferdinando Gorges (q.v.), and it has been suggested that he perhaps returned to New Eng. as a spy in Gorges's employ. Having angered John Endecott, who had recently visited Merry Mount (which he renamed "Mount Dagon") and had ordered the destruction of the eighty-foot maypole there, Morton was again arrested and ordered returned to Eng. While on ship, Morton watched his house being burned to the ground as a final expression by the Puritan leaders of the contempt in which they held him.

After a short term in a British jail, Morton was again freed and soon thereafter was working, along with Gorges, for the revocation of the Mass. charter and the establishment of a different form of government for New Eng. It was during this period of his life that Morton wrote his *New English Canaan*, a work that both extols the benefits to be gained from British colonization of New Eng. and points out the problems he perceived in allowing the Puritans to execute that colonization.

In Aug. of 1643, after writing his will, Morton made a third and final voyage to New Eng., where he was immediately ordered by the authorities of Massachusetts Bay to depart from that colony. After a sojourn in R.I., Morton turned up in Mass. and was arrested on charges of conspiracy against the colony. Imprisoned for a year under harsh conditions and broken in health, Morton was freed from jail and fined 100 pounds. Described by John Winthrop (q.v.) as "old and crazy," Morton then left Mass. for the more tolerant environment of Maine, where he died less than two years later.

Critical Appraisal: The subject of much controversy and debate, Thomas Morton's *New English Canaan* has angered, delighted, and baffled readers during the more than two centuries since its publication in Holland in 1637. Enraged by Morton's audacious attack on the "Saints" of seventeenth-century New Eng., William Bradford (q.v.) dismissed the *New English Canaan* as "an infamous and scurillous booke against many godly and cheefe men of the cuntrie; full of lyes and slanders, and fraight with profane calumnies against their names and persons, and the ways of God." During the twentieth century, however, Morton's book has come to be seen as "a minor American epic" and a brilliant satire of the staunch piety and stern authoritarianism often associated with early New Eng.

If Morton's *New English Canaan* remains enigmatic and difficult to interpret with certainty, such difficulties arise at least in part from the fact that he wrote the book for a variety of often quite complex reasons. Like such works as Captain John Smith's (q.v.) *Description of New England* (1616) and William Wood's (q.v.) *New England's Prospect* (1634), Morton's book was designed to encourage British colonists to settle North America. As a result, the *New English Canaan* is replete with sumptuous descriptions of the earthly "paradice" awaiting the British colonist courageous enough to venture across the ocean to New Eng. To counter rumors to the contrary, the Indians of New Eng. are described as the innocent children of a munificent nature, and the potential of the land for future development is emphasized. "If this Land be not rich," states Morton, "then is the whole world poore." According to Morton, "The more I looked, the more I liked it."

In addition, Morton wrote the *New English Canaan* at least in part, as his seventeenth-century antagonists have charged him, to discredit the work of the Puritans in New Eng. As an ally of Sir Ferdinando Gorges and others who wished to end the Puritan domination and had much to gain personally from so doing, Morton used the treatment he received at the hands of the Puritan autocracy as a means of undermining the credibility of the American Puritans in Eng. Consequently, passages in the *New English Canaan* describing the cruelty and intolerance of the Puritan officials, particularly toward Church of England rituals and policies, were designed to attract the attention of British leaders such as Archbishop William Laud who were suspicious of Puritans in general and who were in a position to influence legislation concerning the future of Puritan New Eng. In New England, writes Morton, "the Book of Common Prayer is an idol, and all that use it idolators."

Finally, Morton wrote the *New English Canaan* as a work of literature, and it is perhaps as literature that the book has its most lasting appeal. An educated man knowledgeable in the literature and literary traditions of the British Renaissance, Morton enlivened his narrative with poetry, Classical allusions, and satire. Described by Donald F. Connors as a veritable "maze of Classical and Biblical allusions representing, allegorically, some contemporary occurrence" of special significance for Morton, "The Poem" by Morton which begins "Rise Oedipus, and if Thou canst, unfould" was, Morton states, so "Enigmatically composed" that "it pusselled the Seperatists," for whom it was left attached to the maypole, "most pittifully to expound it." Other of Morton's poems, such as those on drinking and festivity, have been likened to similar works by poets such as Robert Herrick.

Morton's skill as a writer is perhaps nowhere more apparent, however, than in the deft satire with which he describes his religious opponents in New Eng. Within the context of Morton's narrative, John Endecott becomes "Captain Littleworth," Samuel Fuller "Doctor Noddy," John Winthrop "Iosua Temperwell," and Miles Standish "Captain Shrimpe," names by which these individuals have subsequently become immortalized. As a consequence of Morton's spirited opposition to religious authoritarianism, his affirmation of personal liberty, his sense of the dramatic, and his skill as a satirist, he and his *New English Canaan* have held a long and irresistible fascination for many later American writers probing the moral depths of their literary and cultural heritage. During the nineteenth century, for example, Morton helped inspire writers such as Washington Irving, Lydia Maria Child, Maria Sedgwick, John Lothrop Motley, John Greenleaf Whittier, Henry Wadsworth Longfellow, and, of course, Nathaniel Hawthorne. During the twentieth century, Morton has been no less significant, appearing in various forms in the works of Stephen Vincent Benet, Robert Lowell, and Richard L. Stokes. No doubt Morton will continue to play a prominent role in the development of American literature, for the image of individualism and vitality that he projected for himself as the infamous "Lord of Misrule" has earned him a permanent position in the American mythology.

Suggested Readings: DAB; DNB; FCNEV; LHUS. *See also* Charles Francis Adams, Jr., ed., *The New English Canaan of Thomas Morton* (1883); Robert D. Arner, "Mythology and the Maypole of Merrymount: Some Notes on Thomas Morton's 'Rise Oedipus,' " EAL, 6 (1971), 156-164; idem, "Pastoral Celebration and Satire in Thomas Morton's *New English Canaan*," *Criticism*, 16 (1974), 217-231; C. E. Banks, "Thomas Morton of Merry Mount," PMHS, 58 (1924), 147-192; Donald F. Connors, *Thomas Morton* (1969); idem, "Thomas Morton of Merry Mount: His First Arrival in New England," AL, 11 (1939), 160-166; Richard Drinnon, "The Maypole of Merry Mount: Thomas Morton and the Puritan Patriarchs," MR, 21 (1980), 382-410; Robert J. Gangewere, "Thomas Morton: Character and Symbol in a Minor American Epic" in Calvin Israel, ed., *Discoveries and Considerations: Essays on Early American Literature and Aesthetics* (1976), pp. 189-204; Minor Wallace Major, "William Bradford Versus Thomas Morton," EAL, 5 (1970), 1-12; William J. Scheick, "Morton's *New English Canaan*," *Explicator*, 31, no. 47 (1973); John B. Vickery, "The Golden Bough at Merry Mount," NCF, 12 (1957), 203-214.

James A. Levernier
University of Arkansas at Little Rock

GEORGE MOXON (1602-1687)

Works: Three Hymns (n.d.).

Biography: George Moxon was born in Yorkshire, Eng., near Wakefield, in 1602. He was educated at Sidney Sussex College, Cambridge, and became chaplain to Sir William Brereton in Chester County. His next appointment, at St. Helen's Chapel near Warrington in Lancashire, lasted until 1637, when his "Nonconformity to Ceremonies" led to a dispute with Dr. Bridgman, the bishop of Chester. A warrant for Moxon's arrest was hung on the door of St. Helen's, and Moxon, in disguise, stole away to Bristol, where he embarked for New Eng. He served as pastor in Springfield, Mass., until 1653, when he returned to Eng. with William Pynchon (q.v.) and shared a Congregational pulpit and parsonage with the Rev. John Machin. The two men alternated Sundays at Astbury and Rushton until the Restoration of Charles II in 1660, when both men were silenced. Moxon continued preaching (illegally, one assumes) at Rushton until 1662, when he moved to Congleton. There he preached privately in his own home until he was granted a license to resume public preaching in 1672. Edmund Calamy called Moxon "a man of blameless conversation, and not of a contentious spirit. He was very useful to persons under spiritual trouble." Moxon continued in his ministry at Congleton until overcome by old age and palsy. He died on Sept. 15, 1687, at the age of 85.

Critical Appraisal: Edmund Calamy described Moxon as "so good a Lyrick Poet, that he could imitate *Horace* so exactly, as not to be distinguish'd without Difficulty." Calamy also noted that at the time of his death, Moxon "had the Notes of some Sermons of *Self-denial* prepared for the Press, but never Printed them, nor any thing else." Harold S. Jantz, who first made mention of Moxon's hymns in 1944, searched for more of Moxon's writings in the British Museum but found none. The only evidence we have of Moxon's skill as a lyric poet rests in three hymns copied out by a William Robie, or Roby, of Boston, on the back and front fly leaves of John Cotton's (q.v.) *The Powring out of the Seven Vials* (1642). Actually, we cannot be certain that these verses are indeed the work of George Moxon or that he wrote them in America, for Robie, a transplanted Yorkshireman, noted below the verses, "Mr. Mossens verses, Novem: 1670." Harold Jantz suggested that "Mossen" is a variant spelling of "Moxon" and that these verses were transcribed by Robie in 1670 around Thanksgiving Day but had been written earlier, during Moxon's sojourn in Springfield, also for a Thanksgiving Day celebration.

All three poems, or hymns, are untitled. The beginning of the first one is missing. Leo Kaiser has described the remaining fragment as consisting of seventeen stanzas. Robie's transcription, however, divides the poem into three stanzas of rhyming couplets in iambic heptameter. The first and second stanzas contain five couplets each, and the third has seven. Like Michael Wigglesworth's (q.v.) "Day of Doom" and Edward Taylor's (q.v.) "God's Determination Touching His Elect," Moxon's poem describes the downfall of the unregenerate and the joy of the elect on Judgment Day. The evil-doers lose all their power in Christ's presence: "Of all their righteousnesse & sin; their stript from top to toe; / All is throne downe by Christ the King; They have no more to sho." The redeemed are urged to "be confident be bold" in their faith and rejoicing. Although they may feel unworthy of redemption, they need not doubt Christ's love and protection: "Hee is become your castle strong; As hee himselfe hath said; / The gates of Hell cannot hurt you; Therefore be not Dismayd." The Gospel and the law are contrasted, and the Gospel is shown to be the stronger, surer way to salvation: "The Law is weake in this Respect; The Apostle true doth say; / The spirit of life in Christ alone; Doth take our sins away." The hymn ends on a peculiarly downbeat note, however: "The Lamb and eake his followers all; Are subjects of great scorn; / Among the Anti Christian Crue; they are in peaces torn." If Moxon did write this hymn in America, perhaps he had his own banishment in mind when he wrote this melancholy conclusion.

The second hymn, again in rhymed couplets of iambic heptameter, consists of twelve stanzas of joyful thanksgiving. In this poem, all of the world is filled with redemption and happiness: "Heares pardon for the guilty soul; The barren, fruitfullnesse; / Strength to the weak, Joy to the sad; To each soul tendernesse. / This Day Doth tell you of God's Love; This Day his praises sound / England, Ireland, Nations all; In Thankfullnesse abound."

The third poem, most clearly meant to be sung, consists of twenty quatrains in iambic tetrameter with a rhyme scheme of "aabb." Each stanza is followed by a two-line rhyming refrain in iambic dimeter. Its imagery is patterned after the triumphal hymns of Moses and Miriam in Exodus 15 and Deborah and Barak in Judges 5. Here Moxon sang the praises of the Old Testament Lord of Hosts: "Jehovah is a man of warr. / His troops & Companies from ffar / With shining sheilds, & glistering speares, / Which stout & strong in feilds Apeares. / ffight valiently, / O jah on high." The song is full of Hebraic war imagery; arrows, steeds, chariots, and golden spoils abound. "Young maids with Timbrills" perform victory dances as did David before the Ark. Here the poet celebrated the martial exploits of God the Father; Christ the redeeming Son never appears. In this hymn, even when describing God's forgiveness, Moxon did not turn to the Gospels. Instead, he borrowed images from the Song of Solomon: "Now Jah shall reign for ever & Aye, / Arise belov'd & Come away. / As pleasant Roe on banks so stay / That we may reign with thee for Aye. / Come away, / Come away."

Calamy's description of Moxon as a skilled imitator is borne out in these three hymns. Following the conventional hymn book meter and borrowing their images from the Bible, these verses are fairly interesting examples of occasional poetry as practiced by the Puritan clergy of New Eng.

Suggested Readings: CCNE; DNB; FCNEV. *See also* Edmund Calamy, *An Account of the Ministers...Silenced After the Restoration in 1660* (1713), II, 128-129; Leo M. Kaiser, "Three Hymns Attributed to George Moxon," EAL, 8 (1973), 104-110 (prints hymns).

Zohara Boyd
Appalachian State University

HENRY MELCHIOR MUHLENBERG (1711-1787)

Works: W. Germann, ed., "Heinrich Melchior Muhlenberg: Patriarch der Lutherischen Kirche Nordamericka's, Selbstbiographie 1721-1743" (1881); Johann Ludwig Schulze, ed., *Nachrichten von den Vereinigten Deutschen Evangelische-Lutherischen Gemeinen in Nord-America, Absonderlich in Pennsylvanien*, 2 vols. (1886, 1895); C. W. Schaeffer, trans., "Muhlenberg's Defense of Pietism," LCR, 12 (1893), 349-370; Theodore G. Tappert and John W. Doberstein, eds., *The Journals of Henry Melchior Muhlenberg in Three Volumes* (1942-1958).

Biography: Henry Melchior Muhlenberg was born in Einbeck in the Duchy of Hanover, Ger., on Sept. 6, 1711. In 1735 he attended the University of Göttingen, where he eventually entered the seminary attached to it to pursue a career in the Lutheran ministry. In 1738 he transferred to the University of Halle, a center of Lutheran pietism where, in addition to his studies, he taught Greek and Hebrew in the theological school and served as an instructor in the orphanage. After his ordination in 1739, Muhlenberg assumed pastoral duties in Grosshennersdorf in Saxony. Then, in Sept. 1741, he accepted a call to the United Congregations of Philadelphia, New Hanover, and Providence in Pa. He arrived in Philadelphia on Nov. 25, 1742, and served in America until his death on Oct. 7, 1787.

During his forty-five-year American ministry, Muhlenberg was mainly concerned with establishing Lutheranism on a firm foundation. First he had to overcome the American phenomenon called "voluntarism" in which the laity dominated the churches by virtue of their immigration before that of a regularly ordained clergy. This he did in 1748 when he created the first Lutheran Synod in America, the Ministerium of Pennsylvania, which, while giving the laity some voice in Congregational affairs, firmly established the primacy of the clergy.

Muhlenberg, despite his pietistic background, pursued a clearly moderate course in theological matters, eschewing the extremes of both left and right. His early actions were geared to excising from his congregations the influence of left-wing radical pietism advocated by Moravians under the leadership of the enigmatic Count Nicholas von Zinzendorf (q.v.). Moravian preachers had infiltrated pastorless Lutheran congregations by posing as Lutheran ministers. Muhlenberg successfully exposed and expelled them. The right-wing threat of scholastic orthodoxy represented by Christoph Wilhelm Berkenmeyer of N.Y. was ended when Muhlenberg assumed control over those congregations. Ultimately, he evolved a middle-of-the-road Lutheran theology that was decidedly ecumenical and whose emphasis on liturgical revivalism kept the denomination from the excesses of the Great Awakening by insisting that revivalistic practices be channeled through the liturgical forms of the institutionalized church. By the time of his death, Muhlenberg's brand of Lutheranism held sway from New Eng. to the Carolinas.

Critical Appraisal: Muhlenberg's extant writings consist of an autobiography, begun in 1782 and covering the years from 1721 to 1743; a "Defense of Pietism," written in 1741, which, although signed only "D. M.," has been ascribed to Muhlenberg writing as Diaconus Muhlenberg; extracts from his journals published in the Halle Reports; and his journals or diaries, now published in three volumes. The journals, covering the years 1743-1787, present several problems. Some of them are missing, for example, those of 1754 and 1773. Others have pages ripped out. Some of this excision was done by Muhlenberg, on one occasion because he needed paper for another project. Others were done by persons and for reasons unknown. The journals were also intended as an official record of his ministry and so are self-serving to a degree. Muhlenberg wrote them with an eye to outside readership if not eventual publication. Moreover, Muhlenberg was an extremely cautious man. He intensely disliked being involved in controversy, most particularly political controversy, so he was Byzantine in what he recorded. One must sometimes read between the lines to understand his position. Extracts of Muhlenberg's journals as reproduced in the Halle Reports are of limited importance, for they were doubly edited, first by Muhlenberg, who was very careful to let his European superiors learn only what he wanted them to know of his activities, and then by Halle, which censored what it considered unedifying or impolitic. Less than one-tenth of his journals were published in the Reports and none from the second half of his ministry.

The style of the journals, which were originally written in German, is clear and lucid, although not elegant. Their importance lies in the wealth of historical detail they give us about life in the Philadelphia area in particular and the Middle Colonies in general during the eighteenth century. Fortunately, Muhlenberg did not confine his entries to official actions. He also recorded all sorts of interesting trivialities that throw much light on everyday life. For example, he reproduced the recipe for a salve to cure rheumatism, an antidote for snake bites, the best way to keep flies off horses and cabbages, and a way to preserve cider. The journals also have numerous entries on the contemporary political situation. Muhlenberg wrote about provincial elections, the struggle for royal government in Pa., the Paxton Boys' uprising, the Stamp Act crisis, and the Revolution. The journals thus give us a valuable insight into how the large German minority in Pa. reacted to the political crises of their day.

For the most part, however, the journals concern themselves with religious matters. They are the most important source we possess for the history of colonial Lutheranism. Although Muhlenberg mainly recorded everyday, factual details of a busy pastoral life, he also faithfully reproduced essential Church documents such as minutes and summaries of Ministerium meetings and Church constitutions. He was also an intimate friend of Gilbert Tennent (q.v.) and William Tennent II (q.v.) and of George Whitefield (q.v.) and in several passages recorded his feelings on the Awakening in which they were deeply involved. Muhlenberg was convinced that excessive emotionalism in religion was wrong. Rather than a manifestation of the workings of the spirit, he saw it as a psychological phenomenon—a reaction to the person of the speaker and his manner of preaching. To avoid such excesses, Muhlenberg insisted that religious revivals be conducted only within the sacramental life of the institutional church. Thus he evolved a form of liturgical revivalism, halfway between orthodoxy and enthusiasm, that enabled Lutherans to avoid the worst excesses of the Great Awakening.

Suggested Readings: CCMC; DAB; DARB; Sprague (IX, 4-13). *See also* William J. Mann, *Life and Times of Henry Melchior Muhlenberg* (1887); Leonard R. Riforgiato, *Missionary of Moderation: Henry Melchior Muhlenberg and the Lutheran Church in English America* (1980); Paul A. Wallace, *The Muhlenbergs of Pennsylvania* (1950).

Leonard R. Riforgiato
The Pennsylvania State University

ROBERT MUNFORD (c. 1737-1783)

Works: *The Candidates* (w. c. 1770; pub. 1798); *The Patriots* (w. c. 1777-1779; pub. 1798); William Munford, ed., *A Collection of Plays and Poems* (1798).

Biography: Robert Munford III—playwright, extensive landowner, politician, soldier—was born at "Whitehall" in Prince George County, Va. Traditionally, Munford's birthdate was given as "no later than 1730"; however, Rodney M. Baine, Munford's biographer, has presented convincing evidence for 1737 as the most probable date. Through his parents, Munford was allied with many prominent Va. families. His mother, Anna (Bland) Munford, for example, was the sister of Richard Bland (q.v.) and the granddaughter of William Randolph of Turkey Island. Munford's father became an alcoholic, however, and drove his once prosperous estates into ruin by the time of his death in 1745. Young Robert was taken in by his uncle William Beverley of Blandfield, reared to the age of 14, and then taken to Eng. with Beverley's children to be educated at Wakefield Grammar School. Beverley died in 1756, leaving no provision in his will for Munford; therefore, he returned to Va. and studied law in the office of his second cousin Peyton Randolph, king's attorney, studies that were interrupted by his service in 1758 as a captain in the French and Indian War.

Upon completion of his law studies, Munford settled in Lunenburg County, married his cousin and childhood playmate Anna Beverley, established his "Richland" plantation, and began his rise to prominence in his county. From the time Mecklenburg County was formed in 1765, Munford served at one time or another in every important office—county lieutenant, chief magistrate, sheriff, burgess (1765-1775), Va. House of Delegates (1779, 1780-1781). Although reluctant to make a violent break with Eng., he worked tirelessly during the Revolution as a recruiter and quartermaster and served in the field for several months in 1781 as commander of the militia from three counties. Although most authorities list the date of his death as 1784, Rodney M. Baine indicated that Munford died between Dec. 16, 1783, and the end of the year.

Critical Appraisal: Robert Munford's literary canon includes a readable translation of the first book of Ovid's *Metamorphoses*, a few poems, and two plays—*The Candidates* (c. 1770) and *The Patriots* (c. 1777-1779). Virtually none of his works—neither of his plays—was published until 1798, when his son

William Munford (q.v.) published *A Collection of Plays and Poems*. His place in American literature rests upon his two plays.

Va. in the eighteenth century provided a varied milieu of quality professional and amateur theater in which Munford could prepare himself for making a significant contribution to the development of American dramatic literature. *The Candidates* is the first real American farce, and *The Patriots* may be termed America's first legitimate comedy; both plays are filled with local allusions to persons and events, and both present perceptive and realistic pictures of certain aspects of Va.'s political life as seen by a participant. Munford's lively, biting satire ridicules those political practices and attitudes that he felt were antithetical to good sense, good morals, and rational patriotism. There is no evidence that the plays were performed during Munford's lifetime; however, they are thoroughly competent, good acting plays that evidently were written to be performed. The plays contain native American characters and themes that would have appealed to local audiences in the eighteenth century and that still seem relevant to a twentieth-century audience.

Munford's *The Candidates* is an entertaining, witty look at colonial Va. elections and the relationships between voters and gentlemen candidates. Although less expertly written than *The Patriots*, it is of great historical interest as the best available contemporary description of a colonial Va. election. The setting of the play is the burgesses election following the death of Governor Lord Botetourt in Oct. 1770, and it is filled with thinly disguised caricatures of Munford's contemporaries. The plot concerns an election for a seat in the Va. House of Burgesses in which an honorable gentleman must face the demagoguery and dishonorable tactics of three unqualified and really objectionable candidates.

At the core of the play lies a serious theme that reflects the attitude of the colonial Va. gentry toward public service and their relationship with the masses of voters. As a ruling class, the Va. gentry had a compelling sense of *noblesse oblige* and a profound aversion to excess and demagoguery in politics. It is assumed in the play that only a gentleman will run for office, that he will be a man of learning and integrity, and that he will vote only on his own good sense and conscience when he goes to the legislature. There are no real issues in the campaign; the election is fought entirely on the basis of personal traits and family prestige. Jay B. Hubbell has astutely noted that the play helps explain why Va. elections produced statesmen such as George Washington (q.v.) and Thomas Jefferson (q.v.).

One minor character in the play has received a great deal of critical attention, perhaps unduly so. Ralpho, a servant in the play, has been cited traditionally as America's first comic stage Negro. Rodney M. Baine has convincingly argued, however, that Ralpho was never intended to be a Negro at all, that internal evidence refutes this idea.

Munford employed in *The Patriots* the traditional five-act complex plot so popular in eighteenth-century comedy. It consists of three romances—the first serious, the second comic, and the third farcical. In the serious plot, Meanwell and Trueman are moderate gentlemen accused of being Tories and must appear before the local Committee of Observation (Safety), a group of radical, close-minded patriots. Trueman is in love with Mira, daughter of Brazen, one of the most irrational of the Committee. The comic plot presents Pickle, servant to Meanwell, who pretends to be Meanwell while trying to seduce Melinda Heartfree, an innocent country girl. In truth, however, Pickle is really a disguised George Worthy, nephew of Meanwell's old friend Worthy, and Melinda is Meanwell's long lost niece. In the farcical plot, Isabella, a female patriot, is obsessed with fighting and dying for one's country, insisting that any lover of hers must be a brave soldier. Colonel Strut woos Isabella, but he proves to be a coward.

As in *The Candidates*, Munford uses the clichés of plotting and characterization of a century of English comedy: romance, mistaken identity, an almost false wedding, recruiting among rustics, the mock duel, the cowardly braggart, the reformation of a rake, and the discovery of a long lost heiress. The speech of the gentlemen is stilted and the Trueman-Mira speeches are sentimental and stilted. Munford rose above the clichés and sentimentality, however, with his witty satire and perceptive picture of the times as he accomplished a complex dramatic unity in the development of a serious universal theme.

The satire is directed at the excesses of radicals, those "violent Whigs" who are intoxicated with "liberty without constraint," and their intolerant attitude toward all who are not as intoxicated as they are. In *The Patriots*, the ugly head of Revolutionary radicalism is seen rising to threaten the enlightened, moderate rule of the educated, altruistic colonial gentry pictured in *The Candidates*. From the very beginning of the play, everything in all three plots contributes to the basic theme of loyalty—the nature of true loyalty and the intolerant judgment of the loyalty of others. The Trueman-Mira romance is intertwined with his being accused of Toryism; Pickle, in the comic plot, is in disguise, because he had been accused of being a Tory and does not wish to embarrass Meanwell; Isabella, in the farcical plot, is a mirror of the Committee's radicalism and a contrast to Mira's moderation.

Munford's *The Patriots* is an important contribution to the development of American literature, because it treats in a perceptive and skillful manner, at the very beginning of the new nation, a problem that has remained a peculiarly American dilemma—the treatment of minorities and those who dissent from the majority opinion. Unique among propaganda plays of the American Revolution, *The Patriots* is concerned with a threefold parochial strife rather than a single colonists-British struggle. It recognizes a triangular conflict between the American Whig, the Tory, and the neutralist. Munford depicted the dangers of an immoderate, witch-hunting patriotism lashing out at minorities, at those who did not mouth their loyalties violently enough, and at those who insisted upon defending the rights of others to voice a dissenting opinion. Although a champion of colonial rights, Munford himself felt the brunt of mob mentality about the time he wrote this play; he was accused of Toryism because of his association with certain friends and relatives and because he insisted upon conservative moderation in politics.

Suggested Readings: DAB. *See also* Rodney M. Baine, *Robert Munford: America's First Comic Dramatist* (1967); Richard R. Beeman, "Robert Munford and the Political Culture of Frontier Virginia," JAmS, 12 (1978), 169-183; Courtlandt Canby, ed., "Robert Munford's *The Patriots*," WMQ, 6 (1949), 437-503 (text and criticism); Jay B. Hubbell, *The South in American Literature, 1607-1900* (1954), pp. 142-148; Jay B. Hubbell and Douglass Adair, eds., "Robert Munford's *The Candidates*," WMQ, 5 (1948), 217-257; Norman Philbrick, ed., *Trumpets Sounding: Propaganda Plays of the American Revolution* (text of *The Patriots* and criticism; 1972), pp. 257-337.

Homer D. Kemp
Tennessee Technological University

WILLIAM MUNFORD (1775-1825)

Works: *Poems and Compositions in Prose on Several Occasions* (1798); Hening and Munford's Reports (1808-1812); Munford's Reports (1812-1818); *The Iliad* (translator; 1846).

Biography: Born in Mecklenburg County, Va., William Munford was the only son of Col. Robert Munford (q.v.), himself a poet and the author of Revolutionary-era satiric plays. His father died when William was only 8 years old, but George Wythe oversaw his education in the grammar school connected with William and Mary College and subsequently in the college itself. After reading law in Wythe's office and admission to the bar, he practiced in the courts and beginning in 1797 represented his home county for three terms in the Va. House of Delegates and for three terms in the Va. Senate. In 1806 he moved to Richmond, where he was appointed to the Council of State and in 1811 became clerk of the House of Delegates, holding that office until his death. With William W. Hening, he reported four volumes of the decisions of the Supreme Court of Appeals and later produced six more volumes on his own. He assisted Benjamin Watkins Leigh in preparing the Code of 1819, and in his spare time, he kept alive the love of the Classics acquired under the tutelage of Wythe by working on the translation of the *Iliad*, which was published twenty-one years after his death in 1825.

Critical Appraisal: In the preface to his *Poems and Compositions in Prose*, William Munford listed among his reasons for publication a desire for money and fame, portraying himself as a "juvenile adventurer, on the great ocean of popular favor." Unfortunately, his poetry was more juvenile than adventurous, despite flashes of wit and intelligence, and popular favor did not respond to his ambitions. His collection does, however, offer a revealing insight on the taste and attainments of a young man with a taste for literature in the Va. of the 1790s. The contents of the volume are by turns patriotic, Classical, sentimentally romantic, and satiric. The opening "Poem on the Defeat of General St. Clair, the Fourth of November, 1791," written when he was 16 and published separately then, adapts somewhat clumsily the ballad form of "Chevy Chase" to an account of St. Clair's defeat by the Indians of the Northwest Territory. The doggerel patriotism of this early effort reappears in rhetorically more dignified and successful garb in the later prose addresses, a Fourth of July oration and a speech calling for the summoning of a constitutional convention. He follows this with several verse translations of Horace and "A Mournful Soliloquy of a Poor Student."

The most ambitious work in the *Poems* is his verse tragedy, *Almoran and Hamet*, based on the novel of the same title by John Hawkesworth. Munford claimed that "Morality and Religion are its chief subject, and one great end is constantly kept in view to shew the evils of arbitrary power." The title characters are twin brothers who share the throne of an oriental kingdom; Almoran, the elder twin, who is infatuated by his arbitrary powers, intends to eliminate the virtuous Hamet and seduce his fiancee, the chaste Almeida. He is ultimately frustrated by the "Genius" that had earlier seemed to abet and encourage his villainy. Despite its fantastic plot and sentimental, overblown dialog, the play is reasonably well structured and paced. There is no record of this play ever having been staged, but Munford took part in amateur theatricals at Sir Peyton Skipwith's estate, Prestwould, and it may have been done there by his friends. He wrote a Prologue to the *Beaux-Stratagem*, included here, and also played the part of Archer in *The Recruiting-Officer* when it was put on at Prestwould.

Forty more pages of *Poems* are given up to versifications of Ossian, and the remainder is filled with a variety of occasional poems. Among the best of them is "The Political Contest, A Dialogue," showing the misadventures of a reasonable man, a supporter of the federal union but an opponent of the Alien and Sedition Laws, who falls into the company of an extreme republican and an enthusiastic federalist. Also of some interest is the humorous sketch of a mismanaged plantation, "The Disasters of Richland, The Authors Place of Residence." *Poems and Compositions in Prose* ended Munford's attempts at making a literary career for himself, but not his interest in literature. His translation of *The Iliad* brought to accomplishment the tentative poetic skills revealed in his 1798 collection, and it received, too late for him to enjoy, the critical praise the earlier volume failed to attract.

Suggested Readings: DAB. *See also* Rodney M. Baine, *Robert Munford, America's First Comic Dramatist* (1967), pp. 91-94; Walter J. Meserve, *An Emerging Entertainment, The Drama of the American People to 1828* (1977), pp. 150-151.

Frank Shuffelton
University of Rochester

JOHN MURDOCK (1748-1834)

Works: *The Triumphs of Love* (1795); *The Politicians* (1798); *The Beau Metamorphized* (1800).

Biography: Although he has been called "one of the most productive playwrights writing for the American theater during the last decade and a half of the eighteenth century," surprisingly little is known about the life and career of John Murdock. Born sometime in 1748, probably in Pa., Murdock was living in Philadelphia at the time when he wrote and published his plays. Evidence within the plays themselves has led scholars to determine that Murdock was probably a barber by profession. A manuscript note in the copy of *The Politicians* owned by the Historical Society of Pennsylvania seems to confirm this conclusion. It states that the play was written "by Jno. Murdock Hair Dresser No. 57. Walnut Street." The title pages of all of Murdock's plays proclaim that they were written by "an American citizen of Philadelphia."

There is no record of Murdock's ever having attended an institution of higher learning, and he was probably self-educated. A prefatory note to *The Beau Metamorphized* contains a self-apology for the author's educational deficiencies: "The Author of this and former essays...does not presume to rank himself among the learned; he is sensible of the disadvantages he labours under in point of education and situation in life." Nonetheless, Murdock's plays reveal an individual of considerable culture and awareness. A keen observer, Murdock understood human behavior, appreciated the theater, and was well versed in dramatic traditions, both British and American. He also understood politics and used his knowledge of the political world to his advantage when writing satire, his main strength as a dramatist. According to Walter J. Meserve, Murdock was "obviously a shrewd man with a good wit, a sense of humor, and a distinct talent for ridiculing society." "Had he possessed friends in the right places or a wealthy patron," continued Meserve, "he would almost certainly have become America's first successful hack playwright."

Unfortunately, however, Murdock never received the acclaim that he felt he deserved and fought to achieve. Of his three plays, only the first, *The Triumphs of Love*, was produced, and that in a severely abridged form. After only one performance on May 22, 1795, the management of the New Theatre in Philadelphia decided not to produce the play again. Apparently, however, the play was a popular success, for it was performed before a crowded house, received laudatory reviews in the local press, and was later printed for a large subscription that included such noteworthies as Governor Thomas Mifflin, Dr. Benjamin Rush (q.v.), John Beale Bordley (q.v.), and Tench Coxe (q.v.), all of whom purchased multiple copies. Feeling that he had "been most shamefully treated by the managers of the new theatre," Murdock presented his case to the public, complaining to the press that the management of the theater was determined "to trample on native productions" because it was less expensive to produce "imported dramas" for which "no premiums" were due than it was to pay royalties to American playwrights.

Confident in his abilities as a dramatist, Murdock published *The Politicians* and *The Beau Metamorphized* at his own expense, boldly stating on the title page of the latter that although the play had been written "by an American Citizen of

Philadelphia" it had been "Rejected by the Managers of the New Theatre, when offered to them for performance." Nevertheless, Murdock's appeals to the patriotic sentiments of the public apparently went unheard, for his plays were never again performed, and he himself disappeared from public view. The details surrounding his death in 1834 remain a mystery.

Critical Appraisal: There was evidently some truth to John Murdock's claim that a conspiracy existed on the part of American theater owners "to trample on native productions." At the time when Murdock was writing, the American theater was largely controlled by Englishmen who had come to America as actors and later took up careers as playwrights and theater managers. Such individuals naturally preferred British productions to American ones, and by repeatedly performing British plays they cultivated a taste for British drama among American audiences from Boston to Charleston. It was into this arena that aspiring American playwrights like John Murdock, William Dunlap (q.v.), Robert Munford (q.v.), and Royall Tyler (q.v.) were forced to submit their productions. During the season, for example, when Murdock's *The Triumphs of Love* was performed, the New Theatre offered only one other production by an American, a statistic which scholars have used to vindicate Murdock's position. Like Charles Brockden Brown (q.v.), another Philadelphia writer, Murdock struggled to create an American artistic tradition based upon native themes and topics, and like many other American writers before and after him, he encountered opposition.

In many respects, Murdock's plays deserved considerably more recognition than they received. As he himself pointed out in the preface to *The Beau Metamorphized*, plays of decidedly dubious merit written by British playwrights were repeatedly performed in American theaters while works like his own were repeatedly ignored. He deserves particular credit for his efforts to create a distinctly American stage tradition. Skilled at creating lively dialog and pointed satire, Murdock enjoyed poking fun at issues of immediate concern to Americans of his day, and he worked hard to structure his productions around uniquely American characters and types. In *The Triumphs of Love*, for example, Murdock satirized Quaker marital customs, particularly the unwillingness of Quakers to allow their children to marry outside the faith. *The Politicians* consists of an extended but lively debate over the various political controversies surrounding the Treaty of 1794 and its consequences for Americans, and *The Beau Metamorphized* is structured around the efforts of an American woman to convert an English traveller to an appreciation of American democracy.

In *The Triumphs of Love* and *The Politicians* Murdock merits recognition as one of the first American playwrights to introduce black characters into his productions. Although these characters are often presented in rather stereotypical terms, they nonetheless assume identities of their own. In fact they serve as moral touchstones against which the actions of the other characters in the plays can be evaluated. In this respect, Murdock's slave Sambo in *The Triumphs of Love* anticipates Mark Twain's portrayal of Jim in *Huckleberry Finn*. In addition, Murdock's skillful use of the vernacular in which his black characters speak anticipates the successful use of the American vernacular by such writers as James Fenimore Cooper and Bret Harte. Moreover, Murdock required that the Quaker master in *The Triumphs of Love* free his slave, an action which at least one scholar has postulated may very well have resulted in the play's early demise.

Although Murdock did not, as one eighteenth-century reviewer would have it, totally "misplace his abilities when they were employed in the production of a dramatic performance," it must, in the end, be acknowledged that his plays certainly were not without their faults, some of which were conspicuous. Commenting on *The Triumphs of Love*, another eighteenth-century reviewer pointed out that the play "shews the writer a man of feeling, and some observation, but who wants the knowledge of the stage, necessary to succeed in dramatic composition." Indeed, as subsequent commentators have indicated, Murdock's greatest problem as a playwright was his seeming inability to sustain a plot, focusing instead on a series of individualized incidents that tend to overextend the interest of an audience. Yet, as Walter J. Meserve quite aptly states, Murdock wrote very well for his time, "creating comic dialogue that ranks with that of Tyler, Dunlap, and Munford." Had Murdock been permitted to continue his craft, he might very well have become a highly accomplished playwright. As he now stands, he deserves recognition for the innovations in character and theme which he brought to the American theater, particularly his insistence on the writing of American plays for American audiences.

Suggested Readings: Charles Durang, *History of the Philadelphia Stage* (1868); Walter J. Meserve, *An Emerging Entertainment* (1977), pp. 157-162; Thomas Clark Pollock, *The Philadelphia Theatre in the Eighteenth Century* (1933), pp. 57-58; Arthur Hobson Quinn, *A History of the American Drama from the Beginning to the Civil War* (1923), pp. 123-126, 332-333; Hugh F. Rankin, *The Theatre in Colonial America* (1965).

James A. Levernier
University of Arkansas at Little Rock

JUDITH SARGENT MURRAY (1751-1820)

Works: *Some Deductions from the System Promulgated in the Page of Divine Revelation* (1782); "Encouraging a Degree of Self-Complacency, Especially in Female Bosoms," *Gentleman and Lady's Town and Country Magazine* (1784); "Reverie, Occasioned by Reading the Vision of Mirza," *Boston Magazine* (1784); "Domestic Education of Children," *Massachusetts Magazine* (May 1790); "Epilogue to Vanity," *Massachusetts Magazine* (1790); "The Equality of the Sexes," *Massachusetts Magazine* (Mar., Apr. 1790); "New Epilogue to the Recruiting Officer," *Massachusetts Magazine* (1790); "Prologue to Vanity," *Massachusetts Magazine* (1790); "Reflections... Occasioned by the Death of an Infant Sister," *Massachusetts Magazine* (Jan. 1790); "Verses Wrote at a Period of the American Contest, Replete with Uncertainty," *Massachusetts Magazine* (Feb. 1790); "Apology for a Prologue," *Massachusetts Magazine* (1791); "Description of Bethlehem; in the State of Pennsylvania," *Massachusetts Magazine* (Jun. 1791); "Prologue to the West Indies," *Massachusetts Magazine* (1791); *The Gleaner Essays, Massachusetts Magazine* (1792-1794); *The Repository Essays, Massachusetts Magazine* (1792-1794); "Occasional Epilogue to *The Contrast*," *Massachusetts Magazine* (1794); *The Medium, or Virtue Triumphant* (1795); *The Traveller Returned* (1796); *The Gleaner* (1798).

Biography: Born in Gloucester, Mass., in 1751, Judith Sargent Murray had the fortune of being a member of a locally prominent, civic-minded family. Her father, a prosperous sea captain, ship owner, and merchant, sided with the Sons of Liberty during the American Revolution, thus establishing his daughter's strong nationalism as expressed through her writings in later years. The eldest of eight children, Murray was particularly fortunate in having a brother, Winthrop, who revealed a native intelligence that pointed his way to Harvard. It was often customary in the eighteenth century for such young men in the smaller New Eng. settlements to receive private tutelage from the local minister, in this case, John Rogers, a Harvard graduate himself and a minister of Gloucester's Fourth Parish Church. Murray, who also evidenced wit and intelligence at an early age, was included in her brother's schooling. Unlike many women of her day, she learned Latin, Greek, and mathematics and later received further guidance in her studies from her brother during his summer vacations from Harvard.

As she developed her intellect, Murray also developed her religious beliefs—both in preparation for a lifetime as a writer. Raised a Congregationalist like most of her New Eng. contemporaries during the late 1770s and 1780s, she and her family became converted to Universalism, a liberal branch of American Protestantism.

In 1769, at the age of 18, Murray married an almost carbon copy of her father, Capt. James Stevens, a seaman and soon-to-be Revolutionary War patriot. Although sharing political and religious beliefs, the couple apparently had no children. In 1786 Stevens went to Jamaica to avoid financial ruin, dying there shortly after his arrival. His death completely changed Murray's life, for two years later, she married the local Universalist minister, the Rev. John Murray. Thereafter she devoted much of her energies and writing to the dissemination of Universalist teachings.

In 1793 Murray moved with her second husband to Boston so that he could establish the first Universalist Church in that city. By this time, Murray had established herself as a writer and was a regular contributor to the *Massachusetts Magazine*. The move to Boston proved propitious for her writing career, for here she supported the budding theatre and had her two plays produced. During the 1780s and 1790s, she evidenced a true independence of mind, fearlessly and publicly expressing her notions on religious matters, political and literary nationalism, the value of the theatre, the moral and intellectual equality of the sexes, and the right of women to a sound education and recognition as writers.

With her second husband, Murray had two children, of whom only one survived infancy. Along with her domestic duties, she passed an active life as
religious proselytizer, poet, playwright, and essayist. She spent her later years,
after 1800, primarily editing her husband's religious writings for publication,
thus abandoning her own writing in favor of her husband's. She died in 1820,
after a rich career as a contributor to the literary and religious life of the early
years of the American Republic.

Critical Appraisal: As a literary figure, Judith Sargent Murray is best
known for her two essay series published in the *Massachusetts Magazine* in the
early 1790s, one that she signed "The Gleaner," the other that she titled "The
Repository." These essays, varying greatly in subject matter, brought Murray a
fair amount of literary notoriety and resulted in the publication of a three-volume
collection, *The Gleaner*, in 1798. Murray began her career as an essayist in the
early 1780s when she published in pamphlet form *Some Deductions from the
System Promulgated in the Page of Divine Revelation* (1782) under the name
Judith Stevens. Although this maiden essay is not distinguished for either style or
sophistication of thought, it clearly indicates two themes to which Murray would
devote much of her more mature literary efforts: a defense of women as spiritual-
intellectual equals and a presentation of the basic beliefs of the Universalist
Church. These subjects, particularly the latter, she expanded upon in imaginative
ways in her "Repository" essays, a short series of sermonic pieces on subjects
such as death, friendship, lying, and charity, subjects, it should be noted, preva-
lent in the writing of women in late eighteenth-century New Eng.

More far-ranging in nature and subject are Murray's 100 "Gleaner" essays.
These essays contain a sentimental quasi novel, lectures on the moral lessons of
history, guidelines for the conduct of women, feminist discussions of women's
education, and diatribes on the current state of American political life. Stylistically, she attempted to copy Joseph Addison's balanced, sophisticated prose with
a certain amount of success; at the same time, she filled her works with Classical
and biblical references, reflections of the success of her childhood studies. Unlike Addison, but like her fellow women writers in New Eng., she eschewed
satire and cynicism, approaching all subjects with a philosophical seriousness.
Primarily, through all of her prose pieces, she attempted to prescribe a code of
behavior for women that is based on a sentimental view of life and guided by
educated reason. She believed all would be well in the world, for mankind was
protected by a benevolent providence.

Because so much of *The Gleaner* series vividly presents feminist ideals as well
as passionate expressions of a deep-rooted patriotism, a critical issue concerning
these essays involves Murray's choice of a male persona as her mouthpiece.
Vigillus, as she called her male mask, introduces himself in "Gleaner No. I" by
stating that he has been "seized with a violent desire to become a writer," which
seems to contradict his routinized quiet life. To gain fame, Vigillus tells his
readers, he expects to compete with writers of both sexes, thereby indicating
Murray's belief in the capabilities of women as litterateurs. Paradoxically, it is

just this belief that led Murray to choose the masculine cover, as she explained in her "Conclusion" to the 1802 edition of *The Gleaner*. Here she revealed that her decision was based on feminist interests: she hid her identity in an attempt to be judged seriously and fairly for her talents, to avoid being ridiculed or praised on the basis of being a woman writer. Because of the prejudice against women writers, she feared her works would not be viewed impartially. A positive reception would indicate clearly that women could be as professional and polished as men in their writings. The popularity of her essays proved her point.

As a poet, Murray also helped to enhance the image of women as writers. She did so by achieving contemporary acceptance, if not continued acclaim, through her verse published in the poets' corner of the *Massachusetts Magazine*. During the early 1790s, under the pen name "Constantia," she shared some literary fame with another New Eng. poetess, Sarah Wentworth Morton (q.v.) ("Philenia"). However, whereas Philenia often published short verse of a sentimental nature, verse whose speakers suffer from severe cases of melancholia, Constantia's speaking voice shows determined concern for a serious subject of public interest: promoting theatre in America. Her pioneering efforts in this area are notable, if much of her versification about the stage is not. Her "Prologue to Vanity" succinctly presents her view, as she noted that *Vanity* is "A moral piece—which tho' not spick and span, / Yet hath its fable, sentiment, and plea." She envisioned the theatre as a tool through which a vast audience could be taught morality and social mores. Other serious lessons in her dramatic "logues" concern patriotism and moderation in personal behavior. In "Prologue to the West Indies," she praised the excellence of American literature, echoing the cultural nationalism that spread through the U.S. in the years following independence and reinforcing a theme that appears in her essays. She praised contemporary literary figures such as Royall Tyler (q.v.) and David Humphreys (q.v.), indicating not only her views but also her familiarity with the current literary scene in America. Praise of America appears in other forms throughout her poetry. Murray's later poetry consists of short sentimental verse written to introduce her essays. Their aphoristic, moralizing tone contrasts sharply with the early verse, in which she spoke as a politically and culturally aware New Eng. woman poet.

Murray's own venture into the writing of dramatic literature made her one of only three women to attempt play writing in New Eng. before 1800. She wrote two plays, neither of which had any success, although both were produced at the Federal Street Theatre in Boston. Evidently the excessive lack of wit and heavy-handed sentimental moralizing in her plays failed to please either the contemporary reviewers or the audiences. But despite adverse receptions, she never lost faith in her dramas, publishing them in her collected works. *The Medium* (1795), retitled *Virtue Triumphant* in 1798, and *The Traveller Returned* (1796) are deliberately modeled on Royall Tyler's *The Contrast*. She chose an American rather than a British work for the basis of her sentimental style, a further example of her literary nationalism. Like Tyler she used dialect to create character types, and also like Tyler her major concern was to depict current American manners and society. *Virtue Triumphant* presents her concept of proper middle-class behavior in late eighteenth-century America. Her delineation is based on her conservative Federalist politics: she presented a society in which status, class, and money are extremely important and espoused a social hierarchy based on the principle that wealth and property are the only acceptable credentials. Indeed the plot of *Virtue Triumphant* involves problems created by a young lady's lack of money, problems that dissolve when a deus ex machina ending reveals her to be an heiress. The play fades out on a note of domestic bliss. Her second play, *The Traveller Returned*, also emphasizes domestic felicity, but is placed against a Revolutionary War setting so that she can also reiterate her patriotism. Both plays are sentimental dramas that outline the proper behavior of women as submissive, if educated, wives.

Contrary to this generally passive vision of the ideal American woman presented throughout her works in prose, verse, and drama, Murray's own persistent, outspoken involvement in literary and cultural nationalism and her participation in the search for American subjects make her a significantly active and prolific figure in the history of women's letters in America.

Suggested Readings: DAB; NAW. *See also* Herbert Ross Brown, *The Sentimental Novel in America* (1940); Pattie Cowell, *Women Poets in Pre-Revolutionary America, 1650-1775* (1981); Vena B. Field, *Constantia—A Study of the Life and Works of Judith Sargent Murray, 1751-1820* (1931); Chester E. Jorgenson, "Gleanings from Judith Sargent Murray," AL, 12 (1940), 73-78; Arthur Hobson Quinn, *A History of American Drama from the Beginning to the Civil War* (1923), pp. 126-127.

Jacqueline Hornstein
The Cathedral School of St. Mary
Garden City, New York

WILLIAM VANS MURRAY (1760-1803)

Works: *Political Sketches* (1787).

Biography: William Vans Murray was born in Cambridge, Md., on Feb. 9, 1760. He received his early education in Md. and studied law at the Middle Temple in London, 1784-1787. While in Eng. he married Charlotte Hughins and also wrote *Political Sketches*, which was dedicated to John Adams (q.v.), then minister to G.B. He returned to Md. in 1787 and began to practice law. He served in the Md. legislature, 1788-1790, and then as a congressman from Md., 1791-1797. A loyal Federalist, he strongly supported his friend Adams and was consulted by George Washington (q.v.). In 1797 Murray was appointed minister to the Neth., where he served ably until 1801. During this period, he also served on the three-man commission to Fr. appointed by President Adams to settle the aftermath of the infamous XYZ Affair and repair relations with Fr. in 1800. Murray was decisively instrumental in the success of this mission. After completing his service at the Hague, Murray spent his remaining years on his farm near Cambridge, where he died on Dec. 11, 1803.

Critical Appraisal: William Vans Murray was noted as an extremely intelligent, effective, and eloquent speaker and writer; and these qualities are evident in his commentary on American government and politics, whether in his letters or in the small quantity of his other writing published during his lifetime. After his death, John Quincy Adams said of him in a memorial sketch in *The Portfolio* for Jan. 7, 1804, that he had "a strong and genuine relish for the fine arts, a refined and delicate taste for literature, and a perservering and patient fondness for the pursuits of science." Adams added that Murray's letters were marked by elegance, simplicity, wit, and variety of style, which "might serve as models of epistolary correspondence," and commented further that Murray's constantly active, but disciplined, observation also embraced "the all enlivening fancy of a poet," keen sensibility, and rapidity of conception. Murray's writing clearly reflects the pleasant, lively, witty man of "original humour" described by Adams. Not only does his *Political Sketches* (96 pages) survive to illustrate the literary qualities commended by Adams, but also newspaper pieces (especially supporting the election of John Adams in 1796), an unpublished diary, both posthumously published and unpublished letters, his commonplace book, and a small amount of verse (published in 1971). Noting Murray's skill at eloquent topographical and social description, Adams mentioned a long and commendable account by Murray of a trip he had made to Hol. in 1784, which Adams hoped someday might be published. Given the attractive quality of Murray's prose, it is unfortunate that more of it is not readily available.

Suggested Readings: DAB. *See also* John Quincy Adams, "William Vans Murray," *Annual Report of the American Historical Association for the Year 1912* (1914), pp. 347-351; Alexander DeConde, "The Diplomacy of William Vans Murray," HLQ, 15 (1952), 185-194, 297-304, and MdHM, 48 (1953), 1-26; W. C. Ford, ed., "Letters of William Vans Murray to John Quincy Adams, 1797-1803," *Annual Report of the American Historical Association for the Year 1912* (1914), pp. 343-715; Peter P. Hill, *William Vans Murray, Federalist Diplomat* (1971); Julian Mason, "William Vans Murray: The Fancy of a Poet," EAL, 6 (1971), 62-68; PAAS, New Series, 12 (1899), 245-255 (has extracts from Murray's diary).

Julian Mason
The University of North Carolina at Charlotte

_ N _____

ROBERT CARTER NICHOLAS (1728-1780)

Works: Letters in the *Virginia Gazette* (1766-1775); *Considerations on the Present State of Virginia Examined* (1774). Nicholas's letters to the *Gazette* can be found through Lester J. Cappon and Stella F. Duff, eds., *Virginia Index, 1736-1780* (1950).

Biography: Robert Carter Nicholas, youngest son of Dr. George and Elizabeth (Carter) Burwell Nicholas, was born in Va. in 1728. His mother, daughter of Robert "King" Carter, was the widow of Nathaniel Burwell. After his studies at the College of William and Mary, Nicholas became a successful planter, outstanding lawyer, staunch defender of the established church, and prominent political leader. During his fifteen years in the House of Burgesses (1756-1761 and 1766-1776), Nicholas was an influential member or chairman of most of its important committees. From 1766 to 1776, he was also treasurer of Va., where he served with scrupulous honesty after exposing the misuse of public monies during the administration of speaker-treasurer, John Robinson. Although Nicholas was a delegate to all of Va.'s Revolutionary conventions, he was a reluctant Revolutionary and has usually been labeled "conservative." In 1775 he objected to Patrick Henry's resolutions for arming the colony and in May 1776, he opposed independence. Yet he worked on committees to execute measures that he had originally opposed or about which he had serious doubts. Following three terms in the House of Delegates (1776-1778), Nicholas was appointed judge of the High Court of Chancery, where he served until his death in 1780. Four of Nicholas's sons—George, John, Wilson Cary, and Philip Norbonne—were active in political life. His daughter Elizabeth married Edmund Randolph (q.v.), Revolutionary son of Loyalist John Randolph.

Critical Appraisal: Because he authored numerous official memorials, remonstrances, addresses, and petitions and engaged in several public debates in newspapers and pamphlets, Robert Carter Nicholas was one of the most important writers in Va. in the second half of the eighteenth century. Early in his career in the House of Burgesses, he was appointed to a committee to draw up an address to the king defending the colony's right to pass certain laws, including the controversial "Two-Penny Act," which had been disallowed by the crown. Thereafter, Nicholas was always appointed to help prepare various addresses to the king, Parliament, and royal governor. He was probably the ablest penman among the burgesses until the emergence of Thomas Jefferson (q.v.).

Nicholas was, however, better known to the Va. public as a respected statesman who engaged in heated and sometimes protracted debates in the *Virginia Gazette*. He never remained silent when a controversy touched him. Consuming at least a full page each, his letters were substantial for one who declared that "to appear in print is, of the things in life, one of the farthest from my ambition." Although usually a lucid writer, he did not hesitate to use harsh language when he was deeply offended.

In 1766 Nicholas initiated one of the colony's earliest newspaper wars when he felt obliged to defend his actions in working to separate the offices of speaker and treasurer while seeking to become treasurer. In a long letter that was impressive for its logic and lucidity, he made a classic statement of the "balance-of-powers" theory of government. Stressing that concentrated power was inimical to independent, uninfluenced thinking, he demonstrated that the union of offices had had dire economic effects on the colony.

In response to provocation, Nicholas used the pages of the *Gazette* in 1773 to publish two long letters stating his economic principles and their relation to Va.'s immediate situation. Although not an enthusiastic supporter of paper currency, he argued for its issuance as a practical necessity. Established upon sufficient funds and properly managed, paper money was a legitimate and useful expedient, particularly for conducting internal business.

The *Gazette*-reading public was privy not only to Nicholas's political and economic views, but also to his religious ideas. Nicholas carried on a prolonged and vituperative public controversy with Samuel Henley (q.v.), a clergyman and professor of moral philosophy at William and Mary. Nicholas twice used his power as an influential vestryman at Williamsburg's Bruton Parish to prevent Henley from becoming rector of the parish. Henley accused Nicholas of being motivated by "private pique and resentment" and challenged him to bring his charges into the open. Nicholas strongly objected to the professor's doctrinal latitudinarianism as well as his views on episcopacy and the church-state alliance. Henley was suspected of being a Socinian, had raised questions about the institution of episcopacy, and had condemned the accepted theory underlying the church-state alliance. By contrast, Nicholas believed that an establishment was necessary if Christianity—most perfectly embodied in the Anglican church—were to have true influence in human affairs. As long as a just policy of toleration existed, Nicholas averred, religious establishment was not incompatible with religious liberty. Thus within the established church itself, on the eve of the Revolution, there was significant public airing of opposing views on the social role of religious establishment.

In May 1774, while his controversy with Henley dragged on, Nicholas introduced a resolution in the House of Burgesses calling for a day of prayer and fasting in response to Parliament's edict closing the port of Boston. The idea had been "cooked up" by Thomas Jefferson and others who believed that Nicholas's "grave and religious character" made him the perfect spokesman for such a proposal. This resolution and the general direction of events in Va. prompted an anonymous pamphlet of strongly Loyalist sentiment, *Considerations on the Present State of Virginia*, authored by Va.'s attorney general John Randolph. Randolph justified the Boston Port Act, harsh and punitive as it was, as necessary to bring the offenders to justice. In lengthy passages, he heaped scorn on the idea of a day of fasting and prayer and on the events of the day itself. He suggested that Nicholas was either a fool or a knave to have participated in the scheme.

Nicholas responded to Randolph's pamphlet with the anonymous publication of *Considerations on the Present State of Virginia Examined*. His critique was thorough and ruthlessly logical. He quoted long passages from Randolph's essay and then exposed the author's errors in reasoning. Nicholas's point of departure was always the British Constitution and the "sacred laws of justice"; he never justified the Americans on the basis of "natural rights." He neither condemned nor defended the Boston Tea Party, but he did condemn the British response as clearly unconstitutional in its failure to distinguish between the innocent and the guilty and in its ex post facto nature. Nicholas suggested that the Boston Port Act affected all of the colonies, for "when my neighbor's house is on fire, it highly behooves me to look to my own."

During the quarter-century of his public life, Robert Carter Nicholas spoke forthrightly and intelligently on controversial issues concerning Va.'s politics, economy, religious establishment, and position within the empire. His reputation as a statesman and a writer is secure.

Suggested Readings: DAB. *See also* Victor Golladay, *The Nicholas Family of Virginia* (Ph.D. diss., Univ. of Va., 1973); Hugh Blair Grigsby, *The Virginia Convention of 1776* (1855), pp. 61-69; Charles F. Hobson, *The Public Career of Robert Carter Nicholas* (M.A. thesis, Emory Univ., 1966); Edmund Randolph, *History of Virginia*, ed. Arthur H. Shaffer (1970); Earl G. Swem, ed., *Virginia and the Revolution: Two Pamphlets* (the pamphlets are those of John Randolph and Robert Carter Nicholas; 1919); William J. Van Schreeven, comp., and Robert L. Scribner, ed., *Revolutionary Virginia: The Road to Independence*, vol. I (includes the pamphlets by Randolph and Nicholas and several public documents authored by Nicholas; 1973).

Mary E. Quinlivan
The University of Texas of the Permian Basin

NATHANIEL NILES (1741-1828)

Works: *Discourses on Secret Prayer* (1773); *The Remembrance of Christ* (1773); *Two Discourses, on I John* (1773); *A Descant on Sinful Pleasure* (1774); *Two Discourses on Liberty* (1774); *The American Hero* (1775); *The Perfection of God* (1778); *The Substance of Two Sermons* (1779).

Biography: Born in South Kingston, R.I., Apr. 3, 1741, Nathaniel Niles

NILES, NATHANIEL   1077

attended Harvard, leaving after a year because of illness. After graduation from
the College of New Jersey (now Princeton Univ.) in 1766, he studied medicine
and law and spent a brief period teaching in New York City before studying
theology under Joseph Bellamy (q.v.). Although never ordained, he preached
throughout his life in Conn. and Vt. Before the Revolution, he married Nancy
Lathrop and settled in Norwich, Conn. There he worked in his wife's father's
wool factory while devoting time to politics, serving in the Conn. legislature
from 1779 to 1781. Within the next two years, he left business and moved to
what soon became West Fairlee, Vt. After the death of his first wife, he married
Elizabeth Watson in 1787. Niles continued his active political life until his death,
Oct. 31, 1828. He was a member of the State Supreme Court (1784-1787), a
member of the federal House of Representatives (1791-1795), and a trustee of
Dartmouth College (1793-1820).

    Critical Appraisal: Best known as a writer during his lifetime for his
popular poem *The American Hero*, Niles combined in his work an interest in
both theology and politics. This single published poem, subtitled a "Sapphick
Ode," suggests the psalms in its long, unrhymed but alliterative lines grouped in
numbered triplets. More like prose than poetry in its biblical rhythms, *The
American Hero* focuses in its first five stanzas on conventional religious subjects
and themes as Niles praised God and reiterated the inevitability of death. In the
last ten of its fifteen stanzas, the poem shifts to the contemporary scene as Niles's
treatment of the Revolutionary War gives rise to both Classical and local frames
of reference; a narrator expresses his theme (*"War*, I defy thee"), calling upon
Mars amid American grapeshot. The blend of patriotism, Classical inspiration,
and New Eng. theology produces an incongruous mixture evidently appealing to
eighteenth-century readers; the poem was set to music during the Revolution and
reprinted in several colonial newspapers. Its final stanza is characteristic: "Life,
for my Country and the Cause of Freedom, / Is but a Trifle for a Worm to part
with; / And it preserved in so great a Contest, Life is redoubled."

    Niles's sermons reveal his abiding concern with both holy and civil, philo-
sophical and actual, law. *Two Discourses on Liberty* is typical; here Niles stated
that "the author's general design is to awaken in his country men proper sentiments and emotions, respecting both civil and spiritual liberty." More satisfying
finally to the modern reader than his poem, his sermons were preached ex
tempore from brief notes and later written with careful attention to style and
rhetoric. They are sophisticated and sensible exhortations, milder than those of
earlier New Eng. divines, tempered by kindness and a more intimate relationship
between preacher and reader. Often drawing equally on Locke and the Bible,
Niles is serious, impassioned but rational, frequently anecdotal, and invariably
competent in explicating Scripture for an increasingly secular New Eng.

    Suggested Readings: CCNE; DAB; P; Sprague (I, 716-718); T₂. *See also* F. M.
Caulkins, *History of Norwich, Connecticut* (1866); J. K. Lord, *A History of Dartmouth
College* (1913); J. G. Ullery, *Men of Vermont* (1894).

Caroline Zilboorg
Lake Erie College

SAMUEL NILES (1674-1762)

Works: *The Sentiments and Resolutions of an Association of Ministers...Concerning the Reverend Mr. George Whitefield* (1745); *Tristitiae Ecclesiarum* (1745); *A Brief and Plain Essay on God's Wonder-Working Providence for New-England, in the Reduction of Louisbourg* (1747); *A Vindication of Divers Important Gospel-Doctrines* (1752); *The True Scripture-Doctrine of Original Sin* (1757); *A Summary Historical Narrative of the Wars in New-England* (w. 1760; pub. 1837-1861); *A Pressing Memorial* (1761).

Biography: Samuel Niles was born on Block Island (R.I.) in 1674. After he received a B.A. from Harvard College in 1699 (M.A., 1759), he studied theology with the Rev. Peter Thatcher of Milton, Mass. In 1711, following two years of preaching on Block Island and a period of missionary work in R.I., he was ordained pastor of the Second Congregational Church in Braintree, Mass. His pastorate was very successful, and local records abound with anecdotes about his powerful and often querulous personality. Niles was a traditionalist: he criticized the new practice of Congregational singing from notes; more significantly, he opposed both the rising influence of rational religion and the evangelical innovations of the Great Awakening. In 1744 he moderated a meeting of ministers that attacked George Whitefield's (q.v.) itinerant missionary work. He died in 1762, still an active minister at the age of 88.

Critical Appraisal: Samuel Niles can best be seen as a defender of traditional New Eng. values, both in religion and politics, at a time when old ways were threatened from many directions. He was raised in a late seventeenth-century world and was 71 when he first published a major work. Some commentators have distinguished between his "religious" and his "literary" writings, but this distinction obscures their thematic (if not stylistic) unity.

In his theological writings, Niles sought to disassociate himself both from the challenges to the old order posed by rational ("Arminian") religion and from those mounted by the evangelical preachers of the Great Awakening. Like the latter, he was a Calvinist in theology and defended the doctrine of predestination against the Arminian idea of unlimited redemption (*The True Scripture-Doctrine of Original Sin*). But he was equally critical of the new evangelism. *Tristitiae Ecclesiarum* is one of the most vigorous and concise statements by a member of the group Edwin Scott Gaustad has described as "Old Calvinists." George Whitefield, Gilbert Tennent (q.v.), and other revivalists emphasized the salvation of the individual, even if it meant traveling as itinerants to proselytize—and perhaps split—the congregations of established ministers. Niles could not accept itinerancy and the possible breakdown of traditional order: for him the primary value was social harmony, which the evangelicals disrupted. The "venerable Fathers" of seventeenth-century Mass. achieved an admirable balance between the rights of the individual and the needs of society, but with an emphasis on the latter: "The Beauty and Strength of a Community (especially Ecclesiastical) consists in nothing more, than in the Harmony of it's Members." He deplored the "Strife and Contention" the itinerants had created and denounced them as deluded men who had mistaken "the Effects of their own over-heated Imaginations" for Divine revelation. Niles was less demanding theologically than the "New Divinity" men of the Awakening whom he opposed. In his concern for maintaining social harmony, he dismissed the importance of intellectual differences among Calvinists: we are agreed on basic doctrine; what is crucial is to realize that "true Religion can never subsist long in a Country without Order."

Although Niles's commitment to the Congregational order as it had developed for a century before the Great Awakening led him into conflict with many of his contemporaries on the questions of church and community organization, another part of his traditional value system was less controversial in the mideighteenth century. This was his view of the historical mission of Protestant American civilization. The idea that America, and especially New Eng., had a unique and heavenly ordained role dated from the founding of Mass. Niles embraced it, and in this case the evangelicals agreed with him.

He developed his vision of Anglo-American destiny most elaborately in his *Summary Historical Narrative* of the colonists' wars with the Indians and the French, published from a manuscript in the nineteenth century. Its episodic construction and occasional chronological confusion give the impression that he never revised it. But it is impressive in its crisp prose, direct narrative style, and colorful detail. Niles started his *Narrative* with the Indian wars of the 1630s and carried it through the fall of French Can. in 1760. The author's intent was to show evidence of God's hand in the Anglo-American victories over the "barbarous and bloodthirsty" Indians and the "Popish" French, "our cruel, designing, fierce enemies." The *Narrative* was based on published histories and captivity stories, Niles's own recollections, and the reminiscences of others. The core of the work is a minute chronicle of the "mischiefs and slaughters committed by the Indians, by the instigation and influence of the French at Canada." Niles had an eye for lurid detail, and spared no pains to describe atrocities. This is a story told in black and white. Unlike Cadwallader Colden's (q.v.) *History of the Five Indian Nations* (1727-1747), there is little sympathy here for the "savages," apart from an occasional nod in the direction of those tribes allied with the colonists, and no understanding of the way in which the European colonizers disrupted the Indians' way of life. Niles was out to prove the historical destiny of Anglo-America and showed scant tolerance for the other cultures with which it contested hegemony. Niles's poem about the capture of Louisbourg by Mass. troops in 1745 (*A Brief and Plain Essay*) may well be "forgettable" as verse, as Clifford K. Shipton once described it. But it too gives an idea of the passions aroused among New Eng. Protestants by the Anglo-French wars: "King George's glory, & their Churches cause, / The Country's Peace, her Liberties and Laws. / These to secure they wisely make a stand / 'Gainst what portends much ruin to our Land."

Samuel Niles's two literary missions—to defend the established Congregational way in religion and the mission of New Eng. in history—were complementary. Although he was unconvinced by the revivalists, he was a strong advocate for a combination of traditional Puritan theology and cultural values that still carried a considerable impact in years of religious and political change.

Suggested Readings: CCNE; DAB; Sibley-Shipton (IV, 485-491); T₁. *See also* Edwin Scott Gaustad, *The Great Awakening in New England* (1957), pp. 70-71, 129-132; Nathan O. Hatch, *The Sacred Cause of Liberty* (1977), pp. 21-54; Warren B. Otis, *American Verse, 1625-1807: A History* (1909), pp. 17-19. See CMHS, 3rd ser., 6 (1837), 154-279; 4th ser., 5 (1861), 309-589, for the text of the *Summary Historical Narrative*.

Douglas M. Arnold
Yale University

OLIVER NOBLE (1733-1792)

Works: *Preaching Christ, the Office-Work of Ministers* (1771); *Regular and Skillful Music in the Worship of God* (1774); *Some Strictures upon the Sacred Story Recorded in the Book of Esther* (1775); *The Knowledge, or Well Grounded Hope* (1781).

Biography: Oliver Noble, son of David and Abigail (Loomis) Noble, was a Congregationalist minister born Mar. 3, 1733, at Hebron, Conn. He graduated from Yale in 1757 and on Jan. 10, 1759, began his ministry at Coventry, Conn., where he remained until 1761. On May 15, 1761, he married Lucy Weld, whose father and grandfather were also ministers. They had seven daughters and two sons. The next year, he settled in Newbury, Mass., and served at the Fifth Congregational Church until 1784. Noble's wife died on May 28, 1781; three years later, he resettled in New Castle, N.H., where he remained as pastor until his death at the age of 59 on Dec. 15, 1792.

Noble was living in Newbury during the events that led to the American Revolution. He delivered *Some Strictures* in 1775 to commemorate the Boston Massacre. About a month later, after Lexington, a false alarm spread through northeast Mass. warning that the British regulars were marching toward Newbury. This caused great consternation and panic, and there is an account of a woman running five miles in an attempt to flee, stopping on Oliver Noble's meetinghouse steps to nurse her baby, and discovering that she had brought the cat instead. Noble was probably away that night with the militia; he served as chaplain with Col. Little's Mass. regiment at the siege of Boston and later in N.Y.

Throughout all of his career, Noble suffered discouragement. At Newbury there was dissension among his congregation, and he spoke of his family "rising into maturity, deprived of the means of a proper education, and the decencies of life." Finally, he asked for and received his dismissal. Earlier, while in Coventry, he had been the center of a strange controversy. He was charged with falsehood by the members of his congregation and dismissed, having given different reasons to different people for wearing a blue cloak with a white cape.

Critical Appraisal: When preaching of things that touched his heart, Oliver Noble could be stirring and very moving. The sections of his sermons that are the most personal vividly express the emotions of a minister whose published works were inspired by specific contemporary events. An ordination of a new minister, the attempt to establish a sacred music school, the fifth anniversary of the Boston Massacre, and the death of his wife were the occasions that prompted Noble to write his published works.

His most memorable and popular sermon was *Some Strictures upon the Sacred Story in the Book of Esther*, delivered in 1775 to commemorate the Boston Massacre. In this work, Noble paralleled the biblical story of Esther with the contemporary situation in America. The oppressed Jews become the oppressed Americans; the naturally benevolent Persian king, deceived into becoming an accessory to tyranny, becomes the British king. Finally, the English ministers and officials have become the despots and oppressors of the Americans as Haman was for the Jews: "To accomplish this dreadful havock of their species, state-jobbers practise upon the imbecilities of princes." Noble's purpose was "to incite in the minds of my countrymen, a prudent steadfastness in the cause of liberty and a pious trust in God under oppression." For Noble, Haman's agents became revenue collectors and inspectors, as Noble alluded to the contempt Americans had for these British officials. He was still hopeful that the British king would realize, as the Persian king did, that his citizens were being oppressed, before it was too late. But he did not really expect this to happen and warned his audience that although God was with them, they must help themselves and prepare to fight: "They have no reason to expect the mighty hand of God working for them, while like asses they crouch down, to take on them burdens."

Although *Regular and Skillful Music* is Noble's least substantial work, it is interesting as an illustration of his belief that all Christians should praise God in song. Preached in 1774, it calls upon the "flourishing, oppulent" town of Newbury to support a free sacred music school open to members of all denominations.

The final pages of his last published sermon, *The Knowledge, or Well Grounded Hope*, show Noble at his most moving. In this funeral sermon on the death of his wife, Noble expressed his personal anguish: her voice will never more "charm my ears or refresh my drooping heart."

Like Noble's last published work, his first sermon is most interesting when he spoke about his personal life. The closing pages of *Preaching Christ*, an ordination sermon delivered in 1771, alluded to the disgrace he suffered ten years earlier at the hands of his former congregation, who dismissed him on the charge of falsehood. After telling the new preacher to pay particular care to the children of his parish, because they "are men in miniature and allow you to see human nature undisguised," Noble pleaded with the congregation to help their new minister and to be kind to him: "Be always tender of his character; be careful of his reputation. Harbor no jealousies, nor ungodly surmises against him."

Suggested Readings: CCNE; Dexter (II, 478-480); Sprague (I, 602). *See also* Joshua Coffin, *A Sketch of the History of Newbury, Newburyport, and West Newbury, 1635-1845* (1852), pp. 246, 251.

David Leslie Newman
University of Houston

JOHN NORTON (1606-1663)

Works: *A Brief and Excellent Treatise Containing the Doctrine of Godliness or Living unto God* (1648); *Responsio ad totam quaestionum syllogen a clarissimo viro domino Gulielmo Apollonio* (1648); *A Discussion of That Great Point in Divinity, the Sufferings of Christ* (1653); *The Orthodox Evangelist* (1654; 1657); *Abel Being Dead Yet Speaketh; Or, The Life & Death of . . . John Cotton* (1658); *The Heart of N-England Rent at the Blasphemies of the Present Generation* (1659; 1660); *A Brief Catechisme* (1660); *Three Choice and Profitable Sermons* (1664).

Biography: John Norton was born in Bishop's Stortford, Hertfordshire, Eng., on May 9, 1606. After being prepared by vicar Alexander Strange of Buntingford, he matriculated at Peterhouse, Cambridge, at age 14. He was graduated B.A. in 1624 and M.A. in 1627. Thereafter, he taught school in Bishop's Stortford and eventually accepted a private chaplaincy in High Laver, Essex, which allowed him to preach publicly on occasion until he was silenced for nonconformity. After a storm-cancelled attempt to emigrate in Sept. 1634, which is described in Thomas Shepard's (q.v.) *Autobiography*, he arrived in Plymouth colony in 1635, where he was well received and was urged to remain. Instead, he accepted a call to the Ipswich church, which he served as teacher until 1653, when he went to Boston to replace the recently deceased John Cotton (q.v.).

Norton had been a popular preacher and pastor at Ipswich, known especially for his intellectual skills and deep learning. He was a participant in important colonial affairs, including both the Anne Hutchinson controversy and the Cambridge Synod. Three times he was chosen to be the spokesman for New Eng. in writing defenses of the basic principles of congregational polity and theology, including a justification of the suppression of the Quakers. Later, he went with Simon Bradstreet as delegate to the English court to obtain Charles II's confirmation of the colony's charter shortly after the Restoration, a mission that was surprisingly successful considering the Puritans' very weak bargaining position at the end of the Commonwealth period. Some colonists, however, saw in the king's reaffirmation of the charter a contingent threat to the ascendancy of congregational polity in New Eng. After a career defending New Eng.'s religious and political order in various official writings and personal service, Norton died on Apr. 5, 1663, under a cloud of unofficial public disapprobation, although an elegy by his Boston colleague, John Wilson (q.v.), affirms his achievements.

Critical Appraisal: As writer and preacher, John Norton was neither as prolific nor as eloquent as fellow elders such as Thomas Hooker (q.v.), Thomas Shepard, and John Cotton. He was, however, one of the most respected and influential men in the first generation of New Eng.'s settlers. Much of his published work was commissioned by the Mass. General Court, and a very small number of his many sermons has survived. Norton's extant writings fall into four categories: polemics, theological exegesis, biography, and pastoral works. Together, these several kinds of works give a clear impression of Norton's mind and political as well as spiritual temperament.

The first category, polemical writings, includes three major publications, each the product of a particular request by the General Court of Massachusetts Bay. In the course of his career, Norton thus became an important spokesman for officialdom in the colony. The first of these writings is a Latin work titled *Responsio ad totam quaestionum syllogen a clarissimo viro domino Gulielmo Apollonio*. This work is now available in an English translation by Douglas Horton titled *The Answer to the Whole Set of Questions of the Celebrated Mr. William Apollonius, Pastor of the Church of Middelburg*. Apollonius, like others in Hol. with ties to the English church, was committed to the Presbyterian form of polity rather than to the newer Independency, later to be known as Congregationalism, which was being advanced by an able minority in the then-convened Westminster Assembly. Apollonius, a friend and correspondent of Robert Baillie, one of the outspoken Scottish Presbyterian delegates to the Assembly, wrote a series of questions for the Independents at the Assembly to answer. Those five men, however, decided to forward the questions to New Eng., where Congregationalism had already been put to a practical test. The New Englanders asked John Norton, whose Latin was known to be incisive and ready, to write the reply. In his *Responsio*, as in later writings, Norton gave an unequivocal endorsement to Congregational polity. Together with contemporary and much longer works by Thomas Hooker and John Cotton, the *Responsio* is one of the key documents in the history of Congregationalism. At the same time, the document expresses a desire for communication and cooperation among the various Protestants. In its learning, its tone, and its broad understanding of ecclesiastical history, it is a model of restrained but forceful debate literature. It is, in effect, argumentative definition.

Two other works of polemics were also written at the request of the General Court. The first was *A Discussion of That Great Point in Divinity, the Sufferings of Christ*, Norton's answer to William Pynchon's (q.v.) *The Meritorious Price of Our Redemption* (1650), which denied that Christ had suffered the torment of hell. The central issue was the imputation of grace and salvation to the elect through the sufferings of Christ, a central tenet of Calvinist thought and one that the New Englanders wanted to affirm forcefully. This Norton did, in the process writing a discourse on central tenets of the faith of New Eng. Puritans. The book thus served as a good preparative to Norton's most famous work, published the next year, *The Orthodox Evangelist*.

The final work of polemics, however, was *The Heart of N-England Rent* (1659). Here he attacked the Quakers, who in the 1650s had been increasingly prominent in New Eng. and whose doctrines were viewed as threatening to the New Eng. orthodoxy in various ways. Norton associated the Quakers of the 1650s with certain German and Dutch "Enthusiasts & Libertines" of the 1520s. In fact, he was more specific in naming the sixteenth-century heretics and their doctrines than he was in dealing with the Quakers, although he was decisive in viewing them as "the ministers of Satan," whose influence in New Eng. was a "sign" of the "evil times" that were upon the colonists. Norton defended the importance of revering "Church Authority" if New Eng. were to survive to fulfill its promise. He urged gentle means in dealing with the Quakers with the stronger measure of banishment to be used only when subtler persuasion has failed. Although Norton has since been identified chiefly with his anti-Quaker writing and practice, it is important to notice that in his own view—and that of his colleagues—he was defending the high principles of colonial as well as scriptural order, higher values as he saw it than liberty of conscience.

Norton's chief work of theology was *The Orthodox Evangelist*, a book that modern scholars such as Norman Pettit and James W. Jones have emphasized in placing Norton as a mediator between the strict preparationists (Hooker, Shepard, Peter Bulkeley [q.v.]) and the antipreparationists (chiefly Cotton). The book begins with considerations of abstract theological notions such as "the Divine Essence" and the Trinity but ultimately settles into a discussion of the stages of redemption. Norton emphasized the need for ministers to encourage hope in sinners, "according as the preparatory work doth increase," but also insisted that the power to bestow grace is God's entirely. The doctrine is firmly predestinarian Calvinist. John Cotton saw fit, shortly before his death, to write a prefatory Epistle to the book, apparently approving its contents more or less, although Norton's account of the process of salvation often sounds more like Hooker's than Cotton's in its stress on progression through a series of stages before as well as after grace.

It is important to remember that Norton also wrote the first separately published biography in New Eng., *Abel Being Dead Yet Speaketh; Or, The Life & Death of. . .John Cotton*. This is the first of many biographies written in the manner of saints' lives, commemorating the deeds and holiness of a passing generation of leaders who had accomplished much and set an example that their successors were increasingly aware was not being matched in the second generation. Norton outlived the giants of New Eng.'s early days—John Winthrop (q.v.), John Cotton, Thomas Shepard, Thomas Hooker, and others—although he identified with them and strove to use their representative figure, Cotton, to body forth to his younger contemporaries a lesson in dedicated living. The spiritual biography initiated in *Abel Being Dead* was most fully developed some forty years later in Cotton Mather's (q.v.) *Johannes in Eremo*, containing a life of Norton as well as Cotton, and, still more, the *Magnalia Christi Americana*.

Finally, a small group of publications represents Norton's career-long work as preacher and pastor. He wrote a simple and fairly standard catechism (1660) and a treatise on "living unto God" (1648), both of which aim at instructing his parishioners in the Christian life. Three of his sermons, all from late in his career, were published posthumously (1664). The latter are of special interest, because, like several of his polemical writings, they stress the value of a respect for order in social and ecclesiastical areas of life. Like other of his works, they bear the marks of Norton's clear and sometimes overriding awareness of the political and historical situation from which he wrote.

Suggested Readings: CCNE; DAB; DNB; FCNEV; LHUS; Sprague (I, 54-59); T_1. *See also* John Ditsky, "Hard Hearts and Gentle People: A Quaker Reply to Persecution," CReAS, 5 (1974), 47-51; Edward J. Gallagher, Introduction to Norton's *Abel Being Dead (1658)* (1978), pp. v-xxvii; Douglas Horton, "The Translator's Preface," *The Answer to the Whole Set of Questions of the Celebrated Mr. William Apollonius*, by John Norton (1958), pp. ix-xxi; James W. Jones, *The Shattered Synthesis: New England Puritanism Before the Great Awakening* (1973), pp. 3-31; Cotton Mather, "Nortonus Honoratus, The Life of Mr. John Norton" in *Magnalia Christi Americana* (1702); A. W. M'Clure, *Life of John Norton* in *Lives of the Chief Fathers of New England* (1846), II, 175-248; Norman Pettit, *The Heart Prepared: Grace and Conversion in Puritan Spiritual Life* (1966), pp. 177-184.

Sargent Bush, Jr.
University of Wisconsin at Madison

JOHN NORTON II (1651-1716)

Works: "A Funeral Elogy, upon...Anne Bradstreet" (pub. as prefatory poem in Anne Bradstreet's *Several Poems*, 2nd ed. 1678); *An Essay Tending to Promote Reformation* (1708).

Biography: Relatively little is known of Rev. John Norton of Hingham, Mass. The nephew of the more famous Rev. John Norton (q.v.) of Ipswich and of Boston, he was born at Ipswich in 1651 to William and Lucy Norton and graduated from Harvard with the class of 1671. Norton was ordained in the church at Hingham on Nov. 7, 1678, and married his wife, Mary, during the same week. The second meetinghouse built in Hingham became Norton's church; at the end of the last century, it still stood and was at that time the oldest church in New Eng. Norton demonstrated in his *Essay* that his theology was orthodox; he sustained as late as 1708 a very real sense of the Puritan pilgrimage to the New World as an "errand into the wilderness." He observed in this sermon "it was no worldly design, but merely on the account of Religion they [the Puritan forefathers] came to these remote Ends of the Earth, a vast and howling Wilderness." Norton died suddenly on Oct. 3, 1716; he was 65 years of age. The *Boston News Letter's* obituary said that he "was a very Excellent Scholar, a sound Divine and a laborious Preacher."

Critical Appraisal: John Norton displayed his scholarship in his sermon *An Essay Tending to Promote Reformation*, as well as in his much earlier elegy. At several points, Norton translated biblical texts from the original Hebrew or Greek. The sermon is a plea for a reformation of morals among his congregation, sparked by Queen Anne's "Royal Proclamation for Punishing Vice and Immoralities." Norton contended that the people of New Eng., not just those of his own congregation, had slipped away from the hallowed ideals and aspirations that had brought them to their new home. But since his congregation was composed of "an Assembly of the Chosen People of the Lord," they could cast off their degenerate spirits and reclaim the purity of their ancestors. Norton also advised his congregation how to select a government representative. In phrases that are timeless in their veracity, Norton maintained that "It would be good to take men that are advantaged by Liberal Education, by knowledge of Affairs abroad, as well as customs at home; and of the Transactions; and what hath passed in former Ages: Without which Knowledge, men will hardly attain to be great States Men."

Albeit Norton's elegy on Anne Bradstreet (q.v.) does not ring in so timeless, or timely, a tone, it is a fine poem that as Moses Coit Tyler remarked, "is something more than mechanic poetry, something other than inspiration of the thumbnail." Written only a year after Norton took a B.A. from Harvard, the poem bespeaks an enthusiasm for Classical learning that is almost wholly absent from his later, more austere sermon. Indeed, this poem marks a rare departure from the usual Puritan elegy; for Norton's elegy is Classical both in style and structure. The poem is heavily imbued with allusions to the ancient world and its mythology; not only did Norton cite, among others, the muses, Virgil, Sol, and Cicero, but he even named "The Persian God, the Monarch of the dayes," no doubt the Zoroastrian god of light, Ahura Mazda. The poem named Apollo (the sun) and his sister Phoebe (the moon) in these affective lines: "Ask not. . . Why that the palefac'd Empress of the night / Disrob'd her brother of his glorious light."

The structure of the elegy closely resembles the ancient Greek "Lament for Bion" and pastoral laments by Theocritus classified by the Greeks as idylls. It employs much of the traditional machinery of the pastoral elegy, including an invocation to the muse (Bradstreet is herself the tenth muse: "I am unblest in one, but blest in nine"), an extensive statement of grief, the participation of nature in the sorrow, and a climactic plea that Bradstreet be dutifully and lovingly remembered by future generations. Out of the ordinary, especially for a young divinity student, are the omissions of the change of mood, consolation, and, as became commonplace in Renaissance pastoral laments, the statement of the deceased's attainment of some sort of immortality beyond mere fame. Instead, Norton conspiciously chose here to remain unconsoled. The elegy also demonstrates Norton's sophistication in prosody. Choosing to ignore the strict metrical demands of the heroic couplet's ten syllables per line, Norton often added a syllable at the ends of his lines, hence loosening the verse form by end line amphibrachs or feminine endings and imparting a grace and femininity appropriate to his subject. Observe, for example, this fine couplet, which opens the poem: "Ask not why hearts turn Magazines of passions, / And why that grief is clad in sev'ral fashions." Would that Norton had left more such excellent poems! It may yet remain for some scholar to unearth more poetry by this gifted poet; for as Moses Tyler remarked, "certainly, the force and beauty that are in this little poem could not have been caught at one grasp of the hand."

Suggested Readings: CCNE; FCNEV; Sibley-Shipton (II, 394-396); T₁. *See also* Harrison T. Meserole, ed., *Seventeenth-Century American Poetry* (1968), pp. 460-463; Perry Miller and Thomas H. Johnson, eds., *The Puritans: A Sourcebook of Their Writings* (1938), II, 580, 583-585, 771. Meserole and Miller and Johnson reprint the "Elogy."

John C. Shields
Illinois State University

JOHN NORTON (1715-1778)

Works: *The Redeemed Captive* (1748).

Biography: John Norton was born in Berlin, Conn., on Nov. 16, 1715. He was the fourth son of John and Ann (Thompson) Norton, pioneer settlers of the region. A 1737 graduate of Yale College, Norton was ordained at Deerfield, Mass., on Nov. 25, 1741, and was shortly thereafter appointed the first pastor of the Congregational Church in neighboring Falltown (Bernardston), Mass. In 1746, Norton was serving as chaplain for the British troops and their families at Fort Massachusetts, near the present town of Williamstown, when on Aug. 20 the garrison was stormed and captured by several hundred French and Indian marauders. Along with the other prisoners, Norton was forced to march to Canada, where he remained in a Quebec jail until his ransom during the summer of 1747. As partial reparation for his captivity, the Connecticut General Assembly awarded Norton 100 pounds. On Nov. 30, 1748, Norton was installed pastor of the church in Middletown (now Chatham), Conn., where he served until his death from smallpox on March 24, 1778. The father of six children, Norton was twice married.

Critical Appraisal: During the eighteenth century, the imperialistic rivalry between England and France for the territories of the New World and the American military campaigns that were the extension of their continental wars resulted in almost continual frontier warfare, with both sides employing Indian warriors. As loyal subjects of the British king, Americans turned vehemently against the French during these conflicts, which they designated collectively as the French and Indian Wars, and individually as King William's War, Queen Anne's War, King George's War, and the Seven Years' War. These border wars with the French and their Indian allies produced a series of Indian captivity narratives, of which John Norton's *The Redeemed Captive* is considered one of the most famous.

Writing at a stage in the development of the captivity tradition when national-istic propaganda was often intermingled with statements of religious devotion, Norton found consolation and even "Joy" in "the many great and repeated Mer-cies" that God showed him during his captivity, but he was also intent on recording the evidence he witnessed of French designs on the American conti-nent. Norton describes, for example, a Frenchman turned savage who mutilates the body of an English soldier, and he details the treachery of a French general who promises to protect the British if they surrender but who later turns them over to his unpredictable Indian cohorts. While taking comfort in the belief that the French and Indians "could do nothing against us, but what God in his holy Providence permitted them," Norton inventories the military might of the French in Can., and he states that it was the French opinion that the people of New Eng. should be brought "into Subjection" to the throne of Fr. and their children returned "to the Church of Rome." Like the captivity narratives of John Gyles (q.v.) and Mary Kinnan (q.v.), Norton's *The Redeemed Captive* can be seen as another step in the process of secularization already underway in the captivity narratives of the early eighteenth century but given impetus by the spirit of nationalism which accompanied the French and Indian and, later, the Revolu-tionary wars.

Suggested Readings: CCNE; Dexter (I, 587-588). *See also* Phillips D. Carleton, "The Indian Captivity," AL, 15 (1943), 169-180; Emma Lewis Coleman, *New England Captives Carried to Canada* (1925), pp. 203-206, passim; James A. Levernier and Hen-nig Cohen, eds., *The Indians and Their Captives* (1977), pp. xx, 47-49; Roy Harvey Pearce, "The Significances of the Captivity Narrative," AL, 42 (1971), 544-546; R. W. G. Vail, "Certain Indian Captives of New England," PMHS, 68 (1952), 113-131; idem, *The Voice of the Old Frontier* (1949), pp. 37, 241; Richard VanDerBeets, ed., *Held Captive by Indians* (1973); idem, "The Indian Captivity Narrative as Ritual," AL, 43 (1972), pp. 548-462; idem, "A Surfeit of Style: The Indian Captivity Narrative as Penny Dreadful," RS, 39 (1971), 297-306; idem, " 'A Thirst for Empire': The Indian Captivity Narrative as Propaganda," RS, 40 (1972), 207-215.

James A. Levernier
University of Arkansas at Little Rock

HENRY NORWOOD (1615-1688)

Works: *A Voyage to Virginia* (1649).

Biography: Henry Norwood was born in 1615 into an aristocratic family in Eng. with loyal ties to the throne. He was a favored son, so it is likely that he followed the family tradition of an Oxford education. His promising military career temporarily ended with the beheading of Charles I, and he fled to Va. where his cousin Sir William Berkeley (q.v.) was governor. There he began his participation in Va.'s affairs, which he continued, although most often in absen-tia, almost until the end of his life. His first appointment, granted by the exiled

Charles II, was as treasurer of Va., but when Oliver Cromwell took control there in 1652, Norwood left the colony and devoted the next three years to the various uprisings on behalf of the king's restoration. Cromwell finally captured Norwood, had him imprisoned in the Tower from 1655 to 1659, and then shipped him to N.J. as a prisoner. When Charles II was restored to the throne, Norwood's position became favored, and he once again regained his rewarding appointment as treasurer of Va. His next return to the New World was in 1664 when he helped to capture New Amsterdam, saw it renamed N.Y., and served so well both in military matters and in overseeing the colony that he was recommended to be governor. But instead the king offered Norwood the governing of the exotic and profitable province of Tangier. Even during his tumultuous tenure in Tangier and through his later years when he was active in government affairs in Eng., Norwood continued to be involved in Va. affairs. One of the most colorful gentlemen-adventurers of his day, Norwood was even to his death at the age of 73 a man of verve and style and an able leader of men.

Critical Appraisal: Henry Norwood's *Voyage to Virginia* is one of the most engaging narratives in all of seventeenth-century American literature. It is a fast-paced adventure story that deftly blends the real, the vivid, and the Gothic while being graced with a romantic touch and spiced with wit and humor. Norwood's Va. narrative reveals impressive literary characteristics seldom found in the era's usual voyage tales, particularly his worldly humor and his flair for evoking the sensuous pleasures he experienced. In an early portion of the narrative, he sauntered on Fyal Island "picking at will the succulent peaches"; much later, after terrifying storms swept Norwood's crew onto the strange new land, they lauded their hospitable rescue by Indians and enjoyed "a lusty, rousing fire," wild turkey, and abundant other "delectables." Like a skilled novelist, Norwood offered striking contrasts of style and mood in his *Voyage to Virginia*. After punishing gales had ruined the passengers' provisions and damaged the ship, the famine became so stark and so little hope was left for the survivors that Norwood advised "converting a dead carcasse into food" for the women. With chill matter-of-factness, he recorded that it was done "to good effect." Such harsh passages serve to render truth to Norwood's descriptions of their many invigorating adventures.

Some critics have accused Norwood of snobbery. But this decidedly questionable charge is refuted by many episodes, including the graceful account of his being sheltered in a humble Indian's home made only of mat and reeds and the bark of trees fixed to poles. But to Norwood, "it had a loveliness and symmetry...pleasing to the eye," holding its own even with "the splendor of Versailles." There is also his resounding rebuke of the upper-class Maj. Stephens for his rancor to the Indians. Moreover, "his habits on shore were scandalously vicious, his mouth always belching oaths." An outstanding characteristic of Norwood's voyage narrative is his wit, ranging from sardonic observations of human nature to delightful, self-effacing comments regarding the Indians' choosing him as the group's leader. "They did me the honour to make all applications to me, as being of largest dimensions, and equip'd in a camlet coat glittering with galoon lace of gold and silver, it being generally true, that where knowledge informs not, the habit qualifies."

The geniality and wit of this action-packed voyage narrative can be found in Norwood's later writings, although unfortunately, they are not readily accessible except to the very diligent. The one piece of writing extant in its entirety, beyond the *Voyage to Virginia*, is a letter to John Thurloe, then secretary of state, written while Cromwell had Norwood imprisoned in the Tower. It is an adroit piece of writing, confirming Norwood's ability with oral rhythms, his easy way with metaphors, and his skilled blending of an appeal for fair treatment with firm tones of dignity. Except for the voyage narrative and the Thurloe letter, Norwood's extant writings, his letters and reports, are in excerpts only, but they show a graceful literacy and an appealing warmth. Most of these excerpts are found in letters to high-born friends or in passages of reports concerning places he was governing. His writings from Tangier, in particular, have a zest and a trenchant eye for the picturesque not found in the official reports by the men who governed that province either before or after Norwood.

Although Henry Norwood's various writings all attest to his literary ability, it is his *Voyage to Virginia* that sparkles above the rest. It is strange that the author of what has been heralded as "the literary masterpiece of the second half of the seventeenth century" remains little known.

Suggested Readings: Richard Beale Davis, *Intellectual Life in the Colonial South, 1585-1763*, 3 vols. (1978), passim; Leota Harris Hirsch, "Henry Norwood and His Voyage to Virginia" in *Essays in Early Virginia Literature*, ed. J. A. Leo Lemay (1977), pp. 53-72; Howard Mumford Jones, *The Literature of Virginia in the Seventeenth Century*, 2nd ed. (1968). For Henry Norwood's narrative see Francis C. Rosenberger, ed., *Virginia Reader: A Treasury of Writings* (1948), pp. 115-171.

Leota Harris Hirsch
Rosary College

SAMUEL NOWELL (1634-1688)

Works: *Abraham in Arms* (1678).

Biography: Samuel Nowell was an unusual figure in seventeenth-century Mass. Although he trained to be a minister, he never held a regular pastorate and distinguished himself in civil affairs instead. In eventually becoming involved in government, he followed his father's example, for Increase Nowell had been an important official from the time he joined the Massachusetts Bay Company in Eng. to the time of his death. Samuel was born in Charlestown, Mass., in 1634 and was graduated from Harvard College in 1653, where he remained as a fellow or tutor. Nowell first came to prominence by serving as a chaplain of the Puritan army at the Great Swamp Fight against the Narragansett Indians in Dec. 1675 during King Philip's War. In 1677 Nowell became a freeman of Mass. and embarked on a political career that included election as an assistant or magistrate, a commissioner of the United Colonies, and colonial treasurer. In the 1680s he was known as one of the strongest defenders of the colonial charter, and he died in London in 1688 on a mission to protest the revocation of the charter and the imposition of the Dominion of New Eng.

Critical Appraisal: As a writer, Nowell is remembered for his Artillery Company Election Sermon of 1678, in which his strong commitment to the colony's autonomy was evident. *Abraham in Arms* remains one of the most stirring and important Puritan sermons of the last half of the seventeenth century and is notable for Nowell's multiple use of the images of war and soldiers.

First, and perhaps least importantly, Nowell used biblical references to justify and understand the recently concluded war against the Indians. He compared the Puritan war effort to that of Abraham, who waged war to rescue Lot in Genesis 14. Later, Nowell argued that God used the Indians to underscore how militarily unprepared the colonists were. Moreover, in Nowell's view, the Indians remained powerful to remind the settlers that God expected them to be prepared.

Military preparedness was urged for apocalyptical reasons in the second development of the military images. Nowell reminded his listeners that at some point they would be called to fight for the Lord at Armageddon. For the preacher, the battle of Christ against Antichrist would be physical, in which humans would play crucial roles. That struggle was on the horizon in Nowell's opinion. To fight the forces of Gog and Magog, New Englanders needed to keep their armies prepared; to do otherwise would be to fail the Lord.

Those New Eng. soldiers could also protect the colonists from threats to their property, especially threats coming from Eng. To protect themselves from English interference was the third reason for military preparedness, although it was only implied. Significantly, Nowell emphasized that the danger posed by Eng. was first to property and only second, it seems, to religious practices. As historian T. H. Breen has argued, this emphasis on property rights was unusual at the time and constitutes one reason why *Abraham in Arms* is a notable sermon.

Nevertheless, Nowell did not fail to see the dangers in material goods. He feared that prosperity would produce men too weak and fearful to fight the Lord's battles or their own. The preacher felt compelled to explain that God's soldiers must be devout and righteous; neither atheists nor libertines made good soldiers in Nowell's view. Similar strictures regarding the moral dangers of prosperity can be found in other sermons of the period, but Nowell differed from other preachers in praising the second generation of New Englanders.

In sum, *Abraham in Arms* includes a number of significant themes. In it Nowell revealed some of the Puritan thinking about Indians and about eschatology. He also suggested the determination of many colonists to defend what they had created in Mass. while indicating that others worried about the moral condition of the settlers.

Suggested Readings: CCNE; Sibley-Shipton (I, 335-342). *See also* T. H. Breen, *The Character of the Good Ruler* (1970), pp. 117-122; Richard Slotkin and James K. Folsom, eds., *So Dreadfull a Judgment* (reprints the sermon with an introduction and annotations; 1978), pp. 258-300.

Timothy J. Sehr
Indiana University Archives

JAMES NOYES (1608-1656)

Works: *A Short Catechism* (c. 1641; 1661); *The Temple Measured* (1647); *Moses and Aaron: Or, The Rights of Church and State* (1661).

Biography: James Noyes was born in Eng. in 1608 to a Puritan family with impeccable credentials: a relative commemorated in John Foxe's *Book of Martyrs*, his father a minister, and his mother's brother the famous divine, Robert Parker. Tutored as a child by his cousin Thomas Parker (q.v.), Noyes later left Brasenose College, Oxford, to teach with Parker. Shortly before the pair emigrated in 1634, Noyes married Sarah Brown of Southampton, and their eight children established a family dynasty in New Eng. Preaching first at Medford, Mass., Noyes rejoined his cousin as teacher of the Newbury church in 1635, where his life was marked by participation in doctrinal and political disputes. He spoke on behalf of John Wilson (q.v.) during the Antinomian crisis and wrote a catechism commissioned by the General Court in 1641. But his policy of open church admission and his Presbyterianism troubled the General Court, which empowered a Synod to investigate Newbury's dispute on ministerial power in 1646. Noyes spent the rest of his years defending his practices in writing while raising his large family in a house shared with Thomas Parker. His long illness and death in 1656 reportedly were occasioned by despair over the execution of Charles I. Known for his tenacious logic, Noyes was eulogized by Thomas Parker as being "among the greatest worthies of this age."

Critical Appraisal: *A Short Catechism* was James Noyes's only American publication, and its popularity is attested by frequent reprintings. The commissioning of this work by the General Court marks the high point of Noyes's orthodoxy in New Eng., for his two English publications on church government opposed the Congregationalism of the New Eng. Way. Noyes is most important for his foreshadowings of what would become the central struggles of the next century of the church. Both *The Temple Measured* and the posthumous *Moses and Aaron* place Noyes solidly on the side of Presbyterianism, with the first volume standing as Noyes's written response to a Synod's investigation of Newbury church policy in 1646. Boston authorities tolerated Presbyterians on the northern frontier, and there is evidence in Thomas Lechford's (q.v.) *Plain Dealing* that the Newbury church was used to temper criticism from English Presbyterians as well as to encourage emigration from Scot. Noyes was, in fact, attacked by

Congregational writers in Eng., including Giles Firmin (q.v.) and John Ellis. He argued that congregations do not have independent power, so a member of one church should be a member of all, and councils of ministers should have authority over individual churches. He went on to deny the authority of church covenants, the foundation of Congregationalism. Such covenants where they exist do not give covenant members authority to discipline church members or to establish criteria for membership. *The Temple Measured* also argued for open admission to church sacraments, anticipating Solomon Stoddard's (q.v.) practices in Northampton; "God only knows the heart," so with a general profession of faith, even children were admitted full communion.

In *The Temple Measured* and *Moses and Aaron*, however, the most significant arguments concern the source of power. In the first work, Noyes conceded that the source of ministerial authority resides in the people's act of election; once elected, the minister may exercise that authority. In the second volume, Noyes retracted this statement to argue that the source of authority is in God's calling, which is independent of the people. The title *Moses and Aaron* recalls John Norton's (q.v.) sermon on the right of civil authority to enforce ecclesiastical rules, delivered to the Synod investigating Newbury in 1646. In its preface, Parker noted that this opinion would have been dangerous to publish before 1661, when the monarchy returned to power. Echoing John Winthrop's (q.v.) position on liberty, Noyes denied people the power to dissolve political or ecclesiastical bonds or to resist authority. "A plea from Gods word, is greater then a plea of conscience," so Presbyters and magistrates alike have power to punish even sins of conscience. Noyes went so far as to advocate the hiding of certain truths from the people to preserve the peace and power of officials. Natural rights do not supersede covenants, even when abused by evil magistrates, for "It is common to usurpe authority under pretence of liberty." While Noyes, like his contemporary Nathaniel Ward (q.v.), embodied the conservative reaction to Congregationalism, his opponents nurtured a democratic spirit that would find spokesmen in preachers such as Benjamin Woodbridge (q.v.), who was hired to preach by dissidents in the Newbury church, and John Wise (q.v.), who would formulate the theories of natural rights and Independency early in the eighteenth century.

Noyes's style is distinguished by its emphasis on logical simplification of statement, with occasional flights of passionate rhetoric in attacks on popery and democracy. Although his catechism never achieved the popularity of John Cotton's (q.v.) *Spiritual Milk for Boston Babes*, which became enshrined in *The New England Primer*, it is noteworthy for its softening of the usual Puritan language of original sin and damnation. His doctrinal works are marked by close logic, a thorough knowledge of Greek, and citations from scriptural and church authorities, and they display tempered arguments no doubt forged in innumerable debates with learned and unlearned parishioners alike. Noyes is refreshing for eschewing the cudgels of Ramist logic, asserting at one point that the writers of the Bible were not schooled in logic and at another point decrying "fleeing to figures" when common sense would do. Noyes's style is also marked by pithy adages, the so-called short knocks that felled his adversaries, according to Thomas Parker. For example, he was especially quick to condemn democracy: "It is safer to know our duty, then to enjoy liberty"; "Pride and independencie are inseperable"; "To give people the casting power, is to make Ministers like blind mens boyes, to set the cart before the horse." Or in a metaphor certain to appeal to the residents of the tidal marshes of Newbury: "Laws are like seabanks imoveable without the same power that made them." Despite the usual Puritan apparatus of biblical citation, Noyes's writings provide a highly readable introduction to the church politics of early New Eng.

Suggested Readings: CCNE; Sprague (I, 43-44). *See also* John J. Currier, *History of Newbury, Mass. 1635-1902* (1902); Cotton Mather, *Magnalia Christi Americana* (1702; rep. 1820), I, 436-440; Henry Erastus Noyes and Harriette E. Noyes, Comps., *Genealogical Record of Some of the Noyes Descendants of James, Nicholas and Peter Noyes*, 2 vols. (1904); John Winthrop, *Winthrop's Journal "History of New England,"* *1630-1649*, 2 vols. (1908 ed.).

David H. Watters
University of New Hampshire

NICHOLAS NOYES (1647-1717)

Works: "A Short Discourse about 66" (1665); "To His Worthy Friend, The Reverend Mr. William Hubbard" (1684); *New England's Duty and Interest* (1698); "A Preferatory Poem on That Excellent Book, Entitled *Magnalia Christi Americana*" (1702); "On Cotton Mather's Endeavors Toward the Christian Education of Negro Slaves" (1706); *To My Worthy Friend Mr. James Bayley* (1706); *Upon the Much Lamented Death of...Mrs. Mary Gerrish* (1710).

Biography: Nicholas Noyes is best remembered for his participation in the Salem Witchcraft Trials of 1692. One of the magistrates charged with hearing and deciding the cases, Noyes has been immortalized in our history as the minister who refused to pray with John Proctor, who excommunicated Rebecca Nurse, and who was cursed by Sarah Good: "and if you take away my life, God will give you blood to drink." He later helped reverse the decision to excommunicate Rebecca Nurse and showed some signs that he changed his original position and repented his previous action. Noyes died of apoplexy in 1717 at the age of 70.

Born in Newbury, Mass., on Dec. 22, 1647, Nicholas entered Harvard at 16 and graduated four years later with "highest honors," apparently well prepared for his first ministry, a prestigious assignment as teacher to the First Church of Salem, which was the oldest church in the colonies. He became an unusually influential member of the Puritan community, serving as commissioner and acting as strong supporter of Cotton Mather (q.v.) in all church matters, especially in Mather's opposition to the Half-Way Covenant.

During his life, Noyes wrote and delivered hundreds of sermons, composed thirteen poems that have been identified and reprinted, and compiled (or collaborated on) hundreds of pages of judicial statements. By 1700 Noyes had been, like his friend Cotton Mather, thwarted in his efforts to defeat the Half-Way Covenant and was observing the community he helped to design move relentlessly and irreversibly into the secular orientation of the Enlightenment. After this battle had been lost, Noyes withdrew from public life, and in so doing, he brought to a close a public life that parallels closely the rise and demise of the Puritan experiment. Like the Mathers, Noyes would accept the secular advances of the age of reason, but when those advances brought with them challenges to the traditional theology, he opted for the old way, the covenant way. As a touchstone, Noyes offered the historian many opportunities to test Capt. Edward Johnson's (q.v.) belief that the life of the state is to be found duplicated in the life of each individual in that state. If there was not the poetry, if there were only the biography, Nicholas Noyes would still remain a central personage in the study of American Puritanism.

Critical Appraisal: Comments on Noyes as poet are plentiful, if not always detached from the pull of his actions as prosecutor in the witchcraft trials. Moses Coit Tyler referred to Noyes as "the most gifted and brilliant master ever produced in America of the most execrable form of poetry to which the English language was ever degraded." He was, of course, referring to Noyes's affinity with the English metaphysical poets. We could, perhaps, agree with Tyler were it not for Edward Taylor (q.v.). But we can agree with Harold Jantz, however, when in 1943 he characterized Noyes's poetry as having "a vitality and originality which keeps it far above dull mediocrity."

A classmate at Harvard praised the student Nicholas for his verses, but before 1702 the most important poem he wrote was "A Short Discourse about 66," in which the poet used images from *Revelations* to contemplate the Apocalypse. In 1702 Noyes included a prefatory poem to Mather's *Magnalia* that has been his most well-known piece. It is one of the most legalistic of all Puritan poems with its concern for those specific traditions that were Puritan. It also defined the nature of history for the conservative Puritan, and it offered comment on the art of composition. It is revealing to compare this poem and its emphasis on the legal and traditional meaning of history with Johnson's *Wonder-Working Providences* and its definition of history as the unraveling of God's providences. In so doing, one can see the secular action that Noyes deplored, since during the fifty years that separate the two works, history had become the major sanction for the authenticity of religion, a reversal from its previous role of servant to theology.

Perhaps no poem so explicitly links Noyes to the metaphysicals as does the verse epistle he wrote to his friend James Bayley, who was suffering dreadfully with an attack of the "stone" (gall stones). To help his friend see God's grace in the affliction, Noyes likened this attack to the stoning of St. Stephen and reminded Bayley that suffering is the fate of all martyrs. Christ took a "harder, heavyer stone" from Bayley's heart, Noyes told his friend, just before the poet began a rapid cataloging of biblical references: the stone on which appears the Ten Commandments; the whetstone; and grindstone; and, climactically, the white stone of Revelation 2:17.

In the same year, Noyes sent to Cotton Mather a note and a poem, both praising Mather's attempts to educate and save his slaves. This poem has gone virtually unnoticed in the history of race relations in America, but it succinctly articulates the Puritan position on the subject.

Noyes's last three poems are probably his most technically accomplished: the elegies on John Higginson (q.v.), his senior ministerial colleague for twenty-six years; Mrs. Mary Gerrish; and Joseph Green (q.v.). These poems reveal the culmination of a growth in poetic craftsmanship to the upper reaches of Puritan verse. Witty, pious, didactic, charming, dramatic, and personal, Nicholas Noyes left only thirteen poems that are definitively his own work. Would that there were that many more.

Suggested Readings: CCNE; FCNEV; Sibley-Shipton (II, 239-246); T₁. *See also* Harrison T. Meserole, ed., *Seventeenth-Century American Poetry* (1968); pp. 269-284; John E. Trimpey, "Nicholas Noyes" in "The Poetry of Four American Puritans" (Ph.D. diss., Ohio Univ., 1969), pp. 85-131; A. Von Muhlenfels, "Nicholas Noyes (1647-1717): Puritan Man of Letters" (Ph.D. diss., Penn State Univ., 1962).

John E. Trimpey
University of Tennessee at Chattanooga

O

URIAN OAKES (c. 1631-1681)

Works: *An Almanack* (1650); *The Unconquerable, All-Conquering and More-Then-Conquering Souldier* (w. 1672; pub. 1674); *New-England Pleaded with* (1673); *An Elegie upon the Death of the Reverend Mr. Thomas Shepard* (1677); *The Soveraign Efficacy of Divine Providence* (w. 1677; pub. 1682); *Oratio Quinta* (w. 1678; pub. in *Humanista Lovaniensis*, 19 [1970]); *A Seasonable Discourse* (1682).

Biography: Born in Eng. around 1631, Urian Oakes came to New Eng. with his parents in the late 1630s. He graduated from Harvard College in 1649, and in 1654, while Oliver Cromwell was still in power, Oakes returned to Eng. to take a position in the ministry at Tichfield. With the Act of Uniformity, however, he was forced to relinquish his clerical position and became headmaster of the Southwark Grammar School. Then upon the death of Jonathan Mitchel (q.v.), minister in Cambridge, New Eng., the parish sent agents to Eng. to invite Oakes to assume the pulpit in their church. He accepted their call, and from 1671 until his death a decade later, Oakes was associated with the Cambridge church, his high standing in colonial affairs attested to both by his position as moderator of the "Reforming Synod" of 1679 and his preaching several sermons on important public occasions. After Leonard Hoar's (q.v.) resignation as president of Harvard College in 1675, Oakes consented to become president *pro tempore*, and when other candidates later declined the post because of the languishing state of the institution, in 1680 Oakes assumed the presidency. He died in Cambridge in 1681.

Critical Appraisal: Oakes's literary reputation rests primarily on his *Elegie* upon the death of his close friend Thomas Shepard, Jr. (q.v.), but his published sermons and extant Latin orations (delivered at the Harvard Commencements during his tenure as chief officer and recorded by John Leverett) offer proof that his was one of the widest-ranging intellects among second-generation New Eng. Puritans. The *Elegie* has rightly been praised as one of the best examples of Puritan incidental verse and displays Oakes's sympathetic knowledge of Classical and Renaissance models for that particular verse form, but Oakes's familiarity with the full range of Classical literature is even more apparent in the various Commencement addresses he delivered at Harvard. These entertaining examples of learning and sharp wit offer an interesting commentary on Harvard's difficulties during this period, as well as a glimpse of Oakes's attitudes toward himself and the position he then held.

Most important for the intellectual historian, however, are Oakes's published sermons, which exemplify the mode of the jeremiad and stand among the most revealing political utterances of the period. Soon after he had returned to New Eng., Oakes was called on to deliver the annual sermon before the Artillery Company of Boston, and his effort, *The Unconquerable, All-Conquering and More-Then-Conquering Souldier*, was deemed so eloquent that the next year (1673), he was asked to preach the even more prestigious annual election sermon. Along with Jonathan Mitchel's *Nehemiah on the Wall* (1667), Oakes's *New-England Pleaded with* ranks as one of the most forceful jeremiads of the dark period just before King Philip's War. Its searching indictment of the evils into which the colony had fallen displays Oakes as one who—despite the delightful wit so evident in his Commencement addresses—profoundly deplored the apostasy into which he believed his generation to have fallen. *The Soveraign Efficacy of Divine Providence*, another address before the Artillery Company, and presented in the aftermath of the violent Indian wars, further reveals Oakes's concern that his countrymen did not fully appreciate how much they had incurred the wrath of their God, especially in their seeming inability to understand how completely He ordered the actions of men as well as of nature.

Suggested Readings: CCNE; DAB; DNB; FCNEV; Sibley-Shipton (I, 173-185); Sprague (I, 141-143); T₁. *See also* T. G. Hahn, "Urian Oakes's *Elegie* on Thomas Shepard and Puritan Poetics," AL, 45 (1973), 163-181; Cotton Mather, *Magnalia Christi Americana* (1702), Book IV, Chapter 5; Samuel Eliot Morison, *Harvard College in the Seventeenth Century* (1936), pp. 415-440; William J. Scheick, "Standing in the Gap: Urian Oakes' Elegy on Thomas Shepard," EAL, 9 (1975), 301-306.

Philip F. Gura
University of Colorado, Boulder

SAMSON OCCOM (1723-1792)

Works: *Ten Indian Remedies from Manuscript Notes on Herbs and Roots* (w. 1754; pub. 1954); "An Account of the Montauk Indians, on Long Island" (w. 1761; pub. 1809); *A Sermon Preached at the Execution of Moses Paul* (1772); *Mr. Occom's Address* (1773); *A Choice Collection of Hymns* (editor; 1774); "Now the Shades of Night Are Gone" (1793); "Waked by the Gospel's Powerful Sound" (1801).

Biography: Samson Occom, the first American Indian known to have written for publication, was a Mohegan, born in 1723 at Mohegan, an Indian village between Norwich and New London, Conn. He is reported to have said that he was "brought up a Heathen" until he was 18. During the Great Awakening, Occom converted to Christianity, having been influenced by the many missionaries who preached to the Indians.

Determined to become a teacher to his tribe, Occom became the first Indian student of Rev. Eleazar Wheelock (q.v.) at Lebanon in 1743 and stayed there for four years. He then spent a year studying with Rev. Benjamin Pomeroy at Hebron. From the two clergymen, Occom acquired a knowledge of English, Latin, and Greek and did some work in Hebrew. He planned to attend Yale, but poor eyesight prevented him from doing so.

Occom taught at New London, in 1748, but he soon left to teach among the Indians at Montauk, Long Island, where he remained for ten years. After some time, he was licensed by the Windham, Conn., Association and began to preach to the local Indians and to neighboring tribes in his own language. Ordained by the Suffolk Presbytery on Aug. 30, 1759, he began missionary work among the Oneidas for the Correspondents of the Society in Scotland for Propagating Christian Knowledge in Jun. 1761.

At Wheelock's request, Occom accompanied Nathaniel Whitaker (q.v.) to Br. in 1765, seeking funds for Moor's Charity School, run by Wheelock. As the first Indian preacher in Eng., Scot., and Ire., he caused quite a stir, preaching 300 to 400 sermons and raising over 12,000 pounds. This money eventually became the basis for the endowment of Dartmouth College.

After his return to America in 1768, Occom lived at Mohegan until 1786 when he removed with other Indians from New Eng. and Long Island to the Brotherton Tract, Oneida County, N.Y. There he spent his last years, mostly at New Stockbridge and at Tuscarora, where he taught. Occom died on Jul. 14, 1792.

Critical Appraisal: Occom's impact on American history was substantial. Besides being the first Native American to write for publication, he was the first to write hymns and the first to preach before an European audience. He was involved in the *Mohegan Land* case, a territorial dispute between Indians and the colony of Conn., and was a leader in the removal of New Eng. Indians to the Brotherton settlement. Occom, his son-in-law Joseph Johnson, and his brother-in-law David Fowler negotiated with the Oneidas who ceded a tract to the New Eng. Indians and later to the Stockbridge Indians. It was his trip to Br. and his reception by the Dissenters and Church of England evangelicals that made Occom famous. But his writing was widely read and well received in America; his sermon preached at the execution of Moses Paul, for example, went into many editions.

In 1761 Occom wrote "An Account of the Montauk Indians, on Long Island," a brief description of their marriage practices; naming ceremonies; concepts of Gods; the medicine men or "powaws' " death, burial, and mourning practices; and their concept of life after death. This description of practices and beliefs of the "ancient" Montauks shows Occom's familiarity with the tribe. More significantly, it clearly indicates that Christianity did not have as complete a hold on Occom as writers in later times have believed. In speaking of the power of the "powaws," he said that he believed it as true as any other kind of witchcraft, including the English variety, and saw it as a "great mystery of darkness."

After his return from Eng. in 1768, Occom had a falling-out with his former teacher, Eleazar Wheelock, who wanted to send him to the Iroquois as a missionary. Wheelock's attempts to reclaim an overpayment of support funds for the trip to Br., Occom's perception that Wheelock had neglected the Indian's family while he was gone, and Wheelock's use of the money raised to found Dartmouth College further strained relations between the two. Occom believed that it was fraudulent to use money raised for the education of Indians at Moor's Charity School for the education of whites at Dartmouth College. Occom was further disappointed by the refusal of the Boston Board, under whose jurisdiction he preached, to give him any support. These disappointments no doubt helped shape his later beliefs regarding the Indian's position in a white-dominated society.

His best-known work, *A Sermon Preached at the Execution of Moses Paul* (1772), gives some of the first clear insights into these beliefs. In revising and expanding it for publication, Occom sought a product unlike the sermons of his white contemporaries and predecessors—one with a distinctly Indian stamp upon it. The work consists of an introduction, explication, and application of the text. Taking for his text Romans 6:23, "For the wages of sin is death; but the gift of God is eternal life through Jesus Christ our Lord," Occom derived two propositions: that sin is the cause of all the miseries in the world, and that salvation and happiness are the free gifts of God. Then he made a three-part application of the text: one to the condemned man, one to the whites, and one to the many Indians in the audience. Moses Paul, an Indian who while drunk killed a white man, Occom depicted as living proof of the text, and the preacher implored him to repent. The whites are asked to continue their struggle against the sinful state of all men. The application directed at the Indians, however, is a long, more specific plea to avoid drunkenness. Here, he insisted upon the ultimate equality of all races, "Negroes, Indians, English, or what nations soever" in their rationality and spirituality. He saw, though, that many of the Indians had undermined that rationality and spirituality through drunkenness. "God made us rational creatures, and we chuse to be fools," he said. Drink contributes to the sad temporal state of the Indian, too, Occom said, and, although the Indian in colonial American society is "a despised creature," he should not contribute to his debasement by taking to drunkenness.

Writers in this century have followed the lead of their nineteenth-century counterparts in emphasizing the Christian rather than the native aspects of Occom's career. They have tended to ignore the sensitivity to Indian concerns that underpins his work, and they have failed to emphasize that his proremoval activities, and possibly even his intemperance in later life, represented to some degree a cultural backlash against European civilization.

Suggested Readings: DAB; DARB; Sprague (III, 192-195); T$_2$. *See also* Harold W. Blodgett, *Samson Occom* (1935); Edwin H. Hatfield, *The Poets of the Church* (1884);

Edwin M. Long, *Illustrated History of Hymns and Their Authors* (1882); William DeLoss Love, *Samson Occom and the Christian Indians of New England* (1899); James Dow McCallum, ed., *Letters of Eleazar Wheelock's Indians* (1932); Edward S. Ninde, *Story of the American Hymn* (1921); Leon Burr Richardson, ed., *An Indian Preacher in England* (1933). "An Account" was printed in CMHS, 1st ser., 10 (1809), 106-111; "Now the Shades" first appeared in Joshua Smith et al., *Divine Hymns* (1794), and "Waked by the Gospel's Powerful Sound" first appeared in Josiah Goddard, ed., *A New. . .Collection of Select Hymns* (1801).

James W. Parins
Little Rock, Arkansas

JONATHAN ODELL (1737-1818)

Works: "Inscription for a Curious Chamber Stove" (1777); "The Word of Congress" (1779); "The Congratulation" (1779); "The Feu de Joie" (1779); *The American Times* (1780).

Biography: Jonathan Odell was born on Sept. 25, 1737, in Newark, N.J. After graduating in 1759 from Princeton (then the College of N.J.), where his grandfather, Jonathan Dickinson had been the first president, Odell served as a physician with the British army. After four years, he left this position to study for the Anglican priesthood in Eng. and in 1767 was appointed rector of St. Mary's Church in Burlington, N.J. In the summer of 1776, the Provincial Congress, suspicious of his Tory sympathies, restricted his travels to the vicinity of Burlington. In Dec. he escaped behind British lines in N.Y., where he remained throughout the war, publishing Loyalist verse, acting with Joseph Stansbury (q.v.) as an intermediary in the Benedict Arnold (q.v.) conspiracy, and working as a secretary to Sir Guy Carleton, commander of the British forces in N.Y. After the war, he settled with his family in New Brunswick, Can., where he served as provincial secretary until his retirement in 1812. He died in Fredericton, New Brunswick, on Nov. 25, 1818.

Critical Appraisal: Although Jonathan Odell composed occasional verse, much of which is still unpublished, he is best known as one of the premier writers of verse satire during the Revolutionary War, primarily on the strength of five poems composed during his stay in N.Y. The earliest of them, "Inscription for a Curious Chamber Stove," originally published in Eng. and later reprinted in America, satirizes Benjamin Franklin (q.v.), cleverly applying imagery associated with his invention of a stove to his Revolutionary activities: "A Spark, that from *Lucifer* came, / And kindled the blaze of *Sedition*." Three other satires—"The Word of Congress," "The Congratulation," and "The Feu de Joie"—appeared in *Rivington's Royal Gazette* in 1779. "The Word of Congress," a long series of personal attacks upon members of Congress, offers up "Some ars'nic verse, to poison with the pen / These rats, who nestle in the Lion's den!" "The Congratulation" and "The Feu de Joie" both celebrate British military successes. In the latter work, he advised the rebels: "Leave those, whom Justice must at length destroy. / Repent, come over, and partake our joy." A fifth satire, *The American Times*, although its ascription has been questioned, is generally considered to be the work of Odell. It is the longest, most ambitious of the poems, consisting of three parts, which, in mock-epic style, present indictments of the Revolutionary leaders. At the end of the poem, St. George exacts justice and returns America to its former relationship with the mother country.

Despite the vigor of Odell's attacks upon the American Revolution, their impact was limited, serving mainly to bolster the morale of Loyalist readers in N.Y. during the war. In a broader sense, however, Odell's contribution to the American literary tradition went beyond his role as wartime propagandist and survived his postwar expatriation. In upholding political order against the threats of rebellion and anarchy, Odell helped to provide a basis for conservative satire that Federalist writers, such as the Connecticut Wits, would later adopt in combating democratic excesses during the early years of the Republic.

Suggested Readings: CCMC; DAB; P; T₂. *See also* Pastora S. Cafferty, "Loyalist Rhapsodies: The Poetry of Stansbury and Odell" (Ph.D. diss., George Washington Univ., 1971), contains texts of unpublished poems by Odell; Winthrop Sargent, ed., *The Loyalist Poetry of the Revolution* (1857, 1972); idem, *The Loyal Verses of Joseph Stansbury and Doctor Jonathan Odell* (1860); Thomas B. Vincent, *Jonathan Odell: An Annotated Chronology of the Poems* (1980).

Charles Modlin
Virginia Polytechnic Institute and State University

THOMAS ODIORNE (1769-1851)

Works: *The Progress of Refinement* (1792); *Ethic Strains on Subjects Sublime and Beautiful* (1821); *Moral Evil No Accident* (1821); *Poems* (1821).

Biography: Thomas Odiorne, a N.H.-born poet, philosopher, and businessman, graduated from Dartmouth in 1791. He sold books in Exeter, N.H., until 1800 and then established an iron manufacturing firm in Malden, Mass., where he died in 1851. In 1792 he published his most important work, *The Progress of Refinement*. This work shows the poetic influence of James Thomson and Mark Akenside and the clear philosophic influence of Locke and the associationalist psychology of David Hartley. The multifaceted philosophical interest in nature expressed in *The Progress of Refinement* establishes Odiorne as a precursor of the Romantic movement.

Critical Appraisal: Thomas Odiorne's central concern in *The Progress of Refinement*, a long poem in three books, is the ethical effect of nature on man's progress toward a state of "pure refinement" characterized by the "harmony of mind with general ends." As Leon Howard pointed out, "The most striking thing about the poem is undoubtedly its display in America of a philosophical interest in nature, and its emphasis upon the importance of nature to human life." Odiorne stressed the mutual adjustment between man and nature. Nature can be appreciated because of man's refined taste and imagination, and nature in turn educates, refines, and heals man: "Her inspiration touches with delight / Poetic, with enthusiasm sweet, / Refines the taste, and meliorates the heart." Anticipating Ralph Waldo Emerson's emphasis on the regenerative influence of nature, Odiorne wrote of her ability to calm and lull the agitated soul to a "tranquil state." According to *The Progress*, the benefits of nature to man are many-sided: "Entertainment is the flower, / Knowledge the fruit, and happiness the end, / Of all her dictates."

The fine arts, the subject of Book Two of the poem, contribute to the refinement that better enables man to appreciate nature. Nature's inspiration prompts a "magic melody of phrase" and produces art that is simultaneously a "beauteous offspring of the original" and an inspiration to search for further "new and wonderous" knowledge in nature. In nature "The Hand Divine" is visible in "every leaf that grows." Virtue, the subject of Book Three, is the final step in the progress toward refinement. When nature and the arts "humanize the mind," virtue "then lives, and every ruder passion dies." Virtue is best expressed in the sympathy of man for man, which is a reflection of the sympathy between man and nature. Thus nature, the fine arts, and virtue "all conspire to. . . accomplish a noble and very desirable end."

Odiorne drew on the philosophy of Locke and David Hartley to show the relationship between man and nature, which, said Howard, indicates that "verse writers in this country were by no means unaffected by the new influences and attitudes found in their English contemporaries." Although the poem is immature, Howard pointed out that it anticipates the poetry of Wordsworth and suggested that the influences that inspired the great English Romantic were operating in America as early as 1792.

Suggested Readings: S. Austen Allibone, *A Critical Dictionary of English Literature and British and American Authors* (1820); Leon Howard, "Thomas Odiorne: An American Predecessor of Wordsworth," AL, 10 (1938-1939), 417-436.

Linda Palmer Young
University of California, Davis

JAMES EDWARD OGLETHORPE (1696-1785)

Works: *The Sailor's Advocate* (1728); *A New and Accurate Account of the Provinces of South Carolina and Georgia* (attributed; 1732); *Select Tracts Relating to Colonies* (compiler; 1732); *A Brief Account of the Establishment of the Colony of Georgia Under General Oglethorpe* (attributed; 1733); "A Curious Account of the Indians" (1733); "State of Georgia" (1739); "Account of Carolina and Georgia" (1752).

Biography: Born to a prosperous English family of Jacobite leanings, James Edward Oglethorpe was educated at Eton and Oxford and saw brief military service before assuming the family estate in Surrey. Elected to Parliament from Haslemere in 1722, he campaigned against the impressment of sailors and led an inquiry into conditions prevailing in debtors' prisons, which led him to adopt a plan to settle debtors in the American colonies. In collaboration with associates of the philanthropist Dr. Thomas Bray (q.v.), Oglethorpe applied for and received in 1732 a charter to settle the new colony of Ga. The trustees of the colony—including, of course, Oglethorpe—intended that it act as a buffer between S.C. and the Spanish settlements in Fla.; give refuge to European Protestants; produce silk, wine, spices, drugs, and other warm-weather commodities; and provide a home for the poor and destitute. Oglethorpe himself led the first group of colonists to Ga.—they addressed him as "Father"—and supervised much of the planning and building of Savannah in 1733. As de facto governor of the colony, he spent the next five years in intermittent trips between Ga. and Eng., defending the colony's reputation, arranging for the immigration of settlers from Salzburg and Moravia, and raising funds. His philanthropic approach to colonization and his personal involvement in the hardships of the colony's first years made him the subject of adulatory speeches and poetry in Eng.

Between 1738 and 1742, Oglethorpe was continuously in Ga., preoccupied with military affairs in the face of a possible Spanish invasion from Fla. during the War of Jenkins' Ear. He led several abortive expeditions against Fla. and successfully repelled a Spanish attack on St. Simons Island in 1742. But this was also a time of criticism by "malcontents" such as Patrick Tailfer (q.v.) and Thomas Stephens, who barraged the British press and the trustees with complaints against the colony's prohibitions of rum and slavery, its system of land inheritance, the misleading claims made for the climate and soil, and what they regarded as Oglethorpe's faulty administration. Despite this criticism and the other trustees' growing disillusion with the colony's inability to produce profitable crops or markedly increase its population, Oglethorpe maintained his idealistic stance, fighting off all appeals for reform of the inheritance system and for the introduction of rum and slaves, and rejecting outright the suggestion that British charity cases might not make the best colonists in an unsettled wilderness.

Oglethorpe left a struggling and dispirited colony in 1743 to return to Eng., in part to defend himself successfully in a court-martial brought by one of his own officers. He never returned to Ga., and his influence on the other trustees waned rapidly as they gradually undercut the idealistic foundations of the colony, finally surrendering their charter to the crown in 1752. The remainder of Oglethorpe's life was spent largely in literary society, in the company of figures such as Johnson, Boswell, and Goldsmith.

Critical Appraisal: Most of the writings attributed to James Oglethorpe were published anonymously, and there is substantial evidence to ascribe those works concerning the colonization effort to Benjamin Martyn (q.v.), secretary of the trustees and author of a number of other promotional tracts published by them. Of the works definitely by Oglethorpe, *The Sailor's Advocate* is a pamphlet summarizing his arguments against impressment, and *Select Tracts* is a compilation of essays by Bacon, Machiavelli, John De Witt, William Penn (q.v.), and Sir Josiah Child, all aimed at support of the colonization effort. The remainder of Oglethorpe's works are brief reports: "A Curious Account" expresses Oglethorpe's hope for the conversion of the Indians because of their well-developed sense of morality and justice; "State of Georgia" is a summary of conditions in the colony addressed to the trustees and later repeated in *A State of the Province of Georgia* by William Stephens (q.v.); "Account of Carolina and Georgia," written for inclusion in Thomas Salmon's *Modern History*, 4th edition, is a balanced and generally optimistic account of landscape and Indian customs in the colony, with an emphasis on its natural resources and agricultural potential.

A *New and Accurate Account* is usually ascribed to Oglethorpe but perhaps is by Martyn alone or by Martyn and Oglethorpe in collaboration. It exemplifies the promotional literature of the Ga. trustees, who maintained for two decades a well-orchestrated public campaign designed to attract support for the colony. The tract begins with a description of the colony, including the claims that its weather is moderated by large fresh-water seas north of the Appalachians, that the soil is so fertile that it needs no manure even after sixty years of cultivation, and that the forests can be cleared easily by girdling trees and waiting "a year or two" for a gust of wind to fell them. A brief description of the Indians is generally sympathetic and open-minded by the standards of the time. The remainder of the tract is an argument in favor of establishing a debtors' colony, asserting that such a colony will help Eng. grow rich, will convert many Indians to Christianity, and will expand Eng.'s trade and its merchant marine. Almost entirely financial rather than philanthropic in its thrust, the argument is dotted with allusions and quotations, fiscal calculations, and comparative references to other nations. Its appeal is largely pragmatic and economic, and its fiscal emphasis marks an important exception to the puffery of much promotional literature. The inflated claims for landscape, climate, and soil occupy a relatively minor place in the tract.

A *Brief Account*, in contrast, is a compilation of assorted reports bearing on the colony's early history: the trustees' designs for the colony (by Martyn), the colonists' arrival in Ga., Oglethorpe's first meeting with the Indians, and his speech before the S.C. Assembly. Almost entirely positive in tone, A *Brief Account* was intended to show the good intentions and hopeful beginning of the colony to the British public.

Most of Oglethorpe's writings are notable for their refreshingly positive view of the Indians. "A manly, well-shaped race," he called them in "Account of Carolina and Georgia," "a generous, good-natured people; very humane to strangers; patient of want and pain. . . .Their public conferences show them to be men of genius, and they have a natural eloquence, they never having had the use of letters." This romantic idealism helped Oglethorpe maintain generally friendly relations with the Indians of Ga. for over a decade. This attitude, and his commitment to a form of yeomanry without slavery that he called "Agrarian

Equality," mark Oglethorpe as anticipating much of a subsequent American idealism. His correspondence demonstrates a stubborn, principled consistency in his conception of the colony's future, and a continuing optimism, despite the Ga. experience, that a colony conceived on philanthropic grounds could succeed.

Suggested Readings: DAB; DNB; LHUS; T₁. *See also* Verner W. Crane, "The Promotion Literature of Georgia" in *Bibliographical Essays: A Tribute to Wilberforce Eames* (1924, 1967), pp. 281-298; Amos Aschback Ettinger, *James Edward Oglethorpe: Imperial Idealist* (1936, 1968); Mills Lane, ed., *General Oglethorpe's Georgia: Colonial Letters, 1733-43* (1975); Randall M. Miller, "The Failure of the Colony of Georgia Under the Trustees," GHQ, 53 (1969), 1-17; Trevor R. Reese, ed., *The Clamorous Malcontents* (1973); idem, *The Most Delightful Country of the Universe* (1972); Phinzy Spalding, *Oglethorpe in America* (1977); Clarence L. Ver Steeg, Introduction, *A True and Historical Narrative of the Colony of Georgia* (1960), pp. ix-xxxiv. *Select Tracts* and *A New and Accurate Account* have been reprinted in *The Most Delightful Country*. *A Brief Account* is in Peter Force, ed., *Tracts and Other Papers*, vol. I (1836, 1947). "A Curious Account" is in CGHS, II (1842), 61-63. "Account of Carolina and Georgia" is partly reprinted in Henry Bruce, *Life of General Oglethorpe* (1890), pp. 80-86.

David H. Stanley
University of Utah

PETER OLIVER (1713-1791)

Works: *A Speech Delivered. . .After the Death of Isaac Lothrop* (1750); *A Poem Sacred to the Memory of the Honorable Josiah Willard* (1757); *A Poem Sacred to the Memory of Mrs. Abigail Conant* (1769); *The Scripture Lexican* (1784); Douglass Adair and John A. Schutz, eds., *Peter Oliver's Origin & Progress of the American Revolution: A Tory View* (1963).

Biography: Born in 1713 to a distinguished Boston family, Peter Oliver so prospered that scarce a decade after graduation from Harvard College, he had sufficient financial means to allow ever-increasing political participation. His chief business venture was an iron slitting mill at Middleborough. There he built Oliver Hall, an imposing showpiece where provincial notables and visiting dignitaries were amiably entertained. A respected dabbler in agriculture, science, colonial history, and poetry, Oliver lived the life of a genial country squire, first entering politics as a justice of the peace and then serving as justice of the Common Pleas Court of Plymouth. Despite a lack of formal legal training, he was promoted to the Superior Court in 1756. Judge Oliver also sat for Middleborough in the House of Representatives in 1749 and 1751, and in 1759 he was honored by election to the Council. There he joined his brother Andrew and friend Thomas Hutchinson (q.v.), he being the lesser light of this Mass. Loyalist triumvirate.

A staunch supporter of crown prerogative and parliamentary policy against adherents to colonial rights and popular rule, Judge Oliver was dropped from the Council in 1766 in the wake of provincial reaction against the Stamp Act. Rather than retire from politics after this rebuff, he continued in the judiciary as an advocate of the Loyalist cause, most notably during the *Richardson* case of 1770 and the Boston Massacre trial. He could with ease accept the Townshend Acts, serve on the Gaspe commission, and justify the Boston Port Bill—under whose provisions he was appointed as a Mandamus councilor in 1774. Two years earlier, Oliver had been elevated to chief justice of the Superior Court, a position he held despite attempts by the House early in 1774 first to impeach and then to indict him criminally for his unpopular stand on payment of Superior Court judge salaries by the crown.

Consistently and stubbornly resistant to the popular will, he was disposed toward a Tory stance by breeding and background, style and temperament, nature and inclination. A companion and associate of well-born and highly placed crown supporters, a dedicated devotee of governmental pomp and ceremony, a sworn upholder of the laws of Eng., Oliver left Boston amidst the British evacuation in Mar. 1776. He adapted easily to life in the mother country, although preferring Birmingham to London just as he had chosen Middleborough over Boston. As for America, a diary entry during the evacuation well expressed his attitude: "I bid A Dieu to that shore, which I never wish to tread again till that greatest of social blessings, a firm established British Government, precedes or accompanies me thither."

Critical Appraisal: Although he was not a prolific writer, Oliver's literary importance stems from his manuscript concerning "The Origins & Progress of the American Rebellion," unpublished until 1961 except for a brief overview that appeared in the *Massachusetts Gazette and Boston Weekly News-Letter*, Jan. 11, 1776. The "Origin" is an account of the causes of the Revolution written by a Loyalist intimately involved in the process and concretely concerned with the outcome of an occurrence that both assaulted his values and taxed his understanding. Rather than originating "from severe oppressions" as had other colonial revolts, here, according to Oliver, was "an unnatural Rebellion" that, "to an attentive Mind, must strike with some Degree of Astonishment," since it evidenced "base Ingratitude" for past tender nurturance and protection provided by mother Eng. His partisan account vividly reveals the indignant and exasperating frustration of a crown supporter witnessing the destruction of a satisfying and stable social order. Oliver seems to write to clarify for himself the question of "why is the sudden Transition made, from Obedience to Rebellion."

To answer this query, Oliver dealt with both long-term and immediate causative factors, chronologically ordering his narrative around the events leading to Revolution, with brief character sketches fittingly interjected to clarify both the nature of the participants and of the struggle itself. Almost inexplicably, he casually glided over what most participants and historians alike had adjudged to be the chief political conflicts leading to rebellion. Oliver dismissed the problem of representation by harkening briefly to natural-law concepts regarding the need for representative institutions in general and the particular suitability of "the English system of Government, so much applauded by Foreigners." Colonial resistance to taxation he described as "base Ingratitude" for past economic stimulation and military protection provided by the mother country. Besides, the people of Mass. had no legal right to protest the imposition of taxes already allowed under charter provisions. As for the dominating question of the nature of the imperial relationship, he perceptively commented: "It is much to be deplored, that the Springs of the English Government too often lost of their Elasticity." But, for Oliver, such elasticity would have resulted in more effective coercion rather than conciliation and thus would "prevent the Power of the People from encroaching upon the royal Prerogative." Although he saw this conflict as endemic in Mass. from founding days onward, Oliver explained it—and its eventual development into "the *Hydra* of Rebellion"—by a conspiracy theory of history. Basing his views on a concept of human nature where power and pelf were the prime motivators, Oliver charged that rebellion in Mass. resulted from the disaffection of James Otis (q.v.) in 1761 after his father had been passed over for the post of chief justice and Thomas Hutchinson appointed instead. In retaliation, Otis, aligned with "a few abandoned Demagogues," deceived and secured the support of "the black Regiment" of dissenting clergymen who jointly spread sedition among the ignorant "generality of the People." Enlisting the aid of opposition forces in Eng., this malevolent faction at length was able to foment rebellion despite strong colonial Loyalist sentiment. Unfortunately, however interesting Oliver's account in its particulars, such a simplified explanation of so complex an event is disappointing in its generalities.

Unastonishing in depth of causative interpretation, the "Origin" remains a rich source of data on particular persons and events of the Revolutionary era. It is also a literary pleasure, written in an easy flowing style. Classical, biblical, poetic, and historical quotes or analogies embellish the narrative. But life is given to form by the forceful directness of Oliver's almost rancorous sarcasm. Although his barbs are usually delivered symbolically or metaphorically, subtle allusion is not his way of dealing with rebels. After presenting a series of short character sketches focusing mainly upon Boston patriots, Oliver observed: "I have done Sir! for the present, with my Portraits. If you like them, & think them ornamental for your Parlour, pray hang them up in it; for I assure You, that most of them justly demerit a *Suspension*." Such levity, often intended to demean his political enemies, calls into question the historical accuracy of Oliver's observations. Since his narrative is also a personal memoir, a bias—at times passionate—is evident. Both at the beginning and end of his account, he claimed strict adherence to accuracy: "I promise You that I will adhere most sacredly to Truth, & endeavor to steer as clear as possible from Exaggeration; although many Facts may appear to be exaggerated, to a candid Mind, which is always fond of viewing human Nature on the brightest Side of its Orb." Full of a judicial sense of integrity, Oliver did strive to present the truth that he saw. Still, the reader cannot but wonder what effect the low-keyed but pervasive note of melancholy in the "Origin" had upon its writing. Perhaps his overdrawn description of the treatment afforded Governor John Winthrop (q.v.) grew from Judge Oliver's perception of his own predicament: "He spent his Estate in the Service of the Colony; but, like many others, who sacrifice all to the publick Welfare, met with publick Ingratitude." Should the image of the American Revolution that Oliver presented be thus distorted by emotion, it is nonetheless a valid vision worth comparing with more plentiful filiopietistic accounts.

Suggested Readings: DAB; Sibley-Shipton (VIII, 737-763); T_1; T_2.

John G. Buchanan
California State University, Long Beach

SARAH OSBORN (1714-1796)

Works: *The Nature, Certainty, and Evidence of True Christianity* (1755); Samuel Hopkins, ed., *Memoirs of the Life of Mrs. Sarah Osborn* (1799); *Familiar Letters, Written by Mrs. Sarah Osborn, and Miss Susanna Anthony* (1807). See also the Sarah Osborn Papers in the American Antiquarian Society and Osborn's manuscript diary in the Newport Historical Society.

Biography: Sarah Haggar (later Osborn) was born in London on Feb. 22, 1714, to Benjamin Haggar and Susanna Guyse. She received a brief formal education, largely religious, at a boarding school near London. Her father had immigrated to America, and in 1722 Sarah and her mother followed him to Boston. By 1729 the Haggars had settled in Newport, R.I. Osborn's spiritual autobiography suggests that she had been an independent child, little restrained by parental discipline. (For example, to illustrate God's providence, she recounted her deliverance from a dangerous nocturnal canoe trip taken without her parents' knowledge and against their wishes.) In 1731 she married Samuel Wheaton, a seaman, also against her parents' wishes. She bore a son, Samuel, in 1732, and her husband died at sea in 1733. The financial strains of widowhood led her to assume the management of a local school, but it soon failed, and she turned to shopkeeping in exchange for board.

She was admitted to full communion with the First Congregational Church of Newport in 1737. Apparently moved by the revivalism of the Great Awakening, she agreed in 1741 to lead a women's religious society, an organization that she directed for the rest of her life. Writing to the Rev. Joseph Fish many years later, Osborn remarked that "all things are carried on in an orderly secret way we have none that devulges to the world what passes amongst us that I Ever Heard off [so] that we enjoy the sweetest freedom with each other."

Shortly after her marriage to Henry Osborn in 1742, he was bankrupted and became physically unable to work. Sarah Osborn opened another school in 1744, supporting her invalid husband until his death. During the revivalism of 1766-1767, she became the focal point of religious meetings for local blacks, as well as for groups of young people. Her evening meetings became so popular that Joseph Fish urged her to discontinue them before she overstepped the proper bounds of "feminine" activity. Osborn chose to go on with her evangelical work but not without becoming, as Samuel Hopkins (q.v.) noted, "greatly cautious, fearing to go beyond her line, as a woman." Ill health and failing eyesight forced Osborn to live on the charity of friends for much of the last twenty years of her life. She died on Aug. 2, 1796, at the age of 83.

Critical Appraisal: Of Sarah Osborn's prolific writings, a single slim volume was published anonymously during her lifetime. Her editor and minister, Samuel Hopkins, remarked that Osborn had "written more than fifty volumes. . . besides letters to her friends and other occasional writing," but *The Nature, Certainty, and Evidence of True Christianity* was the only work she saw in print. Her *Memoirs* were published posthumously in 1799, and some *Familiar Letters* to Susanna Anthony appeared in 1807, but both volumes were selected more with a view to the spiritual edification of readers than to an accurate or complete representation of the author.

Much of Osborn's published work takes the form of spiritual autobiography. *The Nature, Certainty, and Evidence of True Christianity*, for example, outlines Osborn's conversion experience for the benefit of a "dear Friend, in great *Darkness, Doubt* and *Concern*." Osborn's *Memoirs* and *Familiar Letters* include spiritual autobiography, religious meditations, brief didactic tracts (for her students, perhaps), accounts of revivalism, and references to the British occupation during the Revolution. Particularly important for contemporary historians are her accounts of the women's religious society in Newport, which she directed from 1741 until her death in 1796. The society met regularly for meditation and prayer, charging its members "not to ridicule or divulge the supposed or apparent infirmities, of any fellow member; but to keep secret all things relating to the society, the discovery of which might tend to do hurt to the society or any individual." Never large in numbers (Samuel Hopkins estimated the membership at sixty in 1769, thirty in 1799), the society apparently exercised a political influence disproportionate to its size. Ezra Stiles (q.v.) noted, for example, that Osborn and her supporters influenced the selection of Samuel Hopkins as minister in 1770 over the opposition of at least half the congregation.

In addition to such public responsibilities, Osborn's writing reveals her private struggles and satisfactions. She discussed, for example, her continual battle for humility. Admitting to a "strong *Propensity* to cleave to the *Covenant of Works*," she prayed to be reminded of her insignificance: "O, for Jesus' sake, suffer me not to do any thing that will tend to puff up self. . . .Lord, I am afraid of this worldly mindedness. . . .Lord, I dread being glued down to the things of time and sense." Other recurring subjects include Osborn's almost constant poverty, her sensitivity to public censure, and her close personal friendships, particularly with Susanna Anthony.

Evading the limited sphere to which gender and financial circumstance would assign her, Osborn defined her calling outside the traditional boundaries of home and family. God had "assignd" her "great Work," and she prayed for the strength to do it: "O, how unequal to the work am I! Lord, help me, and qualify me for the business to which thou in thy providence hast called me." The sheer bulk of Osborn's writings may suggest how persistently she pursued her evangelical mission. In the process, she left important records of revivalism, education, and women's organizations in eighteenth-century America.

Suggested Readings: Mary Sumner Benson, *Women in Eighteenth-Century America* (1935), pp. 119, 260-262; Jacqueline Hornstein, "Sarah Osborn" in *American Women Writers*, ed. Lina Mainiero (1981), III, 310-311; Mary Beth Norton, *Liberty's Daughters: The Revolutionary Experience of American Women, 1750-1800* (1980), passim; idem, "'My Resting Reaping Times': Sarah Osborn's Defense of Her 'Unfeminine' Activities, 1767," *Signs*, 2 (1976), 515-529; Ezra Stiles, *The Literary Diary of Ezra Stiles*, ed. Franklin B. Dexter (1901), I, 43-44.

Pattie Cowell
Colorado State University

JAMES OTIS (1725-1783)

Works: *The Rudiments of Latin Prosody* (1760); *A Vindication of the Conduct of the House of Representatives* (1762); *The Rights of the British Colonies Asserted and Proved* (1764); *Brief Remarks on the Defense of the Halifax Libel* (1765); *Considerations on Behalf of the Colonists* (1765); *A Vindication of the British Colonies* (1765).

Biography: James Otis was born in West Barnstable, Mass., Feb. 5, 1725, the eldest son of Col. James and Mary Allyne Otis. He took an A.B. at Harvard in 1743 and then studied law in Boston with Jeremiah Gridley. A fine Classical scholar, Otis in 1760 published a treatise on Latin prosody and is thought to have written one on Greek prosody that remained unpublished. His law practice was extensive, but it seems to have been characterized from the beginning by violence and inconsistency.

As advocate general of the Vice-Admiralty Court, an office to which he had been appointed by Governor Pownall, Otis was expected to support the Writs of Assistance, but instead he resigned and represented the Boston merchants in the dispute. Elected to the legislature in 1761, Otis continued to attack the crown officials. He was largely responsible for effecting a coalition of "country" people and Boston merchants to form the popular party. In 1762 and 1764, he published two of the most significant documents of the period, *A Vindication of the...House of Representatives*, and *The Rights of the British Colonies*; however, two tracts published in 1765 in response to Martin Howard, Jr.'s (q.v.) Halifax Letters reveal his occasional irrationality and violent temperament.

Otis attended the Stamp Act Congress and continued active in public affairs, although his frequent changes of position and abusive speeches and writings brought him under attack by both Whigs and Tories. From 1769 until his death May 23, 1783, Otis suffered from extended spells of irrationality, and although he occasionally participated in public meetings and was appointed to the Boston Committee of Correspondence in 1772, he was no longer a factor in Mass. politics.

Critical Appraisal: James Otis's first political pamphlet, *A Vindication of the Conduct of the House of Representatives* (1762), was an early and forceful statement of the principles argued more fully after 1765. The occasion was the outfitting, at the colony's expense, of a ship to protect the New Eng. coast from French privateers. This trivial incident enabled Otis to remind his readers of other instances of the governor and Council making financial commitments without the consent of the House, "taking from the house their most darling priviledge, the right of originating all taxes." In a clear statement of his premises, Otis presented basic Whig political theory: "1. God made all men naturally equal. 2. The ideas of earthly superiority, preheminence, grandeur, are educational, at least acquired, not innate. 3. Kings were (and plantation Governors should be) made for the good of the people, and not the people for them." After praising the British constitution and the king, Otis argued that the governor's action could lead to "annihilating one branch of the legislature, and making the government arbitrary."

Otis is probably best known for his 1764 pamphlet, *The Rights of the British Colonies Asserted and Proved*. Presenting the principles of natural law, natural rights, and the compact theory of government that were to be echoed innumerable times in the succeeding two decades, he affirmed that "an original supreme Sovereign, absolute, and uncontroulable, *earthly* power *must* exist in and preside over every society; from whose final decisions there can be no appeal but directly to Heaven," and that this sovereign is the people. Nevertheless, Otis acknowledged Parliament's authority to make laws for the general good to which the colonists, as well as British citizens within the realm, were equally bound. The pamphlet was praised and condemned, both in the colonies and in Eng., and remained for a long time the subject of debate by historians. The problems arose from Otis's attempt to claim, at the same time, that Parliament was the supreme legislature of the colonies and that it had no right to tax them. Formally, the pamphlet appears to have a logical structure, but the four sections are not evenly balanced, with the first, "of the Origin of Government," and fourth, "of the...Rights of the British Colonists," greatly emphasized. In addition, there are digressions, apparent irrelevancies, and sections of ponderous documentation. Occasionally, the writing seems to have no logic or coherence, but there are sections of rhythmic and graceful prose.

A Vindication of the British Colonies and *Brief Remarks on the Defense of the Halifax Libel*, both written in 1765, are part of the controversy that involved Martin Howard, Jr., and Governor Stephen Hopkins (q.v.) of R.I. In his Halifax letters, Howard had stated the case for parliamentary authority. In *A Vindication*, Otis repeated many of his earlier arguments but was also much more inflammatory. He attacked *ad hominem*, finding in the *Halifax Letter* "inaccuracies in abundance, declamation and false logic without end; *verse* is retailed in the shape of *prose*, solecisms are attempted to be passed off for good grammar, and the most indelicate fustian for the fine taste." In *Brief Remarks*, he continued his violent attack, accusing Howard of belonging to "the little, dirty, drinking, drabbing, contaminated knot of thieves, beggars and transports, or the worthy descendents of such, collected from the four winds of the earth, and made up of Turks, Jews and other Infidels, with a few renegado Christians and Catholics." Yet he did admit the power and authority of Parliament to impose taxes, both external and internal, on the colonies. *Considerations on Behalf of the Colonists in a Letter to a Noble Lord* (1765), originally published as letters in the Boston *Gazette*, was an answer to Soame Jenyns's *Objections to the Taxation of our American Colonies*. Otis's tone was not so much inflammatory as complaining. He seems to have taken a position halfway between that of the Halifax tracts and *Considerations*, arguing against the idea of virtual representation but avoiding the question of Parliament's right to tax the colonies.

James Otis was, according to John Adams (q.v.), the Isaiah and Ezekiel of the American Revolution. His writings are significant documents in the history of that important period and deserve attention for what they reveal of the colonists' struggle in the 1760s to reconcile their loyalty to the crown and the British constitution with what they believed to be their natural rights as free men under natural law.

Suggested Readings: DAB; LHUS; Sibley-Shipton (XI, 247-287); T$_2$. *See also* Bernard Bailyn, *Ideological Origins of the American Revolution* (1967); idem, *Pamphlets of the American Revolution* (1965), I, 409-482; Charles F. Mullett, "Some Political Writings of James Otis," UMS, 4 (1929), 257-432; Stephen E. Patterson, *Political Parties in Revolutionary Massachusetts* (1973); William Tudor, *Life of James Otis* (1823).

Elaine K. Ginsberg

West Virginia University

GORONWY OWEN (1723-1769)

Works: Robert Jones, ed., *The Poetical Works of the Rev. Goronwy Owen*, 2 vols. (1876); J. H. Davies, ed., *The Letters of Goronwy Owen, 1723-1769* (1924).

Biography: The Welsh poet Goronwy (or *Gronow*) Owen was born on Jan. 1, 1723, in Anglesey, Wales. He was educated in local schools and attended Jesus College, Oxford, from Jun. 1742 to Jan. 1744. In 1745 he was ordained deacon and made curate of his home parish, Llanfair. After marrying in 1747 and serving over the next decade as minister or schoolteacher in various villages in western Eng., Owen in 1757 accepted a position as master of a grammar school attached to William and Mary College in Va. His wife died during the arduous crossing, and Owen remarried within the year. In 1760 he was obliged to resign his mastership, soon thereafter becoming minister of St. Andrew's in the frontier county of Brunswick, Va. There he died in 1769, survived by his third wife, Joan, and his five children.

Critical Appraisal: Welsh poet, Classical scholar, and minister—Goronwy Owen spent the last twelve years of his life in Va. Although he did write occasionally in English, as a number of his letters testify, virtually all of his slim output of poetry was written in his native Welsh. Owen's poetry derives primarily from two literary traditions, that of the Classical literature of Greece and Rome and that of his native Wales. Never a prolific poet, Owen published only some fifty poems, of which a number are in Latin and several more are translations from the Greek. Virtually all of his original work is in the old Welsh *cywydd* form. He continued to write poetry in his native Welsh—always adhering to the intricate native forms and meters—throughout his long sojourn in America. Owen's best-known lyric and one of the major Welsh poems is his *cywydd* to the Last Judgment ("Cywydd y Farn Fawr") composed in the early 1750s. The best-known piece from his American years is the eulogy on his friend Lewis Morris, "Marwnad Lewis Morys." This intricate and ambitious poem of over 200 lines, composed in each of the twenty-four bardic meters, has been called "one of the greatest feats in the Welsh language."

In 1757 Owen tried to publish his works. Although his initial attempt failed, just a few years later, in 1763, a volume of his poems did see publication through the efforts of friends. Two further editions of the poems were subsequently published in 1817 and 1876. The poet's correspondence was published in 1860, 1895, and 1924. Because Owen was a highly assiduous and knowledgeable correspondent, his letters convey considerable information not only about the literary life of eighteenth-century Wales, but also about political, social, and economic matters.

Suggested Readings: CCV; DNB. *See also* John Gwilym Jones, *Goronwy Owen's Virginian Adventure: His Life, Poetry, and Literary Opinions, with a Translation of His Virginian Letters* (1969); Weldon Thornton, "Goronwy Owen" in *Southern Writers: A Biographical Dictionary*, ed. Robert Bain et al. (1979), pp. 334-335; Edwin T. Williams, "Goronwy Owen: A Welsh Bard in Virginia," VC, 9 (1959), 42-47; William D. Williams, *Goronwy Owen* (1951).

Robert Colbert
Louisiana State University in Shreveport

JOHN OXENBRIDGE (1609-1674)

Works: *A Quickening Word* (1670); *New-England Freemen Warned and Warmed* (1673).

Biography: The life of John Oxenbridge exemplifies the difficulties confronted by Puritan ministers during the seventeenth century. Born in Eng. in 1609, Oxenbridge was admitted to Emmanuel College, Cambridge, in 1626 but soon transferred to Magdalen Hall, Oxford, where he earned a B.A. in 1628 and an M.A. in 1631. He remained at Magdalen Hall as a tutor until 1634, when Archbishop William Laud deprived him of that office for showing contempt of college statutes by drawing up his own code of conduct for his students. Oxenbridge then traveled to Bermuda, where he served as a minister until 1641, returning to Eng. as the civil wars began. He preached at various places in Eng. and Scot. in the 1640s and 1650s and was made a fellow of Eton College in 1652. With the Restoration in 1660, he was ejected from Eton and then silenced by the Act of Uniformity in 1662. He once again left Eng., arriving eventually in Boston, Mass., after stops in Surinam and Barbados. In early 1670, he was admitted to the First Church in Boston and soon after became its copastor. Oxenbridge quickly commanded respect as his selection to preach the election sermon in 1671 demonstrates. He died suddenly on Dec. 28, 1674.

Critical Appraisal: Both of John Oxenbridge's published sermons reveal his deep commitment to the notion of a Puritan errand into the wilderness. Although much of what Oxenbridge said was conventional by the 1670s, he spoke with an eloquence, breadth of knowledge, and fervor unusual for the period. In both sermons, the minister reminded his listeners of their covenant with God and their failure to live up to its terms while he assured them that it was not too late to reform. Such themes dominated the jeremiads preached by second-generation ministers. What distinguished Oxenbridge's sermons was their tone; one can detect in his works an anguish arising from his personal tribulations.

Oxenbridge delivered *A Quickening Word* to his Boston congregation as part of a series of sermons on Isaiah 55:6, which calls on the Jews to seek the Lord while he is near. For the Boston pastor, the verse applied to the position in which the New Englanders lived. Christ was calling his people and offering them salvation, and the people should not ignore his call. On the whole, Oxenbridge was optimistic that it was not too late to turn to a loving Christ, who is called a kinsman knocking at the door. In a recurring metaphor, the minister compared the situation to a marketplace transaction; Christ was offering a bargain that a wise trader would take advantage of. The image should have appealed to his Boston congregation, which contained a number of merchants. However, Oxenbridge also earnestly warned those merchants not to let business concerns stand in their way.

New-England Freemen Warned and Warmed had a different audience. Oxenbridge addressed the members of the General Court or legislature on the annual day of election and instructed them regarding their responsibilities. In part, the sermon contributed to an ongoing bitter debate over the Half-Way Covenant and the founding of the Third Church in Boston, and on those issues Oxenbridge faced a hostile audience. More generally, the pastor was pleading that New Englanders remember their fathers' commitments to God. He warned against any surrender of ecclesiastical or civil rights and any compromise with Eng. Reminding his listeners how unusual it was for them to be able to elect their own civil officials, Oxenbridge urged them to elect saintly men so that the magistrates would not surrender their liberties to English officials, who would threaten the colonists' freedom to worship God properly. In an effort to unify the people, the minister argued that no serious divisions existed in the colony; all settlers were devoted to New Eng.'s mission according to Oxenbridge. To support this argument, he relied on numerous biblical quotations, allusions to Greek history and Cicero, and references to previous election-day preachers such as Samuel Danforth (q.v.) and William Stoughton (q.v.) and to first-generation New Eng. ministers such as John Cotton (q.v.) and Thomas Shepard (q.v.).

Suggested Readings: CCNE; DNB; Sprague (I, 170-171). *See also* Emory Elliott, *Power and the Pulpit in Puritan New England* (1975), pp. 140-142; Cotton Mather, *Magnalia Christi Americana* (1702), Book 3, Pt. 4, Ch. 6; Robert Pope, *The Half-Way Covenant* (1969), pp. 176-177.

Timothy J. Sehr
Indiana University Archives

P

PHILIP PAIN (c. 1647-c. 1667)

Works: *Daily Meditations: Or, Quotidian Preparations for, and Considerations of Death and Eternity* (1668).

Biography: All that is known of Philip Pain is this volume of poems, the title page of which reads: "Begun *July* 19. 1666. By *Philip Pain*: Who lately suffering Shipwrack, was drowned." The date of his death is inferred from this statement and the publication date; publication occurred sometime before Sept. 3, 1668, when the printer Marmaduke Johnson referred to the volume in a deposition before the governor and Council of Mass. inquiring into violations of licensing. Since the sequence and "A Postscript to the Reader" indicate that the author was young, a birth date making him about 20 when he died is generally accepted. No Philip Pain [*Paine, Payne*] has been discovered among appropriate colonial or English records. In addition to the name on the title page, the introductory poem, "The Porch," is signed "P. P.," and there is a Donnean pun in Meditation 50. Nonetheless, the author's name has been called into doubt because of the lack of biographical evidence, Harold Jantz asking, "Is it possible that the *Philip* is an erroneous resolution of the initial P., on the part of the editor of the first edition?" and Harrison T. Meserole adding in the face of both the name and the signature "the possibility that a printer's error is responsible for the initial 'P.'" Inferences from the poem have cast the author as one of Arminian persuasion rather than as strict orthodox Calvinist. It is more likely that he was Anglican or one tending toward that end of the religious spectrum.

Critical Appraisal: The 1st edition of *Daily Meditations* was published in Cambridge by Marmaduke Johnson; a Huntington Library facsimile was printed in 1936. A new edition, with some textual changes, appeared in 1670 from the press of S[amuel] G[reen] and M[armaduke] J[ohnson]; a Massachusetts Historical Society facsimile was printed in 1936. A 3rd edition, called the second on the title page, came out in 1682. "A Postscript to the Reader" was signed "J. T." in edition 1 but "M. J." in edition 2. Leon Howard speculated that this "may represent either a confession or a pretense to authorship by Marmaduke Johnson." Otherwise "J. T." remains unidentified.

The volume may be the first poems published in the colonies written by a native American. It consists of an introductory poem, "The Porch"; sixty-four six-line stanzas of iambic pentameter, each labeled "Meditation" and numbered consecutively; and "A Postscript to the Reader," a poem in seven six-line stanzas of iambic pentameter, rhyming *ababcc*. The rhyme in the meditations is couplet, including near rhymes (for example, "time / thine," "God / abode") as well as nonrhymes (for example, "beneath / bereave," "Harps / hearts"). In the last line of Meditation 7, the rhyme word *heart* is printed as a picture. Each page, presenting four meditations, is headed by a date (*"July* 19. 1666" through *"August* 3."* in sequence) and a designation in relation to the weekday (*"The fifth day"* for Thursday; *"The first day"* for Sunday). At the foot of each page is an iambic pentameter couplet (except for Jul. 22, Meditations 13-16, where a third part-line is given), which completes that day with an admonition or aphoristic statement.

What little attention has been paid to these poems has emphasized the concern with death, the restiveness of the author's faith, the poetic insufficiencies (such as the rhyme), and the minimal metaphoric pattern. The evaluation has generally been negative, the poems being viewed as versified doctrine, conventional, and poetically limited. Three clear poetic influences are John Donne, George Herbert, and Francis Quarles, the latter two creating discussion about the more extensive influence. Specific borrowings from all three authors are observable, and the daily concluding couplet derives from emblematic literature (for example, Quarles's *Emblemes*).

The organization of "Porch" and "Church" (the place wherein the meditations are pursued) derives from Herbert's *The Temple*, progress through which will bring one to be the Temple of God. So here the series of meditations in Pain's Church will bring one to accept death and to achieve salvation; the title page cites Job 30:23 and Ecclesiastes 12:1. The function of meditation, which contemplated matters such as mortality, sin, and means to union with God, was to achieve understanding of the self and its relationship with God. For the Puritan, only a plain style of expression, one eschewing elaborate and extended metaphors, was appropriate. Contrary to the criticism of recent commentators, the meditative act did not seek to add to God's glory, which would indeed have been sacrilegious and impossible; it sought understanding of the individual in the scheme of things. The result of these meditations is to recognize that "To live's a Gift, to dye's a Debt," and thus we must "look / Death in the face." One's sense "Of guilt & sin" that makes it "so hard to dye" must be broken down to achieve "for aye...Joyes everlasting, Everlasting joy." "The Porch" has laid forth the message of the poetic sequence to follow, which will contemplate human concepts of death such as are suggested in the introductory poem, with the vacillation of spirit that man is subject to. There is not a "yearning for death," but an acceptance of its reality; there is not an "unqualified rejection of the world," but a rejection of its significance. Man both fears and contemns death, is concerned with time, and is bothered by mutability. In comparison with Michael Wigglesworth (q.v.), Pain is not stiff or pedantic; he is sensitive to words, despite some repetition, and personal. The last line of "The Porch" is a chiasmus, an X, signifying Christ. A design printed around the poem figures a door, through which we step into the Church.

The four daily meditations are organized around a "week" consisting of four days each, dividing the sequence into four weeks, or a month, since four is the number of man and mortality; the scheme is thus $4 \times 4 \times 4 = 64$. The first sixteen meditations move through contemplations of eternity, death, and time, each day ending with an admonition except the last (the three-line verse), which concludes that he continues to live through God's mercy. The second "week," Meditations 17-32, proposes an acceptance of death's reality by all people. The couplet following, at the center of the sequence, is a prayer that the poet be ready when death comes. The third "week," Meditations 33-48, examines the conquering of death by Christ and explores the ways in which man, following Christ, may conquer sin and vanity, praise God, and receive God's mercy. The last "week," Meditations 49-64, moves to contemplation of heaven (contrasted with hell) and salvation and to a recapitulation of his need to be ready and thus to conquer death. The final couplet summarizes both the last "week" and the poem.

Some words and phrases have struck critics as fillers for a line or a stanza, and the minimal metaphor has labeled the verse at times flat thematic statement. But nautical, the world-as-theater, temporal, and biblical imagery are employed throughout, and although commonplace, Pain's handling of this imagery is poetically sound and successful, and memorable lines come through. The techniques of repetition (as in No. 56), of allusion (for example, "This Pearl being lost," No. 42, Matthew 13:45-46), of image (for example, "Death is a surly Sergeant," No. 60), and of accented rhythm (for example, "Drown'd in this Deluge of Security," No. 8) suggest that Pain's poetry deserves higher evaluation than it often has received.

Suggested Readings: FCNEV. *See also* Robert Daly, *God's Altar* (1978), pp. 137-139; Norman Farmer, Jr., "The Literary Borrowing of Philip Pain," N&Q, 11 (1964), 465-467; Theodore Grieder, "Philip Pain's *Daily Meditations* and the Poetry of George Herbert," N&Q, 9 (1962), 213-215; Leon Howard, ed., *Daily Meditations* (1936), Introduction, pp. 5-12; Thomas E. Johnston, Jr., "American Puritan Poetic Verses: Essays on Anne Bradstreet, Edward Taylor, Roger Williams, and Philip Pain," DAI, 29 (1969), 3141-3142A; Ph.D. diss., (Ohio Univ., 1968); Harrison T. Meserole, ed., *Seventeenth-Century American Poetry* (1968), pp. 285-286; Donald E. Stanford, "The Imagination of Death in the Poetry of Philip Pain, Edward Taylor, and George Herbert," SLitI, no. 2 (1976), 53-67; Roger B. Stein, "Seascape and the American Imagination: The Puritan Seventeenth Century," EAL, 7 (Spring 1972), 28; Yvor Winters, *Forms of Discovery: Critical and Historical Essays on the Forms of the Short Poem in English* (1967), pp. 107-108.

John T. Shawcross
University of Kentucky

JOHN PAINE (1661-1731)

Works: "Deacon John Paine's Journal" (w. 1695-1718; pub. in *The Mayflower Descendant*, 8 [1906], 180-184, 227-231; 9 [1907], 93-99, 136-140).

Biography: John Paine was born in Eastham, Mass., on March 14, 1661. His parents were Thomas and Mary (Snow) Paine, the daughter of Nicholas and Constance (Hopkins) Snow. Although there seems to be no record that Paine ever attended college, he was an active and influential leader in his community, serving for many years as deacon of Eastham. John Paine was twice married. In 1691 he married Bennet Freeman, daughter of Major John and Mercy (Prence) Freeman, and after his first wife's death on May 13, 1716, he married Alice Mayo, daughter of Nathaniel and Hannah (Prence) Mayo. By his first wife, Paine fathered thirteen children. He died in Eastham in 1731, at age 70.

Critical Appraisal: Like many pious New Eng. Puritans of the seventeenth and early eighteenth centuries, including John Winthrop (q.v.), Cotton Mather (q.v.), and Samuel Sewall (q.v.), John Paine kept a commonplace book or journal in which he recorded, with appropriate commentary, events in his life which he deemed of providential significance. The year in which Paine began keeping his journal and the year in which he discontinued the practice are unknown. Only a fragment of his journal, that written between 1695 and 1718, has survived. For the most part typical of extant Puritan journals of the time, Deacon Paine's journal possesses one feature of significance to literary historians: its author occasionally tried his hand at the writing of poetry. Within the pages of the journal can be found fourteen poems, ranging in length from two to thirty-two lines, on a variety of topics.

Of these fourteen poems, seven are elegies written about the deaths of relatives and friends, and the remainder are occasional poems written to commemorate events such as the births of children, his wife's recovery from a prolonged and serious illness, and the poet's own birthdays. Personal yet pious, simple and plain yet direct and moving, Paine's elegies reflect his sincere grief at the death of relatives and friends. About the death of his mother on April 28, 1704, for example, Paine lamented: "A faithfull wife She ever was unto her dearest mate / Whom Shes constrained now to leave in Solitary State / . . . in the various troubles of the world Shees had her part / She hath had marthas trouble yet had also mary's heart." At the same time that Paine anguishes over the loss of loved ones, however, he also expresses confidence that death has brought them a spiritual reward that is far greater than any joy they could have experienced on earth. About his son Benjamin, who died on Jan. 14, 1717, Paine comments: "I hope in heaven my precious Babe is blest / and that with Jesus he is now at rest / The lord gives and the lord takes away / Blessed be the name of the lord."

Of greater interest, perhaps, are the more introspective poems that Paine was fond of writing on the occasion of his birthdays. Like the elegies, Paine's birthday verses are pious and often didactic: "So many years the which are past & gone / [I] truly Say as he did Spake of old / My years are past Like as a tale that's told / lord help me to improve the little Space / which yet is granted me of thy free grace." Unlike the elegies, however, these poems express, in often painful terms, the author's nagging doubts about his individual worth and election: "A wreched Sorry fruitless worm am I / unfit to live and therefore not fit to die."

While in retrospect it is admittedly easy to dismiss the poetry of John Paine as the inconsequential prattle of an amateur poet with an overly religious sensibility, his poetry and the poetry of others like him reveal a significant dimension of Puritan aesthetic theory as it was perceived and practiced in early New Eng. Confronted with death and mortality on a daily basis and beset with doubts about their own worthiness, the Puritans of seventeenth- and eighteenth-century America found consolation in their faith, and they often turned to poetry as a means of expressing that consolation.

Suggested Readings: FCNEV. *See also* Emory Elliott, "The Development of the Puritan Funeral Sermon and Elegy: 1660-1750," EAL, 15 (1980), 151-164; Robert Henson, "Form and Content of the Puritan Funeral Elegy," AL, 32 (1960), 11-27.

James A. Levernier
University of Arkansas at Little Rock

ROBERT TREAT PAINE (1773-1811)

Works: *Federal Orrery* (1794-1796); *The Prize Prologue; Spoken in the Character of Apollo, by C. Powell, at the Opening of the First Theatre* (1794); *The Invention of Letters: A Poem, Written at the Request of the President of Harvard University* (1795); *Rise Columbia!* (1796); *The Ruling Passion: An Occasional Poem* (1797); *Adams and Washington, a New Patriotic Song* (1798); *Dedicatory Address; Spoken by Mr. Hodgkinson...at the Opening of the New Federal Theatre* (1798); *The Green Mountain Farmer, or Washington and Victory* (1798); *The Two Patriotic Songs of Hail Columbia, and Adams and Liberty* (1798); *To Arms Columbia* (1799); *An Oration, Written at the Request of the Young Men of Boston...in Commemoration of the Dissolution of the Treaties Between France and the United States* (1799); *An Eulogy on the Life of General George Washington* (1800); *Monody on the Death of Sir John Moore* (1811); *The Works in Verse and Prose* (1812); *The Hasty-Pudding* (1815).

Biography: Christened Thomas, Robert Treat Paine, Jr., was born in Taunton, Mass., on Dec. 9, 1773. He was the second son of Robert Treat Paine, signer of the Declaration of Independence, and Sally (Cobb) Paine, sister of the Revolutionary Gen. David Cobb. After graduating from Harvard in 1792, where he excelled in Classical languages and composition, Paine became a clerk for James Tisdale. His main interests, however, were in bohemian theater life and the poetical correspondence he carried on with Sarah Wentworth Morton (q.v.) in the *Massachusetts Magazine*. In Oct. 1794 Paine left Tisdale's employment and started a biweekly newspaper, the *Federal Orrery*. But because he neglected his editorial responsibilities, the paper did not thrive, and he sold it in Apr. 1796. Having married Eliza Baker, a 16-year-old actress, in 1795, he began to study law with Theophilus Parsons in 1798. Admitted to practice in 1802, he showed genuine promise as a lawyer but once again neglected his business and became an alcoholic. In 1805 he had a severe attack of dysentery from which he never fully recovered. He died destitute on Nov. 13, 1811, survived by a daughter, two sons, and his wife.

Critical Appraisal: The history of Robert Treat Paine's literary reputation was accurately summed up by Chief Justice Theophilus Parsons in his *Memoir* (1859) and is still applicable: "Robert Treat Paine was the poet of his day, and in that day enthusiastically admired," the old judge wrote. "He was then praised beyond his merits, and now his actual merit is forgotten." During his lifetime, Paine was the most popular poet in Boston, and his poems demanded extraordinarily high prices. He was best known for his patriotic odes and songs, the most famous being "Adams and Liberty" (1798), which may be the first poem-song by a native American to gain genuine nationwide popularity. Today, its unabashed and somewhat naively optimistic patriotism is badly dated, but lines such as "'Mid the reign of mild peace / May your nation increase, / With the glory of Rome and the wisdom of Greece" still testify that Paine knew how to arouse popular sentiments. The lines also identify Paine's debt to the neo-Roman school of thought, which, perhaps under the influence of the Augustan metaphor that so many eighteenth-century British authors employed, sought to interpret America's history and future aspirations in terms of Classical history. Paine's patriotic works are heavily influenced by this school of poetry, partly because he knew the Classics intimately and partly because his favorite poets, Dryden and Pope, relied heavily on the same metaphor.

Paine's patriotic prose is somewhat less readable than his poetry. Weighted down with rhetorical flourishes, his sentences frequently lumber along without the wit, variety, or intelligence that inform the prose of Addison or Johnson, his ostensible models. In his *Eulogy on Washington*, for example, he was capable of writing that "Born to direct the destiny of empires, his character was as majestic as the events, to which it was attached, were illustrious. In the delineation of its features, the vivid pencil of genius cannot brighten a trait, nor the blighting breath of calumny obscure."

In addition to suffering from uninspired rhetoric, some of Paine's work also shows the unfortunate influence of the *Della Crusca* school of the mideighteenth century. Such works tend to be sentimental, pretentious, and frequently silly. Paine's letters to Sara Wentworth Morton in the *Massachusetts Magazine* are self-consciously poetic in this fashion.

But if Paine's contemporary reputation was not entirely deserved, neither, as Theophilus Parsons noted, is his present obscurity. Two of his accomplishments are worthy of notice. First, and perhaps of lesser interest to literary historians, Paine could write excellent satiric heroic couplets. A good example may be found in this character sketch from *The Ruling Passion* (1796):

> See, the lank book-worm, piled with lumbering lore,
> Wrinkled in Latin, and in Greek fourscore,
> With toil incessant, thumbs the ancient page,
> Now blots a hero, now turns down a sage!

O'er Learning's field, with leaden eye he strays,
'Mid busts of fame, and monuments of praise
With Gothick foot he treads on flowers of taste,
Yet stoops to pick the pebbles from the waste.

Unlike the lines of many minor authors who attempted such satiric couplets in imitation of John Dryden and Alexander Pope, here the wit, imagery, and originality of rhyme keep pace with the rhetoric of the couplet. Similarly, Paine's knowledge of the tropes and figures of Classical rhetoric stand him in good stead. Paine is in firm control of these lines thanks to his skill with isocolon, chiasmus, and various alliterative patterns. The work deserves to be remembered as one of the better examples of typical eighteenth-century satire produced by an American.

Perhaps Paine's most significant accomplishment was made as a drama critic. His drama criticism, as preserved in the 1812 edition of his collected works, dates mostly from 1808 and was originally published in a weekly miscellaneous periodical, the *Times*. The reviews are unusually lengthy and detailed. Occasionally, they are weighted down with a pompous show of scholarly learning, but unlike many of his contemporaries, Paine is not a carping critic, and his criticism is always constructive rather than abusive. He dwells upon character analysis and details of acting such as elocution and stage business. In short, the reviews are a virtual gold mine of information for historians of early American acting and the stage, even though many of the plays Paine reviewed are now unknown even to specialists.

The faults with Paine's literary endeavors were those of his time and not of his undoubted genius. Some of his poetry and his drama criticism deserve better of modern scholars than they have been willing to bestow.

Suggested Readings: DAB; LHUS; T₂. *See also* Philip Hale, "A Boston Critic of a Century Ago," PMHS, 59 (1925-1926), 312-324; Vernon Louis Parrington, *Main Currents in American Thought* (1927), II, 288-295.

Carl R. Kropf
Georgia State University

SOLOMON PAINE (1698-1754)

Works: *A Short View of the Difference Between the Church of Christ, and the Established Churches of the Colony of Connecticut* (1752).

Biography: Solomon Paine was born the third of four sons in 1698 at Eastham on Cape Cod. His father was a prominent man in that town and also in Canterbury, Conn., where he moved his family about 1706 and helped to form the Canterbury church in 1711. His mother's ancestors included Deacon John Doane, one of the early magistrates of Plymouth colony.

Solomon was always under the shadow of his brother Elisha, with whom he professed religion in a conversion experience during the Windham revival of 1721. Elisha was considered to be more astute than his bullish brother, and although it was Solomon who became the pastor of the Canterbury Separate Church on Sept. 10, 1746, this was only after brother Elisha declined the position, feeling instead impelled toward an itinerant ministry among the Separatist churches. Solomon was already hailed as an exhorter, recognized as sound in his faith (although of lesser abilities than his brother), and deemed acceptable as a preacher of the word. The Canterbury Separate Church under Solomon Paine was a strong body professing a high degree of spirituality. His career as pastor was highlighted by his involvement in the great schism between the Pedabaptists and the Baptists, wherein he earned the reputation of being "the radical preacher of Canterbury." Having earned a reputation as a mystic among the New Eng. Separatists, Paine died on Oct. 25, 1754.

Critical Appraisal: Solomon Paine's only publication was an apology written at the height of the conflict between the established Old Light churches and the New Light Separatist churches. With his brother Elisha, Paine became one of the primary advocates of the right to be separate, if one's conscience dictated, without fear of reprisal from the established churches. In a preface to his essay, Paine described in detail the spiritual passion that forced him out of his reluctance to publish the message God was causing to well up inside him "to the point of bursting," comparing his experiences to those of the prophets Amos and Ezekiel. The text itself starts with an appeal to the Conn. General Assembly, imploring them to abstain from persecuting all who felt conscience bound to dissent from the established church. Paine argued that following the dictates of one's own conscience is an inalienable right and that even kings and queens allowed the Church of England freedom to organize and freedom from censure. He compared the present situation of the Separates with the civil situation of the colonies and promised obedience in all civil matters while soliciting tolerance in matters of conscience. Paine also called upon the Council to repeal all ecclesiastical laws that might abridge Americans' religious liberty as granted by God and tolerated by the king. His appeals having been refused, he recounted the subsequent inner turmoil stemming from his disinclination to pursue the matter further for fear of reprisal. He excused himself on two grounds: he did not have a sufficient gift to be spokesman for this political cause, and he feared neglecting his own preaching. Nonetheless, he felt prodded incessantly by voices inside his head begging him to risk fines, imprisonment, and even death.

Paine vividly described his conflict as a fire burning in his heart and as a tormenting sleeplessness filled with voices giving him no rest until he finally gave in to the will of God by beginning to write one more appeal. At that point, not only did his health return, but the spiritual life of his preaching doubled, causing him to fall into an ecstasy of love for God and his church. He was overcome by this manifestation of God's movement in his life, which made him a humble and willing servant instead of a reluctant and fearful one. Unfortunately, this new petition was also refused, so the Separates at this point turned their attention to Eng. to carry their appeal to King George himself. Paine and Ebenezer Frothingham (q.v.) were chosen to carry it to Eng. and make the presentation, but Paine's death in 1754 halted the plans. By the time the Separates finally were able to achieve relief and a measure of acceptance, they were disintegrating into Shakerism and fanaticism, and they finally died out as a major sect altogether.

Suggested Readings: CCNE. *See also* Richard L. Bushman, *The Great Awakening: Documents on the Revival of Religion, 1740-1745* (1970); Edwin Scott Gaustad, *The Great Awakening in New England* (1957); C. C. Goen, *Revivalism and Separatism in New England, 1740-1800* (1962); Alan Heimert, *Religion and the American Mind* (1966); Alan Heimert and Perry Miller, eds., *The Great Awakening* (1967).

Peggy McCormack
Loyola University of New Orleans

THOMAS PAINE (1737-1809)

Works: *The American Crisis* (1776-1783); *Common Sense* (1776); *Public Good* (1780); *The Rights of Man* (1791-1792); *The Age of Reason* (1794-1796).

Biography: Thomas (Tom) Paine, the son of a Quaker stay-maker, was born in the small town of Thetford, Eng., in 1737. The first 37 years of his life were undistinguished and involved a series of abortive occupations: a brief stint as a sailor, off and on employment as a stay-maker, a short term as a teacher, and two periods of work in the Excise Service. His first wife died shortly after their marriage; his second marriage, which was never consummated, ended in a legal separation. In Oct. 1774, equipped with letters of introduction from Benjamin Franklin (q.v.), whom he had met that summer in London, Paine set sail for America; in Jan. 1776 he arrived in Pa., where he established himself as the leading propagandist of the American Revolution with the publication of *Common Sense*. Throughout the War of Independence, Paine continued to write on behalf of the patriot cause and served as secretary for a number of congressional committees; he also worked with Robert Morris in the founding of what became the Bank of North America, and in 1781 he accompanied Col. Henry Laurens to Fr. to negotiate a loan. In 1787 he again returned to Europe, this time to seek support for the construction of an iron bridge he had designed. During his sojourn abroad, he also wrote his two most extensive works: *The Rights of Man* and *The Age of Reason*. The former occasioned Paine to be charged with treason against Eng.; the second part of the latter was written during his incarceration in a French prison, the arrest having been made on the grounds that he was a citizen of a hostile nation. Partly because of the radicalism of these two works and partly because of his outspoken censure of George Washington (q.v.) and other founding fathers, Paine was socially ostracized when he returned to America in 1802.

Also, because of his atheistic opinions, upon his death in 1809, sacred ground was denied him, and he was buried on his farm in New Rochelle, N.Y.

Critical Appraisal: Despised and denigrated throughout much of the nineteenth century as a malcontent, infidel, and reprobate, Thomas Paine was rehabilitated about the turn of this century, and today he is popularly regarded as "America's First Liberal," as "Freedom's Apostle," as a "Man of Reason," and as "America's Godfather." Reexamining the causes and the contexts of the American Revolution and the intellectual climate of the time, however, modern scholars have concluded that although Paine does deserve a prominent place in American history and eighteenth-century culture, it is not for the reasons his early champions claimed. He was not an original thinker but rather an influential popularizer of the intellectual trends of his time. Similarly, the forces that led to the American Revolution were in operation long before he arrived on the scene, and thus his role in determining the course of American history must be viewed as ancillary. But Paine was also, without a doubt, the most brilliant of the Revolutionary pamphleteers and one of the most colorful figures of the period.

What enabled Paine to articulate so powerfully the sentiments of the patriots, however, was not great knowledgeability of the state of American affairs or any altruistic adaptability; instead, the secret of his success is to be found in the extent to which America had come to symbolize the archetypal dream of a New World and a second chance. In the situation of the colonies, Paine saw the objective correlative of his own personal frustrations and ambitions, and it was these things that he articulated in his propaganda. Hence characterizing his writing is its *ad hominem* quality, imputation of motivations, and discussion of political issues in psychological terms—hence also his disenchantment with the founding fathers when his own fortunes began to decline. But that the cause of America was thus furthered by a man who wrote out of his own hopes and fears also makes Paine of special importance for the humanistic light that the paradox sheds on the meaning of the phrase "the American dream."

Common Sense, a classic in the art of demagoguery, was published in Jan. 1776—just a year after Paine's arrival in America and six months before the Declaration of Independence. Initially unsigned, the pamphlet was first thought to be the work of various patriots, including Benjamin Franklin, John Adams (q.v.), and Samuel Adams (q.v.), although it is unlikely that any politically astute or established American would have expressed himself as Paine did. *Common Sense* is not merely a call for revolution but also a scornful denunciation of everything British and an unqualified proclamation of America's ability to be autonomous. Formally structured as a four-part philosophical inquiry into the origin and nature of government, the work is really an erratic tirade designed to remove the two emotional obstacles that made many colonists reluctant to revolt. The first was loyalty toward Br. as the mother country, and here Paine's tactic was to argue that if Br. had acted like a true parent, no colonist would have dreamed of rebellion; to remain loyal in view of the way Br. had treated the colonies was not to be a dutiful child but rather an imbecile who did not realize that Br. was jesuitically promoting this very sense of loyalty to keep the colonies in a state of subjection. To overcome the second emotional obstacle—the fear that the colonies had more to lose than to gain by separating from Br.—one of Paine's strategies was to shame those who advocated reconciliation either as persons ignorant of the cruelties that Br. had perpetrated in America or as self-serving sycophants. Another device was to evoke truisms whereby seeming disadvantages are shown to be advantages. The argument that the colonies were outnumbered by the British forces, for example, was overturned by the axiom that the smaller the group, the more unified the effort.

Thus the rhetorical techniques that Paine employed throughout *Common Sense* belie his repeated protestations that his arguments were based on plain facts and reason. The work's tremendous impact must be traced in part to the climate of the times: Americans would not have responded to Paine's propaganda if they had not been psychologically disposed to do so. At the same time, to burn with resentment is not automatically to fight with fervor; and if by Jan. 1776 Americans were angry, they were also confused. *Common Sense* served to abolish the confusion by justifying the anger and giving it a glorious name: "The cause of America," Paine exhorted, "is in a great measure the cause of all mankind."

Similar to *Common Sense* in style and theme is *The American Crisis*, the collective title given to the series of sixteen essays that Paine wrote during the war to keep the fight going and bring it to a victorious conclusion. Since each essay was also written in response to a specific critical issue, if read chronologically, they provide an interesting index to the struggle's problems and progress. "Crisis I" begins with the oft-quoted statement: "These are the times that try men's souls." Washington is reported to have ordered all of his corporals to read this "Crisis" to their troops, and according to legend, it was largely responsible for his successful movement on Trenton on Christmas Day 1776.

Public Good (1780), Paine's other major piece of American propaganda, is stylistically very different from his other writings, although characteristically the explanation is to be found in his personal involvement in the issue at hand. Designed to persuade Va. to cede to federal control her claims to the unsettled western lands, a prerequisite insisted upon by Md. before that state would ratify the Articles of Confederation, *Public Good* could not be penned in Paine's usual flamboyant style if he were not to run the risk of alienating his Virginian friends, chief among them at the time being Thomas Jefferson (q.v.). Thus untypically, *Public Good* is devoid of wild analogies and unscrupulous invective and consists instead of a closely reasoned argument based upon analysis of historical documents.

In *The Rights of Man*, however, the characteristic Paine style is again to be found. A two-part work, published in 1791 and 1792, respectively, *The Rights of Man* is best described as Paine's attempt to do for Englishmen what he believed *Common Sense* had done for Americans. As such, the work is a plea for Englishmen to overthrow the monarchy and has for its basic premise the Rousseauistic and Lockean theory that government originates in a "social compact" and exists for the purpose of guaranteeing the "natural rights" of the individual. *The*

Rights of Man is also Paine's attempt to correct the errors he believed Edmund Burke had made in his *Reflections on the Revolution in France*, an attempt that proceeds mainly through ridicule of Burke's aristocratic style.

Ridicule is also one of Paine's major strategies in *The Age of Reason*, which explains to a great extent why his last extensive work occasioned Paine to become notorious in a free-thinking age as "a filthy little atheist." Not at all that radical in "the age of enlightenment," Paine's argument in the first part of the work is that the knowledge of God that man acquires through his reason and contemplation of the laws of nature does not accord with the traditional image of the Deity; the second part intends to prove that the Bible cannot be regarded as an infallible document because of its many inconsistencies. Paine's method of argumentation, however, has a destructive quality, and his tone is abrasively arrogant: "My mind," he asserted, "is my own church."

Overall, therefore, Paine's importance is to be found less in his ideas than in his power of expression. It is for this very reason, however, that his writings, unlike so many political discourses, have not become dated but are as vibrant today as they were 200 years ago.

Suggested Readings: DAB; DNB; LHUS; T$_2$. *See also* Bernard Bailyn, *"Common Sense"* in *Fundamental Testaments of the American Revolution* (1973), pp. 7-23; Moncure D. Conway, ed., *The Writings of Thomas Paine*, 4 vols. (1894-1896); Eric Foner, *Tom Paine and Revolutionary America* (1976); Philip S. Foner, ed., *The Complete Writings of Thomas Paine*, 2 vols. (1945); David Freeman Hawke, *Paine* (1974); Evelyn J. Hinz, "The 'Reasonable' Style of Tom Paine," QQ, 79 (1972), 231-241; Cecilia M. Kenyon, "Where Paine Went Wrong," APSR, 45 (1951), 1086-1099; Sidney Warren, *American Freethought, 1860-1914* (1953); Jerome D. Wilson, "Thomas Paine in America, An Annotated Bibliography, 1900-1973," BB, 31 (1974), 133-151, 180.

Evelyn J. Hinz
University of Manitoba

ELIHU PALMER (1764-1806)

Works: *An Enquiry Relative to the Moral & Political Improvement of the Human Species* (1797); *The Political Happiness of Nations* (1800); *Principles of Nature* (1802); *The Prospect* (editor; 1803-1805); *Original Sin, Atonement, Faith, &c.* (1806).

Biography: Elihu Palmer, one of the most noted religious heretics of eighteenth-century America, was born in Canterbury, Conn., on Aug. 7, 1764. He attended Dartmouth College, where he was a member of Phi Beta Kappa, graduating in 1787. Hoping to become a minister he moved to Pittsfield, Mass., to study divinity under the Rev. John Foster. Foster later became a Universalist, and Palmer apparently began to develop his skepticism toward orthodox Christianity during his stay at Pittsfield. Palmer accepted a call to be pastor of a Presbyterian

Church at Newtown, Long Island, N.Y., in 1788 but left after six months because of his liberal opinions. He then became a Baptist and moved to Philadelphia but soon was disowned by the Baptists when he advertised to deliver a public sermon attacking the divinity of Christ.

Palmer then decided to abandon the ministry and study law; he was admitted to the Philadelphia bar in 1793. That same year, however, he lost both his wife and his sight during a yellow fever epidemic. Following this tragedy, Palmer became an itinerant Deist preacher, moving to Augusta, Ga., in 1793 and then to New York City in 1794, which became his home. From 1794 until his death, he founded a number of Deistic societies and preached regularly in New York City, as well as occasionally in Philadelphia and Baltimore. He contributed many essays to the Deist newspaper *The Temple of Reason* between 1801 and 1803 and later published his own Deist weekly, *The Prospect; Or, View of the Moral World*, between 1803 and 1805. He died of pleurisy in Philadelphia on Apr. 7, 1806.

Critical Appraisal: Palmer was a tireless Deistic speaker and writer who was influenced by the writings of early eighteenth-century English Deists like Matthew Tindal and John Toland, as well as contemporary authors like Rousseau, Volney, Condorcet, William Godwin, Thomas Paine (q.v.), and Joel Barlow (q.v.). He expressed his militant Deism through his newspaper essays, two Fourth of July orations delivered in N.Y. in 1797 and 1800, and his major work *Principles of Nature*, published in 1802. For Palmer, as for most late eighteenth-century Deists, the central theme of the age was the perfectibility of man. This tenet, he believed, had been hidden from man by a conspiracy of kings and priests, but the time had now arrived for Deism to triumph. The opening blow had come in the American Revolution, which Palmer asserted in 1797 had been the first step in "the inevitable ruin and virtual destruction of those unnatural institutions and corrupt principles which have so long disgraced the character of man, and robbed him of his highest happiness." The American and French Revolutions had broken the hold of kings and priests on the minds of men, and the whole vicious fabric of Christianity was on the brink of final destruction. Deism, which would then replace Christianity, would be simple and benign; its triumph would usher in the universal reign of peace, justice, and reason throughout the world.

Palmer, like Thomas Paine, considered the destruction of Christianity to be his initial task; as he put it in *Principles of Nature*, he intended to destroy "pious and holy fanaticism." He singled out the major Christian doctrines of original sin, the Trinity, the Virgin birth, and atonement for withering and sarcastic attack. Evil, Palmer was convinced, lay not in original sin or human depravity but in corrupt institutions; man would be perfect when despotism and superstition were destroyed. Palmer devoted much of his writings to attacks on the Bible, ridiculing miracles and prophecies. In *The Prospect* he attempted to write a series of articles commenting critically on every chapter of the Bible; he had reached the thirty-fifth chapter of Exodus when the paper ceased publication.

Personally fearless, Palmer's sense of being persecuted by orthodox religious leaders made him fanatically anti-Christian. He was an eloquent spokesman for the small but significant strain of militant Deism that emerged in America during the 1790s. None of the various Deistic societies he founded lasted more than a few years, and his writings probably reached only a handful of Americans. Nevertheless, Palmer was an important critic of established religion, and his career demonstrates the impact of war and political upheaval on traditional Christianity in America.

Suggested Readings: DAB. *See also* Roderick S. French, "Elihu Palmer, Radical Deist, Radical Republican," in *Studies in Eighteenth-Century Culture*, ed. Roseann Runte (1979), pp. 87-108; G. Adolf Koch, *Republican Religion: The American Revolution and the Cult of Reason* (1933), pp. 51-73; Henry F. May, *The Enlightenent in America* (1976), pp. 231-232; Herbert M. Morais, *Deism in Eighteenth-Century America* (1934), pp. 128-138.

John F. Berens
Northern Michigan University

JOHN PARKE (1754-1789)

Works: *The Battle of Bunker's-Hill* ("Prologue," by Hugh H. Brackenridge; 1776); *The Death of General Montgomery* ("Prologue," by Hugh H. Brackenridge; 1777); "Reply to Rev. Jacob Duché" (pub. in *Letters from Gen. Washington to Several of His Friends;* 1778); *Lyric Works of Horace* (1786); *Virginia: A Pastoral Drama* (1786).

Biography: John Parke, the leading colonial poet of Del., was born at Dover, Apr. 7, 1754, the son of Thomas and Ann Parke. His father was a prosperous hat maker and county official. After attending Newark Academy and Newark College, John graduated from the College of Philadelphia in 1771 with an A.B. and in 1775 with an A.M. Following law studies with Thomas McKean, he joined the Continental Army at the beginning of the Revolution and with the recommendation of McKean and Caesar Rodney was appointed assistant quartermaster general at Cambridge, Mass. Ten months later, in N.Y., he was appointed lieutenant colonel of artificers; apparently he was with George Washington (q.v.) at Valley Forge in the winter of 1777-1778. On Oct. 29, 1778, he resigned from the army; one can only speculate why he resigned after two years' service. But his strongly expressed patriotism, his advancement in the service, and his comparative youth all argue against a voluntary severance. Presumably unmarried (as indicated by deeds in which his name appears), he retired to his estate "Poplar Grove" in Kent County, Del., where he lived until his death, Dec. 11, 1789.

Critical Appraisal: If one seeks in Lt. Col. Parke's major writings reflections of his experiences during the first two years of the American Revolution, one will be disappointed, for even when the themes of his verse touch upon contemporary affairs, the sentiments are unoriginal, and the imagery is bombastic. Most of the verse in the *Lyric Works of Horace*, his major work, attempts to adopt Horace's Classic Roman mode to persons and events in colonial America. One gathers that he would have heartily approved of Horatio Greenough's heroic statue of Washington (1832) attired in Roman toga, which to most Americans, then as now, never seemed to come off as planned. Parke, taken with Washington as a resurrected Caesar Augustus, dedicated *Lyric Works* to his commander and substituted him and "Chaste Martha" for Augustus and his spouse in his paraphrase of Horace's 14th Ode from his Third Book, titled "On the Return of Augustus from Spain." In his versions of Horace's odes, epodes, and epistles, Parke either substituted American public figures for Roman and applied descriptions and allusions to local and contemporary history, or more directly imitated Horace, or attempted literal translations, with American dedications in the titles. As Everett Duyckink observed, the names appearing in the dedications of these poems comprise a "catalogue of the worthies of the time." Some are obviously his friends—one translation is addressed to his waiter in the army and another to his publisher, Eleazor Oswald. But one suspects that the hundred or so names in these poems are either name dropping (as with one to Louis XVI) or attempts to win preferment, as with the many dedications to Revolutionary political and military figures.

Most of the poems in *Lyric Works* are in the spirit of Horace—complimentary, offering encouragement, celebrating triumphs, or otherwise singing of love, friendship, or festivity; in fact, Parke omitted the satires, because they "might offend." Some of the odes and epodes, addressed to women, are less good-humored; one insults a "Lewd Old Woman," another castigates "Jilts of All Descriptions," and a translation of the Fifth Ode of Book II advises a friend in love with a "Green Girl" to wait for her to ripen: "Then pluck not the grape ere 'tis fit for your use; / Soon autumn shall paint it and ripen its juice."

The full title of Parke's major work is a misnomer. *The Lyric Works of Horace...to Which Are Added a Number of Original Poems* should include a disclaimer to "original," because those poems that do not imitate Horace do imitate contemporary English neo-Classic verse. Many of the elegies, fables, distichs, epigrams, and rebuses are by hands other than Parke's. Like the pastorals, with their Philanders and Corydons, most are unworthy of notice. But John Wilcocks's "Parody on Mr. Pope's Ode to Solitude" sparkles, and William Prichard's "Beauties of Harrowgate," a spa or "local" poem, happily holds up the American resort as Philadelphia's answer to Bath or Buxton. Parke's masque, titled *Virginia: A Pastoral Drama*, and addressed to the governor of Del., is sometimes cited as an uncommon application of the masque form to a native American setting: Strephon, Flavia, and other hunters and huntresses hold forth in song from "a cottage with a view of the Potomac" to welcome Washington's return to Mount Vernon, his "blest retreat."

Suggested Readings: DAB. *See also* Stanley J. Kunitz and Howard Haycraft,

American Authors, 1600-1900 (1938); *Magazine of History*, extra no. 91 (1923); J. T. Scharf, *History of Delaware*, vol. II (1888).

Eugene L. Huddleston
Michigan State University

JAMES PARKER (c. 1714-1770)

Works: *A Letter to a Gentleman in the City of New-York* (1759); *Conductor Generalis* (1764); *An Humble Address to the Publick* (1766).

Biography: James Parker was born in Woodbridge, N.J., sometime around 1714. After the death of his father, he was apprenticed to William Bradford (q.v.), a N.Y. printer (1727). In 1733 he ran away to Philadelphia and gained employment with Benjamin Franklin (q.v.), returning to N.Y. in 1742 to set up a press in silent partnership with Franklin. A year later, he established the *New-York Weekly Post-Boy* (later published under other titles). He was also public printer for the provincial government, but this did not prevent him from becoming embroiled in several political controversies, most notably when the governor censured him for printing an unfavorable remonstrance by the Assembly in 1747.

Parker's business interests continually expanded. He founded several newspapers and was responsible for the training of many prominent printers. In 1751 he established N.J.'s first permanent printing office at Woodbridge; in 1755 he set up John Holt as publisher of the *Connecticut Courant* in New Haven; in 1765 he founded a printing press in Burlington, N.J. During his career, he was printer for the government of N.J. and Yale College; he also published some famous periodicals, including the *Independent Reflector*, edited by William Livingston (q.v.) (1752-1753), and the *New American Magazine*, edited by Samuel Nevill (1758-1760).

In addition to his businesses, Parker served as a British postal agent (after a recommendation by Franklin, the deputy postmaster general for America); librarian of the Corporation of the City of New York; and judge of the Court of Common Pleas for Middlesex County, N.J. (from 1764). He supported the colonial side during the controversy with Br. until his death in 1770.

Critical Appraisal: According to Victor H. Paltsits, James Parker was "a better printer than Bradford or Franklin." Ward L. Miner has written that "he was aware, as few colonial printers were, that there was such a thing as typographical excellence." However, his considerable talents as typesetter, editor, publisher, and entrepreneur were greater than his own literary skills.

Parker's style is labored and tedious. His personal mark is most often found in broadsides and newspaper essays defending the rights of printers. In 1759 he protested a N.Y. stamp act as "a very grievous Burden upon the Printers in general." In a private letter to Franklin (1765), he denounced the new British stamp duty as "the fatal *Black-Act*." However, he was not committed to absolute freedom of the press: on several occasions, he revealed the names of "scurrilous" writers to the authorities and modified his editorial practices when criticized by the government.

Parker's most famous work is actually a compilation. Using English sources, he assembled the *Conductor Generalis*, a lengthy manual of procedure for justices of the peace, sheriffs, and other civil magistrates. This book went through many printings before the end of the eighteenth century and was one of the most influential guides of its type. Parker, with a characteristic eye for business, assured his readers that it was "the cheapest and most useful" of those available.

Suggested Readings: DAB. *See also* Leonard W. Labaree et al., eds., *The Papers of Benjamin Franklin* (1960), II, 341-345; XI (1967), 37-38n, 251-252n; XII (1968), 175; Leonard W. Levy, *Legacy of Suppression: Freedom of Speech and Press in Early American History* (1960), pp. 45-47, 79-82, 142-143; Douglas C. McMuntrie, *A History of Printing in the United States* (1936), II, 149-150, 227-233; Ward L. Miner, *William Goddard, Newspaperman* (1962), pp. 13-14, 50-52; Lyon N. Richardson, *A History of Early American Magazines, 1741-1789* (1931), pp. 75-76, 83-86, 87-90, 99, 123-126; Arthur M. Schlesinger, "The Colonial Newspapers and the Stamp Act," NEQ, 8 (1935), 65-66, 69-70.

Douglas M. Arnold
Yale University

THOMAS PARKER (1595-1667)

Works: *Theses Theologicae de Traductione Hominis Peccatoris ad Vitam* (1617; rep., 1657, 1658); *The True Copy of a Letter Written by Mr. T. Parker...Declaring His Judgment Touching the Government Practised in the Churches of New England* (1644); *The Visions and Prophecies of Daniel Expounded* (1646); *The Copy of a Letter...to His Sister, Mrs. Elizabeth Avery* (1650).

Biography: Born at Newbury, Berkshire, Eng., on Jun. 8, 1595, Thomas Parker was the son of one of the founders of Congregationalism, lauded by Cotton Mather (q.v.) as "the father of all the *non-conformists* in our age." Thomas probably followed his father to the Neth. in 1607, when Robert Parker fled prosecution before the Court of High Commission for his Separatist activities. The young Parker may have completed part of his grammar school education at Leyden, but he matriculated from Trinity College in Dublin in 1610 and from Oxford in 1613, failing to take a degree at either university. Returning to Leyden in 1614, he studied theology at the University of Leyden. He did not earn his master of philosophy until 1617, at the University of Franeker. As Samuel Eliot Morison observed, Parker "enjoyed the most varied academic education among the 130 or more university alumni who came to New England in the Great Emigration."

He also enjoyed notoriety for a series of seventy supralapsarian theses he published about the time he took a degree. Parker himself never participated in the major controversy his *De Traductione Peccatoris* stirred in the Neth. and in Ger.; but two of his tutors, Johannes Maccovius and William Ames, were drawn into a bitter dispute over the orthodoxy of the theses with the Dutch theologian Sibrandus Libbertus. The dispute placed Maccovius and his student under suspicion of heresy, and the theses came to the attention of the Provincial Deputation of the Estates of Friesland and the Synod of Dort, which acquitted the accused and laid the controversy to rest. Nevertheless, Libbertus opposed Parker's ordination into the Presbytery (according to Cotton Mather, "out of a secret grudge"), and although Maccovius finally persuaded him to give his approval, Parker had already returned to Newbury to apply himself "with an invincible industry unto the study of 'school divinity.' " Wearying of his study of scholastic theology, he assisted the Newbury minister and served as the town's schoolmaster until 1633-1634, when he joined the families who immigrated to New Eng. on the *Mary and John*. There, Parker settled briefly at Ipswich. In 1635 he founded the settlement of Newbury (adjoining Ipswich) with his cousin James Noyes (q.v.) and his nephew John Woodbridge (q.v.).

After his move to Newbury, Parker suffered what Mather called "a miserable defluxion of rheum upon his eyes" and went blind. Nevertheless, his renown grew from his ministry, sometimes controversial writings, and careful preparation of boys for Harvard. The most famous of his pupils was the Puritan diarist Samuel Sewall (q.v.), whom Parker grounded so well in Latin and Greek that he was examined for admission to Harvard at 15. Parker took no wages for his teaching, but Ola Winslow maintained that his traditional school "kept the English ideal of education before every parent and freeman." This basic conservatism extended to Parker's political and religious views and embroiled him in controversy with his own congregation and with the Westminster Assembly. Parker was a Royalist, enthusiastic about the restoration of Charles II and skeptical of democratic principles, especially when they influenced church administration. He was also a biblical literalist: fascinated by the Book of Revelation, he encouraged his students to read the Bible and biblical prophecies as literal and inerrant evidence of God's dispensation and to practice religion not "as an unfolding experience in each individual life," but as "the biblical word unchanged . . . as a mandate for living." In 1661 Parker's stern orthodoxy triggered a long dispute with the covenanted membership of Newbury, whose democratic participation in the management of church affairs Parker discouraged. In spite of his Congregationalist background, he leaned toward a strict form of Presbyterianism and stubbornly conducted a form of religious service a portion of his congregation found intolerable. Although he appeared in person before the New Eng. Synods of 1643 and 1662, Parker's beliefs were never officially sanctioned; but as Morison observed, he "eventually wore out and outlived his opponents," dying on Apr. 24, 1667.

Critical Appraisal: According to Samuel Eliot Morison, Parker was as well known in Eng. for his American writings as he was in the colonies. The most controversial work written after his immigration to New Eng. was *The True Copy of a Letter Written by Mr. T. Parker...Declaring His Judgment Touching the Government Practised in the Churches of New England*, a critique of Congregationalism intended for the Westminster Assembly. Parker's strategy in the letter was subtle: his denunciation of democratic forces within the church was preceded by a humble, pious petition to his family and delivered in the elegant, measured style of the Declaration of Independence: "although wee hold a fundamentall power of government in the people, in respect of election of Ministers; yet we judge, upon mature deliberation, that the ordinary exercise of government must be so in the Presbyters, as not to depend upon the express votes and suffrages of the people." Parker aired his conservatism more bluntly in 1650 with *The Copy of a Letter...to His Sister, Mrs. Elizabeth Avery*, whom he reprimanded for embracing Quakerism. "Your printing of a Book, beyond the custom of your Sex," he declared, "doth rankly smell; but the exaltation of your self in the way of your opinions, is above all." The rest of Parker's canon consists of his interpretations of Bible prophecies. Only *The Visions and Prophecies of Daniel Expounded* was printed; it was probably the first book prepared for publication in the town of Newbury.

Suggested Readings: CCNE; DAB; DNB; Sprague (I, 41-43). *See also* Cotton Mather, "The Life of Mr. Thomas Parker" in *Magnalia Christi Americana* (1852, rep. 1967), I, 480-488; S. E. Morison, "The Education of Thomas Parker of Newbury," PCSM, 28 (1932), 261-267; *The Puritan Pronaos* (1936); T. B. Strandness, *Samuel Sewall: A Puritan Portrait* (1967); Ola Elizabeth Winslow, *Samuel Sewall of Boston* (1964).

Eliza Davis
The University of Alabama in Huntsville

EBENEZER PARKMAN (1703-1782)

Works: *Zebulun Advised* (1738); *Reformers and Intercessors* (1757); *The Love of Christ* (1761); *The Diary of Ebenezer Parkman, 1719-1755* (1974).

Biography: Ebenezer Parkman was born in Boston, Mass., Sept. 5, 1703, the son of an undistinguished but very religious shipwright. His early schooling was with John Barnard (q.v.) at the North Latin School; thereafter he went to Harvard College, graduating in 1721. Between college sessions, he taught school here and there, but by inclination and training his life's work was to be in the ministry. After serving as a supply pastor in a number of pulpits, he was called to Westborough, Mass., where he was ordained the first minister of the church, Oct. 24, 1724. Parkman was the pastor of this church until his death Dec. 9, 1782.

In the early days of his pastorate, in a frontier community, there were occasional Indian scares and other hazards encountered on the edge of the wilderness. A minister in those days had to supplement a meagre salary from the town by working the ministerial farm on which he had been "settled"; Ebenezer Parkman was no exception to this rule.

During the Great Awakening, when many towns were convulsed and parishes sometimes split, Westborough's minister was conservative and much opposed to the hysterical shriekings and outbursts that accompanied revivals. Yet Parkman knew and admired Jonathan Edwards (q.v.), and he invited the great evangelist George Whitefield (q.v.) to preach in Westborough. When the dispute with G.B. before the Revolution developed, Parkman deplored violence and riots and hoped for a reconciliation. Although these views were increasingly unpopular, respectful townspeople kept their beloved pastor in their pulpit to the end.

Critical Appraisal: The published occasional sermons of Ebenezer Parkman show his firm attachment to the old theology with doctrines such as justification by faith and the idea of original sin. The sermons were long and scholarly, somewhat more characteristic of the seventeenth than the eighteenth century. By far the most important of Parkman's writings was his great diary, begun in college and kept for sixty-two years. Parts of this have been lost, but large portions of the manuscript are preserved in the American Antiquarian Society and the Massachusetts Historical Society. This very lengthy document reveals in unique detail the happenings in town and colony, giving a full view of all aspects of life. The minister faithfully recorded day by day the enormous work in building a new town as well as the numerous tribulations of a young minister in raising a rapidly growing family. Parkman's wide interest in all sorts of events makes his diary an indispensable source of information for the social history of eighteenth-century New Eng.

Suggested Readings: CCNE; Sibley-Shipton (VI, 510-527). *See also* Francis G. Walett, ed., *The Diary of Ebenezer Parkman, 1719-1755* (1974), Introduction.

Francis G. Walett
Abington, Massachusetts

WILLIAM PARKS (c. 1698-1750)

Works: *The Maryland Gazette* (1727-1735); *The Virginia Gazette* (1736-1750).

Biography: Although not much is known about William Parks's early life, his biographers concluded that he was born in Shropshire, Eng. First records of his work include three brief appointments: as publisher of *The Ludlow Post Man* (1719-1721); as printer in Hereford of two books, including a translation of Bunyan (1721); and as editor of *The Reading Mercury* (1723).

In 1725, however, Parks directed his attention toward the colonies. Hired by the Md. Assembly to inform the inhabitants of that province about world events and to report the proceedings of the Assembly, Parks set up his printing office in Annapolis in 1726. In addition to beginning the "Journals of the Assembly" and printing "The Compleat Body of the Whole Laws" of Md., Parks initiated the first newspaper printed in the South—*The Maryland Gazette*. The *Gazette* was published from 1727 to 1734 and included news items as well as poems and essays.

While maintaining his official duties as Public Printer of Md., Parks negotiated with Va. in 1728 to set up a second print shop in Williamsburg and to perform similar duties for that colony. In 1730 he began printing at his Williamsburg office, becoming public printer of Va. and, in 1733, publishing "All the Acts of Assembly Now in Force in the Colony of Virginia." After moving from Annapolis to Williamsburg, Parks published *The Virginia Gazette* from 1736 until his death. Aside from a brief, hostile encounter with the Va. House of Burgesses stemming from inflammatory accusations made against the House in "The Journal of the Council" printed by Parks, the printer's career in Williamsburg was exemplary. An outstanding citizen, Parks was elected alderman and then mayor for two terms. William Parks died Apr. 1, 1750, aboard the *Nelson*, while en route to Eng. He was survived by his widow Eleanor and a married daughter.

Critical Appraisal: Often referred to as the most important colonial printer after Benjamin Franklin (q.v.), Parks is also credited with inaugurating "the first flourishing of Maryland literature." Among the early poets that Parks set in print were Ebenezer Cooke (q.v.) and Richard Lewis (q.v.). Lewis's translation of Edward Holdworth's *Mouse Trap, or The Battle of the Cambrians and the Mice*—one of the first examples of belletristic literature printed in the colonies—was published by Parks in Md. in 1728. In 1730 Parks printed Ebenezer Cooke's *Sotweed Redivius* and, in 1731, reprinted this famous satire of early Md. with additions in a collection of Cooke's works, titled *The Maryland Muse*. While printing in Williamsburg, Parks also published John Markland's (q.v.) *Typographia: An Ode on Printing* (1730) and William Dawson's (q.v.) *Poems on Several Occasions* (1736).

Other important works printed by Parks in Md. and Va. include Daniel Dulany's (q.v.) *The Right of the Inhabitants of Maryland to the Benefit of English Laws* (1728)—the earliest American essay series; Edward Blackwell's *A Compleat System of Fencing* (1734); E. Smith's *The Compleat Housewife* (1742)—the first colonial cookbook; and William Stith's (q.v.) monumental *History of the First Discovery and Settlement of Virginia* (1747). In Williamsburg Parks added to his reputation as an outstanding printer by constructing, with the aid and encouragement of Benjamin Franklin, the first paper mill south of Pa.

As publisher of *The Maryland Gazette* and *Virginia Gazette*, Parks also performed important services for early American culture. Like their English antecedents—Joseph Addison and Richard Steele's *Tatler* and *Spectator*—these newspapers stimulated literary output in the region and furnished a forum for political debate. In extant copies of *The Maryland Gazette*, one can find poems as disparate as the scatological "Tale of the T . . . d" and the occasional piece

"Verses on St Patrick's Day." One can also find fiery opposition, as in the exchange between Rev. Jacob Henderson and Daniel Dulany over clergy's salaries, or eloquent debate, as in Henry Darnall's contribution to the quarrel between colonial planters and merchants, "A Letter to the Inhabitants of Maryland." Notable in the issues of *The Virginia Gazette* are the "Monitor" series, a group of satiric essays poking fun at contemporary society, and poems like Joseph Dumbleton's (q.v.) "The Paper Mill," which, although it makes fun of the relationship between printer and poet in general, praises Parks as the "Poet's Friend."

It is questionable whether Parks himself wrote any of the material appearing in his papers. The first two numbers of the "Plain Dealer" essay series, which appeared in *The Maryland Gazette* in 1729 and were later reprinted in Franklin's *Pennsylvania Gazette*, have, on occasion, been attributed to Parks. These two essays demonstrate affinities in theme and technique with essays of contemporary English essayists. The first essay stresses the neo-Classical dictum to practice "good sense" in the matters of life and has led critics to speculate about Parks's Deistic leanings. The second essay also summons a recurrent theme from the work of the English Augustans—fame and the author—and concludes that an author's fame is more enduring than a politician's.

Suggested Readings: DAB; LHUS. *See also* Alfred O. Aldridge, "Benjamin Franklin and *The Maryland Gazette*," MdHM, 44 (1949), 177-189; Robert D. Arner, "The Short, Happy Life of the Virginia 'Monitor,'" EAL, 7 (1972), 130-147; Jay B. Hubbell, *The South in American Literature, 1607-1900* (1964); J. A. Leo Lemay, *Men of Letters in Colonial Maryland* (1972), pp. 111-125; Lawrence C. Wroth, *The Colonial Printer* (1922); idem, *William Parks: Printer and Journalist of England and Colonial America* (1926).

A. Franklin Parks
Frostburg State College

JONATHAN PARSONS (1705-1776)

Works: *A Needful Caution* (1742); *Wisdom Justified* (1742); "Account of the Revival of Religion in the West Parish of Lyme," *The Christian History* 2 (1745), 118-162; *The Doctrine of Justification* (1748); *Manna Gathered in the Morning* (1751); *Good News from a Far Country* (1756); *A Rejoinder to the Reverend Mr. Robert Abercrombie's Late Remarks* (1758); *The Connection* (1759); *Infant Baptism* (1765); *Infant Baptism...Second Edition* (1767); *A Funeral Sermon...of Ebenezer Little* (1768); *Communion of Faith Essential* (1770); *To Live Is Christ* (1770); *Freedom from Civil and Ecclesiastical Slavery* (1774); *Sixty Sermons on Various Subjects*, 2 vols. (1779-1780).

Biography: The seventh child of Ebenezer Parsons and his wife, Margaret, Jonathan Parsons was born in West Springfield, Mass., Nov. 30, 1705. Apparently self-educated in his earlier years, Parsons was graduated from Yale College in 1729 but stayed on to study theology with Rector Elisha Williams (q.v.) and serve as college butler during the ensuing year. Subsequently, he studied with the Rev. Jonathan Edwards (q.v.) in Northampton before becoming pastor of the First Church in (Old) Lyme, Conn., in 1731.

A man of volatile spirit, Parsons was, according to his own testimony, at first "a violent Arminian," but the preaching of the Rev. George Whitefield (q.v.) awakened him in 1740, and after some struggles, he finally experienced what he took to be a saving conversion in 1741 while meditating on his Bible alone in the fields. He then became an ardent worker in the New Light or Calvinist faction of the Great Awakening movement, began itinerant preaching in eastern Conn. with some success, and significantly enlarged the church membership at Lyme. In 1742 he was invited to preach the Thursday lecture in Boston, an occasion he utilized to defend the revival movement and warn off its opponents in his sermon, *Wisdom Justified*. In 1744 he furnished a substantial account of the revival in his parish, including his personal experiences, to *The Christian History*, and the publication of this piece precipitated a division within his church. Although the opposition consisted of a mere handful, they were intransigent, vociferous, and they seem to have been sustained by the Old Light ministers of two neighboring churches. For a time, Parsons held on, but finally, he asked to be dismissed rather than see his church torn apart by dissension, and the church dismissed him after a council in 1745.

Parsons was not long adrift, however, for his good friend, the Rev. Whitefield, introduced him to a group in Newbury, Mass., who had seceded from two Congregational churches there to found a New Light church. In 1746 Parsons was installed as pastor of the (now) Newburyport Presbyterian Church, he and his flock having adopted the Presbyterian form to avoid the legal problems that would have resulted from trying to establish a second Congregational Church in one parish. Parsons remained in this congregation for the rest of his life, and under his leadership, it became one of the largest churches in New Eng.

A New Light and supporter of Whitefield to the end, Parsons had the peculiar honor of having the great evangelist die in his home in 1770. The next day, Parsons preached a funeral sermon, *To Live Is Christ*, to a huge crowd that had been awaiting Whitefield, and Whitefield was buried before the pulpit in Parsons's meetinghouse (where Parsons joined him six years later).

An excellent Classical scholar, learned in history and medicine, Jonathan Parsons also had considerable native talent as an orator and public figure. The appreciation of his people is reflected in the two massive volumes of his ordinary sermons, which they published posthumously in 1779 and 1780. The sermons testify to his mental vigor and extraordinary homiletics.

Critical Appraisal: Virtually all of the printed writings of Jonathan Parsons were written after the beginning of the Great Awakening and reflect his primary concern with religious issues that became prominent around1740. Thus there is a consistent preoccupation with Calvinistic theology, the evangelical mission exemplified in the career of George Whitefield, and the peculiar emphasis upon the doctrine of God's sovereignty notably espoused by Jonathan Edwards. Although an outspoken partisan of the New Lights, Parsons stressed the need for restraint and rational balance on all sides and particularly on the part of the clergy, when he preached *A Needful Caution* to his congregation at Lyme in 1742 during the first bloom of the Awakening. Later the same year, preaching the Thursday lecture in Boston, Parsons still stressed the theme of restraint, but in the public lecture, he took a much more partisan position himself and addressed much of the sermon to those who were either indifferent or in opposition to the movement. *Wisdom Justified* makes clear that there is no middle way between support of what Parsons presented as the Way of Christ and the various currently popular heresies such as Arianism, Arminianism, and Pelagianism. One way leads to heaven, the rest to hell. In this sermon, he also identified the issue of God's sovereignty as the touchstone of orthodoxy.

Six years later, when the momentum of the Awakening had slowed and critics indicted the movement as a destroyer of churches, Parsons attempted again to focus the public's attention on the central theological issue with *The Doctrine of Justification by Faith*, three lectures that clearly define his own lifelong theological stance and, incidentally, reiterate the essentials Jonathan Edwards had published just ten years before in a sermon of the same title. Again Parsons attacked the Arminians, insisting that even the most limited concept of human merit denies the sovereignty of God and, in practical terms, leads to penances and other practices of the Church of Rome. A more comprehensive statement followed in *Good News from a Far Country*, a substantial sermon in seven installments treating the many facets of the concept of redemption through grace and discussing the specific questions and needs of many different types of people. In the conclusion of that sermon, he noted that Arminians and enthusiasts of the opposite extreme are *equally* the enemies of Christ—a new emphasis for Parsons.

A sermon on *Infant Baptism*, published in 1765 and reissued in 1767 with a large polemical appendix relating to a Baptist opponent, is significant in the context of the period of awakenings in the early 1760s, including the rise of the Baptists in New Eng. and the separations in many churches. Most important is Parsons's explicit statement that the old threat of Arminianism had been replaced by the threat from the other extreme: Baptists and wild enthusiasts. Indeed, in the appendix to the 2nd edition, Parsons acknowledged that he had been accused recently of *Arminian* leanings. By 1770 he was ready to publish an anonymous "letter," *Communion of Faith Essential to the Communion of Churches*, pleading for a union of churches with commitments to Calvinist theology and urging that matters of church government and even liturgy be put aside. Faced with faction and disintegration wherever he looked, Parsons seems to have wanted to salvage the faith from the churches.

However, lest anyone suspect that Parsons was losing his poise in his last years, *Freedom from Civil and Ecclesiastical Slavery* fully attests to his willingness to engage dangerous issues with as much vigor as ever just two years before his death. Preached on the fourth anniversary of the Boston Massacre, the sermon virtually forecasts the Revolution and plays upon the spirit of the times by insisting that a Mass. law requiring the citizens of a parish to support a church they do not want to attend is also unfair taxation, that ecclesiastical freedom is just as important as secular freedom, and that *internal* justice should be as important as any. He even averred that arms are appropriate to defend oppressed religion as well as civil bodies.

According to John Searle's funeral sermon, Jonathan Parsons possessed most of the gifts of a great orator; perhaps his literary gifts were less extraordinary, although his prose is clear, flexible, vivid, with a variety of apt imagery, and the intelligence investing it is learned, disciplined, yet sensitive to the varieties of nuance. His limitation seems to be an inadequate sense of the larger structures in prose rhetoric, resulting in a certain lack of tension and incisiveness or a tendency to prolixity. Still, *The Doctrine of Justification* does not compare much to its detriment with that of Jonathan Edwards, and the two volumes of posthumously published sermons, *Sixty Sermons*, reflect a high degree of homiletical art in Parsons's weekly sermons.

Suggested Readings: CCNE; Dexter (I, 389-393); Sprague (III, 47-52). *See also* William Allen, *The American Biographical Dictionary*, 3rd ed. (1857), pp. 638-639; Edwin S. Gaustad, *The Great Awakening in New England* (1957); C. C. Goen, *Revivalism and Separatism in New England, 1740-1800* (1962); Alan Heimert, *Religion and the American Mind* (1966); Alan Heimert and Perry Miller, eds., *The Great Awakening* (1967), p. 35-40, 187-191, 196-200; John Searle, "The Character and Reward of a Good and Faithful Servant of Jesus Christ" in *Sixty Sermons*, by Jonathan Parsons (1779-1780), I, iii-lxvi; Joseph Tracy, *The Great Awakening* (1842), pp. 133-155.

Wilson H. Kimnach
University of Bridgeport

FRANCIS DANIEL PASTORIUS (1651-c.1720)

Works: *Henry Bernhard Koster, William Davis, Thomas Rutter and Thomas Bowyer* (1697); *A New Primmer* (1698); *Umständige Geographische Beschriebung der zu Allerletzt Erfundenen Provintz Pensylvaniae* (1700); "The Monthly Monitor" (Ms. commonplace book, The Historical Society of Pennsylvania; 1701); "Francis Daniel Pastorius His Hive, Melliotrophium, Alvear or Rusca Apium, Begun A. D. 1696" [the "Bee-Hive"] (Ms., Univ. of Pa., n.d.).

Biography: Francis Daniel Pastorius was born Sept. 26, 1651, at Sommerhausen, Franconia, in Ger., the only child of Magdalena and Melchior Adam Pastorius, the author of many German and Latin religious works. After studies at the Windsheim Gymnasium and the University of Altdorf, Pastorius traveled to Strasbourg, Basal, Jena, and Ratisbon to study law and government. He then returned to Altdorf, where he received a doctor of law degree in 1676.

From 1676 to 1680, Pastorius practiced law at Windsheim and Frankfurt; for the next two years, he traveled throughout Europe as the tutor to a young nobleman, Herr Vonn Rodeck. Upon his return to Frankfurt, Pastorius, now interested in the religious thought of the Pietists and concerned about the future of Europe, became the agent for a group of Quakers who wanted to purchase land in Pa. Pastorius sailed from London in late spring of 1683 and arrived in Philadelphia in Aug., when he met William Penn (q.v.) and purchased additional land from him. The settlement of Germantown was organized in Oct. of that year, and Pastorius served the community during the next twenty-five years, as mayor, clerk, keeper of records, scrivener, member of the Provincial Assembly, and leader of the 1688 protest against slavery. Also in 1688 Pastorius married Ennecke Klostermanns, by whom he had two sons. During these years between his arrival and his death in the winter of 1719-1720, Pastorius spent much of his time studying, writing, and accumulating one of the largest libraries in the province. From 1698 to 1700, he taught at the Friends' School in Philadelphia and later was master of a school in Germantown from 1702 until shortly before his death.

Critical Appraisal: Unlike many of his contemporaries in colonial Pa., Francis Daniel Pastorius has long held a firm place in history as one of the foremost scholars in the colonies and as the organizer of the first German immigration to America. Until fairly recently, however, he has not been recognized as a major contributor to American literary history.

Consider these evaluations: "He wrote punning Latin verses, one or two books of little importance that were published, and an unpublished manuscript of a thousand pages." "The works of the linguist, jurist, and mystic of the wilderness are all forgotten, save his Latin 'Ode to Posterity.' " "This work [Bee-Hive] is a proof of the industry and diligence of the author, if it testify little as to the literary value of his work." Ellis Oberholtzer added, however, that Pastorius was observant, humorous, sincere, and wide ranging. George Genzmer noted that "the best of his German verse is direct, sincere, and melodious," but he made no comment on Pastorius's work in English. Even DeElla Toms in the one dissertation devoted to Pastorius, "The Intellectual and Literary Background of Francis Daniel Pastorius," admitted that "Pastorius' poetic talent was a modest one; his literary significance lies in his position as one of the earliest nature poets of a new type in Germany and as a pioneer poet in colonial Pennsylvania."

Pastorius, however, has not been without more fervent admirers. John Greenleaf Whittier eulogized him as "The Pennsylvania Pilgrim" (1872), and Marion Dexter Learned, Pastorius's biographer, praised the "Bee-Hive" as the "Magna Charta of German culture." John Stoudt supplied perhaps the fullest evaluation of Pastorius's verse, which he called sentimental, didactic, allegorical, clever, alliterative, rational, conventional, yet "fresh and pleasing even in its ponderous rhythms." Stoudt went one step further: Pastorius was "perhaps even the first ranking literary figure of his time in Colonial America, surpassing even Cotton Mather." Harrison Meserole provided a more tempered and more authoritative critique than Stoudt in his introduction to a selection of Pastorius's poems:

His wealth of garden and herbal imagery, his rollicking humor, his regularly gentle but occasionally sharp satire, and his experiments in rhythms, structures, and rebus effects establish him not only as the first poet of consequence in Pennsylvania but also as one of the most important poets in early America.

Certainly, many of the poems from the "Bee-Hive" (reprinted in Meserole's anthology) bear witness to his interest in nature and, in particular, his own garden. "On His Garden Book," "If Thou Wouldest Roses Scent," "I Have a Pretty Little Flower," and several of his epigrams draw chiefly upon garden imagery. "If any be pleased to walk into my poor Garden" combines this same imagery with humor and diction one might not expect from such a scholar:

Put nothing in thy mouth;
But freely Fill thy Nose and Eyes
With all my Garden's growth.
For, if thou imitate the Apes,
And Clandestinely steal my grapes,
One wishes thee the Belly-Gripes,
An other hundred Scaffold-Stripes, &c.

In a similar vein, Pastorius noted that to improve the rose's scent, one should "Plant Garlic to their stem":

Likewise, if a Friend of thine
Should to Goodness so incline,
As to lead a Vertuous life,
Let him take a Scolding Wife:
Thus Natura works, you see
Sometimes by Antipathy.

Not all of Pastorius's poems move so lightly: "Thy Garden Orchard, Fields" and "To God Alone, the Only Donour" are closer to the great Lutheran hymns than to comic verse. So, too, do many of his other religious poems, epigrams, and observations reveal his far-ranging scholarship and deep religious commitment.

In total, Pastorius wrote six books and pamphlets and left an imposing collection of manuscripts (many now lost): one folio, fourteen quartos, twenty-two octavos, and six duodecimos. When Harold Jantz's work on the largest of them, the folio "Bee-Hive," is complete, we will have the basis for thorough scholarship. Until then, we can acknowledge Pastorius as one of the foremost literary figures in colonial America, if not its foremost literary craftsman.

Suggested Readings: DAB; DARB; LHUS. *See also* Marion Dexter Learned, *Francis Daniel Pastorius, The Founder of Germantown* (1908); Harrison T. Meserole, ed., *Seventeenth-Century American Poetry* (1972); John J. Stoudt, *Pennsylvania German Poetry, 1685-1830* (1955).

Timothy K. Conley
Bradley University

HENRY PATTILLO (1726-1801)

Works: *The Plain Planter's Family Assistant* (1787); *Sermons* (1788); *A Geographical Catechism, to Assist Those Who Have Neither Maps nor Gazetteers* (1796).

Biography: Henry Pattillo was born "of pious parents" near Dundee, Scot. The surname was originally spelled "Pattullock." With his brother George, he immigrated to Va. in 1740 and became a mercantile clerk but later turned to teaching. In 1751 he was invited by the "eminent" Samuel Davies (q.v.) to live with him in Hanover and study for the Presbyterian ministry. There he pursued a "classical and theological course," and in 1758, at the time he was licensed to preach, was examined in geography and astronomy and in Latin, Greek, and Hebrew. He and his wife, Mary Anderson, whom he married in 1755, reared a large family. In 1765 he moved to N.C., preaching at Hawfields, Eno, and Little River in the central part of the colony. Beginning then, he pursued the life of the schoolmaster, and wherever he went thereafter, his home served as both dormitory and classroom. In 1768 royal Governor William Tryon called on him to restrain the insurgent Regulators, but by 1775, when he was elected a delegate to the first N.C. Provincial Congress, he had become an ardent patriot. In 1780, after six years during which he held no pastorate, he accepted a call to the Granville County congregations of Nutbush and Grassy Creek, remaining in the vicinity as both teacher and preacher until his death during a visit to Va. in 1801.

Critical Appraisal: Henry Pattillo's love of books, it was said, was exceeded only by his love of religion. His writings were either theological or instructive. The miscellaneous selections in *The Plain Planter's Family Assistant* begin with a message "To Heads of Families," offering advice to Christian fathers and mothers. Among the book's several catechisms, the only unusual one is "The Negroes Catechism" of fifty questions followed by answers to be memorized. For example, "Q.40" asks whether or not a slave is happier than his master. Yes, for a slave has no heavy responsibilities; his "humble station" is preferable to that of his master, who must worry about "debts" and "taxes" and the need to "provide victuals and clothes for his family." Pattillo was careful to point out the equality of slave and master in God's sight. Another composition to be memorized is "Prayer for a Negroe."

In the preface to the *Sermons*, the chauvinistic author "hopes for the indulgence of his country-men, for whom, only, he writes." First of the three sermons is "On the Divisions Among Christians," in which, after a history of how the various sects developed, Pattillo extended the Presbyterian hand of fellowship to all, especially the Methodists; for "Though the people of Christ are divided in name, they are one in will and affections." The theme of "On the Necessity of Regeneration to Secure Happiness" is that man must "be born again" to be saved. The third sermon, "The Scripture Doctrine of Election Asserted, and Objections Answered," disdains John Wesley's "Free Grace" and cites biblical passages to prove and justify predestination. Following these three sermons is "An Address to the Deists," a lengthy diatribe against "a set of creatures worse than Atheists." Pattillo traced the literature of Deism from Matthew Tindal. Although Deists are "destroyers," Christians must continue to labor patiently "to convince and reclaim the infidel." *Sermons* concludes with a list of over 500 names of paid subscribers to the volume.

A Geographical Catechism is composed entirely of 104 questions and answers. Pattillo intended that the "three young lads" at that time under his care "should commit it to memory." A formidable task it would have been, even in a day of mechanical recitations. The book was planned both as a school text and as a reference work in which "honest farmers and their families" could identify the geographical names mentioned in newspapers. He also hoped the publication would bring in "a few dollars." In spite of his emotional anti-Deism, Pattillo's comments on the harmony of the universe and on the work of "the great CREATOR" who had "stockt every Moon in the system with creatures capable of enjoying his goodness, and adoring his wisdom and power" show that he was influenced by the intellectual climate of the age. He happily accepted without question what he believed to be scientific discoveries, expounding at length on planets and comets and "fixt stars." In addition to the expected survey of countries and oceans and continents, Pattillo took up matters such as the signs of the Zodiac. As for words of British origin on the map of the U.S., this tempestuous American patriot would begin immediately to "annihilate those names of places that insult our ears with discarded [English] royalty."

Two undated titles listed by Samuel Allibone—*Leland's Deistic Writers, Abridged* and *Sermon on the Death of Washington*—have not been cited and may never have been published.

Suggested Readings: CCV; Sprague (III, 196-199). *See also* William Henry Foote, *Sketches of North Carolina, Historical and Biographical* (1846), pp. 213-226; Drury Lacy, *A Sermon Preached on Occasion of the Death of the Rev. Henry Pattillo* (1803); Durward T. Stokes, "Henry Pattillo in North Carolina," NCHR, 44 (1967), 373-391.

Richard Walser
North Carolina State University at Raleigh

ROBERT PAXTON (d. 1714)

Works: Ms. sermon book.

Biography: Relatively little is known of Robert Paxton's life in America. Born in Scot., he was licensed to preach in the colonies on Oct. 21, 1709, and served, according to an entry in his sermon book, four years at a church at "Keckatoun on James River" in Va. until his death on Mar. 25, 1714. Existing records, however, do not connect him with the parish. A record does exist of his being asked to preach at Bruton Parish, Williamsburg, Va., in 1710, and William Byrd of Westover's (q.v.) diary contains an entry for Nov. 1711 that "Mr. Paxton gave us a sermon that was very good." Apparently none of Paxton's sermons was published in America or Eng., even though he collected them into a sermon book and left instructions that the manuscript be sent to his father, John Paxton, a schoolmaster in Scot. The manuscript, which is in the Harvard-Houghton Library, is representative of typical pastoral and doctrinal sermons preached to rural congregations in southern colonial America.

Critical Appraisal: Of Robert Paxton's forty-eight sermons, one is on fasting, three are on the sacrament, and there is one each on incarnation, Christ the Redeemer, the nature of Christ, the Holy Ghost, and the Gospel light. Other sermon topics include repentance, living a good life, moderation, Godliness, anger, humility, patience, salvation, the burden of sin, and love. A representative example of each general type, doctrinal and pastoral, reveals the essential characteristics of all of Paxton's sermons.

"Of Moderation," a pastoral sermon addressed to the individual, calls for restraint in "the affection for earthly things." Taken from Philippians 4:5, "Let your moderation be known unto all men, the Lord is at hand," the sermon itself is moderate in tone. Paxton did not conjure up fire and brimstone to frighten his parishioners into repentance of their material desires, nor did he argue for an immediate divorce from earthly attractions. In a simple and logical manner, Paxton pointed out that in the physical state, there is a tendency to neglect the inner spirit or to confuse physical and spiritual desires. His solution referred the individual to the example of the early Christians who retired from "the noise and tumult," thereby gradually weaning themselves from the world so that at the moment of physical death, the soul dropped into eternity like "ripe fruit from the tree."

Typical of Paxton's doctrinal sermons is "Of the Lord's Supper," preached from Acts 2:42. Paxton explained the sacraments, "briefly the Name, Meaning, Parts, Efficacy, Number, and necessity of them by which we may understand all that is necessary for us to know concerning them." He began by comparing Christ and his disciples to Roman officers and their soldiers. "Faithful soldiers" always follow the commands of "Christ the Captain of our Salvation." He continued the analogy by presenting the Roman meanings and uses of the term *sacrament* and proceeding to the Christian meanings. His sermon generally, then, reveals how the outward rituals and symbols of the sacrament correspond to inward spiritual grace and harmony.

Paxton's style befits his service as a rural preacher. He based the text upon a biblical verse but seldom sprinkled further scriptural references or quotes throughout the sermon. His language is very plain and straightforward, even more so than that of many later eighteenth-century sermons whose authors were influenced by the plain, scientific writing style of the period. Paxton used few metaphors, and when he did, they were clear and direct. In "Of Moderation," he said, "our affections ... like colored glass represent all objects in our own hue and complexion," and without moderation "we are as unfit to judge of divine and spiritual enjoyments as a country man is to be a master in the schools." His congregation would have easily understood either metaphor. Paxton's sermons only further reinforce the recent evidence that an eloquent, careful, and reasonably plain style was commonly used by Anglican preachers in southern colonial America.

Suggested Readings: CCV. *See also* Richard Beale Davis, *Intellectual Life in the Colonial South, 1585-1763* (1978), II, 582, 727-730, 731; Tom D. Kilton, "Post Restoration English Commemorative Sermons," JLH, 14 (1979), 297-318; Rolf P. Lessenich, *Elements of Pulpit Oratory in Eighteenth-Century England (1600-1800)* (1972); Bishop Meade, *Meade's Old Families, Ministers, and Churches of Virginia* (1900).

Leonard C. Butts
Florida Southern College

EDWARD PAYSON (1657-1732)

Works: *A Small Contribution to the Memorial of That Truely Worthy and Worthily Man of God Mr. Samuel Phillips* (1696); *Pious Heart-Elations* (1728).

Biography: Edward Payson was born in Roxbury, Mass., on Jun. 20, 1657. A graduate of Harvard College (A.B., A.M., 1677), Payson began preaching at Rowley in 1680, and in 1682 he was ordained Rowley's fourth minister, sharing the pulpit for a time with his future father-in-law, Samuel Phillips. In addition to his work as a minister, Payson taught in the local Latin school. Payson remained in Rowley for the rest of his life. According to one biographer, "during the thirty-six years of his ministry after the death of his colleague, two hundred and seventy-one persons were added to the church, sixty of them immediately after the earthquake in 1727."

Payson was twice married: to Elizabeth Phillips in 1683 and to Elizabeth Whittingham in 1726. Although records on the subject vary, he was reportedly the father of twenty children, only half of whom outlived him. Payson died in Rowley on Aug. 22, 1732, after a lengthy illness which had left him incapacitated and unable to speak. According to an obituary in the *Boston News-Letter*, Payson was a man of "unaffected Godliness and true Holiness."

Critical Appraisal: Edward Payson wrote only two published works: a sermon titled *Pious Heart-Elations* and a lengthy elegy titled *A Small Contribution*. Typical of the jeremiad literature of the day, *Pious Heart-Elations* was written in response to the earthquake which shook New Eng. on the morning of Dec. 3, 1727. As did most of the ministers who preached on the subject, Payson interpreted the event as an "Awful Providence" from God that the people of New Eng. had strayed from the ways of piety and were in need of reformation. While there is nothing unusual about Payson's sermon, it assumes significance as one of many sermons addressed to the subject of the earthquake and is an indication of the providential significance which Puritans like Samuel Sewall (q.v.), Increase Mather (q.v.), and Cotton Mather (q.v.) tended to place on unusual occurrences such as floods, severe storms, and earthquakes.

Of greater significance, perhaps, to the literary historian is Payson's *Small Contribution*, a lengthy elegy he wrote as a "memorial" for his colleague and father-in-law Samuel Phillips, who died in Rowley on April 22, 1696, at the age of 71. Nearly 150 lines in length, Payson's *Small Contribution* was written in five parts, each of which was intended to summarize a particular aspect of Phillips's contributions to his country and his family. According to Harold Jantz, Payson's *Small Contribution* is "obviously the work of an amateur who under the stress of deep emotion labored valiantly to put his grief into rhyme." Although Jantz condemns the first four sections of the poem as "One of the most movingly awkward and inept elegies" ever published in New Eng., he praises the fifth part, "Mr. Phillips Buried," in which Phillips's predecessors at Rowley address their successor in death, as a virtual miracle of "naïve and perfect folk poetry." For this reason, if for no other, Edward Payson deserves to be remembered.

Suggested Readings: CCNE; FCNEV; Sibley-Shipton (II, 514-518). *See also* Emory Elliott, "The Development of the Puritan Funeral Sermon and Elegy: 1660-1750," EAL, 15 (1980), 151-164; Robert Henson, "Form and Content of the Puritan Funeral Elegy," AL, 32 (1960), 11-27. For a reconstruction of Payson's *Small Contribution*, see Thomas Gage, *History of Rowley* (1840), pp. 79-84. No copy of the original broadside seems to have survived.

James A. Levernier
University of Arkansas at Little Rock

EDWARD PAYSON (1783-1827)

Works: Asa Cummings, ed., *The Complete Works of Edward Payson, D.D.*, 3 vols. (1846).

Biography: Born in North Rindge, N.H., on Jul. 25, 1783, Edward Payson received his education at home from his father, Rev. Seth Payson, and at the academy in New Ipswich, entering Harvard as a sophomore in 1800 and graduating in 1803. From that year until 1806, he taught school in Portland, Me. After preaching for three months in Marlboro, N.H., he was ordained in 1807 as a Congregational pastor, becoming the colleague of Rev. Elijah Kellogg at the Second Congregational Church in Portland. From 1811 until his death, Payson served this congregation as sole minister. He married Ann Louisa Shipman in 1811. In 1821 he received the degree of doctor of divinity from Bowdoin College. He died, probably of tuberculosis, in Portland, on Oct. 22, 1827.

Critical Appraisal: Only three of Edward Payson's sermons appeared during his life: *The Bible Above All Price* (1814), *A Thanksgiving Sermon* (1820), and *An Address to Seamen* (1821). He was, however, a popular and powerful

Calvinist preacher whose intense humility prevented his seeking publication. He deserves notice now not only for his many extant sermons, available in *The Complete Works*, but for the numerous excerpts from his letters and from his diary that Asa Cummings included in the "Memoir," a lengthy biography that comprises most of the first volume.

Payson's sermons are characterized by passion and effective control of extended metaphors with frequent biblical sources. His sincere and fundamental approach to the interpretation of the Bible is rhetorically persuasive, relying more on emotion than on cold logic, and often expressed in long, carefully constructed sentences that combine dramatic hyperbole with balanced propositions. His *Address to Seamen*, for example, is typical in its clever elaboration of the central conceit: the individual as God's vessel navigating past the Rock of Intemperance and the Gulf of Perdition, through the Straits of Repentance and the Bay of Faith to the Port of Heaven.

Similarly emotional, Payson's diary, begun early in life as "a check upon the misemployment of time," soon becomes a record of religious experience that echoes an earlier age in its emphasis on spiritual autobiography and on the writer's doubts and unworthiness: the entries suggest Thomas Shepard's (q.v.) introspection and self-abnegation as Payson declared "I am entirely stupid," and like Cotton Mather (q.v.), the author recorded his literal prostration during private prayer; he noted with accuracy that his "disposition is naturally so ardent, that I can enjoy nothing with moderation." Payson also shared Jonathan Edwards's (q.v.) struggle with a language commensurate with his personal religious feeling and like Edwards repeatedly chose words such as *ravishing, delightful*, and *sweet*. Payson's compelling letters similarly reveal a reflective self-concern that establishes him as a divine firmly of the century in which he was born rather than a minister of the century in which he died.

Suggested Readings: DAB; Sprague (II, 503-512). *See also* Asa Cummings, "A Memoir of the Rev. Edward Payson, D.D." (1830) in *The Complete Works of Edward Payson, D.D.*, vol. I (1846); E. L. Janes, *Mementos of Rev. E. Payson, D.D.* (1873); William B. Sprague, *Our Pastor; Or, Reminiscences of Rev. Edward Payson, D.D.* (1855).

Caroline Zilboorg
Lake Erie College

OLIVER PEABODY (1698-1752)

Works: *An Essay to Revive...Military Exercises* (1732): *That Ministers Are to Separate Men for Ministry* (1736); *The Foundations* (1742).

Biography: Oliver Peabody was born in Boxford, Mass., on May 7, 1698. Despite his family's disapproval and serious financial difficulties, he began his education at Harvard in the spring of 1717. During his junior year, he was awarded a scholarship with the stipulation that he qualify for and devote himself to pastoral work among the Indians. After his graduation from Harvard in 1721, the church to which Peabody was assigned to preach was extinct, so he returned to college for two more years and earned an M.A. in 1723.

As a result of the efforts of the prospective Indian parishioners, he was called to the Natick English and Indian Congregational Church in 1723. The initial difficulties were severe. Although he had been granted a parcel of land, there was little money for his subsistence, for the building of a parsonage, or for any other necessities. In addition, there was a controversy concerning whether the church should be established as Indian or as English and Indian. In 1729 the English and Indian church was finally established, and Peabody was ordained the same year. Although little information survives to document his work among the Indians, enough exists to suggest that he was liked and respected and that he effectively promoted the moral, cultural, and economic well-being of the local Indians. Few white families lived within his parish, but those that did testified that he discharged his pastoral duties with "great renoun," was a model of social life, and was preeminent in universality and benevolence.

Disruptions within the parish, missionary work among the Indian tribes, and efforts to ensure the parish's survival each affected Peabody's weak constitution and contributed to his death at 53. He was survived by his wife and nine of their twelve children. His final words perhaps serve best as his epitaph—"I have fought a good fight, I have finished my course, I have kept my faith."

Critical Appraisal: Oliver Peabody was consistently said to be aligned with the Old Lights of the Great Awakening. Yet he is also said to have approved of the Awakening as he saw it work in Natick. His sermons, however, provide no evidence that he did approve of the movement; in fact, he was critical of some of its manifestations. The criticisms are neither consistent nor strong, but they are present. In *The Foundations*, he warned against "hearing many different preachers." In the same sermon, he warned against the danger of hearing "every Wind of Doctrine." These minor instances might be taken as a protest against the excesses and influence of the itinerant preachers. The looser structure of church authority and the alterations in doctrine that were manifestations of the Great Awakening are also subject to limited criticism in *That Ministers Are to Separate Men for Ministry*. Unlike the itinerants, Peabody insisted on a proper and orderly procedure for the ordination of pastors. He did not, however, stand out as a strong proponent of either faction in the controversy.

Although his duties involved work among the Indians, Rev. Peabody had little to say about this aspect of his pastoral care. The Indians are mentioned several times in *An Essay to Revive...Military Exercises*, but only once in reference to any religious activity, when he suggested that "proper and qualified missionaries" should be sent to work among them. Peabody also criticized the current treatment of Indians by suggesting that justice might be preferable to "spiritous liquors" in winning them over. But most of his comments upon the Indians are directed at their use and value as models for military training.

Written for oral delivery, a sermon's power could be increased or diminished in proportion to the force of its delivery. When read, Peabody's sermons are occasionally repetitious; however, we cannot judge how the sermons were heard.

Suggested Readings: CCNE; Sibley-Shipton (I, 529-534).

George Craig
Edinboro State College

DEUEL PEAD (d. 1727)

Works: *A Sermon Preached at James City in Virginia* (w. 1686; pub. 1960); *Jesus Is God* (1694); *Jesus Is God* (1694); *The Wicked Man's Misery* (1699); "The Converted Sinner" (1701); many other occasional sermons.

Biography: The date and exact place of Deuel Pead's birth are unknown. Baptized in London at Westminster Abbey on Apr. 18, 1663, and educated at Trinity College, Cambridge (A.B., 1664), Deuel Pead came to Md. from Eng. in 1682 and preached before the Md. Assembly the following year. He remained in Md. for only a short time, however, and in Nov. 1683 became minister of Christ Church, Middlesex County, Va. While at Christ Church, Pead began a series of Saturday afternoon sermons to guide the church members to a greater understanding of the Lord's Supper celebrated on the next day. In 1686 Pead was summoned to preach at Jamestown on the annual Apr. 23 celebration of James II's ascension to the throne. The anniversary was also labeled a "Cockney Feast" by Va. Governor Lord Effingham. Why Pead was asked to preach is uncertain, although he did suggest in the sermon that he grew up and perhaps was born in London. Whatever the reasons, Pead's sermon is one of the few surviving Anglican sermons from the seventeenth-century south. Pead served for seven years at Christ Church and returned to Eng. in 1690. His sermon was sent to Eng. to be published but was never printed because of the change of political climate.

After his return to Eng., Pead was appointed minister of St. James's, Clerkenwell, London, in 1691 and remained in this position until his death. From 1694 to 1709, he preached his most interesting series of occasional, doctrinal, and moral sermons. He was a staunch supporter of the status quo, shifting loyalties from the Catholic Stuarts to William and Mary with ease, and he became one of the more popular ecclesiastical commentators upon events of his time. Deuel Pead died in Eng. on Jan. 12, 1727, and was buried at Clerkenwell.

Critical Appraisal: As an American author, Deuel Pead's most important work is the only surviving sermon he preached in Va., *A Sermon Preached at James City*. The sermon is based on the text of Psalm 122:6, "Pray for the peace of Jerusalem / They shall prosper that love thee," from which Pead developed an extended comparison between Jerusalem and London. He began by explaining the biblical history of the text, followed by a discourse on the necessity for prayer. Ignorance of prayers is no excuse, Pead warned, for everyone in America has reference to *The Book of Common Prayer* "so graciously distributed by the King." Prayers should be for peace, specifically "for the peace of Jerusalem." For "Jerusalem" one can read "London" throughout the sermon, for although Pead declared that London was more fortunate and more civilized than Jerusalem in its day, the sermon was aimed at those who defied the right of the Stuarts to rule: "pray for all that irreligion and prophaneness, all disloyal and antimonarchial principles may cease from amongst the citizens." Pead asked for prayers for the peace and unity of king, church, and citizenry. He directly referred to the attempts of Shaftesbury, "That cursed Achitophel," to return a Protestant king to the throne and derided the Puritans for their pretense of piety and peace while so openly interrupting justice and inventing insurrections. Pead ended the sermon by asking for moderation in celebrating James II's anniversary as in all things.

Pead's sermon is similar in many ways to his works later preached and published in Eng. He quoted liberally from Hebrew and Latin and clearly supported king, church, high morals, and peace. Pead's language is somewhat more ornamental in the James City sermon than in his later works; yet throughout his life, he showed a prevailing tendency to change his pace and style to fit the subject and occasion of his sermons. They range from the straightforward, plain Puritan style of *The Wicked Man's Misery* to the *Jesus Is God* compendium of sermons that are highly doctrinal and fall into scriptural references, discussions of etymology, and Hebrew quotations.

The difference between the James City sermon and later works may also be that Pead's style was not yet fully developed and appears somewhat stiff in this early sermon. The most interesting aspect of the James City sermon is Pead's use of nautical imagery, derived either from his own experience as chaplain in the British navy in 1671 or from his knowledge that the less learned in the gathering at James City, a seaport, could more easily follow nautical images than more complex or esoteric language. He managed to make several smooth and convincing transitions from common seafaring rhetoric to the lofty and sublime figures of the sea in the *King James Bible*. Pead, although quick to reveal his learnedness, always tried to keep his rhetoric and style under control. He was usually logical and precise. His surviving sermons reveal a man whose loyalties lay with the church and state as institutions, not with individual personalities representing them.

Suggested Readings: CCMDG; CCV. *See also* Richard Beale Davis, *Intellectual Life in the Colonial South, 1583-1763* (1978), II, 582, 716-720; Tom D. Kilton, "Post Restoration English Commemorative Sermons," JLH, 14 (1979), 297-318; Rolf P. Lessenich, *Elements of Pulpit Oratory in Eighteenth-Century England (1660-1800))* (1972); Bishop Meade, *Meade's Old Families, Ministers, and Churches of Virginia* (1900). *A Sermon Preached at James City* has been edited by Richard Beale Davis, WMQ, 17 (1960), 373-394.

Leonard C. Butts
Florida Southern College

EBENEZER PEMBERTON (1672-1717)

Works: *The Souldier Defended & Directed* (1701); *A Christian Fixed in His Post* (1704); *Advice to a Son* (1705); *A Sermon Preached in the Audience of the General Assembly* (1706); *A Funeral Sermon on the Death of. . .the Reverend Mr. Samuel Willard* (1707); *The Divine Original and Dignity of Government Asserted* (1710); *A True Servant* (1712); *Brief Account of the State of the Province* (1717); *A Discourse Had Previous to the Ordination of the Reverend Mr. Joseph Sewall* (1718); *Sermons and Discourses on Several Occasions* (1727).

Biography: One of the most respected New Eng. ministers of the early eighteenth century, Ebenezer Pemberton grew up in Boston and received a Harvard B.A. in 1691. He remained at the college for the next nine years, first as a graduate student, then as librarian and tutor. During these years, he became an ally of his fellow tutors, John Leverett and William Brattle (q.v.), in their theological and political struggle with President Increase Mather (q.v.). This marked Pemberton as a theological liberal and opponent of the Mathers but did not prevent his appointment to the pulpit of Boston's Old South Church in 1700. Pemberton's years at the Old South were happy and productive. Many of his parishioners objected to his theological liberalism, but he compromised by accepting the conservative Joseph Sewall (q.v.) as his colleague in 1713. Since his was one of the province's most important pulpits, he was invited to preach election and artillery sermons and had access to the press for his other writings as well. Pemberton seldom hesitated to speak his mind, whether on theological matters or on the wearing of wigs and hats to Sunday services, which he strongly opposed. Despite his often rancorous temper, most Bostonians considered him a great and learned man. When he died unexpectedly in 1717, even his adversary Cotton Mather (q.v.) admitted that he was "a man of greater Abilities than many others; and, no doubt, a pious man."

Critical Appraisal: Ebenezer Pemberton's writings are good examples of the mainstream of Congregational orthodoxy during the first decades of the eighteenth century. Pemberton's reputation as a theological liberal resulted more from his friendship with Leverett and Brattle than from any original doctrinal thinking on his part. Like most of his generation of New Eng. clergymen, he wrote primarily on secular themes. His published sermons on the duties and responsibilities of soldiers, magistrates, and ministers illustrate how the Puritan concept of calling had evolved by 1710. They also reflect the new professional self-image that New Eng.'s ministers developed after 1690.

In his 1701 artillery sermon, *The Souldier Defended & Directed*, and in his 1710 election sermon, *The Divine Original*, Pemberton defined the deportment that God, and New Englanders, expected of civil authorities. In the former, he outlined the historical and biblical precedents for military readiness, praised the militia for its public service, and counseled his audience to treat their duties with the gravest seriousness. Above all, he emphasized that soldiering, like all of man's callings, demanded not only specific skills but also a solid commitment to Christ. His election sermon nine years later applied the same themes to the political rulers of Mass. Pemberton took his text from the Psalm 82:6—"I have said, Ye are Gods" —and delineated the godly attributes required in magistrates. Wisdom, righteousness, justice, tact, and forebearance were all essential to the ruler's calling, he asserted, for nothing could bring more rapid ruin to a state than ungodly magistrates. Unlike his seventeenth-century predecessors, Pemberton issued no specific political directives to the province's soldiers and magistrates. Attesting his ignorance of military and political affairs, he stressed that he sought only to apply the general truths of Christianity to these callings. In so doing, he demonstrated the ministry's decreasing interest and power in the political affairs of New Eng.

These two sermons are notable not for their eloquence, but for the similarity of their message and tone to other clerical writings of the first quarter of the eighteenth century. Pemberton's descriptions of the good soldier and the good ruler are interchangeable with those of Cotton Mather, Benjamin Colman (q.v.), and other prominent clergymen. These descriptions reflect the ministry's consensus, not only on the role of civil authorities in provincial New Eng., but on their own role as well. Through spokesmen like Ebenezer Pemberton, the clergy spoke with one voice on matters of state, a voice not of didactic harangue, but of respectful counsel.

Pemberton's writings on the duties and responsibilities of his own calling reveal another clerical consensus of the early eighteenth century. His 1707 sermon at the funeral of his colleague, Samuel Willard (q.v.), presented a characterization of the good minister that was often repeated in the pulpits of New Eng. Willard, Pemberton declared, was dedicated, pious, diligent, and, above all, learned. From his life, the young minister could learn how to behave and what to expect in his career. Like almost all clerical writing on this topic between 1690 and 1750, Pemberton's sermon on Willard defined the academic qualifications and standards of behavior his profession required. It also included a plea for better ministerial salaries, a theme that was beginning to become common by 1707. These sentiments, which after Pemberton's death were echoed throughout New Eng., demonstrated the almost obsessive concern of ministers with the affairs of their calling. They also illustrated how narrow this concern was, and this narrowness contributed greatly to the worsening relationship of ministers and their congregations in the years before the Great Awakening.

Although Pemberton's sermons do not even begin to approach the scholarly range of Cotton Mather's or the rhetorical brilliance of Jonathan Edwards's (q.v.), they are competent, if unexciting, expositions of the most common clerical themes of the day. Yet Pemberton was among the most influential and respected of his generation of ministers, and his writings are important because they typify the concerns and style of that cautious and conservative generation. In his sermon at Willard's funeral, Pemberton compared ministers to owls who "if they would not be hooted at" should "keep close within the tree and not Perch upon the upper bows." In his career and writings, Pemberton exemplified this advice; in so doing he set an example that New Eng. ministers emulated for decades.

Suggested Readings: CCNE; Sibley-Shipton (V, 107-112); Sprague (I, 250-251); T_1. *See also* Perry Miller, *The New England Mind: From Colony to Province* (1953), pp. 447-448, 453, 458.

James W. Schmotter
Cornell University

SAMUEL PENHALLOW (1665-1726)

Works: "Mission of Penhallow and Atkinson. . . to the Penobscot Indians" (w. 1703; pub. 1880); *The History of the Wars of New-England with the Eastern Indians* (1726).

Biography: Born in St. Mabyn, Cornwall County, Eng., Samuel Penhallow trained for the ministry but chose a career in N.H. politics. He enrolled in Rev. Charles Morton's (q.v.) school in 1683, but when English officials closed it down two years later for its Dissenter leanings, Penhallow followed his tutor to Mass. in 1686. The Mass. Council offered him a three-year subsidy to learn the Narragansett language and promised him sixty pounds a year for as long as he served the Christian Indian inhabitants of one of the Praying towns. Instead, Penhallow migrated to Portsmouth where within a year he had married Mary Cutt, the daughter of N.H. province's president, thus ushering him into the province's highest social and political circles. The beginning of Penhallow's political career began in 1699: he became a justice of the peace in Aug., speaker of the General Assembly in Sept., and provincial treasurer in Dec. Penhallow served in a variety of other political posts, including recorder, counselor to the governor, and, most notably, chief justice of the province's Supreme Court, where he served—except for a two-year hiatus (1717-1719) occasioned by an internal power struggle between the governor and lieutenant governor—until his death.

Critical Appraisal: Samuel Penhallow's history is a detailed narrative of the events concerning two early eighteenth-century Indian wars (the first occurring during Queen Anne's War, the second erupting in 1722 and lasting until 1726) in what is now N.H. and Maine. Penhallow claimed that he consulted the available official records and that he interviewed many of the white participants to confirm his account. Unfortunately, these efforts did not translate into complete accuracy. Penhallow saw all Indians as "bloody pagans" and "monsters" who instigated these wars with such vengeance that even "their greatest benefactors have frequently fallen as victims to their fury." Penhallow, therefore, put Indian actions and motivations in the worst possible light while justifying the settlers' acts of violence as necessary defensive responses. For example, Indians are invariably condemned for scalping their victims, but scalp bounties paid to whites are approved because they get results. Penhallow also misrepresented certain incidents: the well-known Pigwacket battle (1726) was not, as Penhallow asserted, a fight between two warring camps, but the slaughter of noncombatant Indians hunting in their own territory.

Penhallow's history, however, still has much historical significance. Above all, it is an example of a captivity narrative writ large. The "fierce and barbarous savages," Penhallow announced early in the volume, were left by God "to be pricks in our ears, and thorns in our sides." As with individual captivity narratives, N.H. and Maine's sufferings came by way of the Indians, because "God has made them a terrible scourge for the punishment of our sins, and probably that very sin of ours in neglecting the welfare of their souls." Thus Penhallow's "memoir" was intended to tell the story of these two wars so "that the generations to come might know them, and set their hope in God, and not forget his works, but keeps his commandments."

Penhallow's narrative is significant in other ways. It offers some valuable insights into Indian motivation in spite of the author's tunnel vision. This is most clear in his description of the advance of English settlement in the years after the Treaty of Utrecht (1714-1721), especially the growth in English activity at the Kennebec River's sturgeon fisheries. They were the first settlements hit in the second war, and as scholars have recently shown, this war broke out principally over an intense competition for food resources. Penhallow's history is also important in American historiography, because it was Francis Parkman's source for his discussion in *A Half-Century of Conflict* (1892) of Anglo-French competition in the region. It is perhaps unfortunate that Penhallow's reputation tends to come through Parkman, for he managed to intensify Penhallow's already hostile depiction of the Native American without providing the context of Penhallow's Puritan ideology.

Suggested Readings: DAB; T$_1$. *See also* Francis Jennings, "A Vanishing Indian: Francis Parkman versus His Sources," PMHB, 87 (1963), 306-323; Kenneth Morrison, "The People of the Dawn: The Abnaki and Their Relations with New England and New France, 1600-1727" (Ph.D. diss., Univ. of Me., 1978); Francis Parkman, *A Half-Century of Conflict*, 2 vols. (1892); P. W. Penhallow, *Penhallow Family* (1885). Penhallow's account of a trade expedition to Penobscot is printed in NEHGR, 34 (1880), 90-93.

Richard L. Haan
Hartwick College

WILLIAM PENN (1644-1718)

Works: *Epicidea Academia Oxoniensis* (1660); *A Declaration from the Harmless and Innocent* (1661); *Ah, Tyrant Lust* (1664); *The Spiritual Base* (1667); *An Answer to a Vain Flash* (1668); *No Cross, No Crown* (1668); *Sandy*

Foundations Shaken (1668); *Words in Earnest* (1668); *Innocency with Her Open Face* (1669); *Exception to the Proceedings* (1670); *A Guide Mistaken and Temporizing* (1670); *A Letter of Love* (1670); *My Irish Journal* (1670); *The Peoples' Ancient and Just Rights Asserted* (1670); *Some Seasonable and Serious Queries* (1670); *Truth Exalted* (1670); *Bill of Injustices* (1671); *A Seasonable Caveat Against Popery* (1671); *A Serious Apology for the People Called Quakers* (1671); *Short Testimony Concerning Josiah Coale* (1671); *A Trumpet Sounded in the Ears of the Dutch* (1671); *Truth Rescued from Imposture* (1671); *A Discourse on the General Rule of Faith and Practice* (1672); *Epistola Consulibus Emdense cum Senatus Dantisci* (1672); *New Witnesses Proved Old Heretics* (1672); *Plain Dealing with a Traducing Anabaptist* (1672); *A Serious Apology for Friends* (1672); *The Spirit of Truth Vindicated* (1672); *A Winding Sheet for Controversies Ended* (1672); *Wisdom Justified by Her Children* (1672); *Answer to "The Spirit of the Hat"* (1673); *Invalidity of John Faldo's Vindication* (1673); *Jeremy Ives Sober Request Proved False* (1673); *Several Tracts* (1673); *The Christian Quaker* (1674); *Counterfeit Christian Confronted* (1674); *Naked Truth* (1674); *Urim and Thummin* (1674); *The Continued Cry of the Oppressed* (1675); *England's Present Interest Discovered* (1675); *Judas and the Jews* (1675); *Saul Smitten to the Ground* (1675); *The Spirit of Alexander the Coppersmith* (1675); *A Treatise on Oaths* (1675); *Description of the Province of West Jersey* (1676); *The Skirmisher Defeated* (1676); *Tender Counsel and Advice* (1677); *Epistle to the Children of Light* (1678); *The Great Case of Liberty of Conscience* (1679); *A Brief Examination* (1681); *An Exalted Distraphas Reprehended* (1681); *The Great Question* (1681); *The Oaths of Irish Papists* (1681); *One Project for the Good of England* (1681); *Protestant's Remonstrance Against Pope and Presbyter* (1681); *Some Account of the Province of Pennsylvania* (1681); *Answer to a False and Foolish Libel* (1682); *Brief Account of the Province of East Jersey* (1682); *The Frame of Government of Pennsylvania* (1682); *Some Sober and Weighty Reasons Against Prosecuting Protestant Dissenters* (1682); *A Testament for His Wife and Children* (1682); *Draft of a Charter of Liberty* (1683); *Information and Direction for Such Persons as Are Inclined to America* (1684); *A Defense of the Duke of Buckingham's Book of Religion* (1685); *Fiction Found Out* (1685); *Further Account of the Province of Pennsylvania* (1685); *Persuasive to Moderation* (1685); *The Quaker Elegy on the Death of Charles* (1685); *Tears Wiped Out* (1685); *The Excellent Privilege of Liberty and Property* (1687); *A Letter Containing Some Reflections on a Discourse Called "Good Advice"* (1687); *Advice in the Choice of Parliament Men* (1688); *The Great and Popular Objection Against the Repeal of the Penal Laws* (1688); *The Reasonableness of Toleration* (1689); *Some Proposals for a Second Settlement on the Susquehanna* (1690); *Just Measures* (1692); *New Athenians No Noble Bereans* (1692); *Essay Toward the Present and Future Peace of Europe* (1693); *Fruits of Solitude* (1693); *An Account of My Journey into Holland and Germany in 1677* (1694); *Introduction to the Journal of George Fox* (1694); *More Work for George Keith* (1696); *Primitive Christianity Revived* (1696); *Plan for a Union of the Colonies* (1697); *A Defense of the Paper Called*

"Gospel Truths" (1698); *An Account of the Blessed End of Gulielma Penn* (1699); *A Brief Account of the Rise and Progress of the People Called Quakers* (1699); *Just Censure of Francis Bugg's Address to Parliament* (1699); *More Fruits of Solitude* (1702); *A Collection of the Works of William Penn*, ed. Joseph Besse (2 vols., 1726); *Fruits of a Father's Love* (w. 1699; pub. 1726). William Penn published more than one hundred fifty titles. A complete list of Penn's works can be found in Joseph Smith, *A Descriptive Catalogue of Friends' Books* (2 vols., 1867) and *Supplement* (1893); Mary Kirk Spence, *William Penn: A Bibliography* (1932); Donald Wing, *Short-Title Catalogue* (3 vols., 1945-1951); and Clifford K. Shipton and James E. Mooney, *Short-Title Evans* (1969). *The Papers of William Penn* are being edited by Mary Maples Dunn and Richard S. Dunn for publication by the University of Pennsylvania Press.

Biography: Quaker leader, founder of Penn., and visionary—William Penn was born in London, Eng., in 1644, the son of Admiral William Penn and his wife, Margaret (Jasper) Penn. As a youth, Penn was brought up in the religion of his parents, who were members of the Church of England, but he early came under the influence of the Puritans and eventually became a Quaker. Although he studied at Oxford, his early connections with the Puritans prevented him from completing his degree. For a time, Penn sojourned at the French court in Paris, and during the Dutch wars he served in the military on the Continent.

Eventually Penn's Quaker beliefs brought him into conflict with the authorities, and he was imprisoned in the Tower of London, where he was held for several months. Throughout his captivity, Penn remained firm in his convictions. It was at this time that he began writing the many tracts and pamphlets in support of the Quaker beliefs and ideals that were to make him famous in Eng. and abroad. After his release from prison in the summer of 1669, Penn began preaching on behalf of the Quaker faith. His travels as a Quaker spokesman took him throughout much of Europe and brought him into contact with several influential Protestant leaders who later proved sympathetic to his mission.

During the late 1670s, Penn began to take an active interest in the colonization of North America. He aided in the settlement of East and West Jersey, and he secured from Charles II the right to establish colonies in the region of what is now Penn. and Del. In 1681, Penn himself came to America, where he drew up documents for the government of Pa. (named in honor of his father), treated with natives, and planned the city of Philadelphia. Although Penn left America for Eng. after only twenty-two months in Pa. and was, except for a brief sojourn between 1699 and 1701, to live the rest of his life in Europe, he remained the driving force behind the colony for the first quarter century of its existence, steering it safely through the troubled political waters of the late seventeenth century.

Penn was twice married, and he was the father of several children. In later life, Penn was beset with financial difficulties, and he was for a time imprisoned for debts. After a long and productive life, the founder of Pa. suffered a stroke in 1712. He remained largely incapacitated until his death in Eng. on July 30, 1718.

Critical Appraisal: Although the works of William Penn embrace a variety of themes and issues, they share several common denominators. As Harry Emerson Wildes, one of Penn's most eminent biographers, has explained, all of Penn's writings "defend the principle of universal peace, freedom of conscience, and toleration of religious beliefs and practices differing from one's own." They uphold, continues Wildes, "what Penn considered the ancient rights of free Englishmen, the rights to liberty, ownership of property, justice, and the dignity of the individual, as well as the equality of all men under the King and before the Lord."

Unlike many of his fellow Quakers, however, Penn did not withdraw himself totally from worldly concerns. Instead, he was a political and a religious activist, and he used his pen to further the ends of his religion and his ideals. To this extent, Penn was atypical of his creed, which downplayed emphasis on the written word as a means of communication. As an American writer, however, he expressed many of the themes that would later become synonymous with the American Dream, and he helped to shape the philosophy and values of an entire nation. In his *Description of the Province of West Jersey, Brief Account of the Province of East Jersey*, and *Account of the Province of Pennsylvania*, for example, Penn beckoned to the weary and downtrodden of Europe, describing the North American continent as an idyllic haven, where the cares and worries of the past could be forgotten and where dreams of freedom and hope could be enacted. In phrases reminiscent of earlier promoters such as Captain John Smith (q.v.) and Samuel Purchas (q.v.), Penn repeatedly praised the natural abundance everywhere to be found in the middle latitudes of North America, and he predicted a prosperous and happy future for this region. In Pa., he believed, men could live in unity with God and nature, and a general spirit of tolerance and benevolence would contribute to the making of a religious utopia, free from unjust persecutions and highly conducive to the attainment of spiritual peace and harmony.

Accordingly, Penn's *Frame of Government of Pennsylvania* guaranteed to pious individuals those rights and privileges which he, as a Quaker and an Englishman, believed God had entitled all human beings to possess. These guarantees included, among other things, the right to own property, a voice in the workings of government, and above all the freedom of worship and thought, and they gave to Pa. an intellectual and political legacy highly significant for the future development of American culture. In the open and free environment of Pa., the ideas of the Enlightenment could easily take root and the shoots of democracy could begin to grow. A love of freedom and a concomitant affirmation of the dignity of the individual were characteristics that William Penn and Benjamin Franklin (q.v.), despite their many other dissimilarities, both held in common.

Throughout his writings, Penn demonstrated a remarkable familiarity with literature and literary tradition. Despite the narrowness of his sectarian allegiances, Penn was interested in almost all areas of human knowledge, and he read widely and sensibly. According to William Comfort, Penn was admirably familiar "with the fields of history, biography, theology, law, government, political philosophy, natural science, and gardening," and he is known to have read the works of writers such as Augustine, Bacon, Boyle, Chaucer, Cowley, Machiavelli, Sir Thomas More, Seneca, Tacitus, and Thucydides. As a youth, Penn dabbled in poetry, and throughout his life he showed a noteworthy fondness for the written word and its potential. There are decidedly poetic passages, for example, in works as diverse as *No Cross, No Crown*, the *Description of the Province of West Jersey*, and the *Brief Account of the Rise and Progress of the People Called Quakers*. The short sayings and maxims in Penn's *Fruits of Solitude* and *More Fruits of Solitude* have been compared to those of La Rochefoucauld, and they also invite comparison with the aphorisms of Franklin. Regrettably, many anthologies of early American literature have neglected the works of William Penn. As history and as literature, they have much to offer the student and scholar of this period.

Suggested Readings: DAB; DARB; DNB; LHUS; T$_1$; T$_2$. *See also* Edward E. Beatty, *William Penn as a Social Philosopher* (1939); Mabel R. Brailsford, *The Making of William Penn* (1930); Edward B. Bronner, *William Penn's Holy Experiment* (1962); Augustus C. Buell, *William Penn: Founder of Two Commonwealths* (1904); James Clarkson, *Memoirs of the Private and Public Life of William Penn* (1814); William W. Comfort, *William Penn, 1644-1718* (1944); idem, *William Penn's Religious Backgrounds* (1944); idem, *William Penn and Our Liberties* (1947); Bonamy Dobrée, *William Penn: Quaker and Pioneer* (1932); Mary Mapes Dunn, *William Penn: Politics and Conscience* (1967); Hans Fantel, *William Penn: Apostle of Dissent* (1974); Melvin B. Endy, *William Penn and Early Quakerism* (1973); John W. Graham, *William Penn: Founder of Pennsylvania* (1916); Mrs. Colquhoun Grant, *Quaker and Courtier: The Life and Work of William Penn* (1907); Elizabeth Janet Gray, *William Penn* (1938); William I. Hull, *William Penn: A Topical Biography* (1937); Joseph E. Illick, *William Penn's Relations with the British Government* (1963); idem, *William Penn the Politician* (1965); Catherine Owens Peare, *William Penn* (1957); Lucy B. Roberts, *William Penn: Founder of Pennsylvania* (1910); Colwyn Vulliamy, *William Penn* (1934); Mason Locke Weems, *The Life of William Penn* (1836); Harry Emerson Wildes, *William Penn* (1974).

James A. Levernier
University of Arkansas at Little Rock

GEORGE PERCY (1580-1632)

Works: *A Discourse of the Plantation of the Southern Colony in Virginia...1606* (w. 1607; partially modernized in *Jamestown Documents*, 1967; first pub. in Samuel Purchas, *Hakluytus Posthumus, or Purchas His Pilgrimes*, 1625); *A Trewe Relacyon of the Procedeinges...in Virginia...1609 vntill 1612* (w. c. 1622-1625; pub. in TQHGM, 3 [1922], 259-282).

Biography: Born on Sept. 4, 1580, and deceased late in 1632, the youngest brother of Henry, ninth earl of Northumberland, George Percy was one of the original colonists of Va., the writer of the first account of the first Va. voyage, and inevitably a competitive contemporary of Capt. John Smith (q.v.).

Independent records and references to him in the Percy muniments and other contemporary sources reveal that he attended Gloucester Hall, Oxford, by the time he was 13 and was admitted to the Middle Temple, London, at 16. But less than two years later, payments began to be made to him "travelling into Ireland." They continued until Mar. 27, 1602, and were resumed a year later for one more year. During the interval, George Percy seems to have been involved in the Neth. War of Independence, at least partly in company with his brother the earl. The next known fact is that he sailed with the first colonists "on Saturday, the twentieth of December," 1606 (he may err by one day in several of his statements). From the outset, possibly at the earl's suggestion, Percy kept a diary that was later published as his *Discourse*, which makes him the premier chronicler of the first Va. voyage. Although never a member of the official "local council of Virginia," he served faithfully in many capacities, and when the colony all but fell apart late in 1609, he was locally elected councilor and deputy governor. After relief came in 1610, he was officially made lieutenant, captain, and eventually deputy governor again. During all of this period, he maintained his diary, until he sailed back to Eng., Apr. 22, 1612, apparently leaving behind a wife named Anne Ffloyd, about whom nothing further seems to be known.

Subsequently, there are few traces of George Percy: a letter from him mentioning a possible expedition to the Amazon, other bits about his interest in the Va. company; and finally his return to the Neth. before 1627, when he was made captain of a company there. On Nov. 5, 1632, the earl died in Eng., and the new earl, George's nephew, is recorded as having dispatched fifty pounds to him soon after. This is the closing entry in the life of George Percy.

Critical Appraisal: Like many another member of an English noble family in the expansive or flamboyant days of Queen Elizabeth I and King James I, George Percy cannot be understood without some notice of his family background. Descended in the eighth generation from Henry Percy, first earl of Northumberland, he was the eighth and last son of Henry, the eighth earl, and brother of the ninth. Among his ancestors was a Henry known as "Harry Hotspur" (made vivid by Shakespeare), another Henry later dubbed "the Magnificent," and his own brother Henry styled "the Wizard Earl" for his mysterious experiments in the Tower of London while he was King James's prisoner for "technical treason" related to the Gunpowder Plot of Nov. 5, 1605. Boundless pride was the chief characteristic of the Percys, along with strong inclinations toward ostentation and quarrelsomeness. Eight of nine Percys in George's direct line died violently: decapitated, assassinated, or slain in battle.

Of a less violent nature, yet typical of the Percys, is the ostentation shown by the earl, and young brother George, on two occasions: the earl, accompanied by George, scandalized the English commander-in-chief in the Neth. in 1602-1603 by the theatrical glamor of his uniform on a visit to the war zone. In 1611, with the earl's blessing, George spent a small fortune on his "reputation (being Gov-

ernor of James Towne) to keepe a continuall and dayly Table for Gentlemen of
fashion"—at the edge of an untamed forest populated by naked natives, only a
year after the "Gentlemen of fashion" had starved to the point of cannibalism
under the same Governor George Percy.

As for Percy's ability with the pen, his style reflects an oil and vinegar
nonmixture that shows an appreciation of the literary English of the day tinged
with childish wonderment over the New World's exotic nature, detached human
interest in his fellow colonists, inhuman disregard for the "savages," and a side
interest in statistics that was rare in his day. His one complete work, *A Trewe
Relacyon*, which exists only in a manuscript copy in the Free Library of Philadelphia and in a printed version of a slightly inaccurate transcription (*Tyler's
Quarterly*), is by far the most revealing of the early accounts of the Jamestown
colony. Among other unbowdlerized details, it contains an immortal story of an
English raid on an Indian village in which all of the male inhabitants were
mowed down by muskets, and the "queen" and children taken captive. The
children were then thrown in the James River and their brains shot out. Governor
Lord De La Warr [Thomas West (q.v.)] next commanded that the queen be
burned alive, but Percy was so tired of bloodshed that he had her put to the
sword—it would be quicker.

Percy's earlier work, the *Discourse*, survives only in the version that was
published by Samuel Purchas (q.v.). This tale of Jamestown's early days is
already well known. Its idyllic accounts of strolls outside Jamestown and visits to
the Indians up the James by boat are classics of their kind, and his necrologies for
1607 are unique in early American literature. But unfortunately, the text is
suspect at the beginning and certainly apocopated at the end. (Purchas had *some*
manuscripts of Percy's in 1613, but did not publish this one until 1625.) However it was, Percy is perhaps superior in his way to the most objective scholar of
today for the simple reason that the Percys were so proud that nothing mortal
seemed strange to them.

Suggested Readings: DAB; DNB; T₁. *See also* G. R. Batho, ed., *The Household Papers of Henry Percy, Ninth Earl of Northumberland (1564-1632)*, Camden Society, 3rd ser., 93 (1962); Gerald Brenan, *A History of the House of Percy*, 2 vols., ed. W.
A. Lindsay (1902); Philip L. Barbour, "The Honorable George Percy: Premier Chronicler
of the First Virginia Voyage," EAL, 6 (1971), 7-17; idem, *The Jamestown Voyages,
1606-1609*, 2 vols., Hakluyt Society, 136-137 (1969); Edward Barrington de Fonblanque,
Annals of the House of Percy, 2 vols. (for private circulation only; 1887); John W.
Shirley, "George Percy at Jamestown, 1607-1612," VMHB, 57 (1949), 227-243.

Philip L. Barbour
Williamsburg, Virginia

NATHAN PERKINS (1749-1838)

Works: *A Sermon, Preached to the Soldiers* (1775); *A Sermon Occasioned
by the Unhappy Death of Mr. Lloyd* (1780); *Letters of Gratitude, to the Connect-*

icut Pleader (1781); *The Reprimander, Reprimanded* (1781); *A Sermon, Preached at the Installation of...Solomon Wolcott* (1786); *A Narrative of a Tour Through...Vermont* (w. 1789; pub. 1920); *A Sermon, Delivered at the Ordination of...Hezekiah N. Woodruff* (1790); *The Pleasantness of True Religion*, pub. in David Austin, ed., *The American Preacher* (1791), I, 355-374; *A Discourse, Delivered at the Ordination of...William F. Miller* (1792); "An Appendix," in Joseph Lathrop, *Sermons on...Christian Baptism* (1793); *Christ the Way, and the Truth, and the Life*, pub. in David Austin, ed., *The American Preacher* (1793), IV, 323-363; *A Discourse, at the Ordination of...Calvin Chapin* (1794); *Twenty-Four Discourses* (1795); *Two Discourses...on...the Christian's Hope* (1800); *The Universality and Perpetuity of the Obligation...to Observe the Rite of Baptism* (c. 1800); *The Character of a Faithful Minister* (1807); *The Duty and Supports of a Gospel Minister* (1807); *The Benign Influence of Religion on Civil Government* (1808); *A Preached Gospel the Great Instituted Means of Salvation* (1808); *A Discourse...at the Ordination of the Rev. Nathan Perkins, Jr.* (1810); *A Discourse...at the Ordination of the Rev. Nathaniel G. Huntington* (1810); *The Gospel Glad Tidings of Good Things* (1810); *The National Sins, and National Punishment in the Recently Declared War* (1812); *A Sermon Delivered at the Interment of the Rev. Timothy Pitkin* (1812); *A Minister of the Gospel Taking Heed to Himself and Doctrine* (1816); *A Sermon Delivered at the Interment of The Rev. Nathan Strong* (1817); *A Discourse...at the Ordination of Reverend Eli Moody* (1818); *Sabbath School Catechism* (1819); *A Half Century Sermon* (1822).

Biography: Minister of the Congregational Church in West Hartford, Conn., for 66 years, Nathan Perkins was born in Lisbon, Conn., on May 18, 1749. The Perkins family was well-to-do, and Perkins received a fine education. After studying under Joseph Lathrop, minister at West Springfield, Mass., Perkins entered the College of New Jersey (now Princeton Univ.) in 1766. His college career was notable in several regards. A brilliant scholar, he placed first in his class and was named Latin salutatorian. His academic accomplishments and conservative political leanings earned him a footnote in literary history as a satiric target in "Father Bombo's Pilgrimage to Mecca," written by Philip Freneau (q.v.) and Hugh Henry Brackenridge (q.v.), both members of the class of 1771 at the college. Finally, Perkins experienced a religious conversion of unusual intensity during his college years, which confirmed his New Light sympathies and his calling to the ministry. After receiving an A.B. in 1770, Perkins studied under Benjamin Lord (q.v.) and then preached at Wrentham, Mass. Refusing a call to the Wrentham church, he instead accepted the West Hartford pulpit that he would hold for the rest of his life. He was ordained on Oct. 14, 1772.

Having inherited money from his parents, Perkins lived comfortably in West Hartford, devoting himself to his ministry and his family. In 1774 he married Catherine Pitkin, daughter of the Farmington, Conn., minister and granddaughter of Thomas Clap (q.v.). The couple were to have nine children. Perkins became a friend of Ezra Stiles (q.v.) and a leader among the New Lights of

Conn. He was a founder of the Connecticut Missionary Society and the Hartford Theological Seminary, and active throughout his long career in the religious associations of the state. His interest in education led him to devote much of his time to teaching and preparing young men for college and the ministry; his most famous student was Noah Webster (q.v.). Princeton recognized his many services by naming him a doctor of divinity in 1801.

An ardent Federalist, Perkins opposed the rise of political liberalism and the decline of the established clergy's power in Conn. He used his pulpit to decry America's declaration of war against Eng. in 1812, preaching *The National Sins, and National Punishment in the Recently Declared War*, wherein he particularly castigated slavery as a threat to national unity. The War of 1812 was unpopular in Federalist New Eng., and Perkins was asked to attend the secret Hartford Convention, which met late in 1814 to propose constitutional revisions reflecting the region's antiwar position. In these political forays Perkins and his followers among the Congregational clergy were defeated by the contrary tides of history, but Perkins continued to devote himself to good works and the revitalization of conservative theology. His long life and ministry ended on Jan. 18, 1838.

Critical Appraisal: Nathan Perkins's writings clearly reflect his religious, political, and educational concerns and his sense of his role as a leader among the Congregationalist ministers of Conn. In his many sermons, he explicated and defended the theology that he studied at the College of New Jersey and that he believed with an intensity that originated in his collegiate conversion experience. Too young to have participated in the Great Awakening, he was nevertheless an intellectual heir of Jonathan Edwards (q.v.), the college's early president; of John Witherspoon (q.v.), its president during Perkins's college days; and of Gilbert Tennent (q.v.) and William Tennent II (q.v.), strong supporters of the college. From Witherspoon's enlightened and wide-ranging curriculum, Perkins may also have acquired some of his breadth of interest and his concern for educational reform.

Like the leaders of the Awakening, Perkins believed in the ministry's duty to encourage religious renewal through missionary tours. His excursion to Vt. in the spring of 1789, "influenced by the Call of duty & Conscience," resulted in a minor classic that may still be read for the pleasure of its shrewd and often acerbic observations. Moreover, *A Narrative of a Tour* is extraordinarily revealing of Perkins's character, for his sense of duty clearly conflicted with his love of domestic comfort and propriety as he traveled through the frontier communities: "people nasty—poor—low-lived—indelicate—and miserable cooks." His eye took in the spiritual and the physical at a single glance. Pittsfield, Mass., for example, he summed up as a town of "loose morals,—loose principles,—good land,—no good fencing timber." Perkins saw the national past made visible in the hard conditions of Vt.: "I can now realize what our forefathers suffered in settling America!" Yet he was ambivalent about the meaning of this glimpse into the past, unsure whether the frontier was simply sinful and uncomfortable ("Slept on a Chaff-bed without covering—a man, his wife & 3 children all in the same nasty stinking room"), or whether it was in its social simplicity a better world from which America had declined: "Woods make people love one another & kind & obliging and good natured. They set much more by one another than in the old settlements." Whatever his momentary doubts, Perkins clearly preferred the civilized world he knew. Vermont's uncomfortable coarseness dismayed him, and he looked forward to the day when the state would be "like Connecticut." Vermont was, after all, the home of Ethan Allen (q.v.), "an awful Infidel, one of the wickedest men that ever walked this guilty globe. I stopped & looked at his grave with a pious horror."

Although Perkins's *Narrative* is of great human interest, it is also untypical of its author. Most of Perkins's published writings are of course sermons, and many of these sermons are occasional, including sermons preached at ordinations or funerals, a lengthy election sermon (*The Benign Influence of Religion on Civil Government*), and a half-century sermon. These works are representative if not exceptional, for Perkins suffered from a weakness for digression.

A Sermon, Preached to the Soldiers, Perkins's earliest publication, shows him melding the minister's religious and civic duties as he retold the myth of an American past where "the glorious light of christianity has dispelled the dark glooms of paganism," defended the patriot ideology, and prepared the recruits for the horrors of battle. Among the funeral sermons, *A Sermon on the Suicide of Mr. Lloyd* is of particular interest. Joseph Lloyd had been a prominent Long Island patriot—and the owner of Jupiter Hammon (q.v.)—who had killed himself after hearing a rumor of an American defeat at Charlestown. Perkins struggled to balance his personal sympathy for Lloyd with an interpretation of the suicide that would be consistent with divine providence.

The sermons of Nathan Perkins illustrate the range of occasional and doctrinal concerns typical of a conservative minister of his period, while his *Narrative* offers modern readers a chance to look behind the public persona of a leading Conn. minister. This brief journal deserves to be better known. Perkins may also have been the author of two anonymous tracts, *Letters of Gratitude* and *The Reprimander, Reprimanded*, although this attribution is doubtful.

Suggested Readings: CCNE; P; Sprague (II, 1-4).

Douglas R. Wilmes
The Pennsylvania State University

EDWARD PERRY (1630-1695)

Works: *A Memorable Account of the Christian Experiences and Living Testimonies of...Edward Perry* (1726).

Biography: Edward Perry was born in Devonshire, Eng., in 1630. He moved to New Eng. in 1649, later settling at Sandwich in Plymouth colony, where he married and lived until his death in 1695. Like many other residents of his town, he became a Quaker in the 1650s. Perry had apparently challenged the authorities even before becoming a Quaker by marrying in an irregular manner in 1654, indicating a dissenting temper for which he and his fellow Sandwich Quakers would be persecuted severely for almost a decade and intermittently thereafter. A leader of Friends in Plymouth colony, he spoke out against persecution and used his residence outside Mass. to launch sharp attacks on that colony. Perry died in 1695.

Critical Appraisal: Edward Perry's writings were collected long after his death in the *Memorable Account* (1726). Consisting of a sketchy journal of his religious life, several exhortations to Friends, and political pieces attacking Mass. and Plymouth, the work usefully informs on the religious views of seventeenth-century New Eng. Friends and their exchanges with the Standing Order.

Perry's journal conforms to the expected Quaker mode, giving little attention to the details of his life other than his searching for a satisfactory religious life and eventually finding it in Quakerism. His religious exhortations are exercises of a seventeenth-century Friend who encouraged his auditors to pay attention to the Christ within, ignore salaried clergy, attend religious meetings regularly and promptly, and observe the Quaker testimony against bearing arms.

Of greatest interest are two manuscripts written and delivered to opponents at times of colonial crisis late in the seventeenth century. Perry wrote the first, "A Warning to New-England," in 1676 during King Philip's War and sent it to the Mass. General Court. The court was not favorably impressed by Perry's argument that Puritan persecution of Quakers brought on God's vengeance via an Indian attack on English settlements. He wrote the second untitled work and delivered it to the Plymouth General Court in 1683. Part of an effort to regain the Sandwich Quakers' civil rights, this work is less strident than the attack on Mass., although it is outspoken in attacking Plymouth's past persecutions of Quakers and in calling for reformation.

Perry's main importance to the twentieth-century historian is that of a New Eng. Quaker who continued to challenge New Eng. colonial governments long after major persecution had lapsed. Much of *Memorable Account* also represents the efforts of later New Eng. Quakers to perpetuate the remembrance of earlier persecutions and to hold up the standard of founding Quakers to later generations of Friends.

Suggested Readings: Douglas Edward Leach, *Flintlock and Tomahawk: New England in King Philip's War* (1958); Arthur J. Worrall, *Quakers in the Colonial Northeast* (1980).

Arthur J. Worrall
Colorado State University

HUGH PETER (1598-1660)

Works: *Milk for Babes, and Meat for Men* (1630, 1641); *A True Relation of the Passages of Gods Providence in a Voyage for Ireland* (1642); *Church-*

Government and Church-Covenant Discussed. In an Answer of the Elders of the Severall Churches in New-England to Two and Thirty Questions, Sent Over to Them by Divers Ministers in England, to Declare Their Judgements Therein. Together with an Apologie of the Said Elders in New-England for the Church-Covenant, Sent Over in Answer to Master Bernard in the Yeare 1639. As Also in an Answer to Nine Positions About Church-Government (compiler; 1643); *New Englands First Fruits* (contributor; 1643); *God's Doings and Man's Duty*, 3 eds. (1646); *Mr. Peters Last Report of the English Wars* (1646); *Good Work for a Good Magistrate* (1651); *The Case of Mr. Hugh Peters. . .Written by His Own Hand* (1660); *A Dying Father's Last Legacy to an Only Child: Or, Mr. Peter's Advice to His Daughter* (1660, 1661, 1683).

Biography: Hugh Peter is significant in American history during 1635-1641, when he was a resident of Mass., and 1641-1645, when he was acting as an agent for the Bay colony in Eng. His publications are more numerous than those given above; cited are items pertinent to his American experience or directly important to biographical matters. He was born in Fowey, Cornwall, Eng., in Jun. 1598, the son of Thomas Dickwood (or *Dyckwoode*) and Martha Treffrey. His father later changed the name to "Peter," and although this is the usual designation that he himself used, "Peters" is frequently recorded. He had a brother Thomas who also immigrated to Mass. He received a bachelor's degree (1618) and a master's degree (1622) from Trinity College, Cambridge, and became a deacon in the Anglican Church on Dec. 23, 1621, and a priest on Jun. 18, 1623. About 1625 he married Elizabeth, widow of Edmand Reade of Wickford, Essex, and daughter of Thomas Cooke of Pebmarsh, Essex; she had eight children and four grandchildren. Elizabeth did not accompany him at first on his removal to Rotterdam and then America, but she had been in Rotterdam, back in Eng., and then in Salem before the end of 1637, where she died within the year. Peter's stepdaughter Elizabeth married John Winthrop, Jr. (q.v.) (1606-1676), who immigrated to Mass. in 1631 and later became the governor of Conn. Peter was constantly in difficulties because of his religious ideas and preaching. He was granted a lectureship at St. Sepulchre's, London, but was jailed in 1626 for assailing the Catholic queen, Henrietta Maria, and his license to preach was subsequently suspended. He was a member of a group of feoffees, organized in 1626, who made attempts to reform the English church internally. Part of his action with the group was to subscribe for fifty pounds in May 1628 to the New England Company (later the Massachusetts Bay Company), and in May 1628 he signed the first instructions to John Endecott, the governor, to establish a godly church in New Eng., if not in Eng. He was not a Separatist, always staying within the Anglican Church, but always acting to purify it. Peter apparently went into a kind of exile to the Low Countries by the beginning of 1628, returning intermittently during the next two years. The reform group ran afoul of Archbishop William Laud from 1630 to its dissolution in 1633, and Peter fled to Rotterdam about 1630, where he remained until leaving for America in Jul. 1635, arriving in Oct.

In Hol. Peter was pastor (with John Forbes) of the Congregation of Merchant Adventurers at Delft in 1631 and preached in Rotterdam several times before Apr. 1633. He gave two farewell sermons at Delft in Oct. 1633, where he was succeeded by Thomas Hooker (q.v.). He helped form an independent English congregation in Rotterdam, where in Jul. 1633 William Ames became his associate, dying, however, in Nov. Peter delivered the funeral sermon. In Oct. 1633 Charles I ordered the restoration of the Church of England liturgy and discipline, and reforming non-Separatist groups were thus weakened. Accordingly, Peter's covenant for the Rotterdam congregation drew much opposition, largely because of the dependence of church membership (participation in the Lord's Supper) on subscription to the covenant. He modified it in 1635 and was reordained under the covenant by Forbes. By this time, he seems to have been the only minister of the old English classis in Hol. Interferences from Laud seem to have been the overt cause of his leaving for America, arriving Oct. 6, 1635.

He was a supporter of the New Eng. Way, that is, of non-Separatist, internally reformed Congregationalism, being admitted a freeman of the Bay colony on Mar. 3, 1636. With Sir Henry Vane (governor in 1636-1637), he tried to heal the split between John Winthrop (q.v.) and Thomas Dudley (q.v.) and was appointed to committees to draft a code of laws on May 25, 1636, and Mar. 12, 1638. Without Vane he called a second reconciliation meeting in Dec. 1636. He became pastor at Salem on Dec. 21, 1636, succeeding Roger Williams (q.v.). The congregation was pulled together again by a covenant similar to the one he had advanced in Rotterdam. He was much caught up in the political-religious life of the colony, encouraging fisheries, trade, shipbuilding, and peaceful relations with Indians. He was on the committee (appointed Nov. 20, 1637) to found what became Harvard College, later acting as an overseer of theses, and he was involved in the examination and trial of Anne Hutchinson in Nov. 1637-Mar. 1638. It was also his duty to excommunicate Roger Williams out of the Salem congregation in 1640 as a Baptist. Sometime before Sept. 1639, he married Deliverance Sheffield, a widow, who bore him a child, Elizabeth (baptized Oct. 1, 1640, in Salem). Deliverance apparently went insane, but survived him. Elizabeth married Thomas Barker, at All Hallows, Londonwall, in 1665, and claimed Peter's Salem estate in 1703. In Jun. 1641 the General Court of Mass. deputed Peter, Thomas Welde (q.v.) (minister at Roxbury and coauthor of the *Bay Psalm Book*), and William Hibbins (a Boston merchant) to make financial arrangements for the colony with English creditors, to act as envoys to congratulate the leaders of the Long Parliament for their actions against the monarchy and Laud, to offer advice "for the settling of the right form of church discipline," to promote the cotton trade with the W. Ind., and to further emigration and investments. They sailed from Boston on Aug. 3, 1641. While en route, Peter was also commissioned to negotiate with the Dutch East India Company concerning boundaries, molestations, transference of territories, and governmental and religious cooperation. John Winthrop called him in his journal "a man of a very public spirit and singular activity for all occasion," and a twelve-line poem by Edward

Johnson (q.v.), in his *Wonder-Working Providence*, talks of "bold Peters" fighting "In Wildernesse for Christ": "It matters not though the world on thee do frown."

Peter immediately got caught up in the Civil Wars and religious reforms that were being waged in Eng., serving as regimental envoy in Ire. (1642) and on several commissions as well as becoming a leader of the Independents. Among the things accomplished as agent for the Bay colony was his publication with Thomas Welde of *New Englands First Fruits*, the aim of which was to attract settlers to New Eng. The work provides descriptions of the land, agriculture, climate, religious life, and Harvard. Peter also compiled the three tracts called *Church-Government and Church-Covenant Discussed*, the first part written largely by Richard Mather (q.v.), the second by Peter, and the third by John Davenport (q.v.), with an introduction. The commission from the colony was successful in obtaining monies for trade, removing duties on goods for home consumption, and acquiring financial backing for Harvard. The attempt to secure a patent for the Narragansett lands (Jul. 1643) led to a forged patent by Welde that unsuccessfully challenged Williams's right to the land. Peter and Welde joined the Corporation for the Promoting of the Gospel of Jesus Christ in New England, created by Parliament on Jul. 27, 1649. A letter from the corporation in 1651 expresses satisfaction with their work. Parliament's vote of financial support for Indians, who might potentially become members of the congregation, in 1654, was opposed by Peter who wanted the money to be used for the needy who were already members of the church. He had been ordered home in 1645, and in 1654 continued hope for his return was expressed by the General Council.

Peter did not return. He became chaplain to Cromwell, and the remainder of his life was spent in trying to establish and further the Interregnum government. He was excepted from the Act of Free and General Pardon, Indemnity, and Oblivion (Aug. 29, 1660), being tried on Sept. 13 and executed on Oct. 16. *Mercurius Publicus* (for Oct. 15-22, 1660, pp. 678-679) reported that his execution "was the delight of the people; which they expressed by several shouts and acclamations, not onely when they saw him go up the Ladder, and also when the Halter was putting about his Neck; but also when his head was cut off, and held up aloft upon the end of a Spear." His head was displayed on a pole on London Bridge; his body was dismembered and hung on the gates.

Critical Appraisal: Hugh Peter's concerns were religious, not theological. His theology was orthodox and simple, and he proposed no system. He was concerned, rather, with the structure and membership of the church, stressing the process of conversion, duty, and Christian liberty, by which he meant an ordered freedom with self-limiting impositions. There was toleration of opposite views, but no acceptance of them within his congregation. Important was ideal law, innate natural law. Like most Puritans of the period, he believed in a providential interpretation of history and English Puritanism as the forerunner of the kingdom of God. His first published work, *Milk for Babes*, is a catechism of spiritual instruction, with marginal guides, in direct language and systematic organization. *God's Doings and Man's Duty* is a sermon laying forth his view of the current political affairs on the eve of the second Civil War. The New Model Army, as saints of the church, had been preserved, and the endeavors of the king and his proud followers had come "to nothing but vanity and emptiness." An aim of the sermon was to head off dissension among the Parliamentarians, not all of whom accepted the ideas of the Independents and the New Model Army. In *Good Work for a Good Magistrate*, the most complete statement of his views, he offered "True Religion Maintained and Advanced by the Magistrate, and Walked in by the People," "True Mercy," and "True Justice and Righteousness" as God's ways and means "to bring any Nation to, and preserve them in, as happy a condition as this world can afford." These last two works indicate Peter's concern with the structures of religion and with the earthly kingdom required before the millennium might advance. *The Case of Mr. Hugh Peters* is a petition to the House of Lords (Jul. 13) for his release from certain execution, with a narration of his activities since his return to Eng. He denied complicity in the beheading of Charles I, but it is clear he was warping the truth. His last work, *A Dying Father's Last Legacy*, is the only publication of his in America before 1800 (dated 1717). His legacy to Elizabeth is his belief in the reformed Church of God and the Gospel of Christ; his advice—avoid the world and embrace union with Christ. Peter's style in all of his works, whether polemical or not, is simple and direct, built on concrete images and almost aphoristic statement. The organization is clear and logical. He was a practical stylist, conditioned by his intents.

Suggested Readings: CCNE; DAB; DNB; FCNEV; Sprague (I, 70-75); T$_1$. *See also* CMHS, 4th ser., VI, 103-108 (letters from Peter); J. B. Felt, *Memoir, or Defence of Hugh Peters* (1851); William Harris, *An Historical and Critical Account of Hugh Peters* (1751); J. R. Hutchinson, "The Ancestry of Hugh Peter or Peters," NYGBR, 48 (1917), 68-75, 180-185; Samuel E. Morison, "Sir Charles Firth and Master Hugh Peter with a Hugh Peter Bibliography," HGM, 39 (1931), 121-140; J. Max Patrick, "The Arrest of Hugh Peters," HLQ, 19 (1956), 348; idem, *Hugh Peters, A Study in Puritanism* (1946); E. P. Peters and Eleanor Bradley Peters, *Peters in New England* (1903); Samuel Peters, *A History of the Rev. Hugh Peters, A.M.* (1807); PMHS, passim, esp. 1st ser., X, 19 (letter from Peter); 2nd ser., VIII, 118-122; 3rd ser., XLII, 219-224, 230-231, 261-266; Raymond P. Stearns, *The Strenuous Puritan: Hugh Peter, 1598-1660* (1954); William Yonge, *England's Shame: Or, The Unmasking of a Politick Atheist: Being a Full and Faithfull Relation of That Grand Imposter, Hugh Peters* (1663).

John T. Shawcross
University of Kentucky

SAMUEL A. PETERS (1735-1826)

Works: *Reasons Why Mr. Byles Left New London* (1768); *A Sermon, Preached at Litchfield, in Connecticut, Before a Voluntary Convention of the Clergy of the Church of England* (1770); "Genuine History of Gen. Arnold by an Old Acquaintance," *The Political Magazine, and Parliamentary, Naval, Military and Literary Journal* (1780); "Account of the Dungeon of Symbury Mines in Connecticut, with an Engraved Sketch of That Rebel Prison for the Loyalists," *The Political Magazine* (1781); *A General History of Connecticut* (1781); "History of Jonathan Trumbull, the Present Rebel Governor of Connecticut," *The Political Magazine* (1781); *Reply to Remarks on a Late Pamphlet. Entitled a Vindication of Governor Parr* (1784); *An Answer to Dr. Inglis's Defense of His Character* (1785); *A Letter to the Rev. John Tyler, A.M. Concerning the Possibility of Eternal Punishments* (1785); *A Sermon Preached at Charlotte Chapel, Pimlico...on the Death of Thomas Moffatt* (1787); *The Will of Man Regulated and Made Perfect by the Wisdom of God* (1788); *A History of the Reverend Hugh Peters* (1807).

Biography: Samuel Andrews Peters was born in Hebron, Conn., on Nov. 20, 1735. After graduation from Yale College in 1757, Peters went to Eng. to receive holy orders in the Anglican Church. Appointed as a missionary by the Society for the Propagation of the Gospel in Foreign Parts, he returned to Hebron, where he served as rector of the Anglican parish from 1760 to 1774. His aggressive high church Anglicanism, political Loyalism, and ostentatious lifestyle provoked suspicion and animosity, and this hostility intensified in the summer of 1774, when he led the opposition against Governor Jonathan Trumbull's request that Conn. towns raise contributions to aid Boston (which was being punished for the Tea Party). After confrontations with patriot groups in Hebron, Peters fled to Boston, where he involved himself in further controversy. In Oct. 1774, he sailed for Eng.

Supported by a small pension from Parliament, Peters devoted much of his time to writing and held no clerical post during the remainder of his life. After struggling unsuccessfully for a Canadian bishopric, Peters was elected bishop of Vt. in 1794 but was unable to gain consecration. In 1804 he lost his pension after a quarrel with Prime Minister William Pitt. Peters's disillusionment with the English church and government led him to return to N.Y. in 1805 to pursue his claim to the Carver land. He had earlier befriended a dying American explorer, Jonathan Carver (q.v.), who bequeathed to Peters an immense tract of land around present-day Minneapolis, which Carver claimed he had received from two Indian chiefs in 1767. Peters's grandiose but unsuccessful schemes for this "Petersylvania" occupied his last twenty years. He died impoverished in N.Y. on April 19, 1826, at the age of 90.

Critical Appraisal: Samuel Peters's writings not only reflected the controversies that filled his life but also provoked further contention. Usually prompted by emotion-laden events and issues, his published works were often polemical and included scurrilous attacks against his enemies—individuals or institutions—and considerable self-glorification, frequently with callous disregard for the truth.

Before his exile in Eng., Peters published a pamphlet, a sermon, and some brief exchanges in newspapers. These writings displayed a strident Anglicanism and a concomitant attack on New Eng. Puritanism. As a Loyalist exile in London, Peters devoted the later years of the American Revolution to propagandizing the British public. His first literary effort was an article on Benedict Arnold (q.v.) in *The Political Magazine*, which specialized in wartime political propaganda. In this biographical sketch, Peters deceptively portrayed himself as an "old acquaintance" of Arnold from pre-Revolutionary Conn. The account was generally complimentary, although Peters noted some character defects. But his pen was far more vitriolic in an essay on Jonathan Trumbull, the governor of Conn. Trumbull, Peters's archenemy, was—according to Peters—responsible for most of the priest's woes. After casting doubt upon Trumbull's legitimacy, financial integrity, and political motivation, Peters described the persecution of Hebron's "extremely popular" missionary, "the Revd. Mr. Peters," and laid the principal blame upon the governor.

Many of the themes from these earlier writings reappeared in the anonymous *History of Connecticut* (1781), Peters's most significant and controversial work. This history, the first significant narrative of the colony, was an attempt to redress the neglect of Conn. by New Eng. historians. In the preface, Peters claimed he had written a dispassionate history, "unbiased by partiality or prejudice," and expressed hope that he would avoid "the danger of being accounted a deceiver." Peters neither achieved the impartiality he claimed nor avoided the epithet "liar" hurled at him by contemporary and later critics. Because of his exaggerations, distortions, and outright fabrications, Peters failed as historian. Nevertheless, he made important contributions to American folklore and literary history. Recent scholarship has emphasized this balanced view of Samuel Peters.

The first portion of the work, which narrated Conn.'s history to the time of the Stamp Act, was replete with muddled and inaccurate accounts of the early settlement and creations of Peters's febrile imagination—such as a purely fictitious triumvirate of Indian kings and the use of germ warfare against them by the missionaries. Despite the many distortions and travesties on historical fact in this part of the *History*, much of the controversy following the book's American publication in 1829 concerned its account of the "Blue Laws." Eventually, Walter Prince concluded in 1898 that Peters was essentially correct concerning the restrictive, Puritanical laws. Prince did not, however, exonerate Peters as historian, for he attributed Peters's numerous blunders to careless note taking and lack of critical reference and training that indicated "slovenly habits of a mind unmethodical in the extreme."

The middle and longest portion of the *History of Connecticut* included descriptions of the various settlements, flora and fauna, and religious and social practices of the colonists. The many tall tales in this section led literary critics to label Peters the Knickerbocker of Conn. and a forerunner of Mark Twain. Perhaps the most valuable service of Peters's *History* was the recording of legends, incidents, and curious customs of colonial Conn. Among the best known is his tale of the large army of bullfrogs that invaded the village of Windham, spreading panic among the inhabitants who believed the "Hideous noise" was an invading army of French and Indians. Peters's lighthearted description and endorsement of *bundling* (New Eng.'s courtship custom of unmarried couples sharing a bed without undressing) will always be delightful reading.

In the final section of the work, which covered the decade following the Stamp Act, Peters returned to his earlier vitriolic tone. He repeated his tale of the villainy of Jonathan Trumbull and predicted a chaotic future for a Conn. bereft of the restraining hand of Mother Country and Anglican Church.

The principal writings of Samuel Peters after the publication of his *History of Connecticut* were vituperative pamphlets against the successful candidate for the Canadian bishopric that Peters so dearly wanted in the 1780s and *A History of the Reverend Hugh Peters*, published after Peters returned to the U.S. In the latter work, he falsely claimed descent from a brother of Hugh Peter(s) (q.v.), the eminent Puritan divine. Much of the book is an analogy between the maligned character of Hugh Peter and the unjust treatment his supposed descendant received from the English church and government.

Samuel Peters's principal contribution to American literary history was his *History of Connecticut*. Although the work cannot be accepted as objective history, the controversy it engendered as well as its positive qualities—its pleasing anecdotal style, ready wit, and delightful tall tales—assure Parson Peters of a minor place in Americana.

Suggested Readings: CCNE; DAB; Dexter (II, 482-487); Sprague (V, 191-200); T_2. *See also* Kenneth W. Cameron, ed., *The Works of Samuel Peters of Hebron, Connecticut: New-England Historian, Satirist, Folklorist, Anti-Patriot, and Anglican Clergyman* (the most complete compilation of Peters's published writings; 1967); Sheldon S. Cohen, *Connecticut's Loyalist Gadfly: The Reverend Samuel Andrew Peters* (1976); Charles Mampoteng, "The Reverend Samuel Peters M.A. Missionary at Hebron, Connecticut, 1760-1774," HMagPEC, 5 (1936), 74-92; Samuel Middlebrook, "Samuel Peters, A Yankee Munchausen," NEQ, 20 (1947), 75-87; Walter F. Prince, "An Examination of Peters's 'Blue Laws,' " *Annual Report of the American Historical Association for the Year 1898* (1899); Lorenzo Sabine, *Biographical Sketches of the Loyalists of the American Revolution* (1864), II, 177-182.

Mary E. Quinlivan
The University of Texas of the Permian Basin

GEORGE PHILLIPS (1593-1644)

Works: *A Reply to a Confutation of Some Grounds for Infants Baptisme* (1645).

Biography: George Phillips was born in 1593, probably at South Rainham in Norfolk, Eng. He received a B.A. (1613) and an M.A. (1617) at Gonville and Caius College, Cambridge, and served as vicar at Boxted in Essex. But pressure to conform led him to join Governor John Winthrop (q.v.) on the *Arbella* bound for New Eng. On Apr. 7, 1630, the day before sailing, Phillips signed, and may have written, *The Humble Request*, a poignant declaration of continuing love for the Church of England and a denial of Separatist motives. Phillips's daughter Elizabeth and son Samuel (later minister at Rowley) survived the voyage, but his first wife died soon after they landed on Jun. 12. Phillips settled in Watertown, Mass., with Sir Richard Saltonstall. The church covenant was signed on Jul. 30, and Phillips served as minister until his death on July 1, 1644.

A learned man who read Latin, Greek, and Hebrew, and who, according to Cotton Mather (q.v.), "*read over the whole Bible six times every Year*," Phillips was also very independent. In 1631 he and church elder Richard Brown pronounced the disquieting view that "the churches of Rome were true churches," which brought Governor Winthrop to Watertown to debate them. In 1632 Phillips and Brown opposed taxation of Watertown by the governor and assistants to help pay for fortification of Newtowne (Cambridge), arguing "that it was not safe to pay moneys after that sort, for fear of bringing themselves and posterity into bondage": to this gesture, H. W. Foote traced "the beginning of representative government in Massachusetts," for although Phillips and Brown publicly recanted on Feb. 17, on May 8 a General Court arranged for "Every town" to select "two men to be at the next court, to advise with the governour and assistants about the raising of a public stock, so as what they should agree upon should bind all, etc."

Phillips is widely credited with being the first minister in Massachusetts Bay to practice Congregational Church polity. When in 1631, for example, Governor Winthrop and other officials were invited to intercede in a controversy over the fitness of Watertown's Elder Brown, Phillips asked them to come not as magistrates, but "as members of a neighbouring congregation only." Phillips displayed this same regard for local autonomy in his own dealings with other churches.

Throughout these episodes, Phillips never lost the respect of the civil authorities or of his colleagues. He was one of a group charged by the General Court with compiling laws for Massachusetts Bay, issued in the "Body of Libertyes" (1641). In 1642 he served on the first Board of Overseers of Harvard College. Thomas Shepard (q.v.), with whom, according to Mather, he had waged "a Controversy" with much "*Reason*, and yet Candor and Kindness" wrote the preface to his only published work. After Phillips's death, Governor Winthrop praised him as "a godly man, specially gifted, and very peaceful in his place, much lamented of his own people and others." His descendants included the founders of Phillips Exeter Academy and Phillips Academy, Andover, and the nineteenth-century abolitionist and orator Wendell Phillips.

Critical Appraisal: George Phillips explained in his introduction to *A Reply to a Confutation of Some Grounds for Infants Baptisme* that he was "provoked" into putting his ideas in print. He was surprised, his account goes, to come upon a book by Thomas Lamb, *A Confutation of Infants Baptisme* (1643), purporting to answer a treatise by Phillips that he had never written. Nathaniel Briscoe of Watertown had, it turned out, once asked Phillips to write down his views on the church and infants' baptism and then, without Phillips's knowledge, sent the notes to London to be refuted by Anabaptists. In *A Reply* Phillips set the record straight on both subjects.

A Reply is especially significant, since it sheds light on Phillips's attitude toward church discipline, ministerial ordination, and the sacraments. Phillips is best known for remarking, soon after he landed in Salem, that "if they will have him stand minister by that calling which he received from the prelates in England, he will leave them." [From Samuel Fuller to William Bradford (q.v.), June 28, 1630]. Scholars usually cite this comment as evidence of Phillips's Separatist bent, an interpretation at odds with his having endorsed *The Humble Request*; others, trying to reconcile these facts, have suggested that by "leave" Fuller meant "permit" or "allow."

Whatever the correct sense of Fuller's quotation, *A Reply* reveals the essential consistency of Phillips's thought. He held that the form of rites and sacraments was less important than the spiritual truth they signified: the imposition of hands, although not required, was "a comely and convenient rite"; "dipping" and "sprinkling" were equally efficacious practices Phillips found pointless to dispute. Like most of New Eng.'s leading divines, he believed that baptism, although no guarantee of grace, was necessary to propagate the churches. Once instituted, the churches remain "true churches, so long as God continues his dispensation towards them"—no matter how "defiled"—until Christ comes to judge the world; "they remain entirely equall among themselves, and all equally subordinate unto Jesus Christ." Thus Phillips squared God's sovereignty and human imperfection with the Congregational way.

Phillips did not live to see *A Reply* published. But his views on extending the benefits of baptism were quoted during the Synod of 1662 as the New Eng. clergy hammered out the Half-Way Covenant. The work of an important shaper of early colonial affairs and Congregational polity, *A Reply* deserves wider attention.

Suggested Readings: CCNE; DAB; DNB; Sprague (I, 15-17). *See also* Henry Wilder Foote, "George Phillips, First Minister of Watertown," PMHS, 63 (1930), 193-227; David D. Hall, *The Faithful Shepherd: A History of the New England Ministry in the Seventeenth Century* (1972), pp. 103-105, 146; E. Brooks Holifield, *The Covenant Sealed* (1974), p. 147; Cotton Mather, *Magnalia Christi Americana* (1702), III, 82-84; Perry Miller, *Orthodoxy in Massachusetts: 1630-1650* (1933), pp. 134, 135, 153, 201, 204; Edmund S. Morgan, *The Puritan Dilemma: The Story of John Winthrop* (1958), pp. 52-53, 98, 107-108; Samuel Eliot Morison, *The Founding of Harvard College* (1935), p. 327; Williston Walker, *The Creeds and Platforms of Congregationalism* (1893, 1960), pp. 251-252, 307.

Wesley T. Mott
University of Wisconsin at Madison

THEOPHILUS PICKERING (1700-1747)

Works: *The Reverend Mr. Pickering's Letters to the Reverend Nathaniel Rogers, Mr. Daniel Rogers of Ipswich and Mr. Reverend Davenport* (1742); *Reply to a Request for a Church Meeting with Regard to Charges Against Him*

(1744); *Short Letter* (1744; rep. in *Letter to the Separated Brethren from the Second Church*, 1748); *Mr. Pickering's Letter to Mr. Whitefield* (1745); *Letter to Ebenezer Cleaveland* (1746); *Bad Omen to the Churches of New England* (1747); *Supplement to Bad Omen* (1747); *Pretended Plain Narrative* (finished by Second Church members after his death; 1748); *Journal* (now lost but quoted in *Two Centuries of Church History*; 1884).

Biography: Theophilus Pickering, son of Salem, Mass., farmers John and Sarah Pickering, was born on Sept. 28, 1700. He graduated from Harvard College in 1719, taught school in Bridgewater for three years, attended Cambridge University for a second degree, and then embarked on a career as a minister. After preaching in Bridgewater in the fall of 1721, he was sent by the province to preach to the unwilling Baptists and Quakers of Tiverton. The following year, he made an unsuccessful attempt at the Charleston pulpit. Pickering was not to get his start until 1725 when the death of John Wise (q.v.) created a vacancy in the Second Church of Ipswich in the Chebacco parish. Pickering served as the Chebacco parish minister for the remaining twenty-two years of his life.

Pickering's ordination at Chebacco on Oct. 13, 1725, signaled the beginning of a successful, but turbulent, ministry. At the root of Pickering's troubles was the Great Awakening: the eighteenth-century religious movement that called for a return to a fire and brimstone theology. Claiming that the followers of the Awakening were enthusiasts who whipped up artificial hysteria, Pickering attempted through public letters and religious tracts to prevent the New Light theologians from invading his parish. He was opposed throughout his attempts by a strong Chebacco faction of New Lights who accused Pickering of neglecting his ministerial duties. He died of a fever in 1747, leaving uncompleted a pamphlet opposing the formation by the New Lights of a Fourth Church in Ipswich.

Critical Appraisal: Through his letters and religious tracts, Theophilus Pickering established himself as one of the foremost opposers of the Great Awakening in the early eighteenth century. From 1742 to 1747, Pickering vehemently and openly opposed the attempt of New Light theologians to set up a church in Ipswich. During much of this time, the security of his ministerial position was in question as a result of his vocal opposition to the New Lights. But Pickering's belief in the danger of New Lightism was so strong that he relentlessly confronted New Light supporters with letters and position papers, some of which were published in the *Boston Gazette* and *Boston Evening Post*. At the center of his argument is the belief that New Light "enthusiasm" was a threat to the Calvinistic teachings of the New Eng. religions.

Pickering's staunch opposition to New Light theology is particularly evident in his argumentative series of five letters in 1742 to Nathaniel and Daniel Rogers and Rev. John Davenport (q.v.). The correspondence to the Rogers clan tried to trap the brothers into admitting that their goals and methods were foreign to the New Eng. Way. In the first letter of the series, Pickering asked the Rogers brothers for a distinction between their religion and that of the New Eng. fathers;

he inquired whether their religious ways were different from Calvinism and whether these differences were explained by the Scriptures. The Rogerses' response was evasive and noncommittal, prompting Pickering to counter with a long series of accusations that filled the subsequent letters. Pickering argued that the New Light theology was contradictory to the New Eng. Way because it depended too much on remarkable occurrences and effects and was too evangelical a religion to be supported by the Scriptures. He called it a religion of "doubtful meaning and dangerous tendency." The final letter in the series registers a protest against the intrusion of the New Light theologian John Davenport in Ipswich. The letter, printed in the *Boston Evening Post*, Sept. 6, 1742, identified Davenport as an itinerant preacher who was escorted out of the Conn. colony for disturbing the peace. At the time of the letter, Davenport was preaching for Nathaniel Rogers in Ipswich; he and the Rogers brothers successfully sustained the New Light base in Ipswich despite Pickering's opposing efforts.

Pickering's subsequent letters and religious tracts reflect a man desperately trying to hold on to his parish by voicing his genuine concern over the dangerous threat posed by New Lightism. A letter in 1745 politely informs George Whitefield (q.v.) that his ministerial ways are dangerously enthusiastic. His 1746 letter to Ebenezer Cleaveland, who was admonished and expelled from Yale for New Lightism, asked Cleaveland why he was invading Pickering's Chebacco parish. A year later, *Bad Omen* and *Supplement* attempted to unify all of the Ipswich churches against the establishment of a Fourth Church, the New Light church. Later in 1747, he began, but did not finish, a pamphlet in protest against the ordination of John Cleaveland (q.v.) over the Fourth Church, the New Light church. After he died, his Second Church parishioners completed and published the tract; in it they add that Pickering was a "learned, orthodox, prudent, faithful Minister of Jesus Christ, tho' not without Failings."

Pickering's contribution of letters and religious tracts places him among the New Eng. ministers of the eighteenth century who attempted to avoid the intrusion of New Light theology. These ministers feared that New Eng. was shifting away from its religious roots. Many of these ministers, like Pickering, failed; New Light factions quickly gained support in New Eng. A few years after Pickering's death, the Second Church, which he ministered for twenty years, reunited with the Fourth Church, the New Light church. Had he been alive, Pickering most certainly would have been expelled by a New Light majority.

Suggested Readings: CCNE; Sibley-Shipton (VI, 289, 309, 331-336, 557-558); Sprague (I, 458-459). *See also* [John Cleaveland], *The Chebacco Narrative Rescu'd* (assigned to Pickering by Charles Evans but probably the work of Cleaveland; 1738, 1748); *Cleaveland Manuscripts*, I, 15; Daniel Giddinge, *Broadside* (on the Chebacco controversy; 1748); *Massachusetts Archives*, XII, 492-501, 554, 620-625, 645-647; *Two Centuries of Church History; Celebration of the Two Hundredth Anniversary of the Organization of the Congregational Church and Parish in Essex* (1884); Thomas F. Waters, *Ipswich* (1917), II, 97.

Donna Casella Kern
Michigan State University

ABRAHAM PIERSON (c. 1608-1678)

Works: "Lines on the Death of Theophilus Eaton" (c. 1658); *Some Helps for the Indians* (1658-1659).

Biography: Abraham Pierson (also spelled *Peirson*) is a somewhat baffling figure to the student of biography, for although the outline of his life is generally known, the details are often mysterious. His birthdate is a case in point. Traditionally assigned as 1608, 1609 seems a likelier date on the basis of his baptismal date of Sept. 23, 1609. Similarly, his place of birth is unknown, although the likelihood is that he was born in Bradford, Yorkshire, Eng., since he was baptized there. He graduated A.B. from Trinity College, Cambridge, in 1632, and later that year was ordained deacon at the Collegiate Church in Southwell, Nottingham. Trinity College was the intellectual home of the most Puritan wing of the Church of England, and it is likely that Pierson learned there the staunchly Puritan religious bias that was never to leave him. In the first of many moves that were to characterize his entire life, he left Southwell for the more bracing Puritan atmosphere of the infant colony of Mass., where he was admitted to the Boston church in 1640. After a short sojourn at Lynn, Mass., he moved in the same year to what would later be Southampton, Long Island, where he became first pastor of the church. His son Abraham was probably born (c. 1645) in Southampton, although again the records are confusing; the boy may have been born as early as 1640 in Lynn. Abraham, Jr., was later to be the first rector of the Collegiate School in the colony of Conn. (1701-1707), later Yale University.

In 1647 Pierson moved to Branford, Conn. (then part of New Haven colony), where he became pastor of the church. The move was apparently brought about by Southampton's decision to join forces with the Conn. colony (previously Southampton had been associated with New Haven), whose more liberal theological views Pierson rejected. From this time on, Pierson was a stalwart opponent of union with Conn., and when the two colonies united in 1665, Pierson and a group of his more conservative parishioners moved (1667) to Newark, N.J. Pierson stayed in Newark as pastor of the church until his death in 1678.

During his lifetime, Pierson was associated with many of the more conservative members of the New Eng. establishment, including the Rev. John Davenport (q.v.), the merchant-administrator Theophilus Eaton (who with Davenport drew up the laws for the infant New Haven colony, and whose death Pierson was to commemorate in verse), and the famous John Eliot (q.v.), "Apostle to the Indians," whose example Pierson was to follow both by preaching to the Indians and in his major work *Some Helps for the Indians* (1658-1659).

Critical Appraisal: Pierson's significance to early Conn. was not primarily literary. Indeed, he published only two works during his lifetime, the poem "Lines on the Death of Theophilus Eaton" (c. 1658) and the prose catechism *Some Helps for the Indians* (1658-1659), both during his long residence in Branford. The "Lines," a long (thirty-one stanza) and complimentary eulogy to his friend Eaton, holds little interest for the contemporary reader. The poem smacks of having been written to order and is conventional to the extreme. Moreover, Pierson had no real genius for poetry, and although the assessment of some later readers that the poem is "doggerel" is perhaps unkind, nevertheless it cannot be considered in any way distinguished.

Some Helps for the Indians is a different matter. This catechism is an interlinear rendering into Quiripi, an Indian dialect, of a series of questions and answers that hopefully will lead the Indians toward acceptance of the Christian faith. The work is redolent of the influence of the "Apostle" Eliot, who may have had a hand in it. Yet it is also a curious mixture of Puritanism with an almost Deistic view of religion, as suggested by the long title, which indicates that the *Helps* will teach the Indians how to use their "natural reason" toward discovery of the true God. *Some Helps* begins with a statement of the so-called Argument from common consent, in which Pierson's Indian audience apparently believed, that God exists because mankind uniformly believes in his existence. From there it works via the Socratic method through various doctrinal points toward the ultimate conclusion that the existence of the Christian God and the Christian religion is the only reasonable conclusion to such theological disputations. Of particular interest is the fact that this work obviously was meant to be read aloud to Indian audiences, presumably by other preachers, whose familiarity with the language was not so extensive as Pierson's. The Quiripi language is rendered phonetically, and aids to its pronunciation are included at the front of the volume. The catechism bears eloquent witness to the strength of the feeling on the part of many New Englanders of the time (a feeling later swept entirely away by the carnage of King Philip's War, 1675-1676) that the first duty of godly Puritans was the salvation of the souls of their Indian brethren. *Some Helps* does not pretend to be a literary masterpiece or, for that matter, to have any purely "literary" content at all. Nor does it; yet it remains an interesting monument to one man's faith and his society's hopes.

Suggested Readings: CCNE; DAB; DNB; FCNEV; Sprague (I, 116-118). *See also* Benjamin Trumbull, *A Complete History of Connecticut, Civil and Ecclesiastical* (1818).

James K. Folsom
University of Colorado at Boulder

CHARLES PINCKNEY (1757-1824)

Works: *Three Letters Addressed to the Public Chiefly in Defense of a Permanent Revenue for the Continental Congress of Confederation* (1783); *Observations on the Plan of Government Submitted to the Federal Convention in Philadelphia on the 28th May, 1787* (1787); *Three Letters, Written, and Originally Published Under the Signature of a South Carolina Planter. The First, on* *the Case of Jonathan Robbins; the Second, on the Recent Capture of American Vessels by British Cruisers; the Third, on the Right of Expatriation* (1799); *Observations to Show the Propriety of the Nomination of Colonel James Monroe to the Presidency of the United States by the Caucus at Washington... by a South-Carolinian* (1816).

Biography: Charles Pinckney was born in S.C. in 1757. His father was a wealthy planter and lawyer and other family members included Charles Cotesworth Pinckney and Thomas Pinckney, who were his second cousins. Pinckney became an attorney and fought for the American cause during the Revolution. After serving briefly in the state House of Representatives, Pinckney became a delegate to the Congress of the Confederation in 1784. A strong nationalist, he played a key role in the calling of a general convention to revise and amend the Articles of Confederation. A delegate to the Constitutional Convention, Pinckney made a significant contribution to the content of the new Constitution, adopted by the Convention in Philadelphia in 1787. Between 1798 and 1808, he was elected to four terms as governor of S.C. During that same period, he was elected to the U.S. Senate (1798-1801) and appointed minister to Spain (1801-1805). During the presidential election of 1800, Pinckney played the decisive role in carrying S.C.'s electors for Thomas Jefferson (q.v.). His opposition to his cousin, Charles Cotesworth Pinckney, for the vice-presidency in this election made him an outcast among many of his relatives. During his last term as governor (1806-1808), Pinckney supported an amendment to the state constitution providing additional representation to the backcountry in the legislature and also initiated another amendment establishing universal white male suffrage. After serving two terms in the General Assembly, Pinckney was elected to the U.S. Congress in 1818. While in Congress, he became one of the leading opponents to the proposed Missouri Compromise. Pinckney declined to run for a second term and died in 1824.

Critical Appraisal: Charles Pinckney's literary contributions were primarily political. A strong nationalist following the Revolution, Pinckney became the leading exponent of Jeffersonian Republicanism in S.C. His first literary pursuits were devoted to pointing out the weaknesses of the Confederation system of government (*Three Letters Addressed to the Public... Confederation*) and defending the new federal constitution (*Observations on the Plan of Government Submitted to the Federal Convention in Philadelphia...1787*). In the latter pamphlet, Pinckney not only expounded the many virtues of the Constitution but also went to great pains to identify himself as the major author of that important document. Although Pinckney was not the principal author of the Constitution, his contributions were significant. Pinckney not only presented one of the major frameworks of the new federal government to the Convention for consideration, but he also made many proposals—of which as many as thirty-two were incorporated as provisions in the final document.

In the summer of 1799, Charles Pinckney wrote a series of letters under the pseudonym of "A South Carolina Planter" that were published in the Charleston newspapers in Aug. of that year. These essays, which were later published as a pamphlet, dealt with the case of Jonathan Robbins. Robbins was a sailor who had been seized from a schooner in Charleston and jailed at the request of the British consul who charged that he was in fact Thomas Nash, an Englishman who was a mutineer on the frigate *Hermione* two years earlier. Robbins swore he was born in Danbury, Conn., and declared that he had been impressed and kept on the *Hermione* against his will until the mutiny. Despite this claim, Robbins was tried without a jury in the federal district court in Charleston and then turned over to the British government, which eventually had him executed. Pinckney took this opportunity to address the problem of the rights of American citizenship. Pinckney stated that the right of citizenship was so powerful that any question concerning it warranted a jury trial. He also took the opportunity to condemn both the English and the French for seizing American ships and seamen, despite treaties to the contrary.

Suggested Readings: DAB. *See also* W. S. Elliott, "Hon. Charles Pinckney of South Carolina," DBR, 33 (1864), 63; Andrew C. McLaughlin, "Sketch of Pinckney's Plan for a Constitution, 1787," AHR, 9 (1904), 735-747; George C. Rogers, Jr., *Charleston in the Age of the Pinckneys* (1969); Francis Leigh Williams, *A Founding Family: The Pinckneys of South Carolina* (1978); John H. Wolfe, *Jeffersonian Democracy in South Carolina* (1940).

George D. Terry
University of South Carolina

ELIZA LUCAS PINCKNEY (c. 1722-1793)

Works: Harriott Pinckney Holbrook, ed., *Journal and Letters of Eliza Lucas* (1850); Eliza Pinckney, ed., *The Letterbook of Eliza Lucas Pinckney, 1739-1762* (1972); *Eliza Lucas Pinckney to C. C. Pinckney, 1785* (1916).

Biography: Eliza Lucas Pinckney was born about 1722, probably in Antigua, W. Ind. Her father was Lt. Col. George Lucas, a wealthy planter, who later became lieutenant governor of that island. After being educated in Eng., she moved with her family to S.C. and settled on Wappoo plantation near Charleston. By 1740 Eliza Lucas's family had returned to the W. Ind., leaving her to manage the Lucas's four plantations in S.C. From 1741, through 1744, she experimented with the cultivation of indigo, assisted by a man her father sent from the island of Montserrat. In 1744, about the same time she was experimenting with the cultivation of indigo, she married Charles Pinckney, a prominent lawyer and wealthy planter. She continued her work with agricultural products including silk, flax, and hemp. Eliza Lucas Pinckney lived to see her sons Thomas and Charles Cotesworth become two of the most famous figures in S.C.'s history. She died in Philadelphia in 1793.

Critical Appraisal: Although none of Eliza Lucas Pinckney's writings were published during her lifetime, her letters and journals are a significant contribution to eighteenth-century American literature. Between 1739 and the time of her death, she wrote a prodigious number of letters to her family and friends. Despite two wars, fires, and other natural disasters that have occurred in the S.C. low country since then, much of her work still survives. As a historical record of life in eighteenth-century Carolina, it is invaluable. In her extremely detailed writings we find letters and notes concerning topics such as her management of her father's four low-country plantations, opinions on marriage, family relationships, difficulties with slaves, social gatherings, and the impact of the American Revolution on S.C. Perhaps the most important letter Eliza Lucas Pinckney ever wrote was one to her son Charles Cotesworth Pinckney in 1785. In it she related to him her recollections of her experiments with the cultivation of indigo. Although this letter was not published until 1916, it was used by contemporary writers such as David Ramsay (q.v.) to glorify her role in the development of indigo as a staple crop. By the time of her death, the legend that she alone was responsible for the introduction of indigo into S.C. was firmly established. This romanticized story has persisted for almost 200 years. Only recently have historians begun to separate fact from fiction and recognize that indigo had been grown in limited quantities in the colony as early as the 1690s. Despite Eliza Pinckney's important experiments with indigo, there were other individuals who also contributed to the crop's success as a staple.

Suggested Readings: DAB; LHUS; NAW. *See also* Sam S. Baskett, "Eliza Lucas Pinckney: Portrait of an Eighteenth-Century American," SCHM, 72 (1971), 207-219; David Leroy Coon, "The Development of Market Agriculture in South Carolina, 1670-1785" (Ph.D. diss., Univ. of Ill. at Urbana-Champaign, 1972); George C. Rogers, Jr., *Charleston, in the Age of the Pinckneys* (1969); Mrs. St. Julien Ravenel, *Eliza Lucas Pinckney* (1896); Francis Leigh Williams, *A Founding Family: The Pinckneys of South Carolina* (1978); Marvin R. Zahniser, *Charles Cotesworth Pinckney: Founding Father* (1967).

George D. Terry
University of South Carolina

ELIPHALET PORTER (1758-1833)

Works: *A Sermon Delivered to the First Religious Society in Roxbury* (1784); *A Discourse, Delivered Before the Roxbury Charitable Society* (1795); *A Sermon Preached at the Ordination of the Reverend John Pierce* (1797); *A Discourse, Delivered at Brookline* (1798); *A Sermon...Occasioned by the Death of His Excellency Increase Sumner* (1799); *An Eulogy on George Washington* (1800); *A Discourse Before the Society for Propagating the Gospel Among the Indians* (1808); *The Simplicity That Is in Christ* (1810).

Biography: Eliphalet Porter was born in 1758 in the North Parish of Bridgewater, Mass., the son of Rev. John Porter. Graduated from Harvard in 1777, he settled in Roxbury, Mass., where he was ordained as minister of the

First Church on Oct. 2, 1782. Porter was a member of the Academy of Arts and Sciences, an overseer of Harvard, an original trustee of the Massachusetts Bible Society, and one of the founders of the State Temperance Society. In 1807 Harvard awarded him a doctor of divinity degree. He died in 1833.

Critical Appraisal: Eliphalet Porter ministered to the First Church of Roxbury, Mass., during the fledgling years of the new nation. He had seen too much social and political change to believe that the new century would be calm. In 1810 he urged a convention of Congregationalist ministers to return to the "simplicity that is in Christ" and to study recent American history as diligently as they studied their Bibles. Throughout his sermons, Porter stressed historical events and common sense more than theology as the roots of human understanding.

In 1783 Porter delivered his sermon on *The First Day of Public Thanksgiving After the Restoration of Peace and the Acknowledgement of [America's] Independence*. Although he referred to the "American Israel" and to the hand of providence, he did not dwell on scriptural precedents or on theological points. Instead, he recounted many of the battles of the Revolutionary War and the injustices he believed the British dealt the colonists. "The increasing population, the growing opulence, and the rising importance of our land excited their avarice," he said. Porter reminded his listeners of the wrongs committed against them and the patriotic spirit with which they overcame difficult obstacles. Americans must not forget the struggles that earned them freedom.

Porter adopted a humble, pastoral tone while addressing his congregation. He did not feign humility so much as practice it, knowing full well that humility is more endearing and persuasive than a condescending tone. Porter's humility had rhetorical effect, but it was not merely a characteristic of his presentation. He believed in the inherent clarity of the Christian message: faith in Christ ensures eternal life. His sermons contained no visions of hell or retribution and avoided theological speculation. His point was simple and sincere: believe in Christ and you will live forever. His arguments were emotional rather than intellectual but did not play on his listeners' fears.

In the eulogy on George Washington (q.v.), delivered to the people of Roxbury a month after Washington's death, Porter melodramatically lamented the loss of the first president, who had "retired beyond the reach of his country's call, at which he so often came to her aid." Porter warned the country against an overt display of sorrow and then proceeded to mourn the dead leader with extravagant praise. Porter dwelled on historical details—Washington's military career and his political achievements.

"It is . . . from our own personal observation and experience of others, recorded in the page of faithful history, that we are most effectively taught the knowledge of human nature; and [learn] the soundest maxims of human conducts," he said in a Thanksgiving Day sermon. Porter's writing was invariably earth-bound. He displayed a wide-ranging knowledge of history, literature, and philosophy. More importantly, he displayed a sure knowledge of human nature. In spite of his assertions that human affairs are often chaotic, governments often corrupt, and sin unavoidable, his sermons were rooted in the present and designed to give his listeners hope for better living conditions in this world. Eternal life was presented as a natural extension of life on earth—a sort of historical event in every Christian's future.

Eliphalet Porter seems to have managed to surmount the challenges of a new country and a new century. His interest in current events and his position as minister would naturally have made him a community leader. Although his late sermons reveal a nostalgia for simpler church rituals, he appears not to have lost his concern for the families of his community and for the leaders of his nation.

Suggested Readings: Sibley-Shipton (XVII, 423); T_2. *See also Appleton's Cyclopaedia of American Biography* (1888), V, 77; *Catalog of Manuscripts of the Massachusetts Historical Society* (1969), V, 804.

Tracy Daugherty
University of Houston

JOHN PORY (1572-1636)

Works: *A Geographical Historie of Africa* (1600); *An Epitome of Ortelius* (1602); newsletters (w. 1606-1633; pub. 1849, 1977); *The Summe and Substance of a Disputation* (1630).

Biography: John Pory was born in Thompson, Norfolk, Eng., in 1572 and was graduated from Gonville and Caius College, Cambridge, in 1592. He studied under and assisted Richard Hakluyt in the preparation of the third volume of *Voyages* and in the same year published his own translation and edition of a history of Africa. As a member of Parliament from 1605 to 1611, he participated in the struggle of the House of Commons for greater power. Following extensive travel abroad, he served on the English ambassador's staff in Constantinople for three years and upon returning to Eng. was employed for a short time by the secretary of state. He traveled abroad again and in 1618 was chosen secretary of the Va. colony by Governor Sir George Yeardley, whose wife was Pory's cousin. At Jamestown in 1619, Pory was speaker of the first American legislature, which he organized along the lines of the English House of Commons. While in Jamestown, he went on several exploratory expeditions, once to the Potomac River and on another occasion down into what was to become N.C. He returned to London in 1623 but was back in Va. briefly the following year on a royal commission to investigate conditions there. After settling in London, he spent the remainder of his life as a newsletter writer, an occupation he had followed from time to time since 1606. He was associated with John Donne, Ben Jonson, and other literary figures in various ways in this and other capacities. Pory was buried at Sutton Saint Edmunds, Lincolnshire, where members of his family had lived for generations.

Critical Appraisal: In 1600 John Pory published his translation and enlargement of *A Geographical Historie of Africa* written before 1518 by Leo Africanus (John Leo). This work remained the standard source of information about Africa in English until early in the nineteenth century. Ben Jonson's *Masque of Blackness*, Shakespeare's *Othello* and *Antony and Cleopatra*, and John Webster's *White Devil* drew upon Pory's volume, and Sir Walter Raleigh cited it in his *History of the World*. Numerous standard words, not heretofore used in English, appear in Pory's translation or in his contributions to the work. His characterization of blacks also influenced English attitudes for over three centuries.

His *Epitome of Ortelius* is a tightly condensed version with maps of the great *Theatrum Orbis Terrarum* (1570) of Abraham Ortelius. It was designed to meet the needs of a rising body of literate people in Eng. who could not read Latin. Like his earlier work, this book was intended to help supply these people with the means of satisfying their new thirst for knowledge.

Perhaps the most significant of Pory's writing was his newsletters. Eng. had no printed newspaper until 1620. Both before and after that date, however, many leading men employed personal writers of news who remained in London if the employer were in the country or who went wherever necessary to gather significant news. From 1606 until near the end of his life, Pory was employed at various times in this occupation. His letters are filled with details of court life, government affairs, the doings of merchants and churchmen, gossip of assorted kinds, and especially of the Thirty Years' War. His letters from Jamestown have long been an important source of information about Eng.'s first permanent American colony, and his report of the proceedings of the first Assembly describes the beginning of representative government in America.

The Summe and Substance of a Disputation was prepared with the cooperation of Ben Jonson and relates a formal disputation between a Protestant and a Roman Catholic in Paris. The formal rules of such an encounter were strictly observed, and witnesses were present for both sides. The subject was one that continued to be discussed for many years: "that the bodie & blood of our Saviour be not in the Eucharist truelie according to the veritie and substance of the thing signified by those names, but the Eucharist is a signe & figure of it onlie."

Suggested Readings: DAB; DNB; T_1. *See also* William S. Powell, *John Pory, 1572-1636, The Life and Letters of a Man of Many Parts* (containing texts of all known letters by Pory, 1606-1633; 1977), printed presentation inscription laid in the copy of his *Geographical Historie of Africa* at Gonville and Caius College; proceedings of the 1619 Va. legislature (1619); Sir Benjamin Rudyerd's speech in Commons (Apr. 28, 1628); Roger Manwaring's submission; His Majesty's speech to Parliament, Jun. 26, 1628; "A true recitall of what hath passed between the Mareshall de Chomberg & the Marques of Santa Cruz when the siege of Casall was raised" (Oct. 30, 1630).

William S. Powell
University of North Carolina at Chapel Hill

THOMAS PRENTICE (1702-1782)

Works: *When the People* (1745); *The Vanity of Zeal for Fasts* (1748); *The Believer's Triumph Over Death* (1755); *Observations Moral and Religious, on the* . . .*Earthquake* (1756); *A Letter to the Rev. Andrew Croswell* (1771).

Biography: Minister of Arundel and Charlestown, Thomas Prentice was born on Dec. 9, 1702, in Cambridge, Mass. His father Thomas, a bookmaker, died in 1709, and his mother, Mary Boston, remarried in 1719. Thomas, Jr., then chose his uncle Solomon Prentice, a farmer, as his guardian. At Harvard he received a ten-pound Hollis Scholarship, became a "Hopkins Scholar" or "Hopkinton Bachelor," and was a "respondent" at the 1726 Commencement, which was "a very considerable scholastic honor." In 1729 he married Irene Emery of Wells, Mass., and was invited to preach at Arundel (Kennebunkport), Maine. After some exchange in which Prentice proved himself a fairly masterful bargainer, he was ordained Nov. 4, 1730. But Prentice acted haughtily among his parishioners and refused to teach the town school as his predecessor had done, although he is credited with introducing the potato to Arundel. On Jul. 19, 1738, he asked to be relieved of his duties, citing lack of security for his family in the face of an impending Indian attack. He was soon invited to become minister at Charlestown, Mass., where he remained. Four of Prentice's seven daughters died in childhood, and his wife, Irene, died Jun. 9, 1745, after delivering his son. He married Mrs. Mary Butman of N.Y. on Nov. 30, 1749.

Prentice opposed the Great Awakening and the itinerant preachers associated with it. He was active in the Society for the Propagation of Christian Knowledge Among the Indians of North America. An overseer of Harvard College, he attacked the college authorities for levity in the Commencement exercises, including the staging of a comedy and the lampooning of professions. Prentice died Jun. 17, 1782, "after tedious confinement from bodily disorders."

Critical Appraisal: The works of Thomas Prentice evidence an orthodox preacher immersed in the issues of his day. Prentice's letter to the Reverend Andrew Croswell supports that minister on the occasion of his being ridiculed by his students at Yale, who apparently mimicked their mentor, calling him "a madman" and "Merry Andrew." Croswell's troubles stemmed from his "extraordinary former conduct" in jumping from row to row and even from the balcony to the floor, and crying to people in the streets. Yet Prentice claimed that all preachers are reproached in the person of Croswell and that it is necessary to defend the character of the "divine Preacher upon whom depends the fate of religion." The letter is signed with a pseudonym: "Your brother in tribulation and patience, Simon, the Tanner."

In *When the People*, a sermon preached in "Thanksgiving. . . for the Taking of Cape Breton," Prentice found biblical parallels for the 1745 New Eng. victory at Louisbourg in the story of Israel's battle with Zabin, king of Canaan. He stated, "That it is a great and noble thing for the people, and particularly for the Rulers and chief Men among them, willingly to offer themselves to a military Expedition against their Enemies when the Safety and Welfare of their Country and Nation call for it." But he also claimed that victory "is of the Lord." In his sermon on *The Vanity of Zeal for Fasts*, Prentice castigated those who made fasts occasions for "low, base, and selfish Designs." He asserted that the genuine human objective should be not fasting, but mercy and righteousness shown to widows and orphans. What is wanted of people is genuine repentance and reformation. These things only can ward off judgment of God, which will break in regardless of fasting, and may be already present in war, the Court House fire, and the destruction of "publick Records of the Province and other useful and valuable writings." Prentice ended with an exhortation to live honestly, admonishing his audience that then "this will be a Fast that the *Lord* hath chosen. . . . And the sorrowful Occasion of our Fasts will be taken away, and they be turned into chearful Feasts."

Suggested Readings: CCNE; Sibley-Shipton (VIII, 81-89).

Virginia Levey
University of Central Arkansas

BENJAMIN PRESCOTT (1687-1777)

Works: *A Letter Relating to the Divisions in the First Church in Salem* (1734); *A Letter to a Friend, Relating to the Differences in the First Church in Salem* (1735); *Mr. Prescot's Examination of Certain Remarks* (1735); *A Letter to the Reverend Mr. Joshua Gee* (1743); *A Letter to the Reverend Mr. George Whitefield* (1745); *A Free and Calm Consideration* (1774).

Biography: Benjamin Prescott was born on Sept. 16, 1687, in Concord, Mass., son of Jonathan and Elizabeth (Hoar) Prescott. His father was a prosperous physician and a captain in the militia. After graduating from Harvard College (B.A., 1709; M.A., 1712), Prescott was ordained on Sept. 23, 1713, as the first minister of the newly gathered Third Congregational Church of Salem, Mass. By reason of changes in town borders, this church became the Second or South Parish of Danvers in 1752 and the South (or Old South) Church of Peabody in 1868. Prescott was married three times and outlived all three of his wives. Prescott's ministry closed with a bitter dispute with his congregation over the payment of his salary in inflated paper currency; on Nov. 16, 1756, he resigned from his pulpit. In 1761 Prescott became a justice of the peace, and he was active in the duties of this office for the rest of his life. He died on May 20, 1777, at Danvers (now Peabody); his estate included one female Negro slave.

Critical Appraisal: Benjamin Prescott's earliest publications deal with a bitter dispute that broke out in the early 1730s in the neighboring First Congregational Church of Salem, where a minority of the congregation accused the minister, Samuel Fiske, of altering the church records by an act of forgery. When

Fiske refused to call a congregational meeting to deal with this accusation, other churches convened a series of three church councils to deal with it. *Mr. Prescot's Examination* is a reply to an anonymous book defending Fiske. Alluding to the difficulties that had been encountered in attempts to persuade Fiske and his adherents to cooperate with the three church councils—Fiske had refused, on the grounds that he had never been given a full list of the offenses with which he might be charged—Prescott wrote: "This brings to my Remembrance the Story of the honest Country Man, who having a desire to pull off his Horse's Tail, stood in vain tugging at the whole of it; till his wiser Neighbour passing by, advis'd him to take a few Hairs at a Time: which good Advice being taken, he soon with ease accomplished his Design." That was how the church councils dealt with the Salem Church case: the members of the third Council agreed that they did not have to be given a full list of all of Fiske's alleged offenses in order to deal with some. Fiske's followers claimed to be shocked that a minister who was a gentleman would tell something as far beneath his dignity as the story of the horse's tail, but if that sort of rustic illustration was rarely used by ministers of the eighteenth century, it has become a staple of a great deal of ministerial discourse since then.

In May 1743 a majority of the Congregational ministers of Massachusetts Bay, at their Annual Convention in Boston, voted approval of a *Testimony* against various errors in doctrine and disorders in practice associated with the revivals of the Great Awakening. Although a clause was added ascribing to God all of the glory for "any special Revival of pure Religion in our Land," Joshua Gee (q.v.) thought that even this added clause stopped short of plainly acknowledging that there had in fact been any such revival anywhere in the land, and Gee published *A Letter to the Reverend Mr. Nathaniel Eels* (Jun. 3, 1743), criticizing the Convention's *Testimony*. Prescott's *Letter to Gee* is a reply to Gee's *Letter to Eels*. Defending the Convention, Prescott accused Gee of quibbling about a number of trivial points, including its designation of itself as consisting of "the Pastors of the Churches in the Province of Massachusetts-Bay," when some ministers from other provinces attended. Prescott pointed out that the outsiders did not affect the stand that the Convention took, since only six outsiders attended, with only two voting. Prescott criticized Gee for abusing those who opposed his viewpoint at the Convention. Gee's leading opponent at the Convention had been Charles Chauncy (q.v.), and Edwin Scott Gaustad declared that "Prescott attempted to discount all of Gee's charges with the affirmation that they were wholly the result of a personal grudge against Chauncy." One of Prescott's arguments in defense of the Convention was that persons living at a distance are in a position to evaluate a report of errors and disorders as factual, but are not in a position to affirm routinely, merely on the basis of other persons' testimonies, whether a reported revival of religion in a given church really is due to the direct influence of God's grace, instead of being a merely human phenomenon. Prescott claimed that the Convention, despite its refusal to endorse any particular case of revival as positively directed by God's Spirit, really did acknowledge the reality of revival in the land in the last paragraph of its *Testimony*. Gaustad took the position that "so much effort and vigorous language was required of Prescott to substantiate this claim that he succeeded only in revealing its absurdity."

In his *Letter to Whitefield*, Prescott joined the ranks of those who directed personal attacks against one of the leading revivalists of the Great Awakening. Interpreting selected passages from George Whitefield's (q.v.) *Life* and *Journals* in the worst possible light, Prescott piled up one *argumentum ad hominem* after another. According to Prescott, Whitefield ascribed to the inspiration of God's Spirit what might just as easily be given natural explanations as desires projected from his own human heart. Prescott suggested that Whitefield had not necessarily undertaken his extensive preaching journeys out of obedience to the clear will of God as revealed in the Scriptures: perhaps he had done so instead out of vanity and personal ambition, to receive applause and accumulate wealth. Most of us will probably agree with Prescott's view of the coincidence that Whitefield was born in an inn as a trivial parallel to the circumstances of the birth of Jesus. On the other hand, few persons living today will accept Prescott's accusation that Whitefield, in changing his course of studies at Oxford without the permission of his tutor, violated God's injunction that Christians "abide stedfast in that Station and Calling wherein God has set them." Prescott's most basic accusation, underlying all others, was that Whitefield was not really a "born-again" Christian: by his own testimony, his conversion to Methodism was not accompanied by spiritual regeneration.

> It appears. . . that you was deeply engaged, and that you approved your self a forward Disciple of Mr. *Wesley*, but however by his Example and Instructions, you might perhaps become a finished Methodist, and as such, a Creature of his forming and fashioning; yet still, if. . . your own Account is to be rely'd upon, you was not a new Creature, in the Gospel Sense. For you all this while was not bless'd with any Measure of true Poverty of Spirit, or that Humility which Christ has enjoin'd.

Whitefield, like his fellow grand itinerants, Gilbert Tennent (q.v.) and James Davenport, accused opponents of the Great Awakening of being unconverted and unregenerate, and Prescott was delighted to find passages in Whitefield's candid autobiographical disclosures suggesting the same of him.

Prescott's *Free and Calm Consideration*, published anonymously, is a collection of letters, 1768-1774, stating American grievances against the British Parliament. On the title page, Prescott identified himself as one born in the Massachusetts Bay Colony before the reign of William and Mary, perhaps to suggest that he was not a young radical. Comparing George III to a father, with Parliament and the American colonists as his children, Prescott interpreted the recent acts of Parliament as an elder brother's unjust interference in the affairs of his younger brothers. Instead of becoming defensive about the Boston Tea Party, Prescott employed the tactic of diversion, castigating the owners of the tea for their failure to seek satisfaction through normal legal channels. In these letters, most of which originally appeared in the *Essex Gazette*, Prescott demonstrated that he kept his mental powers intact in his old age.

Prescott's writings are flawed by occasional grammatical errors, as when he habitually wrote "you was" instead of "you were"; this particular lapse is especially jarring in his *Letter to Whitefield*, where it occurs many times. Emerson Davis called Prescott "a man of talent and an excellent pastor"; perhaps it should be added that he had a propensity for controversy. All of his published works were written and printed, sometimes anonymously, as acts of participation in ecclesiastical or political controversies, and a controversy over his salary cost him his pastorate. In his writings, he delighted in detecting and refuting the errors of his opponents. His reasoning was often that of the debater, with more zeal for winning points than for maintaining objectivity.

Suggested Readings: CCNE; Sibley-Shipton (V, 485-491); Sprague (I, 313). *See also* Emerson Davis, *Biographical Sketches of the Congregational Pastors of New England*, typescript, from a nineteenth-century ms., deposited in the Congregational Library, Boston, V, 65-66; Edwin Scott Gaustad, *The Great Awakening in New England* (1957), p. 64; Edward M. Griffin, *Old Brick: Charles Chauncy of Boston, 1705-1787* (1980), pp. 75-78; Harold Field Worthley, *An Inventory of the Records of the Particular (Congregational) Churches of Massachusetts Gathered 1620-1805*, HTS, 25 (1970), 472-475. On Samuel Fiske, see Davis, *Biographical Sketches*, IV, 351-352, and Sibley-Shipton (V, 413-424).

Richard Frothingham
University of Arkansas at Little Rock

BENJAMIN YOUNG PRIME (1733-1791)

Works: *The Unfortunate Hero* (1758); *The Patriot Muse* (1764); *A Song for the Sons of Liberty* (1765); *The Fall of Lucifer* (1781); *Columbia's Glory* (w. 1784; pub. 1791); *Muscipula sive Cambromyomachia* (1840).

Biography: Benjamin Young Prime (at birth his middle name was *Youngs*, his mother's maiden name, but he dropped the "s" as a young adult) was born in 1733 at Huntington, Long Island, N.Y. As an only child, he received an early personal and varied education from his father, Rev. Ebenezer Prime. This training prepared him well for the College of New Jersey (now Princeton University), then at Newark, where he continued his studies in language and science, the two fields that were to occupy him throughout his life. After graduation in 1751, he studied medicine as an assistant to Dr. Jacob Ogden of Jamaica, N.Y. In 1754 his alma mater awarded him an honorary M.A., and he spent the 1756-1757 academic year as a tutor at the college, which had been moved to Princeton since his student days. In the next few years, he practiced medicine in East Hampton and then in Huntington, and in 1760 he was awarded an honorary A.M. by Yale, largely in recognition of his continued scholarly pursuits in languages.

In 1762 Prime went abroad for study and travel, first receiving advanced training at St. Guy's Hospital in London and later taking the M.D. degree in 1764 from the University of Leyden. While abroad, he also continued his literary pursuits, publishing *The Patriot Muse* in London in 1764. By the end of that year, he resumed his medical practice in New York City, but by the early 1770s, he had returned to Huntington, partly because of his father's failing health. Forced to flee Long Island when the British gained control of part of the island, he and his family spent the war in New Haven, Conn., where they lacked both a permanent residence and a stable income. Despite the hardships, Prime remained a strong supporter of the colonial quest for independence, but a recurrent circulatory ailment prevented him from serving in the army.

At the end of the war, Prime returned to his ancestral home in Huntington only to find that it had been looted and extensively damaged by British troops. With deteriorating health and a diminished estate, he devoted his final years, with only partial success, to the recovery of his property and to the support of his wife and five children. In 1791 he died of apoplexy before his 58th birthday.

Critical Appraisal: As a writer of poetry for four decades, Benjamin Young Prime published approximately 200 pages of verse during his lifetime and left a comparable amount in manuscript form (his private papers are in the Prime Family Collection at the Speer Library of the Princeton Theological Seminary). As a whole, his writings mirror closely the times that produced them. In form, Prime generally followed the neo-Classical British poets, most often writing in heroic couplets or in what he, resembling Abraham Cowley, called "Pindaric odes." In subject matter, he wrote verses on the central figures and events of the two major wars during his lifetime. If his writings are conventional in form and often lack imagination, they, nonetheless, provide a poetical account, by an intelligent and well-educated observer, of the shift in colonial allegiances away from Br. Combining scholarship, patriotism, and piety, Prime's poems occupy a significant position in the literature of the Revolution and also serve, as C. Webster Wheelock has asserted, to fill a gap in American poetry between the Puritan poets and the Connecticut Wits.

Although he wrote poems as early as his college days, Prime did not publish any of his work until 1758, when *The Unfortunate Hero* appeared, containing two patriotic odes supporting Br. against Fr. The title poem, written in ten irregular stanzas, with many Classical allusions and conventions, praises the military exploits of Lord George Howe and laments his death in battle near Carillon. Accompanying this poem was "An Ode on the Surrender of Louisbourg," written in thirty-four six-line stanzas. Besides the differences in form, this poem varies considerably from the Howe ode in tone and mood, for it celebrates a British victory, not a British death. In the second poem, Prime emphasized that God is on the side of the British, exulting that "Our Cause is still the Care of Heav'n." This practice of discerning God's support for his side was to continue throughout Prime's career.

These two odes were printed again in 1764 as parts of a larger, more varied collection, *The Patriot Muse*. Most of the nineteen separate pieces of this collection show Prime's continued strong support of Br. against Fr. Several of the poems, such as "On General Braddock's Defeat" and "On the Surrender of Fort William-Henry," recount events of the recent war from the British perspective, the most partisan being "Britain's Glory, or Gallic Pride Humbled" on the British capture of Quebec in 1759. The collection ends with "On the Peace of Fontainebleau," in which Prime vehemently condemned the treaty as an "inglorious peace" and praised William Pitt for denouncing it. In addition to these poems on the war are several poems that show the experimentation and versatility of the young poet: "The Lamentation of Louis XV" in both French and English, two hymns, two elegies (one on N.J. Governor Jonathan Belcher and college president Aaron Burr (q.v.); the other on George II), two Latin translations from the Old Testament, and an acrostic on Pitt's name (for which Prime apologized in his preface). Prime also included in this collection a short poem in heroic couplets "On the Liberty of the Press," in which he advocated "the golden mean."

Although a strong supporter of Br. in *The Patriot Muse* in 1764, Prime began to shift his views during the Stamp Act crisis of 1765. In *A Song for the Sons of Liberty*, a broadsheet that apparently appeared several times in slightly different forms, Prime condemned the Stamp Act as an instrument to enslave the colonies. Full of internal rhyme and incremental repetition, this popular ballad made Prime a well-known rebel, for in it he strongly defended colonial freedoms and denied allegiance to Parliament, although granting the ultimate sovereignty of the king. The final stanza demonstrated both the form and theme of the work:

> The Birthright we hold, Shall never be sold,
> But sacred maintain'd to our Graves;
> Nay, and ere we'll comply, We will gallantly die,
> For we *must not* and *will not* be Slaves; *Brave Boys*,
> We *must not*, and *will not* be Slaves.

Curiously, after the relative success of this broadsheet ballad, Prime did not publish another work until 1781, when *The Fall of Lucifer* appeared. This poem of 104 quatrains in iambic pentameter is a thorough condemnation of Benedict Arnold (q.v.), comparing his fall to those of Cain and Judas as well as to Lucifer's. Although the meter is often rough and the tone perhaps overly vehement, the poem clearly demonstrates again Prime's combination of patriotism and theology, although now his allegiance is explicitly against the British. Apparently, in Prime's mind, when his allegiance turned from Br., so did God's. This poem also praises George Washington (q.v.) as a leader protected by heaven and predicts the ultimate glory and freedom of the colonies.

Prime developed these themes more fully in his most ambitious single poem, *Columbia's Glory, or British Pride Humbled*, which recounts the Revolutionary War and is a conscious parody of his earlier poem, "Britain's Glory." Written in 1784, but not published until 1791, this poem was Prime's only publication during his lifetime to appear under his name. Although lacking economy and imagination, it is partially successful. Over a fourth of its 1,441 lines are devoted to a moving tribute to Washington, full of historical and Classical allusions. The poem's ending plea for universal peace and freedom and an earlier speech by Columbia (the new nation personified) are also especially effective. In its vision of America's future and its stress on Divine Providence as the source of the recent American victory, the poem provides, as C. Webster Wheelock has noted, an early statement of the manifest destiny doctrine.

Columbia's Glory seems the high point of Prime's poetical career, but at his death, he left many diverse works among his papers. Approximately a dozen of these minor works appeared in 1840 in a collection edited by his son Nathaniel Scudder Prime, titled *Muscipula sive Cambromyomachia*. The title poem of this collection is Prime's Latin translation of Edward Holdsworth's mock epic on how the invention of the mousetrap saved Wales from a great invasion of mice.

Overall, Prime's poetry seems to merit attention more on historical and cultural than on literary grounds. As works that chronicle many crucial events in our nation's early political and military history and that also show how quickly colonial allegiances shifted, Prime's poems certainly deserve to be preserved.

Suggested Readings: DAB; P; T$_2$. *See also* L. M. Kaiser, *"Carmen Gratitudinis*: A Latin Tribute to President Aaron Burr by Benjamin Young Prime (1751)," HumLov, 26 (1977), 228-235; C. Webster Wheelock, "Benjamin Young Prime, Class of 1751: Poet-Physician," PULC, 29 (1968), 129-149; idem, "The Poet Benjamin Prime (1733-1791)," AL, 40 (1969), 459-471.

John S. Hardt
Ferrum College

THOMAS PRINCE (1687-1758)

Works: *Carmen Miserabile. A Solemn Lacrymatory* (1708); *God Brings to the Desired Haven* (1717); *Sermon Delivered by Thomas Prince* (1718); *An Account of a Strange Appearance in the Heavens* (1719); *Earthquakes the Works of God and Tokens of His Just Displeasures* (1727); *Morning Health No Security Against the Sudden Arrest of Death Before Night* (1727); *A Sermon on the Sorrowful Occasion of the Death of...King George* (1727); *Civil Rulers Raised Up by God* (1728); *The Departure of Elijah Lamented* (1728); *The Grave and Death Destroyed* (1728); *The People of New-England* (1730); *A Sermon at the Public Lecture in Boston* (1730); *The Vade Mecum for America: Or, A Companion for Traders and Travellers* (1731); *The Dying Prayer of Christ* (1732); *The Faithful Servant* (1732); *Young Abel Dead, Yet Speaketh* (1732); *Precious in the Sight of the Lord* (1735); *Christ Abolishing Death* (1736); *A Chronological History of New England*, 2 vols. (1736, 1755); *A Funeral Sermon* (1738); *The Sovereign God* (1744); *Extraordinary Events the Doings of God* (1745); *The*

Pious Cry to the Lord for Help (1746); *The Salvations of God in 1746* (1746); *A Sermon Delivered...in Boston* (1746); *The Fulness of Life* (1748); *The Natural and Moral Government and Agency of God* (1749); *God Destroyeth the Hope of Man* (1751); *Be Followers of Them, Who...Inherit the Promises* (1755); *Improvement of the Doctrine of Earthquakes, Being the Works of God, and Tokens of His Just Displeasure* (1755); *The Case of Heman Considered* (1756); *The Character of Caleb* (1756); *Psalms, Hymns, and Spiritual Songs of the Old and New Testament* (1758); *Extract of a Sermon* (1774); *Six Sermons* (1785); *Dying Exercises of Mrs. Deborah Prince* (1789).

Biography: Thomas Prince was born in Sandwich, Mass., on May 15, 1687. His father, Samuel Prince, was a merchant, and his mother, Marcy (Hinckley) Prince, was the daughter of Governor Thomas Hinckley (q.v.) of Plymouth colony. Tutored first by his parents, particularly his mother, and then by his maternal grandfather, Prince began early to show marked precocity, a trait that took him through several preparatory schools to Harvard, which he entered in 1703 at age 17. At Harvard several of Prince's early interests—especially history, theology, and the ancient languages—persisted, and several new interests—notably geography, astronomy, and medicine—developed. To serve these diverse interests, Prince soon began developing a great library, remnants of which now belong to the Boston Public Library.

Following graduation from Harvard in 1707, Prince returned to Sandwich and began teaching school, a job he soon found tiring. In Mar. 1709 he began a long journey that took him through Barbados to Eng., from there to Madeira and Barbados again, then back to Eng., where he decided to remain. In Eng. he visited London occasionally and preached in several churches, mainly in the south and east. In Jul. 1717 he returned to Boston, and in Oct. 1718 he was ordained as Joseph Sewall's (q.v.) colleague in the ministry of the Old South Church, Boston, where he continued to serve until his death in 1758. In Oct. 1719 he was married to Deborah Denny, a young woman he had met in Eng. and brought to Mass.

Although Prince remained conservative on all major theological issues, he retained his interest in science and regularly imported books on recent developments in science, medicine, and philosophy, adding them to a library that was already strong in literature, theology, and history. In addition to carrying out some experiments of his own, Prince became one of Boston's strongest advocates of inoculation against smallpox. On matters pertaining to polity and ritual, he also proved flexible. He supported the introduction of singing by note, reduced the number of sermons, and advocated religious toleration. Despite public and private pressure from other ministers and the press of Boston, he defended the Great Awakening and invited George Whitefield (q.v.) to preach at the Old South Church. Despite the controversies that his stand on such issues evoked, and the pain of seeing four of his five children die, he remained a loyal minister and a prolific writer. He died on Oct. 22, 1758, survived by his wife, Deborah, and a daughter, Sarah.

Critical Appraisal: Thomas Prince's published sermons are unusually erudite and elaborate, even for an age in which sermons were expected to show great learning and engage in careful "demonstrations." Among them are a variety of "occasional" sermons preached on days of thanksgiving or humiliation and a variety of "ceremonial" sermons preached at ordinations or funerals, including two preached for his own children. In the mid-1740s, he greeted news of British victories by writing a remarkable series of sermons that recounted recent European history for the purpose of demonstrating God's support of his chosen people. His edition of *The Bay Psalm Book*, which came late in his life, is noteworthy on two counts: it is based on faithfully literal, scholarly translations, and it is virtually unsingable. Like it, Prince's treatise on earthquakes and his pieces on other strange occurrences are museum pieces whose primary interest is that they show clearly the impact of enlightened ideas on the New World.

Prince's most distinctive work, and still his chief claim to our attention, is his unfinished *Chronological History of New England*. In it his purpose, as defined in his elaborate introduction, was to present in "orderly succession" the chief "Transactions and Events" of human history beginning with Adam, "year one, first month, sixth day." Shunning interpretation, he sought to make a "naked REGISTER" of "Facts in *Chronological Epitome*," without "artificial Ornaments" or other interpretive schemes that might "raise the imagination and affections." In addition, he proposed to rely, not on other interpreters, but only on original records and sources. Still, although it is clear that Prince's work represented vast effort sustained over many years, the judgment of his achievement has never been better than mixed. In part because the scale of his project was so grand and in part because the reception of his first volume, published in 1736, was so disheartening, he was twenty years publishing the second volume. Since his story as written ends in 1633, it ends near the beginning of the seventh great period of history that he delineated—namely, New Eng.'s climactic entrance— and so makes scant use of the unique collection of local materials he had so carefully gathered. Even so, his place among our early historians is secure, not only because of the vast scholarship that went into his work but also because he made clear the importance New Eng. attached to her own grand entrance upon "the stage of History."

Suggested Readings: CCNE; DAB; LHUS; Sibley-Shipton (V, 341-368); T₁. *See also* Sacvan Bercovitch, *The American Jeremiad* (1978), pp. 89-91; Benjamin B. Wisner, *The History of the Old South Church in Boston* (1830), pp. 22-31.

David Minter
Emory University

SAMUEL PURCHAS (1575-1626)

Works: *Purchas His Pilgrimage* (1613, 1614, 1617, 1626); *Purchas His Pilgrim* (1619); *Hakluytus Posthumus, or Purchas His Pilgrimes*, 4 vols. (1625); 20 vols. (rep., 1905).

Biography: Samuel Purchas was born into a prominent family in Thaxted, Essex, Eng., in 1575. He attended St. John's College, Cambridge, earning the M.A. in 1601, the bachelor of divinity in 1615. In 1601 he married Jane Lease and became curate of Purleigh, Essex; in 1604, he was appointed vicar of Eastwood; in 1614, when his new eminence as a writer gained him royal favor, he became chaplain to the archbishop of Canterbury and rector of St. Martin's, Ludgate. He died in 1626, one of the best known and most popular writers of his time.

Critical Appraisal: Samuel Purchas is now known chiefly for his *Pilgrimes*, a monumental, if badly flawed, work. His first publication, the *Pilgrimage*, however, was very influential. It quoted (in the 4th edition) nearly 1,400 sources, attracting the patronage of Sir Walter Raleigh, The East India Company, and King James, who read through its nearly 800 folio pages at least seven times. Moreover, the *Pilgrimage* inspired the romantic visions of both William Wordsworth and Samuel Taylor Coleridge and has been cited as one of the strongest defenses of British-Protestant expansionism ever written. The work aspired to survey all known religions "from the Creation unto the Present," and it attempted, awkwardly, to relate each faith to the geographical and historical circumstances of its founding. For this purpose, Purchas borrowed and paraphrased John Rolfe's (q.v.) *A True Relation of the State of Virginia in 1616*. The *Pilgrimage* clearly convinced thousands of fascinated Englishmen that America, in particular, deserved to be saved from barbarism and the spread of Catholicism (then being vigorously promoted by Spain and Portugal).

Purchas's next major work was the less successful *Pilgrim*, which purported to be no less than "the Historie of Man," and was designed to illustrate the "Wonders of his Generation," the "Vanities of his Degeneration," and the "Necessity of his Regeneration." This sort of parallelism and light wordplay is characteristic of a style that mingles Ciceronian ornateness with stern but plain moral exhortations and parenthetical prayers. Purchas made no effort to separate his primary passion for preaching from his avocation as a student of nature and travel; he admitted frankly to having traveled byways rather than highways in his works. The *Pilgrim*, finally, is a long and inconsequential work.

Purchas His Pilgrimes, originally published in four large volumes, deserves to be criticized for its moralizing, censorious tone, and countless instances of botched editing involving priceless sources. Having received all of Hakluyt's remaining manuscripts, plus the archives of the East India Company, Purchas altered them as he chose, usually for reasons of expense. Some of these abridgments were justified, but most were based on moral and political judgments unacceptable to most historians. Although history must be a "sworne witnesse" to truth, Purchas declared in "A Note Touching the Dutch" (vol. I), he would omit certain Dutch atrocities so as not to appear an "uncharitable Tale-bearer" or cause "discord betwixt Neighbors." He felt constrained as well to reword offensive reports or speeches, mainly when they were apt to give joy to the enemies of "our State and Religion."

It comes as no suprise, then, that the many narratives in the *Pilgrimes* that touch on America and its near neighbors are annotated copiously with Purchas's own moral evaluations: the Indians are barbarians, if superior to their would-be Catholic conquerors, and their culture contains no hint of civility, learning, or ethics. Purchas even feared that the Indians, who respect "little else but sensuality," shall multiply geometrically and take over the world. Buried inside the nineteenth volume of this enormous work is one of the few pieces written entirely by Purchas himself, "Virginias Verger, or A Discourse Showing the Benefits Which May Grow to the Kingdome from American-English Plantations." This remarkable essay reads like a sermon; it argues that Eng. has a moral duty to convert savages to her church. Now "more brutish than the beasts they hunt," the original Virginians, by giving up the riches of their land to the conquering English, shall profit more (spiritually, at least) than they ever dreamed possible. The very wealth of Va., and the fact of Br.'s access to it, are certain signs that Eng. has been chosen to lead the barbarians out of the wilderness. Purchas, a journalist and preacher, rather than a scholar, had a very large public and taught it well.

Suggested Readings: DNB; LHUS; T_1. *See also* Philip L. Barbour, *The Three Worlds of Captain John Smith* (1964); Alexander Brown, *The Genesis of the United States*, 2 vols. (1890); Douglas Bush, *English Literature in the Earlier Seventeenth Century*, 2nd ed. rev. (1962); George Brunder Parks, *Richard Hakluyt and the English Voyages* (1928); Boies Penrose, *Tudor and Early Stuart Voyaging* (1962); E.G.R. Taylor, *Late Tudor and Early Stuart Geography: 1583-1650* (1934; rep., 1962); Louis B. Wright, *Religion and Empire: The Alliance Between Piety and Commerce in English Expansion, 1558-1625* (1943).

James Stephens
Marquette University

WILLIAM PYNCHON (c. 1590-1662)

Works: *The Meritorious Price of Our Redemption* (1650); *The Jewes Synagogue* (1652); *The Time When the First Sabbath Was Ordained* (1654); *A Farther Discussion of. . .the Sufferings of Christ* (1655); *The Covenant of Nature Made with Adam* (1662).

Biography: William Pynchon was probably born about thirty miles northeast of London, near Springfield, in Dec. 1590. His family was Norman, and Pynchon's grandfather fixed his descendants' status among the landed gentry by marrying the daughter and heiress of Sir Richard Empson. The eldest of his family, William Pynchon inherited his father's Springfield property, married the daughter of an old Warwickshire family, and for his first forty years lived the life of a country gentleman, serving as churchwarden of his parish and as justice of the peace. But in May 1629, he became one of the original twenty-six patentees of the Massachusetts Bay Company and one of eighteen assistants named in the Charter to the Governor and Company of Massachusetts Bay in New Eng. Like John Winthrop (q.v.), with whom he sailed to New Eng. in 1630, Pynchon was a large landowner and a Puritan, pressed to emigrate, perhaps, for social and economic reasons.

Once in New Eng., Pynchon and his family settled first in Dorchester and then in Roxbury, where Pynchon (the town's principal founder) became a prominent farmer and fur trader. His success with the peltry trade led him in 1635 to purchase a site for a new colony on the west bank of the Connecticut River, where he could trade directly with the Indians. The new settlement, Agawam, flourished; in 1641 it was named Springfield in honor of its founder's English home.

Pynchon proved to be a strong but controversial leader in the economic and social history of western Mass. A member of the first Court of Assistants and the first General Court in Mass., he served as treasurer of the Bay colony from Aug. 1632 until May 1634 and administered justice in the Conn. and Bay colonies until 1651. The settlement at Springfield reflected his Puritan values and his staunch individualism: as Samuel Eliot Morison pointed out, it was "a proper godly plantation. . . and no mere trucking post"; and as its magistrate and judge, Pynchon paid about half the town taxes, owned the most land, and imported the town's Cambridge-bred minister, George Moxon (q.v.). Yet he was not an orthodox member of the Puritan oligarchy that supervised the river towns in the Conn. and Bay areas. "Impatient of ecclesiastical and political trammels," he ran athwart of the General Court's economic and religious policies and was ultimately forced to return to Eng. His first fall from grace occurred in 1638, when the Conn. General Court enforced the Mass. system of granting a monopoly in the beaver trade to one or two outstanding leaders in each town in return for a tax on each skin. In one of his more famous letters, Pynchon contended that it could not "well stand with the public good and the liberty of free men to make a monopoly of trade." Pynchon, of course, already possessed a monopoly of the beaver trade in Agawam, but his reputation as "a conscientious magistrate who respected the English tradition of justice, and who denied it not to the poorest and most pestiferous man under his jurisdiction" suggests that his motives were more than economic. Another dispute, in which Pynchon opposed the paternalism of the Conn. General Court in its regulation of the corn trade between the river settlers and the Indians, ended in 1641 with his unpopular decision to remove Springfield from the jurisdiction of the court and make it part of the Massachusetts Bay government. Although Pynchon was elected to his former position with the Court of Assistants in 1642, his reputation as something of a renegade probably survived to abet the General Court's denunciation of his 1650 declaimer against Calvinistic theology, *The Meritorious Price of Our Redemption*.

The source of William Pynchon's formal education is a mystery, but he was well versed in Latin, Greek, and Hebrew and so well read in theology that he was highly regarded as a "gentleman of learning." His theological expertise led him, in his later years, to articulate his moderate Puritanism. In *The Meritorious Price of Our Redemption*, he obdurately denied the Calvinistic supposition that Christ paid for Adam's disobedience and man's sins by enduring the torments of hell and the wrath of God. The General Court denounced the book, ordered it burned, proclaimed a day of fasting and humiliation in the wake of the burning, and ordered three clergymen to offer rejoinders if Pynchon did not recant. Ironically, Pynchon appeared at the court immediately after presiding at what may have been the first witchcraft trial in Mass. Historians agree that he judged the case of Mary and Hugh Parsons rationally and mercifully (by the standards that were to be set in Salem) and may have prevented Springfield from joining Salem as a center of intolerance and inhumanity. But Pynchon himself became the victim of what Morison called "the narrowest, most bigoted period" of Mass. history. Appearing before the court in 1651, Pynchon felt the necessity to convince his peers that he was in a "hopefull way to give good satisfaction." He never made a full retraction, and even published two more editions of his controversial book in 1655. But he published them in Eng., where he and his wife surreptitiously retired in Sept. or Oct. of 1651. Pynchon devoted the last ten years of his life to study and scholarship at his estate near Runnymede and died there in 1662.

   Critical Appraisal: William Pynchon's most famous and accessible work is his controversial treatise *The Meritorious Price of Our Redemption*, a quarto volume of 158 pages. Growing out of an argument Pynchon had heard from a friend thirty years earlier, it directly counters the espousals of the Westminster Assembly, which sat from 1643 to 1647. Since Pynchon was probably a nonconformist rather than a Separatist, he chafed under the Calvinistic assumption that Christ suffered "Hell Torments" to make what the Assembly called "a proper, real, and full satisfaction to his Father's justice in [man's] behalf." The treatise is arranged as a discourse between "a Trades-man and A Divine," and its central argument is that Christ earned man's redemption by his perfect obedience and was crucified not as a sign of God's anger, but because Satan was intent on revenge. Its central characteristics are stylistic eloquence, clear reasoning, and logical argumentation. E. H. Byington contended that "the most vigorous part of the Book" is Pynchon's exegesis of those scriptural texts used to prove the imputation of human sin to Christ. Pynchon's polemicism never degenerates into invective: his "close and logical" exegesis is followed by a rigorous definition of what he conceived as the genuine basis of man's redemption.

   Pynchon's argument is noteworthy for its dependence on the authority of tradition and scholarship: he drew on the Hebrew and Greek texts of the Bible, carefully compared passages in the Geneva Bible with their counterparts in the Tyndale and King James translations, and consistently cited great theologians, from Augustine to Ainsworth (with whom Pynchon corresponded), for support of his ideas. His other, more obscure works suggest the same probing, scholarly revaluation of theology, dealing as they do with subjects such as the worship customs of the Jews and "The Manner how the First Sabbath was Ordained." As a Springfield historian suggested, Pynchon was "a profound scholar, a logical writer, and an independent thinker," and although his writings had very little impact on the religious climate of seventeenth-century Eng., they are significant expressions of the spirit of enlightened inquiry and protest that eventually flourished in New Eng.

Suggested Readings: DAB; DNB; T$_1$. *See also* H. M. Burt, *The First Century of the History of Springfield* (1898); E. H. Byington, *The Puritan in England and New England* (1896); Philip F. Gura, "'The Contagion of Corrupt Opinions' in Puritan Massachusetts: The Case of William Pynchon," WMQ, 39 (1982), 469-491; Samuel Eliot Morison, "William Pynchon, Founder of Springfield," PMHS, 64 (1932), 67-108; Joseph H. Smith, "Legal and Historical Introduction to the Pynchon Court Record," in *Colonial Justice in Western Massachusetts (1639-1702): The Pynchon Court Record* (1961).

Eliza Davis
The University of Alabama in Huntsville